Envisioning Brazil

Envisioning Brazil

A Guide to Brazilian Studies in
the United States, 1945–2003

~

EDITED BY

MARSHALL C. EAKIN

and

PAULO ROBERTO DE ALMEIDA

THE UNIVERSITY OF WISCONSIN PRESS

The University of Wisconsin Press
1930 Monroe Street
Madison, Wisconsin 53711

www.wisc.edu/wisconsinpress/

3 Henrietta Street
London WC2E 8LU, England

1   3   5   4   2

Printed in the United States of America

Library of Congress Cataloging-in-Publication Data
Brasil dos brasilianistas. English
Envisioning Brazil: A guide to Brazilian studies in the United States /
edited by Marshall C. Eakin and Paulo Roberto de Almeida.
p. cm.
"The essays were updated by the various authors in late 2003
for this English-language edition"—ECIP Ch. 1.
Includes bibliographical references.
ISBN 0-299-20770-6 (cloth: alk. paper)
1. Universities and colleges—Curricula—United States. 2. Brazil—
Study and teaching (Higher)—United States. 3. Brazil—Study and teaching
(Higher)—Great Britain. 4. Brazil—Study and teaching (Higher)—
France. 5. Brazil—Bibliography. I. Eakin, Marshall C. (Marshall Craig),
1952– II. Almeida, Paulo Roberto de. III. Title.
F2520.7.E58 2005
981'.0071'073—dc22
2005001336

In memory of Robert M. Levine

1941–2003

CONTENTS

PREFACE
Brazilian Studies in the United States: A Project in Development
RUBENS ANTÔNIO BARBOSA   ix

INTRODUCTION
Envisioning Brazil and Brazilianists
MARSHALL C. EAKIN *and* PAULO ROBERTO DE ALMEIDA   xiii

PART 1
The Development of Brazilian Studies in the United States

1. Trends, Perspectives, and Prospects
PAULO ROBERTO DE ALMEIDA   3

2. Research on Brazil in the United States
ROBERT M. LEVINE   30

3. Teaching Brazil in U.S. Universities
THEODORE R. YOUNG   52

PART 2
Perspectives from the Disciplines

4. Brazilian Portuguese Language and Linguistics
CARMEN CHAVES TESSER   73

5. Literature, Culture, and Civilization
K. DAVID JACKSON   93

6. Arts and Music
JOSÉ NEISTEIN 133

7. Brazilian History in the United States
JUDY BIEBER 162

8. Anthropology of Amazonia
JANET M. CHERNELA 203

9. The Brazilian Economic System through U.S. Lenses
WERNER BAER *and* ROBERTO GUIMARÃES 241

10. Political Science and Sociology
MARSHALL C. EAKIN 264

11. International Relations
SCOTT D. TOLLEFSON 288

12. Geography
CYRUS B. DAWSEY III 309

PART 3
Counterpoints: Brazilian Studies in Britain and France

13. The British Contribution to the Study of Brazil
LESLIE BETHELL 347

14. Comparative Development of the Study of Brazil in
the United States and France
EDWARD A. RIEDINGER 375

PART 4
Bibliographic and Reference Sources

15. A Chronology of U.S.–Brazil Relations and
Academic Publications, 1945–2003
PAULO ROBERTO DE ALMEIDA 399

16. Brasiliana in the United States: Reference Sources and Documents
ANN HARTNESS 424

17. Selective Bibliography and Chronology
PAULO ROBERTO DE ALMEIDA 460

NOTES ON CONTRIBUTORS 485
INDEX 491

~

Brazilian Studies in the United States

A Project in Development

Rubens Antônio Barbosa

Even before I came to Washington as the Brazilian ambassador to the United States in June 1999, I had already decided to build and maintain a strong working relationship with the academic community in the United States. I saw this not only as an opportunity to create new momentum for Brazilian studies in the United States but also as a way of expanding the intellectual cooperation between U.S. scholars of Brazil and their Brazilian counterparts. I was fully and personally aware of the long tradition of Brazilian studies in the United States, as has been manifested in the hundreds of high-quality academic studies that constitute a category that we Brazilians would call "Brazilianism."

This idea became a reality almost immediately, through a meeting held at the Brazilian embassy in October 1999. In the beginning, the plan was to bring together those (few) responsible for Brazilian studies programs and the directors of the main academic centers for Latin American studies at major universities in the United States, for what would be the first gathering for networking, discussing the field of study, and, above all, planning new initiatives and activities that could result in the expansion of Brazilian studies in those academic centers. The news that the Brazilian embassy in Washington was planning to hold an exploratory, and therefore understandably modest and tentative, meeting spread like wildfire. The Brazilianist community across the United States soon became aware of the event and started requesting invitations for other directors of centers for Latin American studies and for new "active academic representatives" of Brazilian studies. Thus a meeting that was intended for fewer than twenty center directors and a few heads of Brazil programs became a gathering of about fifty Brazilianists and Latin Americanists, something that had never taken place as part of the official Brazilian diplomatic activities in the United States. As would be expected with any premiere, expectations for the meeting were high.

Aside from its other practical results, the meeting was a success simply because it was held, opening the way for a productive dialogue between the Brazilian embassy and those responsible for academic studies, especially the many "interpreters of Brazil" from outside Brazil (in fact, many had lived in Brazil for long periods of time and spoke Portuguese without any accent). For the purpose of this book, it is important to highlight that the proposition of making a survey of the Brazilianist work produced in the United States after the Second World War was welcomed with enthusiasm, even if with the analytical mind-set that is to be expected of any academic community that insists on methodological skepticism when faced with any broader attempt to produce an overview.

The project for the book proceeded as planned with the selection of the researchers and the preparation of tentative chapters, as well as the expected and necessary changes of approach and methodological adaptations (such as the inclusion of language studies, for instance, which is of negligible importance in Brazil, for obvious reasons, but that could be considered strategic in terms of the future of Brazilian studies in the United States). A second meeting with Brazilianists, this time dedicated specifically to discussing the chapters of the future book, was again held at the embassy in December 2000, with the enthusiastic participation of about fifty scholars as special guests and the same number of other experts in Brazil and Latin America, along with many others who shared an interest in this type of academic discussion.

What you are about to read in this compilation of essays, which I am pleased to introduce, is the result of an intense cross-fertilization process between U.S. Brazilianists and Brazilian scholars who came in large numbers to critically analyze texts written by their colleagues (many of whom had been friends for a long time, although this did not reduce the intensity of the debates). It would be impossible to summarize here the high quality of the interaction that took place then. Many of those who were present will remember the depth, intensity, and seriousness of some exchanges that occurred among the experts, the same way that I recall pleasant conversations I had with several scholars present, the majority of whom are well known by generations of Brazilian social science students and also by the Brazilian public in general. In a way, one could say that, during those two days in December, in the conference room of the Brazilian embassy and also later at the Brazilian ambassador's residence in Washington, those responsible for the best-known portion of the U.S. bibliography on Brazilian studies appeared in person, something like half the Brazilianist "GDP" of the second half of the twentieth century.

The results of this productive academic interaction between Brazilianists and Brazilians are shown in this book, which promises to mark, deservedly, this important stage in the specialized U.S. academic production about Brazil. In fact, this book is the first overall assessment ever done of the contribution by U.S. scholars to the knowledge about Brazil in the second half of the twentieth century. Most works were originally prepared in English, but the book was first published in Portuguese (in early 2002), thanks to the interest demonstrated by publisher Fernando Gasparian, from the Brazilian publishing house Paz e Terra, who is probably the most frequently used and well-known publisher of American Brazilianists in Brazil.

This book is only a small part of all the endeavors that have been set in motion by the Brazilian embassy in Washington since 1999, accomplished so far through various academic initiatives. Several of the projects include, among others, the establishment of a Brazilian studies center at Columbia University in New York, a Brazilian studies program at Georgetown University, the "Brazil Project" at the Woodrow Wilson Center for International Scholars, both in Washington, D.C., along with a series of other initiatives aimed at elementary and middle school students—such as "Discover Brazil"—and the decision to begin publishing Brazilian books ("Brasiliana") in the United States, in association with the Duke and North Carolina university presses. The embassy has taken a proactive role in that we have not only continued to support existing agreements with public institutions but also have sought to expand and intensify the links, both formal and informal, between Brazilian and U.S. entities, especially toward the creation of Brazilian studies programs and academic centers, wherever possible. Because government funding is insufficient, great attention has been given to engaging both the U.S. and the Brazilian private sectors in those activities.

One program that should continue to promote cooperation between the academic communities in Brazil and the United States over the next few years is the Brazilian History Recovery Project in the U.S. Archives (Resgate-EUA). This project, coordinated by the Brazilian embassy in Washington, is aimed at identifying, cataloging, and recovering, to the greatest extent possible, documents about Brazil that are located in U.S. institutions, particularly at the National Archives and Records Administration.

These documents are important for research on Brazil's bilateral relations, regional foreign policy, and international relations, as well as for the study of the country's political, social, economic, and military history. Once identified and reproduced in an electronic format, these documents will be made available to Brazilian archives (the Brazilian Ministry of Culture's National Library and Diplomatic History Archive, both located in Rio de Janeiro), along with other research centers.

These are some of the initiatives taken since I became the Brazilian ambassador to the United States, and they are aimed at strengthening and expanding Brazilian studies in the United States and at increasing the awareness in Brazil of the resources and academic studies available in the United States about our country. This book is a concrete result of those efforts. My goal is that it will be the first of a series of other new products that will further enhance the positive academic relationships that have historically existed between the United States and Brazil.

Washington, D.C.
October 2002

INTRODUCTION

≈

Envisioning Brazil and Brazilianists

Marshall C. Eakin
and
Paulo Roberto de Almeida

Origins

This edited volume emerged from an idea put forth by Ambassador Rubens Barbosa shortly after his arrival in Washington, D.C., in October 1999. The ambassador convened a meeting at the Brazilian embassy of Brazilianists from academic institutions across the United to discuss ways to promote Brazilian studies here, among them this book. Shortly thereafter Ministro-Conselheiro Paulo Roberto de Almeida took charge of the project, and Marshall C. Eakin came aboard as coeditor. They then commissioned all the essays, the majority of which were presented at a two-day seminar at the Brazilian embassy on December 6–7, 2000. More than one hundred people attended and participated in the critique and discussion of the papers. The presenters then had the opportunity to revise their essays during the first half of 2001. The Portuguese-language version of this book was published in Brazil in 2002 as *O Brasil dos brasilianistas: um guia dos estudos sobre o Brasil nos Estados Unidos, 1945–2000* (São Paulo: Paz e Terra). The authors updated their essays in late 2003 for this English-language edition.

Objectives

Our principal objective has been to assemble the most comprehensive and sweeping assessment ever attempted of the patterns and characteristics of Brazilian studies in the United States. This volume is an overview of the writings on Brazil by U.S. scholars since 1945. It is not a comprehensive bibliography but rather an effort to assess trends and perspectives. We have focused on synthesis and interpretation. The effort to provide an overview of the intellectual production by U.S. scholars has led us to make some important editorial decisions. The first has been the delimitation of what we mean by a "U.S." scholar. The essays focus on scholars who have made their careers primarily in the United States, but the reader will see that our definition at times includes foreign scholars who have spent most of their career at U.S. institutions. Second, although the aim is to survey U.S. scholarship, all the essays make (sometimes frequent) reference to Brazilian scholarship and scholars. In particular, it is often impossible to understand the directions in U.S. scholarship without an understanding of the academic and political trends in Brazil since 1945.

Although this overview is not entirely comprehensive, we believe that it is the single most thorough analysis ever produced of U.S. scholarship on Brazil. The attentive reader will, however, notice some important gaps, the most prominent of which are urban anthropology and the performing arts. The former is covered to some extent in the discussions of ethnology (chapter 8) and sociology (chapter 10). The latter, unfortunately, receives very little mention here.

OVERVIEW OF THE BOOK

We have divided this book into four parts. Part 1, "The Development of Brazilian Studies in the United States," contains three chapters on large themes and patterns. In chapter 1 Almeida surveys Brazilian studies in the United States since 1945. Chapter 2 follows with the late Robert Levine's overview of the development of Brazilian studies here, with special attention to institutions and research trends. As a complement to Levine's emphasis on research, Young's essay in chapter 3 provides a look at how the teaching of Brazil developed at U.S. universities.

Part 2, "Perspectives from the Disciplines," moves from the sweeping overview of part 1 to surveys of various academic disciplines. In chapter 4 Tesser provides a wonderful analysis of the long but uneven development of the teaching of Portuguese in the United States. She shows that despite its long history, the teaching of Portuguese occupies a small place within the teaching of foreign languages in the United States. Like the teaching of most foreign languages, instruction in Portuguese language has been dwarfed by the explosion of interest in Spanish. The dominance in Latin American studies of Spanish and Spanish America is a theme that runs throughout many essays in this volume. In chapter 5 Jackson turns to what has perhaps been the most developed of all the disciplines in Brazilian studies—literature. A strong group of scholars has written about Brazilian literature for decades. The excellence of Brazilian literature since 1945 has helped bring attention to the work of these scholars, just as their literary studies and translations have helped bring Brazilian literature to the attention of readers and literary scholars in the United States Neistein's essay in chapter 6 is a double survey, of both art and music. Although not as well known in the United States as Brazilian literature, Brazil's art and music have received attention by a small but dedicated group of scholars.

The next series of essays turns to the social sciences. U.S. historians of Brazil have perhaps the longest tradition and the most highly developed literature next to that of the literary scholars. Bieber's excellent survey in chapter 7 demonstrates the breadth and depth of historical studies of Brazil in the United States. From a small cohort of scholars in the 1950s, the field grew dramatically in the 1960s and 1970s, experienced declining numbers in the 1980s, and is once again growing in size and in the quantity and quality of published work. With a firm grounding in fieldwork in archives in Brazil, historians are perhaps in the strongest position (along with literary scholars) to maintain their identity as a subdiscipline within history and Latin American studies in the United States.

Anthropology is another discipline deeply rooted in extensive fieldwork in Brazil. Like the literary scholars and historians, anthropologists have strong linguistic skills and deep local experience. Chernela's essay in chapter 8 concentrates on the long and highly developed field of Amazonian ethnology. She shows how studies by U.S. anthropologists have at times shaped the very direction of the discipline, both in the United States and in Brazil. At the same time the changing nature of the discipline—from traditional community studies to structuralism and discourse analysis—has shaped these anthropological studies. In chapter 9 Baer and Guimarães provide a detailed survey of the main patterns in economics. Many of the key works that they discuss arose out of the collaboration of U.S. and Brazilian scholars, and much of the literature has developed around the key problems that have faced Brazil's economy since 1945.

Eakin's essay in chapter 10 is also a double feature, surveying both political science and sociology. Both disciplines have roots that go back to the 1930s and 1940s but did not really develop until the 1960s. Although sociology had a strong early start, especially in the area of race relations, it has failed to develop a strong subdisciplinary identity around Brazilian studies, and the number of sociologists studying Brazil today is small. Political science developed an impressive group of scholars, and they were especially interested in the study of authoritarianism from the 1960s to the 1980s. Although a strong and impressive group of scholars continues to write about Brazil, the larger developments in the discipline (in particular the move away from "area studies" and toward theory) may threaten the survival of political science within Brazilian studies. Tollefson's essay in chapter 11 follows with a synthesis of studies on international relations with a Brazilian focus. In chapter 12 Dawsey presents an interesting look at geographers who chose to focus on Brazil. As with some of the other disciplines, the changing nature of geography has meant profound shifts in its studies—whereas the field focused on countries and their regions in the 1950s and 1960s, today it concentrates on larger questions of theory and problems.

Part 3, "Counterpoints: Brazilian Studies in Britain and France," offers two essays that help place the U.S. contributions in perspective. In chapter 13 the eminent British historian of Brazil, Leslie Bethell, looks at the contributions of British historians to the development of Brazilian studies. Edward Riedinger then compares the development of Brazilian studies in the United States and France in chapter 14.

Part 4 consists of three chapters on bibliographic and reference sources. Almeida's chapter is a chronology of key publications by U.S. Brazilianists placed alongside key developments in U.S.–Brazilian relations. In chapter 16 Hartness provides a thorough guide to reference sources on Brazil. As is the case in some of the other chapters, we can see the digital age's reshaping of the traditional emphasis on print sources toward comprehensive and accessible electronic data. This book ends with a selective bibliography compiled by Almeida.

A key contributor to the book, and one of the foremost Brazilianists, Robert M. Levine, died in April 2003. He was probably the most prolific U.S. scholar of things Brazilian, and he was among the pioneering generation of U.S. Brazilianists. We have dedicated this volume to this renowned scholar, who did so much to promote the study of Brazil in the United States.

PART 1

∼

The Development of Brazilian Studies in the United States

CHAPTER 1

◌

Trends, Perspectives, and Prospects

PAULO ROBERTO DE ALMEIDA

INTRODUCTION
The Birth of the Brazilianist

The foreign student of subjects related to Brazil, usually called a "Brazilianist," was an essential part of the process leading to the emergence and affirmation of the social sciences in Brazil in the second half of the twentieth century. Although a contemporary figure, she has been for all intents a much older and continuous presence throughout the country's history. In fact, the "accidental Brazilianist," that is, one who left a written record of his presence, first appeared in the garb of a traveler or temporary resident, whether an adventurer in search of easy wealth, a naturalist fascinated by the exuberance of its flora and fauna, a businessman seeking great profits, or a missionary dedicated to saving souls. During the period when the state was created and the nation established, he was converted more systematically into a contemporary chronicler of historical events of Brazilian history, an interpreter of the specifics of its nature, its human characteristics, and its social institutions, including slavery, which has so influenced modern Brazil. The participation of the external observer, to some extent "objective" vis-à-vis the "biases" of Brazilian nationals, in the progressive development of reflections on the realities found in a new country like Brazil, dates back several centuries. Moreover, Brazil has been under construction continuously from the colonial period to the present.

The concept of the Brazilianist obviously did not exist during the initial phases of the formation of the Brazilian nation. It is likely that the founding father and initiator of this trend was the English historian

3

Robert Southey, who is still influential in Brazilian social theory, despite its contemporary "emancipation" from foreign analytical formulas and methodologies. At the height of the independence period, this shrewd observer of the Portuguese colonial empire, who anticipated the broader studies of Charles Boxer, wrote a history of Brazil (Southey, 1817–22) that served as a unique reference work in that discipline until the first truly national historian appeared, the diplomat Francisco Adolfo de Varnhagen. During the nineteenth century, there were several other Brazilianists, including two Germans, Von Humboldt and Von Martius, the latter of whom wrote the first guide on how to write the history of Brazil, Handelmann (who, like Southey, never visited Brazil), the Swiss Louis Agassiz, and the French, Gobineau and Louis Couty, to cite only the best known.

Despite these illustrious ancestors, the concept of the Brazilianist per se first appeared much later, during the Cold War, amid concerns about imperialism that involved the possible destabilization of the principal country in South America. According to bibliographic research, the term *brasilianista* was first used in Brazil in 1969 by Francisco de Assis Barbosa "to describe a foreigner who is a specialist in Brazilian matters" (Massi and Pontes, 1992: 91). The concept was applied to U.S. historian Thomas Elliot Skidmore in the preface to the Brazilian edition of his *Politics in Brazil* (1967). This certainly was not the first use of the term, since it was being used in the early 1960s by the group of scholars who benefited from fellowships and other forms of support from the U.S. government, which was reacting to the Cuban Revolution in its desire to encourage the study of Brazil. To distinguish themselves from other specialists on Latin America, the Brazil specialists began calling themselves "Brazilianists." This was not even the first generation of U.S. students of Brazil, nor the first application of the suffix "-ist" to students of other cultures, since the notion was already present in the academic universe of European historians and social scientists in the nineteenth century, as demonstrated by whole generations of "Latinists" or "Germanists," for example. The use of this term by Assis Barbosa, however, provides a conceptual point of departure for those who came to be known in U.S. academic circles and in Brazil's universities and the media as students of Brazilian society, its historical formation, and its economic and social development. Again, in this case we do not have a genuine substantive innovation, since, beginning with Thévet and Léry, passing through the travelers and naturalists of the eighteenth and nineteenth centuries, up to the most modern "specimens" of this academic family, the lands and people of Brazil were always visited by, explained, and "revealed" to the outside world by this peculiar genre of "interpreter" of things Brazilian, the foreign scholar. But it was with the U.S. Brazilianists that, from the mid-1960s on, the conceptual and terminological universe of Brazilian social sciences came to incorporate and interact with the production of these new visitors and observers.

In fact, until the 1960s and 1970s the twentieth century had never seen such a rapid development and advantageous proliferation of foreign specialists in Brazilian topics as occurred after passage of the National Defense Education Act of 1958. Title VI of this act, as approved by the U.S. Congress, provided generous funding to U.S. universities for teaching and research on Latin American subjects. From that time on, the famous "Brazilianists" appeared in U.S. academia as a subspecies of the more abundant Latin Americanists.

For a time during the 1970s, in view of the large proportion of U.S. academics among foreign scholars, the Portuguese term was often written in English, indicating an almost natural dominance of the United States in this field of studies. Gradually, however, the term was loosened from its original connotation, becoming wholly Brazilianized, and came to designate all representatives of the species, both contemporaneously and retrospectively. Consequently, a bibliography from the late 1980s, on Brazilianist research translated and published in Brazil from 1930 through the date of the bibliography, showed a 60 percent predominance of specialists born, graduated (and naturalized), or working in the United States, followed at some distance by individuals from the United Kingdom, France, and Germany. Among the latter were some who had spent what were in some cases lengthy periods at U.S. universities (Massi and Pontes, 1992: 113–15).

THE BEGINNINGS
The Founding Fathers

It would be an error, however, to suppose that Brazilianists appeared like a lightning bolt in the blue skies of Brazil at the height of the Cold War and the military dictatorship. In both Brazil and the United States, there was concern about the effects of the Cuban Revolution on a society in the process of social and economic modernization, and still subject to continual eruptions of political instability. To find the origins of the U.S. variant of Brazilianist that would proliferate in the United States only in the second half of the twentieth century, one need not go back to the works of a near "amateur" like William H. Prescott (who published *Conquest of Mexico* in 1843 and *Conquest of Peru* in 1846), or a military adventurer and naval officer, William Lewis Herndon (*Exploration of the Valley of the Amazon*, 1854). In fact, the appearance of the first U.S. Brazilianist may be dated to 1916 when Latin Americanist historians met during a conference of the American Historical Association (AHA) and founded the *Hispanic American Historical Review* (*HAHR*), which was first published in 1918, almost twenty-three years after the appearance in 1895 of the *American Historical Review* (Iggers and Parker, 1979: 365).

The journal of this group of Hispanists in the AHA, interrupted between 1922 and 1926, had a precarious existence in its first twenty-five years of life. It survived, thanks to "disinterested" donations from sponsors interested in the region, such as the Rockefellers and the Duke family, with investments in Mexico and other regions in the Americas. *HAHR* counted on several intellectual Brazilian diplomats, like Manuel de Oliveira Lima, "the Fat Don Quixote," in the words of Gilberto Freyre, among its first contributors. Oliveira Lima may legitimately be considered one of the first U.S. Brazilianists, if not their founding father. He participated in many conferences and gave numerous lectures (later published) in U.S. academic circles. He engaged in rigorously academic research in comparative studies of Brazil and its hemispheric neighbors. Were it not that he was preceded historically by the man who is known as "the father of the Brazilian press," Oliveira Lima also might have been considered the first of a rare breed, the Brazilian Americanist, traveling about the country during the full bloom of Rooseveltian and Wilsonian triumphalism and developing his own view about the strength of the powerful United States.

In fact, a century before Oliveira Lima, Hipólito José da Costa traveled along the East Coast of the United States long before he fled the Portuguese inquisition, established himself in England, and published his *Correio Brasiliense* from London. He wrote the little-known *Diário de minha viagem para Filadélfia, 1798–1799*, found in manuscript in the Biblioteca de Évora by Alceu Amoroso Lima and published by the Academia Brasileira de Letras in 1955. In fact, this was not an academic study. The Portuguese youth (he was twenty-four), born in Colônia do Sacramento and raised in Rio Grande, was traveling in the service of the minister of foreign relations, the future Count of Linhares. In fact, Costa produced a detailed report of his observations on agriculture, industry, and plants in the United States. But this is certainly one of the first works about the United States, written from the perspective of a Brazilian observer, concerned with bringing to the Lusitanian colony in the Americas the plant and animal species and technical improvements he judged would contribute to the improvement of his homeland.

Precisely one century after Hipólito da Costa, as a result of more than three years of his own travels and observations, Oliveira Lima published his pioneering *Nos Estados Unidos* (1899). He expressed his "social and political" impressions (according to the subtitle) of the great expansion then underway in the powerful northern nation. Perhaps anticipating Brazilian reactions in the following century, Oliveira Lima began the introduction to the book by stating that "in Brazil one speaks either very well or very badly of the United States" (1). Later, however, he notes, "I merely observed the United States with Brazilian eyes, that is, constantly seeking that which is useful . . . from examination and comparison" (5). Beginning his comparative view of the critical contemplation that Brazilian intellectuals would expend on the causes of the country's (non)development during the modernist period, Oliveira Lima confesses that "in North America I was seized by, and shortly almost obsessed by, a strong impression of our backwardness, which I had never experienced in Europe, accustomed as we are to consider it an ancient field of experiences and progresses. On the other side of the Atlantic, however, in a country with a civilization as modern as that of Brazil, comparison is irresistible, to our grave discredit, with its train of psychological and sociological considerations" (17). His book, which utilized material published from 1896 through 1899 in the *Revista Brasilia* and the *Jornal do Comércio*, is, indeed, a sampling of sociological commentaries (some strongly impressionistic) on the reasons for U.S. progress in contrast with Brazilian backwardness.

A little more than decade later, Oliveira Lima collected a series of lectures, which he had given at a U.S. university, in *The Evolution of Brazil Compared with That of Spain and Anglo-Saxon America* (1914). This is an essentially historical treatment, but he included sociological commentaries on the different paths of political, social, and economic development followed in the different parts of the hemisphere, with a customary deference to the racialist theories then in vogue. In his memoirs, Oliveira Lima would remember that he had learned more about the United States during the two months he had spent as a lecturer in twelve U.S. universities in 1912, and in the six months when he was a professor at Harvard in 1915–16, than in the four years before (which he had spent as secretary of legation, working under Joaquim Nabuco, another patron of Brazilian Americanists, elevated by Rio Branco in 1906 to be the first ambassador of Brazil in the United States). In the then-sparse U.S. bibliography on Brazil and the equally sparse Brazilian one, Oliveira Lima is a kind of intellectual bridge between the two countries, an example, moreover, rarely repeated during the twentieth century.

In any case, the effort of Oliveira Lima, and the few other Brazilians who came after him, did not prevent Hispanic or Latin American studies in the United States from being dominated by a research and publishing emphasis on Mexico, as is still the case, leaving Brazil in an honorable second place. Writing after the Second World War on the first thirty years of the *HAHR*, a Hispanist provided statistics on the space occupied by the different countries and groups of countries under review: Mexico was in first place with 24 percent, followed by Brazil and the Caribbean, both with 11.5 percent each, proportions that are probably not much different today from the geographic and academic distribution of U.S. interests regarding "southern" hemispheric topics (Simpson, 1949). If one considers, and admits, the special situation of Mexico or the Caribbean's status as a kind of mare nostrum in the geopolitical projections of the United States, this distribution of interests in academia becomes understandable, which only strengthens the position of Brazil in the panorama of area studies.

After pioneering examples on the East Coast at the beginning of the twentieth century, Latin American studies, with little emphasis on Brazilian topics, expanded reasonably well on the West Coast in the 1930s and 1940s and then in the second half of the century literally exploded across the United States. Important steps in the development of Latin American studies in the United States (within which Brazilian studies were inevitably included) were made with the founding in 1928, within the AHA, of the Committee on Latin American History, which gave decisive impetus to the creation, a few years later, of the *Handbook of Latin American Studies (HLAS)*, which even today is still considered an exceptional bibliographic undertaking, without equivalent in any other geographic area in the humanities and social sciences.

HLAS first appeared in 1936 under the sponsorship of the Committee on Latin American Studies of the American Council of Learned Societies, with financial support from the Social Science Research Council of New York. The Rockefeller Foundation supported several early volumes. The Library of Congress took over management, beginning with volume 9, and is still in charge of its editorial direction, as part of its Hispanic Division. Four years later, in 1940, the University of Texas created the Institute of Latin American Studies, which would become the largest and best equipped of the study centers specializing in the region, along with those in California, which were more oriented toward Mexico, Central America, and the Caribbean. In the same year the universities of Wisconsin and New Mexico began teaching Portuguese and Brazilian studies, making them the oldest programs in the United States. *HLAS* was published by Harvard University up to volume 13 (1948), when the publication moved to the University of Florida Press, in Gainesville. Since 1966 it has been published annually by the University of Texas Press in Austin, alternating in odd years with materials related to the humanities (art, music, literature, and history, among others) and in even years with bibliography on the social sciences (anthropology, economics, sociology, political science, international relations, etc.). The presence of Brazil in its pages is, in principle, modest, but few contemporary reviewers of *HLAS* know, for example, that the famous historian, economist, and businessman Roberto Simonsen was a contributing editor in the area of Brazilian economy for volumes 6 to 11 (1941–46).

The Second World War may have affected the normal flow of cultural and academic exchanges between the north and south in the Americas, but it seems in no way to have damaged the development of Ibero-American studies in the United States. On the contrary, the need to secure the goodwill of governments in common cause against the Nazi-fascist enemy and of maintaining a regular provisioning of primary strategic products, led to the sending of goodwill missions, several of which were led by university specialists; in the case of Brazil this was true of the Cooke Mission, which was oriented toward elevating Brazil's economic potential. The Brazilian novelist Érico Veríssimo also made trips to the United States. This warming of relations allowed, for example, for the translation and publication in the United States of some classic works of Brazilian thought during the first half of the twentieth century, such as Euclides da Cunha's epic *Rebellion in the Backlands* (1945). In this same year Gilberto Freyre was preparing a collection of readings on Brazil, published under the title *Brazil: An Interpretation*. His innovative *Casa-grande e senzala* (*The Masters and the Slaves*) would appear the following year. A significant figure during this period was the economist João Frederico Normano, long a resident of the United States, who published in 1931 a work on economy and ideology in Latin America (*The Struggle for South America*) and in 1935 a study on the long-term economic development (focused on product cycles) of his native Brazil, *Brazil, A Study of Economic Types*.

DEVELOPMENT AND THE INITIAL CHARACTERISTICS OF POSTWAR BRAZILIAN STUDIES IN THE UNITED STATES

In the postwar period, Latin American studies began to develop in U.S. universities. This occurred with the establishment of specialized interdisciplinary sections in humanities departments or, where applicable, in centers dedicated exclusively to Latin American studies. This was the case, for example, at the universities of Texas and North Carolina, at Tulane, and especially at Vanderbilt, where the focus was specifically on Brazil. In the beginning, these programs had no government support, which was consistent with the strategic concerns of the U.S. administration in this initial phase of the Cold War. Latin America appeared in the directives of the National Security Council as a region of lesser importance in the external security plans of the United States, which, in fact, merely confirms the generally marginal role of the Americas in international relations.

This situation did not prevent the appearance of some works of recognized high quality on Latin America, with Brazil continuing to occupy a secondary position, behind Mexico, but nevertheless a significant position in studies of the region. Immediately after the Second World War, Brazilian elites, confronting Argentina and nourishing an expectation of political dividends from Brazil's participation in the war, were obsessed with the myth of a special relationship with the United States. They proposed bilateral aid mechanisms and multilateral financing, a sort of Marshall Plan for Latin America (an idea raised during the Inter-American Meeting in Bogotá, 1948). The most they achieved was the creation of the Joint Brazil–United States Economic Development Commission in 1949, which published a report in 1954. The decade following the end of the Second World War has been described as one of the "Americanization" of Brazil (Haines, 1989), and, in fact, the two countries' political alignment in foreign affairs has never before or since been as strong as in those years.

Academic production, which during that period could be described as "pre-Brazilianist," began to grow in parallel with the ebbs and flows of Brazil-U.S. relations in the political, military, and economic areas. Sociologist Donald Pierson, for example, in 1945 published a preliminary survey of literature on Brazil in his discipline, *Survey of the Literature on Brazil of Sociological Significance Published up to 1940*. In 1946, two of the first general introductions to Brazil were published, T. Lynn Smith's *Brazil, People and Institutions*, and Preston E. James's *Brazil*. The 1950s were dominated by these three social scientists, who were responsible for several studies published by university presses. To their names we can add anthropologists Charles Wagley and Marvin Harris, as well as historians Alexander Marchant, Stanley Stein, and Richard Morse, the latter two extremely active in the following decades. Economists Werner Baer and Nathaniel Leff and political scientist Ronald Schneider also appeared on the scene. Their methods and research topics were quite traditional, but their methodological seriousness in the collection of data and the dexterity with which the U.S. researchers set out in search of original sources deeply impressed their Brazilian academic colleagues, who at that time were in the pioneering phase of establishing social science courses in Brazil's most important universities (in São Paulo and Rio de Janeiro). Consequently, several of their titles quickly became required reference books in Brazilian courses in their respective disciplines. This was also true of the French "*brésiliennistes*" (who, of course, did not use this term), who had participated in the creation of the Universidade de São Paulo.

At this juncture, amid an exacerbated hegemonic competition between the United States and the Soviet Union, which had just launched *Sputnik*, defiantly challenging U.S. supremacy in the space race, there arose the accidental element of the Cuban Revolution, which undoubtedly was to become the great stimulus for the development of Latin American studies in the United States in the second half of the twentieth century. Many Latin Americanists have proposed, tongue in cheek, to erect a statue to Fidel Castro, since his initiatives, immediately identified with the cause of world socialism, caused the U.S. government to finance a variety of programs designed for the "prevention and cure" of the ills of Latin America. In the political and diplomatic fields, examples of these initiatives would include the Peace Corps (not restricted to the hemisphere) and the Inter-American Development Bank, a regional development-financing institution (first proposed decades before). These initiatives, in fact, had been proposed earlier by countries like Brazil and Chile. Brazil had proposed an "Operation Pan America" in 1958. Later, there was also the Alliance for Progress, with the aim of financing social projects, which was a direct result of the combined Cuban-Soviet threat in terms of development models. In that regard, it is noteworthy that the developmental and industrial efforts of the United Nations Economic Commission for Latin America (ECLA), which until 1964 was run by the Argentine economist Raúl Prebisch, emphasized to some extent the role of the state and the virtues of centrally guided planning and a directed allocation of foreign investments. In education, the U.S. government began expanded financing of Latin American studies programs in various universities, the most immediate consequence of which was a stimulus for the study of Spanish and Portuguese and the awarding of a significant number of fellowships for research in Latin America. In the private sector, efforts like those of the Ford Foundation, aimed at financing graduate studies in the social sciences, complemented those already in place, whether from the government (the Fulbright and Fulbright-Hays programs, for example) or from other private institutions (Rockefeller Foundation).

The figure of the Brazilianist as a social scientist—that is, the figure of the professional researcher who is primarily focused on the study of Brazil-related topics and is so identified by the Brazilian academic community—was born during the intense period of social ferment that corresponded with the end of the Kubitschek government and the series of political-military crises of the Quadros-Goulart governments. This was true even if the individual did not have to teach his students specialized courses on Brazil as part of a regular degree program in his own institution. The production of original works on Brazil from this time forward, in the form of theses and dissertations, was always more voluminous than the titles actually published for the general public, whether in English by U.S. university presses or in Portuguese versions distributed by publishing houses in Brazil. It is also noteworthy, especially in the period from the end of the Second World War to the mid-1960s, that the Brazilianist "species" was never quite purebred, since a number of Latin Americanists who were important researchers on Brazilian topics should not be overlooked, as is illustrated by the case of Robert Alexander, who always included chapters or substantive analyses on Brazil in his many books on political leaders and parties, as well as on the Communist and labor movements in Latin America (see his books of 1957, 1962, and 1965, among other titles).

THE RISE OF THE BRAZILIANIST IN THE AUTHORITARIAN PERIOD

Interest in Brazil grew exponentially in the United States during the transition from the Eisenhower to the Kennedy administrations. This was manifested both in the many new candidates for university specializations aimed at research on Brazilian topics and in the search for new sources of information in Brazil. This period was marked by attempts to overcome the frequent misunderstandings between the previous Republican administrations and Latin American governments. Symptomatic of these problems was the disastrous visit by Vice President Richard Nixon to South America, which was followed by President Kubitschek's proposal of "Operation Pan America," which in 1960 would lead to the creation of the Inter-American Development Bank. This period was also marked by a fragmentation of the "monopoly" of the old-line U.S. Latin Americanists such as John J. Johnson, a specialist in military issues, and the previously cited Robert Alexander, among others. Their analytical generalizations did not allow for inclusion of subregional situations and national characteristics or differences. This does not mean that Latin American studies were neglected in U.S. universities. On the contrary, in fact, research centers multiplied and previously existing centers expanded. It also does not mean that regional specialists no longer published compendiums covering all the countries to the south of the Rio Grande, but nevertheless a recognition emerged that continental uniformity (until then, under the stereotype of the sombrero and the despotic caudillo) concealed specific situations that needed to be studied.

In one trend, that of subregional specialization in individual countries, there was a new and more vigorous wave of "explorers" of the new research terrain, which would motivate the publication of guides or research manuals designed to serve as guidebooks for the new specialized studies. In this camp were the books by Harry Hutchinson (*Field Guide to Brazil*, 1960) and William Jackson (*Library Guide for Brazilian Studies*, 1964), as well as the compilation, directed and edited by Robert Levine, of the first research guide to identify the characteristics of the Brazilian "laboratory": *Brazil: Field Research Guide in the Social Sciences* (1966).

Another trend was the intensification of translation and publication in the United States of representative titles by Brazilian social scientists. Sociologist Gilberto Freyre, who had visited U.S. universities since the 1910s, was one of those who benefited most from this growth in academic demand and university curiosity about everything Brazilian. Indeed, in addition to the publication of his *Masters and Slaves* soon after the end of the war (an immediate classic), his defense of the Brazilian racial model, *New World in the Tropics: The Culture of Modern Brazil,* was published in 1959, followed by *The Mansions and the Shanties,* his "urban" follow-up to *Masters and Slaves,* in 1963. Freyre's racial theories had a major impact on the debate in the United States about slavery in the Americas, but were later challenged by a new generation of scholars in both Brazil and the United States.

In the years immediately preceding and following the military intervention that ended the cycle of elected Brazilian governments since 1945, several other Brazilian researchers were translated and published by different university presses or commercial publishing houses in the United States. In fact, between 1963 and 1967 the following important Brazilian academic works were published in English: Celso Furtado, *The Economic Growth of Brazil,* and Pandiá Calógeras, *A History of Brazil* (both in 1963); Vianna Moog, *Bandeirantes and Pioneers,* and Cruz Costa, *A History of Ideas in Brazil* (in 1964); Celso Furtado, again, in 1965 (*Diagnosis of the Brazilian Crisis*), along with José Honório Rodrigues, *Brazil and Africa* (1965) and *The Brazilians* in 1967; Josué de Castro became internationally influential with the publication of *Death in the Northeast* in 1966. Historical studies with completely different methodological approaches appeared such as José Maria Bello's traditional *A History of Modern Brazil, 1889–1964* (1966), and Caio Prado Jr.'s Marxist treatise, *The Colonial Background of Modern Brazil* (1967).

It was in the context of the modernizing authoritarian regime established by the military in 1964 that the Brazilianist was born, a figure that was nothing more than an invention of Brazilians themselves, according to Robert Levine, one of the most respected and influential members of this small community of scholars. This community, at first a restricted one, would dominate the panorama of research on Brazil in the United States for the three decades that followed. The best-known representative of this small tribe of researchers, in both countries, is probably Skidmore, author of *Politics in Brazil, 1930–1964* (1967). The book's subtitle, *An Experiment in Democracy,* in accordance with the times, expressed a certain skepticism regarding the possibilities of political stability and representative democracy in Brazil. Soon translated and published in Brazil, first by the small publishing house Editora Saga in 1969, *Brasil: de Getúlio Vargas a Castelo Branco, 1930–1964* became what is certainly the most frequently republished book by a Brazilianist (now issued by Paz e Terra) ever to appear. Skidmore's success, which rapidly converted him into an unofficial representative of U.S. Brazilianists (Massi and Pontes, 1992), should not obscure the work of the previous generation of scholars. Some of Skidmore's predecessors, for example, were Charles Wagley, whom I have already mentioned; the "biographer" of São Paulo, Richard Morse; and Stanley Stein, whose study on the coffee economy in *Vassouras* (1957) has been in print in Brazil since 1961.

Some Brazilianists have attempted to describe Brazilian history as a whole, as was done by Skidmore himself in his two books on Brazilian political history (the second volume, *The Politics of Military Rule in Brazil, 1964–85,* published in 1988, describes the years of the military regime). Other important overviews are Bradford Burns's *A History of Brazil* (1970), and Richard Graham's *A Century of Brazilian History Since 1865* (1969). Many scholars during the 1960s and 1970s, however, preferred to create a division of labor by selecting a limited time period or geographic region for their study. In some cases, these efforts were effectively coordinated, such as a series of regional studies conducted by Joseph Love (*Rio Grande do Sul and Brazilian Regionalism, 1882–1930* [1971]; *São Paulo and the Brazilian Federation, 1889–1937* [1980]); John Wirth (*Minas Gerais in the Brazilian Federation, 1889–1937* [1977]); and Levine (*Pernambuco in the Brazilian Federation, 1889–1937* [1978]). In other cases, the studies were undertaken independently, as in the projects of Warren Dean (*The Industrialization of São Paulo, 1880–1945* [1969]) and Eul-Soo Pang (*Bahia in the First Brazilian Republic* [1978]).

A focus on policies or economic decision-making processes, at times combined with regional issues, also received the attention of researchers in projects conducted at this time. Representative examples of this approach are studies by John Wirth (*The Politics of Brazilian Development, 1930–1954* [1970]), Warren Dean (*Brazil and the Struggle for Rubber* [1987]), and Peter Eisenberg (*The Sugar Industry in Pernambuco* [1974]).

From the end of the 1960s to the mid-1970s, Brazil experienced one of the most dramatic periods of its political history, with many Brazilian researchers condemned to exile or intimidated by the machinery of repression. During this period, Brazilian studies in the United States experienced what was probably its time of greatest prestige and unquestioned academic acceptance, either because of the manner in which the political problems of the time were addressed or because of its research into the origins of the contemporary state of affairs. Several authors, such as Ronald Schneider (*The Political System in Brazil* [1971]) and Alfred Stepan (*The Military in Politics* [1971]), analyzed the authoritarian regime and the manner in which it operated. Stepan also coordinated another frequently cited volume on the subject during those years of military rule: *Authoritarian Brazil* (1973). In other cases, the analytical scalpel exposed civil society itself, as in Philippe Schmitter's study of interest groups from a historical perspective, *Interest Conflict and Political Change in Brazil* (1971), or another study by Schneider, *Brazil: Foreign Policy of a Future World Power* (1976).

Other works focused more narrowly on social or religious groups, such as Ralph Della Cava's works on popular religion in the Northeast (*Miracle at Joaseiro* [1977]) and Skidmore's study on the "whitening" initiative conducted by the Brazilian elites in the postabolition period, *Black into White* (1974). In a more traditional style of political history, it is indispensable to mention the substantial work of John W. F. Dulles, who combined archival research with personal testimonies of important figures in recent Brazilian history to produce an impressive series of titles on the country's political history and its labor and Communist movements.

The modernizing-repressive period of the military regimes in the 1970s also brought the academic equivalent of the import-substitution model that was then being applied in Brazil's industrial sector, in the form of expanded funding provided to Brazil's universities and research laboratories in order to increase the number of degrees granted and make new research projects possible. Greatly increased funding for professional training led to an exponential growth of fellowships granted for graduate degree programs abroad. The gradual return of these researchers led to a proportionate expansion in the volume of rigorous studies published in specialized academic journals, thus increasing the quality and professionalism of the social sciences in Brazil. Universities and other institutions of higher learning in the United States and Europe hosted a significant number of these graduate students, candidates for both masters and doctoral degrees. There were some concentrations in certain disciplines, since these institutions offered obvious comparative advantages in the sciences and economics. In fact, a significant proportion of the higher echelons of private and public entities in Brazil in recent years, as well as among senior officials of the Brazilian federal government, have had diplomas from—and doctoral dissertations that were defended at—some of the best U.S. universities. Among these have been ministers responsible for the economy and presidents of the Central Bank.

In the other direction, that of "exporting" ideas and theories from Brazil to the United States, the most conspicuous and noteworthy example has perhaps been dependency theory, an important part of the academic work of Fernando Henrique Cardoso. This theory led to a critical trend in U.S. sociological theory regarding the problems of developing countries, particularly in Latin America. Even though its principal proponent has several times added qualifications to his understanding of the concept of "dependency," this notion was so well accepted by U.S. scholars that the author felt compelled to write a critique of the "consumption of dependency theory in the United States" (Cardoso, 1977). The community of "consumers" became quite divided about dependency's merits and intrinsic limitations, attributing to the "theory" greater qualities and greater analytical importance than it actually had in its country of origin.

Once the gestation and growth of the social sciences in Brazil was completed, by the early 1980s, that is, once "import substitution" had been achieved in the areas of the social sciences, the role of the Brazilianists was no longer seen through the magnifying glass of their technical superiority and greater access to funding for research in primary sources. This does not mean that Brazilian social sciences have ended their journey toward the internationalization of procedures and research standards but rather that their "dependence" on former standards and "ideal" norms established by the Brazilianists during the formative period no longer seemed to be crucially important to Brazilian researchers. As Brazil advanced through the 1980s in step with the processes of political democratization and social mobilization, which themselves were the subjects of significant studies by Brazilianists, such as Stepan (1989), a new generation of Brazilianists emerged. This generation has different concerns and new research topics, less concerned with broad societal studies and more focused on groups, and more sector specific, with a wide variety of research topics as diverse as Brazilian and U.S. societies.

In some ways, the 1980s can be seen as a transitional period between the pioneers of "traditional" Brazilian studies from the Cold War era and the new academic scholars focused on the theoretical refinement of the social sciences and humanities. During this period the "large" comprehensive explanations about Brazilian society and politics were being replaced by research more focused on specific topics. The correlation with topics and trends found in the social sciences in Brazil is also quite noteworthy. The generation of great Brazilian academic scholars and influential Brazilian intellectuals of the 1950s and 1960s—who began their intellectual production in the 1930s and 1940s and were not content to merely explain or interpret Brazil, but were equally interested in transforming the country— was made up of the same thinkers who influenced the work of Brazilianists and other foreign scholars, figures such as Gilberto Freyre, Sérgio Buarque de Holanda, Caio Prado Jr., Celso Furtado, Florestan Fernandes, and others. In contrast, the new generation of Brazilianists that began to form in the 1980s did not find many Brazilian interlocutors who were both public figures and intellectuals but instead found myriad Brazilian academic scholars whose research is now focused on narrower topics.

THE RECENT DIVERSIFICATION AND FRAGMENTATION OF BRAZILIAN STUDIES
Is It the End of the Road for Brazilianists?

The history of academic Brazilian studies in the United States reveals a series of periods of concentration on topics and interests in the areas of the humanities and social sciences. The pioneers of the 1950s and 1960s, especially in history and political science, flourished during a period when the social sciences in Brazil were still "accumulating capital" in terms of their methodological sophistication. The new generation of Brazilianists was somewhat more concerned with topics in specific sectors, rather than broad historical interpretations or comprehensive essays about Brazilian society, as had been the case during the earlier years of exploring the research terrain. Institutionally, support for research continued to be dominated by a healthy "anarchy" and the dynamics of attracting funds through centers for Latin American studies at the major U.S. universities, which maintained—and continue to maintain—direct contacts with Brazilian universities, research centers, and professors, stimulating a continuous flow of academics in both directions. Nevertheless, persistent deficiencies in Portuguese-language programs at U.S. universities, as well as the naturally stronger ties with Spanish-speaking countries geographically closer to the United States, continued to constitute important obstacles to a greater expansion of Brazilian studies programs in the centers for Latin American studies at U.S. universities.

In terms of academic disciplines, history has always been the preferred field for many of the U.S. academics whose research was focused on Brazil, accounting for roughly a third of all such researchers in the humanities and social sciences. Economists have played an equally prominent role in terms of the "Brazilianist" output, but they have always played a more narrowly defined role in academic Brazilian studies, having generally been more reluctant to participate in meetings of specialized (yet interdisciplinary) associations, such as the Latin American Studies Association and the Brazilian Studies Association. Over the years, Brazilian studies in the United States has gone through a process of diversification and enrichment of research topics. The emergence of new areas of research that were previously neglected has been closely correlated with general trends and developments among U.S. academics (i.e., gender, ethnic studies, minority groups, human rights, etc.). A survey of published works in the 1980s and 1990s would show several notable names that appear repeatedly, as well as the emergence of a new generation of Brazilianists, whose studies are more narrowly focused on a wide range of new topics.

In the field of history, the pioneering generation of the 1960s continued to publish prolifically in the decades that followed. Scholars such as Stanley Hilton (*Hitler's Secret War in South America* [1981] and *Brazil and the Soviet Challenge* [1991]); A. J. R. Russell-Wood (*The Black Man in Slavery and Freedom in Colonial Brazil* [1982]); Robert Conrad (*Children of God's Fire* [1983]); Stuart Schwartz (*Sugar Plantations in the Formation of Brazilian Society* [1985]); Neill Macaulay (*Dom Pedro* [1986]); Warren Dean (*Brazil and the Struggle for Rubber* [1987] and *With Broadax and Firebrand* [1995]); Tom Skidmore (*The Politics of Military Rule in Brazil* [1988] and *Brazil* [1999]); Bob Levine (*Vale of Tears* [1992] and *Brazil* [1999]); and John W. F. Dulles (*Brazilian Communism, 1935–1945* [1983] and his biographies of Castelo Branco [1978, 1980] and Carlos Lacerda [1991]) are excellent examples of Brazilianists from the 1960s generation who remained active in publishing into the 1990s.

Several new and prominent scholars (although not all of them young authors) also appeared in the field of history, beginning in the 1980s, such as Jeffrey Needell (*A Tropical Belle Epoque* [1987]); Steven Topik (*The Political Economy of the Brazilian State* [1987] and *Trade and Gunboats* [1996]); Roderick Barman (*Brazil: The Forging of a Nation* [1988] and *Citizen Emperor* [1999]); Gerald Haines (*The Americanization of Brazil* [1989]); Marshall C. Eakin (*British Enterprise in Brazil* [1989], *Brazil* [1997], and *Tropical Capitalism* [2001]); Ruth Leacock (*Requiem for Revolution* [1990]); Joseph Smith (*Unequal Giants* [1991]); Sandra Lauderdale Graham (*House and Street* [1988]); Thomas Holloway (*Policing Rio de Janeiro* [1993]); Eugene Ridings (*Business Interest Groups in Nineteenth-Century Brazil* [1994]); Jeffrey Lesser (*Welcoming the Undesirables* [1995] and *Negotiating National Identity* [1999]); Barbara Weinstein (*The Amazon Rubber Boom* [1983] and *For Social Peace in Brazil* [1996]); Kim Butler (*Freedoms Given, Freedoms Won* [1998]); Robin Anderson (*Colonization As Exploitation in the Amazon Rain Forest, 1758–1911* [1999]); and William Summerhill (*Order Against Progress* [2003]).

In history, sociology, and political science, the pattern has been the continued productivity of several experienced scholars and analysts of Brazilian politics and society, as well as the emergence of new scholars guided by concerns and topics different from those of their predecessors of the 1960s. The first group includes June Hahner, Laura Randall, Peter McDonough, Ronald Chilcote, Richard Graham, Joseph Page, and Ronald Schneider, among others, who are well-known observers of Brazilian society. The second group includes Reid Andrews (who updated a study by Florestan Fernandes in *Blacks and Whites in São Paulo, 1888–1988* [1991]), David Plank, Michael Hanchard, James Green, and David Foster, among many other prominent new scholars of the social sciences and humanities in the United States with a special interest in Brazil.

During this recent period, some of the topics studied, time periods selected, and analytical methodologies used have become common among both Brazilian and U.S. academics, demonstrating an intellectual osmosis that is more than welcome after several years of discrepancies between the analytical approaches used in Brazil and the United States. Perhaps "dependency theory" has played a role in this interactive process, given that many among the new generation of social scientists in the United States were attracted by the not-so-subtle charm of this conceptually elegant analytical framework, which has strong political credentials. In fact, the dialogue between the communities of researchers in Brazil and the United States intensified during the 1980s and 1990s. Because of the positive results achieved through programs financed since the mid-1990s by private organizations, such as the Ford Foundation, as well as the expansion of the system of Brazilian public-sector scholarships for graduate study, the traditional French (and European) domination of the social sciences in Brazil began to be overcome and superseded, at least in part, by a new excellence in the humanities and social sciences in the United States.

Nevertheless, the institutional ties between universities in the United States and Brazil have been hindered because the United States does not have centralized entities that support and sponsor research, similar to Brazil's Council for Advanced Professional Training and National Council for Scientific and Technological Development, or similar to the ministries of education in most European countries, which are based on the same government-centered tradition as Brazil's. The many Brazilian candidates for graduate studies in the United States always assume the roles of "individual clients" of the U.S. university establishment, which makes it more difficult to conceptualize and establish joint academic programs between corresponding entities in both countries, along the lines of what has been done between Brazil and Europe, under the auspices of joint bilateral education commissions or partnerships created by interested universities (as has been done with Germany and France, for example). Even though the United States has received the largest number of Brazilian scholarship recipients outside Brazil, generally on an individual basis, it is possible that a larger number of bilateral projects have been developed between Brazilian and European universities. In any case, a survey of the relevant data from the Brazilian Ministry of Education and Culture (i.e., scholarships granted for studies abroad, by country and by category) would be able to elucidate some of the characteristics of educational cooperation between these regions, noting concentrations in academic subject areas and how these have evolved over time, as well as a comparative examination of increases and decreases over the years and other interesting details.

One noteworthy detail is that many of the top economic policy makers in the Brazilian government since the mid-1960s have obtained their graduate degrees or done postgraduate research in economics at major U.S. universities, which for years have been the preferred choice and favorite destination for Brazilian economists who pursue graduate studies. A survey of the locations where Brazilian government ministers and senior policy makers in the areas of economics, technology, and science received their master's and doctoral degrees would easily confirm this assertion, and the same would also probably be true for high-level private-sector managers.

CONCLUSION
Brazilian Studies in the United States Reaches Maturity

Obviously, a critical assessment of Brazilian studies in the United States cannot be based solely on published books, as I have done in this essay. In order to be balanced and comprehensive, such an assessment would need to also address academic instruction and research at universities and think tanks, the output of which can be measured mainly through articles published in specialized journals and in graduate theses and dissertations, which is beyond the scope of this overview. The panorama described here, however, has made it possible to follow the development of the principal areas of research and identify the most important works published since 1945, describing some analytical continuities while also noting a few turning points of discontinuity and transformation.

In fact, unlike the studies of other countries (especially France, for example), the field of Brazilian studies in the United States did not really begin to take shape until after the Second World War. In its initial period, Brazilian studies merely seemed to reproduce the pattern that had already been established by previous generations of those who studied the Americas, which involved a simple presentation and systematic description of the noteworthy and "exotic" aspects of the country in question, describing its history, natural characteristics, and people to foreign readers. What was different about studies done by the new breed of U.S.-based Brazilianists, especially after the expansion of foreign culture and language studies in the United States, facilitated by the National Defense Education Act of 1958, was a systematic concern with explaining Brazil on its own terms, even if from the implicitly comparative perspective of a Western, or "modern," template. After 1960, understanding "politics" in Brazil became the main focus of these scholars, which turned them into points of reference for domestic debates about political and social institutions, economic problems, authoritarian phenomena, the roles of the military, the elite, and religious groups. In the end, this discussion turned many of these scholars into participants in the process of the emergence and affirmation of the social sciences in Brazil.

Obviously, Brazil was not the only country studied in this way, given that the imperatives of the Cold War and pressure from the Cuban Revolution led to the use of U.S. university researchers to project "hegemonic interests" into Latin America and other continents. Nevertheless, the interactions between these U.S.-based Brazilianists and Brazilian universities and publishing houses during a time of restrictions on political freedoms and the restructuring of Brazil's national research system had the effect of giving these scholars a unique status and even transforming them into symbolic figures in the world of academia. The "import substitution" model that was applied to the social sciences in Brazil in the 1970s and 1980s—with financial support from U.S.-based foundations—had the effect of making Brazilianists more numerous, although without diminishing any of the prestige they continued to enjoy in academia and among the well-educated public in general. In recent years, we have finally seen a growing diversification of Brazilian studies in the United States, with the introduction of greater specialization in narrower subject areas, with researchers focusing on specific sectors. This pattern seems to closely mirror the ambiguities found in the U.S. university establishment itself, rather than a concern with systematic descriptions, as was characteristic of the "Fidel-inspired" generation of Brazilianists who wanted to analyze Brazil's role as a player on the world stage.

Moreover, there are hardly any—if any—Brazilian universities that maintain a research institute or curriculum devoted to studying the United States (or even international relations and foreign policy, in general). The increasingly significant role played by the Brazilian economy in international economics—as well as the continued expansion of globalization and regional integration—may yet have an effect on the global economic landscape that contributes to the establishment of new ties and the creation of better-structured programs of cooperation between the academic institutions of the two countries.

In conclusion, it is worth noting that the vast scientific and economic infrastructure of the United States, which has made it the world's "universal brain-drain pump," has similarly served as a powerful brain-drain pump for several generations of Brazilian scientists (and other foreigners, in general), attracting a significant number of Brazilian "brains" into the U.S. scientific establishment, as well as into the activities of U.S.-based state-of-the-art private enterprises focused on technological research. In several areas beyond the scope of this essay, such as medicine and high technology, it is quite likely that Brazil will continue to supply highly skilled labor to many private U.S.-based companies, research institutions, and university hospitals in the United States on a scale that has never been suitably documented. In any event, the traditional methods used in awarding grants from Brazilian institutions that sponsor research have had to be revised precisely because of the troubling phenomenon of Brazilian financing that was providing the support for state-of-the-art research conducted in the United States.

This does not appear to be happening in the social sciences and humanities, because of the specific ways in which university professionals enter the workplace in their respective countries. Contemporary Brazilianists, in any event, no longer enjoy the same unique status in the landscape of Brazilian social sciences as was conferred upon their predecessors in the 1960s and 1970s. The social sciences in Brazil finally seem to have shaken off their former chains of subservience to foreign "masters" and methodological imports. Intellectual relationships, or, more accurately, interactions, have in fact become much more equitable, and the typical U.S.-born Brazilianist—especially when seen as one who merely "accumulated capital" during the period when the social sciences were still being established in Brazil—may now have disappeared. The study of Brazil still provides a livelihood for Brazilianists in an inconspicuous corner of the social sciences in the United States and appears to have a bright and promising future. So, long live the scholarly study of Brazil by Brazilianists!

References

Alexander, Robert J. 1957. *Communism in Latin America.* New Brunswick, N.J.: Rutgers University Press.

———. 1962. *Labor Relations in Argentina, Brazil, and Chile.* New York: McGraw-Hill.

———. 1965. *Latin American Politics and Government.* New York: Harper and Row.

Anderson, Robin L. 1999. *Colonization as Exploitation in the Amazon Rain Forest, 1758–1911.* Gainesville: University Press of Florida.

Andrews, George Reid. 1991. *Blacks and Whites in São Paulo, 1888–1988.* Madison: University of Wisconsin Press.

Barman, Roderick J. 1988. *Brazil: The Forging of a Nation, 1798–1852.* Stanford, Calif.: Stanford University Press.

———. 1999. *Citizen Emperor: Pedro II and the Making of Brazil, 1825–1891.* Stanford, Calif.: Stanford University Press.

Bello, José Maria. 1966. *A History of Modern Brazil, 1889–1964.* Trans. James Taylor, with a new concluding chapter by Rollie E. Poppino. Stanford, Calif.: Stanford University Press.

Burns, E. Bradford. 1970. *A History of Brazil.* New York: Columbia University Press.

Butler, Kim D. 1998. *Freedoms Given, Freedoms Won: Afro-Brazilians in Post-Abolition São Paulo and Salvador.* New Brunswick, N.J.: Rutgers University Press.

Calógeras, João Pandiá. 1963. *A History of Brazil.* Trans. Percy Alva Martin. New York: Russell and Russell. Original edition: *Formação histórica do Brasil.* Rio de Janeiro: P. de Mello, 1930.

Cardoso, Fernando Henrique. 1977. "The Consumption of Dependency Theory in the United States." *Latin American Research Review* 3, no. 12: 7–24.

Castro, Josué de. 1966. *Death in Northeast*. New York: Random House. Original edition: *Sete palmos de terra e um caixão; ensaio sôbre o Nordeste, área explosiva*. São Paulo: Editora Brasiliense, 1965.

Conrad, Robert Edgar, comp. 1983. *Children of God's Fire: A Documentary History of Black Slavery in Brazil*. Princeton, N.J.: Princeton University Press.

Costa, Hipólito José da. 1955. *Diário de minha viagem para Filadélfia, 1798–1799*. Rio de Janeiro: Publicações da Academia Brasileira.

Cruz Costa, João. 1964. *A History of Ideas in Brazil: The Development of Philosophy in Brazil and the Evolution of National History*. Trans. Suzette Macedo. Berkeley: University of California Press.

Cunha, Euclides da. 1945. *Rebellion in the Backlands*. Trans. Samuel Putnam. Chicago: Chicago University Press.

Dean, Warren. 1969. *The Industrialization of São Paulo, 1880–1945*. Austin: University of Texas Press. Brazilian edition: *A Industrialização de São Paulo, 1880–1945*. São Paulo: Difel, 1971.

———. 1987. *Brazil and the Struggle for Rubber: A Study in Environmental History*. Cambridge: Cambridge University Press.

———. 1995. *With Broadax and Firebrand: The Destruction of the Brazilian Atlantic Forest*. Berkeley: University of California Press. Brazilian edition: *A Ferro e fogo: a destruição da floresta atlântica*. São Paulo: Companhia das Letras, 1997.

Della Cava, Ralph. 1970. *Miracle at Joaseiro*. New York: Columbia University Press. Brazilian edition: *Milagre em Joaseiro*. Rio de Janeiro: Paz e Terra, 1977.

Dulles, John W. F. 1978. *President Castello Branco: The Making of a Brazilian President*. College Station: Texas A&M University Press. Brazilian edition: *Castelo Branco: o caminho para a presidência*. Trans. R. Magalhães Jr. Rio de Janeiro: Editora José Olympio, 1979.

———. 1980. *President Castello Branco: A Brazilian Reformer*. College Station: Texas A&M University Press. Brazilian edition: *Castelo Branco, o presidente reformador*. Trans. Heitor A. Herrera. Brasília: Editora da UnB, 1983.

———. 1983. *Brazilian Communism, 1935–1945: Repression During World Upheaval*. Austin: University of Texas Press. Brazilian edition: *O Comunismo brasileiro, 1939–1945: repressão em meio ao cataclismo mundial*. Trans. Raul de Sá Barbosa. Rio de Janeiro: Nova Fronteira, 1985.

———. 1991. *Carlos Lacerda, Brazilian Crusader*. College Station: Texas A&M University Press. Brazilian edition: *Carlos Lacerda: vida de um lutador*. Trans. Vanda Mena Barreto de Andrade. Rio de Janeiro: Nova Fronteira, 1992.

———. 1996. *Carlos Lacerda, Brazilian Crusader: The Years 1960–1977*. College Station: Texas A&M University Press.

Eakin, Marshall C. 1989. *British Enterprise in Brazil: The St. John d'el Rey Mining Company and the Morro Velho Gold Mine, 1830–1960*. Durham, N.C.: Duke University Press.

———. 1997. *Brazil: The Once and Future Country*. New York: St. Martin's.

———. 2001. *Tropical Capitalism: The Industrialization of Belo Horizonte, Brazil.* New York: Palgrave.

Eisenberg, Peter. 1974. *The Sugar Industry in Pernambuco: Modernization Without Change, 1840–1910.* Berkeley: University of California Press. Brazilian edition: *Modernização sem mudança: a indústria açucareira em Pernambuco, 1840–1910*, Rio de Janeiro: Paz e Terra, 1977.

Freyre, Gilberto. 1945. *Brazil: An Interpretation.* New York: Alfred A. Knopf.

———. 1946. *The Masters and the Slaves: A Study in the Development of the Brazilian Society.* Trans. Samuel Putnam. New York. Alfred A. Knopf. Original edition: *Casa-grande e senzala.* Rio de Janeiro: J. Olympio, 1933.

———. 1959. *New World in the Tropics: The Culture of Modern Brazil.* New York: Alfred A. Knopf.

———. 1963. *The Mansion and the Shanties.* Trans. Harriet de Onís. New York: Alfred A. Knopf. Original edition: *Sobrados e mocambos.* Rio de Janeiro: J. Olympio, 1946.

Furtado, Celso. 1963. *The Economic Growth of Brazil: A Survey from Colonial to Modern Times.* Berkeley: University of California Press. Original edition: *Formação econômica do Brasil.* São Paulo: Companhia Editora Nacional, 1959.

———. 1965. *Diagnosis of the Brazilian Crisis.* Berkeley: University of California Press.

Graham, Richard. 1969. *A Century of Brazilian History Since 1865.* New York: Borzoi Books.

Graham, Sandra Lauderdale. 1988. *House and Street: The Domestic World of Servants and Masters in Nineteenth-Century Rio de Janeiro.* Cambridge: Cambridge University Press.

Haines, Gerald K. 1989. *The Americanization of Brazil: A Study of U.S. Cold War Diplomacy in the Third World, 1945–1954.* Wilmington, Del.: Scholarly Resource Books.

Herndon, William Lewis. 2000. *Exploration of the Valley of the Amazon, 1851–1852.* Edited and with a forward by Gary Kindir. New York: Grove Press. Original edition: Washington, D.C., 1854.

Hilton, Stanley E. 1981. *Hitler's Secret War in South America.* Baton Rouge: Louisiana State University Press. Brazilian edition: *A Guerra secreta de Hitler no Brasil: a espionagem alemã e a contra-espionagem aliada no Brasil, 1939–1945.* Rio de Janeiro: Nova Fronteira, 1983.

———. 1991. *Brazil and the Soviet Challenge, 1917–1947.* Austin: University of Texas Press.

Holloway, Thomas H. 1993. *Policing Rio de Janeiro: Repression and Resistance in a 19th-Century City.* Stanford, Calif.: Stanford University Press.

Hutchinson, Harry W. 1960. *Field Guide to Brazil.* Washington, D.C.: National Research Council.

Iggers, Georg G, and Harold T. Parker, eds. 1979. *International Handbook of Historical Studies.* Westport, CT: Greenwood Press.

Jackson, William Vernon. 1964. *Library Guide for Brazilian Studies.* Pittsburgh: University of Pittsburgh Book Center.

James, Preston E. 1946. *Brazil.* New York: Odyssey Press.

Joint Brazil–United States Economic Development Commission. 1954. *The Development of Brazil.* Washington: Institute of Inter-American Affairs.

Leacock, Ruth. 1990. *Requiem for Revolution: The United States and Brazil, 1961–1969.* Kent, Ohio: Kent State University Press.

Lesser, Jeffrey. 1995. *Welcoming the Undesirables: Brazil and the Jewish Question.* Berkeley: University of California Press. Brazilian edition: *O Brasil e a questão judaica: imigração, diplomacia e preconceito.* Rio de Janeiro: Imago, 1995.

———. 1999. *Negotiating National Identity: Immigrants, Minorities, and the Struggle for Ethnicity in Brazil.* Durham, N.C.: Duke University Press.

Levine, Robert M. 1978. *Pernambuco in the Brazilian Federation, 1889–1937.* Stanford, Calif.: Stanford University Press. Brazilian edition: *A Velha usina: Pernambuco na federação brasileira, 1889–1937.* Rio de Janeiro: Civilização Brasileira, 1980.

———. 1992. *Vale of Tears: Revisiting the Canudos Massacre in Northeastern Brazil, 1893–1897.* Berkeley: University of California Press.

———. 1999. *Brazil: A History.* Westport, Conn.: Greenwood.

———, ed. 1966. *Brazil: Field Research Guide in the Social Sciences.* New York: Columbia University Press, Institute of Latin American Studies.

Love, Joseph. 1971. *Rio Grande do Sul and Brazilian Regionalism, 1882–1930.* Stanford, Calif.: Stanford University Press. Brazilian edition: *O Regionalismo gaúcho e as origens da Revolução de 1930.* São Paulo: Perspectiva, 1975.

———. 1980. *São Paulo and the Brazilian Federation, 1889–1937.* Stanford, Calif.: Stanford University Press. Brazilian edition: *A Locomotiva: São Paulo na federação brasileira, 1889–1937.* Rio de Janeiro: Paz e Terra, 1982.

Macaulay, Neill. 1986. *Dom Pedro: The Struggle for Liberty in Brazil and Portugal, 1798–1834.* Durham, N.C.: Duke University Press.

Massi, Fernanda Peixoto, and Heloísa André Pontes (com a colaboração de Maria Cecília Spina Forjaz). *Guia biobibliográfico dos Brasilianistas: obras e autores editados no Brasil entre 1930 e 1988.* São Paulo: Editora Sumaré–FAPESP, 1992.

Moog, Clodomiro Vianna. 1964. *Bandeirantes and Pioneers.* Trans. L. Barret. New York: Braziller. Original edition: *Bandeirantes e pioneiros: paralelo entre duas culturas.* Porto Alegre: Livraria O Globo, 1954.

Needell, Jeffrey D. 1987. *A Tropical Belle Epoque: Elite Culture and Society in Turn-of-the-Century Rio de Janeiro.* Cambridge: Cambridge University Press.

Normano, João Frederico. 1931. *The Struggle for South America, Economy and Ideology.* Boston and New York: Houghton Mifflin.

———. 1935. *Brazil, A Study of Economic Types.* Chapel Hill: University of North Carolina Press. Brazilian edition: *Evolução econômica do Brasil.* São Paulo: Companhia Editora Nacional, Brasiliana, 1939.

Oliveira Lima, Manuel de. 1899. *Nos Estados Unidos: impressões sociaes e políticas.* Leipzig: Brockaus.

————. 1914. *The Evolution of Brazil Compared with That of Spain and Anglo-Saxon America*. Edited with introduction and notes by Percy Alvin Martin. Stanford, Calif.: Stanford University Press. Brazilian edition: *América latina e América inglesa: a evolução brasileira comparada com a Hispano-Americana e com a Anglo-Americana*. Rio de Janeiro: Garnier, n.d.

Pang, Eul-Soo. 1979. *Bahia in the First Brazilian Republic: Coronelismo and Oligarchies, 1889–1934*. Gainesville: University Presses of Florida. Brazilian edition: *Coronelismo e oligarquia (1889–1934): a Bahia na Primeira República brasileira*. Rio de Janeiro: Civilização Brasileira, 1979.

Pierson, Donald. 1945. *Survey of the Literature on Brazil of Sociological Significance Published up to 1940*. Cambridge, Mass.: Harvard University Press.

Prado, Caio, Jr. 1967. *The Colonial Background of Modern Brazil*. Trans. Suzette Macedo. Berkeley: University of California Press. Original edition: *Formação do Brasil contemporâneo*. Vol. 1, *Colônia*. São Paulo: Livraria Martins, 1942.

Prescott, William H. 1843. *History of the Conquest of Mexico*. 3 vols. New York: Harper and Brothers.

Ridings, Eugene. 1994. *Business Interest Groups in Nineteenth Century Brazil*. Cambridge: Cambridge University Press.

Rodrigues, José Honório. 1965. *Brazil and Africa*. Berkeley: University of California Press. Original edition: *Brasil e África: outro horizonte*. Rio de Janeiro: Civilização Brasileira, 1961.

————. 1967. *The Brazilians: Their Character and Aspirations*. Trans. Ralph Edward Dimmick. Austin: University of Texas Press. Original edition: *Aspirações nacionais: interpretação histórico-política*. Rio de Janeiro: Civilização Brasileira, 1963.

Russell-Wood, A. J. R. 1982. *The Black Man in Slavery and Freedom in Colonial Brazil*. New York: St. Martin's Press.

Schmitter, Philippe. 1971. *Interest Conflict and Political Change in Brazil*. Stanford, Calif.: Stanford University Press.

Schneider, Ronald. 1971. *The Political System in Brazil: Emergence of a "Modernizing" Authoritarian Regime, 1964–1970*. New York: Columbia University Press.

————. 1976. *Brazil: Foreign Policy of a Future World Power*. Boulder, Colo.: Westview Press.

Schwartz, Stuart. 1985. *Sugar Plantations in the Formation of Brazilian Society: Bahia, 1550–1835*. New York: Cambridge University Press. Brazilian edition: *Segredos internos: engenhos e escravos na sociedade colonial brasileira, 1550–1835*. São Paulo: Companhia das Letras–CNPq, 1988.

Simpson, Lesley Byrd. 1949. "Thirty Years of the *Hispanic American Historical Review*," *Hispanic American Historical Review* 29, no. 2: 188–204.

Skidmore, Thomas E. 1967. *Politics in Brazil, 1930–1964: An Experiment in Democracy*. New York: Oxford University Press. Brazilian editions: *Brasil: de Getúlio Vargas a Castelo Branco, 1930–1964*. Rio de Janeiro: Saga, 1969; 10th ed.: São Paulo: Editora Paz e Terra, 1996.

————. 1974. *Black into White: Race and Nationality in Brazilian Thought*. New York: Oxford University Press. Brazilian edition: *Preto no branco: raça e nacionalidade no pensamento brasileiro*. Rio de Janeiro: Paz e Terra, 1976.

————. 1988. *The Politics of Military Rule in Brazil, 1964–85*. New York: Oxford University Press. 3d Brazilian edition: *Brasil: de Castelo Branco a Tancredo Neves*. Rio de Janeiro: Paz e Terra, 1989.

————. 1999. *Brazil: Five Centuries of Change*. New York: Oxford University Press.

Smith, Joseph. 1991. *Unequal Giants: Diplomatic Relations Between the United States and Brazil, 1889–1930*. Pittsburgh: University of Pittsburgh Press.

Smith, T. Lynn. 1946 (rev. ed. 1963). *Brazil, People and Institutions*. Baton Rouge: Louisiana State University Press. Brazilian edition: *Brasil: povo e instituições*. Trans. José Arthur Rios. Rio de Janeiro: Bloch-AID, 1967.

Southey, Robert. 1817–22. *History of Brazil*. 3 vols. London: Longman, Hurst, Rees, Orme and Brown.

Stein, Stanley. 1957. *Vassouras, A Brazilian Coffee County, 1850–1900*. Cambridge, Mass.: Harvard University Press. Brazilian edition: *Grandeza e decadência do café no Vale do Paraíba. com referência especial ao Município de Vassouras*. São Paulo: Brasiliense, 1961.

Stepan, Alfred. 1971. *The Military in Politics: Changing Patterns in Brazil*. Princeton, N.J.: Princeton University Press. Brazilian edition: *O Militares na política: as mudanças de padrões na vida brasileira*. Rio de Janeiro: Artenova, 1975.

————, ed. 1973. *Authoritarian Brazil: Origins, Policies and Future*. New Haven, Conn.: Yale University Press.

————, ed. 1989. *Democratizing Brazil: Problems of Transition and Consolidation*. New York: Oxford University Press. Brazilian edition: *Democratizando o Brasil*. Rio de Janeiro: Paz e Terra, 1988.

Summerhill, William R., III. 2003. *Order Against Progress: Government, Foreign Investment, and Railroads in Brazil, 1854–1913*. Stanford, Calif.: Stanford University Press.

Topik, Steven. 1987. *The Political Economy of the Brazilian State, 1889–1930*. Austin: University of Texas Press.

————. 1996. *Trade and Gunboats: The United States and Brazil in the Age of Empire*. Stanford, Calif.: Stanford University Press.

Varnhagen, Francisco Adolfo de. 1978. *História geral do Brasil*. 3 vols. São Paulo: Edições Melhoramentos.

Weinstein, Barbara. 1983. *The Amazon Rubber Boom, 1850–1920*. Stanford, Calif.: Stanford University Press. Brazilian edition: *A borracha na Amazonia: expansão e decadência, 1850–1920*. Trans. Lolio Lourenço de Oliveira. São Paulo: Hucitec-EDUSP, 1993.

————. 1996. *For Social Peace in Brazil : Industrialists and the Remaking of the Working Class in São Paulo, 1920–1964*. Chapel Hill: University of North Carolina Press. Brazilian edition: *(Re)formação da classe trabalhadora no Brasil*. São Paulo: Cortez Editora–Universidade São Francisco, 2001.

Wirth, John D. 1970. *The Politics of Brazilian Development, 1930–1954.* Stanford, Calif.: Stanford University Press. Brazilian edition: *A Política de desenvolvimento na era Vargas.* Rio de Janeiro: Editora da FGV, 1973.

———. 1977. *Minas Gerais in the Brazilian Federation, 1889–1937.* Stanford, Calif.: Stanford University Press. Brazilian edition: *O Fiel da balança: Minas Gerais na federação brasileira, 1889–1937.* Rio de Janeiro: Paz e Terra, 1982.

CHAPTER 2

❧

Research on Brazil in the United States

ROBERT M. LEVINE

Few Americans knew much about Brazil before the mid-nineteenth century. The first scientific expedition to the Amazon was undertaken in 1736 by the French Academy of Sciences, which was seeking to test Newton's theories about the size and shape of the earth. Naturalists Alexander von Humboldt and Aimé Bonpland explored the Amazon in 1799, but neither trip had much impact in North America. In the next century, worldwide interest in Brazil expanded but much more in Europe than in United States. The exceptions were naturalists James Orton, William Henry Edwards, and Frank Michler Chapman. The Swiss-born Louis Agassiz, who taught zoology and geology, led Harvard University's Thayer expedition to the Amazon in search of fossil fish and other specimens to test the theory of evolution.[1] Scientists and naturalists from the United States explored the Brazilian subcontinent, but their work went publicly unnoticed. Much of the western part of North America remained uncharted, and it was perhaps natural that Americans looked westward rather than south in those years.

One of the first U.S. researchers personally to work in Brazil was Stanford University geologist—and later university president—John Casper Branner. In the 1850s the U.S. Navy carried out surveys of Brazil's forests, in search of wood for ship construction as well as to bring back seeds or specimens that might be transplanted to Florida or Hawaii. Lieutenant Lewis Herndon, the leader of the expedition, published a book in 1854 extolling the riches and beauty of the Amazon. In 1857, the Reverends D. P. Kidder and James C. Fletcher published *Brazil and the Brazilians*, based on their travels. This book, a description of the authors' wonderment at what they saw, whetted the appetite of Americans for information about Brazil. By 1866, *Brazil and the Brazilians* had gone through five editions. One of its lasting contributions was to change readers' ideas about the effects of subtropical climate on human life. Fletcher and Kidder's account was so optimistic that some Americans emigrated to Brazil (including slave owners from the defeated Confederacy) and others, including the writer Samuel Clemens (Mark Twain), made plans to visit the Amazon.

The images of Brazil that lodged in the minds of ordinary Americans, however, were more likely based on small *carte de visite* photographs, sold widely in sets to collectors, and, by the 1890s, available in stereopticon slides that gave the impression of three-dimensionality. Because the buying public preferred natural wonders and "exotic" themes, more often than not the images of Brazil available in the United States were limited to waterfalls, jungle flora and fauna, and slaves. Newspapers in large U.S. cities sometimes ran feature stories on Emperor Dom Pedro II, who enjoyed a good press. In 1876, in fact, Pedro, dressed in a three-piece gabardine suit and a felt hat, cut the ribbon to open the Philadelphia Centennial Exposition. It is not known if those who attended the ceremony saw irony in the fact that Pedro was the hemisphere's sole monarch. Some American engineers and economists visited Brazil after the proclamation of the Republic in 1889. Overall, however, research-based scholarship in the modern sense barely existed.

BRAZILIAN STUDIES IN THE UNITED STATES

In most academic research fields in the humanities and social sciences, professionalization emerged after the turn of the century when U.S. universities adopted the German model of research-based higher education. The Johns Hopkins University in Baltimore offered the first doctoral degrees in history, requiring years of study under research professors and the completion of a rigorous and original dissertation of hundreds of pages. Graduate students did not specialize in narrow fields, though. Over the years, one trained to be an economist or a sociologist or a historian. Students were required to learn all languages relevant to their study, but even though they wrote dissertations on China or Africa or Mexico, neither they nor the departments that hired them once they completed their degrees considered them exclusively "Sinologists" or "Africanists" or "Mexicanists." This distinction has survived and is the reason that the term "Brazilianist," coined by Brazilians in the 1960s, is sometimes based on misleading assumptions. A scholar in the United States may spend an entire career researching Brazil. But in the employer's eyes—typically a four-year college or a university offering both undergraduate and graduate degrees—faculty members are expected not only to teach subjects well beyond their research field but to keep up with their discipline broadly. "Brazilianists" whose professional activity involves Brazil alone are rare birds indeed.

According to A. J. R. Russell-Wood, developments about the time of the First World War helped set the stage for scholarly interest in Brazil in the United States. The Andrew Carnegie Endowment funded the creation of libraries not only in the United States; in Latin America it established depository libraries to encourage hemispheric cooperation. This effort, in turn, helped fuel a sense of Pan-Americanism, along with interest in scholarship. Doctoral dissertations began to be written on Latin America. The *Hispanic American Historical Review* started publication in 1918, with "Hispanic" rather than "Latin" chosen for the title in order to include Portugal within its scope. Still, only a handful of articles on Brazil appeared during the next several decades. By the 1940s, however, three scholars— Manoel S. Cardozo, Alexander Marchant, and Robert C. Smith—established themselves by publishing essays and monographs on colonial Brazil.[2]

Before the 1930s, persons seeking to do research *in* Brazil in almost all cases had to be able to pay their own expenses or be supported by non-academic institutions. In 1913, former president Theodore Roosevelt, with financial support from the American Museum of Natural History in New York City, led an expedition to the Amazon. Accompanied by Colonel Cândido Rondon, the group traveled 629 miles down a river linking the Paraná River in Mato Grosso to the Amazon. Previously unknown to cartographers, the river was later named after Roosevelt (Roosevelt, 1914).

Things changed as World War II approached. Before and during the war, a number of U.S. graduate students and scholars were recruited by the Office of Strategic Services to report on conditions and to watch for Japanese or German activities. Some of these young scholars later entered the academic world when the war came to a close, and research funds began to become available. Still, the numbers of researchers in the United States who were working on Brazilian subjects before 1950 remained very small, especially in comparison to the number of U.S. scholars working in Mexico. Anthropologists and sociologists did most of the significant work in Brazil, along with a few historians and political scientists. Dartmouth College's Karl Loewenstein published a harsh critique of Getúlio Vargas's Estado Novo, before Brazil entered the war in 1942 on the side of the Allies. The period from 1930 to 1950 also saw the field studies of

Louisiana State University's T. Lynn Smith (who helped during the first years of the Universidade de São Paulo), Columbia's Ruth Landes, and Donald Pierson (Pierson, 1945; Smith, 1946). Yet scholarly books on Brazil remained rare. Wartime government agencies subsidized the publication of such general texts as Stefan Zweig's *Brazil: Country of the Future* and a number of descriptive works aimed at educating Americans about their Brazilian allies.

Published scholarship on Brazil between the world wars and through the 1950s emphasized studies of conventional topics (biography, diplomatic and political history, economic development). Their focus was narrow, leading to monographs written for professionals. More speculative writing—on the model of the books and essays by such Brazilians as Paulo Prado and Maria Isaura Pereira de Queiroz—was avoided. Many researchers, moreover, relied on their reading and digesting the works of Brazilian scholars rather than upon lengthy original research carried out in Brazil. Some specialists on Latin America had only rudimentary Spanish or Portuguese, although such pioneers as Pierson, Alexander Marchant, Charles Wagley, Stanley J. Stein, and Barbara Hadley Stein learned Portuguese thoroughly. Others did not, including Harvard's Clarence Haring and Columbia's Frank Tannenbaum. As a result, their scholarly contacts in Brazil were limited to intellectuals who spoke English. This surely limited the opportunities for these scholars to learn more than what elites told them. This held true for industrial and agricultural researchers as well, usually contracted for their expertise in bridge building or irrigation, not for their knowledge about Brazil or its society.

Beginning in the early 1960s, more academic departments at colleges and universities in the United States began to identify Brazil as a subject deserving full-time research coverage, although when hired, these specialists were expected to teach courses on other topics as well. Scholarship on Brazil, like scholarship conducted in most "area studies" programs, tended to follow trends in individual disciplines rather than having a life of its own. Thus the large numbers of research projects during the 1960s on regionalism or on Brazilian slavery came more as a by-product of interest in such topics among social scientists and humanists in general than as a decision by "Brazilianists" among themselves. Before the 1960s, most academic departments had only one specialist on Latin America; after this turning point, many added one or even two faculty lines for coverage of the colonial and national periods and sometimes U.S.–Latin American relations. Whether a department hired a Brazilian specialist or someone specializing in another Latin American country tended to be a result of who was the strongest candidate in the pool of applicants, although some universities—Texas, Stanford, Columbia, Princeton, Yale, and Vanderbilt— sought always to have a specialist in Brazil because of the focus of their programs.

On the whole, scholarship at U.S. universities following the Second World War reflected the tensions of the Cold War. The mainstream majority of researchers carried out traditional research, while a much smaller group, more often than not Marxist, identified with progressive causes. In the still-small academic field of Brazilian studies, research methodology across the disciplines remained mostly traditional. Barbara Weinstein, in her 2001 talk, "Buddy, Can you Spare a Paradigm?" to the Conference on Latin American History, stated:

> At that time, I fervently believed that a worldwide socialist transformation was a historical possibility. And I felt that Latin America would be in the vanguard of this global revolutionary process. I regarded as elitist or hidebound my peers who opted to study U.S. political history or European intellectual history. In contrast, my choice of Latin America highlighted my political identification with the Third World over the First. (Weinstein, 2001: 453)

By the early 1970s the balance did shift, although only a minority of academic specialists on Brazil considered themselves to be politically radical. Older scholars (with such notable exceptions as Princeton's Stanley J. Stein) tended to avoid political involvement, while younger academics, some of whom had participated in the civil rights movement or had served in the Peace Corps, now became activists in the campaign against the expanding Vietnam War. They tended to sympathize with the goals of the Cuban Revolution, and disparaged U.S. foreign policy in the hemisphere (support for dictators in Haiti, Central America, Paraguay, and elsewhere; the invasion of the Dominican Republic in 1965; immediate recognition of Brazil's military government in 1964). By the late 1960s, and especially after the increase of repression in Brazil after 1968, many, if not most, of the young foreign researchers in Brazil sympathized with the regime's opponents. Not coincidentally, many researchers on Brazil now pursued nontraditional topics: studies of Christian-based communities, the failure of land reform, the assault on the tropical rain forest, race and class relations, the history of slavery. The work of women scholars— including Daphne Patai's collection of oral histories, *Brazilian Women Speak*, Nancy Scheper-Hughes's controversial *Death without Weeping*, and Candace Slater's *Stories on a String* and *Dance of the Dolphins*—"added thematic and conceptual breadth to the traditional patriarchal portrayal of Brazilian reality."[3]

Before the 1960s, only in rare cases did U.S. scholars engage in serious debate with their Brazilian counterparts. Brazilian university professors tended to come from upper-class backgrounds. (In the absence of major research libraries outside Rio de Janeiro and São Paulo, scholars had to build their own private libraries; even many scholars in the major cities built collections of thousands of books and journals.) Occasionally, visiting U.S. scholars (Ruth Landes, Donald Pierson, T. Lynn Smith) built close professional ties during their extensive research stays in Brazil, but by the 1960s, except in the disciplines of political science, economics, and to some extent anthropology, contact stayed mostly at the social level. Collaboration between Brazilians and North Americans began only in the late 1970s, and successful examples remain relatively rare.

Under Brazil's military regime (1964–85), some Brazilian scholars, intimidated by arbitrary denunciations of scholars as fellow travelers, became angry at what they considered to be the cavalier attitude of some Brazilianists. The Universidade de São Paulo's José Carlos Sebe Bom Meihy, for example, remembers the dismay shared with Brazilian colleagues at what they considered to be Thomas E. Skidmore's matter-of-fact admission that during the 1964 coup he kept in contact with Ambassador Lincoln Gordon.[4]

Some Brazilian scholars continued to dismiss Brazilianists and their work, for example, literary critic Wilson Martins, who after more than two decades at New York University, returned to Curitiba and started writing acerbic and sometimes insulting syndicated newspaper columns. Other damage was done by Brazilian reporters, who were writing provocative articles about Brazilianists.[5] A cottage market of master's theses and articles analyzing the work of Brazilianists (and finding them, in an author's words, naive and poorly informed) emerged during the early 1970s and continued on sporadically. Some U.S. researchers suspected that when newspapers and magazines ran interviews or stories about their work, the editors deliberately selected the most unflattering photograph as a form of derision.[6]

Attacks on individual Brazilianists continued. In 2000, reporter Paulo Moreira Leite singled out Stanley Hilton, Stuart B. Schwartz, and me as "Americans dedicated to Brazilian Studies who attained greatest notoriety during the military government" (Moreira Leite, 2000), as if it were immoral to have come to Brazil during the mid-1960s, when these three young academics happened to complete their doctoral qualifying examinations and went to Brazil for dissertation research. A year earlier, the

prestigious *Folha de São Paulo* published a story by Marcos Augusto
Gonçalves, the section's editor, in its Sunday edition that disparaged historian Jeffrey Lesser's newly translated book this way:

> The new generation of Brazilianists . . . is paying less attention to traditional
> history and political science and substituting more narrow topics, such as
> race, sex, and religiosity. Danger! Race, sex and religiosity are themes treated
> very differently in Brazil and in the United States. The two societies evolved
> along different paths . . . running the risk that [a North American's work]
> will be contaminated by the author's own experience or his supposed "solu-
> tions." Jeffrey Lesser . . . seems convinced that the multicultural ideology in
> vogue in the United States is the model to follow. This results in the im-
> pression that Brazil, for not miming this ideology, finds itself in a "back-
> wards" stage.

On the other hand, the presence of North Americans as long-range or
permanent scholars in Brazil (political scientist David Fleischer; historians Michael Hall, Peter Eisenberg, Judith Hoffnagel, Marc Hoffnagel,
Robert Slenes, and Nancy Naro; linguist Tony Naro) muted anti-American
feeling among their colleagues and students. Still, some foreign scholars
chafed at obstacles that they felt were placed in their path. One wrote:

> I've just been rejected in my request for a federal Brazilian grant, a stan-
> dard handout to productive scholars in the Brazilian system. I had contested
> the brief initial rejection and consequently got a more thorough rejection
> subsequently. From my subjective point of view I found it pretty xenopho-
> bic. . . . The self-defensive rant made it clear that the perception was that
> as outsiders the Brazilianists should read the real experts—Freyre/Buarque/
> Prado . . . Walnice Galvão, and so on. I have often come up against an in-
> stitutional lesson here that there's only enough funding to take care of a few
> pre-established interests (that always receive most of the funding). The
> tone, however, reminded me of the basic outsider dilemma, incurable, and
> only offset by the fact that much good research by Brazilians is conducted
> in the US/Europe. After all, outside of USP, it is pretty much impossible to
> conduct, or rather to execute all the standard necessities, of international
> quality research.

Newly minted Brazilianists tend to have better language skills than their
predecessors and in many cases have fit more effortlessly into the Brazilian university world than members of the preceding generations. Unlike

earlier times, research today on Brazilian subjects embraces the academic trend toward interdisciplinary studies across the humanities and social sciences.[7] Through the late 1990s, many (but not all) academic scholars, especially in political science, literature, and economics, studied their subjects narrowly. The new trend, Piers Armstrong notes, finds scholars conversant with broader disciplinary issues:

> The study of Brazilian literature in ignorance of the country's popular culture (including its music) or of national economic structures without reference to Brazilian social conditions seems inconceivable. Ethnomusicologists must incorporate socioeconomics, history, anthropology, and aesthetics. Moreover, Brazilianists frequently cross the substantial psychological barriers between the social sciences and the humanities.[8]

Brazilianists as Interlopers

While some Brazilians expressed dismay at the seeming incursions of graduate students and other academic specialists from the United States in the mid-1960s, in reality the number of U.S. researchers in Brazil at the height of the research "explosion" never exceeded more than a few dozen. Still, there were enough researchers in Rio de Janeiro, at least, to start an informal group that met from time to time to discuss research findings and to offer suggestions to newcomers. In late 1964, anthropologist Charles Wagley of Columbia University's Institute of Latin American Studies, visiting Brazil for the Ford Foundation, approached members of the group and suggested that information on research opportunities be compiled and published by Columbia for the use of future researchers. The result was the *Brazil: Field Research Guide in the Social Sciences* (1966), with chapters by Albert Fishlow on economics, Paul Mandel on geography, Ralph della Cava on history, and Robert Packenham on political science. Wagley, whose pioneering research in the Amazon during the 1940s had become known to novelist Jorge Amado, may well have been the model for the blond, blue-eyed U.S. professor, James D. Levenson, a character in *Tent of Miracles* (1971) noted for his suave manner and appreciation of *mulatas*.[9]

The timing of the arrival of several dozen foreign researchers (not only from the United States but also from Canada, the United Kingdom, Australia, Israel, Japan, Norway, and Portugal, among other countries) coincided with Brazil's 1964 military coup, something that many did not consider accidental. "Brazilianists," further, were linked—in most cases, inaccurately—to the CIA, or to the CIA-backed "Project Camelot" in Chile, or to USAID contracts with Michigan State University and the University of Southern California to recast Brazilian education along U.S. lines. Those coming to Brazil to study indigenous languages, moreover, were identified as being connected to the Summer Institute of Linguistics (now Languages), some of whose affiliates later were revealed as U.S. spies. An *Istoé* journalist, Kátia Mello, interviewed Gerard Colby and Charlotte Dennett, whose research claimed that the CIA had attempted to "overthrow" presidents Getúlio Vargas and João Goulart during the 1950s and 1960s.[10] Still, no one acknowledged that most graduate students and researchers from the social sciences and humanities sympathized passionately (and with some risk) with those Brazilians who had been branded enemies of the military regime. Later, after the repression tightened in 1968, many U.S.-based scholars actively aided their Brazilian counterparts who had been exiled from their country. Even so, for many, the term "Brazilianist" conjured up distrust and suspicion.

From the 1960s through the late 1970s, research on Brazil at universities in the United States turned, in many cases, to socially conscious topics: race, gender, slavery, poverty, resistance to authority. More often than not, however, the projects followed the traditional research methods of each discipline. Some North American graduate students had studied Marxism—often not as part of their coursework but in student-run study groups—but dissertation advisers did not welcome this kind of analysis, and as a result graduate students tended to follow their advisers' lead. In any case, North American students of Brazil during this period tended to be skeptical of (if not hostile to) U.S. foreign policy and equally unhappy with the repression in Brazil under the military dictatorship, but these feelings did not carry over into their dissertations. Even senior scholars took fewer chances and often were reluctant to innovate. One exception was the ebullient cultural and intellectual historian Richard M. Morse. He became so well accepted by his Brazilian counterparts that he got away with parodying Mário de Andrade's modernist classic *Macunaíma* (Morse, 1990, 1994). Most other "Brazilianists" attempting this would have been unceremoniously escorted to the airport.

Although some U.S. scholars grounded their work in theory (models ranged from Antonio Gramsci to the British socialist E. P. Thompson to mega-thinkers Immanuel Wallerstein and E. J. Hobsbawm), scholarship on Brazil in the United States remained largely empirical, relying on field research and the exhaustive use of formal documentation. Except for labor historians and students of dependency theory, most U.S. researchers did not pay much attention to matters of theory. This had an unfortunate result. To suspicion of "Brazilianists" now was added the charge that U.S. research lacked theoretical sophistication and was therefore irrelevant or even useless. This unpleasant debate lasted for years and still crops up in allegations that U.S. research on Brazil is naive (and, among some U.S. researchers, that Brazilian scholarship, based on theoretical conjecture and not "real" research, was equally lacking in merit). Scholars at the top of their fields in both countries disregarded these statements as foolish, but among many Brazilians at the local academic level, they were accepted as fact. One result was that for several decades, Brazilians preferred to study abroad in Europe, especially France, rather than take degrees in the United States.

The late 1970s in U.S. universities saw a near-paradigm shift among a moderate number of publishing scholars throughout the humanities and, to a lesser extent, in the social sciences. Elegant narrative history and descriptive social science were rejected by academics contemptuous of studies purporting to study society but in reality looking only at elites and the powerful. Now attention fell on ordinary people—workers, miners, domestics, nonwhites, factory workers, fishermen, and women. Researchers now sought to document "agency" through a fusion of social and political analysis viewed not from above but from below. Influenced by such thinkers as Gramsci, Humberto Eco, Salman Rushdie, Walter Benjamin, Michel de Certeau, Edward Said, and Michel Foucault, this wave turned some into converts to the postmodernist (PoMo) movement. As such, they shifted their emphasis from studies of the links between politics and society (or, in a more theoretical vein, agency and hegemony) to the links between politics and culture. PoMo gained influence in some U.S. academic circles, although it was staunchly resisted elsewhere. In a broader way, advances in linguistics and anthropology influenced historians to examine case studies of politics as culture, seen not only from below but also from all levels of society. Gender issues, so-called queer studies, and studies of sexuality came to the fore, almost dominating the seasonal catalogs of the university presses of California, Duke, and Chicago.[11] Scholars who traditionally submitted manuscripts to traditional journals now published in *Critical Inquiry, Comparative Studies in Society and History,* and the women's studies journal, *Signs.*

The postmodern cultural studies movement rejected the entire canon of traditional scholarship. Researchers who based their analysis on exhaustive use of documents and primary source evidence were dismissed as "materialist readers, in which the historicity of the text, its placement, its production, its use, are foregrounded" and therefore invalid.[12] The problem, however, for many academics was that while the PoMos raised valid points of criticism, their own scholarship was entirely removed from "valid" research. Worse, anti-PoMo scholars claimed, cultural studies shrouded itself in a meaningless infrastructure of arcane vocabulary: heteroglossia, situated voices, hybridity, and so on. The result was that although cultural studies may have seemed relevant—especially in its subfield of postcolonial studies—only some scholars in the United States in comparative literature specializing on Brazil embraced it entirely.

The majority of U.S. researchers on Brazil, on the other hand, remained unaffected by PoMo scholarship, and many dismissed it. This position widened the gap between Brazilian scholars influenced by cultural studies and the "Brazilianists" whose empiricism the Brazilian scholars always had mistrusted in any case. A few U.S.-based researchers (Sueann Caulfield, Peter Beattie, Daryle Williams, Barbara Weinstein, and James Green, for example) addressed postmodern issues without heavy use of jargon and buzzwords. Overwhelmingly, Brazilian specialists in the United States, more so than many of their Spanish American counterparts, preserved their sense of the uniqueness of their region and the need to apply practical approaches. Rather than engage in semiotics or debates over deconstruction, Brazilian specialists saw emerging interest in new methodologies surface: oral history, for example, pioneered in Brazil by José Carlos Sebe Bom Meihy, encouraged North Americans to use similar methods, both by use of one-on-one interviewing (Tobias Hecht's [1998] graphic and compassionate work with street children, for example) and soliciting responses via the Internet.

The rift persisted within Brazilian studies in the United States as well. Yet even if often self-congratulatory ("my dissertation adviser doesn't have a clue about poststructuralist feminist theory"; or, "in the old days graduate students didn't know Portuguese as well as we do"; or "they used clumsy, racist terms like 'discovery'"; or "they only used traditional archival sources"), the PoMos have a point. To be intellectually engaged requires keeping up with new developments in one's broader field. Exposure to stimulating debates about military history or cultural studies or postmodernism often moves doctoral candidates and even older scholars working on Brazil to adapt such approaches to their own field research.

External events worsened the tensions within academia. The dramatic fall of the Berlin Wall and the subsequent near-universal embrace of free-market economics produced shock waves in the academic world, although less so among Brazilian specialists than among specialists on Mexico and other parts of the world. Marxist theory, which had taken hold in many departments in the United States among younger scholars (and throughout Latin America as well as in Western Europe and, of all places, Japan), faced harsh reassessment. Academics in the United States erupted in controversy over research models. Debate in some disciplines grew so acrimonious that professional historians, disenchanted with what they called the smothering effect of postmodernism, nontraditional topics, and political correctness, broke away from the 114-year-old American Historical Association in the mid-1990s and formed the Boston-based Historical Society, dedicated to traditional empirical scholarship (www.bu.edu/historic).

FUNDING

By the early 1960s, educational and philanthropic foundations as well as federal agencies contributed significant sums of money to research on Latin America. The private agencies were anchored by the Ford Foundation's Social Science Research Council (SSRC), which provided both dissertation fellowships and project grants to more senior researchers. The Ford Foundation Latin American program established an office in Rio de Janeiro—which still operates—sponsoring programs in community development and educational reform. SSRC selection panels included not only U.S. scholars but distinguished scholars from Latin American countries, one of whom was the sociologist Fernando Henrique Cardoso. Other private granting agencies included the Henry L. and Grace Doherty Foundation, the Wenner-Gren Foundation (providing stipends for anthropologists), the Guggenheim Foundation, the National Geographic Society, and the Rockefeller Brothers Fund (and, later, the Rockefeller Foundation) for medical and health-related studies. In recent years, however, the number of fellowships and grants from private agencies has dwindled to almost nothing. Ford and other foundations increasingly have shifted their priorities away from research to more socially proactive projects. The Foreign Area fellowship program of the SSRC has lumped competition for Latin American grants in with all others areas in the world. The effect has been that at most only one or two stipends annually go to researchers in Brazilian studies. The two Guggenheim foundations (one devoted exclusively to problems of world peace and security) sometimes award stipends to specialists on Brazil, as does the American Philosophical Society of Philadelphia and, in theory, the MacArthur Foundation, but given that these competitions are open to all applicants from all fields (MacArthur does not accept any applications at all but bestows grants on the basis of internal procedures), the number of winners for Brazilian projects each year from private sources rarely exceeds more than a handful.

The Fulbright foreign fellowship program, named for the former Rhodes scholar and Arkansas senator J. William Fulbright, starting in 1949 provided stipends for scholars at different levels to study in countries around the world. At first, most of the fellowships went to recent recipients of bachelor's degrees, but in time, the Washington, D.C.–based Fulbright-Hays Commission initiated programs for research scholars and for graduate students seeking support for their research in the field. From 1949 through 1998, 140 scholars from the United States received fellowships for Brazil, along with 757 lecturing scholars, 85 teachers participating in exchanges, and 386 students, some recent graduates holding bachelor's degrees, other graduate students.[13] While the Fulbright awards remained the best known, other U.S. government agencies started smaller programs to support research abroad. These included, but were not limited to, the departments of education, agriculture, and labor as well as the Alliance for Progress and the Agency for International Development.

Under President Ronald W. Reagan, granting agencies such as the National Endowment for the Arts (NEA), the National Endowment for the Humanities (NEH), and the Fulbright program, always even-handed but now accused by Republicans of being too liberal, became politicized. In addition, federal funding programs for research outside the United States faced downsizing or wholesale cancellation. After the fall of the Berlin Wall in 1989 and the subsequent evaporation of the Cold War, area studies programs in U.S. universities faced similar cuts in revenue allocations. In the late 1990s, the Fulbright program shifted emphasis from dissertation research to recent graduates of undergraduate institutions in the United States. Fellowships formerly provided by the U.S. Office of Education also dropped in number, as did awards from the NEA, and NEH, the major granting agency for historians, language and literature scholars, and political scientists interested in Brazil. Programs ranging from translation projects to sponsorship of exhibitions to collaborative research to proposals for documentary film making to summer study institutes all are fielded by the NEH, whose reduced funding has made competition stiffer than ever. In 2000, conservative Republican members of Congress prepared to launch an even more draconian campaign of budget cuts targeting National Public Radio, the National Endowment for the Arts, and other cultural agencies. Prospects for a return to funding levels of old seemed remote.

THE NEW FACE OF BRAZILIAN STUDIES

The spurt in research activity in the United States on Brazilian topics, then, formed part of a larger opening within North American universities for specialists on countries in the "Third World." Until the 1960s, most academic departments in the United States and Canada heavily emphasized the history of antiquity; medieval, Renaissance, and modern Europe; and the history of their own countries. Only the largest universities hired specialists in Latin America, and, if they did, they were assigned to teach about all of Latin America as well as to lead "survey" courses in U.S. history or in European-centered "Western civilization." During the late 1960s and early 1970s, some U.S. universities hired two Latin American specialists, typically one in the colonial and the other in the modern period. Among these were scholars whose research centered on Brazil, but as often as not they specialized in Mexico or Argentina or Cuba or the Andean republics.

Since then, more academic departments have identified Brazil as a niche necessitating full-time coverage, although when hired, these specialists almost always teach courses on other topics as well. The Brazilian assumption that "Brazilianists" focus exclusively on Brazil, then, is inaccurate. Nor it is widely understood that scholarship follows trends in individual disciplines rather than, in the case of the Brazilianists, having a life of its own. Thus the large numbers of research projects during the 1960s on regionalism or on Brazilian slavery came more as a by-product of interest in such topics among social scientists in general than as a decision by "Brazilianists" in isolation.

To understand the successive evolution of topics and methodological approaches of "Brazilianists," one must realize that every new generation of graduate students as a group is influenced by the trends of the academic discipline in which doctoral apprenticeships take place. This does not stop when young scholars have their doctoral degrees in hand. To the contrary, it increases. The brightest and most successful new "Brazilianist," like any assistant professor in the U.S. university system, becomes attuned to his or her discipline's trends and emphases. Whenever seminal articles or books in their field appear, young scholars, faced with the challenging task of crafting syllabi for the courses they teach, often assign such works for their students to read and discuss before their older (and perhaps more staid) department colleagues do.

Young scholars listen, as well, to senior colleagues from fields undergoing major transitions: medieval history, for example, newly concerned with issues of gender and sexuality; subaltern studies, originating in India, and its companion trend, postcolonial studies. They listen to presentations given by job candidates in their departments; they attend (sometimes more frequently or with greater enthusiasm than their departmental elders) professional meetings where panels often deal comparatively with research topics. At the Chicago meeting of the American Historical Association in January 2000, for example, attendees could choose among 151 AHA-sponsored panels as well as dozens more sponsored by affiliated societies ranging from the American Society of Church History to the Association of Bibliography for History to the Peace History Society. More often than not, such panels deal with new and emerging trends in scholarship: the impact of globalism, for example, or "National Security as Cultural Product," or "Regional Perspectives on Indigenous Policy and Resistance," or "Minorities and the Construction of Political Communities," a panel that included presentations on Mauritania, Latin America, and colonial India. At meetings such as the Social Science History Association or the Latin American Studies Association or conferences on millenarianism or sexuality and gender or the history of medicine or the Oral History Association, opportunities for cross-disciplinary fertilization are even greater. U.S. specialists on Brazil have played major roles in all these associations, exposing them to new ideas and ways of approaching scholarship.

As we have seen, research in the United States following the Second World War reflected the tensions of the Cold War. Individuals tended to fall into one of two camps. The mainstream majority carried out traditional research, which the small left wing of specialists on the Third World criticized as "historical materialism." This group pursued Marxist agendas, writing for such publications as *Radical History* and *Latin American Perspectives*. In the small academic field of Brazilian studies, however, research methodology across the disciplines for the most part remained traditional. By the mid-1970s, however, the balance had shifted. The new generation of graduate students, typified by Weinstein (and more center-left colleagues) differed from the elders in their field. The new generation tended to political activism. Many had been involved in the civil rights campaign or with the growing anti–Vietnam War movement. They felt and expressed solidarity with Cuba and attacked U.S. foreign policy in the hemisphere. Especially after 1968, when the level of repression by the military regime ratcheted up, many, if not most, of the younger foreign researchers in Brazil sympathized with the regime's opponents.

Having to do research in Brazil under the dictatorship had its unpleasant side for Americans—although never to the extent faced by Brazilians.

In rare cases, Americans became caught up in events. Economist Werner Baer (now at the University of Illinois but then at Vanderbilt University) and political scientist Riordan Roett (now at Johns Hopkins School of Advanced International Studies but then at Vanderbilt) were briefly abducted by unidentified, machine gun–wielding thugs. This is how Baer remembers it:

> Riordan and I shared an apartment in Rio in the summer of 1970. During the kidnapping of the German consul general, lots of suspects were rounded up. We were picked up in our apartment by armed men in civilian clothes, blindfolded, and driven somewhere. We wound up being questioned about what we were doing in Brazil and with whom we worked. I was working at that time as an advisor to the Ford Foundation. After about six or seven hours, we were released. Through the Ford Foundation we reported the incident to the U.S. Consulate, who made inquiries. In the end, it turned out that our abductors were from the intelligence services of the army. I never found out why we were suspects.[14]

The most anxiety-provoking part of the kidnapping, Werner Baer said shortly after their release, was that the Americans had to guess whether their abductors were on the right or on the left. Answers that would have satisfied one group would have enraged the other. In the end, they guessed correctly: they had been picked up not by urban guerrillas but by agents of the military regime. Had they guessed wrong, the two scholars might not have been present at the Brazilian embassy in Washington in December 2000 to receive the Order of the Southern Cross from Ambassador Rubens Antônio Barbosa.

Some Americans received harsher treatment. Political scientist and Protestant minister Brady Tyson was expelled from Brazil for having close contacts with the liberation theology wing of the Roman Catholic Church. Journalist and scholar Fred Morris was arrested in Recife and tortured for several days as an alleged Communist. He was freed only after personal intervention by First Lady Rosalind Carter, who took a courageous stand against human rights abuses in Brazil. Sometimes intimidation took milder (but still worrisome) forms: researchers visiting the archdiocese residence of the progressive archbishop Dom Helder Câmara had their photographs taken twice by police agents, once on entry and again on departing. Sometimes the visitors were tailed for weeks by plainclothes agents in their gray Volkswagens; others had their mail opened (and resealed clumsily) and their telephones tapped.

Mostly, though, U.S. researchers enjoyed access to resources not enjoyed by Brazilians. I arrived in Brazil only weeks after the coup and eventually gained the use of the archives of the political police in Rio de Janeiro, Recife, and Natal, for a dissertation on the left-provoked insurrections of 1935. Frank McCann and I received access to Getúlio Vargas's papers through his daughter Alzira. One reason for her decision was that the armed forces regime had made Vargas a "nonperson," ignoring his role in relatively recent Brazilian history. Americans, Alzira reasoned, would have an easier time publishing their work on Vargas than Brazilians, and therefore she offered her cooperation.

Access given to foreign researchers at a time when Brazilian universities faced purges and many progressive intellectuals faced exile, understandably generated suspicion and hostility to "Brazilianists," even if the allegations against them were unwarranted. U.S. researchers were belittled as unfairly privileged and in many cases suspected of connections to the "U.S. Intelligence Service."[15] Hostility toward "Brazilianists" peaked in the late 1970s. By the 1990s, although many Brazilians still misunderstood the U.S. university environment, "Brazilianist" once again became a neutral term. One sign of the acceptance of U.S. scholars in Brazil was the opening of the Fernand Braudel Center in São Paulo during the 1980s. This think tank, founded by journalist and scholar Norman Gall, brought together Brazilians and Americans in seminars and other projects dealing with economic, social, and political issues. Aided by information e-mailed weekly by David Fleischer of the Universidade de Brasília, one of several dozen North Americans working in Brazil, researchers in the United States have been able to keep as up to date as possible on developments in the fast-changing world of Brazilian politics. Leading Brazilian print media such as the *Folha de São Paulo* and *Veja* are available on line. Comprehensive sites such as the University of Texas's Latin American Center's UT-LANIC post dozens of links to the sites of other important Brazilian publications on politics and economics.

The interest among younger scholars to follow new trends stemmed from the research climate in the United States. The most successful assistant professors in U.S. colleges and universities keep their antennae out in their departments and at professional meetings. They peruse new journals: *Colonial Latin American Review* (founded in 1995), *Post-Colonial Studies* (1998), *Rethinking History* (1997), *National Identities* (1999), *Critical Inquiry* (1974), *Journal of Architecture* (1997), or *Journal of Iberian and Latin American Studies* (1994). They also read journals whose editors have struck out in new directions (the *Hispanic American Historical Review*'s embrace in the 1990s of cultural studies, for example, or the special thematic issues of the *Luso-Brazilian Review* or studies published in *Rural History*).

In the mid- through late 1990s, this new generation of scholars on Brazil began to win entry-level positions in colleges and universities. Influenced by such European postmodern theorists as Michel de Certeau, Jacques Derrida, and Foucault, among others, they embraced the postmodernist rejection of all previous research, including the published works of the radical historians typified by Ronald Chilcote, Barbara Weinstein, and Teresa Meade, as "left-wing" Orientalism. The phrase, popularized by Columbia University's Edward Said, a Palestinian nationalist, denoted foreign scholars who impose their value system, rooted in imperialist feelings of cultural and social superiority, on fields of study involving the Third World. So Latin Americanists in general and Brazilianists in particular felt under double-barrel pressure: from non-Latin Americanists who questioned the choice of their field specialization, and from the linguist-based postmodernists, who scorned them as behind the times. Now subfields began to replace the older (but pioneering) fields of the previous generation: gender studies split off from women's studies, queer studies from gay history. This shift, Weinstein argues, "has allowed us to move beyond the recuperation of the historical (and often heroicized) experiences of supposedly marginal groups to establishing how central these categories are to the construction of power (whether political or economic), meaning, and identities at every level of Latin American society" (Weinstein, 2001: 462).

To the PoMos (postmodernists), North Americans working outside their "home" cultures are "agents exiled from any fixed identity."[16] Those not intimidated by postmodernists look at their choice to work in other cultures to be a means of personal self-education: when one studies another society in depth, one is forced to consider one's own values and unconscious suppositions and expectations. The decision to devote one's academic life to Brazilian studies (or Mexican or Chinese or African studies) brings the opportunity not only to embrace the best of both cultures but to work unencumbered by the contentious academic politics of the host country. Few scholars enjoy this luxury.

CONCLUSION

Expectations among readers in Brazil and in the United States of studies by scholars on Brazilian subjects differ greatly. Brazilians who purchase academic books and journals tend to know their country's history well.

They feel comfortable with theory and do not mind if the books they buy lack indexes or dozens of pages of citations, discursive comments about sources, and lists of document sources. Readers in the United States, on the other hand, usually know much less about Brazil and therefore need much more background. They are less interested in theory than Brazilians, look for lucid (and uncomplicated) writing, and consider intellectual flourishes to be annoying.

I think that the claim that Brazilianists have become dinosaurs is based on the misleading assumption that all Brazilianists share the same motives, methodologies, and scholarly goals. Brazilian studies remains in constant flux, challenged especially by relative newcomers to the field (for example, Gail Triner, on the history of banking; Peter Beattie, on the mentality behind the ways Brazil's nineteenth-century military elites attempted to "civilize" lower-class enlisted men; Cristina Mehrtens-Peixoto on the interplay between the public and private sectors in the urban and architectural history of São Paulo; Tobias Hecht on street children, prostitutes, and transvestites in the cities of the Northeast, and so on).

It is, of course, much easier to publish a book or study in Brazil than one on Brazil in the United States. A scholarly study of Euclides da Cunha or of Catholic base communities or on police violence might sell ten thousand copies or more in Brazil. Brazilian students sometimes publish their master's theses, usually at their own expense, although at times through a university press or a government agency. Banks and other commercial firms frequently subsidize the production of handsome "coffee table" books on art or photography or natural history.

Some have managed to find advantage from the outsider status given to Brazilianists. Historian Barbara Weinstein addressed the issue this way: "My outsider status in Brazil . . . allows me to engage in Brazilian intellectual life while remaining aloof from most academic squabbles . . . [it allows me] the pleasures of being a liminal figure, someone who can be simultaneously insider and outsider" (2001: 464–65). During the perilous period for Brazilian higher education during the late 1990s and early 2000s, when scores of distinguished scholars retired from their university positions to secure their generous pension benefits without, in many cases, being replaced, being an outsider obviously had advantages. On the other hand, for many the gap between Brazilian scholars and Brazilianists widened. The high cost of journals and monographs published in the United States limited their dissemination, and the absence of a national Brazilian scholarly journal limited reviewing to the cultural pages of a few leading newspapers. The gap grew even wider at Brazil's inadequately funded second- and third-tier universities, even though some of the newly retired professors started second careers in such places.

Studies written and published by mature scholars tend to have much more in common than popular books or short master's theses. While scholars in Brazil and in the United States may likely differ in their format and possibly in their use of sources, their work is usually as complementary as it is erudite. They are concerned with similar issues and apply high standards to the search for proof of their hypotheses. This holds less true, on the other hand, for popular works or for studies produced on the basis of sparse research. The best studies on Brazil, regardless of the nationality of their authors, draw on all the best analyses of their subject. This is the model, and it should be pursued by researchers at all levels.

NOTES

1. Louis Agassiz and Elizabeth Cabot Agassiz, *A Journey in Brazil* (Boston: Ticknor and Fields, 1868).

2. A. J. R. Russell-Wood, "United States Scholarly Contributions to the Historiography of Colonial Brazil," *Hispanic American Historical Review* 65, no. 4 (November 1985): 688–99.

3. Piers Armstrong, "The Brazilianists' Brazil: Interdisciplinary Portraits of Brazilian Society and Culture," *Latin American Research Review* 35, no. 1 (2000): 229.

4. José Carlos Sebe Bom Meihy, interview by author, February 3, 2001.

5. For example, Paulo Moreira Leite, "O fim do brasilianismo," *Gazeta Mercantil*, 8 December 2000, 2; and Paulo Sotero, "Guia reaviva polêmicas sobre brazilianistas" [*sic*], *O Estado de São Paulo*, 4 December 2000, A13.

6. One North American Brazilianist, who asked to remain anonymous, stopped giving permission to be photographed, but the magazine that ran his interview found an unflattering picture in its files and used it, although it was more than ten years old.

7. See Armstrong, "The Brazilianists' Brazil."

8. Ibid., 227.

9. Levenson, some argue, may have been a composite of Wagley and fellow Columbia anthropologist Marvin Harris.

10. Gerard Colby and Charlotte Dennett, *Seja feita a vossa vontade* (São Paulo: Record, 2000).

11. See, for example, Richard Parker, *Bodies, Pleasures and Passions: Sexual Culture in Contemporary Brazil* (Boston: Beacon, 1991).

12. See John Lye, *Cultural Studies vs. Close Reading*, ENGL 4F70, June 11, 1999, www.brocku.ca/english/courses/4F70/cs-close.html (November 29, 2004).

13. In return, 2,348 Brazilians received Fulbright awards to come to the U.S., including 556 research scholars and 1,246 students. Source: Fulbright Association, Washington, D.C., e-mail, 16 February 2000.

14. Werner Baer, e-mail to author, 20 January 2000.

15. Those making the charges confused the American CIA with the British Intelligence Service.

16. Vicente Rafael, talk to the Conference on Latin American History, Boston, 6 January 2001, quoted in Weinstein, 2001.

References

Agassiz, Louis Agassiz and Elizabeth Cabot. 1868. *A Journey in Brazil.* Boston: Ticknor and Fields.

Amado, Jorge. 1971. *Tent of Miracles.* Trans. Barbara Shelby. New York: Alfred A. Knopf.

Armstrong, Piers. 2000. "The Brazilianists' Brazil: Interdisciplinary Portraits of Brazilian Society and Culture." *Latin American Research Review* 35, no. 1: 227–242.

Cardozo, Manoel da Silveira Soares. 1940. "A History of Mining in Colonial Brazil," Ph.D. dissertation, Stanford University.

Colby, Gerard, and Charlotte Dennett. 2000. *Seja feita a vossa vontade.* São Paulo: Record.

Gonçalves, Marcos Augusto. 1999. "Caderno Mais!" *Folha de São Paulo,* 6 June, pp. 1–6.

Hecht, Tobias. 1998. *At Home in the Street: Street Children of Northeast Brazil.* Cambridge: Cambridge University Press.

Herndon, William Lewis. 2000. *Exploration of the Valley of the Amazon.* Edited, with a foreword by Gary Kindir. New York: Grove Press. Original edition: Washington, D.C., 1854.

Kidder, Daniel P., and James C. Fletcher. 1857. *Brazil and the Brazilians Portrayed in Historical and Descriptive Sketches.* Philadelphia: Childs and Peterson; New York: Sheldon, Blakeman.

Levine, Robert, ed. 1966. *Brazil: Field Research Guide in the Social Sciences.* New York: Columbia University Press, Institute of Latin American Studies.

Loewenstein, Karl. 1942. *Brazil Under Vargas.* New York: Macmillan.

Marchant, Alexander. 1942. *From Barter to Slavery: The Economic Relations of Portuguese and Indians in the Settlement of Brazil, 1500–1800.* Baltimore: Johns Hopkins University Press.

Mello, Kátia. 2000. "Em nome dos EUA" Interview. *Istoé,* 29 November, pp. 9–10.

Moreira Leite, Paulo. 2000. "O fim do brasilianismo," *Gazeta Mercantil,* 8 December, p. 2.

Morse, Richard M. 1990. *A Volta de McLuhanaíma: cinco estudos solenes e uma brincadeira séria.* São Paulo: Companhia das Letras.

————. 1994. *New World Soundings: Culture and Identity in the Americas*. Baltimore, Md.: Johns Hopkins Studies in Atlantic History and Culture.

Parker, Richard. 1991. *Bodies, Pleasures and Passions: Sexual Culture in Contemporary Brazil*. Boston: Beacon.

Patai, Daphne. 1988. *Brazilian Women Speak: Contemporary Life Stories*. New Brunswick, N.J.: Rutgers University Press.

Pierson, Donald. 1945. *Survey of the Literature on Brazil of Sociological Significance Published up to 1940*. Cambridge, Mass.: Harvard University Press.

Roosevelt, Theodore. 1914. *Through the Brazilian Wilderness*. New York: C. Scribner's Sons.

Russell-Wood, A. J. R. 1985. "United States Scholarly Contributions to the Historiography of Colonial Brazil." *Hispanic American Historical Review* 4, no. 65 (November): 688–99.

Scheper-Hughes, Nancy. 1992. *Death without Weeping: The Violence of Everyday Life in Brazil*. Berkeley: University of California Press.

Slater, Candace. 1982. *Stories on a String: The Brazilian Literature de Cordel*. Berkeley: The University of California Press.

————. 1994. *Dance of the Dolphins: Transformation and Disenchantment in the Amazonian Imagination*. Chicago: University of Chicago Press.

Smith, Robert C. 1945. *The Colonial Art of Latin America*. Washington, D.C.: Library of Congress.

Smith, T. Lynn. 1946 (rev. ed. 1963). *Brazil, People and Institutions*. Baton Rouge: Louisiana State University Press. Original edition: *Brasil: povo e instituições*. Trans. José Arthur Rios. Rio de Janeiro: Bloch-AID, 1967.

Weinstein, Barbara. 2001. "Buddy, Can You Spare a Paradigm?" *Americas* 4, no. 57: 453–66.

Zweig, Stefan. 1941. *Brazil: Country of the Future*. New York: Viking.

~

CHAPTER 3

Teaching Brazil in U.S. Universities

Theodore Robert Young

This essay discusses the teaching of Brazil in institutions of higher learning in the United States, primarily within the context of Latin American Studies programs. It consists of an overview that attempts to draw general conclusions about these programs and suggest areas for further discussion within the academy, in particular, the role of key scholars in the efforts to institutionalize Brazilian studies, and what constitutes a Brazil specialist. It also addresses in passing Portuguese-language programs and the language and literature departments and their role in efforts to make Brazilian studies a more permanent presence in U.S. universities.[1] Throughout this chapter, the specific institutions mentioned serve as examples of the issues presented, and they are usually typical of numerous other institutions. This is especially true in the section on summer programs and study abroad, as well as majors and minors in Portuguese. In no way are the names listed meant to be definitive or exhaustive in identifying programs or models of the areas treated.[2]

~

The institutionalization of the study and teaching of Brazil in the United States generally originates in two areas: programs of Latin American studies, and the teaching of language and literature in Portuguese. Similarly, the study of Brazil historically has been a product of a larger Latin American studies project, as outlined by Robert Levine in chapter 2. Overall, when the institutionalization of the teaching of issues relating to Brazil in academic institutions is considered as a whole across the United States (as opposed to, for example, the teaching of history), Brazil's presence is sporadic and unstructured, a not-necessarily large element within area studies programs or language and literature programs. However, specific pockets of greater emphasis exist, frequently developing around one or two individuals, outstanding scholars who draw students and resources to their programs. This is the way in which the still strong program on Brazil at the University of California, Los Angeles, developed around historians Ludwig Lauerhass and the late E. Bradford Burns, along with literature professor Claude Hulet. Similarly, Brown University's exceptional degrees in Portuguese and Brazilian studies coalesced around historian Thomas Skidmore and literature professors Luiz Valente and Nelson Vieira, in addition to Onésimo Almeida. The program on Brazil at the University of Texas, Austin, grew around Fred P. Ellison and produced many of the faculty now directing the teaching of Brazil in the United States. On a smaller scale, Jon Tolman was the heart of the University of New Mexico's courses on Brazil, while Robert Levine and William Smith anchored the efforts at the University of Miami. This reliance on building programs around a small group of eminent scholars raises serious questions about the institutionalization of the teaching of Brazil studies. While few universities would ever consider closing a history program after the exit of the department's foremost scholar, programs on Brazil face the very real threat of languishing if they have not been institutionalized through the creation of degrees or certificates bearing the name "Brazil," through the renewal of the faculty by means of new hires, or through the establishment and maintenance of an active faculty group that bridges disciplinary lines.

The current trend in U.S. academia appears to be moving away from "area studies" programs, such as Latin American studies or East Asian studies, toward transnational and comparative studies, linked to the much-commented phenomenon of globalization. This redefinition of fields of study does not bode well for Brazil programs per se. The reasoning behind the comparativist impetus reflects the interconnectivity of such events as the economic crises of Japan/Asia, Russia, and Mexico; the similarities of transitions from authoritarian regimes to democracy, be it in the former Soviet states, Latin America, or South Africa; or the issues surrounding environmental destruction in tropical rain forests from Malaysia to the Congo to the Amazon. The perceived underlying commonalities of these phenomena may lead to insightful "cross-fertilization" and pooling of resources. Global economists address the financial effects that ripple across continents, causing foreign investors to pull out of specific emerging markets as a reaction to losses in other emerging markets. Political scientists identify patterns of turbulence in young political systems through similarities in other systems. Environmental activists become aware of specific endangering practices and the true scope of threats to global ecology when studying the use of pesticides in discreet ecosystems. Teaching about Brazil within this context will have to result from innovative interdisciplinary and transregional approaches.

TEACHING THE PORTUGUESE LANGUAGE

One of the largest audiences in North American universities and colleges devoted exclusively to Brazil appears within the programs of Portuguese language and Lusophone literature. While continental (and Azorean) Portuguese dominates in areas around New England and parts of California (especially around Artesia, near Los Angeles, and the San Joaquin Valley), a majority of Portuguese-language programs teach Brazilian Portuguese. The language is taught in the context of Brazil's culture, as evidenced in such textbooks as *Travessia* (1988) and *Brasil! Língua e Cultura* (1992), two of the very few Portuguese-language texts produced in the United States. Most Portuguese programs exist within either a department of Spanish and Portuguese or a department of Romance or modern languages. The University of Massachusetts–Dartmouth's relatively new (fall 2000) Department of Portuguese is a notable exception resulting from a combination of demographics and dedicated faculty. While there are thousands of undergraduate programs in Spanish, fewer than one hundred exist in Portuguese. Frequently, the reasoning offered refers to the great number of Spanish-speaking countries compared to the limited number of Lusophone countries. This argument obviously ignores the demographic and economic realities of Latin America, not to mention other Portuguese-speaking nations in Africa, Asia, and Europe. A more plausible justification is the dominance of Spanish-speaking populations within the United States—including both recent immigrants and heritage populations—and the shared border with Mexico. Course offerings thus reflect both the actual, immediate demand of the student clientele and the perceived importance generated by the various academic departments involved in language teaching and Latin American studies at large. Significantly, among the most popular topics for professional development workshops for the American Association of Teachers of Spanish and Portuguese, as cited in its fall 2000 bulletin, was: "How to incorporate Brazil into Latin American Studies programs" (*Enlace*). Similarly, Lúcia Helena Costigan, of the Department of Spanish and Portuguese at Ohio State University, organized a faculty seminar for summer 2001 entitled "The Invisible Giant: The

Place of Brazil in Latin American Studies," funded by a $177,000 National Endowment for the Humanities grant. However, given the widespread presence of Spanish in the United States and the geographic distance to Brazil, in the field of language instruction Portuguese will likely always remain in the shadow of Spanish.

Modern-language pedagogies address language instruction within a cultural context, an obvious example of which is the text *Brasil! Língua e Cultura*. Consequently, Brazil is "taught" along with the language in most Portuguese programs throughout the country. Moreover, the construction of a Portuguese undergraduate major regularly includes both "culture" classes offered by the language department as well as related courses from outside the department. An example of this is the Luso-Brazilian Languages and Literatures major at the University of California, Berkeley. As is increasingly common in the United States, this major requires courses not only in language and literature (taught in Portuguese) but also courses in related areas outside the major (see http://spanish-portuguese.berkeley.edu/). The list of courses outside the department comes from fourteen different disciplines and includes the history of Brazil, as well as numerous courses on Latin America from the fields of anthropology, political science, sociology, and so on. For art and history of art the department accepts "anything pertaining to Spain, Portugal, or Central and South America" (http://ls.berkeley.edu/dept/span/undergrad/optionb.html). Significantly, not only does the Portuguese major include courses not taught in the language and that address Brazil (or Portugal) only in larger regional contexts, it also allows for two related courses in literature, linguistics, or culture taught in Spanish, reinforcing Brazil's position within a Latin American context in the North American academic sphere. At the same time, it is important to note the offering of "culture" courses taught by language/literature faculty. Typically, these include Brazilian (or Luso-Brazilian) culture, addressing a wide range of issues drawing from humanities and social sciences beyond the field of literature. Berkeley is far from alone in its structure. Almost all Portuguese majors in the United States include at least an option for nonlanguage/literature coursework, and even those that do not allow for such an option do have a requirement for the study of culture. For example, the Department of Spanish and Portuguese at Yale University explains that an undergraduate major is "intended to develop competence in the Portuguese language and provide students with a comprehensive knowledge of the literatures and cultures of Portugal, Brazil, and African and Asian lands of Portuguese language or influence" (http://www.yale.edu/span-port/portuguese.html).

BRAZIL IN LATIN AMERICAN STUDIES PROGRAMS

Of the more than forty universities featuring programs in Latin American studies that include Brazil, fewer than fifteen have specific degrees or certificates on Brazil or Brazilian studies, although a much larger number have Portuguese-language majors or minors that may focus on Brazil, as mentioned earlier. Brown University stands alone with its Department of Portuguese and Brazilian Studies, offering degree programs through the doctoral level, and the University of Massachusetts–Dartmouth has a newly created Department of Portuguese. More commonly, a student at either the undergraduate or graduate level must major in Latin American studies with a focus on Brazil or in Luso-Brazilian literature and culture, although Arizona State University offers an undergraduate major and minor in Brazil studies leading to a master's or doctoral degree in Latin American studies. As of December 2003, the institutions that have specific Brazilian studies groups comprised of faculty who work with Brazil, and who would oversee the curricula of those studying the country, included Arizona State University, the University of Arizona, Brown University, Berkeley, UCLA, the University of Florida, Florida International University, Harvard University, the University of New Mexico, the University of Pittsburgh, Stanford University, Tulane University, the University of Texas at Austin, and the University of Wisconsin–Madison. The existence or not of a specifically identified program on Brazil in no way guarantees a strong and well-developed curriculum at either the graduate or undergraduate level; indeed, many institutions that do not explicitly offer a Brazil program may have excellent resources for the teaching of Brazil. An example of this ambiguity would be a comparison of the programmatic output (in terms of undergraduate and graduate students focusing on Brazil and/or writing theses and dissertations on Brazil) of Harvard University's thirty-six faculty members who include Brazil among their specializations vis-à-vis that of the four fellows at Notre Dame University's Kellogg Institute. Nevertheless, as stated elsewhere in this essay, a program on Brazil that lacks institutionalization runs the risk of disappearing with the departure of the key faculty members who have developed and maintained the curriculum.

DISCIPLINARY FOCI

As is true of all area studies programs in U.S. universities, most programs focusing on Brazil are anchored in the disciplines of history, political science, sociology or language and literature. By law, centers for Latin

American studies that receive federally funded Title VI grants must include language components in their curriculum, and this requirement is an important stimulus for the creation of Portuguese-language courses and the teaching of Brazilian studies. Faculty who teach courses on Brazil come from a cross-section of academic disciplines, primarily in the humanities and social sciences, with some faculty in professional schools. For example, Stanford University's program includes the Joaquim Nabuco Chair in Brazilian Studies and a Brazil Working Group comprised of faculty, advanced graduate students, and visiting scholars from Stanford and other Bay Area universities; a study trip to Brazil under the auspices of the graduate school of business; language and literature courses from the Department of Spanish and Portuguese; a Brazilian writer-in-residence program; and other interdisciplinary coursework under the auspices of the Center for Latin American Studies (www.stanford.edu/group/las/about/index.html).

Small programs usually teach Brazil almost exclusively within the content of a more general course or program on Latin America. The University of Massachusetts–Amherst, for example, offers specific courses on Puerto Rico, Venezuela, Colombia, Cuba, and Haiti in a number of disciplines but includes Brazil in introductory classes such as "Latin American Civilization." The exception there, and at most other universities in the United States that deal with Brazil, is in the Department of Spanish and Portuguese, which features such courses as "Brazilian Civilization," "Brazilian Women Writers," "Brazilian Literature," "Brazilian Film and Fiction," and more. Similarly, the Center for Latin American Studies at Ohio State University emphasizes Brazil and Mexico as its primary teaching and library strengths, along with an even greater stress on Central America. Nevertheless, besides the culture and literature courses of the Portuguese program, in the spring of 2005 it offered only one class exclusively devoted to Brazil ("History of Brazil").

Harvard University is typical of a pattern at large Latin American studies programs. Its large concentration of specialists on Brazil—three dozen faculty—have their primary appointments in professional schools. Of the thirty-six faculty members who work on Brazil (including two retired professors but excluding visiting faculty, fellows, and graduate assistants), twenty-five say that Brazil is their primary field and six focus exclusively on Brazil, at least within the context of Latin America. Most surprising, however, is the disciplinary concentration: one-third of Harvard's Brazil specialists are in the School of Medicine, working with tropical diseases and/or public health issues. Similarly, the University of Illinois at Urbana-Champaign includes among its nineteen faculty members who specialize on Brazil a physiological and conservation ecologist, an environmental sociologist, a plant biologist specializing in phytochemistry, and a geologist.

This raises the question of the constitution of Brazilian studies as an interdisciplinary or multidisciplinary field. Traditional "Brazilianists" have come from the social sciences as well as the humanities. Most designated programs on Brazil consist of faculty from such disciplines as language and literature, history, political science, economics, sociology, and anthropology. A commonly held opinion among these academics is that others not specializing in such "core" disciplines, especially those from the "hard sciences," are not really "teaching Brazil." Following this rationale, a geologist just studies the rocks, not "the country itself." Nevertheless, Stephen Marshak, a professor of geology at the University of Illinois at Urbana-Champaign, teaches both structural geology and the geology of Brazil and has published "Tectonic Implications of Precambrian Sm-Nd [sic] Dates from the Southern São Francisco Craton and Adjacent Aracuaí and Ribeira Belts" as well as *Brazil: Precambrian Research*. Is this professor any less involved with the teaching of Brazil than is a political scientist whose primary field is Mexico, speaks no Portuguese or only "Portuñol," and has never been to Brazil but offers a survey course on Latin American politics and is interested in authoritarian regimes and the transition to democracy? The reality is that while a very significant majority of specialists on Brazil come from the traditional fields, all programs on Brazil in the United States draw upon faculty resources from a wide range of disciplinary foci. The "teaching of Brazil" is by its very definition an interdisciplinary approach. Constituent faculty must represent a multitude of disciplines as is the case with all area studies, gender studies, ethnic studies, or similar programs.

The issues for evaluating the quality of a program, especially for prospective students at both the graduate and undergraduate levels, must include several items: quantity of courses dedicated solely to Brazil; quantity of courses that include Brazil (e.g., "History of Latin America"); how frequently these courses are offered; numbers of faculty members whose primary field of research is Brazil, especially but not exclusively in the student's major field; number of other related faculty (especially important for completing graduate committees); degrees offered (Ph.D., M.A., undergraduate major, undergraduate minor, etc.); enrollments (this pertains to sustainability of the courses and of the program); graduation rates (informs as to the institutional support for the student, especially at the graduate level, as well as the difficulty of completing the program of study, which may reflect personnel issues, availability of required and elective courses, etc.); and job placement.

To a large extent, the frequency of course offerings is even more important that the quantity of courses listed in the catalog. As new courses are constructed and approved, catalogs can swell to a remarkable size. Universities and colleges purge these lists much less frequently. Some institutions state which faculty members teach specific classes and the terms during which they are offered, but even this useful information can be outdated or exaggerated (for example, if the catalog indicates that a given professor regularly offers six courses each term, one can assume that the list is not accurate). The presence of faculty who do research on Brazil is essential, not just for the courses that the student may take but also for mentoring and directing theses and dissertations. While the greatest importance obviously is within the student's own major, the presence of other researchers focusing on Brazil allows students to expand their critical thinking beyond strictly disciplinary horizons and may function along with faculty from fields related to Brazil as a pool from which students may draw committee members. At some institutions with one or two very active professors, students may eventually complete a degree with a wide range of class subjects but may run the risk of "majoring in Professor X." This is not to say that such programs are devoid of value, and indeed some such programs may be more enriching for the students than others with more faculty names and less faculty participation. However, as with any program of study, the teaching of Brazil ideally includes multiple perspectives that stimulate critical debate.

BENCHMARK TEXTS

Among the many texts frequently employed in the teaching of Brazil, several works distinguish themselves for their widespread use among U.S. college courses. The following discussion, with the exception of Portuguese-language textbooks, consists only of books written in English that could be considered standard texts for courses about Brazil. These titles come from required readings in courses offered at various universities in the United States. It consequently reflects to some extent more of a "bestseller" list than a critical selection or endorsement of any specific text. It is in no way exhaustive or definitive but merely a sample of the texts most commonly used to teach about Brazil. Although grouped by approximate academic discipline, faculty across many disciplines regularly utilize quite a few of these books. These are not necessarily the most recent texts, but rather they are among the most commonly taught books, especially for introductory or general courses on Brazil.

The most frequently used language textbooks for Brazilian Portuguese are Claude E. Leroy, *Português para principiantes* (1993); Thomas A. Lathrop and Eduardo Mayone Dias *Brasil! Língua e Cultura* (1992); Jon Tolman, John Jensen, Ricardo Paiva, and Nivea Parsons, *Travessia* (1988), and Emma Eberlein O. F. Lima and Samira A. Lunes, *Falando, Lendo, Escrevendo Português* (1981). For the history of Brazil the most frequently used texts are Boris Fausto, *A Concise History of Brazil* (1999); Robert Levine, *Brazilian Legacies* (1997); Marshall C. Eakin, *Brazil: The Once and Future Country* (1997); Leslie Bethell, *Brazil: Empire and First Republic, 1822–1930* (1989); Emilia Viotti da Costa, *The Brazilian Empire: Myths and Histories* (1985); E. Bradford Burns, *A History of Brazil,* 3rd ed. (1993); and Charles Wagley, *An Introduction to Brazil* (1971).

In courses on sociology and race relations, some of the more frequently used texts are Jeffrey Lesser, *Welcoming the Undesirables: Brazil and the Jewish Question* (1994); Nancy Scheper-Hughes, *Death Without Weeping: Violence of Everyday Life in Brazil* (1993); George Reid Andrews, *Blacks and Whites in São Paulo, Brazil, 1888–1988* (1991); Stanley J. Stein, *Vassouras: A Brazilian Coffee County, 1850–1900: The Roles of Planter and Slave in a Plantation Society* (1985); and Carl Degler, *Neither Black nor White: Slavery and Race Relations in Brazil and the United States* (1971). In economics, some examples are Stephen Haber, ed., *How Latin America Fell Behind: Essays on the Economic Histories of Brazil and Mexico, 1800–1914* (1997); Maria Willumsen and Eduardo Giannetti da Fonseca, eds., *The Brazilian Economy: Structure and Performance in Recent Decades* (1997); Stephen Kanitz, *Brazil: The Emerging Economic Boom, 1995–2005* (1995); Maria D'Alva Kinzo and Victor Bulmer-Thomas, eds., *Growth and Development in Brazil: Cardoso's Real Challenge* (1995); Bertha K. Becker and Claudio A. G. Egler, eds., *Brazil: A New Regional Power in the World Economy— A Regional Geography* (1992); Joseph S. Tulchin and Werner Baer, *Brazil and the Challenge of Economic Reform* (1993). In political science, Ronald Schneider, *"Order and Progress": A Political History of Brazil* (1991); Alfred Stepan, ed., *Democratizing Brazil: Problems of Transition and Consolidation* (1989); Thomas E. Skidmore, *The Politics of Military Rule in Brazil: 1964–1985* (1988); Maria Helena Moreira Alves, *State and Opposition in Military Brazil* (1985).

Some texts that appear frequently on syllabi for cinema courses are Robert Stam, *Tropical Multiculturalism: A Comparative History of Race in Brazilian Cinema and Culture* (1997); Randal Johnson and Robert Stam, *Brazilian Cinema* (1995); Randal Johnson, *The Film Industry in Brazil* (1987). In music and dance, Peter Fryer, *Rhythms of Resistance: The African*

Musical Heritage of Brazil (2000); Charles Perrone, *Masters of Contemporary Brazilian Song MPB, 1965–1985* (1989); Alma Guillermoprieto, *Samba* (1990); Chris McGowan and Ricardo Pessanha, *Brazilian Sound: Samba, Bossa Nova and Popular Music of Brazil* (1998).

SUMMER PROGRAMS IN THE UNITED STATES

One of the most common ways of fostering the teaching of Brazil at U.S. colleges and universities is through summer school classes. Usually offered by departments of language and literature, these summer programs frequently combine instruction in the Portuguese language at beginning and, sometimes, intermediate levels, coupled with (Luso-) Brazilian culture. Most Latin American studies programs with a Title VI National Resource Center (NRC) offer some form of summer program to meet the requirements of the federal grant. Moreover, many graduate programs in Latin American studies at schools that offer Portuguese include a second language requirement that can be satisfied by these summer classes. Universities that regularly offer Portuguese-language and Brazilian studies summer programs on campus include the University of California (Berkeley, Los Angeles, and Santa Barbara), the University of Florida, Florida International University, the University of Wisconsin–Madison, the University of Massachusetts-Amherst, the University of Texas at Austin, Middlebury College, and many more.

The University of California at Santa Barbara (UCSB) has one of the most developed summer programs, including an array of language, literature, and culture classes at both the undergraduate and graduate levels. To enhance the students' experience, UCSB runs a Portuguese-language house concurrent with the summer classes where students are immersed in language and culture throughout the day. Run by the Department of Spanish and Portuguese, the language house activities for the length of the summer term include a weekly newsletter, films, skits, guest speakers, and a minicolloquium that brings in scholars for relatively informal panels on any subject related to Brazil, Portugal, and the diaspora. Although run by a language and literature program, the speaker series and colloquium draw from a variety of disciplines. Students are encouraged to speak only Portuguese at all times within the language house and at summer institute functions. While efforts are made to be inclusive of all Lusophone regions, the program run by the UCSB Center for Portuguese Studies was made possible by an endowment from the Calouste Gulbenkian Foundation. Consequently, UCSB offers bachelor of arts and master of arts degrees in Portuguese and a doctoral degree in Hispanic languages and literatures with a specialization in Luso-Brazilian literature with only three faculty members (as of January 2005), two of whom specialize in Portugal, not Brazil. Nevertheless, the summer program stands as a model for other institutions.

SUMMER ABROAD PROGRAMS

Many colleges and universities have or have had summer programs in Brazil, but only a very limited number have existed for more than a decade. The University of Florida's program (now the Florida Consortium for Brazil), which has run continuously for more than twenty years, is unusual in its longevity. Traditionally, summer programs have consisted of a language component and a culture component and are administered by faculty from a language department. Following this model, a couple of faculty members, or even a single professor and some teaching assistants, may organize a summer program in conjunction with a Brazilian institution, either a university or a language school. There are two primary groups of programs: those taught by U.S. faculty to a group while in Brazil, and others taught by instructors from a Brazilian institution in collaboration with the study abroad program. Even schools with relatively small programs dealing with Brazil may sometimes promote a summer course in Brazil, teaching the typical language and culture classes. The University of South Florida (USF) is an example of a newer and smaller institution that greatly enhances its teaching about Brazil with two summer abroad programs, both in conjunction with the Universidade Federal do Paraná. A key aspect of the program was its location outside the Rio de Janeiro–São Paulo–Salvador triangle, specifically based in Curitiba and capitalizing on the interest in that city's status as an innovative center of urban planning. Like numerous other institutions, USF chose to avoid the more common attraction of Rio's tropical beaches, which lure many students to programs from across academia; São Paulo's draw for business and professionally oriented students; and Salvador's emphasis on Afro-Brazilian culture—taken together, these three constitute the majority of summer abroad programs in Brazil. The USF courses offered included Portuguese-language classes, Portuguese for business, Brazilian cinema or culture, and the urban ecology of Curitiba.

Schools seeking to develop new summer programs in Brazil, or to bolster existing ones, follow paths similar to that chosen by USF. The University of New Mexico, whose Portuguese program consists of two regular faculty members (Margo Milleret and Leila Lehnen), runs its summer program in Fortaleza. It includes a single course on Brazilian popular culture designed to improve students' language competency through the use of "authentic materials and communicative activities." Similarly, while the University of Maryland–College Park offers neither an undergraduate degree in Brazilian studies nor a major in Portuguese, it does have several faculty members who work with Brazil, notably in language and literature, and in Afro-American studies. These areas of interest merge in the university's three-week *winter* program (January) in Salvador, Bahia, entitled "Cultura Afrobrasileira" and led by two faculty members from the Department of Spanish and Portuguese. Taking a slightly different tack, the University of Florida has added "Business in Brazil" as a component of its long-standing program in Rio de Janeiro. Promoted through its Center for International Business Education and Research, the new program caters to MBA students and others with career interests in Latin American business. Students participate in the same morning language classes as all other participants, but instead of Brazilian culture seminars in the afternoon they attend a "Business in Brazil" course at the Rio de Janeiro campus of the Pontifícia Universidade Católica.

Year or Semester Abroad Programs

Many universities enhance the educational opportunities for their students with study abroad programs at foreign universities. These tend to fit into the same two primary groups as the summer programs: faculty-led programs and exchange programs. Normally, faculty-led study abroad courses function pedagogically and administratively as if they were regular classes taught at the U.S. institution, only the instruction takes place in a foreign country. Classes may be taught in Portuguese or, less commonly, in English.

Most semester or year abroad programs, however, are direct exchanges with a foreign university. U.S. students attend regular university classes and, in some special instances, courses for foreign students at the host institution. Exchange programs typically require a certain level of proficiency in the language of the chosen country. Most of these universities normally do not offer summer courses. An example of a strongly established program following this pattern is the University of California's program at the Pontifícia Universidade Católica in Rio de Janeiro (formerly at the Universidade de São Paulo). This program has existed through various affiliations with Indiana, Stanford, and other universities for several decades. It formerly was part of the Inter-university Study Program at the Universidade de São Paulo (ISP-USP). ISP-USP is currently administered by the Council on International Educational Exchanges, a consortium of eighty-two institutions of postsecondary education in the United States with overseas programs throughout the world (see www.ciee.org). In both programs, students enroll along with the Brazilian students in host institution classes from almost any discipline and complete all the same coursework. Grades are normally transferred to the home institution by an on-site coordinator, who may or may not be a member of the U.S. university's regular faculty. The coordinator serves as administrator for program activities, including preprogram orientation, local enrollment and registration, advising, housing issues, procurement of federal temporary resident identification cards, and grade adjustment and transfer. The latter require an understanding not only of simple grade scales (e.g., ten-point versus four-point scales) but also of the relative weight of grades within each system, which frequently is not a simple mathematical conversion.

Institutions with a small or no direct program on Brazil may offer opportunities abroad to supplement their curricula. St. John's University in New York offers a single course with emphasis on Brazil ("Cross-cultural Psychology," which includes lectures on the differing systems of racial classification in the Americas, especially in Brazil) yet maintains academic exchange agreements with the Universidade de São Paulo (especially its Faculdade de Economia e Administração), the Universidade Católica de Brasília, and the Pontifícia Universidade Católica of Rio de Janeiro. All study abroad programs, large and small, serve to enhance the teaching of Brazil in U.S. institutions and at times are essential elements of both undergraduate and graduate programs of study.

TITLE VI AND FOREIGN LANGUAGE AND AREA STUDIES

The U.S. Department of Education's Title VI programs allow postsecondary institutions to compete for significant grants to foster both undergraduate and graduate education in numerous fields, including Latin American studies. Title VI-D grants are two-year, start-up awards directed exclusively at undergraduate education. The larger and more competitive Title VI-NRC grants cover an extensive array of activities, including undergraduate, graduate, and postgraduate education, community outreach, and research. A subunit of the Title VI program is the Foreign Language and Area Studies (FLAS) award, which targets students who are permanent residents of the United States for instruction in specific languages, including Portuguese. This program provides academic year and summer fellowships to institutions of higher education to assist graduate students in foreign language and either area or international studies. The goals of the fellowship program include (1) assisting in the development of knowledge, resources, and trained personnel for modern foreign-language and area/international studies; (2) stimulating the attainment of foreign-language acquisition and fluency; and (3) developing a pool of international experts to meet national needs. When linked to a Latin American studies center, the FLAS awards frequently foster the study of Portuguese and of Brazil. With no disciplinary restrictions, these grants cultivate interest in Brazil among graduate students and serve as a significant tool for the enhancement of Brazilian studies programs through recruitment and retention of the best graduate students. For the fiscal years of 2000–2002 (August 15, 2000 to August 14, 2003), the U.S. Department of Education funded 176 FLAS awards for Latin America (104 for the regular academic year and 72 for summer programs in the United States and abroad for advanced students) to 31 U.S. universities (some award centers are consortium programs such as those at Duke University and the University of North Carolina, or San Diego State University and the University of California, San Diego).

Conclusion

In spite of the enormous geographical, demographic, political, and economic importance of Brazil in the western hemisphere, the teaching of Brazil in U.S. colleges and universities remains peripheral to that of the twenty Spanish-speaking countries in Latin America and the Caribbean. This reflects both student-body and faculty demographics, given the significant population of Hispanics and Latinos in the United States. The long-term demographic and cultural realities of the U.S. Southwest (Hispanic/Mexican American), southern Florida (Cuban/Cuban American), and New York (Puerto Rican/Nuyorican) create a linguistic facility for the study of Spanish America and have further facilitated the inclusion of more recent immigrant groups such as Central Americans and Colombians. Access to primary sources in the language increases scholarship of a given region; the presence of more scholars leads to increased emphasis in the teaching at both graduate and undergraduate levels. The front line for teaching about Brazil remains the Portuguese-language programs, as is evident in such programs as those at Georgetown's (and many other universities), where the Department of Spanish and Portuguese offers "Topics in Afro-Luso-Brazilian Culture"; New York University, where the Latin American studies major itself is offered by the Department of Spanish and Portuguese; or the University of California, Berkeley, whose Department of Spanish and Portuguese offers a master of arts degree in Luso-Brazilian studies. Truly successful efforts to educate students about Brazil must bring together faculty from a variety of disciplines.

Florida International University, for example, has programmatically developed a focus on Brazil through the hiring of Brazil specialists in the fields of anthropology, dance, economics, education, history, labor relations, language and literature, political science, and sociology. The University of Wisconsin–Madison has a similar focus group. As is the case in almost all programs, the individual professors' teaching assignments include other general courses in their field. However, the presence of a defined Brazil studies faculty group allows for the regular offering of a variety of core courses on Brazil. Similar initiatives exist at numerous institutions, such as Arizona State University, the University of Arizona, Berkeley, the University of Florida, the University of New Mexico, the University of Pittsburgh, the University of Texas at Austin, and Stanford University. Coordination and communication among faculty and a proactive approach to the teaching of Brazil—including encouraging students to enroll in related Brazil-focused courses across disciplinary lines—are essential to the growth of any true program on Brazil. Unfortunately, as this essay shows, most faculty who study and teach Brazil work in relative isolation within their institution, usually within a traditional discipline (e.g., history) or broader program (e.g., Latin American studies). Brown University remains exceptional in its ability to offer a wide range of courses in a variety of disciplines on a regular basis. Without efforts to coordinate a core of courses on Brazil, Brazil studies will continue to be an all-too-often-neglected subset of Latin American studies.

Many colleges and universities in the United States have an educational interest in Brazil, as evidenced by the thirty-five U.S. institutions participating in the 1999 U.S.-Brazil Partnership for Educational Binational Dialogue. The meetings included such traditional centers of academic interest in Latin America as the University of Pittsburgh but also smaller schools such as Knox College (Illinois), and these meetings foster a dialogue between educational institutions in both Brazil and the United States. Through the kinds of creative initiatives discussed in these meetings, through student and faculty exchanges, combined ("sandwich") degree programs, and distance learning technologies, among others, teaching about Brazil in the United States may gradually become accessible to a much greater number of faculty and students.

The importance of Brazil in the academic curricula of U.S. institutions of higher learning, and in the current context of global and comparative studies, will depend upon scholars' making disciplinary linkages across regional lines (such as urbanization in São Paulo, Mexico City, and Tokyo) and interdisciplinary approaches to specifically Brazilian issues that produce a more complete understanding of particular phenomena (such as climatic, social, economic, and political studies of poverty in Brazil's Northeast). These approaches will have to be brought from field research and scholarly publications into the classroom. For in the final analysis, the study of Brazil in U.S. universities will have to include the expansion of undergraduate and graduate courses on Brazil, as well as cutting-edge research. U.S. scholars who research Brazil must also teach Brazil in order for Brazilian studies to survive and thrive.

Notes

1. This essay does not cover the evolution of Latin American studies (and of area studies in general) from World War II through the Cold War, including the political ideologies that shaped the conceptualization of these "strategic areas." Other authors in this volume discuss these issues. A detailed discussion of Portuguese-language programs and of Brazilian literature programs is the subject matter of Carmen Tesser's essay (chapter 4).

2. A more complete listing of institutions, programs, and faculty appears on the web pages that served as the principal sources of the data for this study. Specific data regarding programs, majors, faculty, and such comes from each institution's published material, either in the form of brochures and pamphlets or, more commonly, websites, which tend to be more current. For greater detail see the website *Directory of Scholars in Brazilian Studies* at http://drclas.fas.harvard.edu/directories/brazil/index.php. It is assumed that all these institutions seek to present themselves in a positive light.

References

Alves, Maria Helena Moreira. 1985. *State and Opposition in Military Brazil.* Austin: University of Texas Press.

Andrews, George Reid. 1991. *Blacks and Whites in São Paulo, Brazil, 1888–1988.* Madison: University of Wisconsin Press.

Becker, Bertha K., and Claudio A. G. Egler, eds. 1992. *Brazil: A New Regional Power in the World Economy—A Regional Geography.* Cambridge: Cambridge University Press.

Bethell, Leslie, ed. 1989. *Brazil: Empire and First Republic, 1822–1930.* Cambridge: Cambridge University Press.

Burns, E. Bradford. 1993. *A History of Brazil.* 3rd ed. New York: Columbia University Press.

Costa, Emilia Viotti da. 1985. *The Brazilian Empire: Myths and Histories.* Chicago: University of Chicago Press.

Degler, Carl N. 1986. *Neither Black nor White: Slavery and Race Relations in Brazil and the United States.* Madison: University of Wisconsin Press.

Eakin, Marshall C. 1997. *Brazil: The Once and Future Country.* New York: St. Martin's.

Enlace: The Newsletter of the American Association of Teachers of Spanish and Portuguese. 2000. 14, no. 2: n.p.

Fausto, Boris. 1999. *A Concise History of Brazil.* Cambridge: Cambridge University Press.

Fryer, Peter. 2000. *Rhythms of Resistance: The African Musical Heritage of Brazil.* Hanover, N.H.: University Press of New England.

Guillermoprieto, Alma. 1990. *Samba.* New York: Alfred A. Knopf.

Haber, Stephen, ed. 1997. *How Latin America Fell Behind: Essays on the Economic Histories of Brazil and Mexico, 1800–1914.* Stanford, Calif.: Stanford University Press.

Johnson, Randal. 1987. *The Film Industry in Brazil.* Pittsburgh, Pa.: University of Pittsburgh Press.

Johnson, Randal, and Robert Stam. 1995. *Brazilian Cinema.* New York: Columbia University Press.

Kanitz, Stephen C. 1995. *Brazil: The Emerging Economic Boom, 1995–2005.* New York: McGraw-Hill.

Kinzo, Maria D'Alva, and Victor Bulmer-Thomas, eds. 1995. *Growth and Development in Brazil: Cardoso's Real Challenge.* London: University of London.

Lathrop, Thomas A., and Eduardo Mayone Dias. 1992. *Brasil! Língua e Cultura.* Newark, Del.: LinguaText.

Leroy, Claude E. 1993. *Português para principiantes.* Madison: University of Wisconsin.

Lesser, Jeffrey. 1994. *Welcoming the Undesirables: Brazil and the Jewish Question.* Berkeley: University of California Press.

Levine, Robert. 1997. *Brazilian Legacies.* Armonk, N.Y.: M. E. Sharpe.

Lima, Emma Eberlein O. F., and Samira A. Iunes, eds. 1981. *Falando, Lendo, Escrevendo Português.* São Paulo: EPU.

McGowan, Chris, and Ricardo Pessanha. 1998. *The Brazilian Sound: Samba, Bossa Nova and the Popular Music of Brazil.* Philadelphia: Temple University Press.

Perrone, Charles. 1989. *Masters of Contemporary Brazilian Song MPB, 1965–1985.* Austin: University of Texas Press.

Scheper-Hughes, Nancy. 1993. *Death Without Weeping: The Violence of Everyday Life in Brazil.* Berkeley: University of California Press.

Schneider, Ronald. 1991. *"Order and Progress": A Political History of Brazil*. Boulder, Colo.: Westview.

Skidmore, Thomas E. 1988. *The Politics of Military Rule in Brazil: 1964–1985*. New York: Oxford University Press.

Stam, Robert. 1997. *Tropical Multiculturalism: A Comparative History of Race in Brazilian Cinema and Culture*. Durham, N.C.: Duke University Press.

Stein, Stanley J. 1985. *Vassouras: A Brazilian Coffee County, 1850–1900: The Roles of Planter and Slave in a Plantation Society*. Princeton, N.J.: Princeton University Press.

Stepan, Alfred, ed. 1989. *Democratizing Brazil: Problems of Transition and Consolidation*. New York: Oxford University Press.

Tolman, Jon M., John Jensen, Ricardo Paiva, and Nivea Parsons. 1988. *Travessia: A Video-based Portuguese Textbook*. Washington, D.C.: Georgetown University Press.

Tulchin, Joseph S., and Werner Baer. 1993. *Brazil and the Challenge of Economic Reform*. Washington, D.C.: Woodrow Wilson Center Press.

Wagley, Charles. 1971. *An Introduction to Brazil*. New York: Columbia University Press.

Willumsen, Maria, and Eduardo Giannetti da Fonseca, eds. 1997. *The Brazilian Economy: Structure and Performance in Recent Decades*. Coral Gables, Fla.: University of Miami, North/South Center Press.

PART 2

∽

Perspectives from the Disciplines

~

Brazilian Portuguese Language and Linguistics

CARMEN CHAVES TESSER

The study of Portuguese language in the United States dates to the 1650s. For three and a half centuries, scholars have struggled to establish the discipline within the academic community. Nevertheless, it would be fair to say that through the ups and downs in interest in Brazil and attention paid to it and to the rest of the Lusophone world, Portuguese-language study has yet to establish a strong foothold in the U.S. academy. On different occasions, depending on the sociopolitical context or educational climate in the United States or in the Lusophone world, Portuguese-language studies have had a definite presence. On other occasions, although Brazilian studies in general has seemed strong, the study of Portuguese has lagged in interest. On yet other occasions, fluctuations in the field of foreign languages and linguistics in the United States have brought about theoretical and practical challenges in scholarship. The puzzle of why the fifth most commonly spoken language in the world seems to be of relatively little interest to the U.S. academy still remains to be solved. The research productivity related to Portuguese language and linguistics in the United States closely mirrors historical events in these disciplines in general.

Early accounts of Brazilian Portuguese study in the United States date to the end of the seventeenth century when a group of Dutch Jews who had settled in Brazil and the West Indies landed in New Amsterdam in 1654. In 1658, they organized New York City's Congregation Shearith Israel, where Spanish, Portuguese, and Hebrew classes were held until the middle of the eighteenth-century; not until the middle of the nineteenth century did the use of English become habitual in the community (Swierenga 1994).

Among the earliest documented evidence of formal instruction in the Portuguese language in the United States can be found in the archives of St. Mary's Seminary of the Society of St. Sulpice in Baltimore. In the cloistered environment of the seminary, the French priest Peter Abad taught the first courses in Portuguese and in Spanish in a U.S. postsecondary school. In 1720, Abad brought out a Portuguese grammar and announced the publication of five volumes to provide "an understanding of the two Iberian languages" (R. C. Smith 1945: 330). By the late nineteenth century, Harvard, the University of Virginia, and Columbia University began listing Portuguese as an option for language courses.

In 1917, Lawrence A. Wilkins called on a group of academics interested in languages "other than German and French" to establish a scholarly organization. Although the organization was initially called the American Association for Teachers of Spanish (Portuguese was not added to the name until 1944), Wilkins remarks that "we are interesting ourselves in Spanish and Portuguese" (Wilkins 1917: 3). The new organization and its journal, *Hispania*, were to strengthen study and scholarship of all the languages of the Americas; nevertheless, Wilkins goes on to describe the need for *Spanish* language instruction and research. In 1919, two years after the organization came into existence, Branner (1919) published "The Importance of the Study of the Portuguese Language" in *Hispania*. In this article, Branner discusses the connection of Portuguese language "with the commercial and other relations between Brazil and the United States" (87). Branner's compelling argument is based on comparative data among the Latin American countries in terms of population, foreign commerce, and geography. He concludes by calling on departments of languages to develop Portuguese programs "and not leave the public any longer to flounder about without proper guidance" (93). Prompted not so much by this call to action but by the national context that brought it about, colleges and universities began offering Portuguese courses as quickly as they could find faculty to teach them. Thus began what Fred Ellison has described as "the ups and downs in the lines of Portuguese development" that have left us "with alternate feelings of euphoria and dejection" (Ellison 1967: 864).

Portuguese instruction in the 1920s reflected the beginning of the "language issue" that would follow the development of the field through its history: would institutions teach, and U.S. scholars investigate European Portuguese and its reflection in the African colonies, or would the emphasis be on the language of Brazil? On the one hand Pan-Americanism gained strength, giving impetus for the study of Brazilian Portuguese. On the other hand, scholars such as Edwin B. Williams of the University of Pennsylvania carried out much early linguistic research in his field of medieval Portuguese linguistics. Williams's tutelage brought about a cadre of young philologists whose interests lay in the Lusophone world but whose teaching had to focus on Brazil due in part to awareness by scholars of the need to focus on inter-American relations. Hand in hand with the early philological and historical research of the Portuguese language came the production of dictionaries and grammar texts that could be used in teaching. In reviewing the early literature on Portuguese language and linguistics in the U.S. academy, we find, for example, that in "Suggestions for the Study of Portuguese," Chester Lloyd Jones (1927) describes newly published grammar texts as well as dictionaries based on the language of the Portuguese-speaking world. Jones concludes the essay by "happily announcing" summer research and study possibilities in Portugal. We also find Jones's "Spanish and Portuguese in American Relations" (1932), in which he argues convincingly for the study of "the dominant languages of the New World," that is, English, Spanish, and Portuguese. The "language issue" becomes an important element in the development of Portuguese language and linguistic research in the U.S. academy, for depending on the context, doctoral programs trained either Lusitanists or Brazilianists, but seldom did they do both. Not until the 1960s did the study of Portuguese language become somewhat synonymous with Brazilian Portuguese language, a direct result of the National Defense Education Act of 1958.

The late thirties and early forties saw a rapid development in the study of Portuguese language in colleges and universities. World events prompted the urgent need for language training. The Pan-American Union survey of 1941 points to forty-seven colleges and universities in the United States that were offering at least elementary instruction in the Portuguese language, and in such states as Massachusetts, California, Michigan, and New York secondary school students were enrolled in the language (Allen 1942). In 1943, James S. Carson, chair of the Education Committee of the National Foreign Trade Council, spoke at the inauguration of the teaching of Portuguese at Central Commercial High School in New York City, calling the occasion one of immeasurable future significance in the history of inter-American relations (Carson 1944, cited in Ellison 1967: 868). As the teaching of Portuguese language became more widespread in the United States, so did academic research into the intricacies of the Portuguese language and into teaching methodology. These developments, coupled with the involvement of professional organizations in the dissemination of research, seemed to forecast success.

In December 1941, the Modern Language Association of America convened the organizational meeting of a "Portuguese Group." William Berrien of the Rockefeller Foundation gave an overview of the field and suggested that this group would form an "ideal starting-point for the serious planning of the development of Portuguese studies in this country" (Berrien 1942: 87). His recommendations, given to a group primarily concerned with literature, included several language and linguistic issues. Some topics that Berrien considered of interest and of usefulness bear repeating here. For example, he points to the need for "well-documented studies on such fundamental problems as the position of object pronouns, the uses of *ser* and *estar*, the personal infinitive, and certain aspects of the subjunctive" (88). He concludes that in the field of syntax, collaborative research may be the best key for yielding "monographs having the advantage of uniformity in design, method, and technique" (88). Berrien calls for scientific investigation in the field of phonetics by suggesting studies conducted in different regions of Brazil. The focus of these investigations, he contends, should be on the palatalized "t" and "d" as well as nasal vowels. Further, he suggests comparative approaches to the study of Portuguese linguistics that would bring together the language spoken "in Portugal, Brazil, and Galicia" (87). Berrien's research agenda, which also included suggestions for the study of literature written in Portuguese, proved prophetic in the development of the discipline.

Fanned by the excitement of war urgency and the euphoria of new areas of research, Portuguese enrollments began to explode throughout the United States. In 1942, 51 postsecondary schools offered the language with a total enrollment of 558 students, in contrast to the 205 students reported by the Office of the Coordinator of Inter-American Affairs the previous year (Ornstein 1950). By 1943, 75 colleges and universities had courses in Portuguese, and in 1944, 92 colleges and universities in 35 states as well as the District of Columbia offered the language (Stewart 1944). The pattern continued until 1948 (1946: 94 institutions and 1,868 students; 1947: 104 institutions and 1,848 students), when the trend reversed and 102 institutions reported a total enrollment of 1,630 students. To try to understand the downturn, Jacob Ornstein surveyed about 30 institutions throughout the country: 23 reported a decline in enrollment; 6 had no change, 2 announced an increase, and one had dropped Portuguese altogether (Ornstein 1950: 251). Ornstein concluded that Portuguese is still "a new field, still under fire. Undoubtedly its fate will depend in no small measure on Luso-Brazilianists themselves" (255). During the 1950s, enrollments fell drastically except at the U.S. Naval Academy (Viera 1992). Although this trend was not particular to Portuguese, its damage to Portuguese-language programs throughout the country was devastating. Many schools discontinued their offerings, and others reduced faculty and limited classes. In 1956, during the Symposium on the Languages and Literatures of Spanish America and Brazil, held in Austin, Texas, Francis M. Rogers reported that only 24 colleges and universities were offering Portuguese courses to a total of 310 students (Ellison 1967: 867). Scholarship in the area of Portuguese language and linguistics tended to turn to survey research of the discipline itself rather than issues of language.

The Modern Language Association of America has recently published a study of foreign-language enrollments in the United States for the 1960s, 1970s, 1980s, and three years in the 1990s: 1990, 1995, and 1998 (Brod and Welles 2000). Enrollments in Portuguese-language courses saw their largest upswing in the sixties, from 1,033 students in 1960 to 5,065 in 1970 (24). This trend is a clear indication of the success of the National Defense Education Act of 1958. Among its many features, the NDEA focused on the "less commonly taught languages," designating six of them as "critical languages." Portuguese received this designation then and still maintains it. The establishment of NDEA institutes that provided Portuguese-language training to Spanish faculty, as well as the establishment of U.S. Department of Education Title VI area studies centers, provided additional boosts to Portuguese enrollments. Portuguese became—and continues to be—essential to local institutions that wanted to secure Title VI funds to develop Latin American area studies. Throughout the United States, Latin American Studies Centers tried to increase Portuguese enrollments by different means, from *feijoadas* to *forró*. Institutions began hiring (or rehiring) a Portuguese-language "specialist." More often than not, the new tenure-track hires were trained in literature but found themselves trying to develop a language program, build enrollment, design new courses, and at the same time establish a research program that would earn them a tenured position. Many a potential career became derailed during the fifties and sixties. The American Association of Teachers of Spanish and Portuguese established the Portuguese Language Development Group in 1963 to study ways to enhance the development of Portuguese-language programs in the United States.

The challenge of building a Portuguese-language program was compounded by the general trend toward the elimination of language requirements in higher education in the 1960s and 1970s. President Jimmy Carter appointed a blue ribbon commission to study foreign-language study in the United States. The 1979 report of the Perkins Commission, known as

"The President's Commission on Foreign Languages and International Studies," found that lack of attention to foreign languages had reached a crisis. Federal funds once again became available for research, program development, and innovation. The field of linguistics developed rapidly and often quite separately from that of language in the context of Portuguese-language learning in the sixties and seventies. The work of Noam Chomsky and his theory of linguistic competence were framed on the notion of a universal grammar—mental structural systems—wired into every human being (Chomsky 1965). Linguists began researching in the field of second-language acquisition and often took advantage of large enrollment programs from which to gather data. Again, enrollment patterns, the ever-present bane of Portuguese studies, became the greatest challenge for those who wanted to pursue empirical research. This challenge has helped formulate an agenda followed by many linguists interested in Portuguese. They relied on field studies in Brazil or another part of the Lusophone world for data collection, on textual data from literary and popular texts, or on comparative data with Spanish or another language.

In 1980, Portuguese enrollments declined to 4,894 students, although Portuguese maintained its position of the ninth most commonly taught language in the United States. Hebrew, the eighth most commonly taught language, had an enrollment of 19,429 in 1980. The 1990s saw a slight improvement in Portuguese-language enrollment patterns. In 1990, 6,211 students studied Portuguese, as did 6,531 in 1995 and 6,926 in 1998. However, in 1998, Portuguese fell to tenth among the most commonly taught languages in the United States. American Sign Language, with 11,420 students, occupied the ninth spot that year (Brod and Welles 2000). Portuguese-language enrollments seem to be in an upward trend once again. This is encouraging, particularly in view of the decline in enrollment in other commonly taught languages, such as French, German, and Russian. However, the total numbers, as well as the rate of growth itself, are rather small, causing difficulties in the publication of pedagogical materials and in the availability of a sizable research pool for linguistic studies.

Along with enrollment and interest fluctuations, Portuguese programs have lived through the many vicissitudes of language-acquisition methodologies that have come and gone from our discipline since the mid-twentieth century. As early as 1945, the National Education Association, funded by the Office of Inter-American Affairs, sponsored twenty-nine regional conferences on the teaching of Spanish and Portuguese. Intended as a way of reflecting on the study and teaching of the two principal languages of Latin America, the conferences sought to engage Spanish and

Portuguese teachers from all levels of instruction in a dialogue addressing issues of common interest, including methods of teaching (Pitcher 1945). Foreign-language teaching in the United States had, at that point, come to one of its many crises as a result of its historical antecedents.

A Necessary Historical Digression

The study of languages in the United States evolved much as the country itself, as a result of immigrant groups that settled in different regions. The concept of "foreign" languages as a discipline worthy of study related to the classical languages, Greek and Latin, in the postsecondary curriculum designed to turn out "right-thinking members of a New England society" (Leavitt 1961: 596). Greek and Latin were not spoken but taught for reading purposes. Students were to read (and translate) the great works that provided the roots for Western civilization. Modern foreign languages were scarcely tolerated, and when they became part of college and university curricula, they had their own utility: German was the language of science; French the language of culture. Again, the purpose of learning these languages was not oral communication but negotiating meaning from a written text: reading/translating. Graduate students studied philology and language history for a better understanding of grammar. The only institution that diverged from this teaching method was the Middlebury Spanish School, established in 1917. The most impressive feature of the teaching in this school was the insistence on spoken language, today the hallmark of the Language Schools at Middlebury College, the Language Pledge. In 1923, as part of a study funded by the Carnegie Corporation, Algernon Coleman of the University of Chicago published *The Teaching of Foreign Languages in the United States*. The most important recommendation of the "Coleman Report" was the reading objective, solidifying the earlier language instruction for reading purposes (Leavitt 1961: 620).

When the United States found itself engaged in war again in the 1940s, the kind of language teaching that took place did not prepare anyone for communicating with anyone else. Mortimer Graves of the American Council of Learned Societies developed the Army Specialized Training Program (ASTP), calling for a concentration on the spoken language being studied. One of the first language courses developed through the ASTP was Brazilian Portuguese. Vicenzo Cioffari describes his experience in developing this method for Portuguese in "Linguistic Experiment in Brazil" (Cioffari 1949). In his summary, he describes the successful learning experiment in which repetition drills and limited grammatical explanations were the preferred methods of instruction. The success of the ASTP prompted many schools to adopt the new methodology in their language classes. They did not, however, take into account some of the key ingredients that contributed to the success of the experiment: first, extrinsic motivation (it behooved our military personnel to understand their Brazilian counterparts); second, total immersion (the program was developed in Brazil); and, finally, total time commitment (classes met for only one hour each day; however, the participants did nothing else for the period of instruction).

In one of those cases of historical irony, in 1949, a young Brazilian linguist who had participated in the first meeting of the Linguistic Circle of New York in 1943 returned to Brazil and proposed as his doctoral thesis a phonemic description of Brazilian Portuguese. The linguist, Joaquim Mattoso Câmara Jr., had formulated his ideas during fruitful conversations with Roman Jakobson and Claude Lévi-Strauss, with whom the Brazilian linguist developed his brand of structuralism. When Mattoso Câmara published *Princípios de linguística geral* in 1954, he set in motion the introduction of structural linguistics to several generations of Brazilian students (Altman 1999). Until the 1960s, the linguistic approach used by Joaquim Mattoso Câmara Jr. was the most common one, and it is still used partially by the Department of Portuguese Language at the Federal University of Rio de Janeiro. In the 1960s the field began to adopt two other theories: the structuralist theory, by the professors who specialized in French authors such as Bernard Pottier; and the formalist theory, identified with the Russian school. Afterward, we begin to see the semiotic approach of Algirdas Greimas, and the generative-transformational theory of Noam Chomsky. In the 1980s, emphasis was put on sociolinguistics and psycholinguistics. In the 1990s, discourse analysis and pragmatics became fashionable.

FOREIGN LANGUAGES AND LITERATURES
Different Cultures, Different Goals, and Different Teaching Methodologies

Many factors contributed to a crisis in the field of foreign languages and linguistics in the late 1940s and early 1950s. There were diverging opinions of the objectives of learning a foreign language. The different cultures in language and literature departments began to take shape. Those who thought language study should progress rapidly to the reading of literary texts found the grammar/translation method more suitable for their objective. Those who believed that language study should be about communicating orally found the ATSP method (later the audiolingual method) more appropriate. Those who were interested in language as an object of study opted for one of the branches of linguistics that were emerging very fast in the late fifties and sixties. For example, scholars specialized in sociolinguistics (language in a sociocultural context; pragmatics); psycholinguistics (language as behavior; language as innate grammar); dialectology (language as regional/geographical marker); applied linguistics (second-language acquisition, methodology). The different specialties meant the perceived need for separate professional organizations, a proliferation of scholarly journals, and a further development of separate agendas. Those interested in Portuguese tended to fall into literature or one of the branches of linguistics.

The 1960s saw the rapid expansion of Portuguese instruction. This was coupled with the availability of federal funds for programs and for the building of language laboratories. Language study in general and the study of Portuguese in particular became more practical and utilitarian. The audiolingual method (ALM) became the accepted mode of instruction. ALM was based on behaviorist psychology, and the underlying assumption was that language was nothing more than a learned set of behaviors— a habit that could be drilled into the heads of students. David Feldman (1963) surveyed eighty-seven institutions that offered Portuguese in 1962 and found that 50 percent were using a language laboratory and were supplementing traditional texts with audio aids and audiolingual materials prepared locally. Feldman pointed out that relatively small enrollments in Portuguese hampered the development of needed materials by major publishing houses (Feldman 1963). It was clear that scholars interested in Portuguese language would need to become engaged in pedagogical issues to produce suitable, ALM-based materials for language classes.

With funds from the Ford Foundation, a team consisting of Richard Barrutia, Francisco Gomes de Matos, Henry W. Hodge, James L. Wyatt, and Frederick G. Hensey, and led by Fred Ellison developed a first-year Portuguese language textbook, *Modern Portuguese,* framed on the ALM. The project was ambitious, and the book featured dialogues and readings by Rachel de Queiroz. Portions of the project were tested throughout the 1960s. It seemed that Portuguese-language educators would have the state-of-the-art textbook that was missing from their programs. However, in 1971, language educators began to notice that the ALM was not producing the bilingual students that they had anticipated. Alfred N. Smith cautioned the profession that "the language student is not a robot to be programmed by the teacher" (A. N. Smith 1971: 87). Ironically that same year, Portuguese programs had at their disposal a true ALM textbook by Ellison and his team, *Modern Portuguese: A Project of the Modern Language Association,* published in New York by Alfred A. Knopf. A year later, *Português contemporâneo,* by Maria Isabel Abreu and Cléa Rameh, was published by Georgetown University Press. With Robert Lado and Joaquim Mattoso Câmara Jr. as consultants, this text was framed on the audiolingual method but included structural explanations of grammatical points. Until the late eighties, these two were the texts of choice for Portuguese-language instruction in the United States. During these twenty years, however, language-teaching approaches changed in view of new developments in linguistics.

PROFESSIONAL ORGANIZATIONS' ROLE IN THE SEPARATION OF LANGUAGE AND LITERATURE

Just as foreign-language teachers became aware of their students' inability to respond like Pavlov's dogs, in linguistics circles Noam Chomsky began challenging traditional views of language development and posed the theory of universal grammar. In a keynote speech to the Northeast Conference on the Teaching of Foreign Languages, Chomsky cautioned the profession against embracing new theories wholeheartedly. "It is the language teacher himself who must validate or refute each specific proposal" (Chomsky 1966: 45). By the late 1960s, another field in language studies— second-language acquisition—was also well established. Researchers in this applied linguistics area tested, validated, and at times refuted language-teaching methods, as Chomsky had suggested. Moreover, attention began to be placed on teaching methodology as a factor in language acquisition. The gulf between language and literature—in research and in teaching practice—at colleges and universities began to widen. The executive council of the Modern Language Association of America (MLA) created the American Council on the Teaching of Foreign Languages (ACTFL), modeled on the American Council on the Teaching of English, which had been created by MLA in 1911. Initial support for ACTFL would come from royalties provided by the audiolingual textbooks developed by *MLA—Modern Spanish* and *Modern Portuguese*. ACTFL would work toward becoming self-sufficient and separate from the MLA. Those interested in literary scholarship would continue to attend MLA meetings. ACTFL, on the other hand, would devote its annual meetings and much of its journal, *Foreign Language Annals,* to matters of language pedagogy and applied linguistics. An unmentioned but palpable hierarchy began to form in the discipline, with those interested in literary research perceived to be at the top. During the seventies, ten dissertations in the area of Brazilian linguistics were completed in the United States. In contrast, a search of *Dissertation Abstracts* during the same time period yields sixty-nine entries on Brazilian literature. The trend continued with a larger number of literary dissertations in the 1980s and 1990s also. In the 1970s, study in Brazilian linguistics was primarily carried out at the University of Wisconsin, Georgetown University, University of New Mexico, Ohio State University, and the University of Texas.

The 1970s then found language programs again in crisis. Not only were approaches to teaching languages in question—ALM did not work; structuralism did not work; grammar/translation did not work—but the split in the discipline meant little dialogue between literary scholars and language scholars. This situation dealt another blow to Portuguese programs, many of which were staffed by one faculty member whose scholarly interests and loyalty often clashed with program development and teaching expectations. Research in second-language acquisition pointed the profession toward the idea that language study has many functions, not the least of which is communication.

The next methodological wave to sweep the country was the functional-notional approach to language teaching. The idea was to introduce "notional categories" (topics that a student needs) and their "functions" (why did they need these topics? how would they be used?). Textbooks should be organized to build on the notional categories and not on grammatical structures. In Portuguese, the only textbook that approached this idea, although not explicitly, was *A Grammar of Spoken Brazilian Portuguese* by Earl Thomas (1974). Although still clinging to a grammatical structural approach, Thomas introduced notions as he had watched children in Brazil learn them. Thus, the future subjunctive and personal infinitives are introduced early in the text as a communicative device. Language practitioners were not convinced by the notional-functional approach, and they continued to organize beginning language classes around grammatical forms. Most Spanish and French textbooks published in the early 1970s, for example, described the concept of notions and functions but framed the material in much the same way that older textbooks had been framed, from basic grammar points to more complex ones. Portuguese students at this time were still memorizing dialogues and going through pattern drills, as prescribed by the audiolingual method, although a great deal of research pointed to the fallacy in the method.

In Portuguese-language studies, another trend began to develop around this time. Scholars who were interested in Portuguese language (as opposed to literature) seemed to become preoccupied with Portuguese immigration patterns and issues of bilingual education in Massachusetts, Rhode Island, and California. Douglas L. Wheeler, writing in *Horizontes: USA*, discusses the shift in interest from Brazil to Portugal in the early seventies (Wheeler 1978). This seems to be the case only in terms of bilingual education issues. Bilingual education in general and its political ramifications in particular became a popular topic of discussion in national language organizations in the seventies. In 1979, Bobby Chamberlain published his *Building a Portuguese Program*, a collection of essays by colleagues in the field who had successful techniques for attracting students, designing programs, planning extracurricular activities, and surviving in a department with other modern languages. Only one of the essays dealt with bilingual education (Mary T. Vermette's "Teaching Portuguese in a Portuguese-American Community"). All others deal with Brazilian Portuguese, and scholars whose primary interest was in literature wrote them. With the exception of a few scholars who studied linguistics and found themselves in charge of building Portuguese programs, the primary interest and publications of the majority of college and university Portuguese faculty in the 1970s was literary subjects. These scholars looked to the Modern Language Association for professional guidance. With the establishment of the American Council on the Teaching of Foreign Languages, the MLA stopped addressing issues of pedagogy at its annual meeting. Very few high schools offered Portuguese. Enrollments were once again beginning to wane, and book publishers were not interested in investing in Portuguese-language materials. It is safe to assume that with very few, but notable, exceptions, those involved in Portuguese-language teaching in the United States missed the beginning of the "comprehension-based" approaches that came into vogue at the late 1970s and early 1980s.

These approaches, based on research in second-language acquisition, included "total physical response" (Asher 1982) and the "natural approach" (Krashen and Terrell 1983). The idea was to teach languages through comprehensible input. The underlying assumption was that whatever approach was adopted or adapted by language teachers, it had to be "communicative." The majority of Portuguese-language teachers had neither the training nor the materials to embark on the newer methodology. Portuguese linguistics research flourished in the eighties, with thirty-two dissertations completed during the decade. More universities were producing linguists with doctoral degrees in Portuguese, but those most active in this type of research were the University of Texas, Georgetown University, the University of New Mexico, and the University of California, Berkeley. At least three of those who received their doctoral degrees in 1980 have continued to produce high-quality scholarly studies in linguistics. Dale Koike (1981) has continued her work at the University of Texas. Her research, although still framed in sociolinguistics, has also branched into Portuguese- and Spanish-language teaching. Antônio Simões (1987) also continues to pursue his interest in empirical linguistic research. In addition, he has developed teaching materials for Portuguese for Spanish speakers and published *Com licença! Brazilian Portuguese for Spanish Speakers* (1992), currently the best text available for this special purpose. Orlando Kelm (1989) has been a leader in the development of materials and methods for teaching business Portuguese and business Spanish. Koike, Kelm, and Simões have also engaged in fruitful collaborative research.

Another important development in 1980 was the National Conference on Professional Priorities, sponsored by the American Council on the Teaching of Foreign Languages, to set an agenda for curriculum development and evaluation for the coming years. One of the issues that was preoccupying educational leaders in the United States was accountability. In the case of language education, the idea was to find a way of measuring language competence. We no longer deluded ourselves into thinking that the usual two-year language sequence would bring about bilingual students. The outcome of this recommendation was the establishment, with funding from the U.S. Department of Education, of the ACTFL Proficiency Guidelines to measure proficiency in five "skills" of language acquisition: speaking, listening, reading, writing, and culture. Federal funding underwrote training for language educators in the administration and rating of oral-proficiency interviews. Since the most developed guidelines and the majority of those trained to administer them dealt with oral proficiency, the ripple effect was that new methodology—"teaching for proficiency"— became synonymous with teaching for "oral" proficiency, bringing back fears of a new audiolingual-type era.

In the 1980s, as Margo Milleret pointed out at the December 2000 meeting at the Brazilian embassy in Washington, D.C., several important events have attempted to improve and enrich the teaching of Brazilian Portuguese language and culture. The first such event, organized by Ricardo Paiva at Georgetown University in December 1984, brought together about 350 individuals. This first congress, funded by TV Globo and the embassies of Brazil and Portugal, featured six well-known novelists. The following year, a second gathering took place in Chicago, although attended by a smaller group; the participants were enthusiastic about the future of Portuguese language and Brazilian studies in the United States. A second initiative of significance was the ALCANCE project at the University of Texas at Austin, underwritten by a grant from the Fund for the Improvement of Post-secondary Education. This project promoted the development of materials, a conference called "Portuguese Language: Teaching and Testing," and the reaching out to Spanish and French teachers, who shared innovations in the latest trends in applied linguistics. A third effort of note was the development of the Simulated Oral Proficiency Interview for Portuguese by the Center for Applied Linguistics, which gave faculty a new tool for evaluating oral language skills for student placement in classes and for judging improvement.

A few Portuguese-language specialists became involved in the proficiency movement early in its development. The late Karin Van den Dool (Stanford University) developed training materials for Portuguese testers. Maria Antônia Cowles became one of the early leaders in developing materials and assessments for business Portuguese and continues to be in the forefront of "teaching for communication" from the Joseph Lauder Institute at the University of Pennsylvania. Funding guidelines for the U.S. Department of Education's Title VI programs called for basing funding decisions, in part, on language instruction in Portuguese that is rooted in the "proficiency-based communicative approach." The communicative approach seeks to develop in students the linguistics skills needed for negotiating meaning and for integrating form and function (Oxford, Lavine, and Crookall 1989).

Just as the profession as a whole moved to the communicative approach, Georgetown University Press published *Travessia* (1988). The beginning language textbook was developed by Jon Tolman, Ricardo Paiva, John Jensen, and Nivea Parsons, with funding from the U.S. government as well as from the Fundação Roberto Marinho. The program includes video-cassettes, audiocassettes, texts, and workbooks. Rich in cultural elements, it still relies heavily on grammar structures. Many faculty members who began using the new material (and finally bestowed museum relic status on *Modern Portuguese*) lacked the training in the new methodologies envisioned in the program. Just as the last elements of *Travessia* became available in 1991 (Laboratory Manual), the foreign language professionals were beginning to embrace the U.S. government's Goals 2000 project.

The project, funded by several government agencies, called for each field to develop content standards for learning in that particular field. Since the project was envisioned as a kindergarten through twelfth-grade endeavor that included the preparation of teachers for these grades, few college and university faculty took notice or cared. Unless the college or

Berrien, Hogue) and continue to produce "well-documented studies on fundamental problems" (Berrien 1942: 90).

Portuguese continues to be listed among the "critical," less commonly taught, languages in the United States. The Brazilian and U.S. governments agree that the language as well as the culture that it embraces are of utmost importance in the new millennium. Study abroad programs conducted in Brazil have augmented the skill level of many language learners and brought them into daily contact with different approaches to teaching. Moreover, new textbooks based on applied linguistics research in the teaching of Portuguese to foreigners have been published in Brazil. From the U.S. side, new materials in the form of CD-ROMs have recently become available to instructors and learners. Language studies are once again fashionable in the United States. Middlebury College, world renowned for language-teaching innovation, inaugurated the Portuguese School in the summer of 2003 as further evidence of growth in the study of Portuguese. Professional associations are teaming up to provide the kind of instruction and language development that is most needed for global understanding. Portuguese language and linguistic studies once again are on the increase. It is up to us to assure that we prepare our students to meet their future professional and cultural challenges.

References

Abreu, Maria Isabel, and Cléa Rameh. 1972. *Português contemporâneo*. Washington, D.C.: Georgetown University Press.

Allen, J. H. D., Jr. 1942. "Portuguese Studies in the United States." *Hispania* 25, no. 1: 94–100.

Altman, C. 1999. "The 'Brazilian Connection' in the History of American Linguistics—The Notebook of Joaquim Mattoso Camara." *Hispania* 26, no. 3: 355–82.

Asher, James J. 1982. *Learning Another Language Through Actions: The Complete Teacher's Guidebook*. 2nd ed. Los Gatos, Calif.: Sky Oaks Productions.

Berrien, William. 1942. "The Future of Portuguese Studies." *Hispania* 25, no. 1: 87–93.

Branner, John Casper. 1919. "The Importance of the Study of the Portuguese Language." *Hispania* 2, no. 2: 87–93.

Brod, Richard, and Elizabeth B. Welles. 2000. "Foreign Language Enrollments in United States Institutions of Higher Education, Fall 1998." *ADFL Bulletin* 31, no. 2: 22–29.

Chamberlain, Bobby J., ed. 1979. *Building a Portuguese Program*. East Lansing, Mich.: Latin American Studies Center.

Chomsky, Noam. 1965. *Aspects of the Theory of Syntax*. Cambridge, Mass.: MIT Press.

————. 1966. "Linguistic Theory." In *Language Teaching: Broader Contexts*, ed. Robert G. Mead. New York: Northeast Conference on the Teaching of Foreign Languages.

Cioffari, Vincenzo. 1949. "Linguistic Experiment in Brazil." *Hispania* 32, no. 1: 185–89.

Ellison, Fred P. 1967. "Portuguese in the First Fifty Years of the AATSP." *Hispania* 50, no. 4: 860–71.

Ellison, Fred P., et al. 1971. *Modern Portuguese: A Project of the Modern Language Association*. New York: Alfred A. Knopf.

Jones, Chester Lloyd. 1927. "Suggestions for the Study of Portuguese." *Hispania* 10, no. 4: 265–69.

————. 1932. "Spanish and Portuguese in American Relations." *Hispania* 15, no. 1: 34–38.

Kelm, Orlando. 1989. "Temporal Aspects of Speech Rhythm Which Distinguish Mexican Spanish and Brazilian Portuguese," Ph.D. dissertation, University of California–Berkeley.

Koike, Dale. 1981. "A Sociolinguistic Analysis of the Infinitive in Colloquial Brazilian Portuguese," Ph.D. dissertation, University of New Mexico.

Krashen, Stephen D., and Tracy D. Terrell. 1983. *The Natural Approach: Language Acquisition in the Classroom*. San Francisco: Alemany Press.

Leavitt, Sturgis E. 1961. "The Teaching of Spanish in the United States." *Hispania* 44, no. 4: 591–625.

Ornstein, Jacob. 1950. "Facts, Figures, and Opinions on the Present Status of Portuguese." *Hispania* 33, no. 3: 251–55.

Oxford, Rebecca L., Roberta Lavine, and David Crookall. 1989. "Language Learning Strategies, the Communicative Approach, and Their Classroom Implications." *Foreign Language Annals* 22: 29–39.

Phillips, June K., ed. 1999. *Foreign Language Standards: Linking Research, Theories, and Practices*. Lincolnwood, Ill.: National Textbook.

Pitcher, Stephen L. 1945. "Conferences on the Teaching of Spanish and Portuguese." *Hispania* 28, no. 3: 370–74.

Simões, Antonio R. M. 1987. "Temporal Organization of Brazilian Portuguese Vowels in Continuous Speech: An Acoustical Study," Ph.D. dissertation, University of Texas, Austin.

————. 1992. *Com licença! Brazilian Portuguese for Spanish Speakers*. Austin: University of Texas Press.

Smith, Alfred N. 1971. "The Importance of Attitude in Foreign Language Learning." *Modern Language Journal* 55: 82–88.

Smith, Robert C. 1945. "A Pioneer Teacher: Father Peter Abad and his Portuguese Grammar." *Hispania* 28, no. 3: 330–63.

Stewart, Charles T. 1944. "Portuguese Courses in the Colleges and Universities of the United States, 1943–44" *Hispania* 27, no. 3: 351–55.

Swierenga, Robert P. 1994. *The Forerunners: Dutch Jewry in the North American Diaspora*. Detroit: Wayne State University Press.

Thomas, Earl W. 1974. *A Grammar of Spoken Brazilian Portuguese*. Nashville, Tenn.: Vanderbilt University Press.

Tolman, Jon M., Ricardo M. Paiva, John B. Jensen, and Nivea P. Parsons. 1988/1991. *Travessia: A Portuguese Language Textbook Program*. Washington, D.C.: Georgetown University Press.

Viera, David J. 1992. "A Selected Annotated Bibliography on the History of Portuguese Language Teaching in the United States." *Hispania* 75, no. 2: 445–53.

Wheeler, Douglas L. 1978. "Portuguese Studies in the United States Today." *Horizontes USA* 111: 194–277.

Wilkins, Lawrence A. 1917. "On the Threshold." *Hispania* (organizational number): 1–10.

REPRESENTATIVE BIBLIOGRAPHY OF PUBLISHED RESEARCH IN
BRAZILIAN PORTUGUESE LANGUAGE AND LINGUISTICS SINCE 1989

Azevedo, Milton M. 1992. "Foreigner Talk as a Stylistic Device in Erico Veríssimo's Fiction." *Hispania* 75, no. 5: 1154–63.

———. 1992. "Linguistic Aspects of the Representation of Foreigner Talk in Brazilian Literature." *Sintagma: Revista de Lingüística* 4: 69–76.

———. 1995. "Linguistic Features in the Literary Representation of Vernacular Brazilian Portuguese." *Hispanic Linguistics* 6: 449–73.

Baxter, Alan N. 1997. *Creole-Like Features in the Verb System of an Afro-Brazilian Variety of Portuguese*. Amsterdam: Benjamins.

Baxter, Alan N. et al. 1997. "Gender Agreement as a 'Decreolizing' Feature of an Afro-Brazilian Dialect." *Journal of Pidgin and Creole Languages* 12, no. 1: 1–57.

Chamberlain, Bobby. 1989. *Portuguese Language and Luso-Brazilian Literature: An Annotated Guide to Selected Reference Works*. New York: Modern Language Association of America.

Clements, J. Clancy. 1992. "Foreigner Talk and the Origins of Pidgin Portuguese." *Journal of Pidgin and Creole Languages* 7, no. 1: 75–92.

Farrell, Patrick. 1990. "Null Objects in Brazilian Portuguese." *Natural Language and Linguistic Theory* 8, no. 3: 325–46.

Feldman, David Morris. 1963. "The Historical Syntax of Modal Verb Phrases in Spanish." Ann Arbor, Mich.: University Microfilms.

Ginway, Elizabeth M. 1991. "Video Use for Portuguese Language and Conversation Classes." *Hispania* 74, no. 3: 775–76.

Hancin, Barbara J. 1991. "On the Phonology-Morphology Interaction in Brazilian Portuguese Vowel Harmony." *Studies in the Linguistic Sciences* 21, no. 1: 39–54.

Jensen, John B. 1996. "Current Studies in Portuguese Linguistics." *Comparative Romance Linguistics Newsletter* 45, no. 2: 23–6.

Jordan, Isolde J. 1991. "Portuguese for Spanish Speakers: A Case for Contrastive Analysis." *Hispania.* 74, no. 3: 788–92.

Kelm, Orlando R. 1992. "The Use of Synchronous Computer Networks in Second Language Instruction: A Preliminary Report." *Foreign Language Annals* 25, no. 5: 441–54.

Kliffer, Michael D. 1991. *From Syntax to Pragmatics: Inalienable Possession in Brazilian Portuguese.* Amsterdam: Benjamins.

Koike, Dale April. 1991. "Tense and Cohesion in Brazilian Portuguese Oral Narratives." *Hispania* 75, no. 3: 647–53.

———. 1992. *Brazilian Portuguese Directives and a Hierarchy of Strategies for Politeness.* Westport, Conn.: Bergin & Garvey.

———. 1998. "A Discourse Approach to the Assessment of Foreign Language Oral Proficiency." *Texas Papers in Foreign Language Education* 3, no. 3: 33–50.

Megenney, William W. 1992. "West Africa in Brazil: The Case of Ewe-Yoruba Syncretism." *Anthropos: International Review of Anthropology and Linguistics* 87: 469–84.

Melo, Cecil L. de Ataide. 1992. "From the Classroom to the Newsroom: A Course-Sheltered Project in Foreign Language Journalism." *Hispania* 75, no. 3: 739–42.

Milleret, Margo. 1990. "Portuguese Program Development: Past, Present, and Future." *Hispania* 73, no. 2: 513–17.

———. 1991. "Assessing the Gain in Oral Proficiency from Summer Foreign Study." *ADFL Bulletin* 22, no. 3: 39–43.

Milleret, Margo, Charles W. Stansfield, and Dorry Mann Kenyon. 1991. "The Validity of the Portuguese Speaking Test for Use in a Summer Abroad Program" *Hispania* 74, no. 3: 778–87.

Pap, Leo. 1992. "On the Etymology of Portuguese SAUDADE: An Instance of Multiple Causation." *Journal of the International Linguistics Association* 43, no. 1: 97–102.

Perroni, M. C. 1993. "On the Acquisition of Narrative Discourse: A Study in Portuguese." *Journal of Pragmatics* 20, no. 6: 559–77.

Sancier, Michele, and Carol Fowler. 1997. "Gestural Drift in a Bilingual Speaker of Brazilian Portuguese and English." *Journal of Phonetics* 25, no. 4: 421–36.

Schmitt, Cristina. 1994. "Accusative Clitic Doubling, Participial Absolutes, and have+ Agreeing Participles." *University of Maryland Working Papers in Linguistics* 2: 178–220.

Simões, Antônio R. M. 1990. "Modeling Shortening and Lengthening in Connected Speech." *Mid-America Linguistics Conference Papers.* Mid-America Linguistics Society.

Stephens, Thomas M. 1994. "Brazilian Portuguese Ethnonymy and Europeanisms." *Hispania* 77, no. 3: 536–43.

Valian, Virginia, and Zena Eisenber. 1996. "The Development of Syntactic Subjects in Portuguese-speaking Children." *Journal of Child Language* 23, no. 1: 103–28.

Wetzels, W. Leo. 1995. "Mid-Vowel Alternations in the Brazilian Portuguese Verb." *Phonology* 12, no. 2: 281–304.

———. 1997. "The Lexical Representation of Nasality in Brazilian Portuguese." *International Journal of Latin and Romance Linguistics* 9, no. 2: 203–32.

Ziegler, Arne. 1998. "Word Class Frequencies in Brazilian Portuguese Press Texts." *Journal of Quantitative Linguistics* 5, no. 3: 269–80.

~

CHAPTER 5

Literature, Culture, and Civilization

K. David Jackson

INTRODUCTION

The study of Brazilian literature and culture in the United States today represents the convergence and interrelationship of diverse historical currents related to U.S. interest in Brazil. These include but are not limited to (1) the work of pioneers in Portuguese language and philology and the literature of Portugal; (2) early writings by missionaries, travelers, and scholars; (3) the development of university studies, courses, and departments that would eventually offer advanced degrees; (4) the presence of Brazilian authors, professors, specialists, and advanced students of Brazilian literature in the United States ; (5) the development of Brazilian studies specialists in history and the social sciences; (6) the development of Brazilian Portuguese–language courses; (7) publishing of literary histories, anthologies, and essays on Brazil; (8) translations of Brazilian books, essays, and literary works; (9) the growth of specialized libraries and collections; (10) international colloquia on Luso-Brazilian studies; and (11) since 1945, the inclusion of Brazil in U.S. area studies of Latin America.

The purpose of this assessment is to review the principles on which the study of Brazilian literature, culture, and civilization (often referred to in the profession as "Portuguese") in the United States has been based historically, its chronological development, and, finally, to evaluate its current directions and dynamics. The historical development of studies of Brazilian literature and culture in the United States may be separated into several phases or stages: "pioneers" (before 1950); "founders" (from 1950 to 1970); and "specialists" (from 1970 to 2000).

Historical Development to 1950

The continental Portuguese language and early literature are the first areas of documented interest. A grammar of Portuguese was published in Baltimore in 1820, eleven years before one would be available for Spanish. A group of eminent philologists, scholars of medieval and Renaissance literatures, constitute the first exponents of literary studies in Portuguese as a field, which these scholars did much to create and advance. Yale professor Henry R. Lang published on Portuguese medieval *cancioneiros* (Dinis, 1894) and lectured on Portuguese literature at the Modern Language Association in the 1890s. Because of his great interest in Brazil, John Casper Branner, president of Stanford University, published *A Brief Grammar of the Portuguese Language* in 1910. Professor John W. Burnam of the University of Cincinnati published transcribed facsimiles of Portuguese manuscripts from 1912 to 1925. Professor J. D. M. Ford of Harvard dedicated much of his career to Camões and the *Lusiads*, which he edited in 1940.

American School of Portuguese Philology and Linguistics

In the period before 1950, research activities in medieval Portuguese linguistics amounted to the creation of a school of U.S. specialists in Portuguese historical philology and linguistics. Professor Lloyd Kasten of the University of Wisconsin–Madison inaugurated the Spanish medieval dictionary project and later directed the Center of Luso-Brazilian Studies. Professor Edwin B. Williams of the University of Pennsylvania taught Portuguese and published the very influential book *From Latin to Portuguese* (1938), textbook to a generation of students. The Pennsylvania Series in Romance Languages and Literatures published paleographic editions of Portuguese texts by scholars such as Richard D. Abraham (*Life of Barlaam and Josaphat*, 1938), Harald J. Russo (*Morphology and Syntax of the Leal Conselheiro*, 1942), Kimberly Roberts (*Orthography, Phonology and Word Study of the Leal Conselheiro*, 1940), and Henry Hare Carter (diplomatic edition of the *Cancioneiro da Ajuda*, 1941). Renowned scholars such as Leo Spitzer and Yakov Malkiel published extensively in the 1930s and 1940s on Portuguese linguistics.

The philological approach also influenced early studies of Brazilian literature, culture, and history. Professor J. H. D. Allen, who published articles on Portuguese linguistics circa 1940, later taught Brazilian literature to a generation of students at the University of Illinois at Urbana. His peers included Norman P. Sacks, who studied Portuguese and Spanish etymologies, Stanley Rose, Hensley C. Woodbridge, Marvin Rainey, and others. Earl W. Thomas, who wrote a dissertation on pronunciation in Minas Gerais (1947), later authored an essay on the history of Brazilian literature (in *Modern Brazil*, 1971), and Gerald Moser studied North American loan words in Brazilian Portuguese (1950), for example, before becoming a specialist on Portuguese Africa. Francis M. Rogers, who received his doctoral degree from Harvard in 1940, joined an interest in phonology with the literary and cultural history of the Portuguese expansion. Linguists continued to make essential contributions to graduate faculties in Portuguese and Romance languages until the 1970s, when advanced study of Romance philology began to fade, replaced by an emphasis on phonology, syntax, and applied linguistics.

Luso-Brazilian Studies

Luso-Brazilian studies is defined as an interdisciplinary grouping of Portugal and Brazil, with emphasis on the humanities (primarily literature, culture, and civilization). "Culture and civilization" refers mainly to intellectual and social history, folklore, and the arts. The teaching of literature, long abandoning its origins in critical editions and philology, has become progressively more interrelated with cultural topics, the social sciences, and other arts, including film, music, dance, plastic arts, and other forms of national expression.

A community of scholars with wide Luso-Brazilian interests identified itself as a field by 1940, as evidenced by several large international colloquia on Luso-Brazilian studies organized in the 1950s and 1960s. The first was organized by Vanderbilt University and the Library of Congress in Washington, D.C. (1950). Eminent American participants in these congresses—representing mainly fields of language and literature, history, art history, politics, and sociology—included J. H. D. Allen (University of Illinois), L. L. Barrett (Washington and Lee), Malcolm Batchelor (Yale), Helen Caldwell (University of California, Los Angeles), Henry Hare Carter (University of Pennsylvania), Bailey Diffie (City College of New York), Ralph Dimmick (Northwestern), Ronald Hilton (Stanford), Lloyd Kasten (University of Wisconsin), Alexander Marchant (Vanderbilt), Charles Nowell (University of Illinois), Francis Rogers (Harvard), Engel Sluiter (University of California, Berkeley), Carlton Sprague Smith (New York University), Robert C. Smith (University of Pennsylvania), T. Lynn Smith (University of Florida), Stanley Stein (Princeton), Charles Wagley (Columbia), Don

Walther (University of North Carolina), Emilio Willems (Vanderbilt), Edwin Williams (University of Pennsylvania), and Benjamin Woodbridge (Berkeley). Many of these figures are included in Martin H. Sable's list of pioneer Latin Americanists in the United States (1989).

Interest in Brazilian literature and culture also benefited from other early specialists in Brazil: Donald Pierson (b. 1900) and Ruth Landes (1908–1991) published pioneering studies of race, religion, and society in Bahia (Pierson's *Negroes in Brazil, A Study of Race Contact at Bahia*, 1942; Landes's *The City of Women*, 1947). Richard Morse (1922–2001) published his history of the city of São Paulo in 1958, while John W. F. Dulles (b. 1913) initiated a series of biographies of statesmen, lawyers, and politicians with his *Vargas of Brazil* (1967). U.S. publications on Brazil can be grouped into four major periods: post–Civil War, treated in Dunn (1866), Kidder (1879), and Elliot (1917); World War II boom reflected in Zweig (1940), Griffin (1940), Loewenstein (1942), Hunnicut (1945), Preston (1946), Smith (1946), Hill (1947), Smith and Marchant (1951); Alliance for Progress and NDEA period, producing Dos Passos (1963), Wagley (1963), Hanke (1967), Poppino (1968), Worcester (1973), Fitzgibbon (1974); and the current New Republic, treated in Page (1995), Eakin (1997), and Skidmore (1999). In one way or another, all of these works foreground the future of Brazil alongside its failure to realize its great potential.

Within Brazil, the field of Brazilian studies was also developing, as seen in the bibliographical manual prepared by William Berrien (Harvard) and Rubens Borba de Moraes (1949), while in the 1980s José Carlos Sebe Bom-Meihy published a book of interviews with U.S. Brazilianists for the Brazilian public (1984) and Fernanda Massi compiled a guide to Brazilianists (1992).

The Portuguese Situation

Essays assessing the situation of "Portuguese" in U.S. universities became a commonplace of professional associations beginning in the 1940s. Albert Lopes wrote "The Importance of the Study of Portuguese in the United States" for *Hispania* (1941). William Berrien (Harvard) contributed an article in 1942 on the future of Portuguese studies in the United States to *Hispania*, and Charles R. D. Miller published "The Place of Portuguese in American Education" in *Education* (1942). In 1950 Henry Hare Carter published a major retrospective on the development of Luso-Brazilian studies in the United States from 1920 to 1950 in the *Acts* of the first international colloquium on Luso-Brazilian studies, sponsored by Vanderbilt

University in Nashville, Tennessee, and the Library of Congress in 1950. One may observe from Carter's data that the study of Brazilian Portuguese language enjoyed a better relative position at that time than it does today. At the 1950 colloquium, Francis Rogers criticized the tendency to specialize in philology and suggested that literary studies develop in contact with the social sciences. Rogers found great spiritual values in the lessons of Portuguese and Brazilian civilizations and literatures, and he encouraged their study and teaching as a moral imperative.

Brazilians are interested as well in information about the teaching of Portuguese and Brazilian literature and culture in the United States. At the Sociedade Brasileira pelo Progresso da Ciência (SBPC) in 1984, I read a paper on the teaching of Brazilian literature in the United States, and in 1997 Regina Igel published a full assessment for Brazilian readers of the teaching of Portuguese language in the United States, noting the historical development and changes affecting the development of the field up to the present.

The main professional organization to support Brazilian literature and culture has been the American Association of Teachers of Spanish and Portuguese, which publishes a newsletter on Portuguese. The Modern Language Association maintains one "Luso-Brazilian" section with three convention sessions, and the Latin American Studies Association actively includes Brazilian topics in its congress and journal as a principal area. Since the 1990s, Brazilian literature has been more exclusively represented by the American Portuguese Studies Association and its journal, *ellipsis*; the Brazilian Studies Association; and a branch of the International Association of Lusitanists and its journal, *Veredas*. Americans also now participate actively in the Brazilian comparative literature association. The International Conference Group on Portugal (based at the University of New Hampshire) includes Brazilian topics in its journal, *Portuguese Studies Review*, as does the new journal of the University of Massachusetts–Dartmouth, *Portuguese Literary and Cultural Studies*.

FIELD OF BRAZILIAN LITERATURE

Brazilian literature as a field of knowledge and study was initially considered part of the interdisciplinary field of Luso-Brazilian studies and as a branch of Portuguese literature. The *Encyclopaedia Britannica* continues to list Brazilian and Portuguese authors together under "Portuguese Literature." The study of Brazilian literature developed mainly in universities, generally within departments of Romance languages and literatures, and later within Spanish and Portuguese departments, where language programs existed. The year 1959 marked the beginning of substantial U.S. government support for the study of Portuguese language.

When the U.S. Department of Health, Education, and Welfare's Language and Area Centers Section began to implement Title VI legislation under the National Education Defense Act (NDEA) of 1958, the agency determined that four foreign languages (French, German, Spanish, and Italian) were in ample supply in the United States and therefore did not require language and area centers, so no Latin American centers were planned. Portuguese was considered a less commonly taught language, however, and, as a result, when the first Title VI centers were funded for the academic year 1959–60, two of the nineteen centers were Luso-Brazilian centers, at New York University and the University of Wisconsin. In the 1960–61 academic year, these were still the only two centers. With the inauguration of the Alliance for Progress (which was a response to the Cuban Revolution of 1959), Spanish was designated a critical language, and the decision was reached to add Latin American centers. Hence, midway through the 1961–62 academic year, five Latin American centers were added (University of Texas, University of Florida, UCLA, Tulane, and Columbia). As of 1962–63, the Luso-Brazilian centers were given additional funding to expand their mission to include Spanish America, and they too became Latin American centers (Bigelow and Legters 1964: 27–28).

While most often studied in conjunction with other subjects, whether Portuguese literature, philology and linguistics, other Romance-language literatures (primarily Spanish), or, eventually, Latin American studies, Brazilian literature and civilization came to exist as a separate subject in many large institutions, particularly the seven with NDEA centers. Support for graduate study has been available through National Defense Education Act (NDEA) and Foreign Language Area Studies (FLAS) fellowships for Latin American area studies, as well as teaching assistantships for language teaching. Research in Brazil is traditionally funded by Ford "Foreign Area Fellowships," Fulbright research grants, and other institutional grants.

Translators, Essayists, and Scholars

In 1922, the year of Brazil's Modern Art Week, Isaac Goldberg (1887–1938)—an editor in Boston and part-time lecturer in Hispanic American literature at Harvard—published the first book on Brazilian literature in the United States, *Brazilian Literature*. Goldberg's translations and other studies include *Brazilian Tales* (1921) and *The Spirit of Brazilian Literature* (1924 and 1925); at the same time, he published a book on Camões (1924). Samuel Putnam (1892–1950) made very significant contributions to the knowledge and study of Brazilian literature and society in the 1940s. Within three years' time, he published translations of three major authors, Euclídes da Cunha (*Os sertões, Rebellion in the Backlands*, 1944), Jorge Amado (*Terras do sem fim; The Violent Land*, 1945), and Gilberto Freyre (*Casa grande e senzala; The Masters and the Slaves*, 1946). Putnam's literary history that followed, *Marvelous Journey* (1948), is the single most significant contribution to the study of Brazilian literature in the United States before the 1960s. Putnam also translated Costa's biography of D. Pedro I (1950). Fernando de Azevedo's encyclopedic work, *Brazilian Culture*, was translated by William Rex Crawford (1950).

The first doctoral degree in Brazilian literature, from 1942, belongs to David Driver (Columbia), who published *The Indian in Brazilian Literature* in New York (1942). Marie Wallis completed a doctoral degree on modern women poets (University of New Mexico, 1947), Don Walther on prose fiction of the Amazon (University of North Carolina, 1948), Hubert Mate on Taunay (Northwestern, 1949), and Benjamin Woodbridge on Machado de Assis (Harvard, 1949).

Other studies of Brazilian literature in the period from 1920 to 1950 include several dozen articles, mostly on selected authors or genres: Mildred Adams (drama), L. L. Barrett (Érico Veríssimo), Margaret Bates (Gregório de Matos), Donald Brown (Aluísio de Azevedo), Ralph Dimmick (Lima Barreto), D. Lee Hamilton (Anchieta), Ronald Hilton (Nabuco), Leo Kirschenbaum (drama), Albert Lopes (novel), Samuel Putnam (social novel), Ernest Stowell (Jorge Amado), Marie Wallis (Adalgisa Nery), Don Walther (Inglês de Souza), Ralph Warner (Afrânio Peixoto), and Clotilde Wilson (Machado de Assis). Author and genre studies would continue to characterize U.S. critical methodology thereafter.

Theoretical and Methodological Orientations in Brazilian Literary Studies
Linguistics, Textual Criticism, and Aesthetics

In terms of theoretical and methodological orientations, Brazilian literary studies were initiated by Romance philologists whose interests extended to Brazilian language and literature. Historical linguistics and textual criticism oriented the first school of U.S. scholars of Brazilian literature, which was a natural development of their work in Portuguese literature.

A second orientation came from translation of Brazilian authors, who illustrated descriptive trends in the social sciences or civilization, particularly following the works of Gilberto Freyre from 1945. Literary and aesthetic studies per se were founded by Samuel Putnam, the work of Helen Caldwell on Machado de Assis, and the poems and translations of Elizabeth Bishop and are strong secondary currents in critical studies.

National and Area Characteristics

With the creation of Latin American centers in 1961–62, Brazilian studies became part of a Latin American area studies approach, with language study as its principal rationale and methodology characterized by the collection of data (literary history), on the one hand, and the interpretation of texts according to national and area characteristics, whether geographical, regional, cultural, linguistic, and the like, on the other. Brazilian literature was organized according to periods, authors, and works following chronological, historical, and even developmental models. The primary texts for this approach were comprehensive Brazilian anthologies, such as the *Presença da literatura brasileira,* edited by Antônio Cândido and José Aderaldo Castelo, or the "Nossos Clàssicos" series of the Editôra Agir. Brazilian literary histories, including those previously translated, were models for information on authors, works, and periods, such as the Editôra Cultrix series, which included Wilson Martins's volume on modernism, later revised and translated to English by Jack E. Tomlins as *The Modernist Idea* (1970), or the histories of Alfredo Bosi, Afrânio Coutinho, Massaud Moisés, Soares Amora, and others. Studies of major authors, movements, or genres characterized the scholarly production at U.S. universities, which attempted to be both comprehensive and descriptive yet without any specific theoretical focus or by using a combination of approaches. Theses were dedicated to informative studies of major twentieth-century authors, including Carlos Drummond de Andrade, Mário de Andrade, Oswald de Andrade, Graciliano Ramos, Murilo Mendes, Osman Lins, Machado de Assis, Lima Barreto, José Lins do Rego, Jorge Amado, Cecília Meireles, and many others. The collection of biographical and bibliographical information was a prime consideration.

The Latin American area approach effectively separated Brazil's literary history from its Portuguese antecedents and from nascent Luso-Brazilian studies, which subsequently failed as a unified field in the U.S. academy. Peninsular Spanish studies were also weakened but survived, whereas philology was largely replaced by applied linguistics. Brazilian literature was recast as a national history of one of the American republics, taught in Spanish departments. In that context, its classification became something of an anomaly, comparable to literatures of the Caribbean, since it was alienated linguistically, culturally, and historically from the Spanish American republics. In the late 1990s, Brazil underwent reevaluation in the academy as perhaps the most important area, in spite of long neglect, in the Latin American sphere. As a consequence, Brazilian studies programs or centers have been instituted or highlighted within the Latin American context in several key institutions, such as the recently formed "Brazil Centers" at the University of Texas at Austin, Georgetown University in Washington, D.C., and Columbia University in New York City.

With its "critical" status as a "lesser-taught" language, comparable to Quechua or Guaraní, Portuguese was offered in departments of Spanish. Literature was taught as an advanced stage of language and area training but without the previous philological or textual traditions, on the one hand, and without any training in world literature, other national literatures, or comparative literature, on the other. Proficiency in the language, however, became the entry for all further advanced work on Brazil, regardless of field.

Largely developed through research and archival work in Brazil and bolstered by the continual presence of visiting professors, advanced programs at U.S. universities came to resemble mini-Brazilian university programs in exile. While this status increased their quality and sophistication, at the same time it made advanced study of Brazilian literature more inaccessible to U.S. students without a high degree of specialization on Brazil and fluency in Portuguese. In all cases, linguistic proficiency was a fundamental prerequisite. Brazilian literature later began to appear in doctorates in comparative literature, in addition to the common split degree with Spanish, while Brazilian cultural topics invaded other departments of humanities and the arts, although with secondary status. Cultural studies as a field, as well as Afro-Romance (Afro-Brazilian and Portuguese African) topics, are secondary areas of teaching and research where Brazil is often represented.

THEMES AND ISSUES

With increasing specialization in the 1980s, studies of Brazilian literature began a slow qualitative shift from descriptive, information-based models to analytical, thematic, or issue-based approaches. This shift is illustrated by studies on myth and ideology, the city, vanguard prose, music, film, satire, formalism, women's issues, race, Afro-Brazilian culture, Indianism, and other thematic, comparative, or sociocultural topics. Sociological orientations are common, as exemplified by the theme of "literature of the dictatorship" that developed after 1985. Comparative studies remain rare, theory is deemphasized, and most advanced studies continue to describe authors and genres. Brazilian authors are still rarely but increasingly discussed in essays originating in other disciplines using the latest concepts and schools of criticism.

The influence of a growing global focus can be seen in U.S. participation in new international associations, such as the Brazilian Association of Comparative Literature (ABRALIC), International Association of Lusitanists, and American Portuguese Studies Association, adding diverse perspectives of scholars from many different countries to the study of Brazilian literature and culture.

GROWTH AFTER MIDCENTURY, 1950–1970

In the 1950s, there followed more doctoral degrees by "founders" of Brazilian literature, including Dorothy Loos (Columbia, 1950), who published *The Naturalist Novel of Brazil* (1963); Fred Ellison (Berkeley, 1952), *Brazil's New Novel: Four Modern Masters* (1954); Raymond Sayers (Columbia, 1953), *The Negro in Brazilian Literature* (1956); Gregory Rabassa (Columbia, 1954), "The Negro in the Brazilian and Hispanic-American Novel of the Twentieth Century" (published in Brazil in 1965); and Alfred Hower (Harvard, 1954), "Hipólito da Costa and Luso-Brazilian Journalism in Exile, London, 1808–1822 (never published)." Timothy Brown (Wisconsin, 1955) studied Monteiro Lobato, and Herman Slutzkin (Columbia, 1957) researched the immigrant. Vianna Moog's *An Interpretation of Brazilian Literature*, from a lecture at the Foreign Office in 1942, was translated by John Knox and published in Rio de Janeiro (1951). Edward Dimmick translated Manuel Bandeira's *A Brief History of Brazilian Literature* (1958). Theodore Rose (New York University, 1959) studied the northeastern novel and Lins do Rego. Professors Ernesto da Cal (Ph.D. 1950) and Alberto Machado da Rosa (Ph.D. 1953) began influential careers, which followed the Luso-Brazilian model, joining Portuguese and Brazilian literatures.

In 1960, Helen Caldwell's book, *Brazilian Othello of Machado de Assis*, changed the critical reading of Machado and remains one of the most significant literary studies of the Brazilian author ever published. The translator of *Dom Casmurro* and *Helena*, Caldwell also published *Machado de Assis: The Brazilian Master and His Novels* (1970). Caldwell's work on

Machado is the first example of a significant contribution to the interpretation of Brazilian literature in the United States. In the same decade, John Nist published *The Modernist Movement in Brazil* (1967), and Gregory Rabassa translated Afrânio Coutinho's *An Introduction to Literature in Brazil* (1969). Many prominent Brazilian literary scholars would begin arriving at U.S. universities in this period, many supported by Title VI funds under U.S. government agencies (see the section of this essay entitled "Interfaces").

Doctoral Theses

A surge in doctoral theses in the 1960s by specialists who would make a significant impact in the field includes Norwood Andrews's thesis on Bernardo Guimarães (Wisconsin, 1964) [now at Texas Tech], Mary L. Daniel's groundbreaking linguistic analysis of Guimarães Rosa (Wisconsin, 1965) [recently retired from Wisconsin], Russell Hamilton's work on Graciliano Ramos (Yale, 1965) [recently retired from Vanderbilt], David T. Haberly's thesis on Luís Delfino dos Santos (Harvard, 1966) [Virginia], Doris Turner's study of Jorge Amado (St. Louis, 1966) [Connecticut College], Joaquim-Francisco Coelho's on Carlos Drummond de Andrade (Wisconsin, 1968) [Harvard], Robert Herron's thesis on Lima Barreto (Wisconsin, 1968) [retired from Washington University], Mark Curran's work on northeastern folk literature (*cordel*) (St. Louis, 1968) [Arizona State], Fred Clark (University of Florida, 1968) on Spanish theater [North Carolina], and Frederick García on the American view of Brazilian letters (New York University, 1969) [U.S. Military Academy]. José Carlos Sebe's book on "Brazilianists" singles out Mary L. Daniel from this generation as a "pioneer." She had a major positive influence on Brazilian literary studies during her distinguished career at Iowa and Wisconsin, which included her editorship of the flagship journal, the *Luso-Brazilian Review*.

The label "Brazilianist" belongs primarily to the generation receiving doctoral degrees from major programs of Luso-Brazilian studies in the late 1960s or early 1970s, a generation born from the early 1930s to mid-1940s. These represent major disciples of the masters of the 1950s, from a handful of universities with doctoral programs in Brazilian literature. While the "Brazilianists" as a category were on the whole social scientists, the study of Brazilian literature produced a generation of future professors who would strengthen the field in a larger number of universities. The 1980s began to produce the work not only of students of the masters but that of the students' protégés as well. During the 1990s there was increased specialization in Brazilian literature, a larger number of Brazilians, and more institutions represented.

From the 1970s until the end of the century, however, constancy and continuity describes the more than seventy doctoral dissertations completed in Brazilian literature in the United States. It remains common for theses to discourse on the complete works of a single author or major work (Williams on Sousândrade, Jackson on Oswald de Andrade, or Dassin on Mário de Andrade). Theses on poetry generally are also full considerations of the work of a single poet, such as Afonso Frederico Schmidt (Tolman), Jorge de Lima (Sovereign, Farias), João Cabral de Melo Neto (Peixoto), Cecília Meireles (Igel, Sadlier), Machado de Assis (Ishimatsu), Manuel Bandeira (Thompson), Carlos Drummond de Andrade (Sternberg), or Cassiano Ricardo (Moreira). Studies of prose fiction likewise have been devoted to single authors, such as Graciliano Ramos (Brown, Courteau), Jorge Amado (Silverman), Érico Veríssimo (Vessels, Young), Antônio Callado (Waldemar), or Clarice Lispector (Slavinsky, Baker). A few theses on the short story also concentrate on Mário de Andrade (Curtis, Schil, Lokensgaard), João Alphonsus, and Aníbal Machado (Lopes). Brazilian theater is surprisingly well represented, as it is rarely taught, with theses on Nélson Rodrígues (Bledsoe), Suassuna (Paiva), Viana Filho (Damasceno), Boal (Anderson), Qorpo Santo (Silvo Filho), social theater (Schoenbach), and troupes or productions (George, Milleret). Autobiography has only recently appeared as a genre study (Borim, Karpa-Wilson).

Thematic or issue-based theses, while much more numerous, are also consistent with those of the first Brazilianists. Roberto Noda's work on Africans in the Americas (1972), for example, connects the early dissertations by Sayers and Rabassa with current African American interest in the cultural heritage of Salvador, Bahia. Most of these theses concern the work of a single author, such as studies of character in Jorge Amado (Silverman), satire in Érico Veríssimo (Vessels), death in Meireles (Igel), or tragedy in Lispector (Slavinsky). Early studies of literary critics of national literature (Dennis, Mac Nicoll) and schools such as structuralism (Mautner) or modernism (Dassin et al.) are complemented by later works on similar themes, for example, self-conscious postmodernity (Barbosa), women and critics (Marchant), or national critiques (Ferreira). Common themes selected for focus range from film (Johnson), death (Igel), and myth (Patai) to violence (Albuquerque), eroticism (Franconi), technology (Ginway), dictatorship (Avelar), female voice (Quinlan), and prophecy (Braga-Pinto).

Regions of Brazil also became topics, such as the Amazon (Maligo), the rain forest (Sá), and the city (Lowe). Cultural movements such as "Tropicalia" are represented (Dunn). Ethnicity or nativism, however, has practically disappeared, represented by a single thesis on ethnic literature (Moniz) and a single comparative work entitled "Afro-Hispanics and Whites in Venezuela and Brazil" (Dixon). The influence of Spanish America on Brazilian literature is very rare, having produced a comparison of Vargas Llosa with Euclídes (Bernucci), novels by Latin America women (Payne), comparative autobiographies (Borim), and a contrast of Guimarães Rosa with Cabrera Infante (Merrim). More typical are comparative studies of Brazilian and U.S. literatures, comparing Guimarães Rosa with Faulkner, for example (Valente), or with other literatures and the Iberian background, such as medieval Iberia/Brazil (Hastings), Camões/Brazil (Meyers), Brazil/Spain (Ayres), or Argentina/Brazil/Portugal (Lopes Jr.).

Comparative studies based on theme also characterize the dissertations. These range from social themes, such as society (Schoenbach), the city (Lowe), violence (Albuquerque), and postdictatorship (Avelar) to theoretical constructs, such as myth (Patai), narrative space (Potter), reader response (Valente), prophecy (Braga-Pinto), and technology (Ginway). The trend to more conceptual, abstract, or theoretical topics becomes stronger in the 1990s, exploring approaches such as fiction and family (Harrison), cultural interspace (Sobral), nation/women/self (Ferreira), or experimental prose in Murilo Mendes (E. Jackson). The appearance of comparative and theoretical topics notwithstanding, the majority of theses continues the author/theme pattern established in the 1950s for U.S. research works on Brazil, reinforcing the documentary or informative model.

Although studies of Brazilian literature were decisively influenced by the area studies approach, they were born out of philological and textual criticism. Given that origin, along with the fact that Brazilian literature has never been taught in a continental Latin American perspective, since the Portuguese language and Brazil's literary background have isolated it from other American literatures, the field has seen neither as much comparative work nor been subject to as much revisionism as is the case of history or the social sciences. There, Brazil functions as part of a wider dynamic, and current historians can indulge in trendy approaches. Brazilian literature is still working to historicize and explicate a basic canon; its comparative studies have very little to do with Latin America and are directed toward areas of historical cultural inheritance, mainly, France, Portugal, Britain, and lately the United States. In the United States, several recent theses on women in Brazilian literary history (Quinlan, Payne,

Marchant) join revisionist attempts to correct or rehistoricize Brazilian literature, but their impact within the U.S. academy has been negligible, as the field of women's studies has yet to sally beyond Clarice Lispector. Traditional approaches to literary studies dominate the field, which evidences both remarkable continuity over half a century and increasing interplay with Brazilian scholarship.

Interfaces
United States and Brazil: Brazilian Authors and Intellectuals in the United States

The presence of Brazilian authors, scholars, and critics has played a major role in encouraging and guiding the development of literary and cultural studies in the United States. Joaquim Nabuco gave a lecture in English at Yale in 1908, "Spirit of Nationality in Brazilian Literature," perhaps his only work written in English. The Oliveira Lima lectures in 1912 were edited by Professor Percy Alvin Martin of Stanford University and published in 1914. As a result of efforts by the Organization of American States and of Franklin Roosevelt's "Good Neighbor Policy" (1936), Brazilian literature came to be more widely known to the U.S. public through the presence of visiting writers, essayists, and scholars. Poet Cecília Meireles was the first Brazilian author to teach courses, sent by Itamarati to the University of Texas at Austin in 1941. Author Érico Veríssimo delivered a series of lectures, first at the University of California, Berkeley, in 1944, and published as a book under the title *Brazilian Literature: An Outline* (1945/1969). Gilberto Freyre lectured at Indiana University (1944), resulting in the book *Brazil: An Interpretation* (1945). Clarice Lispector's lecture at the University of Texas at Austin ("A Literatura de Vanguarda no Brazil," 1963, unpublished) signaled an ever-increasing presence of Brazilian writers and scholars in university programs of Portuguese. A visiting writer program is still active under a Brazilian Ministry of Culture writer-in-residence program at six universities. This program has recently brought Milton Hatoum, Moacyr Scliar, Marina Colasanti, João Gilberto Noll, Silviano Santiago, João Silvério Trevisan, Nélida Piñón, and others to the United States.

Visiting and Relocated Professors

Brazilian literary studies developed under the tutelage of Brazilian professors. Initially supported by Luso-Brazilian Centers and the Title VI program, a wave of Brazilian scholars who came to teach in the United States beginning in the 1960s, whether short or long term, contributed decisively to the development of studies of literature and culture. Sérgio Buarque de Holanda visited the State University of New York at Stony Brook for a semester in 1966, and Afrânio Coutinho had already been active in New York. Chief among those who continued their academic careers in the United States was Jorge de Sena, Portuguese writer and Brazilian citizen, who trained a generation of U.S. scholars at the University of Wisconsin from 1965 to 1970 and later at the University of California, Santa Barbara, from 1970 to 1978. After teaching at Wisconsin, Wilson Martins began a long career at New York University that would last for almost thirty years, while Heitor Martins taught at Tulane University and at Indiana University. Other Brazilian visitors who remained for extended periods were Fábio Lucas, Oswaldino Marques, Luiz Costa Lima, and Carlos Felipe Moisés. Researchers and postdoctoral students included Afrânio Coutinho, Roberto Schwarz, Leyla Perrone-Moisés, and many others. American universities also appointed Brazilians without U.S. degrees as professors in programs of Brazilian language and literature, a group that includes Almir Campos Bruneti, Luiz Costa Lima, Carlos Felipe Moisés, Norman Potter, Roberto Reis, Mônica Rector, Antônio Salles, Elide V. Oliver, Ivana Versiani, and others. Because of this widespread Brazilian presence, programs of Brazilian literary studies in the United States have developed with a notably Brazilian character and in close contact with Brazilian materials, cultural perspectives, and critical methods.

Distinguished visiting professors were assiduously sought by a number of U.S. universities, beginning in the 1960s and 1970s. Antônio Cândido was at Yale (1960s), as were João Alexandre Barbosa (1960s), Haroldo de Campos (1978), and Silviano Santiago (1996). Antônio Soares Amora, Massaud Moisés, Francisco de Assis Barbosa, Dante Moreira Leite, Clemente Segundo Pinho, and Adolfo Casais Monteiro—among others— came to Wisconsin (1960s), while Texas invited Joel Pontes (1960s), Affonso Romano de Sant'Anna (1976), Silviano Santiago (1977), Walnice Nogueira Galvão (1978), João Alexandre Barbosa (1986), Benedito Nunes (1980), Augusto de Campos (1970), and Haroldo de Campos (1970, 1981), for example. The 1980s and 1990s were marked by an increase in visiting professors of literature, including Jorge Schwartz, Raul Antelo, Luísa Lobo, Nicolau Sevcenko, Heloísa Buarque de Hollanda, Cleonice Berardinelli, Flora Sussekind, Roberto Schwarz, and numerous others. Recently, Jorge Schwartz has been at Texas (1998) and Johns Hopkins, Luiz Costa Lima at Johns Hopkins (1999), Affonso Romano de Sant'Anna at North Carolina

(1999), Flora Sussekind at Berkeley, and Roberto Schwarz at Harvard (1999). The distinguished writer Nélida Piñón holds an endowed professorship (the Stanford Chair in the Humanities) at the University of Miami and spends one semester each academic year in Coral Gables during the 1990s. She was recently visiting at Georgetown (1999) and Harvard (2000).

BRAZILIAN STUDENTS IN U.S. PROGRAMS OF BRAZILIAN LITERATURE

From the 1960s, doctoral studies of Brazilian literature attracted students from Brazil who completed their work here and remained in the United States to teach in programs of Portuguese. Principal among these is Joaquim-Francisco Coelho, who studied at Wisconsin with Lloyd Kasten and Jorge de Sena. Coelho presently holds a chair at Harvard. Brazilians with U.S. degrees who are or have been on the faculty of U.S. university programs include Severino João Albuquerque [Wisconsin], Ana Luiza Andrade, Idelber Avelar [Tulane], Miriam Ayres [NYU], Maria Somerlate Barbosa [Iowa], Leo Bernucci [Texas], Joanna Courteau [Iowa State], Cristina Ferreira Pinto [Texas], Rodolfo Franconi [Dartmouth], Regina Igel [Maryland], Sabrina Karpa-Wilson [Indiana], Maria Angélica Lopes [South Carolina], Francisco Caetano Lopes Jr. [Stanford], Pedro Maligo [Michigan State], Naomi Hoki Moniz [Georgetown], Luci de Biaji Moreira [College of Charleston], Luiza Moreira [Princeton], Celso de Oliveira [South Carolina], Ricardo Paiva, Marta Peixoto [NYU], Lúcia Sá [Stanford], Enylton de Sá Rego [Texas], Patrícia Sobral [Harvard], Ricardo Sternberg [Toronto], Luiz Valente [Brown], Renata Wasserman [Wayne State], and others.

U.S. STUDENTS IN BRAZIL

U.S. graduate students of Brazilian literature have consistently conducted research in Brazil. They have formed affiliations with Brazilian colleagues and their institutions, whether universities, research institutes, libraries, or archives, such as the Instituto de Estudos Brasileiros, the Casa Rui Barbosa, the Centro Interdisciplinar de Estudos Contemporâneos, the Fundação Joaquim Nabuco, and many others. Some have traveled to Brazil under Fulbright research grants, others with Ford Foundation or other agency scholarships, or with support from their home institutions. In all cases, their work has benefited enormously from contact with Brazilian professors and researchers. One could say that when in Brazil they worked alongside Brazilian cohorts, under the codirection of Brazilian advisers, with research based on Brazilian sources. To this extent, the U.S. students adapted to a Brazilian context and, to a greater or lesser degree, identified with the concerns and methods of their Brazilian colleagues in the study of national literature. Indeed, in the 1960s, when it was easier to do so, some Americans remained in Brazil to teach at Brazilian universities. U.S. students show a large degree of assimilation to Brazil, especially notable for fluency in language and familiarity with cultural practices.

Between the United States and Europe

Until recently, there had been relatively little contact between U.S. and European scholars of Brazilian literature, perhaps because European libraries lag far behind the United States. The scant contact was true of Latin America as a whole, as evidenced in Carmelo Mesa-Lago's review of Latin American studies in Europe (1979). In the days of Luso-Brazilian studies, when legendary figures such as the British historian Charles Boxer taught in the United States, Brazilian cultural and to a certain extent literary topics were included within their scope. Boxer's controversial study of racial relations, for example, compared Portuguese culture in Asia, Africa, and Brazil (1963), while Harold Livermore's *Portugal and Brazil* (1953) continued a comprehensive view of Luso-Brazilian history and culture. Raymond Sayers (1968) and Nelson H. Vieira (1991) published comparative literary and cultural studies of Portugal and Brazil, while Alfred Hower and Richard A. Preto-Rodas edited a volume on the Portuguese empire in the time of Camões that follows the Luso-Brazilian comparative model in the United States (1985).

Jorge de Sena was the only Portuguese author and intellectual with an encyclopedic knowledge of Brazilian literature to teach in the United States, starting in 1965. He later invited Arnaldo Saraiva, one of the few Portuguese specialists on Brazilian literature, to Santa Barbara as a lector. After Sena, the greatest European scholar to teach Brazilian literature in the United States is without a doubt Luciana Stegagno Picchio of Rome, author of a distinguished history of Brazilian literature (revised and enlarged in 2004), who taught in the Jorge de Sena Center at Santa Barbara and was visiting professor and lecturer at other universities. In Germany, Hans Flasche of Hamburg published articles on Brazilian literature in his journal, which was open to Americans. Dietrich Briesemeister, of the Iberoamericanisches Institut in Berlin, taught in the United States and later edited several volumes on Brazilian literature. Henry Thorau, a specialist on Brazilian literature at the University of Trier, where he holds a chair in

Portuguese, has recently lectured in the United States, as did the Austrian linguist Dieter Messner (University of Salzburg). At the University of Utrecht, Paulo de Medeiros, who previously taught in the United States and has a U.S. degree, is promoting international congresses and a reevaluation of the field. Notwithstanding Paul Teyssier's lectures in the United States in the 1979, there has been little contact between U.S. Brazilianists and French scholars and centers of Brazilian studies. The late Mário Carelli's research archive on French-Brazilian literary history and relations could be a model for U.S. Brazilianism, however, U.S-Brazilian studies is not only much more recent but also much more fragmented across fields and interests.

Only recently has there been renewed active cooperation between British and American scholars through the newly formed Centre of Brazilian Studies at Oxford, directed by the distinguished historian Leslie Bethell, and through journals, edited volumes, and academic conferences; the Oxford center conducted a joint seminar on poet Haroldo de Campos with Yale University in 1999. British translations have proved useful, particularly the work of Giovanni Pontiero, while John Gledson's books on Machado and David Brookshaw's studies of race and Indianism are well known. David Treece of King's College has taught in the United States, while the journal *Portuguese Studies* [issued by the Department of Portuguese and Brazilian Studies, King's College, London] has joined the *Luso-Brazilian Review* as one of the most important publications in the field. With these notable exceptions, however, there has been relatively little contact between U.S. and European studies of Brazilian literature. The International Association of Lusitanists is the main forum promoting the international study of Brazil and Portugal, with representatives from about forty countries present at the last congress (Brown University, 2002). The second and third congresses of the American Portuguese Studies Association (Madison, Wisconsin, October 2000; University of Maryland, October 2004), attracted scholars from Britain, Austria, Sweden, and the Netherlands, as well as a large contingent from Portugal and Brazil. The European associations are evidence that the field is again swinging back to its original Luso-Brazilian focus, united by the Portuguese language in the world, with very little evidence of any specifically Latin American or American continental focus.

Significant Works Produced in the United States

Works produced in the United States that have added significantly to the study of Brazilian literature and culture include (1) reference and research materials (bibliographies, guides, dictionaries, catalogs, recordings); (2) journal articles, special issues, and the like; (3) anthologies and translations; (4) literary histories and monographs, including comparative studies: (5) communication arts and media; and (6) doctoral theses (see appendix 1).

I. REFERENCE AND RESEARCH

The single most significant U.S. contribution to Brazilian studies has been the publication of general reference and research materials, which include the areas of literature and culture. The principal publication in this area is Ann Hartness's *Brazil in Reference Books, 1965–89: An Annotated Bibliography* (1991), an indispensable guide to research. (For information on general research materials, bibliographies, dictionaries, catalogs, and other research materials, see chapter 16, "Brasiliana in the United States: Reference Sources and Documents.") Other materials prepared for studies of Brazilian language, literature, and culture, after J.D.M. Ford et al.'s early guide to Brazilian belle letters (1931), include José Manuel Topete's working bibliography of Brazilian literature (1957), William Jackson's library guides (1964, 1977), David S. Zubatsky's index to Luso-Brazilian journals (1971), Maria Luisa Nunes's list of resources for Brazilian literary studies (1976), Dorothy Burnett Porter's list of Afro-Braziliana (1978), Jon Tolman and Ricardo Paiva's cultural and literary outline series (1985), Irwin Stern's dictionary of Brazilian literature (1988), Bobby J. Chamberlain's selected lists of reference works (1993, 1996), Paula Covington's guide to research sources (1996), and Mônica Rector's dictionary of Brazilian writers (2003). Published catalogues to important collections include the *Catalog of the Oliveira Lima Library* (1970).

II. ACADEMIC JOURNAL ARTICLES AND SPECIAL ISSUES

Journals have played a very important and prominent role in providing information, critical readings, and reference materials on Brazilian literature. These include the flagship *Luso-Brazilian Review* at Wisconsin (since 1965); *Brasil/Brazil* (Brown); *Espelho* (Purdue), which is dedicated to studies of Machado de Assis; and *ellipsis: Journal of the American Portuguese Studies Association*. Brazilian materials have been included in the professional journal of the American Association of Teachers of Spanish and Portuguese, *Hispania*, as well as in those of other associations and institutions, particularly the *Latin American Literary Review*, *Chasqui*, and the *Revista Iberoamericana*. Others include *PMLA, Portuguese Studies Review, Books Abroad, Comparative Literature, Hispanic Review, Amazonian Literary*

Review, Kentucky Romance Quarterly, Latin American Theater Review, Romance Notes, Studies in Short Fiction, and many others.

Brazilian topics have attracted increasing recent critical attention in journals. The *Nuevo Texto Crítico* of Stanford University dedicated a special issue to Oswald de Andrade and his celebrated *Cannibal Manifesto* in 1999 that was subtitled "Anthropophagy Today?" and edited by João Cezar de Castro Rocha and Jorge Ruffinelli. *Portuguese Literary & Cultural Studies* (University of Massachusetts–Dartmouth) produced a massive special number in English to celebrate the five-hundredth anniversary of the discovery of Brazil, presented at the Library of Congress in April 2001 and also edited by João Cezar de Castro Rocha. This latest publication represents a turning point in the publishing of critical essays on Brazil in English. The volume was presented at a public ceremony at the Library of Congress, and marks a Brazilian critical presence in the United States. Of its sixty-five essays, six are by U.S. Brazilianists and the remainder by Brazilian specialists in translation. Brazilianists in this case have been well integrated into the work of their Brazilian colleagues, without distinction.

III. ANTHOLOGIES

Isaac Goldberg published two early anthologies of short stories, *Brazilian Tales* (1921) and *Brazilian Short Stories* (1925). Leonard Downes published *An Introduction to Brazilian Poetry* (1944) in São Paulo for the Brazilian Poetry Club. Anthologies would be revived only as part of a renewed interest in Latin American area studies after 1958, with Harriet de Onis's *The Golden Land: An Anthology of Latin American Folklore in Literature* (1961), and John Nist's *Modern Brazilian Poetry: An Anthology* (1962), *Modern Brazilian Stories* (1967), and *Triquarterly Anthology of Contemporary Latin American Literature* (1969). Both poetry and prose are included in the general area anthologies, such as *Modern Latin American Literature* (1975), *Borzoi Anthology of Latin American Literature* (1977), and *Latin American Literature Today* (1977). Brazilian theater, scarcely represented, is the subject of Wilson Martins and Seymour Menton's *Teatro brasileiro contemporâneo* (1966) [in Portuguese], and Elzbieta Szoka and Joe Bratcher's *Three Contemporary Brazilian Plays* (1988). Silviano Santiago published a useful anthology for teaching, *Brasil: poesia e prosa* (1969) in Portuguese, with a wider selection than Alfred Hower and Ricardo Preto-Rodas's original *Crônicas brasileiras* (1971), another Portuguese text, although there is now a new edition (1994) with Charles Perrone as second author, *Carlos Drummond de Andrade: quarenta historinhas* (1985), also a Portuguese text. Interest in poetry is strong in this period, as shown in Elizabeth Bishop and Emanuel Brasil's *An Anthology of Twentieth-Century Brazilian Poetry* (1972), José Neistein's *Poesia brasileira moderna: A Bilingual Anthology* (1972), and Emanuel Brasil and William J. Smith's *Brazilian Poetry, 1950–1980* (1983). The new Brazilian Concrete Poetry movement is featured in Mary Ellen Solt's *Concrete Poetry: A World View* (1968) and Emmett Williams's *Concrete Poetry* (1968). Specialized or thematic anthologies with Brazilian authors are a feature of the 1990s, including *Hammock Beneath Mangoes* (1991), *One Hundred Years from Tomorrow* (1992), the *Penguin Book of Short Stories* (1992), and *Nothing the Sun Could Not Explain* (1997). *Outras praias/Other Shores* (1998), a bilingual poetry anthology published in Brazil, is available in the United States. Brazilian works now appear more frequently as subsections or special issues in U.S. journal anthologies, such as *Fiction International 28* (1995), *Grand Street 61* (1997), and *The Dirty Goat* (1999).

IV. TRANSLATIONS

Alongside reference works, translations constitute one of the most significant U.S. contributions to knowledge of Brazilian literary studies. The translation of Brazilian literature in the United States has a long and varied history. The Brazilian embassy in Washington, D.C., prepared a useful mimeographed bibliography of translations, "Relação das Obras de Literatura Brasileira Editadas em Inglês" (1988).

A. Novels

Approximately one hundred Brazilian novels were published in the United States between 1920 and 1985. Novels chosen for translation do not constitute a history or survey of Brazilian literature in any systematic fashion; rather, titles chosen for translation may represent either a translator's preference, the discovery of an excellent writer or overlooked talent, a style of the moment, a publishing success, or a personal connection. Many major writers, however, have been widely and successfully translated, such as Jorge Amado (15 titles), Carlos Drummond de Andrade (4 books of poetry), Clarice Lispector (5 titles), Machado de Assis (12 titles), Moacyr Scliar (6 titles), and Érico Veríssimo (6 titles). Others are represented only by selected works, such as Mário de Andrade (2 titles), Oswald de Andrade (2 titles), Ivan Ângelo (2 titles), Lima Barreto (3 titles), Antônio Callado (2 titles), Autran Dourado (2 titles), Rubem Fonseca (2 titles), Osman Lins (2 titles), Rachel de Queiroz (2 titles), Graciliano Ramos (4 titles), José Lins do Rego (2 titles), João Guimarães Rosa (3 titles), Márcio Souza (3 titles), Lygia Fagundes Telles (3 titles), and J. J. Veiga (2 titles).

The chronology of published translations may be as striking for its unusual choices as it is for its coverage of major works. The oldest translation listed as published in the United States is Graça Aranha's *Canaan* (1920), followed by two marginal works scarcely mentioned in Brazilian literary histories, Paulo Setúbal's *Domitila: The Romance of an Emperor's Mistress* (1930) and Mário de Andrade's *Fraulein*, both interests of Margaret Richardson Hollingsworth, who also attempted *Macunaíma* but never completed it. Jorge Amado's *Suor* was published as *Slums* (1937) in the same period as Érico Veríssimo's *Crossroads* (1943). Taunay's *Inocência*, which had come out in London (1889), was retranslated (1945). Next appeared Euclides da Cunha in Samuel Putnam's translation (1944) and José Lins do Rego with a minor work, *Pureza* (1948). Machado de Assis came on the scene with three titles in succession, *Epitaph of a Small Winner* (1952), *Dom Casmurro* (1953), and *Philosopher or Dog?* (1954). Almeida's *Memoirs of a Militia Sergeant* (1959/1999), was followed by a string of Jorge Amado successes, which included *Gabriela, Clove and Cinnamon* (1962), *Home Is the Sailor* (1964), *Shepherds of the Night* (1967), and *Dona Flor and Her Two Husbands* (1969). The northeastern novel was in vogue, and Graciliano Ramos's *Barren Lives* (1965) became the most widely read Brazilian novel in English, still in print after more than thirty-five years. *Anguish* and *St. Bernard* would follow in 1972 and 1975, respectively. At this time, Rachel de Queiroz's *The Three Marias* (1965) and Lins do Rego's *Plantation Boy* (1966) also appeared. João Guimarães Rosa's masterpiece, *Devil to Pay in the Backlands* (1963), was the major disappointment of the day, in a failed translation that turned the greatest work of fiction in this century into a "spaghetti Western," in the phrase of Haroldo de Campos, and squandered its potential place in comparative literature. This was, however, Érico Veríssimo's moment of glory, with *Consider the Lilies* (1969), *The Rest Is Silence* (1969), and *Time and Wind* (1969). Autran Dourado began a series of novels with *A Hidden Life* (1969).

The 1970s saw a continuation of some classics, such as Machado's *Counselor Ayres' Memorial* (1972) and *Yaya Garcia* (1976), Azevedo's *A Brazilian Tenement* (1976), Lima Barreto's *Clara dos Anjos* (1977) and *Life and Death of M. J. Garcia de Sá* (1979), alongside titles by modernist writers, from Oswald de Andrade's *Sentimental Memoirs of John Seaborne* (1972) and *Seraphim Grosse Pointe* (1979) to Antônio Callado's *Don Juan's Bar* (1972), João Ubaldo Ribeiro's *Sergeant Getúlio* (1978), and Lúcio Cardoso's *Threshold* (1975).

In the 1980s, Osman Lins's *Avalovara* received a masterful translation by Rabassa, to be followed within a few years by the greatest variety of

Brazilian fiction ever to be published in the United States. Within five years' time, one sees Márcio Souza *(Emperor of the Amazon,* 1980), Ivan Ângelo *(Celebration,* 1982), Ledo Ivo *(Snake's Nest,* 1981), Ignácio de Loyola Brandão *(Zero,* 1983), Mário de Andrade *(Macunaíma,* 1984), Darcy Ribeiro *(Maíra,* 1984), Moacyr Scliar *(Centaur in the Garden,* 1985), Lygia Fagundes Teles *(Marble Dance,* 1986), Clarice Lispector's *Apple in the Dark* (1986), *Hour of the Star* (1986), and *An Apprenticeship* (1986), along with Rubem Fonseca's *High Art* (1987), among others. Unfortunately, the translation of *Macunaíma*—one of the essential works of the literature—was a failure, and attempts to retranslate it have been stymied by copyright restrictions. The translations of Clarice Lispector, an essential author, also vary greatly in quality. Lispector is the only Brazilian author whose complete works of fiction are now available in English. This is a reflection of her international reception and of her promotion begun by French feminism. Other authors have had less success in the academy and market because of the lack of a critical context, their brief periods in print, and the isolation of Brazilian literature from a Latin American market niche.

Since 1985, the remaining works of Lispector have appeared, along with major works by such influential living writers as Nélida Piñón, Silviano Santiago, and João Ubaldo Ribeiro, who translated his own novel, *An Invincible Memory* (1991). Other selected classics continued to appear, such as Azevedo's *Mulatto* (1990), Piñón's *Caetana's Sweet Song* (1992), Patrícia Galvão's *Industrial Park* (1993), Alencar's *Senhora* (1994), and Osman Lins's *Queen of the Prisons of Greece* (1995). The recently inaugurated, privately financed "Oxford Latin American Library" has begun a more chronological and scholarly approach, with the retranslation of selected major works, with Almeida's *Memoirs of a Militia Sergeant,* Machado's *Dom Casmurro, Posthumous Memoirs of Brás Cubas, Quincas Borba,* Azevedo's *Slum,* and Alencar's *Iracema* already in print. Because this is a continent-wide series, however, the number of Brazilian titles will be limited, whereas the ideal would be a separately constituted "Brazilian library" of classics. Recent translations include Caio Fernando Abreu's *Whatever Happened to Dulce Veiga* (2000) and Hatoum's *The Brothers* (2002).

Along with these better-known authors, many others have also published at least one novel in English, including Cecílio Carneiro (*The Bonfire,* 1971), Josué de Castro (*Of Men and Crabs,* 1970), Gustavo Corção (*Who If I Cry Out,* 1967), Antônio Olinto *(The Water House,* 1985), Antônio Olavo Pereira (*Marcore,* 1970), Marcos Rey (*Memoirs of a Gigolo,* 1987), and José Mauro de Vasconcellos (*My Sweet Orange Tree,* 1970). Judging from dates of publication, U.S. presses were most willing to expand their coverage of Brazilian literature in the period from 1970 to 1985.

Many of these translations are to the credit of professional translators and editors such as Thomas Colchie, Clifford Landers, Margaret A. Neves, Harriet de Onís, Samuel Putnam, Gregory Rabassa, Barbara Shelby, and Ellen Watson. They are supported by the work of more than fifty published U.S. translators, mostly academics, including L. L. Barrett, Albert I. Bagby, Linton L. Barrett, Emmi Baum, Pamela G. Bird, Elizabeth Bishop, Albert Bork, Harry W. Brown, Helen Caldwell, Ralph E. Dimmick, John P. Dwyer, E. Percy Ellis, Fred P. Ellison, Earl E. Fitz, John Fostini, Adria Frizzi, Eloah F. Giacomelli, William L. Grossman, Dorothy Heapy, Susan Hertelendy, Rod W. Horton, Alfred Hower, Lori Ishimatsu, Jean Neel Karnoff, Kerry Shawn Keys, Edgar G. Knowlton, John Knox, Kern Krapohl, Elizabeth A. Jackson, K. David Jackson, L. C. Kaplan, Henry Keith, E. A. Lacey, Helen R. Lane, Dorothy Loos, Elizabeth Lowe, Richard Mazzara, Edgar H. Miller, Ralph Niebuhr, John Nist, Lori A. Parris, Charles Perrone, Dudley Poore, Dillwyn F. Ratcliff, Stanley Richards, Edward Riggio, J. T. W. Sadler, John Saunders, Raymond Sayers, Jack Schmitt, Ronald Souza, Mark Strand, James L. Taylor, L. L. Taylor, Jack E. Tomlins, Willis Wager.

Despite the published titles mentioned earlier, Brazilian literature remains relatively unknown. Brazilian novels do not find a natural readership in the Hispanic or Latin American categories to which they are assigned, and there is little or no secondary literature to accompany their publication in English. Comparative literature courses do not generally select Brazilian works to represent Latin America. Titles do not remain long in print, and almost half the titles translated could be considered minor works. There is no history of Brazilian literature now available in English. The third volume on Brazilian literature of the 1996 Cambridge *History of Latin American Literature* (Roberto González Echevarría and Enrique Pupo-Walker, eds.), however, was largely the work of U.S. Brazilianists (Haberly, Albuquerque, Daniel, Jackson, Peixoto, Slater, Skidmore).

B. Short Stories

Short story collections were published much more selectively, beginning with an early collection by Monteiro Lobato (1925, trans. Anon.). The stories of Machado de Assis contributed *The Psychiatrist* (1963, trans. Grossman and Caldwell) and *The Devil's Church* (1977, trans. Schmitt and Ishimatsu), while Jorge Amado's novela *The Two Deaths of Quincas Wateryell* (1965, trans. Shelby), João Guimarães Rosa's *Sagarana* (1966, trans. Onís) and *Third Bank of the River* (1968, trans. Shelby), Clarice Lispector's *Family Ties* (1970, trans. Pontiero) and *Foreign Legion* (1986, trans. Pontiero), and Osman Lins's *Nine, Novena* (1995) represent classic publications. Other collections are by J. J. Veiga (*Misplaced Machine,* 1970, trans. Bird), Dalton Trevisan (*Vampire of Curitiba,* 1972, trans. Rabassa), Murilo Rubião (*The Ex-Magician,* 1979, trans. Colchie), and Lygia Fagundes Teles (*Tigrela,* 1986, trans. Neves). More recent collections include Darlene Sadlier's *One Hundred Years After Tomorrow* (1992) and Cristina Ferreira Pinto's *Urban Voices* (2000). Brazilian authors continue to be included in the Cambridge anthology of the *Latin American Short Story* (Roberto González Echevarría, ed.) and other anthologies in journals (*The Literary Review; Grand Street*).

C. Poetry

Only six Brazilian poets have individual anthologies or books of their works in English. They are all part of the modernist movement, with the exception of João Cabral de Melo Neto, who represents the "Generation of 1945" and was the major poetic voice of modernism in the last half of the twentieth century. The poets represented are Jorge de Lima (*Brazilian Psalm,* 1941, trans. Wager; *Poems,* 1952, published in Brazil), Carlos Drummond de Andrade (*In the Middle of the Road,* 1967, trans. Nist; *Souvenir of the Ancient World,* 1976, trans. Strand; *The Minus Sign,* 1980, trans. Virgínia de Araújo; *Traveling in the Family,* 1986, trans. Bishop, et al.); Mário de Andrade (*Hallucinated City,* 1968, trans. Jack E. Tomlins); Cecília Meireles (*Poems in Translation,* 1977), João Cabral de Melo Neto (*A Knife All Blade,* 1980, trans. Keys); *Selected Poems,* 1994, trans. Richard Zenith, et al.), and Manuel Bandeira (*This Earth, That Sky,* 1986, trans. Candace Slater).

D. Theater

Brazilian plays are all but confined to midcentury, with Martins Pena's *The Rural Justice of the Peace* (1948, trans. Willis Knapp Jones), Antônio Callado's *Frankl* (1955, trans. Anon.), Pedro Bloch's *Enemies Don't Send Flowers* (1957, trans. Fostini), Guilherme Figueiredo's *The Fox and the Grapes* (1957, trans. Fostini and Jorge Cardoso Aires), and Ariano Suassuna's *The Rogue's Trial* (1963, trans. Ratcliff). Oswald de Andrade's "The Dead Woman" (unpublished 1968 ms., trans. Luiz Galiza) was staged at Berkeley, while Roberto Athayde's *Miss Margarida's Way* (1977) toured U.S. universities. Brazilian theater is the subject of articles in the University of Kansas journal *Latin American Theater Review.*

E. Diaries

Brazilian diaries include Helena Morley's *Minha vida de menina* (1957), translated by Elizabeth Biship as *The Diary of "Helena Morley"* (1977). Carolina de Jesus's *Quarto de despejo* (1962), translated by David St. Clair as *Child of the Dark* (1962), was reprinted in England as *Beyond All Pity* (1990). Interest in Carolina de Jesus has been revived in Robert Levine and José Carlos Sebe Bom Meihy's *The Life and Death of Carolina Maria de Jesus* (1995). The collaborative project between José Carlos Sebe Bom Meihy and Levine, started in 1990, produced nine books on Carolina Maria de Jesus in English and in Portuguese, including *The Unedited Diaries* (1999), an analysis of her original diary entries heavily edited by Audálio Dantas (by cutting, not rewriting) and including unknown diary entries up to 1965.

V. DIDACTIC WORKS

Only recently have early translations of Brazilian books on literature and culture by Veríssimo, Freyre, Bandeira, Moog, and Coutinho been followed by substantive critical essays by prominent Brazilian literary figures in translation. Two early examples are José Bettencourt Machado's *Machado of Brazil* (1953) and Wilson Martins's influential book on modernism revised in translation, *The Modernist Idea* (1970, trans. Tomlins). Recent titles include Luiz Costa Lima's *Control of the Imaginary* (1988, trans. Ronald W. Sousa), José Maia Neto's *Machado de Assis, the Brazilian Pyrrhonian* (1994), Antônio Cândido's *On Literature and Society* (1995, trans. Howard S. Becker), and Flora Sussekind's *Cinematograph of Words* (1997, trans. Paulo Henriques Brito). Since most journals publish original articles in Portuguese, translated essays by Brazilian specialists are few, usually confined to edited collections.

A. Collected Essays

Essays by literary scholars have increasingly appeared in collected, edited volumes, both in the United States and England. Randal Johnson's *Tropical Paths* (1992), in honor of Fred P. Ellison, includes a range of Brazilian specialists. I published *Transformations of Literary Language in Latin American Literature: From Machado to the Vanguards* (1987), a volume in honor of João Alexandre Barbosa; *One Hundred Years of Invention: Centenary of Oswald de Andrade* (1992); and *Experimental, Visual, Concrete: Avant-Garde Poetry Since 1960* (1995), with essays on Augusto and Haroldo de Campos. Recent British volumes include Hilary Owen's *Gender, Ethnicity,*

Class, Bernard McGuirk's *Brazil and the Discovery of America*, and Claudia Pazos-Alonso's *Women in the Portuguese World*. American volumes include David Sheinin and Lois Baer Barr's *Jewish Diaspora in Latin America: New Studies on History and Literature* (1996), Robert DiAntonio and Nora Glickman's *Tradition and Innovation: Reflections on Latin American Jewish Writing* (1993), Marjorie Agosin's *Passion, Memory, Identity: Jewish Latin America* (1999), and Paul Franssen's *The Author as Character: Representing Historical Writers in Western Literature* (1999), for example.

B. Literary Histories

Very few histories of Brazilian literature have been written in the United States since Goldberg's and Putnam's. Gerrit De Jong published *Four Hundred Years of Brazilian Literature: Outline and Anthology* (1969). Claude Hulet published a three-volume history-anthology, *Brazilian Literature* (1974–75) in the style of the Brazilian *Presença da literatura brasileira* series, which has never been superseded, although Frederick G. Williams is author of a highly regarded unpublished collection of bilingual texts used for teaching. The most reliable guide now in print in English is the Cambridge *History of Latin American Literature*, vol. 3.

C. Monographs Published in the United States

Books in English published in United States on Brazilian literature constitute one of the major contributions to the field. Many titles represent published doctoral theses or revisions. The subjects and critical orientation of these books are a significant indication of the state and quality of literary studies, as well as the nature of U.S. contributions to perspectives on Brazilian literature. The main orientations of these studies are principal authors and works.

Monographs on single authors have produced descriptive overviews prepared for Twayne and other series (Earl Fitz on Clarice Lispector, 1985, and Machado de Assis, 1989; Jon Vincent on Guimarães Rosa, 1978), as well as comprehensive studies. The latter include Ricardo Sternberg on Carlos Drummond de Andrade (1986), Helen Caldwell on Machado de Assis (1960, 1970), Malcolm Silverman on Dinah Silveira de Queirós (1979), Fred Clark on Nélson Rodrígues (1991), and Richard Mazzara and Celso de Oliveira on Graciliano Ramos (1974, 1988). Highly focused thematic and critical studies are illustrated by Marta Peixoto's study of passion in Clarice Lispector (1994), Paul Dixon on ambiguity in Machado de Assis (1983, 1989), and Stephanie Merrim on language in Guimarães Rosa, 1983.

Brazilian theater has received increasing attention in studies of authors (Fred Clark on Nelson Rodrigues, 1978; Elzbieth Szoka on Plínio Marcos, 1995), troupes (Leslie Damasceno, 1996), or themes (Severino Albuquerque on violence, 1991; David S. George on cannibalism, 1992). The novel is a staple of author and thematic studies (Loos on naturalism, 1963; Mac Adam on narrative style, 1977), while poetry has also been treated in studies of individual authors or movements (Lori Ishimatsu on Machado de Assis, 1984; Darlene Sadlier on Cecília Meireles, 1983; Charles Perrone on twentieth-century poetry, 1996).

Brazilian modernism received its first book-length treatment by John Nist (1967), before the revised English translation of Martins's *The Modernist Idea* (1970). Randal Johnson (and Robert Stam) studied the film industry (1989, 1993), while Nelson Vieira compared Portuguese and Brazilian cultural traditions (1989). Mark Curran collected and studied the folk literature of the Brazilian Northeast (1973, 1981, 1998), as did Candace Slater (1982), who also worked on Amazonian folk tales (1994).

Emir Rodríguez Monegal promoted Spanish American and Brazilian comparative studies (Mário de Andrade-Borges, 1978), while Stephanie Merrim compared Guimarães Rosa and Cabrera Infante (1978). Elizabeth Lowe studied urbanization (1983), while Daphne Patai analyzed myth and ideology (1982), Darlene Sadlier studied imagery (1982), and Roberto Di Antonio studied utopian and dystopian fiction (1989).

David Driver's pioneering dissertation on Indianism (1943) found a contemporary counterpart in Renata Wasserman's work on North American and Brazilian romantic Indianist fiction (1994). Raymond Sayers's early work on the Negro in Brazilian literature (1956) was continued in Ricardo Preto-Rodas's book on the theme of negritude (1970), now the topic of wide interest in cultural and political studies of race, slavery, and Afro-Brazilian politics. Ethnicity in Brazilian society is treated in works by David T. Haberly (miscegenation, 1983), Nelson Vieira on Jewish writers (1985), and Maria Luiza Nunes on national identity (1987).

While feminist studies began to be applied to Brazilian literature through Clarice Lispector (see Peixoto, 1994), other recent monographs and reprints more fully apply feminist criticism to the canon of Brazilian literature (Susan Quinlan, 1991, 1996, 1999; Peggy Sharpe, 1996 (org.), 1997, 1999; Judith Payne, 1993).

While regionalism is a strong basis for the interpretation of Brazil, the classic work remains Fred P. Ellison's (1954) on the northeastern novel, recently complemented by Pedro Maligo on Amazonian fiction (1998).

While introduced by J. Freels's work on political literature (1966), political themes are largely restricted to the period of the military dictatorship, such as Nancy Baden on the writer and authoritarianism (1999).

D. Monographs of U.S. Scholarship Published in Portuguese in Brazil

Books on Brazilian literature that were prepared in the United States for publication in Portuguese in Brazil constitute a significant outlet for U.S. scholars. These books characterize the professional nature of these studies and their interface with Brazilian scholars and scholarship.

1. Books by Non-Brazilians

This category includes Mark Curran (cordel literature, 1973, 1991, 1998); Leslie Damasceno (theater, 1994); Mary L. Daniel (Guimarães Rosa, 1968); Joan Dassin (Mário de Andrade, 1978); David George (theater, 1990); K. David Jackson (Oswald de Andrade, 1978); Randal Johnson (Macunaíma, 1982); Charles Perrone (popular music and literature, 1988), Susan Quinlan (women's studies, 1996, 1999); Emir Rodríguez Monegal (Borges-Mário de Andrade, 1978); Peggy Sharpe (women's studies, 1996, 1997, 2000); Malcolm Silverman (novel, 1978, 1987); Frederick G. Williams (Sousândrade, 1970, 1976, 1978), and Theodore Young (Érico Veríssimo, 1998). Of these, Mary L. Daniel's book on Rosa had a major impact in Brazil and remains an obligatory reference for studies of Rosa. Many other titles published by Brazilianists in Brazil remain in print and are well known.

2. Brazilian Authors

Books published in Brazil by Brazilian "Brazilianists" (Brazilians with U.S. degrees or teaching in the United States) include Anoar Aiex (Tobias Barreto, 1989, 1990); Ana Luiza Andrade (Osman Lins, 1987); Leo Bernucci (Euclides da Cunha, 1989, 1995); Joaquim-Francisco Coelho (Carlos Drummond de Andrade, 1973; essays, 1975; Manuel Bandeira, 1981, 1982); Cristina Ferreira-Pinto (novel, 1985, 1990); Rodolfo Franconi (eroticism, 1997); Regina Igel (Osman Lins, 1988; Jewish writers, 1997); Vasda Landers (Jeca Tatu, 1988); Heitor Martins (essays, 1973, baroque, 1983); Wilson Martins (essays and history, 1976, 1986, 1991); Naomi Hoki Moniz (Nélida Piñón, 1993); Marta Peixoto (João Cabral, 1983), and Enylton de Sá Rego (Machado de Assis, 1989).

3. Other Countries

U.S. Brazilianists have published in other languages and countries, including books such as Erdmute Wenzel White's *Les Annés vingt au Brésil*

(1977), published in France. European academic journals and books, such as the *Quaderni Portoghese*, have published studies by U.S. Brazilianists in different languages, while studies of Brazilian literature and culture frequently appear in Portugal.

VI. COMMUNICATION ARTS AND MEDIA

U.S. interest in Brazilian music, cinema, and television has been the work of a mere handful of scholars, although these areas are receiving increasing attention in terms of national cultural studies and even literary expression.

A. Film

The major U.S. books on Brazilian film are Randal Johnson and Robert Stam, eds., *Brazilian Cinema* (1982); Johnson's *Cinema Novo x 5: Masters of Contemporary Brazilian Film* (1984), *The Film Industry in Brazil: Culture and the State* (1987); Stam's *Tropical Multiculturalism: A Comparative History of Race in Brazilian Cinema and Culture* (1997); and Ismail Xavier's *Allegories of Underdevelopment: Aesthetics and Politics in Modern Brazilian Cinema* (1997).

Early connections between the United States and Brazil have promoted some research on Orson Welles and Carmen Miranda. The Brazilian scholar Heloisa Buarque de Holanda was in the United States in the 1980s to research filming in Brazil by Welles as a director. His experimental *It's All True* is now available in video. The presence and influence of Carmen Miranda are the subject of Gil-Montero's commercial publication *Brazilian Bombshell: The Biography of Carmen Miranda* (1989).

B. Music

Scholarship on Brazilian art music resulted from the work of area specialists on Latin American music, particularly Gilbert Chase at Tulane University. His protégé Gérard Béhague (*The Beginnings of Musical Nationalism in Brazil,* 1971) is currently the editor of *Latin American Music Review* (University of Texas), which publishes studies of Brazilian music. Béhague has worked extensively on Afro-Brazilian music *(Music and Black Ethnicity: The Caribbean and South America,* 1994). David P. Appleby is author of the only published general history, *The Music of Brazil* (1983), although Béhague authored major comprehensive essays on Brazil and published *Music in Latin America* (1979). Béhague also wrote a prize-winning book on Villa Lobos, *Heitor Villa Lobos: The Search for Brazil's Musical Soul* (1994), followed by Lisa M. Peppercorn's *The World of Villa-Lobos in Pictures and*

Documents (1996) and Appleby's *Heitor Villa-Lobos: A Life* (2002). Recent dissertations include André Cavazotti Silva's "The Sonatas for Violin and Piano of M. Camargo Guarnieri: Perspectives on the Style of a Brazilian Nationalist Composer" (1998).

The use in Disney films of the 1940s of Brazilian popular music, such as Ary Barroso's "Aquarela do Brasil," is covered in *Brazilian Popular Music and Globalization* (2001), edited by Charles A. Perrone and Christopher Dunn. There is evidence of New York interest in performing Brazilian popular music of the time in *Piano Music of Brazil* (1942), edited by Oscar Lorenzo Fernandez et al. Brazilian popular music, with its political and often literary discourse, is a subject of increasing interest as the subject of theses (Stephen Thomas Walden's "*Brasilidade:* Brazilian Rock in the Context of National Cultural Identity," 1997) and books, the most important of which are Perrone's *Masters of Contemporary Brazilian Song* (1989) and Dunn's *Brutality Garden: Tropicália and the Emergence of a Brazilian Counterculture* (2001). Many Brazilian musicians and musicologists study at conservatories or graduate programs in the United States, and composer-musicians such as Tom Jobim cultivated contacts in New York City.

C. Television

Brazilian television, which has yet to attract much attention in the United States, is studied mainly by Brazilian students. Sérgio Mattos wrote *The Impact of the 1964 Revolution on Brazilian Television* (1982) at the School of Communications at the University of Texas, and the dissertation of Raul Franco dos Reis is entitled "The Impact of Television Viewing in the Brazilian Amazon" (1999). Amelia Simpson published the only book on a Brazilian TV personality, *Xuxa* (1990), accompanied in the same year by two analytical studies, Conrad Phillip Kottak's *Prime-Time Society: An Anthropological Analysis of Television and Culture* (1990), and Maria de Magalhães Castro's *Television and the Elites in Postauthoritarian Brazil* (1990). There is a growing corpus of journal articles.

COMPARATIVE THEORY AND GLOBALIZATION

The most creative work being done at present in U.S. universities privileges theoretical or interpretive models in studies of authors and texts, in such recent examples as "belonging and displacement," "literature and drought," "impossibility in literature," "negativity and avant-gardes," and so on. U.S. scholars now regularly participate in Brazilian associations, and they constitute perhaps the most active international constituency—

along with the English—for the study of Brazilian literature and culture. Brazil, Europe, and the United States are now rapidly becoming more integrated, with the global communication resources that the Internet has made available.

APPENDIX
Doctoral Degrees

American doctoral degrees in Brazilian literature begin with David Driver (Columbia, 1942), Marie Wallis (New Mexico, 1947), Don Walther (North Carolina, 1948), Hubert Mate (Northwestern, 1949), and Benjamin Woodbridge (Harvard, 1949). They continue in the 1950s with Dorothy Loos (Columbia, 1950), Fred Ellison (Berkeley, 1952), Raymond Sayers (Columbia, 1953), Gregory Rabassa (Columbia, 1954), Alfred Hower (Harvard, 1954), Timothy Brown (Wisconsin, 1955), Herman Slutzkin (Columbia, 1957), and Theodore Rose (New York University, 1959).

Dissertations in the 1960s include those by Norwood Andrews (Wisconsin, 1964), Mary L. Daniels (Wisconsin, 1965), Russell Hamilton (Yale, 1965), David T. Haberly (Harvard, 1966), Doris Turner (St. Louis, 1966), Joaquim-Francisco Coelho (Wisconsin, 1968), Robert Herron (Wisconsin, 1968), Mark Curran (St. Louis, 1968), Fred Clark (University of Florida, 1968), and Frederick García (New York University, 1969).

Doctoral degrees in Brazilian literature surged in the 1970s (their holders' places of employment are noted in brackets) including those held by Joanna Courteau (Wisconsin, 1970) [at Iowa State], Jon Tolman (New Mexico, 1970) [retired from New Mexico], Robert Bledsoe (Wisconsin, 1971), Gerald Curtis (New Mexico, 1971) [University of Miami, retired], Malcolm Silverman (Illinois, 1971) [San Diego State], Marie Sovereign (Texas, 1971) [retired], Frederick G. Williams (Wisconsin, 1971) [Brigham Young], Ron Dennis (Wisconsin, 1972), K. David Jackson (Wisconsin, 1973) [Yale], Peter Schoenbach (Rutgers, 1973), Renata Mautner Wasserman (Brandeis, 1973) [Wayne State], Jack Schmitt (Wisconsin, 1973) [California State University, Long Beach], Regina Igel (New Mexico, 1973) [Maryland], Joan Dassin (Stanford, 1974) [Ford Foundation], Elizabeth Lowe (CCNY, 1975) [University of Florida], Celso de Oliveira (South Carolina, 1976), Randal Johnson (Texas, 1977) [UCLA], Murray MacNicoll [deceased] (Wisconsin, 1977), Daphne Patai (Wisconsin, 1977) [University of Massachusetts–Amherst], Marta Peixoto (Princeton, 1977) [NYU], Darlene Sadlier (Wisconsin, 1977) [Indiana], Ricardo Sternberg (UCLA, 1978) [Toronto], and Naomi Hoki Moniz (Harvard, 1979) [Georgetown].

Dissertations from the 1980s include those by Maria Angélica Lopes (Wisconsin, 1980) [University of South Carolina], William Brow (Wisconsin, 1980), Ricardo Paiva (Indiana, 1980), Norman Potter [deceased] (Minnesota, 1981), David George (Minnesota, 1981) [Lake Forest College], Maria-Odilia Leal McBride (Texas, 1981), Ramon Magrans (Texas Tech, 1981), Peggy Sharpe (New Mexico, 1981) [Florida State], Ana Luiza Andrade (Texas, 1982) [Universidade Federal de Santa Catarina, Florianópolis], Lori Ishimatsu (Indiana, 1982), Linda Chang (Indiana, 1982), Vanda Bonafini Landers (NYU, 1982), Luiz Valente (Brown, 1983) [Brown], Enylton de Sá Rego (Texas, 1984) [Texas], Severino Albuquerque (North Carolina, 1984) [Wisconsin], Charles Perrone (Texas, 1985) [University of Florida], Susan Quinlan (New Mexico, 1986) [Georgia], Leopoldo Bernucci (Michigan, 1986) [Texas], Margo Milleret (Texas, 1986) [New Mexico], Sandra Dixon (Brown, 1986), Leslie Damasceno (UCLA, 1987) [Duke], Rodolfo Franconi (Vanderbilt, 1987) [Dartmouth], Adria Frizzi (Texas, 1988) [Texas], Francisco Caetano Lopes Jr. [deceased] (Pittsburgh, 1988), Gary Vessels (Santa Barbara, 1989), Cristina Ferreira-Pinto (Tulane, 1989) [Texas], Joyce Carson-Leavitt (New Mexico, 1989), Elizabeth Ginway (Vanderbilt, 1989) [University of Florida], and Douglas Thompson (UCLA, 1989), among others.

In the 1990s those awarded doctoral degrees include Elizabeth A. Jackson (Texas, 1990) [Wesleyan], Pedro Maligo (Texas, 1990) [Michigan State], Maria Somerlate Barbosa (North Carolina, 1990) [Iowa], Robert Anderson (North Carolina, 1990) [University of North Carolina–Latin American Studies], Mary Schil (Wisconsin, 1991), Judith Payne (Penn State, 1991), Eva Paulino Bueno (Pittsburgh, 1991), Luiza Moreira (Cornell, 1992) [SUNY-Binghamton], Thomas Waldemer (Berkeley, 1992), Barbara Slavinsky (Stanford, 1993), João Camillo Penna (Berkeley, 1993), Eurídice Silva Filho (North Carolina, 1994) [Tennessee-Knoxville], Theodore Young (Harvard, 1994) [Pasadena City College], Kim Hastings (Yale, 1995), Robert Meyers (Yale, 1995), Miriam Ayres (Yale, 1995) [NYU], Marguerite Harrison (Brown, 1995) [Smith College], Elizabeth Marchant (NYU, 1995), Luci Moreira (Illinois, 1995) [College of Charleston], José Farias (Indiana, 1995), Christopher Dunn (Brown, 1996) [Tulane], Jerome Branche (New Mexico, 1996), Idelber Avelar (Duke, 1996) [Tulane], Steven Walden (Georgia, 1996), Patrícia Sobral (Brown, 1997) [Harvard], Lúcia Sá (Indiana, 1997) [Stanford], Dario Borim (Minnesota, 1997) [University of Massachusetts–Dartmouth], Sabrina Karpa-Wilson (Harvard, 1998) [Indiana], Mark Lokensgaard (Brown, 1999) [Trinity, San Antonio], Niyi Afolabi (Wisconsin, 1997) [Tulane], Leonardo Pinto Mendes (Texas, 1998) [UERJ, Rio de Janeiro], César Braga-Pinto (Berkeley, 1999) [Rutgers], Kimberly

DaCosta Holton (Northwestern, 1999) [Rutgers–Newark], Vivaldo Santos (Berkeley, 1999), and Débora Ferreira (University of Georgia, 1999).

Doctoral degrees awarded after 2000 include those won by Steven Butterman (Wisconsin, 2000) [University of Miami], Bryan Kennedy (North Carolina, 2000), Magda Silva (North Carolina, 2000), Cynthia Baker (Texas, 2000), Kathryn Sanchez (Santa Barbara, 2000) [Wisconsin], Emanuelle Karen Felinto de Oliveira (UCLA, 2001) [Missouri-Columbia], Loida Pereira Peterson (North Carolina, 2001), Marilu Perez (Indiana, 2002), Robert Moser (Brown, 2002) [University of Georgia], Richard Allen Gordon (Brown, 2002), João Cezar de Castro Rocha (Stanford, 2002) [UERJ, Rio de Janeiro], Mônica Prata (North Carolina, 2002), Suzanne Schadl (New Mexico, 2002), Regina Rogerio Felix (Illinois, 2003) and Maria Ana Quaglino (UCLA, 2003).

References

Agosin, Marjorie. 1999. *Passion, Memory, Identity: Jewish Latin America*. Albuquerque: University of New Mexico Press.

Appleby, David P. 1983. *The Music of Brazil*. Austin: University of Texas Press.

Atas do Colóquio Internacional de Estudos Luso-Brasileiros. Washington, D.C., 15–20 de Outubro de 1950). 1953. Nashville, Tenn.: Vanderbilt University Press.

Azevedo, Fernando de. 1950. *Brazilian Culture*. Trans. William Rex Crawford. New York: Macmillan.

Baden, Nancy. 1999. *Muffled Cries: The Writer and Literature in Authoritarian Brazil, 1964–1985*. Lanham, Md.: University Press of America.

Bandeira, Manuel. 1958. *A Brief History of Brazilian Literature*. Washington, D.C.: Pan-American Union.

Béhague, Gérard. 1971. *The Beginnings of Musical Nationalism in Brazil*. Detroit, Mich.: Information Coordinators.

———. 1979. *Music in Latin America: An Introduction*. Engelwood Cliffs, N.J.: Prentice-Hall.

———. 1994. *Heitor Villa Lobos: The Search for Brazil's Musical Soul*. Austin, Tex.: Institute of Latin American Studies.

Benedict, Saint, Abbot of Monte Cassino. 1911. *An Old Portuguese Version of the Rule of Benedict*. John W. Burnam, Ed. Palaeographical ed. from the Alcobaca ms no. 300 (agora 231) in the Bibliotheca publica of Lisbon. Cincinnati: Ohio University Press.

Berrien, William, and Rubens Borba de Moraes, eds. 1949. *Manual bibliográfico de estudos brasileiros*. Rio de Janeiro: Gráfica Editora Souza.

Bigelow, Donald N., and Lyman H. Legters. 1964. "NDEA Language and Area Centers: A Report on the First Five Years." USHEW, Office of Education, OE-56016,

Bulletin 1964, no. 41:, U.S. Government Printing Office, Washington. 27–28, a publication of the Office of Education, U.S. Department of Health, Education and Welfare, OE-56016.

Bishop, Elizabeth, and Emanuel Brasil. 1972. *An Anthology of Twentieth-Century Brazilian Poetry.* Middletown, Conn.: Wesleyan University Press.

Bom Meihy, José Carlos Sebe. 1984. *Introdução ao nacionalismo acadêmico: os brasilianistas.* São Paulo: Brasiliense.

Boxer, Charles. 1963. *Race Relations in the Portuguese Empire, 1415–1825.* Oxford: Oxford University Press.

Branner, John Casper. 1910. *A Brief Grammar of the Portuguese Language with Exercises and Vocabularies.* New York: H. Holt and Company.

Brasil, Emanuel, and William J. Smith. 1983. *Brazilian Poetry, 1950–1980.* Middletown, Conn.: Wesleyan University Press.

Brazilian Embassy. 1988. "Relação das obras de literatura brasileira editadas em inglês." Mimeographed bibliography. Washington, D.C.

Caldwell, Helen. 1960. *Brazilian Othello of Machado de Assis.* Berkeley: University of California Press.

———. 1970. *Machado de Assis: The Brazilian Master and His Novels.* Berkeley: University of California Press.

Cândido, Antônio. 1995. *On Literature and Society.* Trans. Howard S. Becker. Princeton, N.J.: Princeton University Press.

Catalog of the Oliveira Lima Library. 1970. 2 v. Boston: G. K. Hall.

Chamberlain, Bobby J. 1993. *Portuguese Language and Luso-Brazilian Literature: An Annotated Guide to Selected Reference Works.* New York: MLA.

———. 1996. "A Consumer Guide to Developing a Brazilian Literature Reference Library," *Hispania* 64, no. 2: 260–64.

Costa, Sergio Corrêa da. 1950. *Every Inch a King, A Biography of Dom Pedro I, First Emperor of Brazil.* Trans. Samuel Putnam. New York: Macmillan.

Coutinho, Afrânio. 1969. *An Introduction to Literature in Brazil.* Trans. Gregory Rabassa. New York: Columbia University Press.

Covington, Paula, ed. 1996. *Latin America and the Caribbean: A Critical Guide to Research Sources.* Westport, Conn.: Greenwood Press.

De Jong, Gerrit. 1969. *Four Hundred Years of Brazilian Literature: Outline and Anthology.* Provo, Utah: Brigham Young University Press.

DiAntonio, Robert, and Nora Glickman, eds. 1993. *Tradition and Innovation: Reflections on Latin American Jewish Writing.* Albany: State University of New York Press.

Dinis, King of Portugal. 1894. *Das Liederbuch des Konigs Denis von Portugal. Zum ersten mal vollständig herausgegeben und mit Einleitung, Anmerkungen und Glossar verschen.* Ed. Henry R. Lang. Halle, Germany: a. S., M. Niemeyer.

Dos Passos, John. 1963. *Brazil on the Move.* Garden City, N.Y.: Doubleday.

Downes, Leonard. 1944. *An Introduction to Brazilian Poetry.* São Paulo: Clube de Poesia.

Driver, David. 1942. *The Indian in Brazilian Literature*. New York: Hispanic Institute in the United States.

Dulles, John W. F. 1967. *Vargas of Brazil*. Austin: University of Texas Press.

Dunn, Ballard S. 1866. *Brazil, the Home for Southerners*. New York: G. B. Richardson.

Dunn, Christopher. 2001. *Brutality Garden: Tropicália and the Emergence of a Brazilian Counterculture*. Chapel Hill: University of North Carolina Press.

Eakin, Marshall C. 1997. *Brazil: The Once and Future Country*. New York: St. Martin's Press.

Elliot, L. E. 1917. *Brazil Today and Tomorrow*. New York: The Macmillan Company.

Ellison, Fred. 1954. *Brazil's New Novel: Four Modern Masters*. Berkeley: University of California Press.

Fitzgibbon, Russell, ed. and comp. 1974. *Brazil: A Chronology and Fact Book, 1488–1973*. Dobbs Ferry, N.Y.: Oceana Publications.

Ford, J. D. M., Arthur F. Whittem, and Maxwell Raphaes I. 1931. *A Tentative Bibliography of Brazilian belles-lettres*. Cambridge: Harvard University Press.

Franssen, Paul. 1999. *The Author as Character: Representing Historical Writers in Western Literature*. Madison, N.J.: Fairleigh Dickinson University Press.

Freyre, Gilberto. 1945. *Brazil: An Interpretation*. New York: Alfred. A. Knopf.

Goldberg, Isaac. 1921. *Brazilian Tales*. Boston: Four Seas, Co.

———. 1922. *Brazilian Literature*. New York: Knopf.

———. 1924. *Camões: Central Figure of Portuguese Literature (1524–1580)*. Girard, Kan.: Haldeman-Julius, Co.

———. 1924. *Spirit of Brazilian Literature*. Girard, Kan.: Haldeman-Julius, Co.

———. 1925. *Brazilian Short Stories*. Girard, Kans.: Haldeman-Julius. Co.

Griffin, Charles, ed. 1940. *Concerning Latin American Culture*. New York: Columbia University Press.

Hanke, Lewis. 1967. *History of Latin American Civilization*. Boston: Little, Brown.

Hanson, Carl A. 1973–74. "Dissertations on Luso-Brazilian Topics: A Bibliography of Dissertations Completed in the United States, Great Britain, and Canada, 1892–1970." *The Americas* 30: 251–67; 373–403.

Hartness, Ann. 1991. *Brazil in Reference Books, 1965–89: An Annotated Bibliography*. Metuchen, N.J.: Scarecrow.

Hill, Lawrence, ed. 1947. *Brazil*. Berkeley: University of California Press.

Hower, Alfred, and Preto-Rodas, Richard A., eds. 1985. *Empire in Transition: The Portuguese World in the Time of Camões*. Gainesville: University of Florida Press.

Hulet, Claude. 1974–75. *Brazilian Literature*. 3 vols. Washington, D.C.: Georgetown University Press.

Hunnicut, Benjamin. 1945. *Brazil Looks Forward*. Rio de Janeiro: Serviço Gráfico do Instituto Brasileiro de Geografia e Estatística.

Igel, Regina. 1997. "Origens e Desenvolvimento do Ensino de Português nos Estados Unidos." In *Cadernos do Centro de Línguas*, no. 1. São Paulo: Faculdade de Filosofia, Letras e Ciências Humanas, Universidade de São Paulo.

Jackson, K. David. 1984. "O Ensino da Literatura e da Cultura Brasileira nos States." Sociedade Brasileira para o Progresso das Ciências, São Paulo.

———. 1987. *Transformations of Literary Language in Latin American Literature: From Machado to the Vanguards.* Austin, Tex.: Abaporu Press.

———. 1992. *One Hundred Years of Invention: Centenary of Oswald de Andrade.* Austin, Tex.: Abaporu Press.

———. 1996. *Experimental, Visual, Concrete: Avant-Garde Poetry Since 1960.* Atlanta, Ga.: Rodopi Press.

Jackson, William V., comp. 1964. *Library Guide for Brazilian Studies.* Pittsburgh, Pa.: University of Pittsburgh Book Centers.

———, comp. 1977. *Catalog of Brazilian Acquisitions in the Library of Congress, 1964–74.* Boston: G. K. Hall.

James, Preston. 1946. *Brazil.* New York: Odyssey.

Johnson, Randal. 1984. *Cinema Novo x 5: Masters of Contemporary Brazilian Film.* Austin: University of Texas Press.

———. 1987. *The Film Industry in Brazil: Culture and the State.* Pittsburgh: University of Pittsburgh Press.

———. 1992. *Tropical Paths.* New York: Garland.

Johnson, Randal, and Robert Stam, eds. 1982. *Brazilian Cinema.* Rutherford, N.J.: Fairleigh Dickinson University Press.

Kidder, Daniel. 1879. *Brazil and the Brazilians.* Boston: Little, Brown, and Company.

Landes, Ruth. 1947. *The City of Women.* New York: Macmillan.

Lima, Luiz Costa. 1988. *Control of the Imaginary.* Trans. Ronald W. Sousa. Minneapolis: University of Minnesota Press.

Livermore, Harold. 1953. *Portugal and Brazil: An Introduction.* Oxford: Clarendon Press.

Loos, Dorothy. 1963. *The Naturalist Novel of Brazil.* New York: Hispanic Insititute.

Loewenstein, Karl. 1942. *Brazil under Vargas.* New York: Macmillan.

Machado, José Bettencourt. 1953. *Machado of Brazil.* New York: Bramerica.

Maligo, Pedro. 1998. *Land of Metaphorical Desires: The Representation of Amazonia in Brazilian Literature.* New York: Peter Lang Publishing.

Martins, Wilson. 1970. *The Modernist Idea.* Trans. and ed. Jack E. Tomlins. New York: New York University.

Massi, Fernanda. 1992. *Guia bibliografico dos brasilianistas.* São Paulo: Sumaré.

Mesa-Lago, Carmelo. 1979. *Latin American Studies in Europe.* Pittsburgh: Center for Latin American Studies.

Moog, Vianna. 1951. *An Interpretation of Brazilian Literature.* Trans. John Knox. Rio de Janeiro: Ministry of Foreign Relations, Cultural Division, Service of Publications.

Morley, Helena. 1977. *The Diary of "Helena Morley".* Trans. Elizabeth Bishop. New York: Ecco Press; distributed by Viking.

Morse, Richard. 1958. *From Community to Metropolis.* Gainesville: University Press of Florida Press.

————. 1965. *The Bandeirantes: The Historical Role of the Brazilian Pathfinders.* New York: Knopf.

————. 1989. *New World Sounding: Culture and Ideology in the Americas.* Baltimore: Johns Hopkins University Press.

Neistein, José, ed. 1972. *Poesia brasileira moderna, A Bilingual Anthology.* Washington, D.C.: Brazilian-American Cultural Center.

Nist, John. 1962. *Modern Brazilian Poetry: An Anthology.* Bloomington: Indiana University Press.

————. 1967. *The Modernist Movement in Brazil.* Austin: University of Texas Press.

Noda, Roberto. 1972. *A Preliminary Bibliography on African Cultures and Black Peoples of the Caribbean and Latin America.* Milwaukee: University of Wisconsin, Dept. of Afro-American Studies.

Nunes, Maria Luisa. 1976. "Resources for the Study of Brazilian Literature." *Neohelicon* (Budapest) 4, nos. 1–2: 225–38.

Onís, Harriet de. 1961. *The Golden Land: An Anthology of Latin American Folklore in Literature.* New York: Alfred A. Knopf.

Page, Joseph A. 1995. *The Brazilians.* Reading, Mass.: Addison-Wesley.

Payne, Judith, and Earl E. Fitz. 1993. *Ambiguity and Gender in the New Novel of Brazil and Spanish America: A Comparative Assessment.* Iowa City: University of Iowa Press.

Peixoto, Marta. 1994. *Passionate Fictions: Gender, Narrative, and Violence in Clarice Lispector.* Minneapolis: University of Minnesota Press.

Peppercorn, Lisa M. 1996. *The World of Villa-Lobos in Pictures and Documents.* Aldershot, England: Scolar Press.

Perrone, Charles. 1989. *Masters of Contemporary Brazilian Song.* Austin: University of Texas Press.

Picchio, Luciana Stegagno. 2004. *História da literatura brasileira.* 2a. ed. rev., e ampliada. Rio de Janeiro: Nova Aguilar.

Pierson, Donald. 1942. *Negroes in Brazil, A Study of Race Contact at Bahia.* Chicago: University of Chicago Press.

Poppino, Rollie. 1968. *Brazil, Land and People.* New York: Oxford University Press.

Porter, Dorothy Burnett. 1978. *Afro-Braziliana: A Working Bibliography.* Boston: G. K. Hall.

Putnam, Samuel. 1948. *Marvelous Journey.* New York: Alfred A. Knopf.

Quinlan, Susan. 1991. *Female Voice in Contemporary Brazilian Narrative.* New York: P. Lang.

Quinlan, Susan, and Fernando Arenas, eds. 2002. *Lusosex: Gender and Sexuality in the Portuguese-Speaking World.* Minneapolis: University of Minnesota.

Quinlan, Susan, and Peggy Sharpe-Valladares. 1996. *Visões do passado, previsões do futuro.* Intro. and notes by Susan C. Quinlan and Peggy Sharpe. Rio de Janeiro: Tempo Brasileiro.

Rabassa, Gregory. 1965. *Negro na ficção brasileira; meio século de história literária.* Tradução de Ana Maria Martins. Rio de Janeiro: Edições Tempo Brasileiro.

Rector, Mônica, ed. 2003. *Brazilian Writers. Dictionary of Literary Biography* v. 307. Farmington Hills, Mich.: Galle.

Rodrígues, José Honório. 1967. *The Brazilians; Their Character and Aspirations.* Trans. Ralph Edward Dimmick. Austin: University of Texas Press.

—————. 1977. *Borzoi Anthology of Latin American Literature.* New York: Alfred A. Knopf.

Sable, Martin H. 1989. *Guide to the Writings of Pioneer Latinamericanists of the United States.* New York: Haworth Press.

Sayers, Raymond. 1956. *The Negro in Brazilian Literature.* New York: Hispanic Institute.

Sayers, Raymond, ed. 1968. *Portugal and Brazil in Transition.* Sixth International Colloquium on Luso-Brazilian Studies, Cambridge, Mass., and New York, 1966.

Sharpe-Valadares, Peggy, org. 1997. *Entre resistir e identificar-se: para uma teoria da prática da narrativa brasileira de autoria feminina.* Florianópolis: Editora Mulheres; Goiânia: Universidade Federal de Goiás.

Sheinin, David, and Lois Baer Barr, eds. 1996. *Jewish Diaspora in Latin America: New Studies on History and Literature.* New York: Garland.

Skidmore, Thomas. 1999. *Brazil: Five Centuries of Change.* New York: Oxford University Press.

Smith, T. Lynn. 1946. *Brazil, People and Institutions.* Baton Rouge: Louisiana State University Press.

Smith, T. Lynn, and Alexander Marchant, eds. 1951. *Brazil, Portrait of Half a Continent.* New York: Dryden Press.

Solt, Mary Ellen. 1968. *Concrete Poetry: A World View.* Bloomington: Indiana University Press.

Stam, Robert. 1997. *Tropical Multiculturalism: A Comparative History of Race in Brazilian Cinema and Culture.* Durham, N.C.: Duke University Press.

Stern, Irwin. 1988. *Dictionary of Brazilian Literature.* Westport, Conn.: Greenwood.

Sussekind, Flora. 1997. *Cinematograph of Words.* Trans. Paulo Henriques Brito. Stanford, Calif.: Stanford University Press.

Tolman, Jon, and Ricardo Paiva. 1985. *Brazilian Literature and Language Outlines.* Albuquerque: University of New Mexico, Latin American Institute.

Topete, José Manuel. 1957. *A Working Bibliography of Brazilian Literature.* Gainesville: University of Florida Press.

Triquarterly Anthology of Contemporary Latin American Literature. 1968–69, 13/14 (Fall/Winter).

Veríssimo, Érico. 1945/1969. *Brazilian Literature: An Outline.* New York: Macmillan.

Vieira, Nelson. 1991. *Brasil e Portugal, a imagem reciproca: o mito e a realidade na espressão literária.* Lisboa : Ministério da Educação, Instituto de Cultura e Lingua Portuguesa.

Wagley, Charles. 1963. *Introduction to Brazil.* New York: Columbia University Press.

Williams, Edwin B. 1938. *From Latin to Portuguese.* Philadelphia: University of Pennsylvania Press.; Oxford: H. Milford, Oxford.

Williams, Emmett. 1968. *Concrete Poetry.* New York: Something Else Press.

Worcester, Donald. 1973. *Brazil, From Colony to World Power.* New York: Scribner.

Zubatsky, David S. 1971. "A Bibliography of Cumulative Indexes to Luso-Brazilian Journals of the Nineteenth and Twentieth Centuries." *Luso-Brazilian Review* 8, no. 2 (1971): 71–81.

Zweig, Stefan. 1940. *Brazil, Land of the Future.* New York: Viking.

Xavier, Ismael. 1997. *Allegories of Underdevelopment: Aesthetics and Politics in Modern Brazilian Cinema.* Minneapolis: University of Minnesota.

≈

CHAPTER 6

Arts and Music

José Neistein

THE ARTS

INTRODUCTION

Initially, the interest in Brazilian visual arts came from scholars in the United States in a wide variety of fields of study. It was only after 1960, however, that a broader interest emerged and an overview was produced. As had already occurred with ethnomusicology, the ethnologists were among the first U.S. scholars to show an interest in Brazilian Indian art from the Amazon and Mato Grosso, as well as from the central and southern regions of Brazil. Roger Bastide, a French sociologist who conducted research in Brazil and taught at the Universidade de São Paulo (USP) for many years, summarized that interest and the status of the research on Brazilian art up through the 1960s in the English version of the *Encyclopedia of World Art* (1960), which was a translation of the Italian *Enciclopedia Universale dell'Arte,* published in 1958. He also included a comprehensive bibliography on the visual arts in Brazil.

Another point of departure for the systematic study of Brazilian arts in the United States were the set of books, articles, and reviews by Robert Chester Smith, published in the United States, Portugal, and Brazil from the 1930s to the 1960s. Robert C. Smith wrote pioneering studies in English on Brazilian colonial architecture, painting, sculpture, and decorative arts, as well as on Brazilian modern architecture of the period from 1940 to 1960, and on Cândido Portinari's paintings. On the occasion of the unveiling of Portinari's large mural paintings at the Hispanic Division of the Library of Congress in Washington, in 1941, Robert C. Smith wrote an essay on the work of the Brazilian artist, with a special emphasis on those murals. That essay was one of the first systematic and consistent studies written outside Brazil about the "boy from Brodósqui" (as the artist was known in Brazil) and was certainly one of the best of its time.

In addition, it was the publication *Modern Architecture in Brazil* (1956), by Henrique E. Mindlin, that launched Brazilian modern architecture onto the international scene, with all of its styles and forms. This systematic study on the aesthetic and technical characteristics of Brazilian architecture remains current as, in addition to being a scholar, the author was also a well-known architect.

HISTORY

1. *General Overviews*

The *Encyclopedia of World Art* featured an introduction to Brazilian colonial and modern art periods written by Mario Barata, accompanied by a bibliography, in conjunction with an entry on "Arte Índia" by Roger Bastide. Ten years later, in 1970, the Brazilian publishing house Livraria Kosmos Editora published *Profile of the New Brazilian Art*, by Pietro Maria Bardi, translated from Italian by John Drummond. The book was intended for international readers. It was the first time an overview of Brazilian arts was published, although with a greater emphasis on the modern period. Thirteen years later, Harper and Row published *The Art of Brazil* (1983), by Carlos Lemos, José Roberto Teixeira Leite, and Pedro Gismonti, translated by Jennifer Clay. *The Art of Brazil*, which was more extensive than Bardi's book, introduced the U.S. reader to a more systematic and detailed perspective on Brazilian arts throughout the country's history, encompassing virtually all areas of visual art creativity and supported by an essential bibliography.

Also in 1983, the Walter Moreira Salles Institute published, in two large volumes, the *História Geral da Arte no Brasil*, containing essays written by a wide variety of authors under the editorial direction of Walter Zanini. This was the first such extensive overview of the Brazilian arts ever published. Although this book was published in Portuguese, it became well known in the United States and had a significant impact on U.S. scholars of the arts in Brazil. This book is still influential, despite being somewhat outdated, since nothing so comprehensive has been published since 1983. Each essay in the *História Geral da Arte no Brasil* has its own bibliography.

2. The Colonial Period (1500–1822)

With the possible exception of the modern period, colonial art has been the most studied of the arts in Brazil, in several different languages and by a wide range of scholars, both in Brazil and abroad. In the United States, Robert Chester Smith's pioneering studies date to the late 1930s, when he published in the *Handbook of Latin American Studies* (coordinated by the Hispanic Division of the Library of Congress) a series of reviews of books and articles on colonial art, most of which had been published in Brazil; this raised the awareness of U.S. scholars of this period of Brazilian creativity. He would later excel in this subject area when he included Brazil in *A Guide to the Art of Latin America* (1948), which he wrote with Elizabeth Wilder. In 1979, the Universidade de Pernambuco published his *Igrejas, casas e móveis, aspectos da arte colonial brasileira*, an extensive series of studies with almost four hundred pages dedicated to the colonial period in the state of Pernambuco. These essays are still models to be followed, because they were based on original documents, and an extensive photographic survey, which added the cunning and conclusive observations of the author to his scientific research. The quality of many of these essays remains unsurpassed.

In 1971, Alfred A. Knopf, publisher of many studies about Brazil as well as several Brazilian literary works, released the first edition of *The Roman Catholic Church in Colonial Latin America,* by Richard E. Greenleaf et al. (Arizona State University published a second edition in 1977). In this book, Brazil is featured within the context of the Counter-Reformation in Latin America. Although more emphasis is given to Spanish America, Brazil is also presented as an example of the relationship between the new theological ideology and the variant forms of the baroque period in the New World, both in architecture and in religious imagery.

In this regard, three other books were published in the United States— two before and one after Richard E. Greenleaf's book. They focus broadly on the baroque and rococo periods in Latin America, always with an emphasis on the history of art and the aesthetics of each period. In these three works, Brazil is analyzed as part of a predominantly Hispanic continental process, with special attention given to the specifics of the Portuguese contributions and Luso-Brazilian expression during those periods. Chronologically, the first was *Baroque and Rococo in Latin America* (1966). Three years later, Praeger published *A History of Latin American Art and Architecture,* by Leopoldo Castedo, translated from Spanish by Phillip Freeman. In 1992, Rizzoli published *History of South American Colonial*

Art, also translated from Spanish, written by Damián Bayón and others, among them, Murillo Mark and Myriam Ribeiro de Oliveira, who were responsible for the part about Brazil. These three books have three hundred pages each, on average, which is not sufficient to cover in depth such a large and varied field of study. Therefore, it is not surprising that these three books are very general surveys based on a study of primary sources and documents. They often rely on direct observations but are not usually original contributions.

Even before these works appeared in the United States, several Brazilian scholars had already published some of their most significant books, which today are considered classics in baroque studies. Sylvio de Vasconcellos, one of the most important authors in this group, had already published *Sistemas construtivos adotados na arquitetura do Brasil* (1951) and *Arquitetura no Brasil, sistemas construtivos* (1961). Among the authors mentioned in the previous paragraph, in their time Damián Bayón and his colleagues were the ones who focused the most on more advanced, enlightened, and well-grounded studies published in Brazil, which raises their *History of South American Colonial Art* to a higher level of erudition and insight. By the end of the 1960s, several issues of the periodical *Revista do Patrimônio Histórico e Artístico Nacional* had already published quite a few articles based on what was then the latest research on colonial architecture, wood carving, painting, and goldsmithery, most of which had been overlooked abroad, including by those in the United States. This was also true of the studies by Lourival Gomes Machado published in the 1950s and 1960s, as well as the magnificent work by Clarival do Prado Valladares, entitled *Aspectos da arte religiosa no Brasil* (1981).

Yet some significant studies of Brazilian colonial art that were based on tireless research and conclusive observations were published in the United States. One of the best examples was *A Portrait of the Dutch Seventeenth Century in Brazil,* by P. J. P. Whitehead and M. Bosleman (1989), which combined historical, political, and economic perspectives with literary, artistic, and scientific ones. Nevertheless, the most prominent U.S. contribution to the study of baroque art in Brazil was Robert Chester Smith's works and his vast photographic survey, which included virtually all visual expressions of Brazilian baroque and that today is maintained by and made available to researchers at the Calouste Gulbenkian Foundation in Lisbon.

3. Brazil's Empire and First Republic: Neoclassic Academicism (1822–1930)

Although fairly well studied in Brazil, the arts from the periods of the Empire and the First Republic have been little studied in the United States, which is not true of Brazilian history in those periods. Among the few books in circulation in the United States about these artistic periods, two are noteworthy, as they were both published in Brazil in English, with the intention of marketing them internationally. One of them was dedicated to Jean Baptiste Debret (1768–1848) and was published in São Paulo in 1960 in conjunction with Hans Staden's report of his (sixteenth-century) trip and Kaspar Van Baerle's writings about the Dutch conquest of Pernambuco (1647), thus covering three different periods. Mario Neme was responsible for the preface and adaptation. The second book, published in 1978, was a facsimile edition of the original drawings by Sir William Gore Ouseley (1797–1866), accompanied by the original text in English and a new translation into Portuguese of *Description of Views in South America, from Original Drawings Made in Brazil, the River Plate, the Paraná &c &c with Notes*. Aside from the works mentioned in the section on general overviews that contain some chapters dedicated to the arts from the periods of the Empire and the First Republic, the U.S. bibliography does not include any original monographs about the subject that could have been published in the United States. The only exception is "Art, Politics and Historical Perception in Imperial Brazil, 1854–1884," by Caren Ann Meghreblian (1990).

4. The Week of Modern Art of 1922

The situation is no different regarding the Week of Modern Art of 1922, an important art event in Brazil. The U.S. bibliography does not list any original study of the Week of Modern Art, widely known in Brazil as "the Week." Except for some chapters dedicated to this subject in the overviews cited earlier, the few books on the subject featured in specialized bibliographies include *Artes plásticas na Semana de 1922*, by Aracy A. Amaral, and the catalog for the exhibit held at the São Paulo Museum of Art in 1972, commemorating the fiftieth anniversary of the Week of the Modern Art of 1922; the catalog was translated into English by Edwina Jackson: *Semana de 22: antecedents and consequences*.

A. Contemporary Art

Contemporary art, the period from the 1940s through the 1990s, has received more attention not only from U.S. and British scholars but also from Brazilian scholars, whose work has been translated into English and published in Brazil, the United States, and Great Britain. Two significant studies of Portinari's paintings were published in 1940 and 1943, respectively: *Portinari of Brazil*, the catalogue for the exhibit held at New York's

Museum of Modern Art and the monograph by Robert C. Smith (1943) released on the occasion of the unveiling of the four large mural paintings at the Hispanic Division of the Library of Congress. The overviews cited earlier also included chapters dedicated to Brazilian contemporary art, which were current when the overviews were published.

In 1962, on the occasion of the exhibit "New Art of Brazil" at the Walker Art Center in Minneapolis, a catalog containing text and illustrations was published. For the exhibit "Art from Brazil in New York," which was in fact a series of avant-garde exhibits held in several galleries, Carlos Basualdo and Paulo Herkenhoff wrote the texts for a catalog published in 1995 by the Brazilian-American Cultural Institute Advisory Board in Washington, D.C. For the 1993 exhibit entitled "Ultramodern: The Art of Contemporary Brazil," held at the National Museum of Women in the Arts, in Washington, D.C., the government of the state of São Paulo published a richly illustrated catalog with texts by Aracy Amaral and Paulo Herkenhoff. In 1984, the London Barbican Art Gallery hosted "Modern Art from the Gilberto Chateaubriand Collection," an exhibit containing a rich selection of Brazilian art from that representative and comprehensive collection. The eighty-page illustrated catalog for the exhibit served as an introduction to Brazilian contemporary art for international readers.

In 1976, the Brazilian Ministry of Foreign Relations published the illustrated book *Brazilian Art*, which was a comprehensive survey also intended for an international audience. For the 1992 exhibit "Body to Earth: Three Conceptual Artists From Brazil," held at the Fisher Gallery of the University of Southern California, Susan M. Anderson, the exhibit's curator, wrote a catalog that included studies on Cildo Meireles, Mário Cravo Neto, and Tunga, the three artists featured in that exhibit. This work is one of the most thoughtful studies of the Brazilian response to international conceptual art and includes bibliographical references.

Edward Sullivan included Brazil in his comprehensive study entitled *Latin American Art in the Twentieth Century* (1996). The material is good and well chosen, although rather limited, as is inevitable in a book of fewer than four hundred pages that covers such a vast topic and such a prolific period. More recently, in 1998, Aracy Amaral wrote the catalog book entitled *Constructive Art in Brazil: The Adolpho Leiner Collection*. This book was designed both for Brazilian and international readers and is the most comprehensive book ever written on Brazilian contemporary art, covering the best collection of this art genre. In her view, Brazil is noteworthy as one of the most creative and original sources of art in the context of international constructivism in the twentieth century. Another universal contribution is the *Catalogue of the Museu de Arte de São Paulo Assis Chateaubriand* (Luiz Marques, 1998).

B. Brazilian Indian Art

The most extensive and comprehensive introduction to Brazilian Indian art ever published in English, in the United States, continues to be Roger Bastide's work, in the *Encyclopedia of World Art.* In addition, several other monographs that are of interest have been published in recent decades. In 1974, Dover Publications published *Amazon Indian Designs from Brazilian and Guianan Wood Carvings,* by Hjalmar Stolpe, a brief study illustrated with drawings of woodcarvings, with many of mostly geometric designs, and others.

Norberto Nícola and a group of contributors wrote a monograph that included several different perspectives about Indian feather art from a great variety of areas and cultures in Brazil. Published in 1982 as an illustrated monography by the Brazilian Ministry of Foreign Relations and the Central Bank in Brasília, this volume accompanied the exhibit "Brazilian Indian Feather Art" and was seen in several countries, including the United States. In 1990, Elaine Brown Sullivan, Susan K. Moore, and Greg Urban wrote the catalog *The Schokleng of Brazil: Artistic Expression in a Changing Forest* for the exhibit by the same name that was held at the Texas Memorial Museum of the University of Texas, in Austin. For the California exhibit held at Sonoma State University's art gallery, Vera Penteado Coelho wrote the catalogue *Drawings by the Waiurá Indians in Alto Xingu* (1991), which was a brief study on the topic. In 1992, the Royal Museum for Central Africa, located in Ghent, Belgium, published a book-catalog by Viviane Baeke, Terence Turner, and Lux Vidal for the exhibit *Kaiapó: Amazonia: The Art of Body Decoration,* which is probably the most comprehensive study on the subject available in print.

C. Afro-Brazilian Traditions

Dorothy B. Porter is the author of the most comprehensive bibliography of Afro-Brazilian studies ever published, both within and outside Brazil. Her *Afro-Braziliana, A Working Bibliography* was published in 1978. The book is almost three hundred pages long and covers more than five thousand titles, many of which are annotated, on a wide variety of topics, including art and folklore. For the 46th Frankfurt Book Fair, in 1994, the theme of which was "Brazil: Confluence of Cultures," Emanoel Araújo and Carlos Eugênio Marcondes de Moura wrote the book *Arte e religiosidade afro-brasileira,* which was published in Portuguese, German, and

English and served as the exhibit's catalog. It was marketed internationally. On the occasion of the exhibit "Face of the Gods: Art and Altars of
Africa and the African Americas," the African Art Museum in New York
published Robert Ferris Thompson's book by the same name, which
served as the exhibit's catalog (1993). In that same year, Athelia Henrietta
Press published *Divine Inspiration: From Benin to Bahia,* with photographs
by Phyllis Galembo and text by Robert Ferris Thompson. In the section
on Bahia, religious articles, artwork, and aspects of *candomblé* (which is
based on a religion brought to Brazil by African slaves) are shown and
analyzed.

In 1988, *The Afro-Brazilian Touch,* written by a group of authors and
translated into English by Eric Drysdale, was published for international
readers, along with the original in Portuguese, *A mão afro-brasileira.* This
book included a wide variety of historical, sociological, ethnographic,
artistic, and folkloric studies of Afro-Brazilian art. For the 1977 Brazilian
exhibit "World Black and African Festival of Arts and Culture," held in
Lagos, Nigeria, Clarival do Prado Valladares wrote the book *African Culture in Brazil,* which served as the exhibit's catalog. In 1989, the California
African-American Museum in Los Angeles hosted the exhibit "Introspectives: Contemporary Art by Americans and Brazilians of African Descent";
the curators, Henry J. Drewal and David C. Driskell, contributed the catalog, which included essays by Luiz Bairros and Sheila Walker.

D. Popular Art

Lucien Finkelstein wrote two books on popular art for the international
market. The first, *Primitivism in Brazilian Art,* coauthored by José Rodrigues Miranda, was published in 1980 and the second, *Brazilian Naïf Art of
Today,* was prepared for the 46th Frankfurt Book Fair in 1994. *Artesão
brasileiro: Folk Art of Northeastern Brazil,* by Beej Nierengarten-Smith, was
the catalog for the exhibit by the same name held at the Laumeir Sculpture Park and Museum in Saint Louis, Missouri, from October 21, 1995, to
January 21, 1996. In 1996 the Saint Louis park and museum hosted another
exhibit, also accompanied by a catalog, "Artesão brasileiro: The Power of
Imagination in Contemporary Folk Art of Minas Gerais." From August to
October of 1978, the Mingei International Museum of World Folk Art in
La Jolla, California, hosted the exhibit "A Cultural Mosaic: The Folk Arts
of Brazil." The catalog for the exhibit was sponsored by the Brazilian-
American Cultural Institute in Washington, D.C.

In 1977, Seldon Rodman published his *Genius in the Backlands: Popular
Artists of Brazil,* a study about the variety and originality of popular forms

of art in Brazil. In 1994, also for the 46th Frankfurt Book Fair, Jacques Van de Beuque wrote *Brazilian Popular Art: Collections of the Casa do Pontal, in Rio de Janeiro*, which was marketed internationally.

E. Industrial Design

In 1994, again for the 46th Frankfurt Book Fair, the Brazilian publishing house Câmara Brasileira do Livro, in conjunction with the São Paulo State Federation of Industries, published *Panorama of Modern Brazilian Graphic Design* in Portuguese, English, and German, with essays by several contributors. This book was marketed internationally.

F. Architecture and Landscaping

The 1956 book by Henrique E. Mindlin mentioned in the introduction was written at the high point of Brazilian modern architecture, and it continues to be the best book of its kind. Fourteen years earlier, also in New York, Phillip Goodwin published, through the Museum of Modern Art, *Brazil Builds: Architecture New and Old, 1652–1942*, with photographs by G. E. Kidder Smith. The book was used as a catalog for an exhibit that today is acclaimed as classical and anthological. David K. Underwood was the author of the extensive monograph *Oscar Niemeyer and the Architecture of Brazil* (1994). Underwood's critical and interpretative style made this work one of the best contributions to the study of this great Brazilian architect, one of the most outstanding names in the field of architecture in the twentieth century. William Howard Adams is the author of *Roberto Burle Marx: The Unnatural Art of the Garden* (1991). This monograph served as a catalog for the exhibit about the remarkable Brazilian landscape architect Burle Marx, also one the most prominent figures in twentieth-century landscaping.

G. Photography

Divine Inspiration: from Benin to Bahia, cited in the section on Afro-Brazilian traditions, must also be noted in this section, because of the high quality of Phyllis Galembo's photographs. In 1991–1992, the Brazilian publishing house Edições Alumbramento of Rio de Janeiro released *Atlantic Rain Forest*, by Luiz Emygdio de Mello Filho, intended for the international market. In 1977, Time-Life Books in Amsterdam published *Rio de Janeiro*, by Douglas Botting, with photographs by Art Kane. A classic work that should also be included here is *Views of the 1876 Centennial Exposition*, published in 1977 in Philadelphia. This book includes 258 photographic prints published by Centennial Photographic Company and features Brazil's participation in the exposition, an important event in the history of the United States.

H. Art Education

The Masrour Association has contributed to the expanding field of art education with the book *Tomorrow Belongs to the Children*, which was the result of an environmental preservation contest in the state of Bahia organized during the 1992 Earth Summit to select the best essays and artwork by children that focused on taking responsibility for the environment. In 1998, Kerry Freedman and Fernando Hernández were the editors of *Curriculum, Culture and Art Education: Comparative Perspectives*, which included Brazil. One of the principal experts on art education in Brazil is Ana Mae Tavares Bastos Barbosa, the author of "Art Education," a section of the *História geral da arte no Brasil.*

I. Miscellaneous

For the 46th Frankfurt Book Fair of 1994, the Brazilian publishing house Câmara Brasileira do Livro in São Paulo released *Images of the Unconscious from Brazil*, by Almir Mavignier. The Tryon Gallery of London published *Flowers of the Brazilian Forests*, by Margaret Mee, with an introduction by Roberto Burle Marx, a preface by Sir George Taylor, and paintings by Margaret Mee. A work that is now of historical interest is *Concerning Latin American Culture: Papers Read at Byrdcliff, Woodstock, New York, August 1939*, edited by Charles Carrol Griffin and published in 1940 by Columbia University Press for the National Committee of the United States of America on Intellectual Cooperation. This book includes Brazil. Joyce Waddel Bailey edited the *Handbook of Latin American Art: A Bibliographic Compilation* (in three volumes), published by ABC-Clio Information Services. Aracy Amaral was responsible for the section on Brazil. In 1997, *Art in Brazil, from the Beginnings to Modern Times, A Selected and Annotated Bibliography*, by José Neistein, was published in Portuguese and English by the Brazilian-American Cultural Institute, in Washington, D.C., and the Brazilian publishing house Livraria Kosmos Editora; it was sponsored by the Hispanic Division of the Library of Congress.

J. Conclusion

Even though U.S. interest in Brazilian art has emerged more recently than the interest in Brazilian music, the *Handbook of Latin American Studies*, published by the Library of Congress, has been the major means to inform U.S. scholars about publications on Brazilian art since the *Handbook* was first published in 1936. Among all fields of study, those that have received the most attention from scholars have been the colonial and contemporary art periods. Among the books and essays on Brazilian baroque art, the most prominent contributions are those by Robert Chester Smith for their comprehensiveness and depth. They are original contributions based on field research and observations, as well as on documents from the period. Regarding the study of contemporary art in Brazil, there has been a predominance of general surveys, usually included in comprehensive overviews of Latin America. Among all art forms, Brazilian architecture has been the focus of the greatest specific interest, particularly during the period of its greatest prominence, in the 1940s, 1950s, and 1960s. Important areas that have attracted less attention from scholars include the arts produced during the periods of the Empire and the First Republic, as well as the Week of the Modern Art of 1922. Since the 1980s, contemporary paintings and sculptures have been the focus of many exhibits held in the United States, generating several catalogs with original essays. Afro-Brazilian traditions have received increasing attention through exhibits and their corresponding catalogs with several original studies. On a smaller scale, popular arts should also be cited. The growing number of both bilingual and multilingual publications with international readerships, as well as the widespread use of the Internet and websites, have caused national borders to become increasingly tenuous. Important and substantial scientific contributions cross borders with ease and gain recognition throughout the world.

MUSIC

INTRODUCTION

The interest shown by U.S. scholars in Brazilian music dates to the beginning of the twentieth century. At that time, their main interest was in ethnomusicology. The great interest in studying the various aspects of Brazilian Indian cultures also attracted the attention of ethnologists and anthropologists to Brazilian Indian music. Later, with the development of African studies, similar attention was paid to Afro-Brazilian studies, in which music was certainly one of the most prominent areas studied. It is worth noting that as early as the third quarter of the nineteenth century, Louis Moreau Gottschalk, now considered one of the fathers of jazz, had already studied both Cuban and Brazilian rhythms. In terms of classical music, he composed and dedicated to Brazilian Emperor Dom Pedro II the *Grand Fantasy on the Brazilian National Hymn*, organized as a theme with variations, initially for the piano and later in an orchestral version. With the development of a methodology for ethnomusicological studies, the interest in both Afro-Brazilian and Brazilian Indian music deepened, intensified, and today continues to be strong, the most significant area of continuous interest among those who study Brazilian music in the United States.

As the production of classical music intensified in Brazil, it has received increasing attention from U.S. musicologists, and even more so as its international prestige has grown stronger. Similarly, Brazilian urban popular music's unique characteristics and strong connections to the record industry led to increased interest by U.S. scholars, whether because of its originality, especially after the appearance of the bossa nova and its links to jazz, or because of its close ties with twentieth-century Brazilian poetry and its depiction of social and political life in Brazil. Studies of classical music started to appear in the early 1930s and multiplied after the Second World War. As for Brazilian urban popular music, studies of it started to emerge during the 1960s and have gradually intensified since the 1970s, as this musical genre has increasingly played a more prominent international role.

Therefore, virtually all varieties of Brazilian music have been listened to, researched, and analyzed in the United States continuously since the mid-1950s, although not always with equal emphasis on all styles. Musicologists from the United States have often read overviews, either in Portuguese or translated into English, published in Brazil and the United States, as well as a number of monographs by Brazilian authors. Based on these readings and also on their personal experience and field research, original studies have been produced in the United States, the most significant of which have become quite well known to Brazilian musicologists and music historians.

AN OVERVIEW OF CLASSICAL MUSIC

In 1934, Eleanor Hague published her *History of Latin American Music*, in which she included Brazil. In 1948, an overview of Brazilian music entitled *Brief History of Music of Brazil*, by Luiz Heitor Corrêa de Azevedo, was published by what was then the Pan-American Union. It is likely that this was the first overview ever published, and it included a general survey of Brazilian classical music production, as well as references to ethnomusicological traditions and folklore. From 1940 to 1943, before Azevedo's overview was published, Gilbert Chase worked as a consultant for Spanish and Latin American music at the Library of Congress, and Brazilian music was included among his functions. In this capacity, he managed to compile the bibliography of Brazilian music of that time, including manuscripts, press items, programs, and early recordings. Based on this work, in 1962, he published the *Guide to the Music of Latin America*, which included Brazil, and an updated bibliography and recent research. From 1963 to 1967, he was in charge of the music section of the *Handbook of Latin American Studies*. From 1964 to 1976, he was the publisher of the *Yearbook of the Inter-American Institute for Musical Research*. In the 1960s, he was the head of the Latin American Studies Department at Tulane University. During those years, he published articles on Hispano-American and Brazilian music, including some articles on ethnomusicology. As a member of the Music Library Association, he also continued his work on the bibliography and wrote commentaries on articles published in the *Revista Brasileira de Música* from 1934 to 1940.

In 1980, Gérard Henri Béhague published an entry on Brazilian music in *The New Grove Dictionary of Music and Musicians*, which is the best and most comprehensive overview of Brazilian music, including all forms of musical expression, ever published in an encyclopedia, whether in Brazil or abroad. Fifteen years later, Béhague rewrote, updated, and broadened this entry in several respects for the encyclopedia *Die Musik in Geschichte und Gegenwart* [Music in History and Today]. The methodology he followed was twofold: he described the development of musical forms in Brazil historically and chronologically, including their social and political contexts, while also analyzing them from the technical and aesthetic perspectives of modern musicology. Béhague is perfectly capable of working with Brazilian music both in its domestic and international contexts because of his own educational background. He studied piano and composition at the National School of Music of the Universidade do Brasil and also at the Brazilian Music Conservatory, both in Rio de Janeiro. He studied musicology at the Musicology Institute of the University of Paris and also studied musicology with Gilbert Chase at Tulane University. Since 1974 he has been a professor of music at the University of Texas and was in charge of the annotated bibliography of music for the *Handbook of Latin American Studies* (1970–1974). He contributed to several publications, including the *Yearbook of the Inter-American Institute for Musical Research*, in the 1970s, and the *Latin American Music Review*, beginning in the 1980s. Another work that should also be included in this overview is *The Music of Brazil*, by David P. Appleby. Yet another important U.S. contribution has been the annotated bibliography of Brazilian music that for several years has consistently been published in the *Handbook of Latin*

American Studies by Robert Stevenson, a professor of music at the University of California, Los Angeles, and a meticulous analyst. In 1945, lexicographer and musicologist Nicolas Slonimsky included Brazil in his *Music of Latin America.*

HISTORY AND FORMS OF CLASSICAL MUSIC

1. Colonial Period

The discovery of information and manuscripts by Francisco Curt Lange about eighteenth-century musical life in the state of Minas Gerais considerably expanded the knowledge of Brazilian music of that period in its history, adding to everything that was already known about musical activities in the states of Bahia and Pernambuco from the sixteenth through the eighteenth centuries and in Rio de Janeiro from 1740 to 1822. The information gathered was consolidated in *A organização musical durante o período colonial brasileiro,* published by F. C. Lange in Coimbra, Portugal, in 1966. In his entry about Brazilian music in *The New Grove Dictionary of Music and Musicians* and, later, in *Die Musik in Geschichte und Gegenwart,* Béhague summarizes and comments on Lange's findings. Béhague also adds a broad introduction to Brazilian music during the colonial period, one of the most cultivated forms of classical music, particularly sacred music, which has been better known, more frequently played, and better researched than secular music. He also introduces the reader to some popular forms of music, mostly of Portuguese origin, in both urban and rural life during the early centuries after Brazil was discovered, and the subsequent creation of musical folklore, which arose out of the contact and symbiosis between these popular forms and the music and instruments used by Brazilian Indian and Afro-Brazilian traditions. Richard Graham wrote a long article, published in the *Latin American Music Review* (1991), about the development of the *berimbau* (a Brazilian musical instrument) during Brazil's colonial period. Although this is a minor aspect of Brazilian colonial music, it is still an interesting form of popular musical expression. In his reviews and comments in the *Handbook of Latin American Studies,* Robert Stevenson has brought to light several important studies by Brazilian authors on classical music in Minas Gerais during the eighteenth and nineteenth centuries, as well as the roots of Brazilian popular music during that period, with an emphasis on the African instruments used in the northeast of Brazil. In his entry "Brasilien," Béhague dedicated a subsection to Afro-Brazilian ethnomusicology of all periods, a field of study to which he devoted special attention for several years.

2. The Nineteenth Century—Opera in Brazil

Antônio Carlos Gomes

In 1938, in Rio de Janeiro, Luiz Heitor Corrêa de Azevedo published his *Relação das óperas de autores brasileiros*, which mainly dealt with the nineteenth century but also included earlier and later operas. This is a subject that has increasingly attracted the attention of scholars in the United States. In *The New Grove Dictionary of Opera* (1992) Robert Stevenson published entries on several Brazilian opera composers, ranging from the colonial period to modern times, such as Carlos de Campos and João Gomes de Araújo. Stevenson also included entries on opera houses in the cities of Belém, Manaus, Salvador, Rio de Janeiro, and São Paulo. In the same dictionary, Gérard Béhague wrote entries not only on Antônio Carlos Gomes and his major operas—*Il Guarany, Fosca, Lo Schiavo,* and *Salvator Rosa*—but also on the operas composed by Camargo Guarnieri. In 1993, William J. Collins's entry on Antônio Carlos Gomes was published in the *International Dictionary of Opera*.

3. Brazil's Empire

Except for the entries by Gérard Béhague published in *The New Grove Dictionary of Music*, cited earlier, and a few other overviews, there is virtually no information in the U.S. bibliography on Brazilian music from the period historically known as the First Reign of Brazil's Empire. The music of the period called the Second Reign of Brazil's Empire is featured in two important essays by Cristina Magaldi. One of them, "José White in Brazil, 1879–1888," was published in the *Inter-American Music Review* (1995) and addresses the presence of that Afro-Cuban musician in Rio de Janeiro. The other study, "Music for the Elite: Musical Societies in Imperial Rio de Janeiro," published by the *Latin American Music Review* (1995), provides abundant information on the concerts and musical life in Rio de Janeiro, the South American capital with the most musical activity in the nineteenth century. Brazilian music from the nineteenth century, however, has only rarely been mentioned in works by U.S. musicologists and historians. One exception was G. H. Béhague's *The Beginning of Musical Nationalism in Brazil* (1971), which describes this important period of Brazilian music from the last decades of the Brazilian Empire through the first decades of the Republic. His focus is on orchestral music, but he also includes several other forms of music, such as the piano, which would become extremely important in Brazilian music, not only from the perspective of the composers but also the interpreters'. It is always worth highlighting the importance of new studies about this period and about composers such as Ernani Braga, Alexandre Levy, and Alberto Nepomuceno, for instance. Failure to grasp the importance of these artists would undermine a full understanding of twentieth-century Brazilian music and creative figures such as Villa-Lobos, Luciano Gallet, Camargo Guarnieri, Francisco Mignone, Lorenzo Fernandez, Guerra Peixe, Cláudio Santoro, and others.

In studies published both in Brazil and abroad, greater attention has been increasingly given to the participation of women in Brazilian musical activities. Irati Antônio and John M. Schechter published an entry on Dinorá Gontijo de Carvalho (1904–1980), and Irati Antônio wrote an entry on Jeonídia Nunes Sodré (1903–1975), both for *The New Grove Dictionary of Women Composers* (1994). However, more extensive and thorough studies in this area are still lacking in the U.S. bibliography.

4. First Half of the Twentieth Century

In the first half of the twentieth century, David P. Appleby produced two important publications: "A Study of Selected Compositions by Contemporary Brazilian Composers," which was his doctoral dissertation in 1956, and *The Music of Brazil* (1983). G. H. Béhague also provided a great overview of this period in his entries published in *The New Grove Dictionary* and in *Die Musik in Geschichte und Gegenwart*. It was only with Villa-Lobos, however, that U.S. and European scholars began to produce studies and monographs on the subject. *Villa-Lobos: Collected Studies,* by Lisa M. Peppercorn (1992), translated from German, is one of the most important contributions in this line of study. In 1996, the Peppercorn released *The World of Villa-Lobos in Pictures and Documents,* and *The Villa-Lobos Letters,* which she translated and annotated, came out in 1994. David P. Appleby wrote *Heitor Villa-Lobos: A Bio-Bibliography* (1988). Gérard Béhague is the author of *Heitor Villa-Lobos: The Search for Brazil's Musical Soul* (1993). Simon James Wright wrote "Villa-Lobos and His Position in Brazilian Music After 1930," which was his 1986 doctoral dissertation, at the University of Wales. The bibliography on Villa-Lobos in English is quite extensive. The only such works mentioned here are those that are broad, historical, analytical, critical, and interpretative, each with a different emphasis but quite complementary as a whole.

Another important composer who has served as a topic for monographs is Camargo Guarnieri. Elisabeth Carramaschi's doctoral dissertation, "A Study of Camargo Guarnieri," at the University of Iowa (1987), is an introduction to the musical works of this composer from the state of São Paulo; it describes the characteristics of his work and offers an analysis of his *Sonata para piano*. Mauricio Alves Loureiro's 1991 doctoral dissertation for the University of Iowa, "The Clarinet in the Brazilian Choro with an Analysis of the Choro para Clarineta e Orquestra," was about the same composer. It includes a bibliography and a reduced version of the score for piano accompaniment.

5. The Second Half of the Twentieth Century

In the early 1950s, as Brazilian music became more diverse in virtually all areas, the musicological bibliography also became more diverse, both in Brazil and abroad. What followed were the years of serial music, concrete and neoconcrete music, random music, electronic music, and, more recently, computer music. The publication of "Manifesto Música Nova" by Gilberto Mendes, Rogério Duprat, and colleagues in the *Revista das Artes de Vanguarda Invenção* (1963) summarized the aesthetic trends of the music played in Brazil during that time while opening the doors to everything that would follow, in terms of both other manifestos and new musicological approaches. In 1984, José Maria Neves published *Música Contemporânea Brasileira*, which was not as much of a statement of principles as the "Manifesto Música Nova" but rather a study of new musical trends. Among the studies published in the United States, it is worth noting *Classical Music of Brazil* by Peter Schoenbach (1984), which is a general overview, addressing mainly the change from nationalism to cosmopolitanism that was underway in music when it was published. Also worth noting is a more recent article, by Gérard Béhague, "Recent Studies of Brazilian Music," published in the *Latin American Music Review* (1995). More recently, the *Computer Music Journal* published Carlos Palombini's "The Fifth Brazilian Symposium on Computer Music: Super and Parallel Computing Applied to Music" (1999), thus launching Brazil onto the international stage for this new musical language.

A. Urban Popular Music

As Brazilian urban popular music has become more diverse and international, it has been the subject of studies that are increasingly extensive and detailed, both in Brazil and abroad. In 1968, Augusto de Campos published *Balanço da bossa*, a pioneering study that would have a great impact both in Brazil and abroad, not only because of the richness of the material gathered and analyzed but also because of the relationship that existed between the newly created bossa nova and contemporary poetry—written, in part, to be the lyrics of bossa nova songs—and because of the depiction that the book offered of political and social life in Brazil. After this study was published, bossa nova traveled around the world, and its impact on U.S. jazz and the corresponding influence of U.S. jazz on bossa nova became evident everywhere. In 1980, Gérard H. Béhague published in the *Journal of Popular Culture* his long article, "Brazilian Musical Values in the 1960s and 1970s, from Bossa Nova to Tropicália," a U.S. version of Augusto de Campos's *Balanço da bossa* but one that was current through the music of Caetano Veloso. His *Recent Studies of Brazilian Music* (1995) included the impact and reach of Brazilian popular music, known in Brazil as MPB. In 1985, Enylton de Sá Rego, together with Charles Perrone, published *Contemporary Brazilian Popular Music,* and, in 1989, Charles Perrone published *Masters of Contemporary Brazilian Song: MPB, 1965–1985,* two works that are essential for an understanding of Brazilian modern urban popular music. Between these two books, in 1987, Samuel Mello Araujo wrote his music master's thesis, "Brega: Music and Conflict in Urban Brazil," presented at the University of Illinois at Urbana-Champaign, focused on a very specific aspect of MPB at that time. In 1991, Chris McGowan and Ricardo Pessanha published *The Brazilian Sound: Samba, Bossa Nova and The Popular Music of Brazil.*

In recent years, the publication of these works has been followed by articles that offer analyses of very specific perspectives on MPB. These essays include "The Fresh Prince of Brazil," about singer and composer Caetano Veloso, in *Spin* (1999), by Ben Ratliff; Joseph Woodward's "Milton Nascimento," in *Jazz Times* (1996); and Cristina Magaldi's "Adopting Imports: New Images and Alliances in Brazilian Popular Music of 1990s," which appeared in *Popular Music* (1999). Because these are articles, a format that allows for more flexibility and current information, these texts—though ephemeral—recorded significant moments and the maturation process of important MPB figures during their careers.

B. Ethnomusicology

Ethnomusicology has been one of the most scientifically studied aspects of Brazilian music since the beginning of the twentieth century and the modernization of ethnographic methodology. The primary focus of that interest was initially Brazilian Indian music, later followed by a similar interest in Afro-Brazilian music, as the study of African music itself intensified.

In his entries on Brazil in *The New Grove Dictionary* and *Die Musik in Geschichte und Gegenwart,* G. H. Béhague dedicates considerable space to various aspects of Brazilian Indian music and ethnomusicological studies of it, supported by a bibliography derived from many sources. Some monographs on ethnomusicology published in the United States and Europe have become required reference sources. One of these is *The Kalopalo Indians of Central Brazil*, by E. B. Basco (1973). Another is *Musical and Other Sound Instruments of the South American Indians*, by K. G. Izikowitz, which was first published in 1935, in Swedish in Göteborg, Sweden, and published in its English translation only much later, in 1970. One of the pioneering Brazilian scholars to write about ethnomusicology was L. H. Corrêa de Azevedo, whose *A música dos índios brasileiros* (1938) has influenced foreign studies on this topic. A similar Brazilian study on ethnomusicology accepted internationally is *Toward a Brazilian Ethnomusic*, by Manuel Veiga Jr. (1989). L. H. Correa de Azevedo also included a brief analysis of Brazilian Indian music and the integration of many of its elements into Brazilian folklore in his "Brazilian Folk Music" entry for *The New Grove Dictionary*. As an illustration of the bibliographical variety on this topic, it is worth citing *Semanticity and Melody: Parameters of Contrast in Shavante Local Expression*, by L. Graham (1988) and A. Seeger's *Why Suya Sing: A Musical Anthropology of an Amazonian People* (1987). Ethnomusicology has been a subject of studies for many years, beginning with the observations by Thévet and H. Staden in the sixteenth century, followed by J. B. von Spix and K. F. P. von Martius, who wrote *Brasilinianischer Volkslieder and Indianische Melodien* [Brazilian Folk Songs and Indian Melodies], which is part of *Reise in Brasilien* [Travel in Brazil], republished in Munich in 1931, analyzed in Béhague.

C. Luso-Brazilian Traditions

Modern studies and field research on Brazilian folklore began with Mário de Andrade. In 1936 he published an extensive article entitled "Folk Music in Brazil" in the *Bulletin of the Pan-American Union*. Also in 1936, and later in 1943, the Imprensa National in Rio de Janeiro published another work by Mário de Andrade, *Popular Music and Song in Brazil*, which was released in English for distribution abroad. In 1959 came the *Dicionário de folclore brasileiro* [Dictionary of Brazilian Folklore], by Luiz da Câmara Cascudo. All these works have had an impact on U.S. scholars. As a result, in 1968, Robert Stevenson published in the *Yearbook of the Inter-American Institute for Musical Research* an article entitled "Some Portuguese Sources for Early Brazilian Music History," which contributed to an understanding of the music and folklore of Brazil from the early centuries after Brazil was discovered. In 1965, T. Tavares de Lima published in the *Boletín Latinoamericano de Música* (1965) "Música Folclórica e Instrumentos Musicais no Brasil," which provided of wide range of information about the Portuguese contributions to Brazilian folklore. In 1942 in Rio de Janeiro, Jayme

Cortesão published his pioneering work, *O Que o povo canta em Portugal*. In 1990, Maria E. da Silva Lucas earned her doctoral degree in ethnomusicology from the University of Texas at Austin, with a dissertation entitled "Gauchos on Stage (Festivals of Native Music)," which focused on Azorean traditions and their strong influence in the folklore of southern Brazil.

D. Afro-Brazilian Traditions

Afro-Brazilian traditions have been the subject of a particularly rich and varied set of studies, field research projects, and publications. M. J. Herskowitz wrote a pioneering and extensive book (477 pages), published in 1944, entitled *Drums and Drummers in Afro-Brazilian Cult Life*. Soon afterward, in 1946, Oneyda Alvarenga, one of Mário de Andrade's students and assistants, published in the *Boletín Latino-americano de Música* an essay entitled "A Influência Negra na Música Brasileira," which today is considered a classic. Many years earlier, in 1935, Arthur Ramos had published *O Folclore negro no Brasil*, a book that for several years served as a guide for many scholars and researchers, both in Brazil and abroad. Gérard Béhague has been studying Afro-Brazilian traditions for many years, and the subsections he wrote on this topic for *The New Grove Dictionary* are truly exemplary. In addition, Béhague published "Notes on Regional and National Trends in Afro-Brazilian Cult Music," in *Tradition in Renewal* (1975), and "Patterns of Candomblé Music Performance and Afro-Brazilian Religious Setting," in his *Performance Practice, Ethnomusical Perspectives* (1984). Other works worth noting are J. J. de Carvalho's "Music of African Origin in Brazil," in M. M. Fraginals's *Africa in Latin America* (1984), and *Shango Cult in Recife, Brazil* (1992); *Angolan Traits in Black Music: Games and Dances of Brazil*, by Gerhard Kubrik (1979); "Songs of Gege and Jesha Cults of Bahia, Brazil," by A. P. Merriam, which ran in *Jahrbuch für Musik Volks und Völkerkunde* (1963); *Contribuição Bantu na música brasileira*, by Kazadi wa Mukuna, published in 1978; *Latin American Percussion: Rhythms and Rhythm Instruments from Cuba and Brazil*, by Birger Sulsbrück (1982) in English; and "Okarité: Yemoja's Icon Tune," by Rita Laura Segato (1993).

E. Music Education in Brazil

Music education in Brazil has been the focus of a growing number of studies. Several doctoral dissertations have addressed different, and sometimes corresponding, aspects of this topic. These dissertations include "Music Education in Brazilian Public Elementary Schools," by Joseidi Gomes Montarroyos, University of Miami (1988); "Music Education in Brazil," by Frederico A. B. Manso, University of Miami (1985); "An Analysis and Adaptation of Brazilian Folk Music into a String Method Comparable to American Models for Use in the Brazilian Music Education System," by Linda L. Kruger, University of Missouri, Columbia (1990); and "Brazilian Choral Directors (Rehearsal Conditions and Methodology)," by David Bretanha Jumber, University of Missouri, Columbia (1990). Several other aspects of musical education in Brazil, and also some related topics, are addressed in doctoral dissertations and master's theses. These include "Brazilian Percussion Compositions Since 1953, an Annotated Catalogue," by John Edward Boulder, American Conservatory of Music (1983); "Early Hymnody in Brazilian Baptist Churches," by Isidoro L. de Paula, South Western Baptist Theological Seminary (1985); and "Dancing to Different Drummers: Rio de Janeiro's Escolas de Samba," by Charles Jonathan Hodel, a master's thesis, University of California, Los Angeles (1990).

CONCLUSION

It has frequently been said that science is supranational; it is not confined within national boundaries. It is also true, however, that there are national approaches to conducting scientific work. The U.S. tradition, like its English counterpart, values the empirical dimension and theorizes only when there is support from sufficient inductive evidence. This does not mean that empiricism is absent from the scientific works done in other countries, but in the United States the desire for evidence is always greater. The vast majority of works on the history of music and musicology in Brazil are characterized, with few exceptions, by exhaustive efforts at collecting data and parsimony in making generalizations and drawing conclusions. On the one hand, this prudence is a virtue. On the other hand, the absence of a deeper engagement deprives us of more value judgments. The final result, however, is positive.

The intensive research and diligent writing of a musicologist like Gérard Béhague, to cite a good example, has singled him out among U.S.-based Brazilianists and set him at par with the most productive Brazilian musicologists, particularly in the study and assessment of classical music and in determining the aesthetics and facts of Afro-Brazilian music. The meticulous, balanced, and critical lexicological and bibliographical work of Robert Stevenson has made Brazilian bibliography available internationally and has helped Brazilian, U.S., and European historians and musicologists better recognize the weaknesses of their own work and thereby overcome those weaknesses. Additionally, it has helped them see their strengths more clearly. It has also allowed us to realize that the results of good work, from any perspective, contribute equally to enhancing the level of knowledge and understanding, taking it beyond the boundaries of national approaches to research.

Opera scholars have assisted in consolidating the international prestige that the work of Antônio Carlos Gomes has always merited and have helped call attention to the role and extent of Brazilian creativity in this area, thus bringing less well-known artists to the forefront. A growing number of scholars of urban popular Brazilian music have enriched the Brazilian perception of this important source of Brazilian creativity while also contributing to the universal understanding of this music and its relationships with modern Brazilian poetry. Some studies of the ethnomusicology of Brazilian Indians have become required reference sources, such as the books by E. B. Basso, K. G. Izikowitz, L. Graham, and M. Veiga Jr.

The collections of Brazilian music recordings in the United States and the quantity and quality of scientific periodicals contribute greatly to research and accelerate the acquisition of knowledge about Brazilian music. Nevertheless, some gaps still persist. The nineteenth century, for instance, continues to be studied and researched only rarely. The interest in Brazilian sacred music and colonial secular music, which are increasingly being researched in Brazil, continues to be quite minimal in the United States. The threatened folklore and the boom in Brazilian country music (*sertaneja*) in Brazil have not received much attention in the United States, either. Finally, the role of women in Brazilian music is another topic that is researched very little in the United States.

References

Adams, William Howard. 1991. *Roberto Burle Marx: The Unnatural Art of the Garden.* New York: Museum of Modern Art.

Alvarenga, Oneyda. "A influência negra na música brasileira." *Boletín Latinoamericano de Música* 6: 357–407.

Amaral, Aracy A. 1992. *Artes plásticas na Semana de 22.* São Paulo: Bovespa.

———. 1998. *Constructive Art in Brazil: The Adolpho Leiner Collection.* São Paulo: Cia. Melhoramentos.

Amaral, Aracy, and Paulo Herkenhoff. 1993. *Ultramodern: The Art of Contemporary Brazil.* São Paulo: Governo do Estado de São Paulo.

Anderson, Susan M. 1992. *Body to Earth: Three Conceptual Artists from Brazil.* Los Angeles: Fisher Gallery, University of Southern California.

Andrade, Mário de. 1936. "Folk Music in Brazil." *Bulletin of the Pan-american Union* 70: 392–99.

————. 1943. *Popular Music and Song in Brazil.* Rio de Janeiro: Imprensa Nacional.

Antônio, Irati. 1994. "Jeonídia Núñes Sodré (1903–1975)." In *The New Grove Dictionary of Women Composers.* New York: W.W. Norton.

Antônio, Irati, and John M. Schechter. 1994. "Dinorá Gontijo de Carvalho (1904–1980)." In *The New Grove Dictionary of Women Composers.* New York: W.W. Norton.

Appleby, David P. 1956. "A Study of Sected Compositions by Contemporary Brazilian Composers." Ph.D. diss., Indiana University.

————. 1983. *The Music of Brazil.* Austin: University of Texas Press.

————. 1988. *Heitor Villa-Lobos: A Bio-bibliography.* New York: Greenwood Press.

Araújo, Emanoel, and Carlos Eugênio Marcondes de Moura. 1994. *Arte e Religiosidade Afro-Brasileira.* São Paulo: Câmara Brasileira do Livro.

Araujo, Samuel Mello. 1987. "Brega: Music and Conflict in Urban Brazil." M.A. thesis, University of Illinois, Urbana-Champaign.

"Artesão brasileiro: The Power of Imagination in Contemporary Folk Art of Minas Gerais." 1996. St. Louis, Mo.: Laumeir Sculpture Park and Museum.

Azevedo, Luiz Heitor Corrêa de. 1938. *A música dos índios brasileiros.* Rio de Janeiro: N.p..

————. 1938. *Relação de óperas de autores brasileiros.* Rio de Janeiro: Serviço Gráfico do Ministério da Educação e Saúde.

————. 1948. *Brief History of Music of Brazil.* Washington, D.C.: Pan American Union.

————. 1989. "Brazilian Folk Music." In *The New Grove Dictionary of Music and Musicians.* London: Macmillan.

Baeke, Viviane, Terence Turner, and Lux Vidal. 1992. *Kaiapó: Amazonia: The Art of Body Decoration.* Ghent, Belgium: Royal Museum for Central Africa.

Bailey, Joyce Waddel. 1984–1986. *Handbook of Latin American Art.* 3 vol. Santa Barbara, Calif.: ABC-Clio Informative.

Barbican Art Gallery. 1984. *Portrait of a Country: Brazilian Modern Art from the Gilberto Chateaubriand Collection.* London: Barbican Art Gallery.

Barbosa, Ana Mae Tavares Bastos. 1983. "Arte-Educação." In *História geral da arte no Brasil.* 2 vols. São Paulo: Fundação Walter Moreira Salles.

Bardi, Pietro Maria. 1970. *Profile of the New Brazilian Art.* Translated by John Drummond. Rio de Janeiro: Livraria Kosmos.

Basco, E. B. 1973. *The Kalapalo Indians of Central Brazil.* New York: Holt, Rinehart and Winston.

Bastide, Roger, with an introduction by Mario Barata. 1960. "Arte Índia; períodos colonial e moderno." In *Encyclopedia of World Art.* Vol. 2: *Brazil.* New York: McGraw-Hill. Translated from the Italian: *Enciclopedia Universale dell'Arte.* Venezia-Roma, 1958.

Basualdo, Carlos, and Paulo Herkenhoff. 1995. *Art from Brazil in New York.* New York: Brazilian-American Cultural Institute Advisory Board.

Bayón, Damián. 1992. *History of South American Colonial Art.* New York: Rizzoli.

Béhague, Gérard H. 1971. *The Beginning of Musical Nationalism in Brazil.* Detroit: Information Coordinators.

———. 1973. "Bossa and Bossas: Recent Changes in Brazilian Urban Popular Music." *Ethnomusicology* 17, no. 2: 209–23.

———. 1975. "Notes on Regional and National Trends in Afro-Brazilian Cult Music." In *Tradition and Renewal*, edited by M. H. Foster. Urbana-Champaign: University of Illinois Press.

———. 1980. "Brazil," In *The New Grove Dictionary of Music and Musicians*, edited by Stanley Sadie. London: Macmillan.

———. 1980. "Brazilian Musical Values in the 1960s and 1970s: From Bossa Nova to Tropicalia." *Journal of Popular Culture* 14: 437–52.

———. 1980. "J.B. von Spix, Brasilianische Volkslieder und indianische Melodie." In *Reise in Brasilien* (with Dr. v. Martins). Munich: N.p.

———. 1984. "Patterns of Candomblé Music Performance, and Afro-Brazilian Religious Settings." In *Performance Practice, Ethnomusicological Perspectives.* Westport, Conn.: Greenwood Press.

———. 1993. *Heitor Villa-Lobos: The Search for Brazil's Musical Soul.* Austin: Institute of Latin American Studies, University of Texas at Austin.

———. 1995. "Recent Studies of Brazilian Music (Review-Essay)." *Latin American Music Review* 16, no. 1.

———. 1995. "Brasilien." In *Die Musik in Geschichte un Gegenwart*, v. 2. Bärenreiter. 99–130.

Beuque, Jacques van de. 1994. *Brazilian Popular Art: Collections of the Casa do Pontal, in Rio de Janeiro.* São Paulo: Câmara Brasileira do Livro.

Botting, Douglas. 1977. *Rio de Janeiro.* Amsterdam: Time-Life Books.

Boulder, John Edward. 1983. "Brazilian Percussion Compositions Since 1953, an Annotated Catalogue." D.M.A. thesis, American Conservatory of Music.

Brazilian Art. 1976. Translated by Dagmar Lagnado. Brasília: Itamaraty.

Câmara Brasileira do Livro e Federação das Indústrias de São Paulo. 1994. *Panorama of Modern Brazilian Graphic Design.* São Paulo: Câmara Brasileira do Livro.

Campos, Augusto de. 1968. *Balanço da Bossa.* São Paulo: Perspectiva.

Carramaschi, Elisabeth. 1987. "A Study of Camargo Guarnieri." Ph.D. diss., University of Iowa.

Carvalho, José Jorge de. 1992. *Shango Cult in Recife, Brazil.* Caracas: Fundef.

———. 1984. "Music of African Origin in Brazil." In *Africa in Latin America*, edited by M. M. Fraginals. New York: Holmes and Meier.

Cascudo, Luiz da Câmara. 1959. *Dicionário de folclore brasileiro.* São Paulo, N.p.

Chase, Gilbert. 1962. *Guide to the Music of Latin America.* Washington, D.C.: Pan American Union.

Coelho, Vera Penteado. 1991. *Drawings by the Waiurá Indians in Alto Xingu.* Sonoma, Calif.: Sonoma State University.

Collins, Williams J. 1993. "Antônio Carlos Gomes." In *International Dictionary of Opera.* Detroit: St. James Press.

Cortesão, Jayme. 1942. *O Que o povo canta em Portugal.* Rio de Janeiro: Livro de Portugal.

Debret, Jean Baptiste. 1960. *Difusão Nacional.* adaptação e prefácio de Mario Neme, São Paulo: N.p.

Drewal, Henry John, and David Driskell. 1989. *Introspectives: Contemporary Art by Americans and Brazilians of African Descent.* Los Angeles: California Afro-American Museum.

Drysdale, Eric, trans. 1988. *The Afro-Brazilian Touch.* São Paulo: Editora Tenenge.

Finkelstein, Lucien. 1994. *Brazilian Naïf Art of Today.* São Paulo: Câmara Brasileira do Livro.

Finkelstein, Lucien, and José Rodrigues Miranda. 1980. *Primitivism in Brazilian Art.* Rio de Janeiro: Imprinta.

Freedman, Kerry, and Fernando Hernández. 1998. *Curriculum, Culture and Art Education: Comparative Perspectives.* Albany: State University of New York Press.

Galembo, Phyllis, and Robert Farris Thompson. 1993. *Divine Inspiration: From Benin to Bahia.* Brooklyn, N.Y.: Athelia Henrietta Press.

Gilberto, Rogério Duprat, et al. 1963. "Manifesto Música Nova." *Revista de Artes de Vanguarda Invenção* 3.

Goodwin, Phillip. 1942. *Brazil Builds: Architecture New and Old, 1652–1942,* photographs by G. E. Kidder Smith. New York: Museum of Modern Art.

Graham, L. 1988. *Semanticity and Melody: Parameters of Contrast in Shavante Local Expression.* Austin: Institute of Latin American Studies, University of Texas.

Graham, Richard. 1991. *Latin American Music Review* 12, no. 1 (spring/summer): 1–20.

Greenleaf, Richard E. 1971. *The Roman Catholic Church in Colonial Latin America.* New York: Alfred Knopf.

Griffin, Charles C., ed. 1940. *Concerning Latin American Culture: Papers Read at Byrdcliff, Woodstock, New York, August 1939.* New York: Columbia University Press.

Hague, Eleanor. 1934. *History of Latin American Music.* Santa Ana, Calif.: Fine Art Press.

Herskowitz, M. J. 1944. "Drums and Drummers in Afro-Brazilian Cult Life." *Musical Quarterly* 30, no. 4: 477–92.

Hodel, Charles Jonathan. 1990. "Dancing to Different Drummers: Rio de Janeiro's Escolas de Samba." M.A. thesis, University of California, Los Angeles.

Izikowitz, K. G. 1935. *Musical and Other Sound Instruments of the South-American Indians.* Gotheburg, Sweden; N.p.

Kruger, Linda L. 1990. "An Analysis and Adaptation of Brazilian Folk Music into a String Method Comparable to American Models for Use in the Brazilian Music Education System." Ph.D. diss., University of Missouri, Columbia.

Kubrik, Gerhard. 1979. *Angolan Traits in Black Music: Games and Dances of Brazil.* Lisbon: Junta de Investigações Científicas do Ultramar.

Lange, F. C. 1966. *A Organização musical durante o período colonial brasileiro.* Coimbra, Portugal, N.p.

Lemos, Carlos, José Roberto Teixeira Leite, and Pedro Manuel Gismonti. 1983. *The Art of Brazil.* Translated by Jennifer Clay, introduction by Pietro Maria Bardi, essay by Oscar Niemeyer. New York: Harper and Row.

Lima, T. Tavares de. 1965. "Música Folclórica e instrumentos musicais no Brasil." *Boletín Latino-americano de música* 49.

Loureiro, Mauricio Alves. 1991. "The Clarinet in the Brazilian Chôro with an Analysis of the Chôro para clarineta e orquestra by Camargo Guarnieri." Ph.D. diss., University of Iowa.

Lucas, Maria E. da Silva. 1990. "Gauchos on Stage (Festivals of Native Music)." Ph.D diss., University of Texas, Austin.

McGowan, Chris, and Ricardo Pessanha. 1991. *The Brazilian Sound: Samba, Bossa Nova and the Popular Music of Brazil.* New York: Billboard Books.

Magaldi, Cristina. 1995. "José White in Brazil, 1879–1888." *Inter-American Music Review* 14, no. 2 (winter/spring): 1–19.

———. 1995. "Music for the Elite: Musical Societies in Imperial Rio de Janeiro." *Latin American Music Review* 16, no. 1 (spring/summer): 1–41.

———. 1999. "Adopting Imports: New Images and Alliances in Brazilian Popular Music of the 1990s." *Popular Music* 18, no. 3: 309.

Manso, Frederico A. B. 1985. "Music Education in Brazil." Ph.D. diss., University of Miami.

Manzolli, Jonathas, and Carlos Cerana. 1995. "Two Reports on the First Brazilian Symposium on Computer Music, Caxambu, Minas Gerais." *Computer Music Journal* 19, no. 2.

Marques, Luiz. 1998. *Catalogue of the Museu de Arte de São Paulo Assis Chateaubriand,* 4 vols. São Paulo: Masp.

Mavignier, Almir. 1994. *Images of the Unconscious from Brazil.* São Paulo: Câmara Brasileira do Livro.

Mee, Margaret. 1969. *Flowers of the Brazilian Forests.* London: Tryon Gallery.

Meghreblian, Caren Ann. 1990. "Art, Politics and Historical Perception in Imperial Brazil, 1854–1884." Ph.D. diss., University of California, Los Angeles.

Mello Filho, Luiz Emygdio, et. al. 1991–1992. *Atlantic Rain Forest.* Rio de Janeiro: Edições Alumbramento.

Merriam, A. P. 1963. "Songs of Gege and Jesha Cults of Bahia, Brazil." In *Jahrbuch für mus., Volks-und Völkerkunde* 1: 100.

Mindlin, Henrique E. 1956. *Modern Architecture in Brazil.* New York: Reinhold.

Mingei International Museum of World Folk Art. 1978. *A Cultural Mosaic: The Folk Arts of Brazil.* La Jolla, Calif.: Mingei International Museum of World Folk Art.

Montarroyos, Joseidi Gomes. 1988. "Music Education in Brazilian Public Elementary Schools." Ph.D. diss., University of Miami.

Mukuna, Kazadi wa. 1978. *Contribuição bantu na música brasileira.* São Paulo: Global Editora.

Museu de Arte de São Paulo. 1972. *Semana de 22: antecedents and consequences.* Translated by Edwina Jackson. São Paulo: Museu de Arte.

Neistein, José M. 1997. *Art in Brazil, from the Beginnings to Modern Times, a Selected, Annotated Bibliography.* Washington, D.C.: Brazilian-American Cultural Institute and Hispanic Division, Library of Congress; Rio de Janeiro/São Paulo: Livraria Kosmos Editora. [Portuguese and English.]

Neves, José Maria. 1984. *Música contemporânea brasileira.* Rio de Janeiro: Ricardi Brasileira.

Nícola, Norberto. 1982. *Brazilian Indian Feather Art.* Brasilia: Itamaraty and Banco Central.

Nierengarten-Smith, Beej. 1995. *Artesão Brasileiro: Folk Art of Northeastern Brazil.* St. Louis, Mo.: Laumeir Sculpture Park and Museum.

Ouseley, William Gore. 1978. *Descriptions of Views of South America, from Original Drawings Made in Brazil, the River Plate, the Paraná &c&c with Notes.* London: T. McLean; Rio de Janeiro: Editora Primor.

Palombini, Carlos. 1999. "The Fifth Brazilian Symposium on Computer Music: Super and Parallel Computing Applied to Music." *Computer Music Journal* 23, no. 1: 82.

Paula, Isidoro L. de. 1985. "Early Hymnody in Brazilian Baptist Churches." D.M.A. diss., Southwestern Baptist Theological Seminary.

Peppercorn, Lisa M. 1996. *The World of Villa-Lobos in Pictures and Documents.* Aldershot, Hants, England: Scholar Press.

———. 1994. *The Villa-Lobos Letters.* London: Toccata Press.

———. 1992. *Villa-Lobos: Collected Studies.* Translated from German. Aldershot, Hants, England: Scholar Press.

Perrone, Charles A. 1986. "An Annotated Inter-Disciplinary Bibliography and Discography of Brazilian Popular Music." *Latin American Music Review* 7, no. 2 (winter): 302–40.

———. 1989. *Masters of Contemporary Brazilian Song: MPB 1965–1985.* Austin: University of Texas Press.

———. 1998. "Popular Music, Brazil." In *Garland Encyclopedia of World of Music,* v. 2. New York: Garland Publishing.

Perrone, Charles A., with Larry N. Crook. 1997. *Folk and Popular Music of Brazil, New Brazilian Curriculum Guide, Specialized Bibliography,* Series II. Albuquerque: Latin American Institute, University of New Mexico.

Perrone, Charles A., and Christopher Dunn. 2001. *Brazilian Popular Music and Globalization.* Gainesville: University Press of Florida.

Plaut, Kimson Frank. 1980. "Samba: The Voice of the Morro: A Historical and Musical Analysis of a Brazilian Popular Form." M.A. thesis, University of Washington.

Porter, Dorothy B. 1978. *Afro-Braziliana, A Working Bibliography.* Boston: G.K. Hall and Co.

Portinari of Brazil. 1940. New York: Museum of Modern Art.

Ramos, Arthur. 1935. *O folclore negro no Brasil*. Rio de Janeiro: Civilização Brasileira.

Rangel, Lucio. 1976. *Bibliografia da música popular brasileira*. Rio de Janeiro.

Ratliff, Ben. 1999. "The Fresh Prince of Brazil (Caetano Veloso)." *Spin* 15, no. 6 (June).

Rego, Enylton de Sá, and Charles Perrone. 1985. *Contemporary Brazilian Popular Music*. Albuquerque: University of New Mexico Press.

Roberts, John Storm. 1999. *The Latin Tinge: The Impact of Latin American Music on the United States*. New York: Oxford University Press.

Rodman, Selden. 1977. *Genius in the Backlands: Popular Artists of Brazil*. Old Greenwich, Conn.: Devin-Odair Company.

Schoenbach, Peter. 1984. *Classical Music of Brazil*. Albuquerque: Latin American Institute, University of New México.

Seeger, A. 1987. *Why Suya Sing: A Musical Anthropology of an Amazonian People*. Cambridge: Cambridge University Press.

Segato, Rita Laura. 1993. "Okarité: Yemoja's icon tune." *Latin American Music Review* 14, no. 1 (spring/summer): 1–19.

Slonimsky, Nicolas. 1945. *Music of Latin America*. New York: Thomas Y. Crowell.

Smith, Robert C. 1979. *Igrejas, casas e móveis, aspectos da arte colonial brasileira*. Recife: Universidade de Pernambuco.

———. 1943. *Portinari*. Washington, D.C.: Government Printing Office.

Smith, Robert Chester, and Elizabeth Wilder. 1948. *A Guide to the Art of Latin America*. Washington, D.C.: Government Printing Office.

Stevenson, Robert. 1968. "Some Portuguese Sources for Early Brazilian Music History." *Yearbook of the Inter-American Institute for Musical Research*. New Orleans: Tulane University.

———. 1992. Various entries. *The New Grove Dictionary of Opera*. New York: Grove's Dictionaries of Music.

Stolpe, Hjalmar. 1974. *Amazon Indian Designs from Brazilian and Guianan Wood Carvings*. New York: Dover.

Sullivan, Edward. 1996. *Latin American Art in the Twentieth Century*. London: Phaidon Press.

Sullivan, Elaine Brown, Susan K. Moore, and Greg Urban. 1990. *The Schokleng of Brazil: Artistic Expression in a Changing Forest*. Austin: University of Texas Press.

Sulsbrück, Birger. 1982. *Latin American Percussion: Rhythms and Rhythm Instruments from Cuba and Brazil*. Translated by Ethan Weisgard. Copenhagen: Den Rytmiske Aftenskoles Forlag.

Thompson, Robert Farris. 1993. *Face of the Gods: Art and Altars of Africa and the African Americas*. Munich: Prestel.

Tomorrow Belongs to the Children. 1992. Salvador, Bahia: Associação Masrour.

Underwood, David K. 1994. *Oscar Niemeyer and the Architecture of Brazil*. New York: Rizzoli.

Valladares, Clarival do Prado. 1977. *African Culture in Brazil*. Brasília: Ministério das Relações Exteriores.

———. 1981. *Arte religiosa no Brasil*. Rio de Janeiro: Spala.

Vasconcellos, Sylvio de. 1951. *Sistemas construtivos adotados na arquitetura do Brasil*. Belo Horizonte.

———. 1961. *Arquitetura no Brasil, sistemas construtivos*. Belo Horizonte.

Veiga Junior, Manue Vicente Ribeiro. 1981. "Toward a Brazilian Ethnomusicology: Amerindian Phrases." Ph.D. diss., University of California, Los Angeles.

Views of the 1876 Centennial Exposition. 1977. Philadelphia: Centennial Photographic Co.

Walker Art Center. 1962. *New Art of Brazil*. Minneapolis: Walker Art Center.

Whitehead, P. J. P., and M. Bosleman. 1989. *A Portrait of Dutch Seventeenth Century in Brazil*. Amsterdam and New York: North-Holland Publishing Co.

Woodward, Joseph. 1996. "Milton Nascimento." *Jazz Times* 26, no. 7 (September).

Wright, Simon James. 1986. "Villa-Lobos and His Position in Brazilian Music after 1930." Ph.D. diss., University of Wales.

Zanini, Walter, ed. 1983. *História geral da arte no Brasil*. 2 vols. São Paulo: Instituto Walter Moreira Salles.

CHAPTER 7

∾

Brazilian History
in the United States

Judy Bieber

I. Introduction

To evaluate a half-century of Brazilianist historical scholarship is both easier and more difficult than it seems. In the United States, the number of scholars who have written dissertations on Brazilian history in the twentieth century has been comparatively few. Historians of Brazil based in the United States do not have independent scholarly associations or journals specifically devoted to Brazilian history. Instead, they have turned to more broadly defined Latin American outlets such as the Conference on Latin American History and the *Hispanic American Historical Review* (hereafter, *HAHR*) to discuss and publish their work. The study of Brazilian history has also found a home in interdisciplinary journals like the *Luso-Brazilian Review,* which has provided ample space for historical contributions and often showcases particular historical themes in special issues.[1] The interdisciplinary Brazilian Studies Association, founded by Jon Tolman and Roberto Reis in 1992, has done much to facilitate international dialogue by holding conferences in the United States, England, and Brazil.[2]

As part of a relatively small and marginal subfield of Latin American history, historians of Brazil in the United States have had to look beyond their borders for intellectual inspiration and context. The North American Brazilianist community is not and never has been hermetically sealed. The works of Francisco Adolfo de Varnhagen, Capistrano de Abreu, José Honório Rodrigues, Gilberto Freyre, Caio Prado Jr., Florestan Fernandes, Fernando Henrique Cardoso, Sérgio Buarque de Holanda, Emília Viotti da Costa, and Carlos Guilherme Mota, among others, represent fundamental *obras chaves* in the training of most, if not all, U.S. historians of Brazil. The *Cambridge History of Latin America*, a basic starting point for many graduate students, was edited by Englishman Leslie Bethell. Our understanding of the colonial era has been influenced incalculably by British historians such as Robert Southey, Charles Boxer, A. J. R. Russell-Wood, and Kenneth Maxwell. Some of the finest works on the empire were written by scholars born elsewhere, namely, Richard Graham, born in Goiás to American parents, and Roderick Barman, originally from England but with an academic career spent in Vancouver, Canada. A strictly nationalist definition of "Brazilianist," therefore, can be misleading.

Although North American scholars may quibble over who invented the term "Brazilianist," how it should be spelled, and to whom it should be applied, Brazilian scholars have adopted more inclusive definitions. In a recent survey of "Brazilianist" works that have appeared in translation, Fernanda Massi and Heloísa Pontes (1992) did not limit their definition of "Brazilianist" to North Americans but included prominent social scientists from Great Britain, France, Germany, Switzerland, Italy, Greece, Spain and Spanish-speaking America, and Greece. Nor did they limit their survey to historians. In his 1990 evaluation of the "brasilianista" community, José Carlos Sebe Bom Meihy also included scholars from a variety of disciplines but limited his sample to scholars who had based their academic careers in the United States, regardless of their birthplace.[3] These more neutral, descriptive definitions seem far more useful and appropriate than the more politically charged term that was applied pejoratively to the generation of scholars that did research in Brazil in the 1960s and 1970s during the height of the Cold War. I would, however, expand it further still to include Brazilians who were trained in the United States and North Americans who chose to make Brazil their academic home, such as Robert Slenes, John Monteiro, and Douglas Libby.

To adopt a more inclusive definition of "Brazilianist" is not inconsistent with the broader goals of this volume. My task is not to provide a comprehensive bibliographical listing of all of the major books and articles produced by U.S. citizens since 1945, a task that already has been ably tackled by others.[4] Rather, this essay will identify works representative of larger trends in a fashion that is selective but, it is hoped, not arbitrary. My aim is to identify major historiographic trends in terms of periodization, subject matter, themes, method, and theoretical approach and to draw comparisons between scholarly trajectories in the United States and Brazil. These trends did not develop in a vacuum but transcend national boundaries and accommodate a plurality of influences.

II. DEFINING THE FIELD

Brazilian history has been an understudied field in the United States compared to other regions of Latin America such as Mexico.[5] Only eight dissertations were written in the United States before 1950, and only two of those saw publication as books: Alexander Marchant's *From Barter to Slavery* (1942) and Alan K. Manchester's *British Pre-eminence in Brazil* (1933).[6] Marchant's study of settler-indigenous relations in the early colonial period was notable for its focus on indigenous agency and material culture.[7] Manchester's work was more conventional, as was Lawrence F. Hill's *Diplomatic Relations Between the United States and Brazil* (1932). (Hill completed a doctoral dissertation on Spanish American history at Berkeley in 1923.) Both, however, became the leading reference works in their respective topics. Hill also collaborated with Manoel Cardozo (1947) on an interdisciplinary volume of essays that included contributions by leading North American and Brazilian scholars.

Interest in Brazilian history began to pick up, albeit gradually, in the 1950s. Fourteen doctoral degrees were awarded in Brazilian history, the majority from the graduate programs of Berkeley, Stanford, Illinois, Columbia, and Catholic University. Although the number produced was still relatively small compared to what was to come, the decade produced four influential scholars who would leave their mark on the field and the next generation of Brazilianists. Stanley Stein, who took his degree from Harvard in 1951, wrote two classics of Brazilian economic history, the innovative *Vassouras: A Brazilian Coffee County, 1850–1900*, and *The Brazilian Cotton Manufacture: Textile Enterprise in an Underdeveloped Area, 1850–1950*, both published by Harvard University Press in 1957. (Stein was trained by C. H. Haring at Harvard.) *Vassouras* was especially noteworthy for its creative use of municipal and notary archives. Stein went on to spend his academic career at Princeton, where he trained a number of prominent successors, including Robert Levine and Kenneth Maxwell. Richard Morse completed his doctoral degree at Columbia in 1952 and spent most of his academic career at Yale (1962–78) and Stanford (1978–84), where he also trained leading figures of the next generation. His *From Community to Metropolis* (1958) also broke new ground and became a classic in the field of urban and labor history. George Boehrer, who graduated from Catholic University in 1952, spent his career at Georgetown University and the University of Kansas and was active for many years in evaluating Brazilian historiography for the *Handbook of Latin American Studies*. Finally, Dauril Alden, the only colonialist of the lot, took his degree from Berkeley in

1959. His research on economic and institutional aspects of colonial life have become standard reference works in the field (1968, 1973, 1996).

Brazil became an increasingly popular historical topic in the 1960s as institutional and financial support became more abundant. Of the 301 dissertations produced since 1930, the majority (272, or 90 percent were completed from 1965 to 2003). Many of the senior Brazilianists who participated in the seminars that led to this volume alluded to the importance of Cold War funding when they referred to themselves as "sons of Fidel Castro."[8] Latin American studies programs proliferated when federal funding became available under Title VI of the National Defense Education Act (NDEA) of 1958. The NDEA also promoted study of Brazilian Portuguese as part of its broader strategic vision of Brazil. Between 1961 and 1969, the Joint Committee on Latin American Studies and the Foreign Area Fellowship Program awarded, respectively, 21 percent and 30 percent of their fellowships to Brazilian projects (Skidmore 1975). In 1968–69 alone, twenty-five North Americans were doing research in Rio (Barman 1990: 377). This abundance of young scholars made possible gatherings such as the "Rio Research Group." Some also were able to obtain access to private archives that Brazilian elites were wary of sharing with local scholars during the repressive military era. One such example was Alzira Vargas de Amaral Peixoto's opening of her father's private papers to Robert Levine (F. D. McCann 2000).

At the beginning of the twenty-first century, the top graduate programs for Brazilian history in terms of completed Ph.D. dissertations in rank order are the University of Texas at Austin; Columbia; University of California, Los Angeles; Stanford; Yale; New York University; University of New Mexico; University of California, Berkeley; University of Florida, Gainesville; and the Johns Hopkins University (see table 7.1). These top ten programs produced 156 dissertations, or 52 percent of the total sample. Fifty percent of those dissertations were published as books. Columbia stands out for having the greatest number of dissertations published: 14 of 21, or 15 percent of all dissertation-based monographs produced by U.S.-based Brazilianists. Many of the most influential figures in the field took their degrees there, including Richard Morse, E. Bradford Burns, Stuart Schwartz, and Joseph Love, who went on to train many of the finest Brazilianists of the next generation. Harvard, although it has been responsible for only three dissertations since the 1930s, produced two of the field's leading figures, Thomas Skidmore and Stanley Stein.

Nearly all the leading Brazilian history programs have had at the helm scholars trained in the 1960s: Richard Graham spent his career at the

University of Texas at Austin, E. Bradford Burns at UCLA, John Wirth at Stanford, Warren Dean at New York University, Richard Morse and Emília Viotti da Costa at Yale, John Russell-Wood at Johns Hopkins, Tom Skidmore at the University of Wisconsin and Brown, Joseph Love at the University of Illinois, Robert Levine at the State University of New York at Stonybrook and the University of Miami, and Stuart Schwartz at the University of Minnesota and Yale. (Although John Russell-Wood received his doctoral degree from Oxford, he has spent his academic career in the United States at Johns Hopkins. Emília Viotti da Costa received her degree from the Universidade de São Paulo.) Neill Macaulay, also trained in the 1960s, turned to Brazilian history after completing his doctoral degree in 1965 and taught at the University of Florida in Gainesville (Macaulay 1974, 1986).[9] Herbert Klein also shifted to a Brazil focus after completing a doctoral degree at the University of Chicago on Bolivian history and went

TABLE 7.1: Top Graduate Programs in Brazilian History 1930–2003

Institution	Number of dissertations	Number published	Percent published
University of Texas at Austin	24	10	42
Columbia University	21	14	57
University of California, Los Angeles	18	6	33
Stanford University	18	12	66
Yale University	16	11	69
New York University	14	4	29
University of New Mexico	13	3	23
University of California, Berkeley	11	7	64
University of Florida, Gainesville	10	5	50
Johns Hopkins University	10	5	50
Catholic University	8	2	25
University of Illinois	8	2	25
University of Indiana	7	1	14
Tulane University	7	2	29
University of Wisconsin—Madison	6	5	83
Princeton University	6	3	50
University of Minnesota	7	2	29
University of California, Santa Barbara	6	1	17
University of Miami	6	1	17
Total for top 10 programs	156	77	50
Total for top 19 programs	216	96	44

on to an academic career at Columbia University. At the beginning of the twenty-first century, many of these well-established programs are in transition as many of these fine senior scholars have retired or died in recent years, with the exceptions of Russell-Wood, Schwartz and Klein.[10]

In contrast, the generation of the 1970s, although the most numerous, has provided a less decisive leadership role in the field. Of the 109 who earned their doctoral degrees in that decade, less than 17 percent published books in the United States[11] The demand for academic jobs far exceeded the supply, and only a minority of that cohort went on to earn tenured positions. Moreover, only Linda Lewin (Berkeley), Thomas Holloway (Cornell/University of California, Davis), Michael Conniff (University of New Mexico/Auburn/University of South Florida), Steven Topik (University of California, Irvine), and George Reid Andrews (University of Pittsburgh) were affiliated with major Latin American history programs. (Andrews originally wrote about Argentina but later shifted to Brazil.) Interest in Brazilian history then slumped in the 1980s but a number of those who earned their doctoral degrees in that decade went on to provide leadership at universities with strong Latin American programs. Jeffrey Needell and Dain Borges, both trained by Richard Morse, went on to teach at the University of Florida in Gainesville and the University of California, San Diego, and the University of Chicago, respectively. Marshall Eakin, a student of E. Bradford Burns, secured a position at Vanderbilt, an institution with a strong commitment to the promotion of Brazilian studies. Activity in the field hit its nadir between 1990 and 1994, when production declined to near-1950s levels. Subsequently, a resurgence has occurred, with fifty-seven dissertations completed in Brazilian history between 1995 and 2003 (see table 7.2).

The presence of women in the field of Brazilian history has lagged behind that of men, both in real and percentile terms (see tables 7.3 and 7.4). For the entire period under study, women represent one-fourth of all Brazilianists trained in the United States. June Hahner was the first woman to make a significant impact upon the field. She earned her doctoral degree at Cornell in 1966 and has spent her academic career at the State University of New York (SUNY) in Albany. Although her first book was on First Republic civil-military relations, she went on to become a leading figure in Brazilian women's history (Hahner 1969, 1978, 1986). Another pioneering woman in the field is Mary Karasch (1987, 2000) who earned her Ph.D. from Wisconsin in 1972. Increasingly visible as a leader in the field is labor historian Barbara Weinstein (1983, 1996), currently a senior editor for the *Hispanic American Historical Review* (2000–2007).

Female Brazilianists became more visible in the late 1970s and attained a peak in the early 1980s (42 percent of the sample), just as overall interest in Brazilian history was beginning to decline. Women have continued to be active, comprising 43 percent of the total doctoral degree–holders trained from 1995 to 2003. However, they still remain a minority in the top ten programs, at just 26 percent of all those awarded doctoral degrees. The percentage of monographs published by female scholars has been proportionate to their presence in the field generally. The programs that have trained the most female Brazilianists are the University of Texas at Austin (Richard Graham/Sandra Lauderdale Graham), Columbia (Herbert Klein), UCLA (E. Bradford Burns), Yale (Emília Viotti da Costa), NYU (Warren Dean), and Johns Hopkins (A. J. R. Russell-Wood). The only female professor who has trained significant numbers of graduate students is Brazilian historian Emília Viotti da Costa, at Yale, who advised, among others, Barbara Weinstein and John French.

III. INSTITUTIONAL COMPARISONS BETWEEN THE UNITED STATES AND BRAZIL

The field of Brazilian history, then, only really began to take off in the 1960s, and even after that period the quantity of North American scholarship

TABLE 7.2: Dissertations Produced in the United States

Year	Number	Number published as books	Percent published
1930s	3	1	33
1940s	5	2	40
1950s	14	8	57
1960–64	8	4	50
1965–69	31	19	61
1970–74	61	17	28
1975–79	48	11	23
1980–84	33	13	39
1985–89	24	12	50
1990–94	17	17	100
1995–2000	41	20	49
2001–2003	16	0	0
Total	301	123	41

Note: Seventeen of the books saw first and only publication in Brazil

Table 73: Analysis of Dissertations on Brazilian History in the United States, 1930–2003

Year	Dissertations produced in the United States				Published as books			
	Number	Male authors	Female authors	Percentage female	Number published	Male authors	Female authors	Percentage female
1930s	3	3	0	0	1	1	0	0
1940s	5	2	3	60	2	2	0	0
1950s	14	14	0	0	8	8	0	0
1960–64	8	7	1	13	4	4	0	0
1965–69	31	27	4	13	19	18	1	5
1970–74	61	54	7	11	17	14	3	18
1975–79	48	36	12	25	11	8	3	27
1980–84	33	19	14	42	13	7	6	46
1985–89	24	15	9	38	12	10	2	17
1990–94	17	13	4	24	17	13	4	24
1995–2000*	41	24	17	41	21	15	6	29
2001–2003	16	8	8	50	0	0	0	0
	301	222	79	26	141	100	25	18

Note: Seventeen of the books in the sample saw first and only publication in Brazil

produced has been relatively small. Of the 301 dissertations written since 1930, 141 (47 percent) were published as books, and only 124 (41 percent) of those appeared in the United States. The number of North American historians who have had translations of their works appear in Brazil is smaller still. A survey of translated "Brazilianist" works from 1930 to 1988 included only thirty-one U.S. historians (Massi and Pontes 1992). (Three additional historians hailed from Great Britain but spent their academic careers in the United States.) Although other important works have been published in translation since, the overall impact of U.S. contributions is perhaps less than we might hope or that Brazilian scholars initially had feared.[12] The relatively minor showing made by North American scholars in the ten-volume *História geral da civilização brasileira* is perhaps indicative of our scholarly weight abroad.[13]

U.S. historians had some advantages over their Brazilian counterparts, primarily in terms of professional and institutional support. The American Historical Association was founded in 1884, the Conference on Latin American History in 1928, and the *Hispanic American Historical Review* in 1918. Universities were established in the eighteenth century. In comparison, Brazilian professional and academic life lagged Although the Instituto Histórico e Geográfico Brasileiro was founded in 1838, it tended to attract self-trained enthusiasts from the social and political elite. However, Brazil began to catch up after World War II when the University of São Paulo began to professionalize the field of Brazilian history. In 1949, it launched

TABLE 7.4: Participation by Women in Top Ten Graduate Programs in Brazilian History

Institution	Number of dissertations	Number of women	Percentage women
University of Texas at Austin	24	6	25
Columbia	21	7	33
UCLA	18	6	33
Stanford	18	2	11
Yale	16	7	43
NYU	14	6	43
Berkeley	11	3	27
University of New Mexico	13	4	31
University of Florida, Gainesville	10	1	10
Johns Hopkins	10	5	50
Total	155	41	26

the *Revista de História*, lauded by Manoel Cardozo as "the best thing that has come out of Brazil in recent years." (Cardozo 1953: 168). The first conference of the National Association of University History Professors (ANPUH) took place in Marília, São Paulo in October 1961 (Boehrer 1963).

The comparatively late appearance of graduate degree programs in Brazil affected the quality of historical scholarship produced there. North American academics who annually summed up the state of Brazilian history in the *Handbook of Latin American Studies* (hereafter, *HLAS*) were harsh, dismissing most works as mediocre, lacking originality and methodological rigor. They bemoaned the preponderance of dilettantes in no uncertain terms. For example, in 1943, Alexander Marchant characterized a genre of Brazilian romantic biographies as follows: "The points by which the breed may be recognized are the use of invented conversations, no great penetration into personality, oversimplified historical and psychological patterns, and a 'literary' if sloppy style. Some such miss the point of a personality or a period so completely as to be bad and misleading" (1943: 292). Manoel Cardozo dismissed the bulk of historical works produced in 1947 as books "hardly worth the paper they are printed on" and characterized journals of local historical societies as "avenues of publicity for antiquarian tidbits and lectures of parochial interest" (Cardozo 1951: 123). In a similar vein, E. Bradford Burns and Colin MacLachlan commented disparagingly as late as 1974, "Regional and municipal studies continue to be popular pastimes. One yearns for a law requiring ex-provincials, residing in the comfort and beauty of Rio de Janeiro, to return to their place of birth for at least a year before affirming their loyalty in print" (Burns and MacLachlan 1974: 306).

The brutal critiques levied by North American scholars may smack of cultural imperialism, but they also point to a larger issue, the numerous financial, political, and institutional constraints that their Brazilian counterparts faced. In Brazil, periods of economic instability and political transitions have limited the publication of serious historical works.[14] At various times from the 1940s through the 1960s, government subsidies that enabled the publication of important scholarly works with a limited audience dried up (Cardozo 1951: 123). During World War II, high-quality paper for academic books was in short supply (Marchant 1946: 304). Periodic inflationary spirals have caused the cost of books to soar beyond the means of the average consumer (Boehrer 1963: 207 and 1964: 122). Finally, the political climate affected choice of subject matter, particularly during the Vargas era (1930–45, 1951–54) and the military regime (1964–85).[15]

The availability of government funding to commemorate centenaries of important events and influential figures also has shaped historical production in Brazil. For example, in 1940, a number of publications coincided with the quadricentenary of the Jesuits, the octo- and tercentenaries of Portugal, and the centenaries of the majority of Dom Pedro II, and the founding of the cities of Porto Alegre and of Petrópolis (Marchant 1941: 305). Another banner year was 1954 with anniversaries of the founding of São Paulo in 1554 and the expulsion of the Dutch in 1654. Centenaries honoring luminaries such as Tiradentes, Rui Barbosa, Joaquim Nabuco, and the Baron of Rio Branco, inspired publications that often stretched on for years beyond the actual event (Marchant 1943: 292–93). More recently, the sesquicentenary of Brazilian independence in 1972, the centenary of the abolition of slavery in 1988, and the quincentenary of 1500 inspired their own outpourings of research.

Brazilian and North American historians began to have more regular opportunities to meet and debate after World War II. A series of international scholarly forums enabled cross-fertilization among scholars from different professional and historiographical traditions. The first International Colloquium on Luso-Brazilian Studies was sponsored jointly by the Library of Congress and Vanderbilt University in 1950. Additional congresses followed in São Paulo (1954), Lisbon (1957), Salvador (1959), and Coimbra (1964) (Cardozo 1950: 169; Boehrer 1960: 203 and 1966: 198). Foreign scholars were also invited to a weeklong seminar held at the Instituto Histórico e Geográfico Brasileiro in August 1963 to commemorate the transfer of Brazil's capital from Bahia to Rio de Janeiro.[16] A small contingent of foreign historians also appears regularly at the annual meetings of the ANPUH and a handful of Brazilians similarly attend conferences of the AHA. In June 2005, the first of a projected series of regular symposia involving North American and Brazilian historians will convene at the Casa Rui Barbosa in Rio de Janeiro.

IV. The Study of Slavery:
Dialog or Missed Opportunity?

A logical place to look for scholarly interchange between Brazilian and North American scholars is the topic of slavery. As former slaveholding nations that held on to the institution well into the nineteenth century, the two cases invite points of comparison and contrast. Yet, surprisingly, little evidence of cross-fertilization exists. If anything, Brazilian scholarship on slavery seems to have had more influence on U.S. scholarship than the other way around. Gilberto Freyre's important work, *Casa grande e senzala* (1933; The masters and the slaves), influenced generations of North American anthropologists, sociologists, and historians and sparked interest in comparative histories of slavery.[17] Notably, Frank Tannenbaum drew extensively on Freyre in his important comparative work, *Slave and Citizen: The Negro in the Americas* (1946). Tannenbaum argued that regional differentiation in slave treatment was grounded in the differences between Protestantism and British common law versus Catholicism and Roman legal traditions. He concluded that Iberian slavery was less harsh than British slavery because of Iberian slavery's more inclusive legal and ecclesiastical protective legislation. His thesis, in turn, was taken up by Stanley Elkins, whose *Slavery: A Problem in American Institutional and Intellectual Life* (1959) sparked even greater interest in the "peculiar institution."[18] Indeed, the 1960s saw an unprecedented outpouring of books about slavery in the United States. Although the initial wave coincided with the emerging civil rights movement, it has continued well into the present.[19]

Brazilianists were also caught up in the field of comparative slavery. Although the topic of slavery could hardly be avoided by anyone studying Brazil's colonial and imperial eras, particular interest in the institution emerged among Brazilianists in the late 1960s and early 1970s. Although a number of dissertations focused on Brazilian slavery, few appeared as books. Robert Toplin (1972) and Robert Conrad (1972) both produced works on abolition, as did Englishman Leslie Bethell (1970). Peter Eisenberg (1974) analyzed the crisis of modernization faced by Pernambuco's sugar plantations in the nineteenth century. Mary Karasch (1987) wrote perhaps the most innovative of these early works as she delved into multiple facets of the slave experience in late nineteenth-century Rio de Janeiro. (Her 1972 dissertation was not published until 1987 and was translated into Portuguese only in 2000.) Also noteworthy were the demographic studies carried out by Robert Slenes (1975) and Donald Ramos (1974, 1979). Ironically, Gilberto Freyre inspired a second wave of scholarship in the 1970s, 1980s, and 1990s that used quantitative methods to challenge his model of the extended patriarchal Brazilian family; this second wave included Ramos, Metcalf (1991), Kuznesof (1986, 1991), and Herbert Klein. Klein, in partnership with Brazilians Clotilde Paiva (1996) and Francisco Luna (2003), has emphasized demographic methodology, like his Brazilian colleague Iraci del Nero da Costa (1979, 1986)

Although interest in slavery continued into the 1980s, comparatively few dissertations and even fewer published books addressed the topic specifically. Sandra Lauderdale Graham's studies of slave and free black women of the late imperial and early Republican eras (1988, 2002), Alida Metcalf's

1992 analysis of slavery in frontier São Paulo, João José Reis's 1993 treatment of the Malês revolt, Kathleen Higgins's 1999 analysis of gender and slavery in colonial Sabará, A. J. R. Russell-Wood's 1982 study of slaves and freedmen in colonial Minas Gerais, Stuart Schwartz's monumental 1985 work on Bahian sugar plantations, demographic studies by Bergad (1999) and Luna and Klein (2003), and Mieko Nishida's 2003 study of manumission in Bahia represent the main published contributions to the study of slavery since the 1980s. All reflect a broader interest in social history methodology and analysis.

Moreover, surprisingly few works published by North American authors have appeared in Portuguese translation in Brazil. Of these, four were classics of U.S. historiography by eminent scholars such as John Hope Franklin and Eugene Genovese (Quarles 1961, Genovese 1976 and 1983, and Franklin and Moss 1989). Of the remaining nine titles, five appeared in the 1970s, including works on abolition by Leslie Bethell (1976), Robert Conrad (1972), and Richard Graham (1979); Carl Degler's comparison of race relations in Brazil and the United States (1976); and Peter Eisenberg's study of Pernambuco (1977). A translation of Stuart Schwartz's important work on Bahia coincided with the centenary of abolition in 1988. Finally, Stanley Stein's *Vassouras,* and Mary Karasch's *Slave Life in Rio de Janeiro* came out in 1990 and 2000, respectively. Perhaps the greatest influence of the U.S. academy on Brazilian scholarship on slavery has taken the form of North American and Brazilian scholars who were trained in the United States and established careers at Brazilian academic institutions. These include Robert Slenes, whose monumental demographic study of Brazilian slavery was completed at Stanford. He subsequently was employed at UNICAMP and has continued to publish on slavery (1999). Roberto and Amilcar Martins, who also contributed to the demographic literature on slavery, helped launch a spirited transnational debate about the nature of slavery and the post–gold boom economy in Minas Gerais in the pages of the *Hispanic American Historical Review* (R. B. Martins 1980; Martins and Martins Filho 1983; Slenes, Dean, Engerman, and Genovese 1984). Douglas Libby, a North American who was trained both in France and in Brazil, became a Brazilian citizen and has contributed actively to the history graduate program at the Universidade Federal de Minas Gerais. He is the author of a series of significant works on slave demography and the regional economy of late colonial and nineteenth-century Minas Gerais (Libby 1984, 1988, 1991). His North American colleague Nancy Naro (Chicago, 1981) researches slavery in Rio (2000). João José Reis (Minnesota, 1983) of the Universidade Federal da Bahia and Marcus Carvalho (Illinois, 1989) of the Universidade

Federal de Pernambuco have also influenced Brazilian slave studies (Reis and Gomes 1996; Reis and Silva 1989; Reis 1988, 1993; Carvalho 1998).

From the 1940s to the present Brazilian historiography on slavery demonstrates a number of thematic and methodological trends, some that ran parallel to developments in the United States and others that emerged independently. Over time, Brazilian historians gradually shifted their attention from top-down institutional, legislative, and economic studies to analyses informed by social history. Particularly from the 1980s on, more historians began to examine the themes of resistance, everyday life, gender, the family, sexuality, and ethnicity. Another factor that has no bearing on U.S. scholarly production but has exerted a major stimulus in Brazil are anniversaries of significant people and events connected with the history of slavery. Notably, the centenary of abolition in 1888 produced an unprecedented outpouring of commemorative scholarship. In contrast, the centenary of the Emancipation Proclamation in the United States did not stimulate a similarly extraordinary number of publications.

The Brazilian historical literature dating from the 1940s was largely institutional. Abolition was a dominant theme, especially in 1949, which marked the centenary of Joaquim Nabuco's birth. The 1950s saw little departure from these basic trends. Of the fifteen books that appeared in that decade, eight had to do with abolition. Flowery titles such as Osvaldo Orico's *O tigre da abolição* (1953), Alfred Valladão's *O evangelista da abolição* (1950), and Roberto Vieira's *Um herói sem pedestal* (1958) suggest that scholarly objectivity was not a priority. Some new trends became apparent in the 1960s. Although abolition continued to be an important theme, it declined with respect to total output.[20] Marxist theory became increasingly influential in academic circles, especially at the Universidade de São Paulo, and informed the landmark studies by Fernando Henrique Cardoso (1962), and Emília Viotti da Costa (1964, 1966). The themes of slave culture and religion also began to receive more treatment (Carneiro 1964, Rodrigues de Carvalho 1967, and Scarano 1969).

Publications on slavery more than doubled in the 1970s with the appearance of fifty-nine titles. Economic and Marxist approaches continued to be popular, as demonstrated by the works of Ciro Flamarion Cardoso (1979), Jacob Gorender (1978), and Paula Beiguelman (1978). The 1970s also marked the peak of Portuguese translations of works on slavery by North American and British scholars (Conrad, Bethell, Graham, Eisenberg). Even here, the emphasis was largely economic. A point of convergence between the two scholarly traditions was evident in the emergence of demographic and quantitative studies. Although this approach quickly fell out of fashion in the United States, Brazilian scholars such as Iraci del Nero da Costa began to further this area of specialization.[21] Another common interest was the theme of slave resistance (Goulart 1972; Pedreira 1973; Freitas 1973, 1976; Queiroz 1977). Race relations also emerged as a topic, with the work of Octávio Ianni (1978), Carlos Hasenbalg (1979), and the translation of Carl Degler's comparative analysis of race in Brazil and the United States (1976). An aspect that distinguished the work conducted by Brazilian scholars, however, was regional breadth. While foreigners have tended to focus on core areas such as Rio de Janeiro, São Paulo, Bahia, and Minas Gerais, Brazilians also examined slavery in Espírito Santo, Pernambuco, Sergipe, Paraíba, Maranhão, Pará, and Rio Grande do Sul.

Interest in Brazilian slavery exploded in the 1980s. A total of 186 publications appeared, more than half published in 1988 alone. Not surprisingly, abolition became the object of renewed scholarly attention, and a number of classics and documentary collections were reprinted. However, economic and quantitative studies also remained important (Luna 1981, Slenes 1988, Iraci del Nero da Costa 1986, Ciro Flamarion Cardoso 1987, Antônio Barros de Castro and Pinheiro 1983). Social history became increasingly popular with studies of slave resistance, sexuality, and daily life and the relationship of slaves to the state (Santos 1980; Moura 1981, 1987; Lima 1981; Freitas 1985; Reis 1987; Reis and Silva 1989; Mott 1989; Schwarcz 1987; Vainfas 1986; Mattoso 1982) . The transition from slave to free labor and attitudes of the Catholic Church toward the institution of slavery received greater attention (Lago 1985; Gebara 1986; Kowarick 1987; J. G. Carvalho 1985, 1987a and b; Balmes and Carvalho 1988). Scholars also began to reassess the validity of Gilberto Freyre's work when *Casa grande e senzala* celebrated its fiftieth anniversary in 1983 (*50 anos* 1983, Medeiros 1984, *Casa-grande* 1985, Fonseca and Portella 1985, Fonseca 1985).

In the 1990s, Brazilian scholarship on slavery continued to grow in sophistication and methodological and theoretical diversity. Regional breadth remained strong, with studies covering fourteen different states. Brazilian scholars also evinced growing enthusiasm in the topic of comparative slavery.[22] As in the United States, social history has become a dominant paradigm, as reflected in the fine works of Sidney Chalhoub (1990, Chalhoub and Pereira 1998), Hebe Maria Mattos de Castro (2000), Keila Grinberg (1994, 2002), Lilia Moritz Schwarcz and Letícia Vidor de Sousa Reis (1996), and Laura de Mello e Souza (1999). Within this rubric, studies of the slave family have begun to go beyond the demographic household approach (Florentino and Góes 1997, Slenes 1999, Motta 1999). In 1995, the tricentenary of the death of Zumbi, the leader of Palmares, produced a flurry of scholarly works (*Do tráfico* 1995, Freitas 1995, Vasconcelos 1995, Reis and Gomes 1996). Finally, the creation of the Prêmio Arquivo Nacional de Pesquisa has led to the publication of noteworthy monographs on Brazilian slavery (Gomes 1995, Castro 1995). Given the high quality of the historical literature on slavery being produced in Brazil, it is unfortunate that more of it is not available in translation.

V. Trends in United States Scholarship

Since the beginning of the Brazilianist boom in the 1960s, a number of historiographical trends have developed.[23] During the 1960s, political history attracted the most attention, particularly in the areas of inter-American relations and the Vargas era (Burns 1966, Skidmore 1967, Levine 1970, F. D. McCann 1973, Hilton 1975). In the latter years of the decade, regional political studies of the First Republic became increasingly popular. The pioneering works of Joseph Love on Rio Grande do Sul, and Ralph Della Cava and Billy Jaynes Chandler on Ceará laid the groundwork for additional monographs in the 1970s that addressed Republican politics in Minas Gerais, São Paulo, Pernambuco, Bahia, and Paraíba (Love 1971, 1980; Wirth 1977; Levine 1978; Della Cava 1970; Chandler 1972; Pang 1979; Lewin 1987). John W. F. Dulles, a politically well-connected mining engineer–turned-scholar, also contributed to our understanding of twentieth-century Brazilian politics with a series of biographies and narrative works (1967, 1970, 1980, 1991).

Economic history also attracted a good bit of interest, particularly for the twentieth century. The theme of economic nationalism was ably taken up by John Wirth (1970) and Peter Smith (1969), while Warren Dean (1969) provided a landmark study of the modernization and industrialization of São Paulo. Richard Graham contributed to our understanding of the commercial relationships between Brazil and Great Britain (1968). The military also commanded the attention of scholars such as June Hahner (1969), who wrote a monograph on First Republic civil-military relations, and Frank McCann (1973), who explored U.S.-Brazilian relations during World War II. The topic of slavery had not yet taken off, although Robert Toplin (1972) and Robert Conrad (1972) both contributed studies on abolition.

In the 1970s, nearly half the dissertations written emphasized politics and economics. Published books on these themes include Barman (1988), Pang (1979), Lewin (1987), Flory (1981), Conniff (1981), and Topik (1987). An important subtheme was foreign relations, with thirteen dissertations examining Brazil's relations with the United States, Great Britain, Portugal,

Peru, the Guianas, and Africa.[24] Other themes that began to receive attention were urbanization (Adelman 1974, Greenfield 1975, Kuznesof 1986), immigration (Pinsdorf 1990, Tsuchida 1978), public health (Blount 1971, Stepan 1981), and labor (Harding 1973, Gordon 1978, Maram 1979). Interest in slavery increased dramatically with twelve dissertations specifically addressing the topic, although only two saw publication as books (Slenes 1999, Karasch 1987).[25] Interest in the colonial period hit its peak with important published contributions on the Inconfidência Mineira by Kenneth Maxwell (1973), household demography by Donald Ramos (1974, 1979), and convent life by Susan Soeiro (1974). North American scholars showed increased interest in the Amazon and environmental history (Sweet 1974, Anderson 1976 [published in 2000], Diekemper 1976, Galey 1977). Social history also began to make gradual inroads, with studies concerning women and the family (Soeiro 1974, Lombardi 1977, Levi 1987, and Kuznesof 1986), criminality and social control (Aufderheide 1976), and regional resistance (Leitman 1979).

Social history increasingly came to define the Brazilianist generations of the 1980s and 1990s. In the area of women and gender June Hahner (1978, 1990, 2003) laid the groundwork with a series of publications both in the United States and Brazil. She was followed by Sandra Lauderdale Graham on domestic servants and slaves (1988, 2002), Muriel Nazzari on the history of the dowry (1991), Kathleen Higgins on gender and slavery (1999), and Susan Besse (1996) on women and economic modernization. Alida Metcalf (1991) took on both male and female gender roles in her study of family strategies on the colonial São Paulo frontier, and John Chasteen (1995) analyzed the construction of masculinity and kinship on the Rio Grande do Sul–Uruguay frontier. Dain Borges (1992) also addressed family structure and norms in his study of Bahia. Linda Lewin offered a meticulous reconstruction of the inheritance laws and practices that are so crucial to the study of the Brazilian family (2003).

In the 1990s, sexuality became a topic of interest—male and female, heterosexual and homosexual. Here North American scholars like Peter Beattie (2001), James Green (1999), Sueann Caulfield (2000), and Suzanne Schadl (2002) are following the earlier lead of Brazilian colleagues affiliated with the Universidade Federal Fluminense like Rachel Soihet (1989), Martha Abreu Esteves (1989), and Magali Engel (1989), who have worked on domestic violence, sexuality, and prostitution, respectively.

Race became a topic of increased academic interest in the 1970s, especially following the publication of Carl Degler's *Neither Black nor White* (1971) and Tom Skidmore's *Black into White* (1974). In the 1980s and 1990s, scholars moved beyond the intellectual history foundation laid by Skidmore to write bottom-up studies focusing on culture, discrimination, and political mobilization (Raphael 1981, Andrews 1991, Simpson 1993, Kraay 1998, Butler 1998, Peard 1999, and Davila 2003). Jeff Lesser has applied the analytical category of race to Brazil's ethnic minorities, including Jews, Middle Easterners, and Japanese people (Lesser 1995, 1998, 2003). The intersection of race, gender, and poverty was systematically explored by Robert Levine in a series of publications related to the life and writings of Carolina Maria de Jesus, author of *Child of Dark (Quarto de despejo)* (Levine and Meihy 1995, Levine 1998). Another theme where race and gender tend to intersect is the history of public health and medicine, as demonstrated in the recent works by Steven C. Williams (1994), Campos (1997), Peard (1999), Smith (1999), and Schadl (2002). The more generalized interest in race within the North American academic community has facilitated the translation of works by Brazilian scholars such as Maria Odila Leite da Silva Dias (1984/1995), Lília Moritz Schwarcz (1999), and a number of social scientists in Renata Reichmann's edited volume, *Race in Contemporary Brazil* (1999).

Brazilianists also began to examine the theme of popular religion more actively from the 1980s on. Ralph Della Cava (1970) was a pioneer in this field. More recently, much of the new research on the colonial period involving inquisition records has been done by Brazilian scholars such as Ronaldo Vainfas (1995) and Laura de Mello e Souza (2003) although Patricia Ann Aufderheide (1973), and Carole Myscofski (1992) also have written articles on this topic. North American scholars have devoted greater attention to the millenarian movements that appeared in Brazil in the nineteenth and early twentieth centuries. Notable contributions include Robert Levine's 1992 reinterpretation of Canudos, Todd Diacon's 1991 analysis of the Contestado Rebellion, and special issues of the *Luso-Brazilian Review* (1991, 1993) that involved participation by Brazilian and North American scholars from a variety of disciplines. Scholars such as Patricia Mulvey (1980), A. J. R. Russell-Wood (1982), Elizabeth Kiddy (1998), John Burdick (1998, 2003), and Rachel Harding (2000) also have explored the racial dimensions of religious expression in Brazil. Finally, Ken Serbin (2000) has provided a provocative analysis of the conflicted role of the Catholic Church during the military period.

The intertwined themes of immigration, urbanization, and labor mobilization have received increased attention since the 1980s. Thomas Holloway (1980, 1993) has examined both state-sponsored migration to São Paulo and mechanisms of social control in Rio de Janeiro while Michael Conniff (1981) provided a fine study on the rise of populist politics in Rio.

Jeff Lesser has written three books about the experience of ethnic minorities that migrated to Brazil (1995, 1999, 2003). Rio de Janeiro and São Paulo have received the most attention from urban historians. Jeffrey Needell provides a fine treatment of Rio's urban renewal in a *Tropical Belle Epoque* (1987), while Teresa Meade (1997) has applied theories of urban space to her analysis of Rio's urban transformation at the turn of the twentieth century. Brazilian historian Sidney Chalhoub has also contributed to the historical dialogue on Rio's development in two books (1986, 1996) that address working-class culture and public hygiene, respectively. For São Paulo, Darrell Levi (1987) provided a portrait of an elite Paulista family. On the other end of the social spectrum, John French (1991, 1992) and Joel Wolfe (1991, 1993) have engaged in a spirited debate about the nature of forms of labor organizing that took place among Paulista workers. Another significant recent contribution is Barbara Weinstein's 1996 analysis of industrialists' attempts to discipline and mold the working class. The middle class is beginning to receive some attention from scholars such as Brian Owensby (1999) and Cristina Peixoto-Mehrtens (2000).

This preference for modern, urban themes is also evident in a spate of recent publications on the Vargas regime, including Robert Levine's *Father of the Poor?* (1997), Daryle Williams's examination of cultural policy (2001), Jerry Dávila's study of Rio de Janeiro's school system (2003), and Bryan McCann's new study of radio propaganda (2004). However, U.S. Brazilianists rarely stray beyond the Rio–São Paulo axis. Notable exceptions are June Hahner in her 1986 comparative study of urban poverty in Brazil and Marshall Eakin's recent book on Belo Horizonte (2001).

Social history also has been reinvigorating traditional topics with new perspectives. For example, studies on the military and the police have been shifting from older, institutional treatments to those that emphasize the class, racial, and ethnic composition of the rank-and-file. Particularly noteworthy in this genre are the recent books by Peter Beattie (2001), Hendrik Kraay (2001), Shawn Smallman (2002), and dissertations by Alexandra Brown (1998) and Zachary Ross Morgan (2001). Finally, Frank McCann has produced a comprehensive new study of Brazil's military during the First Republic and the early Vargas years (2004).

VI. Patterns in Brazilianist Scholarly Production

Although both Brazilian and Brazilianist historians have embraced social history in recent years, a number of differences distinguish the two scholarly traditions. The first is periodization. North American scholars have focused very heavily on the national period, which accounts for 74 percent of all dissertations produced. Nearly half the dissertations address the post-1889 period. Only 18 percent have focused exclusively on the colonial period, and the remaining 8 percent bridge both eras. Interest in the colonial period peaked in the 1970s, when thirty-nine doctoral dissertations were completed. Only eleven works on this period appeared in the 1980s, and numbers have declined further since. Colonialists face a number of constraints, including limited availability of academic jobs, greater difficulty in getting a manuscript accepted by an academic press, and the challenges of mastering paleography. In contrast, interest in the colonial period is booming in Brazil, where scholars have better access to the multitude of archival sources currently available. Unfortunately, few North Americans are actively participating in the vibrant and sophisticated literature now being written. In A. J. R. Russell-Wood's 2001 select bibliography of works published between 1983 and 1999, only four of the forty-nine scholars listed are based in the United States. A few notable exceptions are regionally based histories by B. J. Barickman (1998), Hal Langfur (1999), and Shawn Miller (2000) and ongoing productivity by Kenneth Maxwell (1995), Stuart Schwartz (2000), and Herbert Klein (Klein and Luna 2003).

Imperial society and politics also have not received a great deal of attention until recently. Stanley Stein's overview of the empire's historiography in the *HAHR* in 1960 listed only four North American scholars. The 1970s saw numerous dissertations on Imperial politics but few publications, Tom Flory's fine 1981 study of the judiciary's being a notable exception. Interest in the empire was renewed in the late 1980s with the publication of two important books, Roderick Barman's *Brazil: The Forging of a Nation* (1988) and Richard Graham's *Patronage and Politics in Nineteenth-Century Brazil* (1990). (Also worth mentioning is Eul-Soo Pang's 1988 study of the imperial nobility.) Since then, additional works have ranged from sophisticated political biographies (Barman 1999, 2002) to regional political histories that examine ideology, discourse, class, and gender (Mosher 1996, Kittleson 1997, Schultz 2001, Bieber 1999, Needell 2001, Kirkendall 2002). The First Republic (1889–1930) has been relatively neglected in recent years with notable exceptions of the economic studies of Topik (1987, 1986), Triner (2000), and Summerhill (2003).

North Americans have also tended to focus their research rather narrowly in regional terms, disproportionately favoring Rio or São Paulo. In part, this may be grounded in a perception that these urban centers offer easier conditions for research and have better-organized archives. Of all the dissertations produced in the United States, only 28 percent have dealt with regions other than Rio or São Paulo. Of that smaller subset, 81 percent were based in the five areas of Pernambuco, Bahia, Minas Gerais, Rio Grande do Sul, and the Amazon. Mary Karasch, who is conducting ongoing research on the history of Goiás, is an exception to the rule. So too are Brazilianists who choose rural themes that are not oriented to the plantation or based on the environment. However, interest seems to be growing here, as suggested by the works of Barbara Weinstein (1983), Warren Dean (1987, 1995), B. J. Barickman (1998), Stephen Bell (1998), Shawn Miller (2000), Gerald Greenfield (2001), and Cliff Welch (1999).

Some have argued that the willingness to engage in interdisciplinary endeavors is one of the defining characteristics of the Brazilianist community. In a recent essay, Piers Armstrong (2000) highlighted this trait among modern-day Brazilianists, especially those combining history, cultural studies, and literary criticism. However, this intellectual flexibility is not unique to North American scholars. Armstrong notes that in this recent turn toward cultural exegeses, North American scholars are following the earlier lead of Brazilian scholars and essayists such as Paulo Prado, Sérgio Buarque de Holanda, Gilberto Freyre, Roberto Schwarz, and Roberto da Matta. Interdisciplinary approaches are also evident in the comparatively new and interrelated fields of ethnohistory, indigenous policy, and nation building. A number of doctoral students (Langfur 1999, Sommer 2000) and established scholars (Garfield 2001, Diacon 2004) have turned their attention to these topics in recent years.[26] Once again, however, North American scholars are a few steps behind their Brazilian colleagues (Chaim 1983, Moreira Neto 1988, Coelho 1990, Pires 1990, Farage 1991, Cunha 1992a and b, Monteiro 1994, *Guia* 1994, Vainfas 1995).

In terms of theory and method, Brazilian and Brazilianist historiography are developing along similar lines. Unfortunately, this convergence cannot be attributed directly to cross-fertilization between two national scholarly traditions. Rather, both owe an intellectual debt to a third source, European theory and historiography. (On Brazilian historiographical trends see Rodrigues [1970, 1978]; Mello e Souza and Freitas [1998].) If North American writers are hard to find in Portuguese translation, not so French historians and theorists such as Ferdinand Braudel, Michel Foucault, Jacques Derrida, and Roland Barthes. The influence of the French Annales school is especially apparent in the fine series *A história da vida privada*, coordinated by Fernando A. Novais and Laura de Mello e Souza (1997).

Unfortunately, institutional and financial constraints have tended to limit the scope of direct intellectual collaboration among Brazilian and North American historians. The International Colloquia on Luso-Brazilian

Studies came to an end in the early 1970s, but the conferences organized by the Brazilian Studies Association beginning in the 1990s have provided new spaces for dialog and debate. Scholars also have organized binational panels for the Conference on Latin American History, the Latin American Studies Association, and ANPUH, but limited travel funds often preclude participation by non-nationals. Scholars like Robert Levine and José Carlos Sebe Bom Meihy demonstrated the rewards involved in joint projects (Levine and Meihy 1994, 1995). Other collaborative efforts include Russell-Wood's edited volume, *From Colony to Nation* (1975), special issues of the *Luso-Brazilian Review* previously cited, and a recent special issue on colonial Brazil in the *Hispanic American Historical Review* (Schwartz 2000). In the past few years, historians Marshall Eakin and Jim Green have been extremely active in promoting collegial relations between North American and Brazilian scholars and activists in venues such as BRASA and the Committee on the Future of Brazilian Studies in the United States.

Another means to promote scholarly interchange would be to promote more translations of significant works. Here Brazilian publishers have the edge on North American academic presses in translating Brazilianist publications. It astonishes that eminent historians and essayists such as Sérgio Buarque de Holanda, Carlos Guilherme Mota, José Murilo de Carvalho, and Evaldo Cabral de Mello have not been translated into English. Capistrano de Abreu's classic work, *Capítulos do Brasil colonial,* did not appear in an English edition until 1997. Nor have the fine works that have received the annual history prize of the Arquivo Nacional been made available to English-speaking audiences. These works deserve to reach a wider readership beyond a handful of Portuguese-speaking specialists in the North American academy.

NOTES

1. The *Luso-Brazilian Review* was founded in 1963. Special issues have been dedicated to millenarian movements (vol. 28, no. 1 [summer 1991]); women and sexuality (vol. 30, no. 1 [summer 1993]), the Canudos war 9 (vol. 30, no. 2 [winter 1993]), the Vargas era (vol. 31, no. 2 [winter 1994]), and nineteenth-century politics (vol. 37, no. 2 [winter 2000]).

2. More information can be found on the BRASA website: www.brasa.org.

3. The study, by José Sebe Bom Meihy, was based on a set of sixty interviews conducted with U.S. scholars in 1988–89. Of the thirty-two individuals who appeared in his book, ten were historians, ranging from elder statesmen of the field such as Stanley Stein, Jordan Young, and Richard Morse, to then relatively junior scholars such as Jeff Lesser (Meihy 1990).

4. The *Handbook of Latin American Studies,* published since 1935 and now searchable on-line at http://lcweb.loc.gov/hlas/, and HAPI (*Hispanic American Periodicals Index*) based at the University of California, Los Angeles, and available on line at http://hapi.gseis.ucla.edu. See also Hartness's interdisciplinary guide (1991). On the historical literature, see Robert Levine's two volumes (1980 and 1983) and Steven Topik (1992). A number of more specialized thematic and topical guides are also available. The Latin American and Iberian Institute of the University of New Mexico (with support from the Brazilian embassy) has published a series of bibliographical guides under the Brazilian Curriculum Guide Specialized Bibliography Series (vol. 2). Contributors include Andrews (1997), Hahner (1998), French and Fontes (1998), and for a general overview of Brazilian history, Bieber (2001). On the colonial period, see Dutra (1980) and Russell-Wood (1985), and on race and slavery, see Conrad (1977). A number of review essays on aspects of Brazilian history (too numerous to be cited here) have also appeared in the *Latin American Research Review.*

5. An evaluation of American contributions to Brazilian history up to 1950 was limited to the work of just a handful of scholars: William R. Sheperd, Leon F. Sensabaugh, Arthur P. Whitaker, Percy Alvin Martin, Alan K. Manchester, Alexander Marchant, Manoel S. Cardozo, and Lawrence F. Hill (Ministério das Relações Exteriores 1967).

6. Statistical information for this section comes from the University of Michigan's *Dissertation Abstracts,* now also available on line at www.umi.com or wwwlib.umi.com/dissertations/gateway and from Barman (1990).

7. For a revisionist interpretation of Marchant see Schwartz (1985).

8. A term also invoked by José Carlos Sebe Bom Meihy to describe the second and largest generation of Brazilianists, in which he includes Thomas Skidmore, Warren Dean, Anani Dzidzienyo, June Hahner, Robert Levine, Kenneth Maxwell, and Mary Karasch.

9. When he retired from the University of Florida, he was succeeded by Jeffrey Needell.

10. This list by no means exhausts the number of scholars produced in the 1960s who went on to publish at least one monograph. Such a list should also include Peter Eisenberg, Stanley Hilton, June Hahner, Frank McCann, Robert Toplin, Robert Conrad, Ralph Della Cava, and Billy Jaynes Chandler, among others.

11. Notable published authors include Eul Soo-Pang, Kenneth Maxwell, Rod Barman, Ron Seckinger, Eugene Ridings, Anne Pescatello, Nancy Stepan, Mary Karasch, Donald Ramos, Tom Holloway, Darrell Levi, Tom Flory, Elizabeth Kuznesof, Linda Lewin, and Steven Topik.

12. Among the important works that have been translated to Portuguese are Hahner (1993, 2003), Lesser (1995a), Karasch (2000), Green (2000), Andrews (1998), French (1995), Levine (1995), and Skidmore (1994). Brazilians' fears about having their history appropriated by the deluge of North Americans that descended upon Brazil in the 1960s and 1970s have proved to be exaggerated. On those fears see Skidmore (1975: 720).

13. There were none in the first five volumes, two in vol. 6 (Richard Graham and John Schulz), none in vol. 7, four in vol. 8 (Joe Love, Bob Levine, John Wirth, and Warren Dean), one in vol. 9, Brad Burns, and none in vol. 10 (Steven Topik, personal communication, January 2000).

14. Some series, such as the Biblioteca Pedagógica Brasileira of the Companhia Editora Nacional; the Coleção Documentos Brasileiros, published by José Olympio; and the Biblioteca de História Brasileira of the Livraria Martins, upheld historical publishing (Marchant 1940: 305).

15. For example, Manoel Cardozo notes the appearance of a "number of 'now-it-can-be-told' books on the Vargas régime" that appeared in 1947 (Cardozo 1947: 123). On publishing constraints during the military period, see Boehrer (1964: 122).

16. Foreign participants included Hernani Cidade and Serafim Leite of Portugal, Charles Boxer of Great Britain, and Manoel Cardozo, Alexander Marchant, and George Boehrer of the United States (Boehrer 1964, 122).

17. Ruth Landes speaks of the excitement generated by Freyre's work among faculty and graduate students at Columbia University, particularly among those advised by Franz Boas. Her cohort included Charles Wagley, Donald Pierson, and Melville Herskovits (Landes 1994).

18. Tannenbaum's work was far less influential abroad. The only foreign translation is a Japanese edition, *Amerikaken no kokujin dorei: hikaku bunkashiteki kokoromi* (Tokyo: Saikosha, 1980). The term "peculiar institution" comes from Stampp (1956). For a critique of Elkins's quantitative methodology see "Review of Stanley M. Elkins' *Slavery*" (1961).

19. When I prepared the initial draft of this essay in 2000, I searched the Library of Congress's on-line catalog (http://newfirstsearch.oclc.org) to chart the volume of the historical literature on slavery and how the tempo of this branch of scholarship has changed over time. It is likely that not all works published on slavery are included, but as this collection represents the holdings of hundreds of university libraries as well as the Library of Congress, it should provide a representative sample of the most significant works. I searched for books on slavery, written in English at decade-long intervals. When I encountered multiple editions of the same work, I eliminated all but the first edition, unless substantial revisions were involved in subsequent editions. I also eliminated works published outside the United States. My search turned up 244 books on slavery published in the United States in the 1940s, 257 in the 1950s, 1,268 in the 1960s, 1,996 in the 1970s, 1,181 in the 1980s, and 1,506 for 1990–2000. Material on Brazil comprises only a tiny fraction of this total output.

20. Eight of the twenty-five works surveyed for the decade dealt with abolition. One even took a less top-down approach (Luna 1968).

21. This trend took off with Fogel and Engerman (1974). They were soon attacked for manipulating and privileging statistical data at the expense of other forms of evidence (Gutman 1975). Brazilian scholars (many of whom were trained in the United States) seem to have avoided such pitfalls (Iraci del Nero da Costa 1979).

22. Few studies on slavery for regions other than the United States have appeared in Brazil. One exception is the translation of Emília Viotti da Costa's study of Guyana (1998). A few comparative syntheses (one in translation), and proceedings from an international conference held at the state university of São Paulo (USP) in 1988, suggest the possibility of increased interest (Klein 1987, Gutiérrez and Monteiro 1990, Pas 1992).

23. The dates for this section refer to when the research was conducted and do not always correspond to the publication date of books or articles. My preference has been to cite published monographs instead of dissertations whenever possible.

24. This information comes from Barman (1990: 386–99). Only one of these dissertations was published as a book (Bartley 1978).

25. The remaining dissertations were written by Howard M. Prince, Rebecca Baird Bergstresser, Clevelend Donald Jr., Lawrence Nielsen, Geraldo da S. Cardoso, Jerry M. Turner, James P. Kiernan, Patricia Mulvey, and Jean Rae Flory.

26. Established scholars who have worked or are currently working on indigenous history include Bert Barickman, Judy Bieber, Todd Diacon, Mary Karasch, Alida Metcalf, Barbara Ann Sommer, and the anthropologist Neil Whitehead.

References

Abreu, João Capistrano de. 1997. *Chapters of Brazil's Colonial History, 1500–1800.* Translated by Arthur Brakel, preface by Fernando A. Novias, and introduction by Stuart B. Schwartz. New York and Oxford: Oxford University Press.

Adelman, Jeffrey. 1974. "Urban Planning and Reality in Republican Brazil: Belo Horizonte, 1890–1930." Ph.D. diss., Indiana University.

Alden, Dauril. 1968. *Royal Government in Colonial Brazil with Special Reference to the Administration of the Marquis of Lavradio Viceroy, 1769–1779.* Berkeley: University of California Press.

———. 1973. *Colonial Roots of Modern Brazil.* Berkeley: University of California Press.

———. 1996. *The Making of an Enterprise: The Society of Jesus in Portugal, Its Empire, and Beyond, 1540–1750.* Stanford, Calif.: Stanford University Press.

Anderson, Robin L. 2000. *Colonization as Exploitation in the Amazon Rain Forest, 1758–1911.* Gainesville: University Press of Florida.

Andrews, George Reid. 1991. *Blacks and Whites in São Paulo, Brazil, 1888–1988.* Madison: University of Wisconsin Press.

———. 1997. *Slavery and Race Relations.* Albuquerque: Latin American Institute, University of New Mexico.

———. 1998. *Negros e brancos em São Paulo, 1888–1988.* Bauru, Brazil: Editora da Universidade do Sagrado Coração.

Armstrong, Piers. 2000. "The Brazilianists' Brazil: Interdisciplinary Portraits of Brazilian Society and Culture." *Latin American Research Review* 35, no. 1:227–29.

Aufderheide, Patricia Ann. 1973. "True Confessions: The Inquisition and Social Attitudes at the Turn of the Century," *Luso-Brazilian Review* 10, no. 2 (winter): 208–40.

———. 1976. "Order and Violence: Social Deviance and Social Control in Brazil, 1780–1840." Ph.D. diss., University of Minnesota.

Balmes, Jaime Luciano, and José Geraldo Vidigal de Carvalho. 1988. *A Igreja Católica em face da escravidão*. São Paulo: Centro Brasileiro de Fomento Cultural.

Barickman, B. J. 1998. *A Bahian Counterpoint: Sugar, Tobacco, Cassava, and Slavery in the Recôncavo, 1780–1860*. Stanford, Calif.: Stanford University Press.

Barman, Roderick J. 1988. *Brazil: The Forging of a Nation, 1798–1852*. Stanford, Calif.: Stanford University Press.

———. 1990. "Brazil and Its Historians in North America: The Last Forty Years." *Americas* 46, no. 3:373–99.

———. 1999. *Citizen Emperor: Pedro II and the Making of Brazil, 1825–91*. Stanford, Calif.: Stanford University Press.

———. 2002. *Princess Isabel of Brazil: Gender and Power in the Nineteenth Century*. Wilmington, Del.: SR Books.

Bartley, Russell H. 1978. *Imperial Russia and the Struggle for Latin American Independence, 1808–1828*. Austin, Tex.: Institute of Latin American Studies.

Beattie, Peter M. 2001. *The Tribute of Blood: Army, Honor, Race, and Nation in Brazil, 1864–1945*. Durham, N.C.: Duke University Press.

Beiguelman, Paula. 1978. *A formação do povo no complexo cafeeiro: aspectos políticos*. 2nd ed. São Paulo: Livraria Pioneira Editora.

Bell, Stephen. 1998. *A Campanha Gaucha: A Brazilian Ranching System*. Stanford, Calif.: Stanford University Press.

Bergad, Laird W. 1999. *Slavery and the Demographic and Economic History of Minas Gerais, Brazil, 1720–1888*. Cambridge: Cambridge University Press.

Besse, Susan K. 1996. *Restructuring Patriarchy: The Modernization of Gender Inequality in Brazil, 1914–1940*. Durham, N.C.: Duke University Press.

Bethell, Leslie. 1970. *The Abolition of the Brazilian Slave Trade: Britain, Brazil and the Slave Trade Question, 1807–1869*. Cambridge: Cambridge University Press.

———. 1976. *A abolição do tráfico de escravos no Brasil: a Grã-Bretanha, o Brasil e a questão do tráfico de escravos, 1807–1869*. Rio de Janeiro: Expressão e Cultura.

Bieber, Judy. 1999. *Power, Patronage and Political Violence: State Building on a Brazilian Frontier, 1822–1889*. Lincoln: University of Nebraska Press.

———. 2001. *History of Brazil*. Albuquerque: Latin American Institute, University of New Mexico.

Blount, John A. 1971. "The Public Health Movement in São Paulo, Brazil: A History of the Sanitary Service, 1892–1918." Ph.D. diss., Tulane University.

Boehrer, George. 1960. "Brazil." In *Handbook of Latin American Studies* 22. Gainesville: University of Florida Press, 202–3.

———. 1963. "Brazil." In *Handbook of Latin American Studies* 25. Gainesville: University of Florida Press, 269–70.

————. 1964. "Brazil." In *Handbook of Latin American Studies* 26. Gainesville: University of Florida Press, 121–23.

————. 1966. "Brazil." In *Handbook of Latin American Studies* 28. Gainesville: University of Florida Press, 198–99.

Borges, Dain. 1992. *The Family in Bahia, Brazil, 1870–1945*. Stanford, Calif.: Stanford University Press.

Brown, Alexandra Kelly. 1998. "'On the Vanguard of Civilization': Slavery, the Police and Conflicts Between Public and Private Power in Salvador da Bahia, Brazil, 1835–1888." Ph.D. diss., University of Texas at Austin.

Burdick, John. 1998. *Blessed Anastácia: Women, Race, and Popular Christianity in Brazil*. New York: Routledge.

————. 2003. *Legacies of Liberation: The Progressive Catholic Church in Brazil*. Burlington, Vt.: Ashgate.

Burns, E. Bradford. 1966. *The Unwritten Alliance: Rio-Branco and Brazilian-American Relations*. New York: Columbia University Press.

Burns, E. Bradford, and Colin MacLachlan. 1974. "Brazil." In *Handbook of Latin American Studies* 22. Gainesville: University of Florida Press, 306–307.

Butler, Kim D. 1998. *Freedoms Given, Freedoms Won: Afro-Brazilians in Post-abolition São Paulo and Salvador*. New Brunswick, N.J.: Rutgers University Press.

Campos, Andre Luiz Vieira de. 1997. "International Health Policies in Brazil: The Serviço Especial de Saude Publica, 1942–1960." Ph.D. diss., University of Texas at Austin.

Cardoso, Ciro Flamarion S. 1979. *Agricultura, escravidão e capitalismo*. Petrópolis: Editora Vozes.

————. 1987. *Escravo ou camponês? o protocampesinato negro nas Américas*. São Paulo: Brasiliense.

Cardoso, Fernando Henrique. 1962. *Capitalismo e escravidão no Brasil meridional: o negro na sociadade escravocrata do Rio Grande do Sul*. São Paulo: Difusão Européia do Livro.

Cardozo, Manoel. 1947. "Brazil." In *Handbook of Latin American Studies* 13. Cambridge, Harvard University Press, 123.

————. 1950. "Brazil." In *Handbook of Latin American Studies* 16. Gainesville: University of Florida Press, 167–69.

Carneiro, Edison. 1964. *Ladinos e crioulos: estudos sôbre o negro no Brasil*. Rio de Janeiro: Civilização Brasileira.

Carvalho, José Geraldo Vidigal de. 1985. *A Igreja e a escravidão: uma análise documental*. Rio de Janeiro: Presença.

————. 1987a. *Escravidão negra: a história da Igreja na América Latina e no Caribe*. Petrópolis, Brazil: Vozes.

————. 1987b. *Sobre a abolição da escravatura: carta aos bispos do Brasil*. 2a edição. Petrópolis, Brazil: Vozes.

Carvalho, Marcus J. M. de. 1998. *Liberdade: rotinas e rupturas do escravismo no Recife, 1822–1850*. Recife, Brazil: Editoria Universitária UFPE.

Carvalho, Rodrigues de. 1967. *Aspectos da influência africana na formação social do Brasil.* João Pessoa, Brazil: Imprensa Universitária.

Casa-grande & senzala: 50 anos depois: um encontro com Gilberto Freyre. 1985. Rio de Janeiro: FUNARTE, Fundação Nacional de Arte.

Castro, Antônio Barros de, and Paulo Sérgio Pinheiro, eds. 1983. *Trabalho escravo, economia, e sociedade: Conferência sobre História e Ciências Sociais, UNICAMP.* São Paulo: Paz e Terra.

Castro, Hebe Maria Mattos de. 1995. *Das cores do silêncio: os significados da liberdade no sudeste escravista, Brasil século XIX.* Rio de Janeiro: Arquivo Nacional.

———. 2000. *Escravidão e cidadania no Brasil monárquico.* Rio de Janeiro: J. Zahar.

Caulfield, Sueann. 2000. *In Defense of Honor: Sexual Morality, Modernity, and Nation in Early-Twentieth-Century Brazil.* Durham, N.C.: Duke University Press.

Chaim, Marivone Matos. 1983. *Aldeamentos indígenas. Goiás, 1749–1811.* São Paulo: Livraria Nobel.

Chalhoub, Sidney. 1986. *Trabalho, lar e botequim: o cotidiano dos trabalhadores no Rio de Janeiro da Belle Epoque.* São Paulo: Brasiliense.

———. 1990. *Visões da liberdade: uma história das últimas décadas da escravidão na corte.* São Paulo: Companhia das Letras.

———. 1996. *A cidade febril: cortiços e epidemias na corte imperial.* São Paulo: Companhia das Letras.

Chalhoub, Sidney, and Leonardo Affonso de Miranda Pereira, eds. 1998. *A história contada: capítulos de história social da literatura no Brasil.* Rio de Janeiro: Editora Nova Fronteira.

Chandler, Billy Jaynes. 1972. *The Feitosas and the Sertão of Inhamuns.* Gainesville: University of Florida Press.

Chasteen, John Charles. 1995. *Heroes on Horseback: A Life and Times of the Last Gaucho Caudillo.* Albuquerque: University of New Mexico Press.

50 anos de Casa-grande & senzala: exposição itinerante. 1983. Recife, Brazil: Sociedade Algodoeira do Nordeste Brasileiro.

Coelho, Elizabeth Maria Beserra. 1990. *A política indigenista no Maranhão provincial.* São Luís, Brazil: SIOGE.

Conniff, Michael L. 1981. *Urban Politics in Brazil: The Rise of Populism, 1925–1945.* Pittsburgh, Pa.: University of Pittsburgh Press.

Conrad, Robert. 1972. *The Destruction of Brazilian Slavery, 1850–1888.* Berkeley: University of California Press.

———. 1972. *Os últimos anos da escravatura no Brasil, 1850–1888.* Rio de Janeiro: Civilização Brasileira.

———. 1977. *Brazilian Slavery: An Annotated Research Bibliography.* Boston: G. K. Hall.

Costa, Emília Viotti da. 1964. *Escravidão nas áreas cafeeiras: aspectos econômicos, sociais e ideológicos da desagregação do sistema escravista.* São Paulo: Universidade de São Paulo, Faculdade de Filosofia, Ciências e Letras.

————. 1966. *Da senzala à colônia.* São Paulo: Difusão Européia do Livro.

————.1998. *Coroas de glória, lágrimas de sangue: a rebelião dos escravos de Demerara em 1823.* São Paulo: Companhia das Letras.

Costa, Iraci del Nero da. 1979. *Vila Rica, população (1719–1826).* São Paulo: Instituto de Pesquisas Econômicas da Faculdade de Economia e Administração da Universidade de São Paulo.

————. 1986. *Brasil, história econômica e demográfica.* São Paulo: Instituto de Pesquisas Econômicas.

Cunha, Manuela Carneiro da. ed. 1992a. *História dos índios no Brasil.* São Paulo: Editora Schwarcz.

————. 1992b. *Legislação indigenista no século XIX uma compilação (1808–1889).* São Paulo: Editora da Universidade de São Paulo.

Dávila, Jerry. 2003. *Diploma of Whiteness: Race and Social Policy in Brazil, 1917–1945.* Durham, N.C.: Duke University Press.

Dean, Warren. 1969. *The Industrialization of Sao Paulo, 1880–1945.* Austin: University of Texas Press.

————. 1987. *Brazil and the Struggle for Rubber: A Study in Environmental History* Cambridge: Cambridge University Press.

————. 1995. *With Broadax and Firebrand: The Destruction of the Brazilian Atlantic Forest.* Berkeley: University of California Press.

Degler, Carl N. 1971. *Neither Black nor White: Slavery and Race Relations in Brazil and the United States.* New York: Macmillan.

————. 1976. *Nem preto nem branco: escravidão e relações raciais no Brasil e nos Estados Unidos.* Rio de Janeiro: Editorial Labor do Brasil.

Della Cava, Ralph. 1970. *Miracle at Joaseiro.* New York: Columbia University Press.

Diacon, Todd Alan. 1991. *Millenarian Vision, Capitalist Reality: Brazil's Contestado Rebellion, 1912–1916.* Durham, N.C.: Duke University Press.

————. 2004. *Stringing Together a Nation: Candido Mariano da Silva Rondon and the Construction of a Modern Brazil, 1906–1930.* Durham, N.C.: Duke University Press.

Dias, Maria Odila Leite da Silva. 1995. *Power and Everyday Life: The Lives of Working Women in Nineteenth-Century Brazil.* New Brunswick, N.J.: Rutgers University Press. Originally published in 1984 as *Quotidiano e poder.* São Paulo: Brasiliense.

Diekemper, Barnabas. 1976. "Some Franciscan Missions in the Amazon Valley: Nineteenth and Twentieth Centuries." Ph.D. diss., University of New Mexico.

Do tráfico de escravos aos quilombos contemporâneos: (coletânea de leis). 1995. Rio de Janeiro: Ministério da Cultura, Fundação Cultural Palmares, Instituto dos Advogados Brasileiros, Commisão de Direito Comunitário e Cidadania.

Dulles, John W. F. 1967. *Vargas of Brazil: A Political Biography.* Austin: University of Texas Press.

———. 1970. *Unrest in Brazil: Political-Military Crises, 1955–1964.* Austin: University of Texas Press.

———. 1980. *President Castello Branco: Brazilian Reformer.* College Station: Texas A&M University Press.

———. 1991. *Carlos Lacerda, Brazilian Crusader.* 2 vols. Austin: University of Texas Press.

Dutra, Francis A. 1980. *A Guide to the History of Brazil, 1500–1822: The Literature in English.* Santa Barbara, Calif.: ABC-Clio.

Eakin, Marshall C. 2001. *Tropical Capitalism: The Industrialization of Belo Horizonte, Brazil.* New York: Palgrave.

Eisenberg, Peter L. 1974. *The Sugar Industry in Pernambuco, Modernization Without Change, 1840–1910* . Berkeley: University of California Press.

———. 1977. *Modernização sem mudança: a industria açucareira em Pernambuco, 1840–1910.* Rio de Janeiro: Paz y Terra.

Elkins, Stanley M. 1959. *Slavery: A Problem in American Institutional and Intellectual Life.* Chicago: University of Chicago Press.

Engel, Magali. 1989. *Meretrizes e doutores: saber médico e prostituição no Rio de Janeiro (1840–1890).* São Paulo: Brasiliense.

Esteves, Martha de Abreu. 1989. *Meninas perdidas; os populares e o cotidiano do amor no Rio de Janeiro da Belle Epoque.* Rio de Janeiro: Paz e Terra.

Farage, Nádia. 1991. *As muralhas dos sertões. os povos indígenas no Rio Branco e a colonização.* Rio de Janeiro: Paz e Terra.

Florentino, Manolo, and José Roberto Góes. 1997. *A paz das senzalas: famílias escravas e tráfico atlântico, Rio de Janeiro, c. 1790–c. 1850.* Rio de Janeiro: Civilização Brasileira.

Flory, Thomas. 1981. *Judge and Jury in Imperial Brazil, 1808–1871: Social Control and Political Stability in the New State.* Austin: University of Texas Press.

Fogel, Robert W., and Stanley L. Engerman. 1974. *Time on the Cross: The Economics of American Negro Slavery.* 2 vols. London: Wildwood House.

Fonseca, Edson Nery da. 1985. *Casa-grande & senzala e a crítica brasileira de 1933 a 1944.* Recife: Companhia Editora de Pernambuco.

Fonseca, Edson Nery da, and Eduardo Portella. 1985. *Novas perspectivas em Casa-grande & senzala: conferências de um ciclo promovido conjuntamente pela Fundação Joaquim Nabuco e pelo Governo do Estado de Pernambuco.* Recife, Brazil: Editora Massangana, Fundação Joaquim Nabuco.

Franklin, John Hope, and Alfred A. Moss. 1989. *Da escravidão à liberdade: a história do Negro norte-americano.* Rio de Janeiro: Nórdica.

Freitas, Décio. 1973. *Palmares: a guerra dos escravos.* Porto Alegre, Brazil: Editora Movimento.

———. 1976. *Insurreições escravas.* Porto Alegre, Brazil: Editora Movimento.

———. 1985. *A revolução dos malês: insurreições escravas.* Porto Alegre, Brazil: Editora Movimento.

———. 1995. *Zumbi dos palmares*. Luanda, Angola: Museu Nacional da Escravatura, Instituto Nacional do Património Cultural, Ministério da Cultura.

French, John D. 1991. "Comments: Practice and Ideology: A Cautionary Note on the Historian's Craft." *HAHR* 71 no. 4 (November): 847–55.

———. 1992. *The Brazilian Workers' ABC: Class Conflict and Alliances in Modern São Paulo*. Chapel Hill: University of North Carolina Press.

———. 1995. *O ABC dos operários: em São Paulo, 1900–1950* . São Paulo: Hucitec.

French, John D., and Alexandre Fortes. 1998. *Urban Labor History in Twentieth-Century Brazil*. Albuquerque: Latin American Institute, University of New Mexico.

Freyre, Gilberto. 1933. *Casa Grande e Senzala*. Rio de Janeiro: Maia e Schmidt.

Galey, John H. 1977. "The Politics of Development in the Brazilian Amazon, 1940–1950." Ph.D. diss., Stanford University.

Garfield, Seth. 2001. *Indigenous Struggle at the Heart of Brazil: State Policy, Frontier Expansion, and the Xavante Indians, 1937–1988*. Durham, N.C.: Duke University Press.

Gebara, Ademir. 1986. *O mercado de trabalho livre no Brasil, 1871–1888*. São Paulo: Brasiliense.

Genovese, Eugene D. 1976. *A economia política da escravidão*. Rio de Janeiro: Pallas.

———. 1983. *Da rebelião á revolução*. São Paulo: Global.

Gomes, Flávio dos Santos. 1995. *Histórias de quilombolas: mocambos e comunidades de senzalas no Rio de Janeiro, século XIX*. Rio de Janeiro: Arquivo Nacional.

Gordon, Eric. 1978. "Anarchism in Brazil: Theory and Practice, 1890–1920." Ph.D. diss., Tulane University.

Gorender, Jacob. 1978. *O escravismo colonial*. São Paulo: Ática.

Goulart, José Alipio. 1972. *Da fuga ao suicídio (aspectos de rebeldia do escravo no Brasil)*. Rio de Janeiro: Conquista.

Graham, Richard. 1968. *Britain and the Onset of Modernization in Brazil, 1850–1914*. Cambridge: Cambridge University Press.

———. 1979. *Escravidão, reforma e imperialismo*. São Paulo: Editora Perspectiva.

———. 1990. *Patronage and Politics in Nineteenth-Century Brazil*. Stanford, Calif.: Stanford University Press.

Graham, Sandra Lauderdale. 1988. *House and Street: The Domestic World of Servants and Masters in Nineteenth-Century Rio de Janeiro*. Cambridge: Cambridge University Press.

———. 2002. *Caetana Says No: Women's Stories from a Brazilian Slave Society*. Cambridge: Cambridge University Press.

Green, James N. 1999. *Beyond Carnival: Male Homosexuality in Twentieth-Century Brazil*. Chicago: University of Chicago Press.

———. 2000. *Além do Carnaval: a homosexualidade masculino no Brasil do século XX*. São Paulo: Editora da UNESP.

Greenfield, Gerald M. 1975. "The Challenge of Growth: The Growth of Urban Public Services in São Paulo, 1885–1913." Ph.D. diss., Indiana University.

————. 2001. *The Realities of Images: Imperial Brazil and the Great Drought.* Philadelphia: American Philosophical Society.

Grinberg, Keila. 1994. *Liberata, a lei da ambigüidade: as ações de liberdade da Corte de Apelação do Rio de Janeiro no século XIX.* Rio de Janeiro: Relume Dumará.

————. 2002. *O fiador dos brasileiros: cidadania, escravidão e direito civil no tempo de Antônio Pereira Rebouças.* Rio de Janeiro: Civilização Brasileira.

Guia de fontes para a historia indígena e do indigenismo em arquivos brasileiros: acervos das capitais. 1994. São Paulo: Núcleo de História Indígena e do Indigenismo.

Gutiérrez, Horácio, and John M. Monteiro. 1990. *A escravidão na América Latina e no Caribe: bibliografia básica.* São Paulo: CELA, Universidade. Estadual Paulista.

Gutman, Herbert G. 1975. *Slavery and the Numbers Game: A Critique of Time on the Cross.* Urbana-Champaign: University of Illinois Press.

Hahner, June E. 1969. *Civilian-Military Relations in Brazil, 1889–1898.* Columbia: University of South Carolina Press.

————. 1978. *A mulher no Brasil.* Rio de Janeiro: Civilização Brasileira, Coleção Retratos do Brasil.

————. 1986. *Poverty and Politics: The Urban Poor in Brazil, 1870–1920.* Albuquerque: University of New Mexico Press.

————. 1990. *Emancipating the Female Sex: The Struggle for Women's Rights in Brazil, 1850–1940.* Durham, N.C.: Duke University Press.

————. 1993. *Pobreza e política: os pobres urbanos no Brasil, 1870–1920.* Brasília: EDUNB.

————. 1998. *Women in Brazil.* Albuquerque: Latin American Institute, University of New Mexico.

————. 2003. *Emancipação do sexo feminine: a luta pelos direitos da mulher no Brasil, 1850–1940.* Florianópolis, Brazil: Editora Mulheres.

Harding, Rachel. 2000. *A Refuge in Thunder: Candomble and Alternative Spaces of Blackness.* Bloomington: Indiana University Press.

Harding, Timothy F. 1973. "The Political History of Organized Labor in Brazil." Ph.D. diss., Stanford University.

Hartness, Ann. 1991. *Brazil in Reference Books, 1965–1989: An Annotated Bibliography.* Metuchen, N.J.: Scarecrow Press.

Hasenbalg, Carlos Alfredo. 1979. *Discriminação e desigualdades raciais no Brasil.* Rio de Janeiro: Graal.

Higgins, Kathleen J. 1999. *"Licentious Liberty" in a Brazilian Gold-Mining Region: Slavery, Gender, and Social Control in Eighteenth-Century Sabará, Minas Gerais.* University Park: Pennsylvania State University Press.

Hill, Lawrence F. 1932. *Diplomatic Relations Between the United States and Brazil.* Durham, N.C.: Duke University Press.

Hill, Lawrence F., and Manoel Cardozo. 1974. *Brazil.* Berkeley: University of California Press.

Hilton, Stanley E. 1975. *Brazil and the Great Powers, 1930–1939: The Politics of Trade Rivalry.* Austin: University of Texas Press.

Holloway, Thomas H. 1980. *Immigrants on the Land: Coffee and Society in São Paulo, 1886–1934.* Chapel Hill: University of North Carolina Press.

———. 1993. *Policing Rio de Janeiro: Repression and Resistance in a Nineteenth-Century City.* Stanford, Calif.: Stanford University Press.

Ianni, Octávio. 1978. *Escravidão e racismo.* São Paulo: Hucitec.

Karasch, Mary. 1987. *Slave Life in Rio de Janeiro, 1808–1850.* Princeton, N.J.: Princeton University Press.

———. 2000. *A vida dos escravos no Rio de Janeiro (1808–1850).* São Paulo: Companhia das Letras.

Kiddy, Elizabeth W. 1998. "Brotherhoods of Our Lady of the Rosary of the Blacks: Community and Devotion in Minas Gerais." Ph.D. diss., University of New Mexico.

Kirkendall, Andrew John. 2002. *Class Mates: Male Student Culture and the Making of a Political Class in Nineteenth-Century Brazil.* Lincoln: University of Nebraska Press.

Kittleson, Roger Alan. 1997. "The Problem of the People: Popular Classes and the Social Construction of Ideas in Porto Alegre, Brazil, 1846–1893." Ph.D. diss., University of Wisconsin.

Klein, Herbert. 1987. *A escravidão africana: América Latina e Caribe.* São Paulo: Brasiliense.

Klein, Herbert S., and Clotilde Andrade Paiva. 1996. "Freedmen in a Slave Economy: Minas Gerais in 1831." *Journal of Social History* 29, no. 4:933–63.

Kowarick, Lúcio. 1987. *Trabalho e vadiagem: a origem do trabalho livre no Brasil.* São Paulo: Brasiliense.

Kraay, Hendrik. 1998. *Afro-Brazilian Culture and Politics: Bahia, 1790s to 1990s.* Armonk, N.Y.: M. E. Sharpe.

———. 2001. *Race, State, and Armed Forces in Independence-Era Brazil: Bahia, 1790s–1840s.* Stanford, Calif.: Stanford University Press.

Kuznesof, Elizabeth. 1986. *Household Economy and Urban Development: São Paulo, 1765–1836.* Boulder, Colo.: Westview.

———. 1991. "Sexual Politics, Race, and Bastard-Bearing in Nineteenth-century Brazil: A Question of Culture or Power?" *Journal of Family History* 16, no. 3:241–60.

Lago, Luiz A. Corrêa do. 1985. *O surgimento da escravidão e a transição para o trabalho livre no Brasil: um modelo teórico simples e uma visão de longo prazo.* Rio de Janeiro: Departamento de Economia, PUC.

Landes, Ruth. 1994. *The City of Women.* Albuquerque: University of New Mexico Press.

Langfur, Harold Lawrence. 1999. "The Forbidden Lands: Frontier Settlers, Slaves, and Indians in Minas Gerais, Brazil, 1760–1830." Ph.D. diss., University of Texas.

Leitman, Spencer L. 1979. *Raízes sócio-econômicas da Guerra dos Farrapos: um capítulo da história do Brasil no século XIX.* Rio de Janeiro: Graal.

Lesser, Jeffrey H. 1995. *O Brasil e a questão judaica: imigração, diplomacia e preconceito.* Rio de Janeiro: Imago.

———. 1995. *Welcoming the Undesirables: Brazil and the Jewish Question.* Berkeley: University of California Press.

———. 1999. *Negotiating National Identity: Immigrants, Minorities, and the Struggle for Ethnicity in Brazil.* Durham, N.C.: Duke University Press.

———. 2003. *Searching for Home Abroad: Japanese-Brazilians and Transnationalism.* Durham, N.C.: Duke University Press.

Levi, Darrell. 1987. *The Prados of São Paulo: An Elite Family and Social Change, 1840–1930.* Athens: University of Georgia Press.

Levine, Robert M. 1970. *The Vargas Regime: The Critical Years: 1934–1938.* New York: Columbia University Press.

———. 1978. *Pernambuco in the Brazilian Federation, 1889–1937.* Stanford, Calif.: Stanford University Press.

———. 1980. *Brazil Since 1930: An Annotated Bibliography for Social Historians.* New York: Garland.

———. 1992. *Vale of Tears: Revisiting the Canudos Massacre in Northeastern Brazil, 1893–1897.* Berkeley: University of California Press.

———. 1995. *O sertão prometido, o massacre de Canudos.* São Paulo: Editora da Universidade de São Paulo.

———. 1997. *Father of the Poor? Vargas and His Era.* Cambridge: Cambridge University Press.

Levine, Robert M., ed. 1983. *Brazil, 1822–1930: An Annotated Bibliography for Social Historians.* New York: Garland.

———. 1998. *Bitita's Diary: The Childhood Memoirs of Carolina Maria de Jesus.* Armonk, N.Y.: M. E. Sharpe.

Levine, Robert M., and José Carlos Sebe Bom Meihy. 1994. *Cinderela negra: a saga de Carolina Maria de Jesus.* Rio de Janeiro: Editora UFRJ.

———. 1995. *The Life and Death of Carolina Maria de Jesus.* Albuquerque: University of New Mexico Press.

Lewin, Linda. 1987. *Politics and Parentela in Paraiba: A Case Study of Family-based Oligarchy in Brazil.* Princeton, N.J.: Princeton University Press.

———. 2003. *Surprise Heirs.* 2 vols. Stanford, Calif.: Stanford University Press.

Libby, Douglas C. 1984. *Trabalho escravo e capital estrangeiro no Brasil. O caso de Morro Velho.* Belo Horizonte, Brazil: Itataia.

———. 1988. *Transformação e trabalho em uma economia escravista. Minas Gerais no século XIX.* São Paulo: Brasiliense.

———. 1991. "Proto-Industrialisation in a Slave Society: The Case of Minas Gerais." *Journal of Latin American Studies* 23, no. 1 (February): 1–36.

Lima, Lana Lage da Gama. 1981. *Rebeldia negra e abolicionismo.* Rio de Janeiro: Achiamé.

Lombardi, Mary. 1977. "Women in the Modern Art Movement in Brazil: Salon Leaders, Artists and Musicians, 1917–1930." Ph.D. diss., University of California, Los Angeles.

Love, Joseph L. 1971. *Rio Grande do Sul and Brazilian Regionalism, 1882–1930.* Stanford, Calif.: Stanford University Press.

———. 1980. *São Paulo in the Brazilian Federation, 1889–1937.* Stanford, Calif.: Stanford University Press.

Luna, Francisco Vidal. 1981. *Minas Gerais, escravos e senhores: analise da estructura populacional e econômica de alguns centros mineratorios (1718–1804).* São Paulo: Instituto de Pesquisas Econômicas.

Luna, Francisco Vidal, and Herbert Klein. 2003. *Slavery and the Economy of São Paulo, 1750–1830.* Stanford, Calif.: Stanford University Press.

Luna, Luiz. 1968. *O negro na luta contra a escravidão.* Rio de Janeiro: Editora Leitura.

Luso-Brazilian Review. 1991. 28, no. 1.

Luso-Brazilian Review. 1993. 30, no. 2.

Macaulay, Neill. 1974. *The Prestes Column: Revolution in Brazil.* New York: New Viewpoints.

———. 1986. *Dom Pedro: The Struggle for Liberty in Brazil and Portugal, 1798–1834.* Durham, N.C.: Duke University Press.

McCann, Bryan D. 2004. *Hello, Hello Brazil: Popular Music in the Making of Modern Brazil.* Durham, N.C.: Duke University Press.

McCann, Frank D. 1973. *The Brazilian-American Alliance: 1937–1945.* Princeton, N.J.: Princeton University Press.

———. 2000. "The Writing of Brazilian History in the United States, 1945–2000." Unpublished manuscript.

———. 2004. *Soldiers of the Pátria: A History of the Brazilian Army, 1889–1937.* Stanford, Calif.: Stanford University Press.

Manchester, Alan K. 1933. *British Pre-eminence in Brazil: Its Rise and Decline.* Chapel Hill: University of North Carolina Press.

Maram, Sheldon. 1979. *Anarquistas, imigrantes e o movimento operário brasileiro, 1890–1920.* Rio de Janeiro: Paz e Terra.

Marchant, Alexander. 1941. "History: Brazil: General Statement." In *Handbook of Latin American Studies: 1940* 6, 304–305.

———. 1942. *From Barter to Slavery: The Economic Relations of Portuguese and Indians in the Settlement of Brazil, 1500–1800.* Baltimore: Johns Hopkins University Press.

———. 1943. "History: Brazil: General Statement." In *Handbook of Latin American Studies: 1942* 8, 292–93.

———. 1946. "History: Brazil: General Statement." In *Handbook of Latin American Studies: 1943* 9, 304–305.

Martins, Roberto Borges. 1980. "Growing in Silence: The Slave Economy of Nineteenth-Century Minas Gerais, Brazil." Ph.D. diss., Vanderbilt University.

Martins, Roberto B., and Amilcar Martins Filho. 1983. "Slavery in a Non-export Economy, Nineteenth-Century Minas Gerais Revisited." *HAHR* 63 (August): 537–68.

Massi, Fernanda, and Heloísa Pontes. 1992. *Guia biobibliográfico dos brasilianistas: 1930–1988 obras e autores editados no brasil.* São Paulo: Editora Sumaré.

Mattoso, Kátia M. de Queirós. 1982. *Ser escravo no Brasil.* São Paulo: Brasiliense.

Maxwell, Kenneth. 1973. *Conflicts and Conspiracies: Brazil and Portugal, 1750–1808.* New York: Cambridge University Press.

———. 1995. *Pombal: Paradox of the Enlightenment.* Cambridge: Cambridge University Press.

Meade, Teresa A. 1997. *"Civilizing" Rio: Reform and Resistance in a Brazilian City, 1889–1930.* University Park: Pennsylvania State University Press.

Medeiros, Maria Alice de Aguiar. 1984. *O elogio da dominação: relendo Casa grande & senzala.* Rio de Janeiro: Achiamé.

Meihy, José Carlos Sebe Bom. 1990. *A colônia brasilianista: história oral de vida acadêmica.* São Paulo: Nova Stella Editorial.

Metcalf, Alida. 1991. "Searching for the Slave Family in Colonial Brazil: A Reconstruction from São Paulo." *Journal of Family History* 16, no. 3:283–97.

———. 1992. *Family and Frontier in Colonial Brazil: Santana de Parnaíba, 1500–1822.* Stanford, Calif.: Stanford University Press.

Miller, Shawn William. 2000. *Fruitless Trees: Portuguese Conservation and Brazil's Colonial Timber.* Stanford, Calif.: Stanford University Press.

Ministério das Relações Exteriores. 1967. *Estudos americanos de história do Brasil.* Rio de Janeiro: MRE, Divisão de Documentação.

Monteiro, John M. 1994. *Negros da terra.* São Paulo: Companhia das Letras.

Moreira Neto, Carlos de Araujo. 1988. *Indios da Amazônia, de maioria a minoria (1750–1850).* Petrópolis: Vozes.

Morgan, Zachary Ross. 2001. "Legacy of the Lash: Blacks and Corporal Punishment in the Brazilian Navy, 1860–1910." Ph.D. diss., Brown University.

Morse, Richard. 1958. *From Community to Metropolis: A Biography of São Paulo.* Gainesville: University of Florida Press.

Mosher, Jeffrey Carl. 1996. "Pernambuco and the Construction of the Brazilian Nation-State, 1831–1850." Ph.D. diss., University of Florida.

Mott, Luiz. 1989. *O sexo proibido: virgens, gays e escravos nas garras da Inquisição.* Campinas: Papirus Editora.

Motta, José Flávio. 1999. *Corpos escravos vontades livres: posse de cativos e família escrava em Bananal (1801–1829).* São Paulo: FAPESP Annablume.

Moura, Clóvis. 1981. *Os quilombos e a rebelião negra.* São Paulo: Brasiliense.

———. 1987. *Quilombos, resistência ao escravismo.* São Paulo: Editora Atica.

Mulvey, Patricia A. 1980. "Black Brothers and Sisters: Membership in the Black Lay Brotherhoods of Colonial Brazil." *Luso-Brazilian Review* 17, no. 2: 253–79.

Myscofski, Carole A. 1992. "Heterodoxy, Gender, and the Brazilian Inquisition: Patterns in Religion in the 1590s." *Journal of Latin American Lore* 18, nos. 1–2: 79–93.

Naro, Nancy. 2000. *A Slave's Place, A Master's World: Fashioning Dependency in Rural Brazil.* London: Continuum.

Nazarri, Muriel. 1991. *Disappearance of the Dowry: Women, Families and Social Change in São Paulo, Brazil, 1600–1900*. Stanford, Calif.: Stanford University Press.

Needell, Jeffrey D. 1987. *A Tropical Belle Époque: Elite Culture and Society in Turn-of-the-Century Rio de Janeiro*. Cambridge: Cambridge University Press.

———. 2001. "Party Formation and State-Making: The Conservative Party and the Reconstruction of the Brazilian State, 1831–1840." *HAHR* 81, no. 2: 259–308.

Nishida, Mieko. 2003. *Slavery and Identity: Ethnicity, Gender, and Race in Salvador, Brazil, 1808–1888*. Bloomington: Indiana University Press.

Novais, Fernando A., and Laura de Mello e Souza, eds. 1997. *História da vida privada no Brasil* vol. 1: *Cotidiano e vida privada na América portuguesa*; vol. 2: *Império: a corte e a modernidade nacional*; vol. 3: *República: da Belle Époque à Era do Rádio*; vol. 4: *Contrastes da intimidade contemporânea*. São Paulo: Companhia das Letras.

Orico, Osvaldo. 1953. *O tigre da abolição. Edição comemorativa do centenário de José do Patrocínio*. Rio de Janeiro: Gráfica Olímpica Editora.

Owensby, Brian Philip. 1999. *Intimate Ironies: Modernity and the Making of Middle-Class Lives in Brazil*. Stanford, Calif.: Stanford University Press.

Pang, Eul-Soo. 1979. *Bahia in the First Brazilian Republic, Coronelismo and Oligarchies, 1889–1934*. Gainesville: University Presses of Florida.

———. 1988. *In Pursuit of Honor and Power: Noblemen of the Southern Cross in Nineteenth-Century Brazil*. Tuscaloosa: University of Alabama Press.

Pas, Maria Verônica da. Organizadora. 1992. *Seminário Internacional da Escravidão*. Vitória: Editora Fundação Ceciliano Abel de Almeida.

Peard, Julyan G. 1999. *Race, Place, and Medicine: The Idea of the Tropics in Nineteenth-Century Brazilian Medicine*. Durham, N.C.: Duke University Press.

Pedreira, Pedro Tomás. 1973. *Os quilombos brasileiros*. Salvador: Prefeitura Municipal do Salvador, Dept. de Cultura da SMEC.

Peixoto-Mehrtens, Cristina. 2000. "Urban Space and Politics: Constructing Social Identity and the Middle Class in São Paulo, Brazil, 1930s–1940s". Ph.D. diss., University of Miami.

Pinsdorf, Marion K. 1990. *German-speaking Entrepreneurs: Builders of Business in Brazil*. New York: Lang.

Pires, Maria Idalina da Cruz. 1990. *Guerra dos bárbaros: resistência indígena e conflitos no Nordeste colonial*. Recife: Companhia Editora de Pernambuco.

Quarles, Benjamin. 1961. *Lincoln e o negro*. São Paulo: Martins.

Queiroz, Suely Robles Reis de. 1977. *Escravidão negra em São Paulo: um estudo das tensões provocadas pelo escravismo no século XIX*. Rio de Janeiro: Livraria José Olympio.

Ramos, Donald. 1974. "Marriage and the Family in Colonial Vila Rica." *HAHR* 54 (May): 200–25.

———. 1979. "Vila Rica: Profile of a Colonial Brazilian Urban Center." *Americas* 35 (April): 495–526.

Raphael, Alison. 1981. "Samba and Social Control: Popular Culture and Racial Democracy in Rio de Janeiro." Ph.D. diss., Columbia University.

Reichmann, Renata. 1999. *Race in Contemporary Brazil: From Indifference to Inequality*. University Park: Pennsylvania State University Press.

Reis, João José. 1987. *Rebelião escrava no Brasil: a história do levante dos malês, 1835*. São Paulo: Brasiliense.

———. 1993. *Slave Rebellion in Brazil: The Muslim Uprising of 1835 in Bahia*. Baltimore: Johns Hopkins University Press.

———, ed. 1988. *Escravidão e invenção da liberdade: estudos sobre o negro no Brasil*. São Paulo: Brasiliense em co-edição com o Conselho Nacional de Desenvolvimento Científico e Tecnológico.

Reis, João José, and Flávio dos Santos Gomes, eds. 1996. *Liberdade por um fio: história dos quilombos no Brasil*. São Paulo: Companhia das Letras.

Reis, João José, and Eduardo da Silva, eds. 1989. *Negociação e conflito: a resistência negra no Brasil escravista*. São Paulo: Companhia das Letras.

"Review of Stanley M. Elkins' *Slavery*." 1961. *American Anthropologist* 53 (June): 579–87.

Rodrigues, José Honório. 1970. *História e historiografia*. Petrópolis: Vozes.

———. 1978. *Teoria da história do Brasil: introdução metodológica*. 4th ed. São Paulo: Companhia Editora Nacional.

Russell-Wood, A. J. R. 1975. *From Colony to Nation: Essays on the Independence of Brazil*. Baltimore: Johns Hopkins University Press.

———. 1982. *The Black Man in Slavery and Freedom in Colonial Brazil*. New York: St. Martin's Press.

———. 1985. "United States Scholarly Contributions to the Historiography of Colonial Brazil." *HAHR* 65, no. 4 (November): 688–99.

———. 2001. "Brazilian Archives and Recent Historiography on Colonial Brazil." *Latin American Research Review* 36, no. 1: 75–105.

Santos, Ronaldo Marcos dos. 1980. *Resistência e superação do escravismo na Província de São Paulo (1885–1888)*. São Paulo: Instituto de Pesquisas Econômicas.

Scarano, Julita. 1969. *Devoção e escravidão: a Irmandade de Nossa Senhora do Rosário dos Pretos no Distrito Diamantino no século XVIII*. São Paulo: Universidade de São Paulo.

Schadl, Suzanne Michele. 2002. "The Woman Question and the Man Answer in Nineteenth-Century Rio de Janeiro, Brazil: Ideas on Race, Class, and Sex in Medicine and Literary Naturalism." Ph.D. diss., University of New Mexico.

Schultz, Kirsten. 2001. *"Tropical Versailles": Empire, Monarchy and the Portuguese Royal Court in Rio de Janeiro, 1808–1821*. London: Routledge.

Schwarcz, Lilia Moritz. 1987. *Retrato em branco e negro: jornais, escravos e cidadãos em São Paulo no final do século XIX*. São Paulo: Companhia das Letras.

———. 1999. *The Spectacle of the Races: Scientists, Institutions, and the Race Question in Brazil, 1870–1930*. New York: Hill and Wang.

Schwarcz, Lilia Moritz, and Letícia Vidor de Sousa Reis. 1996. *Negras imagens:*

ensaios sobre cultura e escravidão no Brasil. São Paulo: Estação Ciência, Universidade de São Paulo: EDUSP.

Schwartz, Stuart B. 1985. *Sugar Plantations in the Formation of Brazilian Society, Bahia, 1550–1835*. Cambridge: Cambridge University Press.

———. 1988. *Segredos internos: engenhos e escravos na sociedade colonial, 1550–1835*. São Paulo: Companhia das Letras.

———. 2000. "Brazil: Ironies of the Colonial Past." *Hispanic American Historical Review* 80, no. 4 (special issue, "Colonial Brazil: Foundations, Crises and Legacies): 681–94.

Serbin, Ken. 2000. *Secret Dialogues: Church-State Relations, Torture, and Social Justice in Authoritarian Brazil*. Pittsburgh, Pa.: University of Pittsburgh Press.

Simpson, Amelia S. 1993. *Xuxa: The Mega-Marketing of Gender, Race, and Modernity*. Philadelphia: Temple University Press.

Skidmore, Thomas E. 1967. *Politics in Brazil, 1930–1964: An Experiment in Democracy*. New York: Oxford University Press.

———. 1974. *Black into White: Race and Nationality in Brazilian Thought*. New York: Oxford University Press.

———. 1975. "The Historiography of Brazil, 1889–1964: part 1." *HAHR* 55, no. 4 (November): 718–20.

———. 1994. *O Brasil visto de fora*. Rio de Janeiro: Paz e Terra.

Slenes, Robert W. 1975. "The Demography and Economics of Brazilian Slavery, 1850–1888." Ph.D. diss., Stanford University.

———. 1988. "Os múltiplos de porcos e diamantes: a economia escrava de Minas Gerais no século XIX." *Estudos Econômicos* 18, no. 3: 449–96.

———. 1999. *Na senzala, uma flor: esperanças e recordações na formação da família escrava: Brasil Sudeste, século XIX*. Rio de Janeiro: Nova Fronteira.

Slenes, Robert, Warren Dean, Stanley Engerman, and Eugene Genovese. 1984. "Slavery in a Non-export Economy: A Reply." *HAHR* 64 (January): 135–46.

Smallman, Shawn C. 2002. *Fear and Memory in the Brazilian Army and Society, 1889–1954*. Chapel Hill: University of North Carolina Press.

Smith, Peter S. 1969. "Petroleum in Brazil: A Study in Economic Nationalism." Ph.D. diss., University of New Mexico.

Smith, Thomas Hunter. 1999. "A Monument to Lazarus: The Evolution of the Leprosy Hospital of Rio de Janeiro." Ph.D. diss., Texas Christian University.

Soeiro, Susan. 1974. "The Social and Economic Roles of the Convent: Women and Nuns in Colonial Bahia, 1677–1800." *HAHR* 54 (May): 209–32.

Soihet, Rachel. 1989. *Condição feminina e formas de violência; Mulheres pobres e ordem urbana, 1890–1920*. Rio de Janeiro: Forense Universitária.

Sommer, Barbara Ann. 2000. "Negotiated Settlements: Native Amazonians and Portuguese Policy in Pará, Brazil, 1758–1798." Ph.D. diss., University of New Mexico.

Souza, Laura de Mello e. 1999. *Norma e conflito: aspectos da história de Minas no século XVIII*. Belo Horizonte, Brazil: Editora UFMG.

————. 2003. *The Devil in the Land of the Holy Cross: Witchcraft, Slavery and Popular Religion in Colonial Brazil.* Austin: University of Texas Press.

Souza, Laura de Mello e, and Marcos Cezar de Freitas. 1998. *Historiografia brasileira em perspectiva.* São Paulo: Contexto.

Stampp, Kenneth M. 1956. *The Peculiar Institution: Slavery in the Ante-bellum South.* New York: Vintage.

Stein, Stanley. 1957. *The Brazilian Cotton Manufacture: Textile Enterprise in an Underdeveloped Area, 1850–1950.* Cambridge, Mass.: Harvard University Press.

————. 1957. *Vassouras: A Brazilian Coffee County, 1850–1900.* Cambridge, Mass.: Harvard University Press.

————. 1960. "The Historiography of Brazil, 1808–1889." *HAHR* 40:2 (May): 234–78.

————. 1990. *Vassouras, um município brasileiro do café, 1850–1900.* Rio de Janeiro: Editora Nova Fronteira.

Stepan, Nancy. 1981. *Beginnings of Brazilian Science: Oswaldo Cruz, Medical Research and Policy, 1890–1920.* New York: Science History Publications.

Summerhill, William Roderick. 2003. *Order Against Progress: Government, Foreign Investment and Railroads in Brazil, 1854–1913.* Stanford, Calif.: Stanford University Press.

Sweet, David G. 1974. "A Rich Realm of Nature Destroyed: The Middle Amazon Valley, 1640–1750." Ph.D. diss., University of Wisconsin.

Tannenbaum, Frank. 1946. *Slave and Citizen: The Negro in the Americas.* New York: Vintage.

Topik, Steven. 1987. *The Political Economy of the Brazilian State, 1889–1930.* Austin: University of Texas Press.

————. 1992. "History of Brazil: Essay." In Paula H. Covington, ed. *Latin America and the Caribbean: A Critical Guide to Research Sources.* New York: Greenwood.

————. 1996. *Trade and Gunboats: The United States and Brazil in the Age of Empire.* Stanford, Calif.: Stanford University Press.

Toplin, Robert Brent. 1972. *The Abolition of Slavery in Brazil.* New York: Atheneum.

Triner, Gail. 2000. *Banking and Economic Development: Brazil, 1889–1930.* New York: Palgrave.

Tsuchida, Nobuya. 1978. "The Japanese in Brazil, 1908–1941." Ph.D. diss., University of California, Los Angeles.

Vainfas, Ronaldo. 1986. *Ideologia & escravidão: os letrados e a sociedade escravista no Brasil Colonial.* Petrópolis, Brazil: Vozes.

————. 1995. *A heresia dos indios: catolicismo e rebeldia no Brasil colonial.* São Paulo: Companhia das Letras.

Valladão, Alfred. 1950. *Joaquim Nabuco, o evangelista da abolição.* Rio de Janeiro, N.p.

Vasconcelos, Selma. 1995. *Zumbi dos Palmares.* Recife, Brazil: Governo do Estado de Pernambuco, Secretaria da Cultura, Fundação do Patrimônio Histórico e Artístico de Pernambuco-FUNDARPE.

Vieira, Roberto Attila Amaral. 1958. *Um herói sem pedestal; a abolição e a República no Ceará.* Fortaleza: Imprensa Oficial do Ceará.

Weinstein, Barbara. 1983. *The Amazon Rubber Boom, 1850–1920.* Stanford, Calif.: Stanford University Press.

——. 1996. *For Social Peace in Brazil: Industrialists and the Remaking of the Working Class in São Paulo, 1920–1964.* Chapel Hill: University of North Carolina Press.

Welch, Cliff. 1999. *The Seed Was Planted: The Saõ Paulo Roots of Brazil's Rural Labor Movement, 1924–1964.* University Park: Pennsylvania State University Press.

Williams, Daryle. 2001. *Culture Wars in Brazil: The First Vargas Regime, 1930–1945.* Durham, N.C.: Duke University Press.

Williams, Steven C. 1994. "Prelude for Disaster: The Politics and Structures of Urban Hygiene in Rio de Janeiro, 1808–1860." Ph.D. diss., University of California, Los Angeles.

Wirth, John D. 1970. *The Politics of Brazilian Development, 1930–1954.* Stanford, Calif.: Stanford University Press.

——. 1977. *Minas Gerais in the Brazilian Federation, 1889–1937.* Stanford, Calif.: Stanford University Press.

Wolfe, Joel. 1991. "Response to John French." *HAHR* 71, no. 4 (November): 856–58.

——. 1993. *Working Women, Working Men: São Paulo and the Rise of Brazil's Industrial Working Class, 1900–1955.* Durham, N.C.: Duke University Press.

CHAPTER 8

⁓

Anthropology of Amazonia

JANET M. CHERNELA

The Amazon basin of Brazil and the peoples who inhabit it have long interested scholars. In 1950 the field of cultural anthropology, a comparative approach to the study of culture, was new to North American academe. Since that time, the anthropology of the Brazilian Amazon by U.S. scholars has both reflected and shaped the discipline of anthropology. The first generation of U.S. anthropologists were students of Franz Boas at Columbia University. Among these students only three specialized in South America: Irving Goldman (1963), who worked among the Colombian Cubeo in 1939–40, Jules Henry (1935, 1941), who worked among the Brazilian Kaingang in the 1930s, and Charles Wagley. One of the most prominent anthropologists of his time, Wagley (1951, 1953) is regarded as the founder of Brazilian anthropology in the United States.

Wagley's earliest studies were based on fieldwork in the central and eastern Brazilian Amazon (1951). These investigations resulted in three important books: *Welcome of Tears: The Tapirapé Indians of Central Brazil* (1977), based upon his 1939–40 study among the Tapirapé; *The Tenetehara Indians of Brazil* (1949, 1961), based upon collaborative work carried out in 1941–42 with Eduardo Galvão; and *Amazon Town: A Study of Man in the Tropics* (1953/1976). The latter, based upon fieldwork first carried out in 1948 among farmers and rubber collectors in the town known as Itá (a pseudonym) on the lower Amazon, is the most widely known of Wagley's works and established his stature in 1953 as a leader in Amazon studies. Although Wagley broadened his research scope beyond the Amazon region in the 1960s, producing in 1963 the standard university textbook *Introduction to Brazil* and a number of important publications on race and class in Brazil,[1] he remained one of the principal forces behind Amazonian scholarship. His 1974 edited volume, *Man in the Amazon,* is testimony to his long-term commitment to Amazon studies.

In a step that was to be followed by many others, Wagley forged important personal and institutional linkages among North American and Brazilian anthropologists. The most well known of these was the long-term collaboration with his good friend and distinguished colleague the Brazilian anthropologist Eduardo Galvão. In 1951 Wagley launched one of the first binational research collaborations in anthropology, the Bahia State–Columbia University Community Study Project. This binational cooperation between Wagley and the Brazilian anthropologist Thales de Azevedo resulted in the edited volume *Race and Class in Rural Brazil* (1952).

Wagley was mentor to both North American and Brazilian anthropologists who would work in every aspect of Brazilian society. From 1946 to 1971 he taught anthropology at Columbia University, directing its Institute of Latin American Studies between 1961 and 1969. Among his Columbia students were a number of prominent anthropologists, including Daniel Gross, Marvin Harris, Maxine Margolis, and Robert Murphy. In 1971 Wagley moved to the University of Florida at Gainesville, where he became Graduate Research Professor of Anthropology and participating faculty in the university's Center for Latin American Studies. There, Wagley continued to inspire a new generation of anthropologists who would specialize in Brazil. Among these were Bill Balée, Mercio Gomez, Judith Lisansky, Emilio Moran, Richard Pace, and Jorge Zarur.

Wagley introduced an important anthropological presence in the center's interdisciplinary Annual Latin American Conference (ALAC). With Wagley's influence, the conference resulted in a number of anthropological publications, including the compendium *Man in the Amazon,* edited by Wagley in 1974. Two volumes of essays have been published in his honor: the first was *Brazil: Anthropological Perspectives,* compiled from one of the ALAC meetings and published in 1979 by Maxine Margolis and William Carter; the second was *Frontier Expansion in Amazonia,* edited in 1984 by Marianne Schmink and Charles Wood. These works, each a tribute to Wagley, show the scope and breadth of Wagley's concerns within Brazilian studies.

Wagley's early initiatives in binational cooperation and institution building between the United States and Brazil have been carried forward in several programs at the University of Florida. In 1980, together with Wagley, Marianne Schmink and Charles Wood founded the Amazon Research and Training Program. In 1985 the center initiated the Tropical

Conservation and Development Program (TCD) with major projects in Brazil. In 1986, the University of Florida and the Federal University of Acre (UFAC) began a program of cooperation focusing on ecological and social aspects of rubber tapping and agroforestry in the western Amazon. In her role as codirector of TCD, Marianne Schmink continues to be a principal force in furthering binational exchanges between Brazil and North America.

Between 1939 and 1949 Wagley's fieldwork was virtually alone in English-language anthropology of this least-known continent. In 1949 the publication of the Smithsonian Institution's *Handbook of South American Indians* edited by Julian Steward, ushered in a new period of South American anthropology. This six-volume compilation of essays by more than ninety international collaborators opened native South American ethnology to comparative review (Steward 1948, 1949). The essays provided source data and impetus for virtually all native South American studies to follow. Moreover, the essays laid the basis for theoretical positions in the field for the next half-century. These include two prominent and contrastive directions in North American anthropology—one structuralist, the other materialist/ecological.

STRUCTURAL ANTHROPOLOGY

Structural anthropology, a school founded by the French anthropologist Claude Lévi-Strauss, dominated the anthropology of the 1960s. Lévi-Strauss's theoretical constructs and elaborations were strongly influenced by his own experiences among indigenous peoples of central and western Brazil (1944, 1949, 1958) as well as by reports produced by the German-born Brazilian ethnographer Curt Nimuendajú (née Curt Unkel). These same reports, as we will see, also provided data for the detractors of the structuralist school.

Nimuendajú, who was not formally trained, maintained important ties to the North American anthropologists Robert Lowie, Alfred Kroeber, and Charles Wagley (all students of Boas's). The collaboration between Nimuendajú and Lowie, begun in the thirties, had a major impact on Brazilian social and cultural anthropological studies. The seminal correspondence, written in German between the two collaborators, with Lowie as scientific adviser and English translator, resulted in the publication of two articles (1937, 1938) and three classic monographs on the Apinayé (1939), the Sherente (1942), and Eastern Timbira (1946). Moreover, Nimuendajú's data provided the source material for several chapters on the Gê-speaking peoples that were attributed to Lowie in *The Handbook of South American Indians* (Lowie 1946a, 1946b). Lowie appears to have assisted Nimuendajú in raising research funds through the Carnegie Institute of Washington and the University of California at Berkeley.

Nimuendajú's work on Gê-speaking societies of central Brazil provided an important baseline for longitudinal studies. One of the longest of these studies is the ongoing research among the Eastern Timbira, begun in 1967 by William H. Crocker of the Smithsonian Institution. In a number of articles, Crocker revised, contributed to, and commented upon Nimuendajú's observations and provided new data and interpretations (see, for example, W. Crocker 1961). His monographs, which he wrote alone (1990) and with his wife, Jean (1994, 2004), are important contributions to Gê studies.

Nimuendajú's Gê monographs were the principal sources of inspiration behind the theories of structuralism of both the French and the North American schools. Although the U.S. scholarship diverged from that of the French, it too contributed to structural studies of central Brazilian indigenous societies. In this important anthropological school, north-south collaboration was again at the heart of the endeavor.

As a student of the Brazilian anthropologist Herbert Baldus at the University of São Paulo in the mid-1950s, David Maybury-Lewis reviewed Nimuendajú's work and revisited several of his original sites. Maybury-Lewis continued this interest into his doctoral research at Oxford University, carrying out fieldwork among the Gê-speaking Sherente and Shavante between 1955 and 1959 (1960, 1965a, 1965b). Soon after, when Maybury-Lewis joined the faculty of the Department of Anthropology at Harvard University, he initiated the Harvard Central Brazil Project. The goals of the project were to carry out comparative studies of social institutions among Gê-speaking peoples and to further binational interchange between Brazilian and North American scholars. (In Brazil, a program on interethnic friction was being carried out under the leadership of Roberto Cardoso de Oliveira at the same time.) Students of the Harvard Gê project included Joan Bamberger (Kayapó), Terence Turner (Kayapó), Roberto da Matta (Apinayé), Julio Cezar Melatti (Krahó), Jean Carter Lave (Krikatí), Dolores Newton (Krikatí), Christopher Crocker (Eastern Bororo), and Cecil Cook (Nambikwara), all of whom began research in Brazil between 1962 and 1966. The Harvard Central Brazil Project continued through 1967 and produced at least eight doctoral theses, numerous conference presentations and articles,[2] and several books. The latter include David Maybury-Lewis's monograph on the Akwe-Shavante (1967), Julio Cezar Melatti's work on the Krahó (1972), Roberto da Matta's monograph on the Apinayé (1982); as well as the compendium *Dialectical Societies*, edited by Maybury-Lewis (1979), to which members of the Harvard Gê project made contributions.

The collaborative investigations into Gê culture resulted in rich ethnographic description, particularly relating to social life and structure. The studies demonstrated the complex interweave of ceremonial moieties and age sets, alignments countered by cross-cutting matri-uxorilocal residence patterns that comprise the complexity of Gê social organizations. The goals of these scholars was to discern the logic underlying the intricate Gê social systems and the meanings associated with them. These authors gave prominence to formal cultural categories over external influences.

A selection from the large corpus of writings by David Maybury-Lewis, written in the mid-1970s, well exemplifies the American structuralist school of the period:

> We are now in a position to consider the cultural categories of the Central Gê. It is clear that the relationship terminologies of the Sherente and the Shavante are very similar. Moreover, they were being similarly used in the mid-sixties even though the Shavante were at that time a recently contacted, seminomadic, hunting-and-gathering people, while the Sherente were a small, settled enclave which had been struggling for a century to avoid being swallowed up in Brazilian society. On the evidence, then, the structure of the relationship terminology demonstrates a fundamental property of these two cultures. Both the Sherente and the Shavante terminologies emphasize a binary division of society. . . . The primary discrimination expressed through the system of relationship categories is the distinction between own side and other side. . . . This bipartition of society is part of a world view which insists on a bipartition of the total universe. (1979: 231)

One of Maybury-Lewis's principal assertions was the independence of the social from the biological: "Levi-Strauss's theory fares no better with the Central Gê than Radcliffe Brown's or Homan's and Schneider's because it is in one important respect the same kind of theory. All of these formulations insist that . . . the heart of kinship systems . . . is determined by the biological facts of procreation. . . . The study of 'kinship' will not emerge from the cul-de-sac where it is at present trapped until we develop theories which deal with social theories or socio-logics, which is what kinship systems are, instead of theories derived from the limiting factors which such systems have to take into account" (1979: 245). (See Dole 1983, who regarded kinship systems as subject to other factors.)

Terence Turner, a student of Maybury-Lewis's, diverged from the mainstream to emphasize how dynamic factors, including structural instabilities, are implicit in social systems. Combining Marxist dialectics and Parsonian theories of social organization with structural-functionalist, developmental, and system-theoretical approaches, Turner went beyond stasis to reveal the internal fissures and contradictions that underlie social structural systems and lead to their change (1979a, 1979b, 1995, 2003). In "Kinship, Household, and Community Structure Among the Kayapó" (1979b), for example, Turner predicts "cumulative drift" (long-term change) and the associated rivalry and conflict that are likely to result when relative balance among corporate groups is not maintained. This, Turner predicts, is expected in single-moiety villages that cannot perform all the functions necessary for the developmental life cycles of men and women and, relatedly, the developmental cycle of the domestic group (1979b).

The structuralist school generated animated debate among anthropologists. Robert Murphy, a student of Wagley's and Steward's at Columbia University and later on its faculty, was one of its principal critics. Murphy, also influenced by Marx and Parsons, was concerned with both structure and practice and the dialectical relationship between the two. Murphy's work among the central Brazilian Mundurucú addresses the tensions that emerge from the contradictions between that which is normative, such as rules of social structure, and the practical, quotidian, and individual (1959, 1960, 1961, 1971, 1979). Murphy's best-known work, *Dialectics of Social Life* (1971), influenced by the sociologist Georg Simmel and the founder of psychoanalytic theory Sigmund Freud, contrasts the culturally prescribed with the unexpected and the unacknowledged: "The sensuous world was an essential ingredient in objectifying and realizing the dialectical propensities of the mind, and these, in turn, were essential to the formulation and articulation of oppositional social relationships. Both mind and reality operate in a dialectical fashion, each having its own locus and needs" (1971: 67).

Murphy, like Freud, recognized a level of collective norm to which people publicly subscribed and a different, less orderly, level of ongoing life that is not necessarily acknowledged by practitioners. If socialization is successful—and this was not to be assumed—individuals submerged their own immediate gratifications for those of the collective. That which is collective, such as norm, is, for Murphy, "delusional." In *Dialectics,* Murphy writes, "Man lives with . . . both hard perception and collective delusion" (1971: 229).

An example of Murphy's subversion of the normative is his classic work *Women of the Forest* (1974), which he coauthored with his wife, Yolanda. The Murphys observed and reported the dissonance between men's and women's views of Mundurucú ritual, values, and even the social universe (1974): "The social perspectives of . . . women and men are different, and [women] do not wholly identify with, nor feel bound by, that from which they are systematically excluded" (1974: 51). Their findings suggested that homogenous, consensual notions of culture were oversimplified and misguided (1974).

According to the Murphys, very different cultural realities may coexist—as they do for Mundurucú men and women—without threatening the coherence of society (1974). Instead, the Murphys' presented social interaction as an ongoing dialectic characterized by misinterpretation, tension, and intrigue. The thirteenth-anniversary edition of the Murphys' *Women of the Forest* (2004) contains a foreword with contributions by Robert Murphy's former students Brian Ferguson, William Balée, Janet Chernela, Judith Shapiro, Orna Johnson, and Thomas Gregor (Ferguson 2004). These comments place the original work in the context of its time and discuss its influence in the field.

The Murphys were among the first to point out that by neglecting the unauthorized participants of society and presenting only the normative perspective, anthropologists uncritically re-represent the essentialized and deproblematized notions of groupness presented to them by a subset of stakeholders. "Because they are excluded from so much of what is reported by anthropologists as 'the culture,' we assume that they [women] do not have one of their own. . . . We seem to have forgotten that the very essence of the relationship between the sexes is struggle, opposition, and socially useful, however, unconscious, misunderstanding. . . . Our description of 'Mundurucú culture' should be understood as a point to the counterpoint of the female realm, a foil for the play of social life" (1974: 52). The Murphys challenged those who confused the formal and normative with the full spectrum of social life. The dynamic view held by the Murphys was a strong counterweight to the stasis of structuralism.

The influence of the Murphys is apparent in the work of Robert Murphy's students. As one of them, I am an example. Robert Murphy was my Ph.D. advisor when I began fieldwork in the northwestern portion of the Amazon basin. Working among the Tukanoan Wanano, I (hereafter Chernela) reported and compared male and female versions of a myth cycle involving appropriation and monopoly of instruments of power (Chernela 1997). A comparison of the texts suggests (insofar as these are representative) that which the Murphys upheld for the Mundurucú—that the differing perspectives of women and men show that the most fundamental dilemmas of existence are not the same for both genders and may produce different narrative configurations of power. The simplest and most powerful reading of these myths reduces each to an essential theft-and-loss in which the tellers call attention to the hidden dangers and treachery of the other sex. Like the studies of the Murphys, this analysis too counters the assumptions that small-scale societies are static rather than dynamic, and homogeneous or consensual rather than diversified. These findings indicate that the realm recognized as "official" is but a portion of a greater and more complex reality encompassing division and varieties of dominance.

Other authors influenced by Robert Murphy emphasize classic Freudian oppositions internal to the individual psyche. Principal among these authors are Waud Kracke and Thomas Gregor. Kracke's *Force and Persuasion in an Amazonian Society* (1978) emphasizes the individual personalities of social actors and their impacts on other people and social outcomes. Examining the interactions of leaders and their respective groups in two different Kagwahiv communities, Kracke makes a convincing case for leadership as an interpersonal phenomenon. Kracke's strong Freudian leanings, together with a Weberian consideration of leadership, contribute to his innovative synthesis. Kracke places himself in the narrative, a practice that was new at the time of his writing. Unlike the prevailing genre in ethnographic monographs, Kracke writes as one human being among others. His thesis—that power is interactively produced—is communicated both through the case of Kagwahiv leadership as well as through his own ethnographic exercise.

Thomas Gregor is also concerned with the inner lives of individuals in his consideration of ritual and drama among the Brazilian Mehinaku (1977, 1985). Gregor reaches through symbolism in myth and dream to find underlying universals regarding pleasure, fear, and desire. Gregor does not exoticize the sexual antagonisms that he finds at the center of Mehinaku society; rather, he places them in the context of all human society.

In placing greater interest in structures and inherent oppositions that are internal to the individual psyche, as opposed to regarding "structure" as a property of social constellations, Murphy, Gregor, and Kracke universalize, rather than particularize, humanity. They find powerful oppositions, however unconscious, enacted in the contexts of ongoing social life. These internal structures articulate with and shape society. They are, however, the basis of commonality rather than difference.

ECOLOGICAL ANTHROPOLOGY

The structuralist movement of the 1960s addressed issues of social structure and ideology—native models by means of which a people understand their own culture and the social norms and relations within it. It was followed in the 1970s by a school of anthropology with roots in the empirical traditions of Karl Popper. This paradigm, known as cultural ecology, or ecological anthropology, applies principles of adaptation to cultural factors to explain cultural variation on the basis of processes *external* to culture itself (see Moran 1979, 1984).

One of the principal adherents of this school, Robert L. Carneiro, evaluated the approach this way, "Ecological interpretations of Amazonian culture history . . . have dominated Amazonian research for the last half-century, with no other point of view being even a serious competitor" (Carneiro 1995: 47). Data that emerged from cultural ecological studies of the 1970s and 1980s formed the basis for the indigenous resource management studies that appeared in the 1990s and continued into the millennium.

Once again, the origins for this movement may be traced to the Smithsonian's *Handbook of South American Indians*. As editor of the immense project that spanned the years 1946 through 1950, Julian Steward's overview of the history of an entire continent led him to diachronic and spatial patterns and comparisons. In 1949 Steward put forth a general theory of state formation based upon the comparative trajectories of New and Old World civilizations. His model attributed the rise of the state in South America to a number of causal factors, including population density and technological change, that in turn brought about warfare and related political consolidation in the western part of the continent. The presence of politically complex forms, including the state, in Andean South America, and the absence of these forms in the Lowlands to the east, challenged scholars of evolutionary and materialist anthropology, who would, for the next five decades, attempt to explain these contrastive phenomena.

The explanation put forth by the archaeologists Betty Meggers, among the first female anthropologists to work in Amazonia, and Clifford Evans was that political complexity could not develop in the rain forest environment because the resource base was insufficient to support population growth and density (Meggers 1954, 1971, 1974, 1985, 1990; Meggers and Evans 1957) . The Amazon rain forest was a "counterfeit" paradise: beneath a façade of abundance lay an environment impoverished in the nutrients necessary to productive soils and critical animal protein sources. Any complex society found in the Amazon must have originated elsewhere, such as the Andes, and would eventually devolve in the lowland tropics.

Meggers's hypothesis, that environmental factors in the lowlands of South America served to limit population concentration and social potential, became the focus of debate for a full half-century, inviting numerous countertheories and propositions. A number of opponents of Meggers, among them Donald Lathrap, William Denevan, Anna Roosevelt, and Robert Carneiro, stressed the high fertility of the floodplains along the Amazon River and the presence there of large, pre-Columbian chiefdoms.

Robert Carneiro was an early opponent of Meggers's position, challenging her both substantially and theoretically (1957, 1960, 1961, 1970a, 1970b). Carneiro, who was also influenced by Steward, based his proposition on the theory that populations develop politically complex institutions under narrowly specified conditions. These conditions require population density and competition for resources that occur only when ordinary processes of population dispersal are obstructed. In the interior of the Amazon basin, Carneiro argued, settlement fissioning and dispersal proceeded without impediment, thus avoiding population pressure and related institutional responses. Following Steward, Carneiro argued that where populations are bounded or "circumscribed," population pressure would lead to competition for scarce resources, prompting technological and organizational advancements, including warfare and state apparatuses.

In a series of publications beginning in 1957 and continuing through 1995, Carneiro challenged Meggers's notions about the limits imposed on Amazonian culture by a rain forest environment. Based on the observations of sixteenth-century Spanish and Portuguese chroniclers, Carneiro made the following points: (1) precontact Brazilian populations were greater in total population and settlement size than contemporary indigenous populations (and see Lathrap 1970); (2) there is strong evidence for protein abundance, rather than scarcity, in both terrestrial and aquatic animal life along the Amazon; (3) the sixteenth-century inhabitants of the Brazilian Amazon were amply able to capture and retain undomesticated animals to the point of holding them in surplus supply; and (4) historic accounts document the existence of large villages and warring chiefdoms that attained levels of political complexity not found in contemporary indigenous societies. Carneiro's argument rests largely on the accounts of Spanish chroniclers, accounts that Meggers calls into question.

Meggers's claim (1954: 807) included the assumption that itinerant slash-and-burn cultivation required settlements to remain small and mobile. Bringing to bear data collected among the Brazilian Kuikuru of the upper

Xingú between 1953 and 1954, Carneiro disputed Meggers's assumptions regarding an upper limit to settlement size and permanence for swidden cultivators. In 1961, calculating from these data, Carneiro estimated that a village of about two thousand slash-and-burn cultivators could live in the Kuikuru territory for the long run without relocating their village (Carneiro 1961: 232).

The argument was furthered in the 1980s and 1990s by the archaeologists Anna Roosevelt and Michael Heckenberger. Carrying the ecological program forward, Roosevelt specifies ecologically favorable conditions along the Amazon mainstem that could support large permanent settlements and complex sociopolitical organizations (1980, 1987, 1989, 1991a, 1991b). Roosevelt suggests that maize, produced along silt-laden rivers, permitted population growth and propelled social and political development. Most recently, Heckenberger found evidence of prehistoric fortification in the upper Xingú and suggests a higher degree of social stratification and warfare than previously supposed for societies living along tributaries away from the main channel (Heckenberger 1996, 2003; Heckenberger et al. 2003).

The view of Meggers and Evans, that Amazonia is an area of poor subsistence where indigenous cultures could not rise above the level of small autonomous villages, persisted throughout the seventies, kept in the foreground of Amazon ethnology by its main proponent, Daniel Gross (1975, 1979, 1983). Ten years after the Harvard Gê project, which focused on the internal logic of social structures, Gross launched a new collaborative Gê project whose aim was to investigate questions relating to production and consumption. His project, proceeding from Meggers's earlier proposition, that protein scarcity accounts for the limitation on cultural evolution in the Amazon, asks how it was possible for an interfluvial, savannah (*cerrado*) environment to support villages of more than one thousand inhabitants, as reported by Nimuendajú.

Gross's Gê project, carried out in conjunction with botanist George Eiten of the University of Brasília's Instituto de Ciências Biológicas, resulted in four collective articles (Gross et al. 1979, Werner et al. 1979, Flowers et al. 1982, Rubin et al. 1986). Two of Gross's former graduate students from the City University of New York, Dennis Werner and Nancy Flowers, continued to work among the Gê and pursued collaborations with Brazilian institutions and researchers. Werner, who joined the faculty of the Federal University of Santa Catarina in Florianopólis, produced a number of articles (Werner 1981, 1982a, 1982b, 1983a, 1983b) and a book (1984). Flowers, whose specialty is medical anthropology (Flowers 1983, 1994), returned to the field in the 1990s with Brazilian colleagues Carlos Coimbra and Ricardo Santos, a collaboration that produced several articles (Santos et al.) and an award-winning book, *The Xavante in Transition* (Coimbra et al. 2002). Between 1975 and 1977, Gross was visiting professor at the University of Brasília (UnB) where his students included Mary Allegretti, later National Secretary for the Amazon in the Brazilian Ministry of the Environment (MMA) and Gustavo Lins Ribeiro, presently professor of anthropology at UnB and former president of the Brazilian Anthropology Association (ABA). (Gustavo Lins Ribeiro returned with Gross to New York and completed his Ph.D. with Eric Wolf at CUNY in New York.)

The rigidly limiting role assigned to environmental factors by Meggers and Gross, and the positive role of environment in pushing forward political complexity, as proposed by Roosevelt, are mutually complementary rather than exclusive, if one considers that one model describes the Amazon mainstem—characterized by resource abundance and complexity of social organization—and the other describes the interfluve—characterized by scarcity of protein resources and simplicity of social organization.

Beginning in the 1980s, Chernela (1982a, 1982b, 1985, 1989, 1993, 1994) challenged the simple dichotomy that associates the interfluvial with protein scarcity and simple egalitarian polities by demonstrating that the eastern Tukanoan-speaking populations of the upriver hinterland exhibit: (1) sufficient fish protein whose capture is limited only by cultural proscription, and (2) greater political consolidation and social ranking than predicted by a model that correlates upriver with organizational simplicity and protein scarcity and downriver with organizational complexity and protein abundance.

Later approaches to human-environmental interactions have also recognized a greater complexity in the relationship and the active, rather than passive, role played by humans. For example, the anthropologists Darrell Posey (1982, 1983a, 1983b, 1984a, 1984b, 1997) and William Balée (1985, 1986, 1987, 1989, 1994) argue that depictions of the Brazilian Amazon rain forests as pristine obscure long histories of human modification. That which appears to be timeless and natural is, instead, a product of history.

For the Gê-speaking Kayapó and the Tupian Ka'apor of the southeastern Amazon basin, Posey and Balée, respectively, emphasize agroforestry management previously unnoticed by Western observers. Posey suggests that forest islands on high savannah are the result of skillful and conscious engineering by the Kayapó (Posey 1983; see also Anderson and Posey 1985 and Parker 1992 for a diverging viewpoint). Balée (1994) finds greater biodiversity in Ka'apor forests *after* felling than before. These studies counter the commonplace view that agricultural production necessarily results in declining fertility and species loss. In arguing that indigenous agroforestry practices enhance forest diversity rather than reduce it, these studies contribute to the ongoing debate regarding the general conservation ethic and management abilities of native Amerindians.

Moreover, these works illustrate the fluidity of forest and field in traditional Amazonian agroecology. When fields are small and short-lived the fallow is an interface, a transitional form between natural areas and agroecosystems. Theorists have long assumed that lands left fallow—that is, left to return to forest—were no longer manipulated for economic ends. Posey and Balée argue that managed fallows contain high numbers of economically relevant tree species and are significant in shaping the contours of future forests. By creating a landscape shaped by human intervention, the managed fallow obliterates the line between garden and forest, as it also obliterates the facile distinction between artifice and nature.

By situating the Ka'apor in time, as well as embedding them as actors in a changing landscape, Balée places Brazilian ecological studies within the larger framework of historical ecology. This research design, building on the works of Crumley, Ingerson, and others, reverses the relationship of culture and nature, so that culture does not so much emerge from the environment as it "projects itself upon it." Balée underscores that most of what we understand as the environment, like society itself, is actually historical construct, as humans have created landscapes since prehistory.

DISCOURSE AND CULTURE

Anthropologists of divergent viewpoints agree that rigor in data collection and transparency in reasoning are critical processes of the scholarly exercise through which a cultural "truth" is approximated. But, whereas structural analysis in anthropology focuses on the logic behind internalized rules for social life, ecological anthropology explores the ways in which both observable behavior and systems of meaning may be instrumental to survival. A third school or subfield of anthropology, arising in the 1980s, shares with the ecological school an emphasis on observational methodologies but applies these to spoken conversation. This field, known as "discourse analysis," approaches representational and other cultural data through narrative and other linguistic products. Unlike either the structural or ecological approaches, in the discourse approach the insider's naturally occurring speech is the focus of study and the route to comparative analysis and pattern identification. Methodologies for approaching culture in this way are based upon empirical investigation of actual instances of discourse usage. In this approach, what is said is both the instrument and the object of analysis.

Once again, the anthropology of native Brazilian societies is at the forefront of advances in the field. The Brazilianist and anthropologist Greg Urban sets out the framework of the approach in his 1991 book, *A Discourse-Centered Approach: Native South American Myths and Ritual.* The discourse-centered approach to culture is founded on a single proposition: that culture is localized in concrete, publicly accessible signs, the most important of which are actually occurring instances of discourse (Urban 1991, 1988a).

This new synthesis, in which communication is the object of study as well as the force driving social relations, contests the spaces occupied by structuralism and cultural ecology at the center of Brazilian anthropology through the end of the 1970s. Besides Urban, the approach is well exemplified in the works of the Brazil-specializing anthropologists Anthony Seeger (1975, 1980, 1981,1987), Ellen Basso (1973, 1985, 1986, 1987a, 1987b, 1995), and Laura Graham (1986, 1995). Practitioners of the approach take as their unit of analysis actual conversational turns within sequences, rather than isolated utterances. The endeavor builds on foundations established in interactional sociolinguistics, conversational analysis, and the ethnography of communication. The method of recording everyday interactions through video or audio tape recordings, and analyzing a stream of talk, emerges from the empirical traditions of conversational analysis and other sociological and ethnographic methodologies that value the attempt to faithfully "capture" behavior with a minimum of "external intervention."

Scholars of the discourse school find in speech performance important insight into the very production of society itself. In *Why Suya Sing,* Seeger writes: "The Suya sang because singing was an essential way of articulating the experiences of their lives with the processes of their society" (1987: 128). Not only are linguistic products viewed as *reflecting* social relations and ideology, they are also viewed as shaping them.

One major contribution of the discourse-centered approach is its recognition that culture is produced by individuals in the course of speaking. This approach avoids the essentialism of a homogeneous cultural consensus or an imagined authoritative voice behind cultural production. It creates a space for the unauthorized and unorthodox in cultural expression. Chernela (2003), for example, argues for the concept of a "speech culture" that combines, but heuristically separates, speech practices and language ideologies. In the Northwest Amazon, where an ideology of language establishes a normative equivalence between linguistic performance and descent group belonging, Chernela finds a contrapuntal process of social relations created in the course of women's naturally occurring speech. Chernela finds that a common ground is constructed through the practices of speakers in different languages. Community in this sense emerges as a dynamic cultural artifact—whose production is largely the work of women in speech interaction—that may be contrasted with the normative, fixed codification of community belonging. The work follows the community of practice approach in cognition and learning pioneered by Jean Lave (of the Harvard Central Brazil project) and Etienne Wenger (1991). It builds on several discussions of weeping in Amazonia advanced by Greg Urban (1988b, 1991) and Laura Graham (1986, 1995). It shares with Urban the point that wailing is the purest form of sociability.

LANGUAGE, CULTURE, AND HISTORY

Methodologies that use indigenous discourse have provided a new means of considering history that is not centered on the memories and perceptions of Western chroniclers. Several works by Ellen Basso, based upon recorded transcripts gathered in the Upper Xingú of Brazil between 1967 and 1982, apply the paradigm of discourse analysis to interpretations of Kalapalo history (Basso 1973, 1985, 1986, 1987). As the Kalapalo tales document, and as Basso's commentary reiterates, history is a discourse concerning war dead and their relations with the living. Recounting warfare, enemies, and cannibals, the Kalapalo tales ostensibly describe an earlier period in the lives of the Kalapalo, allowing them to distinguish themselves from violent others and a violent past. In contrast to their "fierce" neighbors—the club-carrying Gê speakers, for example—the restrained Kalapalo are, as they say, a people who fight only "with words" (Basso 1995: 15).

The Kalapalo tales illustrate the role of violence in boundary marking and the changing of parameters of self and other over time as the narratives of warfare reflect an ideological shift in the changing boundaries delineating the moral community. Violence as it is practiced by one group against another, or against an insider who has gone against his or her own, as in witchcraft, dramatizes inclusion and exclusion, the human community and its delimitations (Randall Collins 1974, Chernela 2001b, Chernela and Leed 2001; also see Whitehead and Wright 2004). The boundaries of the group mark the limit beyond which violence is allowed.

In 1961, when Brazil's showcase indigenous reserve, the Xingú National

Park (Parque Indígena do Xingú), was created, The Carib-speaking Kala-palo were brought into the proximity of formerly hostile groups. Basso demonstrates how an ideology and a discourse of reconciliation were constituted over time. The Kalapalo went from perceiving their neighbors as dangerous adversaries, against whose potential advances the Kalapalo had to defend themselves, to recognizing commonalities and describing their neighbors as being "like" the Kalapalo. The Kalapalo category *angikogo*, translated by Basso as "fierce," shifted the parameters of refer-ence as new communities and allegiances formed and the distinctions between one's own community and those of former strangers and ene-mies became blurred.

Basso emphasizes individuality in the construction of a dynamic "Native South American history." Today there are no palisaded villages, no violent battles, no torture of captives, no cannibalism, no grotesque muti-lations, and no trophy taking. "What we learn from Kalapalo stories about the past is that some [who were]. . . involved in warfare attempted to alter the patterns of raiding, kidnapping, and cannibalistic blood feuding by expanding the locus of ethical judgment so as to redefine themselves and their enemies as members of a single moral community" (1995: 21).

In several works Basso considers authorship in the production of cul-ture and history (1973, 1985, 1986, 1987, 1995). For Basso, the production and construction of narrative, like the production and construction of history, are emotionally charged processes in which meanings are negoti-ated, resisted, and debated by individual speakers. She recasts the relations and distinctions between society and the individual; her exploration con-cerns "voices and the cohesion and coherence that are created between them: how the narrators' descriptions of actions are connected to each other to form an intersubjective, emergent narrative process" (1995: 294). Basso rejects theories in which stories of the past represent "collectively accepted images that animate social life" (1995: 304). By foregrounding the personal life and performative goals of the speaker of the narrative, rather than presenting stories as though they were without individual authorship, she avoids presenting any one version as a generalized cultural product.

Yet another ethnologist who uses the products of speech in construct-ing several kinds of "histories" of native Brazilian societies is Robin Wright. Finding thematic commonalities in the speech products of the Baniwa of northern Brazil, including myth, curing chants, initiation chants, oral histories of contact, and life histories, Wright examines inter-nal ethnopoetic features as well as external features. Wright is particularly concerned with notions of temporality as they are found and expressed in these discursive forms. He finds three modalities of time, "primordial time," mythic time, and human history. In contrast to the French structuralist Lévi-Strauss's position, that indigenous peoples perceived histories as repetitive and cyclical, Wright finds that the world order as perceived and created by the Baniwa is not an eternally repeated cycle but "a constantly expanding and globalizing socialization of otherness within its domain" (1998: xiv). This point demonstrates how Baniwa mythic consciousness can explain Baniwa historic consciousness and the ongoing, historically designated definitions of self and other.

By examining "cosmic history" performed from memory in narratives and chants, Wright takes up the relationship between language, memory, and history to explore the millenarian consciousness of the Baniwa and the relationship of these beliefs to social action-history. Both mythic and historic narratives, then, provide the parameters of meaning for political strategies; among these political strategies Wright includes millenarian and messianic movements (see Pollock 1993).

For Wright, written European texts, as sources through which to understand mythic imagery, are essential to the interpretation of spoken narratives. Catastrophic visions in cosmic histories capture catastrophes in fact experienced by the Baniwa. In this way a deconstruction of European sources provides a means with which to understand the historic problems confronted by them and thereby the language of the millenarianists who would solve problems through utopian and miraculous solutions.

The historically oriented work of William Fisher exemplifies the new synthesis of the fin de siècle. Fisher combines economic, historical, and discursive data to return to a study of Gê social institutions and practice. Taking the Gê-speaking Kayapó as his example, Fisher (1996, 1998) argues that ideological and organizational features, formerly considered structurally fixed, or explained on the basis of adaptations to environmental features, must instead be situated historically. Social organization, Fisher argues, is an artifact of history.

Fisher attributes Kayapó social formations to what he calls a "politics of subsistence"—articulation within the larger context of frontier extractivism, characterized by boom-and-bust economic conditions. Fisher discusses the way in which Xikrin Kayapó collective institutions, outwardly timeless and traditional, have developed to engage with broader social networks under conditions of sporadic articulation or disarticulation (Fisher 1998). Fisher writes, "Xikrin are forced to collectively shoulder their isolation from access to goods under conditions that make such goods increasingly necessary. . . . Villagers do not suffer from ever-increasing market encroachment but from radical swings, as the extractivist economy of a particular locale expands or evaporates" (1998: 196). Dependence on Western manufactured goods plays a central role in Kayapó involvement in mining and logging their own lands. This dependency, however, is regarded by Fisher not as the attraction of an intrinsically superior Western technology nor as a corruption of traditional forms but as a form *generated* by the Kayapó themselves within a broader context of extractivism and reservation life.

Fisher's most recent book (2000) places the Gê peoples squarely within what Morton Fried referred to as the "tribal" context—a historic space created by contact between a state and a peripheral nonstate society. Thus, in a divergence from both the structuralist and adaptionist approaches to Gê before him, Fisher's analysis of the Xikrin Kayapó world sees social forms as responses to larger systems of power. Fisher argues that the contemporary system of men's societies and chiefly authority—considered by traditional Gê theorists before him to be "authentic" and "traditional"—requires Western manufactured items and their redistribution for its existence and reproduction. Fisher points to a continuity of Kayapó strategies at work in both commodity and discourse exchange.

A different paper that considers the place of indigenous peoples in emerging international politics also shows the analytic power and breadth of the discourse approach. In "The Shifting Middle Ground: Amazonian Indians and Eco-Politics" (1995), Beth Conklin and Laura Graham discuss emergent ideologies produced in the context of transnational and transcultural encounters as local Brazilian Amazonian struggles undergo processes of internationalization. Conklin and Graham find a useful analogy in Richard White's depiction of Indian-white relations in North America's Great Lakes region in the seventeenth through nineteenth centuries. There, White develops the concept of a "middle ground"—a mutually constructed arena of meaning born from the interactive communication processes of confrontation and negotiation (White 1991).

While it too produces creative innovation and collaboratively constructed meanings, the contemporary middle ground presented by Conklin and Graham is not anchored in the pragmatics of geography, economic interests, or national identities, as was that of White. Instead, the contemporary middle ground is a symbolic space in which images, rather than face-to-face encounters, mobilize political action and realign diverse actors across wide distances, languages, and cultures.

The authors identify a "new politics of the eco-Indian" that relies on a representation of the Brazilian Indian of the 1980s. In this system of signification, which joins native landscapes with native cultures, the idea of the Indian gained symbolic capital through international attempts to conserve diversity—both natural and cultural. In it indigenous people have become key symbols as well as participants in developing ideologies and organizational networks that link local Amazonian conflicts to international issues and social movements. This new middle ground, the authors argue, is forged in perceptions of the Other and the extent to which the Other can serve goals of joint political action. While the new Indian-environmentalist alliance in Brazil has benefited both environmentalist and indigenous interests, Conklin and Graham warn that the relationship, based as it is on strategic misrepresentation, is inherently unstable. It poses risks for indigenous peoples and their rights.

Conklin and Graham's insights into the potential for mutual opportunism in the indigenist/environmentalist alliance is based, in large part, on the Kayapó case. In 1988–89, working with the anthropologist Darrell Posey, the Kayapó were able to garner support from international environmental nongovernmental organizations (NGOs) in order to halt a hydroelectric project that would have inundated their territories (Fisher 1994; Rabben 1999, 2004). In a number of important publications Turner, whose work among the Kayapó spans four decades, discusses the creation of symbolic capital by the Kayapó for eloquent and skillful employ in political and economic negotiation. Turner demonstrates that Kayapó success in controlling their own representation surpasses mimesis as the Kayapó effectively produce "noble ecological rhetoric for . . . eco-patrons while secretly negotiating mahogany concessions" (1997: 120). Turner refers to Kayapó pragmatism as a "mixed portfolio" approach: "The Kayapó see as their best option . . . exploiting all opportunities for strengthening themselves economically, politically, and territorially through all available forms of trade, aid, and political action" (Turner 1997: 98). His analysis lends strong support to the arguments made by Conklin and Graham. No example better demonstrates the power accrued through acts of signification than Kayapó management of imagery and media representation.

Consideration of the linkage between indigenous peoples and the lands inhabited by them is not without consequence. The roles played by indigenous peoples in protecting their own lands are recognized in international instruments that protect their rights to these lands (including the UN–International Labour Organization convention 169 and the UN Draft Declaration on the Rights of Indigenous Peoples). With regard to the indigenous peoples of Brazil, the World Bank document "Integrated Project for the Protection of Indigenous Peoples and Land in the Amazon," authored in part by the anthropologist Judith Lisansky, links indigenous peoples and land in this manner: "traditional populations are an important part of a mosaic of solutions needed to promote environmental protection and sustainable development in the Amazon and other tropical forest regions" (World Bank 2002: 12).

Considering the fragility as well as the importance of the indigenous/ environmentalist alliance, Chernela (2001a) calls attention to the potential dangers when indigenous and environmental interests are pitted against one another to the advantage of economic ones. Chernela reviews Brazilian federal policies of the 1980s, when two conservation units were superimposed on indigenous lands in Roraima, creating bureaucratic ambiguities and allowing entry by commercial interests, including mining and tourism, into areas that would otherwise be off-limits to these activities (2001a).

LANGUAGE AND THE PRODUCTION OF HISTORY

Who makes culture? Who or what causes it to change? And, how is change perceived? Taking speech as their starting point in locating culture and culture change, the works of Basso, Fisher, Graham, Urban, and Wright use discourse to offer a new historical and ethnological synthesis with which to consider native South American society. The works address questions concerning the creative influences and emergent processes that contribute to a dynamic notion of culture, produced and reproduced by language. These works merge several strands of theory to capture the transitions, formations, and transformations of culture in time. Through a methodology centered on the act of listening, these works illustrate the extent to which history is representational, created in the practice of talk, and dependent upon the perspective of the speaker. The methodology provides an approach to culture as an ever-changing phenomenon.

Basso and Wright trace cultural reconfigurations over time and examine the role played by discourse in generating new meanings in oral traditions of the past when conditions force new and untried situations. The followers of the discourse approach are influenced by the historian Hayden White (1978), who contributed to the breakdown of the distinction between the so-called myths of nonliterate peoples and factual representations of Western histories. The discourse-centered approach emphasizes morphological features (the medium, not the message) as communicative in their own right. Insofar as the discourse-centered approach is concerned with language as a process through which individuals evolve and create social configurations, "experiencing time through social change" (Basso 1995:

294), Basso, Wright, and Fisher show it to be an especially appropriate analytic tool with which to explore the processes of historical consciousness.

As anthropology finds itself in a new millennium, peoples formerly portrayed by its scribes as "outside" or "without history" are now regarded as producers of history. The making of history may be described as a gastronomic process, or endocannibalism in which a speaker/writer consumes the past and produces it, anew, as "history." Authorship is either recalled or erased, depending upon custom and circumstance. The retrospective text will reveal the vantage point of the speaker, while the dialogic of speaker-listener (or writer-reader) re-creates the present and transforms a group's identity and juxtaposition in the world. The new product, history, sheds light on the present and bears consequence for the future. It is a kind of ethnophagy in which a people creates itself through memory, language, interpretation, and invention.

ABERTURA

At the close of the century, the relations of concern were no longer intra-community but, rather, the relations that link local levels with global ones. Works considering global processes and their impact on local communities began in the 1970s and increased in frequency through the 1990s. One of the earliest and most important of these is Shelton Davis's *Victims of the Miracle* (1977), an analysis of the penetration of economic development on Brazil's frontier in the decade before democratization. Davis describes the uneven distribution of benefits from the rapid growth of the Brazilian national economy during the 1970s, a phenomenon known as the "economic miracle." While this impressive growth advantaged large private, state, and multinational corporations, Davis argues, it neglected or adversely affected local populations, including Brazilian Indians, peasants, dispossessed migrants, and the urban poor. A related casualty of the unchecked growth of this period was the environment.

In 1979, João Figueiredo, then the president of Brazil, declared a public *abertura*, or opening, a period of public freedom of expression to accompany the gradual democratization of Brazil after nearly twenty years of military rule. The period provided a space for a new literature of reflection and criticism within the social sciences.

In his book *Before the Bulldozer* (1989), David Price closely examines a large development project of this period and its implications for local indigenous peoples, migrant farmers, and the forest. With the movement of the nation's capital to Brasília in the 1960s, the construction of new roads northward from that city in the 1970s and 1980s, and a population newly displaced by growing export agribusiness in the south, the population of the early 1980s pushed northward into the Amazon. Brazil Road 364, between Brasília and Porto Velho, capital of the western state of Rondô-nia, reduced costs of commercial transport and made new lands in the northwest accessible to ranchers and settlers. The paving of the road, completed in the 1980s, was linked to a large resettlement project that would bring unprecedented numbers of displaced landless people into the Amazonian state. The project brought with it devastating impacts on the indigenous tribes of the region, who were poorly prepared for the vast influx of newcomers brought into their midst through federal incentive programs. Conflicting claims by settlers and Indians over the same lands led to outbreaks of violence. Western diseases brought about epidemics and rapid population decimation among the newly contacted indigenous tribes. In the late 1980s, the colonization project, designed to improve the lives of the poor, resulted in high mortality and morbidity of indigenous people, frequent rates of crop failure by settlers, and the highest rates of deforestation ever recorded in Brazil. The project, known as Polonoroeste, brought worldwide criticism from development, environmental, and indigenous advocacy organizations. Price's firsthand account of Polonoroeste and his role as intermediary between the native Nambiquara, whose populations were devastated by the project, and national and international policy makers, remains one of the outstanding case histories, or "ethnographies," of a development project.

Among the groups most affected by BR 364 were the Wari, or Pakaa Nova, whose response to the impact of the development project is the subject of Beth Conklin's book, *Consuming Grief* (2001). Conklin recounts how contact with government-sponsored expeditions between 1956 and 1969 exposed the Wari to an onslaught of infectious diseases. In two to three years after sustained contact, hundreds of Wari died, leaving the population depleted by 60 percent. In this context, Conklin considers transformations in concepts and practices related to death, particularly cannibalism, a key symbol and organizing principle underlying Wari thought. While enduring the relentless presence of death during this period, the Wari were prohibited from practicing ritual cannibalism, a mortuary practice regarded by them as a "loving and compassionate way to deal with death and bereavement" (2001: xxviii). Conklin's sensitive review of one case of decimation and loss combines symbolic and interpretive approaches to convey the profound impact on systems of knowledge, relationships, and emotion wrought as a consequence of displacement by large projects such as BR 364.

During the period of *abertura,* many North American anthropologists followed their Brazilian colleagues in turning toward an "anthropology of engagement." A number of publications by Anthony Seeger, many in collaboration with students and colleagues at the Museu Nacional in Rio de Janeiro during his tenure there, exemplify a reflective scholarship in the service of practice (Seeger 1980, Viveiros de Castro et al. 1979). The growing involvement by anthropologists in global development discourse also drew many into advocacy roles. North American anthropologists worked closely with Brazilian colleagues in efforts to demarcate indigenous lands; to improve the access of indigenous peoples to educational, health, and other services; and to increase the political voice of indigenous people. Robin Wright, for example, collaborated with the local indigenous associations ACIRA[3] and FOIRN[4] in the recovery and publication of native-language narratives (ACIRA and FOIRN 1999). The anthropological linguist Gale Goodwin Gomez worked closely with the Brazilian organization CCPY,[5] first campaigning for the demarcation of Yanomami lands and later developing an innovative literacy program in the new Yanomami territories. In another north-south collaboration, Terence Turner and his students Catherine Howard and Lêda Martins actively participated in the defense of the Yanomami. Other anthropologists, including Shelton Davis, founder of the Anthropology Resource Center; David Maybury-Lewis, founder of Cultural Survival; Steve Schwartzman of the Environmental Defense Fund; Linda Rabben of Amnesty International; Jason Clay of the World Wildlife Fund (formerly of Cultural Survival); and David Cleary, of the Nature Conservancy, brought anthropology actively into the sector of international NGOs.

Motivated by an expectation that anthropologists can impart specialized knowledge that would improve the performance and accountability of multilateral development agencies, a number of anthropologists, including Shelton Davis, Daniel Gross, and Judith Lisansky, joined the multilateral banking sector. Davis, Gross, and Lisansky have contributed to World Bank policies and documents on indigenous peoples. Lisansky, for example, contributed to the World Bank–administered Integrated Project for the Protection of Indigenous Peoples and Lands in the Amazon, with links to FUNAI, the National Indian Foundation of Brazil. Since its inception in 1994 this collaboration resulted in the demarcation of fifty-nine indigenous territories covering a total area of forty-five million hectares. It is hoped that the application of anthropologerrey in public, policy-making arenas, from monitoring bank practices to influencing development policy, has served the interests of local indigenous communities that are affected by the policies.

Collapsing Frontiers

The case of BR 364 was observed internationally, but it was not unique. A process of technological transfer, road building, and geographic displacement that paralleled the case of BR 364 with equally, if not more, far-reaching consequences is recorded for the eastern Amazon basin by Marianne Schmink and Charles Wood. Their book *Contested Frontiers in Amazonia* (1992) traces economic and political changes brought about by the paving of the Belém-Brasília highway, PA 279. Whereas Brazil Road 364 started in Brasília and proceeded northwest, the Belém-Brasília highway proceeded northeast from Brasília, following the Atlantic coast of Brazil and linking previously disconnected rural areas with urban ones. One of the areas reached by the road was São Felix do Xingú, a small Amazon town in the southern part of the state of Pará. The fourteen-year study, coinciding with the end of the military regime, encompasses one of the most conflict-ridden periods of Brazilian frontier history. Documenting mining, migration and colonization in the northeast section of the Amazon basin, Schmink and Wood's 1992 book provides a scrupulously detailed account of the forces involved in the movement of growth-oriented capitalism to this remote region.

The book recounts events in the 1980s when tens of thousands of prospectors from the impoverished northeast invaded the productive gold deposits at Serra Pelada, located in an area under control of the then state-owned conglomerate Companhia Vale do Rio Doce. As the discovery of rich gold deposits set in motion a rush of new migrants, towns, and infrastructure across southern Pará, confrontations between peasants and ranchers over land gave way to conflicts between prospectors, Indians, and powerful mining companies over mineral exploration rights. The book describes confrontations between prospectors, mining companies, and Kayapó Indians over rights to gold deposits on state and reservation lands (see Cleary 1990). Schmink and Wood describe social and political transformations that resulted from the struggle by the Kayapó Indians to defend their lands, material also taken up in William Fisher (1996, 1998, 2000). Schmink and Wood's 1992 study closes with the explosive showdown between miners and the armed forces in 1984.

This period of Amazonian history, involving intense conflict over public lands, geographical displacement, private colonization, and massive gold rushes, profoundly transformed the social and economic character of the region. (See Lisansky 1990 and Moran 1981, 1983 for related discussions of the impact of migration and spontaneous colonization on small farmers along the Amazon's frontier.) These transformations are powerfully shown in the demographic, economic, and social changes brought about in the community of São Felix do Xingú during this period. The town of São Felix do Xingú is by no means atypical.[6] Not surprisingly, Schmink and Wood (1992) liken São Felix do Xingú to the Amazon community in the same state described by Wagley in his 1953 classic study, *Amazon Town*.

Coming Full Circle

A half-century of Brazilian anthropology closes where it began, with local-global integrations and interactions in which the local Amazonian community is a site exemplar.

When Charles Wagley published *Amazon Town: A Study of Man in the Tropics* in 1953, he intentionally obscured the name of his research site, using the pseudonym Itá, because he intended it to represent and stand for all Amazon towns. In describing one small underdeveloped community, Wagley believed that he was describing a region. We now know this town to be Gurupá. Wagley emphasized "lethargy" and "backwardness" in his depictions of Itá. He predicted, "People cannot continue to be illiterate, hungry . . . and deprived . . . without seeking in desperation for . . . rapid change" (1968 [1953]: 311). The last words of Wagley's *Introduction to Brazil* reiterate a Brazilian slogan of the era: "Brazil is rich but Brazilians are poor" (1968: 312). If Richard Pace's 1998 work, *The Struggle for Amazon Town: Gurupá Revisited*, is reliable, Wagley's observations were prescient and insightful. Pace—whose mentors included Wagley, as well as Wagley's student Marianne Schmink, and Conrad Kottak—is an appropriate bearer of the Wagley legacy.

In the twenty-five years that mark the separation of visits by Wagley and Pace, Gurupá experienced dramatic transformations. If Itá was passive, as portrayed by Wagley, Gurupá as portrayed by Pace is a town wrought with political upheaval. The two representations may be understood, as Pace regards them—not as the different perspectives of different researchers, each living within the intellectual context of his time, but rather as exemplifying two different sociological moments in the history of a town. In this sense, Wagley may be said to have "captured" one period, Pace another.

The studies of Gurupá and São Felix do Xingú make for relevant historical comparisons. Like the Schmink and Wood volume, Pace's book is about change itself. Pace follows the long-term processual changes from the 1950s to the 1980s, then the very specific changes that occurred between

1983 and 1991, the years of Pace's fieldwork. During that eight-year span, Pace writes, "Amazon town" had erupted into "a complex mosaic of social and environmental changes stemming from development programs, migration, deforestation, and social conflict" (1998: 3). Over less than a decade, the Amazon reverberated from the impact of massive development projects: "highways through virgin forest, colonization settlements, timber extraction, hydroelectric dams, cattle ranches, and mines" (1998: 3). The same conflicts, violence, and environmental destruction that ensued and are described in Schmink and Wood, affected Gurupá profoundly.

Pace examines the rise and fall of agriculture, ranching, and extractive industries, including rubber (*hevea brasiliensis*), cacao, lumber, and palm hearts (*Euterpe oleracea*). Each attempt at development was short-lived. In the transition between Itá and Gurupá, a large sawmill, a hearts-of-palm processing plant, and the state oil company opened, flourished temporarily, and went into decline. By the time of Pace's study, each of these had left the area. Overharvesting of extractive resources led in some cases to depletion of resources; in others market forces caused declines in product demand and reduced prices. A road, begun in the 1970s with the hope of connecting it to the Trans-Amazonian Highway, two hundred kilometers to the south, was canceled. Poverty, then, is the persistent feature, the common thread uniting the Itá of Wagley and the Gurupá of Pace. The time periods studied by each are characterized by high unemployment and underemployment. Together the two studies bracket, like two bookends, a period of greater prosperity than either of them witnesses.

To what extent is Itá/Gurupá representative of the Amazon? Does it reflect the processes and problems underlying its relation to the larger Brazilian society and to forces beyond national borders? May we treat Gurupá as the Amazonian case par excellence? If not, why? The area in and surrounding Wagley's "Amazon Town" is one of longest settled in the Amazon basin. Gurupá is located midway between the two largest concentrations of archaeological remains and early population density in the Amazon: Marajó Island and Santarém. This area shows the earliest known evidence of pottery making in the Americas. Permanent occupation of Gurupá can be traced to between 6000 and 4000 B.C. There is evidence that by 2000 B.C. the population cultivated numerous crops, including manioc, corn, rice, beans, sweet potatoes, peanuts, fruits, cotton, and tobacco. According to the findings of archaeologists, the population possessed large public works, including burial mounds, ceremonial art, specialization of labor, social ranking, and consolidated chiefdoms. This former Gurupá bears little resemblance to the Gurupá of today, but its import cannot be discounted. Itá/Gurupá, then, stands for the massive historical transitions experienced in the Amazon basin: both the indigenous communities that once thrived there and the contemporary populations, in part recipients of that population's genes and customs, that today "have adapted to the social conditions of poverty and underdevelopment" (Pace 1998: 161).

Perhaps due less to the typicality of Itá/Gurupá than to its visibility, problems there have been presented with a starkness that is muted elsewhere. Gurupá has seen development come and go. In many "Amazon towns" that better typify the region, it rarely, if ever, comes. Inhabitants there remain, in the words of Stephen Nugent, "the invisible people" (1993).

DISCUSSION AND CONCLUSION

Taking as the vehicle of its thesis one community in the Brazilian Amazon, each of the works reviewed here considers the question of societies long regarded as "peoples without history"—that is, small-scale societies lacking written historic documentation. Each of the treatments exemplifies a prevailing approach within the contested arena of anthropological authority. The ecologically grounded approaches of Meggers, Carneiro, Gross, and Roosevelt; the structuralist approaches of Maybury-Lewis and others of the Harvard Gê project; the psychosocial theorists Murphy, Kracke, and Gregor; the discourse approaches of Basso, Seeger, Urban, and Graham; the historical-development approaches of Fisher, Price, and Schmink and Wood represent refinements and advancements within a disputed field.

To bring "meaning" to a chain of events is as much a goal of Basso's narrative speakers as it is of Meggers, Maybury-Lewis, and other authors whose works are discussed here. Each is a well-made story with great depth of time and breadth of subject matter. The authors distinguish between events worthy and unworthy of reporting, as they collapse difference into similarity and find cause in event sequences to persuade the reader toward a moral or pedagogical position. Each author attempts to persuade by means of argumentation and draws upon evidence to substantiate or convince. However, the questions considered by each author, and, relatedly, the relevance of that which is considered "evidence," differs among them. Each author positions herself/himself vis-à-vis the subject matter as proximate or distant. Meggers, Carneiro, Gross, and Roosevelt, even in opposition to one another, exemplifying the "etic" behaviorist school, provide evidence of that which is "seen" and "heard" to convince the listener-reader of the argument. Facts are presented as though they speak for themselves or stand alone. In this "absence" of a narrator, the author gains authority. Least credence is awarded the native "insiders" because, as actors in their own narrative, their interests obscure their potential for insight.

For other anthropologists, the objects of investigation are the publicly and collectively subscribed-to models that societies produce to make sense of their own situations. Whereas a structural analysis deconstructs with care the underlying rules and categories of social thought and behavior, critics of structuralism would point to the tensions and dynamics within social systems, finding them in irreducible pluralities and oppositions inherent in social processes. In the discourse-centered approach, that which is the subject of analysis is the event as it exists in and through the performance of speech: what is said is the artifact of the event and the focus of analysis. For Basso and Wright, the problem is how people reconstruct the dead and the past and, in so doing, how they make history. We learn of death, dying, and killing from the point of view of victors and victims. In Basso's examples, warfare is a talked-about, highly personalized violence, embodying communicational and ritual aspects absent in the battles of states. Both Basso and Wright describe the attitudes of a people for whom death is always at the shoulder.

Anthropologists are translators of signs of many kinds. A linguistic distance separates an act, a code (linking meanings to sign vehicles), and the anthropologist's textual language—a "metacode," or a code about codes used to communicate "findings" to colleagues. Among the dangers of the long-distance approach is that relevant differences are collapsed into a constructed similitude. Social groups and actions, including fights with axes and without them, are organized into sets to achieve coherency of argument and minimize differences among them.

In the discourse approach, two fundamental problems are confronted: the production of culture and the production of the anthropological narrative. Addressing both issues has become crucial in contemporary anthropology. Focusing on the words and figures of speech employed by speakers to talk about their own situation may bridge, in part, the lacuna that regularly plagues anthropological description and analysis. By including as much material in closely worked translation as possible, and by paying greater attention to the translation process, the discourse approach attempts to give the data and the interpretation greater transparency.

The anthropological performance, like that of the oral historian, places conflict at the center of narrative, attempting to manage mortality through language and memory. That which is at stake on the anthropological battleground is nothing less than a violation of integrities. A collapse of boundaries between the disciplines of history and anthropology, linguistics and anthropology, and a number of other recent mergers and acquisitions, results in new syntheses that alter former arguments, alignments, and allegiances.

Acknowledgements

An earlier, Portuguese-language version of this paper was published in *O Brasil dos Brasilianistas* (2002 Editora Paz e Terra). The author wishes to thank organizers and editors of that volume, Rubens Antônio Barbosa, Marshall C. Eakin, and Paulo Roberto de Almeida.

Notes

1. Wagley's later work, concerned with race and class in Brazil, includes *Minorities in the New World: Six Case Studies* (1958, with M. Harris); *The Latin American Tradition: Essays on the Unity and Diversity of Latin American Culture* (1968); and *Race and Class in Rural Brazil* (1952/1964).

2. There is not ample opportunity to mention all publications resulting from this productive school. I mention but four: Bamberger 1986; J. A. Crocker 1977; Lave 1972; and Newton 2000.

3. ACIRA is the acronym for Associação das Comunidades Indígenas do Rio Aiarí, the Association of Indigenous Communities of the Aiarí River.

4. FOIRN is the acronym for Federação das Organizações Indígenas do Rio Negro, the Federation of Indigenous Organizations of the Rio Negro

5. CCPY is an acronym for Comissão Pro-Yanomami, a Brazilian NGO.

6. For other community studies see O'Reilly Sternberg's 1998 classic study of an Amazon island community; Nugent's 1993 political economy of an Amazon town based on extractive exports; Chernela's 2003b study of a central Amazon community that mobilizes, successfully, to protect its fisheries from export; and Kottak 1998 for a longitudinal study of change in a costal community.

References

ACIRA (Associação das Comunidades Indígenas do Rio Aiari) and FOIRN (Federação das Organizações Indígenas do Rio Negro). 1999. *Waferinaipe Ianhenke: a sabedoria dos nossos antepassados. Histórias dos Hohodene e dos Walipere-Dakenai do Rio Aiari. Coleção Narradores Indígenas do Rio Negro.* Vol. 3. São Gabriel da Cachoeira (AM): ISA/FOIRN.

Anderson, Anthony B., and D. A. Posey. 1985. "Manejo de cerrado pelos indios Kayapó." *Boletin Museu Paraense Emilio Goeldi*, Botanica 2, no. 1:77–98.

Balée, William. 1985. "Ka'apor ritual hunting." *Human Ecology* 13, no. 4:485–510.

———. 1986. "Cultural Forests of the Amazon." *Garden* 11, no. 6:12–14, 32.

———. 1987. "A etnobotanica quantitativa dos indios Tembe (Rio Gurupi, Para)." *Boletin Museu Paraense Emilio Goeldi*, Botanica 3, no. 1:29–50.

———. 1989. "Cultura na vegetação da Amazônia brasileira." Belém: Coleção Eduardo Galvão. Museu Parense Emilio Goeldi.

———. 1994. *Footprints of the Forest: Ka'apor Ethnobotany—The Historical Ecology of Plant Utilization by an Amazonian People.* New York: Columbia University Press.

Bamberger, Joan. 1986. "Naming and the Transmission of Status in a Central Brazilian Society." *Ethnology* 13:363–78.

Basso, Ellen B. 1973. *The Kalapalo Indians of Central Brazil.* New York: Holt, Rinehart and Winston.

———. 1985. *A Musical View of the Universe.* Philadelphia: University of Pennsylvania Press.

———. 1986. "Quoted Dialogues in Kalapalo Narrative Discourse." In *Native South American Discourse*, ed. Joel Sherzer and Greg Urban. Berlin: Mouton de Gruyter.

———. 1987a. *In Favor of Deceit.* Tucson: University of Arizona Press.

———. 1987b. "Musical Expression and Gender Identity in the Myth and Ritual of the Kalapalo of Central Brazil." In *Women and Music in Cross-Cultural Perspective*, ed. Ellen Koskoff. Westport, Conn.: Greenwood.

———. 1995. *The Last Cannibals: A South American Oral History.* Austin: University of Texas Press.

Carneiro, Robert L. 1957. "Subsistence and Social Structure: An Ecological Study of the Kuikuru Indians." Ph.D. diss., University of Michigan.

———. 1960. "Slash-and-Burn Agriculture: A Closer Look at Its Implications for Settlement Patterns." In *Men and Cultures*, ed. Anthony F. C. Wallace. Philadelphia: University of Pennsylvania Press.

———. 1961. "Slash-and-burn Cultivation Among the Kuikuru and Its Implications for Cultural Development in the Amazon Basin." In *The Evolution of Horticultural Systems in Native South America: Causes and Consequences*, ed. Johannes Wilbert. *Antropológica*, supp. no. 2:47–67.

———. 1970a. "A Theory of the Origin of the State." *Science* 69:733–38.

———. 1970b. "The Transition from Hunting to Horticulture in the Amazon Basin." *Proceedings of the Eighth International Congress of Anthropological and Ethnological Sciences,* Tokyo and Kyoto.

———. 1995. "The History of Ecological Interpretation of Amazonia: Does Roosevelt Have It Right?" In *Indigenous Peoples and the Future of Amazonia: An Ecological Anthropology of an Endangered World*, ed. Leslie Sponsel. Tucson: University of Arizona Press.

Chernela, Janet. 1982a. "Estrutura Social do Uaupés Brasileiro." *Anuário Antro-pológico/81* (Rio de Janeiro), ed. Roberto Cardoso de Oliveira. 81:59–69.

———. 1982b. "An Indigenous System of Forest and Fisheries Management in the Uaupés Basin of Brazil." *Cultural Survival Quarterly ("Deforestation: The Human Costs")* 6, no. 2: 17–18.

———. 1987. "Pesca e hierarquisação tribal no Alto Uaupés." In *SUMA: Etnológ-ica Brasileira.* Vol. 1, *Etnobiologia.* 2 edição. Darcy Ribeiro ed., (coord. Berta Ribeiro). Petrópolis: FINEP/Vozes.

———. 1989. "Managing Rivers of Hunger: The Importance of the Blackwater River Margin." In *Resource Management in Amazonia: Indigenous and Folk Strate-gies,* ed. William Balée and Darrell Posey. New York: New York Botanical Garden.

———. 1993. *The Wanano Indians of Brazil: A Sense of Space.* Austin: University of Texas Press.

———. 1994. "Tukanoan Know-how: The Importance of the Forested River Margin to Neotropical Fishing Populations." *National Geographic Research & Exploration* 10, no. 4:440–57.

———. 1997. "Ideal Speech Moments: A Woman's Narrative Performance in the Northwest Amazon." *Feminist Studies* 23, no. 1:73–96.

———. 2001a. "Fractured Lands: The Politics of Conservation in North-Central Brazil." *Entrecaminos: An Interdisciplinary Journal of Latin American Affairs* 6:27–40.

———. 2001b. "Piercing Distinctions: Making and Remaking the Social Contract in the North-West Amazon." In *Beyond the Visible and the Material: The Amer-indianization of Society in the Work of Peter Rivière,* ed. Laura M. Rival and Neil L. Whitehead. Oxford: Oxford University Press.

———. 2003a. "Language Ideology and Women's Speech: Talking Community in the Northwest Amazon." *American Anthropologist* 105, no. 4:794–806.

———. 2003b. "Innovative Local Protected Area Governance: Silves in the Cen-tral Brazilian Amazon." In *Innovative Governance: Indigenous Peoples, Local Communities, and Protected Areas,* eds. Hanna Jaireth and Dermot Smyth. New Delhi: IUCN, Ane Books.

Chernela, J., and E. Leed. 2001. "As Perdas da História." In *Pacificando o branco,* ed. Alcida Ramos and Bruce Albert. Brasília: Universidade de Brasília.

Cleary, David. 1990. *Anatomy of the Amazon Gold Rush.* Iowa City: University of Iowa Press.

Collins, Randall. 1974. *The Basics of Conflict Theory.* New York: Academic Press.

Coimbra, Carlos E. A. Jr., Nancy Flowers, Francisco M. Salzano, and Rocardo V. Santos. 2002. *The Xavante in Transition: Health, Ecology, and Bioanthropology in Brazil.* Ann Arbor: University of Michigan Press.

Conklin, Beth. 2001. *Consuming Grief: Compassionate Cannibalism in an Amazon-ian Society.* Austin: University of Texas Press.

Conklin, Beth A., and Laura R. Graham. 1995. "The Shifting Middle Ground: Ama-zonian Indians and Eco-Politics." *American Anthropologist* 97, no. 4:695–710.

Crocker, J. A. 1977. "My Brother the Parrot." In *The Social Use of Metaphor*, ed. J. D. Sapir and J. C. Crocker. Philadelphia: University of Pennsylvania Press.

Crocker, William. 1961. "The Canela Since Nimuendajú." *Anthropological Quarterly* 34, no. 2:69–84.

———. 1990. *The Canela (Eastern Timbira): An Ethnographic Introduction*. Smithsonian Contributions to Anthropology, 33. Washington, D.C.: Smithsonian Institution Press.

Crocker, William, and Jean Crocker. 1994. *The Canela: Bonding Through Ritual, Kinship and Sex*. New York: Harcourt Brace College.

———. 2004. *The Canela: Kinship, Ritual, and Sex in an Amazonian Tribe*. 2nd ed. Belmont, Calif.: Wadsworth.

Da Matta, Roberto. 1982. *A Divided World: Apinayé Social Structure*. Harvard Studies in Cultural Anthropology, 6. Cambridge, Mass.: Harvard University Press.

Davis, Shelton. 1977. *Victims of the Miracle*. Cambridge: Cambridge University Press.

Dole, Gertrude. 1983. "Some Aspects of Structure in Kuikuru Society." *Anthropologica* 59–62: 309–29.

Ferguson, R. Brian. 2004. "Forward." In *Women of the Forest* (thirtieth anniversary edition). New York: Columbia University Press.

Fisher, William H. 1994. "Megadevelopment, Environmentalism, and Resistance: The Institutional Context of Kayapó Indigenous Politics in Central Brazil." *Human Organization* 53, no. 3:220–32.

———. 1996. "Native Amazonians and the Making of the Amazon Wilderness: From Discourse of Riches and Sloth to Underdevelopment." In *Creating the Countryside: The Politics of Rural and Environmental Discourse*, ed. Melanie Dupuis and Peter Vandergeest. Philadelphia: Temple University Press.

———. 1998. "The Teleology of Kinship and Village Formation: Community Ideal and Practice Among the Northern Gê of Central Brazil." *South American Indian Studies* 5:52–59.

———. 2000. *Rain Forest Exchanges: Industry and Community on an Amazonian Frontier*. Washington, D.C.: Smithsonian Institution Press.

Flowers, Nancy M. 1983. Seasonal Factors in Subsistence, Nutrition, and Child Growth in a Central Brazilian Indian Community. In *Adaptive Responses of Native Amazonians*. R. B. Hames and W. T. Vickers, ed. New York: Academic Press.

———. 1994. Subsistence Strategy, Social Organization, and Warfare in Central Brazil. In *Amazonian Indians from Prehistory to the Present*. Anna C. Roosevelt, ed. Tucson: University of Arizona Press.

Flowers, Nancy M., Daniel R. Gross, Madeline Ritter, and Dennis Werner. 1982. Variation in Swidden Practices in Four Central Brazilian Societies. *Human Ecology* 10: 203–17.

Goldman, Irving. 1963. *The Cubeo*. Urbana-Champaign: University of Illinois Press.

————. 2004. *Cubeo Hehénewa Religious Thought: Metaphysics of a Northwestern Amazonian People.* New York: Columbia University Press.

Graham, Laura. 1986. "Three Modes of Shavante Vocal Expression: Wailing, Collective Singing, and Political Oratory." In *Native South American Discourse,* ed. J. Sherzer and G. Urban. Berlin: Mouton de Gruyter.

————. 1995. *Performing Dreams.* Austin: University of Texas Press.

Gregor, Thomas. 1977. *Mehinaku: The Drama of Daily Life in a Brazilian Indian Village.* Chicago: University of Chicago Press.

————. 1985. *Anxious Pleasures: The Sexual Lives of an Amazonian People.* Chicago: University of Chicago Press.

Gross, Daniel. 1975. "Protein Capture and Cultural Development in the Amazon Basin." *American Anthropologist* 77:526–49.

————. 1979. "A New Approach to Central Brazilian Social Organization." In *Brazil: Anthropological Perspectives,* ed. M. Margolis and W. Carter. New York: Columbia University Press.

————. 1983. "Village Movement in Relation to Resources in Amazonia." In *Adaptive Responses of Native Amazonians,* ed. Raymond B. Hames and William Vickers. New York: Academic Press.

Gross, D. R., G. Eiten, N. Flowers, M. F. Leoi, M. Ritter, and D. Werner. 1979. "Ecology and Acculturation Among Native Peoples of Central Brazil." *Science* 206:1043–50.

Heckenberger, Michael J. 1996. "War and Peace in the Shadow of Empire: Sociopolitical Change in the Upper Xingu of Southeastern Amazonia, A.D. 1400–2000." Ph.D. diss., University of Pittsburgh.

————. 2003. "The Enigma of the Great Cities: Body and State in Amazonia." *Tipití* 1, no. 1:27–58.

Heckenberger, M., Afukaka Kuikuro, Urissaapá Tabata Kuikuro, J. Christian Russell, Morgan Schmidt, Carlos Fausto, and Bruna Franchetto. 2003. "Amazonia 1492: Pristine Forest or Cultural Parkland?" *Science* 301:1645–46.

Henry, Jules. 1935. "A Kaingaing Text." *International Journal of American Linguistics* 8:172–218.

————. 1941. *Jungle People: A Kaingang Tribe of the Highlands of Brazil.* New York: Vintage.

Kottak, Conrad. 1998. *Assault on Paradise: Social Change in a Brazilian Village.* New York: McGraw Hill College Division.

Kracke, Waud. 1978. *Force and Persuasion: Leadership in an Amazonian Society.* Chicago: University of Chicago Press.

Lathrap, Donald. 1970. *The Upper Amazon.* London: Thames and Hudson.

Lave, Jean. 1972. "Some Suggestions for the Interpretation of Residence, Descent, and Exogamy Among the Eastern Timbira." *Proceedings of the 38th International Congress of Americanists* 3:341–45.

Lave, Jean, and Etienne Wenger. 1991. *Situated Learning: Legitimate Peripheral Participation.* Cambridge: Cambridge University Press.

Lévi-Strauss, Claude. 1944. "On Dual Organization in South America." *América Indígena* 4:37–47.

———. 1949. *Les Structures élementaires de la parenté*. Paris: Presses Universitaires de France.

———. 1958. *Anthropologie structurale*. Paris: Plon.

Lisansky, Judith. 1990. *Migrants to Amazonia: Spontaneous Colonization in the Brazilian Frontier*. Boulder, Colo.: Westview.

Lowie, Robert H. 1946a. "The Indians of Eastern Brazil," *Handbook of South American Indians*, Smithsonian Institution Bureau of American Ethnology, Bulletin 143, vol. 1:381–97.

———. 1946b. "The Northwestern and Central Ge." *Handbook of South American Indians*, Smithsonian Institution Bureau of American Ethnology, Bulletin 143, vol. 1:477–521.

Maybury-Lewis, David. 1960. "The Analysis of Dual Organizations: A Methodological Critique." *Bijdragen tot de Taal-, Land- en Volkenkunde* 116:17–44.

———. 1965a. *The Savage and the Innocent*. Cleveland: World.

———. 1965b. "Some Crucial Distinctions in Central Brazilian ethnology." *Anthropos* 60:340–58.

———. 1967. *Akwe-Shavante Society*. Oxford: Clarendon.

———. 1979. *Dialectical Societies: The Gê and Bororo of Central Brazil*. Cambridge, Mass.: Harvard University Press.

Margolis, Maxine, and William Carter. 1979. *Brazil: Anthropological Perspectives*. New York: Columbia University Press.

Meggers, Betty. 1954. "Environmental Limitation on the Development of Culture." *American Anthropologist* 56:801–24.

———. 1971. *Amazonia: Man and Culture in a Counterfeit Paradise*. Chicago: Aldine-Atherton.

———. 1974. "Environment and Culture in Amazonia." In *Man in the Amazon*, ed. Charles Wagley. Gainesville: University of Florida Press.

———. 1985. "Aboriginal Adaptation to Amazonia. *In Key Environments: Amazonia*, ed. G. T. Prance and T. E. Lovejoy. Oxford: Pergamon.

———. 1990. "Reconstrução do comportamento locacional pre-histórico na Amazônia." *Boletim do Museu Paraense Emilio Goeldi, Antropologia* 6, no. 2:183–203.

Meggers, Betty, and Clifford Evans. 1957. "Archeological Investigations at the Mouth of the Amazon." *Bureau of American Ethnology Bulletin*, 167. Smithsonian Institution, Washington, D.C.

Melatti, Julio C. 1972. *O Messianismo Krahó*. São Paulo: Editora Herder.

Moran, Emilio F. 1979. *Human Adaptability: An Introduction to Ecological Anthropology*. North Scituate, N.J.: Duxbury Press.

———. 1981. *Developing the Amazon*. Bloomington: Indiana University Press.

———. 1983. *The Dilemma of Amazonian Development*. Boulder, Colo.: Westview.

———. 1984. *The Ecosystem Concept in Anthropology*. Washington, D.C.: American Association for the Advancement of Science.

Murphy, Robert F. 1959. "Social Structure and Sex Antagonism." *Southwestern Journal of Anthropology* 15:89–98.

———. 1960. *Headhunter's Heritage: Social and Economic Change Among the Mundurucu Indians.* Berkeley: University of California Press.

———. 1961. "Deviancy and Social Control, I: What Makes Waru Run?" In *Native South Americans*, ed. Patricia Lyon. Boston: Little, Brown.

———. 1971. *The Dialectics of Social Life.* New York: Basic Books.

———. 1979. "Lineage and Lineality in Lowland South America." In *Brazil: Anthropological Perspectives, Essays in Honor of Charles Wagley*, ed. M. Margolis and W. Carter. New York: Columbia University Press.

Murphy, Robert, and Yolanda Murphy. 1954. "As condições atuais dos Mundurucu." Instituto de Antropologia e Etnologia do Pará, pub. 8. Belém do Pará.

———. 1974. *Women of the Forest.* New York: Columbia University Press.

Newton, Dolores. 2000. "Coleções e expedições vigiadas: os etnólogos no Conselho de Fiscalização das Expedições Artísticas e Científicas no Brasil." *Revista de Antropologia* 43, no. 1.

Nimuendajú, Curt. 1939. *The Apinayé.* Washington, D.C.: Catholic University of America.

———. 1942. *The Sherente.* Los Angeles: Southwest Museum.

———. 1946. *The Eastern Timbira.* Berkeley: University of California Press.

Nugent, Stephen. 1993. *Amazonian Caboclo Society: An Essay on Invisibility and Peasant Economy (Explorations in Anthropology).* London: Berg.

O'Reilly Sternberg, Hilgard. 1998. *A Agua e o homem na várzea do Careiro.* Belém, Pará: Museu Paraense Emilio Goeldi.

Pace, Richard. 1998. *The Struggle for Amazon Town: Gurupá Revisited.* Boulder, Colo.: Lynne Reinner.

Parker, E. 1992. "Forest Islands and Kayapó Resource Management in Amazonia: A Reappraisal of the Apete." *American Anthropologist* 94, no. 2:406–28.

Pollock, Donald. 1993. "Conversion in Amazonia." In *Conversion to Christianity: Anthropological and Historical Perspectives on a Great Transformation*, ed., Robert Hefner. Berkeley: University of California Press.

Posey, Darrell. 1982. "Keepers of the Forest." *New York Botanical Garden Magazine* 6, no. 1:18–24.

———. 1983a. "Indigenous Knowledge and Development: An Ideological Bridge to the Future." *Ciência e Cultura* 35, no. 3:877–94.

———. 1983b. "Indigenous Ecological Knowledge and Development of the Amazon." In *The Dilemma of Amazonian Development*, ed. E. Moran. Boulder, Colo.: Westview.

———. 1984a. "A preliminary report on diversified management of tropical forest by the Kayapó Indians of the Brazilian Amazon." *Advances in Economic Botany* 1:112–26.

———. 1984b. "Ethnoecology as Applied Anthropology in Amazonian Development." *Human Organization* 43, no. 2:95–107.

———. 1997. "The Kayapó." In *Indigenous Peoples and Sustainability: Cases and Actions.* IUCN Inter-Commission Task Force on Indigenous Peoples. Utrecht: International Books.

Price, David. 1989. *Before the Bulldozer: The Nambiquara Indians and the World Bank.* Cabin John, Md.: Seven Locks.

Rabben, Linda. 1999. *Unnatural Selection: The Yanomami, the Kayapó, and the Onslaught of Civilization.* Seattle: University of Washington Press.

———. 2004. *Brazil's Indians and the Onslaught of Civilization: The Yanomami and the Kayapó.* Seattle: University of Washington Press.

Roosevelt, A. 1980. *Parmana: Prehistoric Maize and Manioc Subsistence Along the Amazon and Orinoco.* New York: Academic Press.

———. 1987. "Chiefdoms in the Amazon and Orinoco." In *Chiefdoms in the Americas,* ed. R. D. Drennan and C. A. Uribe. Lanham, Md.: University Presses of America.

———. 1989. "Resource Management in Amazonia Before the Conquest." *Advances in Economic Botany* 7:30–62.

———. 1991a. *Moundbuilders of the Amazon.* San Diego, Calif.: Academic Press.

———. 1991b. "Determinismo ecológico na interpretação do desenvolvimento social indígena da Amazônia." In *Origems, adaptações, e diversidade biológica do homem nativo da Amazônia,* org. Walter Neves. Belém: Museu Paraense Emilio Goeldi: Coleção Emilie Snethlage.

Rubin, Joshua, Nancy M. Flowers, and Daniel R. Gross. 1986. "The Adaptive Dimensions of Leisure." *American Ethnologist* 13, no. 3: 524–36.

Santos, Ricardo V., Nancy M. Flowers, Carlos E. A. Coimbra Jr., and Silvia A. Gugelmin. 1997. "Tapirs, Tractors, and Tapes: The Changing Economy and Ecology of the Xavánte Indians of Central Brazil." *Human Ecology* 25: 545–66.

Schmink, Marianne, and Charles H. Wood. 1984. *Frontier Expansion in Amazonia.* Gainesville: University of Florida Press.

———. 1992. *Contested Frontiers in Amazonia.* New York: Columbia University Press.

Seeger, Anthony. 1975. "By Gê out of Africa: Ideologies of conception and Descent." Paper presented to the 74th annual meeting of the American Anthropological Association. Reprinted in Seeger 1980.

———. 1980. *Os índios e nós: estudos sobre sociedades tribais brasileiras.* Rio de Janeiro: Editora Campus.

———. 1981. *Nature and Society in Central Brazil: The Suya Indians of Mato Grosso.* Cambridge, Mass.: Harvard University Press.

———. 1987. *Why Suya Sing: A Musical Anthropology of an Amazonian People.* New York: Cambridge University Press.

Steward, Julian. 1948. "Culture Areas of the Tropical Forests." *Handbook of South American Indians.* Smithsonian Institution Bureau of American Ethnology, Bulletin 143, vol. 3:883–900.

———. 1949. "South American Cultures: An Interpretive Summary." *Handbook of*

South American Indians. Smithsonian Institution Bureau of American Ethnology, Bulletin 143, vol. 5:669–772.

Turner, Terence. 1979a. "The Gê and Bororo Societies as Dialectical Systems: A General Model." In *Dialectical Societies: The Gê and Bororo of Central Brazil*, ed. David Maybury-Lewis. Cambridge, Mass.: Harvard University Press.

———. 1979b. "Kinship, Household, and Community Structure Among the Kayapó." In *Dialectical Societies: The Gê and Bororo of Central Brazil*, ed. David Maybury-Lewis. Cambridge, Mass.: Harvard University Press.

———. 1995. "Social Body and Embodied Subject: The Production of Bodies, Actors and Society Among the Kayapó." *Cultural Anthropology* 10, no. 2:143–70.

———. 1997. "Self-representation, Media, and the Construction of a Local-Global Continuum by the Kayapó of Brazil." In *Indigenous Cultures in an Interconnected World*, ed. Claire Smith and Graeme Ward. Fulbright Symposium, July 24. Vancouver, B.C.: University of British Columbia Press.

———. 2003. "The Beautiful and the Common: Inequalities of Value and Revolving Hierarchy Among the Kayapó." *Tipití* 1, no. 1:11–26.

Urban, Greg. 1988a. "The Linguistic Anthropology of Native South America." *Annual Reviews of Anthropology* 17:283–307.

———. 1988b. "Ritual Wailing in Amerindian Brazil." *American Anthropologist* 90: 385–400.

———. 1991. *A Discourse-centered Approach to Culture: Native South American Myths and Rituals*. Austin: University of Texas Press.

Viveiros de Castro, E., A. Seeger, and E.B.V. Castro. 1979. "Terras e territórios indígenas no Brasil." *Revista Civilização Brasileira* 12, nos. 1–2: 101–14.

Wagley, Charles. 1951. "Cultural Influences in Population of Two Tupi Tribes." *Revista do Museu Paulista*, NS, 5:95–104.

———. 1953. *Amazon Town: A Study of Man in the Tropics*. New York: Macmillan. Reprinted 1976, New York: Oxford University Press.

———. 1968. *The Latin American Tradition: Essays on the Unity and Diversity of Latin American Culture*. New York: Columbia University Press.

———. 1971 [1963]. *An Introduction to Brazil*. New York: Columbia University Press.

———. 1972 [1952]. *Race and Class in Rural Brazil*. New York: Russell and Russell.

———. 1977. *Welcome of Tears: The Tapirape Indians of Central Brazil*. New York: Oxford University Press (translated to Portuguese 1988).

Wagley, Charles, ed. 1952. *Race and Class in Rural Brazil*. Paris: UNESCO.

———. 1974. *Man in the Amazon*. Gainesville: University of Florida Press.

Wagley, Charles, and Eduardo Galvão. 1949. *The Tenetehara Indians of Brazil: A Culture in Transition*. New York: Columbia University Press.

———. 1961. *Os índios Tenetehara (uma cultura em transição)*. Rio de Janeiro: Ministério de Educação e Cultura.

Wagley, Charles, and Marvin Harris. 1958. *Minorities in the New World: Six Case Studies.* New York: Columbia University Press.

Werner, Dennis. 1981. "Are Some People More Equal Than Others? Status Inequality among the Mekranoti of Central Brazil." *Journal of Anthropological Research* 37, no. 4: 360–73.

———. 1982a. "Leadership Inheritance and Acculturation among the Mekranoti of Central Brazil." *Human Organization* 41, no. 4: 342–45.

———. 1982b. "Chiefs and Presidents: A Comparison of Leadership Traits in the United States and among the Mekranoti-Kayapó of Central Brazil." *Ethos* 10, no. 2: 136–48.

———. 1983a. "Fertility and Pacification among the Mekranoti of Central Brazil." *Human Ecology* 11: 227–45.

———. 1983b. "Why Do the Mekranoti Trek?" In *Adaptive Responses of Native Amazonians.* R. B. Hames and W. T. Vickers, eds. New York: Academic Press.

———. 1984. *Amazon Journey: An Anthropologist's Year Among the Mekranoti Indians.* New York: Simon and Schuster.

Werner, Dennis W., Nancy M. Flowers, Madeline Ritter, and Daniel R. Gross. 1979. "Subsistence Productivity and Hunting Effort in Native South America." *Human Ecology* 7: 303–15.

White, Hayden. 1978. *Tropics of Discourse: Essays in Cultural Criticism.* Baltimore: Johns Hopkins University Press.

White, Richard. 1991. *The Middle Ground: Indians, Empires, and Republics in the Great Lakes Region, 1650–1815.* New York: Cambridge University Press.

Whitehead, Neil L., and Robin Wright. 2004. *In Darkness and Secrecy: The Anthropology of Assault Sorcery and Witchcraft in Amazonia.* Durham, N.C.: Duke University Press.

World Bank. 2002. *Lessons from the Rain Forest: Experiences of the Pilot Program to Conserve the Amazon and Atlantic Forests of Brazil.* World Bank Brazil Rain Forest Unit.

Wright, Robin. 1998. *Cosmos, Self, and History in Baniwa Religion: For Those Unborn.* Austin: University of Texas Press.

CHAPTER 9

~

The Brazilian Economic System
through U.S. Lenses

WERNER BAER *and* ROBERTO GUIMARÃES

Since 1945 the number of U.S. economists who have concentrated on the study of Brazil has been relatively small, even in periods when development economics was a popular field and area studies were getting substantial financial support from U.S. foundations and government agencies (such as the U.S. Agency for International Development). Many economists who devoted their research to Brazilian economic problems were associated with universities that had active centers for Latin American studies and/or economics departments that supported development economics as a field of specialty. Most prominent among such universities were Berkeley, Columbia, Illinois, Stanford, Texas, Vanderbilt, and Yale (through its Economic Growth Center).

The language barrier might be one explanation for the small number of U.S. economists who have concentrated their efforts on Brazil. One thus finds a much larger number of development studies devoted to countries whose official primary or secondary language is English. More important, however, is the bias against area studies among economists. The profession lays great weight on analytical techniques and specialization in fields (such as industrial organization, public finance, international trade, etc.). This has resulted in the perception by many economists that geographical area or country specialization would hinder professional advancement. This perception grew during the 1970s and 1980s. However, the rising interest in the 1990s in what has been called the "new institutionalism" in economics may in time lead to a more receptive climate toward those professionals specializing in a geographical area.

Despite these circumstances, it is remarkable that a small group of talented economists have devoted a large proportion of their professional activities to the study of the Brazilian economy. The attraction of Brazil's society and its institutions were stronger than professional ambitions, and in most cases the Brazilianist economists have had successful professional careers.

The bulk of Brazilian studies by U.S. economists and economic historians has concentrated on themes that originated with Brazilian scholars and/or criticizing Brazilian interpretations of some of the major economic issues arising during Brazil's development in the twentieth century. We shall review the U.S. contributions to the study of the Brazilian economy by dividing the topic according to some major issues. This chapter is organized as follows: in section 1 we concentrate on the economic history of Brazil; this is followed by a review of U.S. scholars' contribution to such postwar issues as industrialization, the role of foreign capital, and protectionism. Next comes an analysis of the literature on macroeconomic achievements and failures, and in the fourth section we look at the contributions to the study of the country's different stabilization programs. Finally, we review some of the major issues that Brazil faced during the last decade of the twentieth century and at the beginning of the twenty-first century, such as globalization, regionalization, and privatization.

1. Economic History of Brazil

Two U.S. economists have delved into certain aspects of Brazilian economic history before the twentieth century. Leff published two volumes of selected essays on the economic history of Brazil (Leff 1982), and some of his main themes reappeared in an essay in 1997 (Leff 1997). In his analysis of the Northeast, he blames the region's problems on the poor export performance of sugar and cotton, the products in which the region traditionally specialized, compared to the dynamism of coffee exports, whose production was located in the southeastern part of the country. Because the domestic resource costs of foreign exchange were lower in coffee than in sugar or cotton, Leff concludes that the Northeast suffered from an early example of the "Dutch Disease." He also raises interesting questions about why Brazil relied on foreign immigrants to supply labor to the booming southeastern coffee economy rather than on migrants from the poor Northeast, suggesting that this may have been because of the absence of capital market institutions to finance such migration and because of racial attitudes.

Leff's thesis about the "Dutch Disease" was disputed by Denslow (1974), who found fault with the nature of the data used and the way Leff interpreted them. Denslow made an important contribution to the study of the origins of regional inequality in Brazil that was originally published in Brazil (Denslow 1978). In a careful empirical study he contrasts the favorable demand and supply conditions for coffee in the Southeast and for sugar and cotton in the Northeast. He found that the decline of the Northeast's competitiveness in the world sugar market resulted from the high internal transportation costs, the low rate of fixed investment in sugar mills and in the ownership structure. In a similar fashion, the Northeast's cotton sector was disadvantaged by high internal transportation costs and by technological backwardness.

One of the major contributions by a U.S. scholar to the economic history of Brazil came from a professional historian—Dean (1969). Before the publication of his book on the industrialization of São Paulo, the standard interpretation of the country's economic history was that Brazil was a primary exporter until World War I. By diminishing imports and thus raising the relative prices of manufactured goods, the shock of the war caused the beginning of the country's industrialization process. Dean convincingly showed that industrial development had already started in the 1890s and that it was financed not only by traditional Paulista coffee planters but also by immigrant merchants. World War I did not result in more investments, as Brazil had no capital goods industry, but rather witnessed the more intensive use of already existing industrial capacity, especially in the textile and food/beverage industries. Later on the U.S.-Brazilian scholarly collaboration of Baer and Villela (1973) showed that despite the substantial early growth of Brazilian industry, one could only speak of "industrial growth" before the 1930s, since industry was not the engine of growth before that time. They stated that if one defines "industrialization" as a period when industry becomes the leading sector of the economy, then this process began only in the 1930s.

Another important study in the economic history of Brazil was made by a professional historian, Haber (1991). He examines the relationship between capital markets development and the industrial structure during the early stages of industrialization, contrasting Brazil, Mexico, and the United States. He shows that constraints placed on the formation of credit intermediaries in Latin America produced greater concentration in the Mexican and Brazilian cotton textile industries than that which developed in the United States. This was, according to Haber, the result of poorly defined property rights and government regulatory policies.

Steven Topik (1987) undertook a pioneering study of the role of the state in Brazil's economy during the late nineteenth century and the first three decades of the twentieth century. He examined the direct and indirect influence of the state in four sectors—finance, the coffee trade, railroads, and industry. Through these four case studies Topik showed that the conflicting interests of factions of among domestic elites and foreign investors led to far greater state participation than any of the participants originally desired.

A notable contribution to the study of Brazil's early industrialization was also made by Fishlow (1972a). He stressed the influence of inflationary finances in the 1890s and the importance of exchange rate fluctuations in stimulating the industrial growth that occurred at that period. He was also among the first economists to point out that World War I stimulated increased industrial output but did not increase industrial production capacity because of the existence of a capital goods industry. The essay also contains many insightful observations about the import-substitution process in the 1930s and during World War II.

2. Brazilian Postwar Development

2.1. Industrialization

The staff of the Cooke Mission from the United States, which visited Brazil in 1942 and 1943, undertook one of the early systematic analyses of the Brazilian economy. For the first time Brazil was analyzed from a spatial point of view, dividing the country into distinct regions. The mission pointed to a number of factors that constituted obstacles to growth (*Missão Cooke* 1949).

The first studies of Brazilian industrialization by U.S. scholars were characterized by controversy. Baer (1965) and Dean (1969) were among those who analyzed the early industrial period. Fishlow (1972a) also examined Brazil's early industrialization, pointing out the effects of inflation and exchange rate policies on the industrial growth during the last decade of the nineteenth century.

Baer (1965) was one of first U.S. scholars to undertake a systematic analysis of the industrialization process in Brazil. In addition to the distinction between industrial growth and industrialization, Baer emphasized the contributions of the Economic Commission for Latin America (ECLA). In his analysis of Brazil's industrialization, Baer sympathizes with ECLA's view of growth promotion: import-substitution industrialization

(ISI). Although he recognizes that in the short-run the ISI strategy tended to create many inefficiencies, some of which will be discussed later, he viewed the ISI as a way to modernize the economy, especially through the diversification of the economic structure. Finally, Baer explores the imbalances that resulted from the ISI period, namely, the worsening of regional imbalances, neglect of agriculture, neglect of the export sector, lack of labor absorption, and worsening of income distribution.

Leff (1968b) produced a study that covered the same period, concentrating on the different groups that influenced policy making with regard to agriculture, foreign capital, and industrialization. Huddle (1969) examined various minute subperiods of the post–World War II industrialization and found that import substitution was mainly concentrated in the middle to the late 1950s.

Other authors were more critical of the ISI process. Joel Bergsman (1970) concentrated his investigation on many of the criticisms described earlier, most notably the impact of exchange rate policies, in particular the role of exchange controls during the post–World War II period. Another in-depth study of exchange rate policies and their impact, both during and right after the ISI period, was done by Coes (1979).

Goldsmith and Wilson (1991) examine the partial industrialization in the Brazilian Northeast. They noted that the region had not overcome its stagnant economy and society. After centuries of isolation and dependence on sugar exports, the Northeast was integrated economically into Brazil between 1930 and 1960, and since then it has been partially industrialized. The regional industrial growth remains keyed to other parts of Brazil, and dependent politics distort the region's relations with Brasília.

Another strand of the literature on the Brazilian industrialization starts with the relative stagnation that took place during the 1960s. Most postmortems of ISI were pessimistic. In particular, orthodox critics viewed ISI itself as one of the major obstacles to the future industrial growth prospects of the economy, while others tended to focus on the problems caused or aggravated by the ISI strategy. Many of these issues are discussed in Baer (1972). An analysis of the achievements of this period is found in Syvrud (1974). He shows that, in contrast to the conventional wisdom, public investment expenditures were never cut back during the stabilization years after 1964, and the government actually increased the available infrastructure, which was dominated by government enterprises. He concludes by saying that it took three to four years until the results of such investments were felt.

2.2. ROLE OF FOREIGN DIRECT INVESTMENT
AND STATE ENTERPRISES

Gordon and Grommers (1962) and Baer (1965) were among the first U.S. scholars to examine the role of foreign capital in the Brazilian economy. The authors argue that Brazil had been open to foreign capital (mainly British) since independence. That capital was initially designed to build a financial, commercial, and transportation infrastructure that would allow the country to export its agricultural products more efficiently to world markets. Dean (1969) and Baer (1995) also noted that European capital was largely available to finance the growth of the textile industry during the early industrialization period.

Baer (1995) shows that during the 1920s foreign capital entered such sectors as cement, steel, and a number of other consumer durables. In addition, the government gave assistance, such as special tax treatment and subsidized loans, to firms in new sectors. During the 1930s the inflow of foreign capital came to a partial halt as the Great Depression unfolded. According to Baer (1995), this partially forced the government to introduce exchange controls and take other drastic actions to deal with the foreign debt.

The growth in foreign direct investment accelerated during World War II but became more significant in the late 1950s, especially with the balance-of-payment pressures that had started earlier in the decade. Baer (1995) also found that the importance of direct foreign loans grew, leading to increasing balance-of-payment difficulties. Accordingly, the early 1960s were a difficult period for foreign capital in Brazil since advocates of nationalist policies became increasingly vociferous and started to exert influence over economic policy. This led to a reduction in the overall level of foreign direct investment and detrimental consequences for the Brazilian economy. Baklanoff (1966) demonstrated that the massive infusion of private capital and know-how from abroad was an indispensable factor that sustained Brazil's industrial growth after 1954. He concluded that the earnings from foreign direct investments in Brazil were a modest price to pay for the powerful, growth-promoting impacts of foreign companies.

The industrialist reaction to foreign capital is reviewed in Baer and Simonsen (1966). After the new regime took over in 1964, the role of foreign capital was diminished in favor of state enterprises and external indebtedness. Nevertheless, the role of multinationals kept increasing throughout this period. The influential studies by Morley and Smith (1971, 1977a and b) compare the operations of U.S. multinationals in their U.S. and Brazilian plants. Morley and Smith found that the former were substantially more automated than the latter. They attributed this to scale differentials rather than cheap labor. In a study of Brazil's electrical technology, Newfarmer and Marsh (1979) compared multinational and domestic firms, and found that the latter employ more labor per unit of capital than the former. Despite the increasing importance of multinationals, foreign direct investment regained a major role only during the 1990s, with the opening of the economy.

Development economists often assert that the economic model adopted by Brazil differs substantially from that of the advanced Western countries because of the expanded role of the state in the economy. According to Baer, Kerstenetzsky, and Villela (1973), this was not the outcome of a preconceived strategy but rather the result of a number of circumstances that led the government increasingly to intervene in the economy. They argue that the initial level of state intervention was necessary, despite its inefficiencies, to promote industrialization and economic development from 1930 to 1960. The presence of state enterprises also provided the necessary infrastructure to make it easier for multinationals and domestic private capital to invest in other areas of the secondary sector. This complementarity of domestic private, public, and foreign capital, also known as *tripé* (tripod), is reviewed in Peter Evans (1979). With the gradual breakdown of the tripod in the 1970s and throughout the lost decade of the 1980s, many started to argue that the government should privatize a large part of its operations. The privatization of state enterprises that took place, some in the 1980s, but especially during the 1990s, is reviewed in Baer and Villela (1994) and by Baer (1995).

2.3. PROTECTIONISM

Protectionism has often been regarded as one of the major historical mistakes in Brazilian economic policy, especially during the ISI period. Most of the analyses of protectionism concentrate on the ISI period. Protectionism in Brazil took many different forms, from the Law of Similars to exchange controls. There were no quantitative restrictions on imports, and foreign exchange was freely available for most capital transactions circa 1945. With the industrialization of the economy and the frequent overvaluations of the cruzeiro, reviewed by Huddle (1964), the overall trend in economic policy became increasingly protectionist. The work by Joel Bergsman (1970) analyzes the role of trade policies in industrialization during this period. Exchange controls were introduced in 1947, and a system of import licensing was used to restrict demand. The consequences of these policies are also analyzed by Gordon and Grommers (1962).

Along with these forms of protectionism, Bergsman (1970) and Huddle (1964) examined in greater detail the introduction of a licensing system that, according to these authors, increasingly discouraged the importation of consumer goods, at that time considered superfluous. Bergsman (1970), Huddle (1964), and Baer (1995) conclude that by 1945–50, the Brazilian government exercised enough control to equilibrate the balance of payments. One of the immediate consequences of this was an increase in allegations of corruption and smuggling, studied by Gordon and Grommers (1962). The conclusions drawn from this period are that the exchange rate policy was in fact one of the main instruments to stimulate the import-substitution industrialization during the 1950s.

Another important policy tool was the Law of Similars, which, according to Gordon and Grommers (1962), was one of the most powerful incentives for foreign investors to move from importing to domestic production. Baer (1995) also discusses the impact of the Law of Similars as an incentive to vertical industrial integration and its role in the capital goods industry.

At a more general level, Bergsman (1970) and Baer (1995) argue that protectionism created obvious inefficiencies throughout the economy. The most remarkable one, emphasized by Baer, is the idea that protectionism inhibits the economy from taking full advantage of specialization, an idea embedded in the theory of comparative advantage. On the other hand, Huddle (1964) focused on the high cost in foreign exchange and the distortion of relative prices. More sophisticated quantitative measures of import substitution were the focus of Morley and Smith (1970). Finally, the role of special plans that targeted specific industries and sectors, best exemplified by the SALTE plan, is examined in Baer (1995).

3. Macroeconomic Problems

3.1. Critical Evaluations of Brazil's Import Substitution

A number of U.S. economists criticized Brazil's exaggerated ECLA approach to import substitution. Bergsman (1970) found that there was a substantial amount of inequality in the inter-industrial structure of protection, so that raw materials and capital goods received a very low or even negative protection, while finished consumer goods received very high protection. At the same time, Brazil seemed to have a high comparative advantage in many raw materials, iron and steel, and many capital goods. Direct government investment, subsidies, domestic procurement requirements, and various special treatments were used to induce investment in the production of many intermediate goods. Bergsman then concludes that "Brazil's experience differs from most other LDCs [Less Developed Countries]. . . . The import-substituting industrialization went beyond the state of consumer durables, where most other LDCs get 'stuck.'" (Bergsman 1970: 173). He noted, however, that many industries in which Brazil was already self-sufficient at the end of the Second World War received very high protection—mostly nondurable consumer goods—and the usual result was a deterioration of efficiency. He also found that high protection of consumer durable goods was shielding high taxes and high costs. The latter could have been avoided with less fragmentation and less complete import substitution. Bergman thus concluded that "removing *all* instances of very high protection could have cost Brazil very little in its industrialization and import substitution, and also could have produced great benefits by forcing older firms to improve their efficiency" (1970: 173).

One of the prevailing criticisms of import-substitution industrialization was that it was capital intensive and contributed to the worsening of Brazil's income distribution, which ultimately would result in a contrasting situation of expanded productive capacity but a low growth of demand. This would lead to long-term stagnation and was used as an explanation of the stagnation that prevailed from 1962 to 1968. Fishlow (1972a and b) was doubtful of this explanation. After examining the 1960s, he concluded that ISI was a cyclical process as "the sharper decline in investment than in income . . . ultimately leads demand to grow up to previous capacity and motivates new capital formation once more" (Fishlow 1972a: 350).

In another evaluation of the ISI process, Morley (1969) made a systematic study of its impact on the import demand function. Morley clearly revealed an increased sensitivity of imports to the country's growth rate and, with the structural changes that had resulted from ISI, a tendency for imports to grow more rapidly than output. He also found that by the 1960s Brazil had a low price elasticity of imports (probably as the country had not yet import-substituted in many sectors that produced inputs to the new industries). Major critics of Brazil's ISI process of the 1950s and early 1960s included Syvrud (1974), who stresses the many social and sectoral imbalances that resulted from the indiscriminate across-the-board industrialization, while agriculture, education, and exports were neglected.

3.2. INDUSTRY STUDIES

Over the decades following Brazil's ISI, a number of U.S. scholars engaged in specific industry studies. The idea of such monographs was to study, on a micro level, the implantation of a new industry—the absorption and adaptation of technology, the factors influencing productivity, and the impact on the rest of the economy. Stein (1957), Leff (1968a), and Tendler (1968) produced the earliest studies, concentrating on the textiles, capital goods, and electric power industries, respectively. Stein, a historian, produced a classic historical study of the textile industry, as it evolved from the middle of the nineteenth century to the middle of the twentieth century. Leff showed how a sophisticated industrial sector was able to achieve viability (lowering costs and increasing labor productivity) in a fairly short period of time. Tendler's study shows how the power sector, which was historically dominated by private firms, grew during the ISI period through the involvement of state enterprises. She also examines how these two ownership sectors coexisted for a long time with a large degree of stability and provided Brazil with increased electric-generating capacity. The study stresses that technology was the overriding variable that shaped the institutional development of the sector.

Baer (1969) produced a study of the country's steel industry. He traced the industry's economic history from being dominated at first by small private firms to becoming a gigantic provider of steel products to new firms established during the ISI period. This occurred mainly on the basis of the creation of large integrated state-owned enterprises. He then examined the impact of the industry on the rest of the economy and also the struggle to improve its efficiency.

The oil price revolution of the 1970s led Brazil to promote a gasoline substitution program by promoting the production of alcohol-driven cars, the alcohol based on sugar cane. This involved a coordinated program to make some technological adaptations to produce alcohol engines, to invest in distilleries, and to use a growing proportion of sugar cane destined for alcohol. Barzelay (1986) provides a study of how the Brazilian state managed to encourage and coordinate the multinationals, the Brazilian private sector, and state firms to produce a viable program in a relatively short period of time. For a while the majority of newly produced Brazilian cars ran on alcohol, until international oil prices began to decline again and made unfeasible a continuance of the program on the previous scale.

Many years after these studies Shapiro (1994) produced a monograph on the Brazilian automobile industry. She concentrated on the policies used by the government to attract multinationals and to stimulate the development of manufacturing of domestic components. Her study also shows how over time the industry's efficiency grew substantially after a precarious beginning.

All of these industry studies suggested that the Brazilian ISI process ultimately produced a viable industrial structure, able to compete on an international level. Doubts remained, however, about the capacity of Brazil to generate as well as absorb industrial technology. This is a topic treated by Amann and Baer (1999).

3.3. AGRICULTURAL STUDIES

G. Edward Schuh, formerly of Purdue University and now at the University of Minnesota, was both an activist scholar, who was most influential in the development of such agricultural training and research centers as Viçosa and Piracicaba, and a pioneer researcher on various aspects of Brazil's agricultural development. His classic work (Schuh 1970) is a mammoth survey of the development of the Brazilian agricultural sector through the 1960s, both its achievements and an analysis of obstacles to its development.

Knight (1971) produced a thorough study of technological change, public policy, and economic behavior in Brazil's agricultural sector. It is based on fieldwork done in Rio Grande do Sul. He found that while there was substantial scope for rapid gains in agricultural productivity, to achieve this would require more than the manipulation of the pricing system for agricultural commodities and inputs. It would require more research resources, better extension services, rural adult education, and, in some cases, land reform. Many of these would be implemented in the last two decades of the twentieth century.

Nicholls (1972) was another U.S. scholar who made some pioneering studies of Brazil's agriculture. He was a strong critic of government policies in the 1950s and early 1960s that neglected investments in agricultural infrastructure. With his Brazilian research partner, Ruy Miller Paiva, Nicholls also undertook a painstaking study of the functioning of Brazilian farms in various parts of the country. The results of this study and its rich supply of micro data are still being used by Brazilian and foreign scholars concerned with agricultural problems of the country (Nicholls and Paiva 1966).

Another influential critique of Brazilian agricultural policies in the 1950s and 1960s was made by Gordon W. Smith (1969). He advanced the thesis that Brazilian agricultural policy had relied excessively on market stimuli while neglecting education, research, land reform, and other structural factors. The analyses of Smith and other U.S. scholars would have a substantial influence on later institutional developments, such as EMBRAPA (Empresa Brasileira de Pesquisa Agropecuária).

In the 1980s Douglas H. Graham and his Brazilian colleagues (1987) updated these previous surveys of Brazil's agricultural sector, including the positive results of some institutional reforms that were made in the 1970s. In the 1990s two American scholars, joined by a Brazilian academic, carried out a pioneering study of property rights, land reform, and the resulting conflicts in Brazil's Amazon frontier (Alston, Libecap, and Mueller 2000). The book examines the institutional development involved in the process of land use and ownership in the Amazon region and shows how this phenomenon affects the behavior of economic agents.

3.4. OTHER INSTITUTIONAL STUDIES

A number of studies by U.S. economists were devoted to institutional developments that occurred during the decades of industrialization. Trebat (1983) produced a systematic analysis of the growth and impact of state enterprises, showing both their strength and weaknesses. An early analysis of financial market reforms was made by Ness (1974). Later on, Welch (1993) undertook a study of the growth of Brazil's capital markets, examining how Brazilian policy makers actively promoted financial market growth. He traced the evolution of the Brazilian capital market before and after the 1964–66 reforms. Welch found that the resulting strong financial market helped Brazil avoid the large capital flight experienced by many Latin American countries during the 1980s and 1990s.

3.5. INCOME DISTRIBUTION

U.S. economists' concern about Brazil's distribution of income had already been expressed in a number of publications in the 1960s. Baer (1965) showed how the ISI process worsened the concentration of assets and income that was inherited from the days when the country was mainly an exporter of primary goods. ISI attracted industries whose capital-labor ratio was much higher than that prevailing in the traditional sectors. Thus the income generated by these new industries was inevitably more concentrated than in the traditional sectors. Baer also called attention to the redistributing impact of Brazil's inflation: usually from the lower-income sectors to the government.

A very influential article on the distribution of income was published by Fishlow in 1972 (Fishlow 1972b). Examining the results of the 1970 census, he showed a pronounced increase in the concentration of income during the 1960s. This came as a shock to the policy makers at the time, since Brazil was in the midst of a boom (known as "the Brazilian miracle"). Fishlow blamed some of his findings on the austerity measures taken by the Brazilian military governments that fell heavily on the wage-earning classes. Fishlow's article had repercussions abroad and was the basis of some harsh criticisms of Brazil's economic policies by Robert McNamara, then-president of the World Bank, who stated that the country had neglected equity in favor of growth. The article caused a substantial debate in Brazil and led to many studies by Brazilian scholars on the topic. One of the best-known rebuttals of the Fishlow article was a book by Carlos Geraldo Langoni (1973); he claimed that most of the increased income concentration resulted from the government's success in promoting growth. This led to a substantial growth of demand for skilled labor, which was in short supply, and thus a large increase in the remuneration to that part of the labor force. This explanation tried to absolve government policies of responsibility for the increased income concentration and advocated the need for greater efforts in increasing investments in education.

Clements (1988) produced an interesting empirical study linking Brazil's trade strategies to employment and income distribution. Although he found that the promotion of nontraditional exports might lead to greater concentration of income, as these new exports had a higher capital-labor ratio than the traditional ones, he also showed that the low share of trade in the economy did not justify attributing much importance to the relation between trade and the distribution of income.

The income distribution question was revived again in the 1990s in connection with the country's adherence to neoliberal economic policies, especially privatization. A major question raised by a number of economists was whether the selling off of many state enterprises to large Brazilian groups and to foreign corporations resulted in an increased concentration of assets and income. Another issue was whether the treatment by regulatory agencies favored the domestic and foreign concessionaires at the expense of the public at large (see Baer and Villela 1994; Baer and Coes 2000).

4. Efforts at Stabilization

4.1. plans and their critics

With the sustained increases in inflation since the late 1950s, the study of the inflationary process became one of the most important topics for those studying the Brazilian economy, in particular the U.S. Brazilianists. In his analysis of the "Plano de Metas," Baer (1995) asserts that even though inflation imposed a cost on the economy, it helped finance the industrialization in this period (1957–59). Detailed studies focused almost exclusively on the inflation that started to flourish during the 1960s. Baer, Kerstenetzsky, and Simonsen (1965) was one of the early contributions to this literature. Baer (1967) analyzed the debate between monetarists and structuralists (a more recent account of this debate can be found in chapter 7 of Baer 1995). Another analysis of Brazilian inflation during the 1960s was by Samuel Morley (1971). He shows how the fight against inflation contributed to the relative stagnation of the Brazilian economy during that period.

Another sector of the literature looked at the propagation mechanisms of inflation, including the oligopolistic nature of some of the key sectors in the Brazilian economy that Baer (1995) studied, and the extensive work on indexation that I review shortly. The social aspects of inflation are discussed by Baer (1991).

The efforts at stabilization by the military regime that took over in 1964 are reviewed in Baer (1995, chapters 5–7). Baer shows that the primary objective of the regime was to bring the rate of inflation down and undertake structural reforms in the financial markets (including indexing). A somewhat similar interpretation is that of Fishlow (1974), while Syvrud (1974) examines the other achievements of the post-1964 policies.

The 1970s were characterized by the reluctance of Brazilian authorities to succumb to the oil shocks that afflicted the world economy. Fishlow (1986) presents a succinct analysis of that period, focusing on the adjustment of the Brazilian economy to the two oil shocks that occurred during the 1970s. Baer (1987) focused on the resurgence of inflation during 1974–86, and he (1995) gives an overview of economic policies and their consequences during the 1970s.

The early 1980s were characterized by stop-and-go in the conduct of economic policy, the increasing difficulties associated with the external debt, and the ever-increasing rate of inflation. The aforementioned work by Baer (1987) looks at this period and sets the stage for a better understanding of the events and circumstances that led to the unfolding of the Cruzado Plan. A comprehensive analysis of this period is also found in Nazmi (1996).

The Cruzado Plan caught the attention of many U.S. scholars who were interested in the study of Brazil's inflation. The Cruzado Plan was scrutinized by Cardoso and Dornbusch (1987), Knight (1987), Baer and Beckerman (1989), and Coes (1995). The authors show that the inability of the federal government to balance the budget was the main reason behind the Cruzado's fall. In addition, the authors argue that the price freeze was a mechanism that allowed the government to postpone possible fiscal adjustments at least until the November 1986 elections. Tanner (1994) also discusses the fiscal problems faced by the Brazilian federal government throughout the 1980s. More recent attempts to explain Brazilian inflation are included in the next two sections.

4.2. INDEXATION

With the persistence of inflation, there was a shift in research efforts, including that of Brazilianists, toward an understanding of the propagation mechanisms of inflation. This brought the experience with indexation in Brazil to the attention of many economists in the United States. Early exploratory contributions include Fishlow (1974) and Baer and Beckerman (1974, 1980). According to Baer and Beckerman, the early experience with indexation, which was supposed to minimize the distortions inherent in the dynamics of any inflationary process, appeared to be positive and even allowed a steady decline of inflation during the late 1960s. With the oil shocks and the growth of external debt in the early to mid-1970s, the authors argue that many of the detrimental impacts of indexation had begun to be felt throughout the economy, all associated with the difficulty of reducing inflation once it began to grow. Furthermore, Baer and Beckerman (1974, 1980) found that indexation was not perceived to be inflationary in the early periods because many other prices were not indexed, but once the fight for shares began, indexation practices rapidly spread throughout the economy, and indexation became a major propagation mechanism of inflation.

McNelis (1988) describes early models of indexing as well as more recent ones that call for less indexation of wages to prices in order to improve price and output stability. He then concentrates on recent experiences, first in countries that have long histories of indexing (including Brazil). Where deindexation worked, the costs of stabilization (involving both deindexation and fiscal correction) were recognized, and the political agreements permitted an acceptable distribution of these costs. Nazmi (1996) discusses indexation and its effects on wages and the exchange rate. In accordance with previous findings, he shows how indexation made it difficult for policy makers to reduce the inflation rate and to deindex the economy.

In an interesting study Smith (1985) examines the indexation of wages in manufacturing during 1964–78. He finds that wage indexation was widespread by the second half of the 1970s and, more important, that average nominal industrial wages kept ahead of inflation until 1978. More recent studies on indexation in Brazil include Coes (1995) and Baer (1995). Coes (1995) found that the Brazilian experience with indexation provided a mechanism for perpetuating the inertial component of inflation. He also argued that the widespread use of indexation throughout the economy forced policy makers to use several measures to deindex. These had limited success. Coes shows that the desired outcomes (reducing inflation, etc.) were harder to achieve than was anticipated. According to Coes, matters were made even more complicated by the large-scale budget deficits and the monetization of those during the period in question. Another important contribution on this can be found in Nazmi (1996).

4.3. RECENT ANALYSES

The post-Cruzado experience is analyzed in detail by Baer (1995), Coes (1995), and Nazmi (1996). The authors study the different attempts to reduce inflation after the failure of the Cruzado Plan. While Baer (1995) provides a somewhat detailed account of each stabilization plan that was implemented, Coes (1995) focuses on the underlying cause of their failure, namely, the lack of consistent fiscal policies in an indexed economy. Nazmi (1996) gives a general overview, focusing on such issues as exchange rate policy and the impact of inflation on public deficit financing. The authors associate the economic environment with the difficulty faced by policy makers in implementing the stabilization measures.

Coes (1995) argues that the Bresser Plan was characterized by the desire of the government (mainly the finance minister) to resume talks with the International Monetary Fund and adjust the government accounts by allowing the currency to depreciate and accepting a lower growth rate for the economy. He also concludes that the Bresser Plan did not propose any deindexation of the economy and, like the Cruzado Plan, relied on price and wage freezes. In addition, Baer (1995) shows that with the political pressures on the government, after the three-month wage freeze ended, wages went up and inflationary forces reappeared.

The next stabilization attempt discussed in the literature is the Verão Plan. According to Coes and Baer, the main difference between the Verão Plan and its predecessor is twofold. First, the new plan was more modest: the main goal was to prevent inflation from rising and gradually reduce the budget deficit. Another attempt to deindex the economy was made, this time according to Baer (1995) and Coes (1995), with very limited success. Shortly after the plan was announced (two months), inflation began to increase. The political implications of this are discussed in Baer (1995) and Coes (1995).

The next chapter in Brazil's recent economic history was the Collor Plan. This episode is discussed in Tanner (1994), Coes (1995), Baer (1995), and Nazmi (1996). Tanner (1994) examines the breakdown of the Brazilian government's budget-balancing mechanism, which it began to use in the mid-1980s. The government was unable to balance its budget through tax increases or expenditure decreases. Evidence presented in Tanner's paper suggests that the government began to rely on unannounced reductions in the indexed inflation compensation on its debt. These reductions can be thought of as an implicit default on domestically held debt. While the "temporary asset freeze" of the March 1990 Collor Plan was highly publicized as an instance of such a default, it was not the first time this occurred. Coes (1995) and Baer (1995) start their analyses with the sequence of events that set the stage for the Collor Plan, in particular how economic events at the end of the Sarney administration affected the outcome of the presidential election. Both authors also discuss the controversies surrounding the launching of the Collor Plan, especially the freeze of 80 percent of the economy's financial assets. According to both authors, without the appropriate resolution of the fiscal imbalances, the Collor Plan had practically failed by late 1990. The next attempt was named the Collor II Plan. The Collor II Plan is discussed by Baer (1995), Coes (1995), and Nazmi (1996). These authors focus on the main imbalances that persisted throughout this period and consequently the ineffectiveness of Collor II to reduce the inflation rate in a consistent fashion.

The latest chapter in the Brazilian stabilization plans, the Real Plan, is analyzed by Baer (1995), Coes (1995), Nazmi (1996), and Amman and Baer (1999). While the first three analyses are very preliminary, they already point to the fact that the success of the plan hinged, among other things, on fiscal consolidation. They also discussed potential problems associated with the real exchange rate appreciation that took place after the introduction of the real. With the benefit of hindsight, the real appreciation of the real is one of the main issues examined by Amman and Baer (1999). The authors describe the stabilization measures that led to the initial success of the real stabilization plan in eliminating inflation. They conclude by asserting that the exchange rate was used as an instrument that allowed structural disequilibria in various subsectors of the economy, in particular a rising current accounts deficit and a persistent public deficit. Finally, Amman and Baer (1999) look at how these factors created a set of contradictions that ultimately led to the eventual collapse of the Real Plan.

5. BRAZIL AND THE GLOBALIZATION TREND

Once Brazilian policy makers realized that there was a limit to ISI and that the country needed to diversify its exports (in the latter part of the 1960s), it set off on a road that would lead toward genuine globalization in the late 1980s. Globalization meant the opening of the economy to trade and investment without restrictions. This did not occur in the late 1960s and 1970s, but Brazil at the time began to use fiscal incentives and subsidized credit to promote export diversification. An early work on the topic was by Tyler (1976), who made a detailed study of the policies that led Brazil to diversify its exports, especially by promoting the export of manufactured goods.

Except for the narrative in Baer (1995), few U.S. writers have done much work on the impact of neoliberalism (i.e., the opening of the economy in the 1990s to both trade and investment) on the Brazilian economy. Baer and Maloney (1997) studied the impact of neoliberal policies on income distribution in Latin America. Their analysis of the immediate concentrating impact of those policies also applied to the Brazilian economy. In a similar fashion, the article by Baer and Hargis (1997), on capital flows to Latin America and the constraints they are placing on policy makers, was based to large extent on such cases as Brazil. Finally, the collaborative works of two Americans and one Brazilian have concentrated on the regional impact (within Brazil) of neoliberal policies (Baer, Haddad, and Hewings 1998; Haddad and Hewings 1998; Haddad, Hewings, and Baer 1999).

EVALUATION

U.S. economists who have devoted their time to the study of the Brazilian economy were part of a small proportion of the profession who were fascinated with the developmental problems of Third World countries. What was to many especially attractive about Brazil was the great variety of its economic problems and the often unorthodox ways in which attempts were made to resolve them. Our survey leads us to classify the U.S. Brazilianist economists into three groups: (a) those who examined Brazil's economic development from a critical efficiency point of view—stressing the distortions that resulted from excessive protectionism and state participation in the economy; (b) those who criticized the Brazilian economic experience from an equity point of view—stressing that both the ISI venture and its successive regimes did not tackle the problem of excessive income and asset concentration but actually worsened it; and (c) those who were less judgmental and were curious to gain a better understanding through their specialized studies of the dynamics of a giant country that is trying to modernize itself. All these approaches enriched the field of economic development and other subdisciplines in the economics profession.

CONCLUSION

Although Brazilianist economists have never been considered to partici-pate in the mainstream of the economics profession, their work has often been cited by mainstreamers who needed empirical examples to provide illustrations of their general insights of the development process and its obstacles. Their findings often changed the analytical focus in various sub-fields of economics, for example, the analysis of the country's experience with indexing; the impact of different exchange rate regimes; techniques of stabilization, and so on. And it is quite possible that the growing field called "the new institutional economics" will increasingly draw upon the type of historical-institutional studies that Brazilianists have undertaken since 1945.

REFERENCES

Alston, Lee J., Gary D. Libecap, and Bernardo Mueller. 2000. *Titles, Conflict, and Land Use: The Development of Property Rights and Land Reform on the Brazilian Amazon Frontier.* Ann Arbor: The University of Michigan Press.

Amann, Edmund, and Werner Baer. 1999. "From Technology Absorption to Tech-nology Production: Industrial Strategy and Technological Capacity in Brazil's Development Process." *Economia Aplicada* (January–March): 109–38.

Baer, Werner. 1965. *Industrialization and Economic Development in Brazil.* Home-wood, Ill.: Richard D. Irwin.

———. 1967. "The Inflationary Controversy in Latin America." *Latin American Research Review* (Spring): 3–25.

———. 1969. *The Development of the Brazilian Steel Industry.* Nashville, Tenn.: Vanderbilt University Press.

———. 1987. "The Resurgence of Inflation in Brazil, 1974–1986." *World Develop-ment* 15, no. 8 (August): 1007–34.

———. 1991. "Social Aspects of Latin American Inflation." *The Quarterly Review of Economics and Finance* 31, no. 3: 45–57.

———. 1995. *The Brazilian Economy: Growth and Development.* 4th ed. Westport, Conn.: Praeger.

Baer, Werner, and Paul Beckerman. 1974. "Indexing in Brazil." *World Development* 2, no. 12 (December): 35–47.

———. 1980. "The Trouble with Indexing: Reflections on the Recent Brazilian Experience." *World Development,.* September 8, no. 9 (September 8): 677–703.

———. 1989. "The Decline and Fall of the Cruzado." *World Development* 34, no. 1: 35–64.

Baer, Werner, and Donald V. Coes. 2000. "Privatization, Regulation and Income Distribution in Brazil." Paper presented at the Congress of the Latin American Studies Association, (LASA), March, Miami, Florida.

Baer, Werner, and Kent Hargis. 1997. "Form of External Capital and Economic Development in Latin America." *World Development* 25, no. 11 (November): 1805–20.

Baer, Werner, Isaac Kerstentzky, and Annibal V. Villela. 1973. "The Changing Role of the State in the Brazilian Economy." *World Development* (November): 23–24.

Baer, Werner, Isaac Kerstentzky, and Mario H. Simonsen. 1965. "Transportation and Inflation: A Study of Irrational Policy-Making in Brazil." *Economic Development and Cultural Change* (January): 188–202.

Baer, Werner, and William Maloney. 1997. "Neo-Liberalism and Income Distribution in Latin America.," *World Development* 25, no. 3 (March): 311–27.

Baer, Werner, and Mario H. Simonsen. 1966. "American Capital and Brazilian Nationalism." In *Foreign Investment in Latin America*, ed. Marvin D. Bernstein. New York: Alfred A. Knopf.

Baer, Werner, and Annibal Villela. 1973. "Industrial Growth and Industrialization: Revisions in the Stages of Brazil's Economic Development." *Journal of Developing Areas* (January): 217–34.

———. 1994. "Privatization and the Changing Role of the State in Brazil." In *Privatization in Latin America: New Roles for the Public and Private Sectors*, ed. Werner Baer and Melissa H. Birch. Westport, Conn.: Praeger.

Baer, Werner, Eduardo Haddad, and Geoffrey Hewings. 1998. "The Regional Impact of Neo-Liberal Policies in Brazil." *Economia Aplicada* (April–June).

Baklanoff, Eric N. 1966. "Foreign Private Investment and Industrialization in Brazil." In. *New Perspectives of Brazil*, ed. Eric N. Baklanoff. Nashville, Tenn.: Vanderbilt University Press.

Barzelay, Michael. 1986. *The Politicized Market Economy: Alcohol in Brazil's Energy Strategy*. Berkeley: University of California Press.

Bergsman, Joel. 1970. *Brazil: Industrialization and Trade Policies*. London: Oxford University Press.

Cardoso, Eliana A., and Rudiger Dornbusch. 1987. "Brazil's Tropical Plan." *The American Economic Review* 77, no. 2 (May): 288–92.

Clements, Benedict J. 1988. *Foreign Trade Strategies, Employment and Income Distribution in Brazil*. Westport, Conn.: Praeger.

Coes, Donald V. 1979. *The Impact of Price Uncertainty: A Study of Brazilian Exchange Rate Policy*. New York: Garland. Publishing, Inc.

———. 1995. *Macroeconomic Crises, Policies, and Growth in Brazil, 1964–90*. Washington, D.C.: The World Bank.

Dean, Warren. 1969. *The Industrialization of São Paulo, 1880–1945*. Austin: The University of Texas Press.

Denslow, David. 1974. "Sugar Production in Northeastern Brazil and Cuba, 1858/1908." Ph.D. diss., Yale University.

———. 1978. "As Exportações e a Origem do Padrão de Industrialização Regional do Brasil." In *Dimensões do Desenvolvimento Brasileiro*, ed. Werner Baer, Pedro Pinchas Geiger, and Paulo Roberto Haddad. Rio de Janeiro: Editora Campus. 21–63.

Evans, Peter. 1979. *Dependent Development: The Alliance of Multinational, State, and Local Capital in Brazil*. Princeton, N. J.: Princeton University Press.

Fishlow, Albert. 1972a. "Origins and Consequences of Import Substitution in Brazil." In *International Economics and Development: Essays in Honor of Raul Prebisch*, ed. Luis Eugenio Di Marco. New York: Academic Press.

————. 1972b. "Brazilian Size Distribution of Income." *American Economic Review* 62, no. 1–2 (May): 391–402.

————. 1974. "Indexing Brazilian Style: Inflation Without Tears." *Brookings Papers on Economic Activity*, vol. 1. Washington, D.C.: Brookings Institution.

————. 1986. "A Economía Política do Ajustamento Brasileiro aos choques do Petroleo." *Pesquisa e Planejamento Econômico* 16, no. 3 (Dezembro): 507–50.

Goldsmith, W., and R. Wilson. 1991. "Poverty and Distorted Industrialization in the Brazilian Northeast." *World Development* 19, no. 5 (May): 435–55.

Gordon, Lincoln, and Engelbert L. Grommers. 1962. *United States Manufacturing Investment in Brazil: the Impact of Brazilian Government Policies, 1946–1960*. Boston, Mass.: Division of Research, Graduate School of Business Administration, Harvard University.

Graham, Douglas H., Howard Gauthier, and Jose Roberto Mendonça de Barros. 1987. "Thirty Years of Agricultural Growth in Brazil: Crop Performance, Regional Profile and Recent Policy Review." *Economic Development and Cultural Change* 36, no. 1 (October): 1–34.

Haber, Stephen H. 1991. "Industrial Concentration and the Capital Markets: A Comparative Study of Brazil, Mexico, and the United States, 1830–1930." *Journal of Economic History* 51, no. 3:559–80.

Haddad, Eduardo, and Geoffrey Hewings. 1998. "Trade Liberalization and Regional Competitiveness in the Brazilian Economy." Paper presented at the 11th Advanced Institute in Regional Science—Summer Institute, Munich, August, München, Germany.

Haddad, Eduardo, Geoffrey Hewings, and Werner Baer. 1999. "Spatial Formation of the Brazilian Economy: Historical Overview and Future Trends." *Geographia Polonica* 72, no. 1.

Huddle, Donald. 1964. "Balança de Pagamentos e Controle de Câmbio no Brasil." *Revista Brasileira de Economia* (March): 5–40.

————. 1969. "Postwar Brazilian Industrialization: Growth Patterns, Inflation, and Sources of Stagnation," In *The Shaping of Modern Brazil*, ed. Eric Baklanoff. Baton Rouge: Louisiana State University Press.

Knight, Peter T. 1971. *Brazilian Agricultural Technology and Trade: A Study of Five Commodities*. New York: Praeger. Publishers.

————. 1987. *A Macroeconomic Evaluation of the Cruzado Plan*. Washington, D.C.: The World Bank.

Langoni, Carlos G. 1973. *Distribuição da renda e desenvolvimento econômico do Brasil*. Rio de Janeiro: Editôra Espressão e Cultura.

Leff, Nathaniel H. 1968a. *The Brazilian Capital Goods Industry, 1929–1964*. Cambridge, Mass.: Harvard University Press.

———. 1968b. *Economic Policy-Making and Development in Brazil, 1947–1964*. New York: John Wiley. & Sons, Inc.

———. 1982. *Underdevelopment and Development in Brazil*. 2 vols. London: George Allen and Unwin.

———. 1997. "Economic Development in Brazil, 1822–1913." In *How Latin America Fell Behind*, ed. Stephen Haber. Stanford, Calif.: Stanford University Press.

McNelis, Paul D. 1988. "Indexation and Stabilization: Theory and Experience." *World Bank Research Observer* (July).

Missão Cooke, A. 1949. Rio de Janeiro: Fundação Getúlio Vargas.

Morley, Samuel A. 1969. "Import Demand and Import Substitution in Brazil." In *The Economy of Brazil*, ed. Howard S. Ellis. Berkeley: University of California Press.

———. 1971. "Inflation and Stagnation in Brazil." *Economic Development and Cultural Change* (January): 184–203.

Morley, Samuel A., and Gordon W. Smith. 1970. "On the Measurement of Import Substitution." *American Economic Review* 60, no. 4 (September): 728–35.

———. 1971. "Import Substitution and Foreign Investment in Brazil." *Oxford Economic Papers* (March): 120–35.

———. 1977a. "The Choice of Technology: Multinational Firms in Brazil." *Economic Development and Cultural Change* (January).

———. 1977b. "Limited Search and the Technology Theories at Multinational Firms in Brazil." *Quarterly Journal of Economics* 91, no. 2 (May): 263–88.

Nazmi, Nader. 1996. "Brazilian Experiences with Inflation: 1964–94." In *Economic Policy and Stabilization in Latin America*. Armonk, N.Y.: M. E. Sharpe.

Ness, Walter L. 1974. "Financial Markets Innovation as a Development Strategy: Initial Results from the Brazilian Experience." *Economic Development and Cultural Change* (April): 453–72.

Newfarmer, Richard S., and Laurence C. Marsh. 1979. "Foreign Ownership, Market Structure and Industrial Performance: Brazil's Electrical Industry." Mimeograph. South Bend, Ind.: Department of Economics, University of Notre Dame, South Bend, Ind.

Nicholls, William H. 1972. "The Brazilian Agricultural Economy: Recent Performance and Policy." In *Brazil in the Sixties*, ed. Riordan Roett. Nashville, Tenn.: Vanderbilt University Press.

Nicholls, William H., and Ruy Miller Paiva. 1966. *Ninety-Nine Fazendas: The Structure and Productivity of Brazilian Agriculture, 1963*. Nashville, Tenn.: Graduate Center for Latin American Studies, Vanderbilt University, Graduate Center for Latin American Studies.

Schuh, G. Edward. 1970. *The Agricultural Development of Brazil*. New York: Praeger. Publishers.

Shapiro, Helen. 1994. *Engines of Growth: The State and Transnational Auto Companies in Brazil*. Cambridge: Cambridge University Press.

Smith, Gordon W. 1969. "Brazilian Agricultural Policy, 1950–1967." In *The Economy of Brazil*, ed. Howard S. Ellis. Berkeley: University of California Press.

Smith, Russell E. 1985. "Wage Indexation and Money Wages in Brazilian Manufacturing: 1946–1978." Ph.D. diss., University of Illinois, Urbana–Champaign.

Stein, Stanley. 1957. *The Brazilian Cotton Manufacture: Textile Enterprise in an Underdeveloped Area, 1850–1950*. Cambridge, Mass.: Harvard University Press.

Syvrud, Donald E. 1974. *Foundations of Brazilian Economic Growth*. Stanford, Calif.: Hoover Institution Press.

Tanner, Evan. 1994. "Balancing the Budget with Implicit Domestic Default: The Case of Brazil in the 1980s." *World Development* 22, no. 1: 85–98.

Tendler, Judith. 1968. *Electric Power in Brazil: Entrepreneurship in the Public Sector*. Cambridge, Mass.: Harvard University Press.

Topik, Steven. 1987. *The Political Economy of the Brazilian State, 1889–1930*. Austin: University of Texas Press.

Trebat, Thomas J. 1983. *Brazil's State-Owned Enterprises: A Case Study of the State as Entrepreneur*. Cambridge: Cambridge University Press.

Tyler, William G. 1976. *Manufactured Export Expansion and Industrialization in Brazil. Kieler Studien*. Institut für Weltwirtschaft an der Universität Kiel. Tübingen: J. C. B. Mohr.

Welch, John H. 1993. *Capital Markets in the Development Process: The Case of Brazil*. Pittsburgh, Pa.: University of Pittsburgh Press.

CHAPTER 10

~

Political Science and Sociology

MARSHALL C. EAKIN

Social science research by U.S. scholars on Brazil dates to the end of the nineteenth century but barely began to develop as an academic enterprise in the 1940s and 1950s.[1] Along with all of Latin American studies, scholarship in political science and sociology experienced a tremendous boom in the 1960s. By the 1970s, a substantial group of political scientists and sociologists working on Brazilian topics had emerged in the United States. This chapter looks at the development of U.S. scholarship on Brazil in political science and sociology, two disciplines that share some common empirical and theoretical interests but that also develop along very different lines.[2] My approach is not that of a practitioner trained in political science and sociology but that of a historian of social science who is reflecting on the rise of both fields as they are applied to the study of Brazil. As is true of the rest of this edited collection, the bias in this chapter is toward published monographs rather than articles and essays. This is somewhat misleading in the social sciences, given their orientation toward publication in article form. I will try to note key articles and edited collections throughout the chapter. Furthermore, the literature produced in the United States has emerged since 1945 in dialog with a much larger production by Brazilian social scientists. Consequently, this description is often like the analysis of one partner in a pair of dancers who are still on the dance floor. The essay is divided into six sections: (1) the "dissimilar origins" of the two disciplines, (2) the professionalization of studies of Brazil in the sixties, (3) the development and impact of dependency theories and authoritarianism on the two disciplines, (4) the evolution of political science since the mid-1980s, (5) the development of sociology during the same period, and, (6) the state of studies of Brazil in both disciplines today.

I. Dissimilar Origins

Although academic studies of government and politics date to the nineteenth century, the study of Latin American government and politics barely began to emerge around the time of the Second World War.[3] The first serious scholarly studies generally focused on government and regime types and relied heavily on the use of documents produced by Latin American governments. The section in the *Handbook of Latin American Studies* dealing with politics, in fact, began in the 1937 edition as "Government," became "Government and International Relations" in the mid-1960s, and split into two sections in the 1973 edition—"International Relations" and "Government and Politics."[4] In the 1940s, J. Lloyd Mecham (University of Texas) and Russell H. Fitzgibbon (University of California, Los Angeles), two of the major figures in the study of Latin American politics, served as coeditors (along with J. B. Childs of the Library of Congress) for these sections of the *Handbook*, with Philip B. Taylor Jr. and C. Neale Ronning sharing these duties across most of the 1950s, 1960s, and into the 1970s. The paucity of materials published in the United States on Brazil (or, for that matter, on Latin America) is striking. In 1945, the section editor, Asher N. Christensen, lamented that he "hoped that succeeding editions of this *Handbook* will be able to note a much wider interest and a more ample scholarly production. Up to now the political scientists of the United States who do not read Spanish have had to rely principally upon the interest, diligence, research, and findings of their colleagues in history, economics, and sociology."[5] The vast majority of the entries in the *Handbook* in the 1940s and 1950s were items published in Latin America.[6] Perhaps the greatest preoccupation of the U.S. scholars in the 1940s was the struggle between fascism, communism, and capitalist democracy, a reflection of the conflicts of the Second World War and the emergence of the Cold War in its aftermath. A sign of the growing professionalization of the field was the formation of the Latin American Conference within the American Political Science Association at the annual meeting in New York.[7]

The first major monograph that might be considered a study of Brazilian politics is Karl Loewenstein's *Brazil under Vargas* (1943). Like much of the early work on government and politics, Loewenstein's book is largely descriptive, historical, and normative. Although the study of Latin American politics by U.S. scholars developed slowly until the 1960s, the lack of work on Brazil is striking, even in comparison to the rest of Latin America. In a landmark book on the state of social science research on Latin America in the early 1960s, the chapter on political science does not list a single monograph on Brazil by a U.S. scholar other than Loewenstein's volume. There was certainly nothing in English to compare with Jacques Lambert's *Le Brésil, structure social et institutions politiques* (1953). Not until the publication of Robert Daland's *Brazilian Planning: Development Politics and Administration* in 1967 did another U.S. political scientist publish a book-length monograph on Brazil! Brazil did play a secondary role in the work of political scientists working on other regions of Latin America, especially those in comparative politics and international relations. The constant refrain of U.S. political scientists in their reviews of work by Latin Americans was the need for more empirical research, greater methodological rigor, and data collection.[8]

Like political scientists, U.S. sociologists were also slow to notice Latin America and to write about the region. The origins of sociological work on Brazil, however, were very different than those of political science. The early volumes of the *Handbook of Latin American Studies* in the 1930s and 1940s do not even have a section on sociology but rather a section on "labor and social welfare." Like the early interest in political science, the bibliographical and research orientation in these decades was on government-generated documentation on issues such as housing, employment, social security legislation, and working conditions. In the early 1950s, when the *Handbook* finally created a "Sociology" section, it was edited by one of the great figures of Brazilian and Latin American sociology in the United States—T. Lynn Smith. He was a key figure in a small but very important group of sociologists that began to take shape in the 1930s, figures who were the pioneers in U.S. social science research on Brazil.

Truly one of the pioneers in the field, Smith did his doctoral work at the University of Minnesota with one of the greatest figures of modern sociology, Pitirim A. Sorokin.[9] After taking a position at Louisiana State University (1931–47), Smith began working in Mexico and in the late 1930s traveled throughout Latin America. In Brazil, he befriended Arthur Ramos and brought him to LSU as a visiting professor in 1940. Ramos taught a course entitled "Races and Cultures of Brazil," which may have been the first sociology course on Latin America taught in the United States. In 1942, Smith went to Brazil as a functionary of the Auxiliary Foreign Service of the U.S. Department of State. The result was *Brazil: People and Institutions* one of the first booklength studies of Brazil by a sociologist in the United

States.[10] Smith returned to Brazil for fieldwork often and befriended or worked with nearly every major figure in Brazilian sociology, including Gilberto Freyre, Manuel Diégues Jr., and Fernando de Azevedo. In 1951, Smith and the historian Alexander Marchant coedited a landmark volume of essays, *Brazil: Portrait of Half a Continent*. The authors of the nineteen essays on everything from geography to education to literature is an all-star list of great intellectual figures in Brazilian studies in both the United States and Brazil at midcentury.[11] In 1947, Smith became one of a handful of Brazilianists hired by Vanderbilt University (along with Marchant) to create the Institute of Brazilian Studies. Smith moved to the University of Florida in 1949, where he remained until his death in 1976.[12]

A group of young U.S. sociologists did fieldwork or taught in Brazil in the 1930s and 1940s. The most important of these was Donald Pierson, a student of Robert E. Park's at the University of Chicago. Park was one of the most influential figures in the development of sociology in the United States. He visited Brazil in the early 1930s and then encouraged Pierson to do his dissertation on blacks as a part of a larger project that Park envisioned, an encyclopedia of the Negro. Pierson did his fieldwork in Bahia (1935–37) and then spent many years teaching at the Escola de Sociologia e Política. His dissertation was published as *Negroes in Brazil* (1940), a landmark book in both U.S. and Brazilian sociology. He also published, among other things, an ethnography of a Brazilian village (Pierson 1951). Pierson played a major role as an intermediary for sociologists in the United States and Brazil. Samuel H. Lowrie and Paul Vanorden Shaw were also key figures in the development of sociology in Brazil through their teaching at the Universidade de São Paulo in the 1930s (Mehrtens 2000).

Like political scientists, U.S. sociologists came to Brazilian studies with questions and methodological approaches that were very United States–centric. The interest in the Brazilian "negro," for example, emerged from the study of race relations in the United States (and, more specifically, Park's own ideological agenda).[13] U.S. social scientists stressed empirical fieldwork over theory, often criticizing Brazilian writers for their obsession with European theorists and the lack of "serious" data gathering through surveys and questionnaires. U.S. social scientists saw countries like Brazil—what would later be labeled "developing nations"—as essentially less developed versions of the United States and Western Europe. Whatever their flaws, these scholars of race relations began a long tradition that continues in the United States, although it now is more cultivated by political scientists and anthropologists than by sociologists (Twine 1998, Burdick 1998, Hanchard 1994).

Until the late 1950s, however, the number of political scientists and sociologists in the United States who did serious work on Brazil (or Latin America, for that matter) was tiny. Loewenstein's book on Vargas, Pierson's work, and Smith's sociological survey of Brazil were the only book-length scholarly studies in political science and sociology. (Surely more widely read and influential in the United States were the translations of Gilberto Freyre's *Casa-grande e senzala* and Euclides da Cunha's *Os sertões*, both published in the mid-1940s.) As late as 1960, perhaps only three or four departments offered a specialization in Latin American politics, and as one observer pointed out in 1967, "If all the books, articles, dissertations and other written efforts, excluding the massive histories of the colonial period and of the 19th century republics were gathered together in an easily accessible collection, a reasonably diligent and able graduate student would be able to read all of them during the typical period of graduate study and research" (Gomez 1967: 4). If that graduate student had been reading just the material on Brazil, she or he could have finished in a very short time. It would take a dramatic set of events in Latin America to get most North Americans to sit up and take notice of the region, and to attract significant numbers of social scientists to do their research there. Clearly, the triumph of Fidel Castro and the Cuban Revolution in 1959 was the defining moment in this transformation and in the rise of Latin American and Brazilian studies in the United States.

II. POLITICAL SCIENCE, SOCIOLOGY, AND THE BOOM

Like Latin American literature, Latin American studies in the United States experienced a boom in the 1960s. The Cuban Revolution, the rise of armed guerrilla insurgencies across the region, and the strenuous efforts of several U.S. presidents to respond to the threat of nationalism and leftist movements were powerful stimulants that helped bring Latin American studies into the mainstream of academia. In the aftermath of *Sputnik* in the late 1950s, Congress established the National Defense Education Act (NDEA), which specifically called for the creation of area studies centers and provided funding (that continues today) for these centers and graduate fellowships. NDEA funds, and monies from a wide variety of agencies and foundations (Ford, Rockefeller, Social Science Research Council, Doherty, Fulbright, Wenner-Gren, Tinker, to name a few) financed the education of hundreds of doctoral students in all fields.[14] At the same time, U.S. universities expanded dramatically with the coming of age of the "baby boomer" generation. Across the country, as universities expanded, they added Latin American specialists in all the traditional departments in the humanities and the social sciences. In this rush to find Latin Americanists, the vast majority of those trained and hired specialized in Spanish-speaking countries, but an important and growing number learned Portuguese and became Brazilianists (Lambert 1984: 9; Eakin 1998: 547–48).

By the late sixties nearly every political science and sociology department in major universities across the country had at least one Latin American specialist. This growth trend continued into the 1970s, and many large state universities (University of California, Los Angeles, and the universities of Texas and Florida, for example) had several Latin Americanists in their sociology and political science departments. Even in these larger programs, however, rarely did more than one of these scholars specialize in Brazil. As in most social science disciplines, the tendency was to hire a Brazilianist to complement the other Spanish American specialists. In political science, the tension that already existed between those who believed in training theorists who could apply their knowledge to any region and those who pushed "area studies" and a deep local knowledge continued in this period of growth. In the 1960s and 1970s the dramatic growth of area studies centers and programs, along with ample funding sources, to some extent attenuated this tension. To a large degree, however, the study of Latin American politics and government in these decades developed along with the subdiscipline of comparative politics.

In all the social sciences during the 1950s and early 1960s modernization theory dominated the intellectual landscape. Essentially, theorists assumed that economic, political, and social development moved inexorably along the path that they believed had been blazed by Western Europe and the United States in the eighteenth and nineteenth centuries. Modernization theory was spurred by the Cold War and the desire of Washington policy makers to remake the world in the image of the United States.[15] The theory was built on a powerful tautology. To become modern (i.e., like the developed North Atlantic nations), Latin American countries needed to become less traditional. They had to adopt the values of the developed world—achievement over ascription, rationality over emotion, rational self-interest, and the profit motive. As Gary Wynia has pointed out, "It was assumed in the 1960s that economic development could be accelerated throughout Latin America and that revolution could be prevented" with assistance from the United States, hence the creation in 1961 by John F. Kennedy of the Alliance for Progress (Wynia 1992: 629). Modernization theory assumed that economic development would engender the development of political democracy. Many of the new scholars turned their attention to studies of political parties and interest groups, in particular, the military and the Catholic Church, as well as students, workers, and peasants.

In the late 1960s and early 1970s a new generation of Brazilianists began to appear in the United States, and book-length monographs became a regular feature of academic publishing in political science. Although much of the fieldwork was undertaken in the 1960s, most of these new books appeared in the early 1970s. In addition to Daland's book on bureaucracy and planning (1967), these included Lawrence S. Graham's work on the Brazilian civil service (1968); both works focus on the fairly traditional concerns of earlier decades—government structures and bureaucracy. In quick succession, books by Ronald M. Schneider (1971), Schmitter (1971), Roett (1972a, 1972b), Stepan (1971), and Bruneau (1974) appeared, analyzing interest groups, the military, the Catholic Church, foreign aid, and the structure of politics in Brazil.[16] Although they were not by political scientists, the works of Wirth (1970) and Page (1972) were also influential in the study of politics. While much of the literature on Latin America in the sixties focused on the rise of revolution, the central preoccupation of much of the work on Brazil was explaining the collapse of democratic politics there in 1964 and an attempt to understand the nature and direction of the military regime. Stepan's work, in particular, was widely read by Latin American specialists and scholars of comparative politics in general.

Despite the early concern of sociologists with Brazil, especially its race relations, sociology was slow to develop a cohort of scholars with a concentration on Brazil. One very prominent sociologist who published on Brazil in the 1960s was Irving Louis Horowitz. A major figure in the discipline in the United States, Horowitz published a volume on the eve of the military coup, ironically entitled *Revolution in Brazil*. A mix of his own analysis and writings by Brazilians, the 1964 book is one of the few book-length sociological studies of Brazil in the 1960s. Of the small group of sociologists who did work in Brazil, most tended to focus on issues of rural development. To some extent, this reflected the interest in development issues of the U.S. government in the postwar era and the priorities of funding agencies. Eugene Wilkening (1968), John Van Dyke Saunders (1971), and Bert Ellenbogen (1964), for example, wrote important books in the 1950s and 1960s on rural issues. Joseph Kahl's work (1968) is an excellent example of the effort to apply modernization theory to Brazil (and Mexico) and to measure the progress of modernity. Even more than the political scientists, the sociologists published their findings as articles and working papers and produced very few books.

By the late 1960s and early 1970s, modernization theory was already under serious attack. Barrington Moore's landmark *Social Origins of Dictatorship and Democracy* (1966) and Guillermo O'Donnell's *Modernization and Bureaucratic-Authoritarianism* (1973) provided powerful intellectual challenges to modernization theory. The collapse of civilian governments and the rise of military regimes all across the region also forced both academics and policy makers to question the logic of modernization theory.

III. The Era of Dependency Theory and Authoritarianism

Along with the boom in Latin American studies in the 1960s, powerful new theories challenged modernization theory as the central paradigm in the social sciences. By the late sixties, a dynamic and innovative intellectual debate arose that eventually gave rise to Latin America's most influential contribution to Western social science—dependency theory. Although it was but one of many theoretical approaches during this period, it was clearly the most influential. The collapse of civilian regimes across the regime, beginning with the military coup in Brazil in 1964, was a powerful force leading to disillusionment with modernization theory's equation of economic development and political democracy. In reality, there emerged a wide variety of dependency theories. To a large degree, they owe their intellectual origins to a variety of influences, in particular, the writings of Raúl Prebisch and the Economic Commission on Latin America (ECLA) in the 1950s, Marxist writings, and theories of imperialism.[17] The single most influential book in the rise of dependency analysis, in fact, was coauthored by the Brazilian sociologist who later became president of Brazil, Fernando Henrique Cardoso (Cardoso and Faletto 1969). By the early 1970s, dependency analysis had become the dominant theoretical paradigm across Latin America, and it had enormous influence among social scientists in the United States. For the first time, work on Latin American politics and sociology influenced the development of the disciplines in the United States. As Arturo Valenzuela has observed, "Rather than being a stepchild of area studies programs and a discipline incapable of generating more universal conceptual insights, Latin American studies would now have a distinct impact on the work in comparative politics and international relations dealing with the Third World. Whereas in the 1960s specialists on Asia and Africa were thought to be the real innovators, in the 1970's the work of Latin Americanists received considerable attention" (1988: 71). In the United States, dependency theory often became a political dividing line in academia with older, more

conservative scholars opposing it and younger, more radical ones enthu-
siastically embracing it.

To some degree, it also exacerbated the old criticism of Latin American social scientists as too theoretical and essayistic, and as not as empirical and data-driven as their North American counterparts. It moved
social science research away from a focus on the individual, the group,
and values (so characteristic of modernization theory) and to much larger
questions:

> Dependency writings called for a broad interdisciplinary perspective to
> explain the major themes of Latin American reality: economic underdevel-
> opment, social inequality, political instability, and authoritarianism. They
> argued that change could best be understood as part and parcel of the glo-
> bal historical process of development. Change could not be understood by
> focusing on individual societies as the basic units of analysis. It was neces-
> sary to situate countries within a global context, stressing the fact that Latin
> America evolved on the periphery of the world system. External factors
> stemming from the international economic order affected in a complex and
> often dialectical fashion domestic factors, conditioning the prospects for
> self-sustained development. (Valenzuela 1988: 71)

This approach reinforced an older Latin American tradition in the social
sciences of collective research projects undertaken in research centers (such
as the Consejo Latinoamericano de Ciencias Sociales), as opposed to the
more individualistic approach of U.S. social scientists.

As Frances Hagopian has pointed out, much of the literature produced
since the 1960s focused on "the causes and consequences of the authoritarian turn of 1964" (1996: 230). One of the most important research
issues to arise from this intellectual transformation was the role of the state
and, more specifically, the rise of what became known as bureaucratic
authoritarianism. As civilian regimes collapsed across the region in the late
sixties and early seventies, social scientists attempted to explain the collapse
of democracy. Guillermo O'Donnell's *Modernization and Bureaucratic-
Authoritarianism: Studies in South American Politics* (1973) initiated more
than a decade of studies of the subject and was probably the second most
influential book published by a Latin American social scientist after Cardoso and Faletto's. The 1964 military coup in Brazil stimulated a series of
studies by U.S. scholars, as discussed earlier, and the Brazilian case was one
of the two (along with Argentina) that formed the focus of O'Donnell's
landmark study.

One of the most ambitious projects to come out of this period was a series of volumes on the "breakdown of democratic regimes" in Europe and Latin America by Juan J. Linz and Alfred Stepan. The authors in this widely read series stressed a "voluntarist" perspective. In the volume for Latin America, Stepan built on his knowledge of the military to analyze the Brazilian case. His analysis of the 1964 coup in Brazil emphasized the "poor civilian political leadership" in the early 1960s (Linz and Stepan 1978). One of the most influential works during this period, *Authoritarian Brazil*, brought together leading U.S. and Latin American scholars to assess all aspects of the Brazilian military regime (Stepan 1973). Along with another edited collection, *The New Authoritarianism in Latin America* (Collier 1973), *Authoritarian Brazil* brought together a group of outstanding essays that sought to understand the rise of authoritarian governments in Latin America, a trend that continued as these volumes appeared.

The turn to bureaucratic authoritarianism also led to a renewed interest in Iberian and Ibero-American patrimonialism and corporatism. For one group of scholars, these new authoritarian regimes simply reinforced the centuries-old corporatist ethos and structures of Iberian and Ibero-American societies. The most forceful advocate of this position was Howard Wiarda, a political scientist eventually associated with the conservative American Enterprise Institute (Wiarda 1977, 1997). Much more influential was Schmitter's *Interest Conflict and Political Change in Brazil* (1971). In the late seventies and eighties, scholars began to analyze the breakdown of authoritarian regimes and the transition to civilian rule (Malloy 1977, Bruneau and Faucher 1981, Stepan 1989, Selcher 1986).

Studies of Brazil under military rule also often blurred disciplinary boundaries. Thomas Skidmore's classic *Politics in Brazil, 1930–64* (1967) drew extensively on the work of political scientists, sociologists, and economists and, in turn, was widely used by them. The same could be said about the follow-up volume, *The Politics of Military Rule in Brazil, 1964–85* (1988). Peter Flynn's *Brazil: A Political Analysis* (1978), although written by a political scientist, is really a political history of post-1889 Brazil. The same could be said of Ronald M. Schneider's more recent *"Order and Progress": A Political History of Brazil* (1991). In some cases, this interest in authoritarian regimes provided new ways to look at old topics. Kenneth Erickson's 1977 work on labor movements, David Fleischer's on political elites (1972), and Peter McDonough's on bureaucratic systems (1981) are good examples of this research.[18]

Sociologists also turned to dependency theory to analyze Brazil. One of the most widely read books in all of Latin American studies since the

1980s is Peter Evans's *Dependent Development* (1979), a sweeping analysis of the "alliance of multinational, state, and local capital in Brazil." Evans consciously draws on the work of Cardoso and Faletto as well as Brazilian sociologists, in particular, Florestan Fernandes (1963), to explain the rise of the so-called Brazilian miracle under military rule in the late 1960s and early 1970s. Evans's global and interdisciplinary dependency analysis owes a greater intellectual debt to Brazilian and Latin American social theorists than to his North American predecessors such as T. Lynn Smith. One unexpected result of the authoritarian rule in Latin America, in retrospect, was greater collaboration and connections among Latin American and North American social scientists. North American scholars often had access to fieldwork conditions that were systematically denied to their Latin American colleagues, and the Latin Americans found themselves teaching in North American universities as they went into exile. Universities, the Woodrow Wilson Center, the Inter-American Foundation, and the Social Science Research Council, for example, provided critical institutional support for making these connections and fostering collaboration (Valenzuela 1988: 74).

Unlike political science, sociology did not develop a strong subspecialty in Latin American studies during or after the boom. As Alejandro Portes describes it:

> Unlike history, anthropology, and, to a lesser extent, political science, North American sociology has never developed a strong subspecialty on Latin America. At the start of the seventies, the field consisted in the United States of two frequently warring groups: first, mainstream scholars who viewed the region primarily as a laboratory to test extant theories of industrial development, political movements, modernization, and the like; second, radical sociologists who identified with the revolutionary project of the Latin American left and attempted to promote it through their personal and scholarly activities. (1988: 124)

The events of the seventies and eighties, he points out, were detrimental to both groups as large data-gathering projects fell into decline and as the left suffered terribly under repressive military regimes in Latin America and during the Reagan years in the United States. The closer connections among scholars across the two regions, however, has helped attenuate the old stereotype of empiricism in the North and theorizing in the South as Latin American sociologists became more empirical in their work and North Americans became more theoretically inclined. (In many cases, the

Latin American social scientists who have a strong empirical orientation did their graduate work in the United States, and those North Americans with a strong interest in theory have often spent a great deal of time in Latin America, beginning with their graduate school training.)[19] Both sociological traditions have become more sophisticated and diverse. Evans's *Dependent Development* (1979) and Stephen G. Bunker's *Underdeveloping the Amazon* (1985) are outstanding examples of this trend among the small group of North American sociologists who wrote about Brazil in the seventies and eighties. Like their Brazilian counterparts, Evans and Bunker take on bigger issues and topics than the typical North American sociologist working on the developed world.

The impact of dependency theory in the United States began to wane by the 1980s and has virtually disappeared from the academic publishing scene. As with the rise and fall of modernization theory, the reasons for the rise and fall of dependency theory are vigorously contested. In some ways, its decline reflects the decline of the influence of grand theories that attempt to explain systems through holistic or structural models. (For an example, see O'Donnell and Schmitter 1986: 4). Many scholars see these schemes as overly deterministic and rigid, and they have moved toward approaches that are more actor centered and process based. The collapse of the Soviet Union, the end of the Cold War, and the crisis of the left in Latin America also contributed to the search for new explanations for political change and development.[20]

IV. POLITICAL SCIENCE AND SOCIOLOGY AFTER DEPENDENCY AND AUTHORITARIANISM

Since the mid- to late-1980s, Brazilian and Latin American studies have been increasingly characterized by a theoretical and methodological eclecticism. A series of factors contributed to this diversity. The end of military regimes across the region and the emergence of democratic politics moved social scientists' interests away from dependency and bureaucratic authoritarianism and to efforts to explain redemocratization. No theoretical approach has emerged with the explanatory force or influence once wielded by modernization and dependency theory. The end of the Cold War and the virtual disappearance of guerrilla insurgencies and civil wars turned scholars' attention away from the military role of the United States and toward economic issues such as trade and regional integration. The surprising strength of democratic politics and the neoliberal economic model, along with the decline of the left (both armed and democratic), have raised important questions about electoral politics, interest groups, and social equity. In the midst of these profound changes in Latin American societies, political scientists and sociologists have pursued a much more diverse and fragmented course than at any time since the 1950s.

In Brazil, the slow but steady process of *abertura,* the return of civilian rule and mass democracy, provided important new social and political developments that social scientists in the United States scrutinized. Studies of interest groups, in particular, the military, business elites, workers, and the Catholic Church became common. Skidmore's history of military rule was one of the first major books to analyze the period as a whole, albeit by a historian. Stepan, who had become a major figure in U.S. political science in the 1970s and 1980s with his work on the military and politics, produced another widely read work as the military regimes across Latin America retreated from power. *Rethinking Military Politics* (1988) also reflected a larger pattern in the discipline as Latin Americanists turned increasingly toward comparative studies of multiple countries. Another major example of this trend is Collier and Collier's *Shaping the Political Arena: Critical Junctures, the Labor Movement, and Regime Dynamics in Latin America* (1991). Hunter (1997) argued that the return to democracy also reflected the weakening of the military's traditional political power, and Hagopian (1996) produced an impressive case study of Minas Gerais that seemed to show that the military had even failed to break the hold of traditional politics and clientelism, despite its efforts to create a technocratic regime over two decades.

Perhaps the most impressive "growth" area in the eighties and nineties was the study of interest groups and the return of electoral politics. The rise of a militant workers' movement in the 1980s received a great deal of attention, especially the rise of Lula and the Partido dos Trabalhadores (Keck 1992, Seidman 1994). The PT has remained (for obvious reasons) an important subject of study (Baiocchi 2003). Reflecting a growing interest in women and gender theory, some social scientists began to produce serious analyses of gender and politics (Alvarez 1990). The rise of mass politics and a vibrant electoral system also has begun to draw political scientists to one of the more traditional areas of North American political science—analysis of elections and the electoral process. Mettenheim's book (1995) is perhaps the best example of this trend. Kingstone and Power's edited volume (2000) is an important look at key political actors and institutions. Samuels (2003) and Nylen (2003) are good examples of recent work on democratic and legislative processes.

The process of *abertura* and the return of civilian politics also generated a group of studies on elites and their role in both the rise of military rule and its decline (Payne 1994, Bartell and Payne 1995, B. R. Schneider 1991, Kingstone 1999). Business and technocratic elites received close attention (Montero 2002). Brazilian studies even came under the influence of rational choice theory, without a doubt the most influential theoretical paradigm in U.S. social science since the mid-1990s. Although she is not a Brazilianist, Barbara Geddes's 1994 study is an example of a sophisticated effort to apply rational choice theory to Brazilian politics. As for other regions of Latin America, political scientists have turned to studies of political parties and, in particular, the political right. Scott Mainwaring's recent book (1999) is a good example of new work on political parties, and Tim Power (2000) has analyzed the political right.

Other studies looked at the role of the Catholic Church in the political process, inspired by its powerful role in challenging the military regime and human rights abuses and by the influence of liberation theology (Bruneau 1982, Mainwaring 1986). This work built on the earlier studies by Bruneau (1974) and Della Cava (1976). Both liberation theology and the rise of evangelical groups stimulated some excellent work by historians and social scientists in the 1980s and 1990s (Hewitt 1991, Burdick 1993, Vasquez 1998). Work on human rights issues has sometimes been collaborative, not only bringing together scholars from Brazil and the United States, but also emerging from the collaboration of nongovernmental organizations and scholars (Dassin 1986). This is an important area where scholars have had an impact on contemporary Brazilian society and politics similar to the works of U.S. social scientists on studies of race in Brazil.

One important area that has been the focus of political scientists and sociologists for some time is the issue of social and economic inequity, certainly one of the most prominent and defining features of Brazilian society and politics. Janice Perlman's classic study, *The Myth of Marginality* (1976), is an early example of work on this topic. More recently, political scientists have focused on poverty, equity, citizenship, and policy (Caldeira 2000). Kurt Weyland's *Democracy Without Equity* (1996) analyzes why democratic governments in Brazil in recent years have failed to achieve redistribution in three key policy areas—taxation, social security, and health care. Although she trained as an economist, Judith Tendler's *Good Government in the Tropics* (1997) is a highly regarded study of efforts in one Brazilian state (Ceará) to respond to basic social needs. Barry Ames's *Political Survival: Politicians and Public Policy in Latin America* (1987) has extensive coverage of Brazil, and it looks at how politicians use spending (on education and the military, among other issues) to stay in power and to advance their electoral clout. Ames has published several other important works on Brazil, including *Rhetoric and Reality in a Militarized Regime* (1973) and *The Deadlock of Democracy in Brazil* (2001). Ames (1986), Hagopian (1990b), and Mainwaring (1991, 1993) are all important essays that advance the study of parties, electoral systems, and voting in Brazil.

Both sociologists and political scientists have continued to show a strong interest in race relations (Fontain 1985, Hanchard 1994). The centennial of abolition in 1988 helped stimulate this long-standing interest. As sociology's interest seemingly withered, a strong contingent of U.S. anthropologists continued the long tradition of studies of race relations that began in the 1930s (Twine 1998, Linger 1992, Hess 1991). Anthropologists, political scientists, and historians also seem to have come to dominate the study of both race and religion as sociologists have gradually disappeared from the scene (Lesser 1999, Pino 1997, Gay 1994, Lovell 1994, Burdick 1998, Marx 1997). The few sociologists who continue to maintain a strong interest in Brazil have (like the political scientists) tended to move on to larger comparative studies. Evans's study of the informatics industry in Brazil, India, and South Korea is an outstanding example of this tendency (Evans 1995). Another example is Seidman (1994). These studies continue a traditional focus on development but with a strong interest in flows of capital, labor, and technology across national boundaries.

If there is one approach that could come to dominate social science work on Brazil in the next decade, the most likely candidate is institutionalism and, in particular, rational choice institutionalism. Like the structural and historical models of earlier decades, rational choice focuses on efforts to develop a more "scientific" approach to understanding social and political phenomena. Unlike these earlier theoretical approaches, the individual is the unit of analysis. Rational choice theorists assume that individuals "are rational in the sense that, given goals and alternative strategies from which to choose, they will select the alternatives that maximize their chances of achieving their goals" (Geddes 1995: 81). Rational choice theory has become the most widely used approach in many of the social sciences since the mid-1980s, in particular, in economics. In Latin American studies it has led to more research on topics that have been neglected, such as electoral politics and legislative processes (Ames 2001, Carey 1996, Mainwaring and Shugart 1997). The approach has been criticized by some scholars of Latin America as "American imperialism in comparative politics" (Wallerstein 2000, Weyland 2000). The prominence of rational choice institutionalism in the U.S. academy will clearly continue to exert an important influence on studies of Latin America and Brazil in the near future.

V. STATE OF THE FIELDS

At the beginning of the twenty-first century, sociologists and political scientists who write about Brazil work in disciplines that have matured dramatically since the 1940s, but they also face the dilemmas created by that maturity. In the 1940s, the number of sociologists and political scientists who wrote about Brazil could be counted (quite literally) on one hand. In the 1960s, their numbers multiplied dramatically into the dozens, with a much stronger cohort in political science than in sociology. With the decline of area studies programs since the mid-1980s, and the growing tendency (especially of political science) to emphasize theory over local knowledge, the very existence of Brazilian studies in these two disciplines is in question. As we have seen, sociology in the United States never developed a strong subfield in Latin American studies, much less Brazilian studies. Much of the earlier interest in Brazil by sociologists has now been taken up by anthropologists. In political science, it has become increasingly detrimental for scholars to identify themselves as country specialists or even regional specialists. Even for those who maintain a strong commitment to Brazilian and Latin American studies, the trend has been to identify themselves as specialists in comparative politics or international relations who also have an interest in the region.

One striking trend that requires comment is the increasing "feminization" of political science. Since the late 1990s, an impressive group of female scholars has been trained and produced important books on Brazilian politics. A young generation of women at some of the most prestigious universities in the United States is now at the associate professor rank, and some have second books appearing or about to appear. Although U.S. academia, in general, has seen a growing number of female faculty since the mid-1980s, the cohort that now works on Brazilian politics is striking not only for its size but also its quality. Frances Hagopian (Tufts/Notre Dame), Margaret Keck (Johns Hopkins), Sonia Alvarez (University of California, Santa Cruz), Leigh Payne (University of Wisconsin), Kathryn Sikkink (University of Minnesota), and Wendy Hunter (Vanderbilt, and now University of Texas) are but a few examples of the rising stars in this generation.

Ironically, sociology and political science in both Latin America and the United States have benefited from the scholarly exchanges of the past few decades, and, to some degree, they have converged. Latin American scholars have become more empirical in their work and U.S. scholars more theoretical, although two distinct traditions continue to exist. Theory in the United States, for example, especially in political science, is much more formalistic and quantitative than among Latin American scholars, and the latter still look more to classical, European social theory for their inspiration than they do to the United States. In many ways, what has been happening in sociology and political science is more akin to recent developments in economics than to those in history or anthropology. The latter two disciplines, especially history, continue to be driven by local knowledge and fieldwork, while economics in the United States has become so theoretical and driven by rational choice theory that it no longer recognizes the need for any deep local knowledge. All countries are simply variations on key themes. If the two disciplines continue to evolve into more theoretical and globally driven paradigms, we will see fewer and fewer sociologists and political scientists who call themselves Brazilianists. In another decade or two we may look back on the 1960s and 1970s as the "golden age" of the study of Brazil by U.S. sociologists and political scientists, an auspicious historical moment when the demand for Brazilianists in both disciplines peaked.

Notes

1. I would like to thank Dain Borges, Wendy Hunter, Anthony Pereira, Tim Power, Andrew Stein, and Kurt Weyland for their perceptive and helpful comments on earlier versions of this essay.

2. *Political science,* as it is used in this essay, includes the study of both government and politics.

3. In an excellent survey of the field, Valenzuela (1988) divides the development of the literature on Latin American politics into four phases: "the public law phase, the modernization phase, the dependency phase, and the new phase of intellectual eclecticism" (65). For another excellent survey of the literature, see Hagopian, 1990a.

4. See volume 27 (1965) and volume 35 (1973).

5. "Government," in *Handbook* (1945), 161. Note that he does not even mention Portuguese.

6. A study by the Library of Congress in 1942 of "investigations in progress" lists just two names under "Brazil—government"—one of which was Bryce Wood's. Under "Brazil—sociology" are just four listings—including Samuel Lowry and Donald Pierson (Marchant and Shelby 1942).

7. *Handbook* (1941), 228.

8. This is particularly true of Kling's chapter in Wagley's *Social Science Research on Latin America* (1964) and the introductory remarks to the relevant sections in the *Handbook.* See, for example, vol. 27, 1965, 356–57.

9. The material for this section comes from chapter 2 in Smith (1974), "Sociology and Sociologists in Brazil and the United States: Some Aspects of Their Interrelationships," pp. 8–24.

10. Published by the Louisiana State University Press, the book went through four editions—1946, 1954, 1963, 1972.

11. Contributors included, Hilgard O'Reilly Sternberg, Preston E. James, Charles Wagley, Arthur Ramos, Carlos Borges Schmidt, José Arthur Rios, Emílio Willems, Reynold Carlson, Dorival Teixeira Vieira, Antônio Candido, A. Carneiro Leão, Roger Bastide, Anyda Marchant, J. V. Freitas Marcondes, Earl W. Thomas, and Gerrit de Jong, Jr. The book is dedicated to the memory of Arthur Ramos (Smith and Marchant 1951).

12. *National Directory of Latin Americanists*, 2nd ed. (Washington, D.C.: Library of Congress, 1971), 517.

13. Park had served as the personal secretary to W. E. B. Du Bois in the early twentieth century he was an active figure in the NAACP, and he worked all his life to promote civil rights for African Americans.

14. The NDEA, among other things, funded graduate fellowships that eventually became today's Foreign Language Area Studies (FLAS) fellowships.

15. An important critique of the "notions of political development" in this period is Packenham 1973. The most influential statements on modernization were Rostow 1963 and Huntington 1968.

16. It should be pointed out that Schneider was the senior member of the group, having begun his academic career in the 1950s.

17. For a fine analysis of the rise of dependency theory, especially in economics, see Love 1996, especially chapter 12, "Paths to Dependency."

18. Although he did his academic training in the United States, Fleischer has spent the last thirty years working in Brazilian universities.

19. An excellent example is Glaucio Dillon Soares, who has spent nearly his entire academic career in the United States, primarily at the University of Florida.

20. The debate about dependency theory also produced a debate about who was responsible for its rise. See, for example, the controversial volume by Packenham (1992) that provoked a debate about the role of Cardoso in formulating dependency theories.

References

Alvarez, Sonia E. 1990. *Engendering Democracy in Brazil: Women's Movements in Transition Politics.* Princeton, N.J.: Princeton University Press.

Ames, Barry. 1973. *Rhetoric and Reality in a Militarized Regime: Brazil Since 1964.* Beverly Hills, Calif.: Sage.

———. 1986. "Electoral Rules, Constituency Pressures, and Pork Barrel: Bases of Voting in the Brazilian Congress." *Journal of Politics* 57, no. 2 (May): 324–43.

————. 1987. *Political Survival: Politicians and Public Policy in Latin America.* Berkeley: University of California Press.

————. 2001. *The Deadlock of Democracy in Brazil.* Ann Arbor: University of Michigan Press.

Baiocchi, Gianpaolo, ed. 2003. *Radicals in Power: The Workers' Party (PT) and Experiments in Urban Democracy in Brazil.* New York: Palgrave.

Bartell, Ernest, and Leigh A. Payne, eds. 1995. *Business and Democracy in Latin America.* Pittsburgh, Pa.: University of Pittsburgh Press.

Bruneau, Thomas C. 1974. *The Political Transformation of the Brazilian Catholic Church.* Cambridge: Cambridge University Press.

————. 1982. *The Church in Brazil: The Politics of Religion.* Austin: University of Texas Press.

Bruneau, Thomas, and Philippe Faucher, eds. 1981. *Authoritarian Capitalism: Brazil's Contemporary Political and Economic Development.* Boulder, Colo.: Westview.

Bunker, Stephen G. 1985. *Underdeveloping the Amazon: Extraction, Unequal Exchange, and the Failure of the Modern State.* Urbana: University of Illinois Press.

Burdick, John. 1993. *Looking for God in Brazil: The Progressive Catholic Church in Urban Brazil's Religious Arena.* Berkeley: University of California Press.

————. 1998. *Blessed Anastácia: Women, Race, and Popular Christianity in Brazil.* New York: Routledge.

Caldeira, Teresa Pires do Rio. 2000. *City of Walls: Crime, Segregation, and Citizenship in São Paulo.* Berkeley: University of California Press.

Cardoso, Fernando Henrique, and Enzo Faletto. 1969. *Dependencia y desarrollo en América Latina: Ensayo de interpretación sociológica.* México: Siglo XXI.

Carey, John. 1996. *Term Limits and Legislative Representation.* Cambridge: Cambridge University Press.

Collier, David, ed. 1979. *The New Authoritarianism in Latin America.* Princeton, N.J.: Princeton University Press.

Collier, Ruth Berins, and David Collier. 1991. *Shaping the Political Arena: Critical Junctures, the Labor Movement, and Regime Dynamics in Latin America.* Princeton, N.J.: Princeton University Press.

Cunha, Euclides da. 1944. *Rebellion in the Backlands.* Trans. Samuel Putnam. Chicago: University of Chicago Press.

Daland, Robert. 1967. *Brazilian Planning: Development Politics and Administration.* Chapel Hill: University of North Carolina Press.

Dassin, Joan, ed. 1986. *Torture in Brazil: A Report.* Trans. Jaime Wright. New York: Vintage.

Della Cava, Ralph. 1976. "Catholicism and Society in Twentieth-century Brazil." *Latin American Research Review* 11, no. 2:7–50.

Eakin, Marshall C. 1998. "Latin American History in the United States: From Gentlemen Scholars to Academic Specialists." *History Teacher* 31, no. 4 (August): 539–61.

Ellenbogen, Bert L. 1964. *Rural Development in Brazil: Perspectives and Paradoxes*. Ithaca: Department of Rural Sociology, New York State College of Agriculture.

Erickson, Kenneth Paul. 1977. *The Brazilian Corporative State and Working-Class Politics*. Berkeley: University of California Press.

Evans, Peter. 1979. *Dependent Development: The Alliance of Multinational, State, and Local Capital in Brazil*. Princeton, N.J.: Princeton University Press.

———. 1995. *Embedded Autonomy: States and Industrial Transformation*. Princeton, N.J.: Princeton University Press.

Fernandes, Florestan. 1963. *A sociologia numa era de revolução social*. São Paulo: Companhia Editora Nacional.

Fleischer, David V. 1972. "Political Recruitment in the State of Minas Gerais, Brazil (1890–1970)." Ph.D. diss., University of Florida.

Flynn, Peter. 1978. *Brazil: A Political Analysis*. Boulder, Colo.: Westview.

Fontain, Pierre-Michel. 1985. *Race, Class, and Power in Brazil*. Los Angeles: Center for Afro-American Studies, University of California.

Freyre, Gilberto. 1946. *The Masters and the Slaves: A Study in the Development of Brazilian Civilization*. Trans. Samuel Putnam. New York: Alfred A. Knopf.

Gay, Robert. 1994. *Popular Organization and Democracy in Rio de Janeiro*. Philadelphia: Temple University Press.

Geddes, Barbara. 1994. *Politician's Dilemma: Building State Capacity in Latin America*. Berkeley: University of California Press.

———. 1995. "Uses and Limitations of Rational Choice." In *Latin America in Comparative Perspective: New Approaches to Methods and Analysis*, ed. Peter H. Smith. Boulder, Colo.: Westview.

Gomez, R. A. 1967. *The Study of Latin American Politics in University Programs in the United States*. Comparative Government Studies 2. Tucson: Institute of Government Research, University of Arizona Press.

Graham, Lawrence S. 1968. *Civil Service Reform in Brazil: Principles Versus Practice*. Austin: University of Texas Press.

Hagopian, Frances. 1990a. "Brazil." In *Handbook of Political Science Research on Latin America: Trends from the 1960s to the 1990s*, ed. David W. Dent. New York: Greenwood..

———. 1990b. "'Democracy by Undemocratic Means'? Elites, Political Pacts, and Regime Transition in Brazil." *Comparative Political Studies* 23, no. 2 (July): 147–70.

———. 1996. *Traditional Politics and Regime Change in Brazil*. Cambridge: Cambridge University Press.

Hanchard, Michael George. 1994. *Orpheus and Power: The Movimento Negro of Rio de Janeiro and São Paulo, Brazil, 1945–1988*. Princeton, N.J.: Princeton University Press.

Hess, David J. 1991. *Spirits and Scientists: Ideology, Spiritism, and Brazilian Culture*. University Park: Pennsylvania State University Press.

Hewitt, W. E. 1991. *Basic Christian Communities and Social Change in Brazil*. Lincoln: University of Nebraska Press.

Horowitz, Irving Louis. 1964. *Revolution in Brazil: Politics and Society in a Developing Nation*. New York: E. P. Dutton.

Hunter, Wendy. 1997. *Eroding Military Influence in Brazil: Politicians Against Soldiers*. Chapel Hill: University of North Carolina Press.

Huntington, Samuel P. 1968. *Political Order in Changing Societies*. New Haven, Conn.: Yale University Press.

Kahl, Joseph A. 1968. *The Measurement of Modernism: A Study of Values in Brazil and Mexico*. Austin: University of Texas Press.

Keck, Margaret E. 1992. *The Workers Party and Democratization in Brazil*. New Haven, Conn.: Yale University Press.

Kingstone, Peter. 1999. *Crafting Coalitions for Reform: Business Preferences, Political Institutions, and Neoliberal Reform in Brazil*. University Park: Pennsylvania State University Press.

Kingstone, Peter, and Tim J. Power, eds. 2000. *Democratic Brazil: Actors, Institutions, and Processes*. Pittsburgh, Pa.: University of Pittsburgh Press.

Lambert, Jacques. 1953. *Le Brésil, structure social et institutions politiques*. Paris: A. Colin.

Lambert, Richard D., ed. 1984. *Beyond Growth: The Next Stage in Language and Area Studies*. Washington, D.C.: Association of American Universities.

Lesser, Jeffrey. 1999. *Negotiating National Identity in Brazil: Immigrants, Minorities, and the Struggle for Ethnicity in Brazil*. Durham, N.C.: Duke University Press.

Linger, Daniel Touro. 1992. *Dangerous Encounters: The Meanings of Violence in a Brazilian City*. Stanford, Calif.: Stanford University Press.

Linz, Juan J., and Alfred Stepan, eds. 1978. *The Breakdown of Democratic Regimes: Latin America*. Baltimore: Johns Hopkins University Press, 1978.

Loewenstein, Karl. 1942. *Brazil Under Vargas*. New York: Macmillan.

Love, Joseph L. 1996. *Crafting the Third World: Theorizing Underdevelopment in Rumania and Brazil*. Stanford, Calif.: Stanford University Press.

Lovell, Peggy. 1994. "Race, Gender, and Development in Brazil." *Latin American Research Review* 29, no. 3:7–35.

McDonough, Peter. 1981. *Power and Ideology in Brazil*. Princeton, N.J.: Princeton University Press.

Mainwaring, Scott. 1986. *The Catholic Church and Politics in Brazil, 1916–1985*. Stanford, Calif.: Stanford University Press.

———.1991. "Politicians, Parties, and Electoral Systems: Brazil in Comparative Perspective." *Comparative Politics* 24, no. 1 (October): 21–43.

———. 1993. "Brazilian Party Underdevelopment in Comparative Perspective." *Political Science Quarterly* 107, no. 4 (winter): 677–707.

———. 1999. *Rethinking Party Systems in the Third Wave of Democratization: The Case of Brazil*. Stanford, Calif.: Stanford University Press.

Mainwaring, Scott, and Matthew Shugart, eds. 1997. *Presidentialism and Democracy in Latin America*. Cambridge: Cambridge University Press.

Malloy, James M. 1977. *Authoritarianism and Corporatism in Latin America*. Pittsburgh, Pa.: University of Pittsburgh Press.

Marchant, Alexander, and Charmion Shelby, eds. 1942. *Investigations in Progress in the United States in the Field of Latin American Humanistic and Social Science Studies. Preliminary Edition*. Washington, D.C.: Hispanic Foundation, Library of Congress.

Marx, Anthony W. 1997. *Making Race and Nation: A Comparison of the United States, South Africa, and Brazil*. Cambridge: Cambridge University Press.

Mehrtens, Cristina Peixoto. 2000. "Urban Space and Politics: Constructing Social Identity and the Middle Class in São Paulo, Brazil, 1930s–1940s." Ph.D. diss., University of Miami.

Mettenheim, Kurt von. 1995. *The Brazilian Voter: Mass Politics in Democratic Transition, 1974–1986*. Pittsburgh, Pa.: University of Pittsburgh Press.

Montero, Alfred. 2002. *Shifting States in Global Markets: Subnational Industrial Policy in Contemporary Brazil and Spain*. University Park: Pennsylvania State University Press.

Moore, Barrington Jr. 1966. *Social Origins of Dictatorship and Democracy: Lord and Peasant in the Making of the Modern World*. Boston: Beacon.

Nylen, William R. 2003. *Participatory Democracy Versus Elitist Democracy: Lessons from Brazil*. New York: Palgrave Macmillan.

O'Donnell, Guillermo. 1973. *Modernization and Bureaucratic-Authoritarianism: Studies in South American Politics*. Berkeley: Institute of International Studies, University of California.

O'Donnell, Guillermo, and Philippe C. Schmitter, eds. 1986. *Transitions from Authoritarian Rule: Tentative Conclusions About Uncertain Democracies*. Baltimore: Johns Hopkins University Press.

Packenham, Robert A. 1973. *Liberal America and the Third World: Political Development in Foreign Aid and Social Science*. Princeton, N.J.: Princeton University Press.

———. 1992. *The Dependency Movement: Scholarship and Politics in Development Studies*. Cambridge, Mass.: Harvard University Press.

Page, Joseph A. 1972. *The Revolution That Never Was: Northeast Brazil, 1955–1964*. New York: Grossman.

Payne, Leigh A. 1994. *Brazilian Industrialists and Democratic Change*. Baltimore: Johns Hopkins University Press.

Perlman, Janice E. 1976. *The Myth of Marginality: Urban Poverty and Politics in Rio de Janeiro*. Berkeley: University of California Press.

Pierson, Donald. 1940. *Negroes in Brazil*. Chicago: University of Chicago Press.

———. 1951. *Cruz das Almas: A Brazilian Village*. Washington, D.C.: Smithsonian Institution.

Pino, Julio Cesar. 1997. *Family and Favela: The Reproduction of Poverty in Rio de Janeiro.* Westport, Conn.: Greenwood.

Portes, Alejandro. 1988. "Latin American Sociology in the Mid-1980's: Learning from Hard Experience." In *Changing Perspectives in Latin American Studies: Insights from Six Disciplines,* ed. Christopher Mitchell. Stanford, Calif.: Stanford University Press.

Power, Tim J. 2000. *The Political Right in Postauthoritarian Brazil: Elites, Institutions, and Democratization.* University Park: Pennsylvania State University Press.

Roett, Riordan. 1972a. *Brazil: Politics in a Patrimonial Society.* Boston: Allyn and Bacon.

———. 1972b. *The Politics of Foreign Aid in the Brazilian Northeast.* Nashville, Tenn.: Vanderbilt University Press.

Rostow, Walter W. 1963. *The Stages of Economic Growth: A Non-Communist Manifesto.* Cambridge: Cambridge University Press.

Samuels, David. 2003. *Ambition, Federalism, and Legislative Politics in Brazil.* Cambridge: Cambridge University Press.

Saunders, John Van Dyke, ed. 1971. *Modern Brazil: New Patterns and Development.* Gainesville: University of Florida Press.

Schmitter, Philippe. 1971. *Interest Conflict and Political Change in Brazil.* Stanford, Calif.: Stanford University Press.

Schneider, Ben Ross. 1991. *Politics Within the State: Elite Bureaucrats and Industrial Policy in Authoritarian Brazil.* Pittsburgh, Pa.: University of Pittsburgh Press.

Schneider, Ronald M. 1971. *The Political System of Brazil: Emergence of a "Modernizing" Authoritarian Regime, 1964–1970.* New York: Columbia University Press.

———. 1991. *"Order and Progress": A Political History of Brazil.* Boulder, Colo.: Westview.

Seidman, Gay W. 1994. *Manufacturing Militance: Workers' Movements in Brazil and South Africa, 1970–1985.* Berkeley: University of California Press.

Selcher, Wayne A. 1986. *Political Liberalization in Brazil: Dynamics, Dilemmas, and Future Prospects.* Boulder, Colo.: Westview.

Skidmore, Thomas E. 1967. *Politics in Brazil, 1930–64: An Experiment in Democracy.* New York: Oxford University Press.

———. 1988. *The Politics of Military Rule in Brazil, 1964–85.* New York: Oxford University Press.

Smith, T. Lynn. 1974. *Brazilian Society.* Albuquerque: University of New Mexico Press.

Smith, T. Lynn, and Alexander Marchant, eds. 1951. *Brazil: Portrait of Half a Continent.* New York: Dryden.

Stepan, Alfred. 1971. *The Military in Politics: Changing Patterns in Brazil.* Princeton, N.J.: Princeton University Press.

———, ed. 1973. *Authoritarian Brazil: Origins, Policies, and Future.* New Haven, Conn.: Yale University Press.

————. 1988. *Rethinking Military Politics: Brazil and the Southern Cone.* Princeton, N.J.: Princeton University Press.

————, ed. 1989. *Democratizing Brazil: Problems of Transition and Consolidation.* New York: Oxford University Press.

Tendler, Judith. 1997. *Good Government in the Tropics.* Baltimore: Johns Hopkins University Press.

Twine, France Winddance. 1998. *Racism in a Racial Democracy: The Maintenance of White Supremacy in Brazil.* New Brunswick, N.J.: Rutgers University Press.

Valenzuela, Arturo. 1988. "Political Science and the Study of Latin America." In *Changing Perspectives in Latin American Studies: Insights from Six Disciplines,* ed. Christopher Mitchell. Stanford, Calif.: Stanford University Press.

Vásquez, Manuel A. 1998. *The Brazilian Popular Church and the Crisis of Modernity.* Cambridge: Cambridge University Press.

Wagley, Charles, ed. 1964. *Social Science Research on Latin America.* New York: Columbia University Press.

Wallerstein, Michael. 2000. "American Imperialism in Comparative Politics." *APSA-CP: Newsletter of the Organized Section in Comparative Politics of the American Political Science Association* 11, no. 1 (winter): 1–3.

Weyland, Kurt. 1996. *Democracy Without Equity: Failures of Reform in Brazil.* Pittsburgh, Pa.: University of Pittsburgh Press.

————. 2000. "Strengths and Limitations of Rational-Choice Institutionalism in the Study of Latin American Politics." Unpublished manuscript.

Wiarda, Howard. 1977. *Corporatism and Development: The Portuguese Experience.* Amherst: University of Massachusetts Press.

————. 1997. *Corporatism and Comparative Politics: The Other Great "Ism."* Armonk, N.Y.: M. E. Sharpe.

Wilkening, Eugene A. 1968. *Comparison of Migrants in Two Rural and an Urban Area of Central Brazil.* University of Wisconsin Land Tenure Center research paper no. 35. Madison: University of Wisconsin Land Tenure Center.

Wirth, John D. 1970. *The Politics of Brazilian Development.* Stanford, Calif.: Stanford University Press.

Wynia, Gary W. 1992. "Politics: Essay." In *Latin America and the Caribbean: A Critical Guide to Research Sources,* ed. Paula H. Covington. Westport, Conn.: Greenwood.

CHAPTER 11

<del>~</del>

International Relations

Scott D. Tollefson

INTRODUCTION

In the new millennium, there seems to be a growing awareness that Brazil is playing a larger role in the international arena. In mid-2000, as Brazil prepared to host the first-ever meeting of South American heads of state, the *New York Times* noted that Brazil was becoming increasingly assertive on the world stage (Rohter 2000). In 2001, a book entitled *Brazil's Second Chance: En Route Toward the First World* captured a heady optimism that has been so recurrent in the study of Brazil's international relations (Gordon and Leone 2001). This essay analyzes the major themes, theoretical orientations, and methodological trends in the study, within the United States, of Brazil's international relations. While the focus of this chapter is U.S. scholarship on Brazil's international relations, it will examine the relationship between scholarship in the United States and Brazil. Finally, it will consider recent trends that affect the study of Brazil's international relations.

The study of Brazil's international relations changed considerably from 1945 to 2003. From 1945 until the mid-1960s, the topic was largely ignored, as the Cold War focused the attention of most U.S. scholars on the Soviet Union and Europe. With Brazil's rapid economic growth from 1968 to 1974, some international relations scholars began to examine Brazil's rise within the international system, and its search for *grandeza* (greatness). At the same time, other scholars, influenced largely by Latin American scholars, used dependency theory or world systems theory to analyze how Brazil's position in the international capitalist system affected its development.

From 1974 to 1985, the limitations of Brazil's economic model and its growing debt crisis had a sobering effect on the literature, which shifted from traditional diplomacy to economic issues, especially the foreign debt crisis. With the collapse of the Soviet Union in 1989, one of the major concerns has been Brazil's position within a changing international system. Since the 1980s, the study of Brazil's international relations has become much more specialized, with the emergence of new themes, such as bilateral relations, regionalism, integration, security, and the environment. With the emergence of comparative foreign policies as a subset of international relations, a larger number of authors have sought to penetrate the "black box" of Brazil's foreign policy-making process (Lincoln and Ferris 1984; Davis and Wilson 1975).

I. Bilateral Relations: The United States and Brazil

Not surprisingly, the most prominent and enduring theme in U.S. scholarship of Brazil's international relations has been U.S. relations with Brazil. Historians have been at the forefront of this literature. The late E. Bradford Burns was one of the most important historians in this area, publishing *The Unwritten Alliance: Rio-Branco and Brazilian-American Relations* (1966). Frank D. McCann Jr. wrote a watershed study, *The Brazilian-American Alliance: 1937–1945* (1973). Stanley E. Hilton, the U.S. historian with the most sustained research on Brazil's international relations, produced an insightful analysis, "The United States, Brazil, and the Cold War, 1945–1960: End of the Special Relationship" (1981). Mark T. Berger, in *Under Northern Eyes: Latin American Studies and U.S. Hegemony in the Americas 1898–1990* (1995), examined how much of U.S. scholarship on Latin America tended to support U.S. relations with the region since the late 1800s. Much of the sophistication of this literature results from the use of archives and other primary sources in Brazil by scholars like Hilton and McCann.

Many political scientists have also focused on the theme of U.S.-Brazilian relations. They include Jan Knippers Black, *United States Penetration of Brazil* (1977); Ruth Leacock, *Requiem for Revolution: The United States and Brazil, 1961–1969* (1990); and Martha Huggins, *Political Policing: The United States and Latin America* (1998). These books are critical of U.S. policy toward Brazil. Additional books in this area include Roger Fontaine, *Brazil and the United States* (1974) and the insightful *The United States and Brazil: The Limits of Influence* (1981), by the late Robert Wesson. Wesson argued that U.S. influence was limited by a number of factors, including Brazil's national interests. In an excellent book, Abraham F. Lowenthal continued in the Wesson tradition and explored Brazil's foreign policy interests vis-à-vis the United States, in *Brazil and the United States* (1986). Lowenthal's approach was a positive development, given that much of the early U.S.-Brazil literature failed to account adequately for Brazil's interests in that relationship.

Very few non-Brazilianists (or non–Latin Americanists) have analyzed Brazil's international relations. One prominent exception is Annette Baker Fox, in *The Power of Attraction: Four Middle Powers and the United States* (1976). Using the comparative method, Fox placed Brazil within the "middle powers" literature. This is a promising approach and one with increasing appeal in the early 2000s, as political science moves toward more cross-regional analyses. In this vein, a new publication, entitled *Foreign Policy in Comparative Perspective: Domestic and International Influences on State Behavior* includes two Latin American case studies (Brazil and Mexico) and various other cases from around the globe (Beasley Kaarbo, Lantis, and Snarr 2001). The comparison focuses on the response of the countries to both domestic and international forces.

Scholarly interest in U.S.-Brazilian relations continued in the 1990s (Cobbs 1992; Smith 1991; Topik 1997), but the theme is less prominent than it was a generation ago, as other themes have emerged. Nonetheless, U.S. policy toward Brazil continues to gain the attention of groups such as the New York–based Council on Foreign Relations. In February 2001, the council released a task force report entitled "A Letter to the President and a Memorandum on U.S. Policy toward Brazil." In its letter to President George W. Bush, the task force made an impassioned plea: "Brazil is the fulcrum. Brazil is too important to everything that is going to happen in South America for a policy of benign neglect. . . . It is time to reenergize U.S.-Brazilian relations. Both nations have much to gain from an enhanced relationship. Now is the time to act" (Council on Foreign Relations 2001: vii).

II. TRADITIONAL DIPLOMACY:
BRAZIL AS A "CONTINGENT POWER"

In analyzing Brazil's international relations, U.S. scholars have been influenced by the foreign policy of the United States. This was particularly true from 1945 to 1964, when the main themes in the study of Brazil's international relations were shaped by the U.S. relationship with the Soviet Union during the Cold War. The first phase of the Cold War virtually coincided with Brazil's 1946 Republic (1946–64), a period in which rapid industrialization, urbanization, and modernization placed enormous strains on Brazil's fledgling democracy. Gerald K. Haines explored some of these themes in *The Americanization of Brazil: A Study of U.S. Cold War Diplomacy in the Third World, 1945–1954* (1989).

The literature of Brazil's international relations during this period reflects the Eurocentric bias of international relations scholarship in the United States. The containment of communism was considered the foremost goal of U.S. foreign policy, and central to that strategy were U.S. efforts to "contain" communism in Central America and the Caribbean. Leading U.S. diplomats and international relations scholars paid little attention to Latin America, except for those areas perceived to be involved in the East-West dispute: Central America and the Caribbean. It is no surprise, for example, that some of the richest literature on U.S. foreign policy during this period focuses on Guatemala and the U.S.-backed intervention in 1954 to "contain communism" in that country. Likewise, the U.S. fascination with Cuba spawned Graham T. Allison's classic study, *Essence of Decision: Explaining the Cuban Missile Crisis* (1971). Though primarily an analysis of U.S. policy, there is no similar study on U.S. relations with Brazil, despite Brazil's prominence in the region. Nor did a single event in Brazil's foreign policy trigger the kind of academic scrutiny brought about by Argentina's war in the Malvinas/Falklands. Brazil is perhaps a victim of its successful foreign policy. Despite sharing a border with ten of twelve South American countries, Brazil has been able to resolve major disputes diplomatically and peacefully. A more bellicose attitude could have spawned a larger interest in Brazil's foreign policy, and a broader literature.

The study of Brazil's international relations during this period was, therefore, often an appendage of the study of U.S. relations with Latin America and the Caribbean. Robert A. Pastor's *Whirlpool: U.S. Foreign Policy Toward Latin America and the Caribbean* (1992) is illustrative of much of the literature in the 1980s and early 1990s: despite its title, the book deals almost entirely with Central America, to the exclusion of South America. During this period, the interest in Brazil by most U.S. international relations scholars in Brazil was a derivative one. Brazil was viewed in relation to Great Power rivalries as a "contingent power." Brazil's power derived from manipulating the Great Power rivalries. Brazil was viewed as important only to the extent that it was relevant to the East-West calculus of power. Rarely did scholars seek to go beyond the notion of Brazil as a pawn in that struggle. There was little understanding of Brazil's foreign policy interests and the internal dynamics that shaped Brazil's foreign policy (Oswald and Strover 1970). Although there are shortcomings in this area, some very sophisticated studies were published, such as Stanley E. Hilton's *Brazil and the Soviet Challenge, 1917–1947* (1991; see also 1975). Hilton's 1991 book is meticulously documented and stands as a classic study. In the late 1980s and early 1990s, many scholars, both in the United States and Latin America, made a conscious attempt to move beyond the Cold War (Selcher 1986; Hartlyn, Schoultz, and Varas 1992).

III. Brazil as an Emerging "Great Power"

For generations, Brazil's size and abundant natural resources have captured the imagination of foreigners, including Americans. In the late 1960s and early 1970s, as Brazil began to experience high rates of economic growth, some of the literature on Brazil's international relations examined Brazil's emergence as a "Great Power." Ronald M. Schneider's *Brazil: Foreign Policy of a Future World Power* (1976) echoed that euphoria, as did William Perry's *Contemporary Brazilian Foreign Policy: The Strategy of an Emerging Power* (1976) and Philip Raine's *Brazil, Awakening Giant* (1974). Capability theory was in vogue among many international relations theorists, especially in the United States. In Brazil, despite the military regime's focus on *grandeza,* only a few scholars embraced capability theory. The most pronounced example of the application of capability theory is that of Ray S. Cline, *World Power Assessment: A Calculus of Strategic Drift* (1980). Cline, quite wrongly and mechanically, ranked Brazil third among the countries of the world in "perceived power." Wayne Selcher provided a rebuttal to Cline, in "Brazil in the World: A Ranking Analysis of Capability and Status," a chapter in *Brazil in the International System: The Rise of a Middle Power* (Selcher 1981). Cline continued to work in this vein with *The Power of Nations in the 1990s* but ranked Brazil a more credible tenth (1994). This optimistic interpretation was challenged, in 1973 and 1974, when the OPEC oil price hike exposed Brazil's Achilles heel—its dependence on imported petroleum. The second oil price hike, of 1979, further eroded the notion of Brazil's "Great Power" status. But even the economic downturns in Brazil could not contain the extreme optimism that was expressed in 1987 by Adrian J. English, in his article, "Brazil: A Super Power in the Making."

By the early 1990s, however, scholars were involved in more sobering analyses of Brazil's position within the international system. No longer was Brazil referred to as a great power or superpower but as a regional power, as in Bertha K. Becker and Claudio A. G. Egler's *Brazil: A New Regional*

Power in the World-Economy (1992). In the conclusion to their book, geographers Becker and Egler borrow heavily from world systems theory: "The process of Brazil's insertion as a semiperipheral country in the capitalist world-economy occurs in the midst of a profound crisis which will be overcome only with a restructuring of that world-economy" (177).

Andrew Hurrell was even more insightful in a superb and theoretically rich chapter entitled "Brazil as a Regional Power: A Study in Ambivalence" (1992). This shift in perspective, from the early 1970s to the mid-1990s, points to some of the shortcomings of capability theory, such as its static character, and its assumption that power can be measured. In fairness to capability theory, it served to point out Brazil's potential for eventually becoming a major actor in the world and generally did not assert that Brazil already was a great power. Whatever one's opinion of capability theory, it sought to call attention to Brazil's importance and its unrealized potential.[1]

IV. Dependency and World Systems Theories: Brazil in the International Capitalist System

In the late 1960s and early 1970s, dependency theory emerged as one of the most important interpretations of international relations. Although many U.S., European, and even African social scientists embraced this approach, it was Brazilian sociologists such as Theotônio dos Santos and Fernando Henrique Cardoso who received some of the greatest attention. Dos Santos and Cardoso were influenced to a large extent by Brazilian economist/historian Celso Furtado and his *Economic Development of Latin America: Historical Background and Contemporary Problems* (1976). Dos Santos's definition of dependency is still the most cited: "By dependency we mean a situation in which the economy of certain countries is conditioned by the development and expansion of another economy to which the former is subjected" (1970: 231).

Based on a historical-structural methodology, Cardoso and Enzo Faletto (from Chile), argued against rigid notions of dependency and pointed instead to "situations of dependency." In their classic study, *Dependency and Development in Latin America* (1979), they wrote:

> We conceive the relationship between external and internal forces as forming a complex whole whose structural links are not based on mere external forms of exploitation and coercion, but are rooted in coincidences of interests between local dominant classes and international ones, and on the other

side, are challenged by local dominated groups and classes. . . . What we affirm simply means that the system of domination reappears as an "internal" force, through the social practices of local groups and classes which try to enforce foreign interests, not precisely because they are foreign, but because they may coincide with values and interests that these groups pretend are their own. (xvi)

Many U.S. scholars embraced this very sophisticated interpretation of dependency. In a parallel and related development, Immanuel Wallerstein's (1974) notion of world systems posited that the emergence, from 1450 to 1640, of a single capitalist world economy created a world division of labor, between the "core" industrial economies and the "peripheral" nonindustrial countries. World systems and dependency theories greatly influenced the U.S. literature on Brazil's international relations. They had a profound impact on scholars such as Richard Graham, the editor of *Brazil and the World System* (1991). The publishing of that book is a good case study of the interaction between Brazilian and U.S. scholars, as they grappled with emerging theory. Using the world systems (Wallerstein) approach, Graham analyzed the relationship between Brazil's development, since colonialism, and the rise of capitalism in Europe. Graham, a professor of history at the University of Texas at Austin, was influenced by Fernando Novais, a professor of history at the Universidade de São Paulo, who was Tinker Visiting Professor of Latin American Studies at the University of Texas at Austin.

In the preface to his book, Graham discusses what he calls the "intellectual interchange" between Graham, Novais, Luis Carlos Soares (professor at the Universidade Federal Fluminense), John R. Hall (professor of sociology at the University of California, Davis), and various others—including Enrique Semo, who was in Austin on a MacArthur Fellowship. And while Graham's book ultimately suffers from the limitations of world systems theory, it is one of the more sophisticated books on Brazil's international relations, because it links the external (multinational corporations, international capitalist system) with the internal (the state and the private sector). The Graham book is exceptional, in that there has been very little collaboration between U.S. and Brazilian scholars on the topic of Brazil's international relations. It points to the important role of foundations, such as Tinker and MacArthur, in funding collaboration. It also serves as a reminder that much more could be done on a collaborative basis between U.S. and Brazilian scholars interested in Brazil's international relations.

In 1979, Peter Evans, a sociologist at Brown University (and later at the University of California at Berkeley), analyzed the interaction between three major actors in Brazil: multinational corporations, the national bourgeoisie, and the state. Heavily influenced by Brazilian scholars, his book, *Dependent Development: The Alliance of Multinational, State, and Local Capital in Brazil* (1979), is one of the most important contributions to the literature on Brazil's international relations and is based on extensive research in Brazil. It too borrowed heavily from dependency and world systems theories.

Whereas capability theory was primarily associated with U.S. international relations theorists, and restricted to that subfield of political science, dependency theory was initially associated mainly with sociologists (many from Latin America) but heavily influenced all the social science disciplines—in Latin America, the United States, Africa, and Europe. By the late 1980s and early 1990s, dependency theory was no longer as influential in the social sciences. The limitations of dependency theory are well documented in Robert A. Packenham's *The Dependency Movement: Scholarship and Politics in Development Studies* (1992). Nonetheless, the influence that Brazilian dependency theorists had on U.S. social scientists is nothing short of remarkable.

V. Geopolitics

Another theme in which U.S. scholars borrowed heavily from their Brazilian counterparts is that of geopolitics. The roots of geopolitical thinking go back at least to the nineteenth century, to European and U.S. theorists. In Brazil, General Golbery do Couto e Silva became one of the world's leading exponents of geopolitical thinking. His books, such as *A geopolítica do Brasil* (1967) and *Conjuntura política nacional: o poder executivo e geopolítica do Brasil* (1981), are among the most important works in the geopolitical literature and unquestionably the most important in Latin America during the latter half of the twentieth century. Many other Brazilians, such as Carlos de Meira Mattos (1977), contributed to the geopolitical literature.

The high mark of geopolitical influence on Brazil's international relations was the military regime period, from 1964 to 1985. Despite such influence in Brazil, that literature had modest repercussions in the United States, in large measure because geopolitics has carried a stigma ever since it was associated with Nazi Germany. Nevertheless, Jack Child published *Geopolitics and Conflict in South America: Quarrels Among Neighbors* (1985). That was followed by Thomas G. Sanders, "Brazilian Geopolitics: Securing the South and North" (1987), and Child and Philip Kelly, editors, *Geopolitics of the Southern Cone and Antarctica* (1988). More recently, Philip Kelly wrote *Checkerboards and Shatterbelts: The Geopolitics of South America* (1997), in which he analyzes the new geopolitical school that he calls "accommodative regionalism." This school focuses less on interstate competition. It places a high value on regional integration efforts and the cooperative relationships that undergird those efforts. The influence of this school of geopolitical thought in Brazil remains unclear.

VI. Inside the "Black Box" of Brazil's Foreign Policy

One of the major developments in the study of Brazil's foreign relations was the emergence of a generation of scholars who were Brazilianists. They conducted research in Brazil, learned Portuguese, and sought to get inside the "black box" of Brazil's foreign policy-making process. This generation focused on *Brazil's* foreign policy interests while recognizing that global conditions and relationships affect those interests. Perhaps the foremost exponent of this approach has been Riordan Roett, who as a graduate student conducted research in the northeast of Brazil that led to his book *The Politics of Foreign Aid in the Brazilian Northeast* (1972). In subsequent years Roett edited books that included chapters on Brazil's international relations, *Brazil in the Sixties* (1972) and *Brazil in the Seventies* (1976). He also wrote the very popular *Brazil: Politics in a Patrimonial Society*, which with the third edition (1984) included a chapter on Brazil's foreign relations. Roett's "The Foreign Policy of Latin America," in Roy C. Macridis's *Foreign Policy in World Politics* (1989), was one of the few chapters on Brazil's foreign policy that was available to undergraduate students in the United States. Roett has continued to be an important player in the study of Brazil's foreign policy, focusing on debt, integration, and broader issues (Roett 1981; Roett and Tollefson 1986; Roett and Purcell 1997).

One of the most prolific authors in this tradition has been Wayne Selcher, who published *Brazil's Multilateral Relations: Between First and Third Worlds* (1978); *Brazil in the International System: The Rise of a Middle Power* (1981); and "Brazil and the Southern Cone Subsystem" (1988). One of Selcher's most important contributions to our understanding of Brazil's foreign policy-making process was "Brazil's Foreign Policy: More Actors and Expanding Agendas," in Jennie K. Lincoln and Elizabeth G. Ferris's *The Dynamics of Latin American Foreign Policies: Challenges for the 1980s* (1984). Selcher identified the domestic actors in Brazil's foreign policy-making process and examined their influence.

Although he is best known for his scholarship on Brazil's Congress, David V. Fleischer, a U.S. professor at the Universidade de Brasília, has played a major role in the study of Brazil's international relations. He has published several chapters and articles on the topic (Fleischer 1985) and wrote an unpublished study and bibliography entitled "Brazil's Foreign Policy and International Relations, 1945–1995." He is an automatic point of contact for most U.S. scholars conducting research in Brasília on Brazil's foreign policy. Fleischer is a walking encyclopedia and Rolodex and has opened many doors for scholars. His weekly *Brazil Report* is sent via e-mail to dozens of professionals interested in Brazil. *Brazil Report* is an excellent summary of events in that country and generally includes a section on Brazil's international relations. Along with Roett, Fleischer is U.S. expert on Brazil's foreign relations quoted most often in leading U.S. newspapers. The books, chapters, articles, and mentoring by Roett, Selcher, and Fleischer influenced a generation of scholars. They paved the way for the more specialized studies that emerged in the 1990s.

An important player in U.S.-Brazilian relations was Lincoln Gordon, who served as U.S. ambassador to Brazil from 1961 to 1966 (which included the 1964 coup) and as assistant secretary of state for inter-American affairs from 1966 to 1968. Gordon is now a guest scholar in foreign policy studies at the Brookings Institution. While best known for his work and publications on Europe, Gordon has continued to write extensively about Brazil. In 2001, he published, with Richard C. Leone, *Brazil's Second Chance: En Route Toward the First World*. The book, historical in scope, assesses Brazil's position within the international system and analyzes its options for assuming a position within the First World. Lincoln Gordon is one of the few U.S. policy makers who have analyzed, in an ongoing manner, Brazil's international relations. This contrasts sharply with Brazilian diplomats, who have a long tradition of publishing on a wide range of topics in international relations. Brazilian diplomats have written the richest, broadest, and most sustained literature on Brazil's international relations.

VII. Diversification of Themes

In the late 1970s and 1980s, the literature on Brazil's international relations became much more diversified. For example, Michael A. Morris focused on maritime concerns in *International Politics and the Sea: The Case of Brazil* (1979). That diversification reflected the growing complexity in the international system, and a realization that transnational actors were becoming more influential. Although Itamaraty retained much of its influence in articulating Brazil's foreign policy, international relations were increasingly viewed as more than mere government-to-government relations.

The diversification in the literature on Brazil's international relations also reflected the rise of neoliberalism in international relations theory, neoliberalism's challenge to neorealism's preoccupation with systemic levels of analysis, and neorealism's focus on security themes. The focus on security often led neorealists to the conclusion that Latin America was not very important, as in Michael C. Desch's *When the Third World Matters: Latin America and United States Grand Strategy* (1993). Neoliberalism analyzed domestic factors that shape international behavior, and was broader in its approach to a variety of themes. The diversification and specialization in themes in international relations literature continues to this day.

A. INTERNATIONAL POLITICAL ECONOMY

In the mid-1980s, much of the literature on Brazil's foreign policy shifted to the economic realm. This reflected the rise of international political economy (IPE) as a subset of international relations theory. It also reflected a growing recognition that the dominant theme of diplomatic history needed to be complemented by economic concerns. Finally, it reflected Brazil's increasing problem with debt. The debt crisis was particularly prominent in the writings of Riordan Roett, who published many articles and chapters on the topic. Some of this literature focused on commercial tensions between the United States and Brazil, such as the study by Ellene A. Felder and Andrew Hurrell, *U.S.-Brazilian Informatics Dispute* (1988). More recently, globalization has accentuated the importance of transnational economic actors. Cross-regional analyses became popular, such as *Capital Control, Financial Regulation, and Industrial Policy in South Korea and Brazil*, by Jessica Gordon Nembhard (1996). Some financial organizations began to analyze Brazil's foreign policy, producing such works as the Global Investment Business Center's *Brazil: Foreign Policy and Government Guide* (2000). This focus on economic issues reveals a changing political reality within Brazil: the rising influence of the economy ministers in the formulation of Brazil's foreign policy.

B. BRAZIL S RELATIONS WITH OTHER COUNTRIES

As the Cold War era came to an end, a growing number of scholars moved beyond U.S.-Brazilian relations and analyzed Brazil's ties with other countries and regions. Riordan Roett and Wolf Grabendorff edited *Latin America, Western Europe and the U.S.: Reevaluating the Atlantic Triangle* (1985).

Peter Coffey and Luiz Correa do Lago edited *EEC and Brazil: Trade, Capital Investment, and the Debt Problem* (1988). John F. Due and Werner Baer published *Brazil and the Ivory Coast: The Impact of International Lending, Investment, and Aid* (1987). Leon Hollerman, an economist, wrote *Japan's Economic Strategy in Brazil: Challenge for the United States* (1988). Stanley E. Hilton turned to a more distant time in "Brazil's International Economic Strategy, 1945–1960: Revival of the German Option" (1986). These studies, while different in focus, underscored Brazil's increasing influence in other regions, particularly in Lusophone Africa but also in the Middle East, where commercial ties become more prominent in the 1980s and 1990s. Brazil's relations with Europe continued to receive attention, and Asia emerged as an important region for Brazil and all of Latin America. In the new millennium, the notion of an Atlantic triangle has reemerged, with discussions for integration of Mercosur, the European Economic Union, and Free Trade Area Agreement.

C. REGIONALISM AND INTEGRATION

In the 1970s, Brazil became more assertive in diversifying its external ties. The end of the Cold War led to an even greater expansion in Brazil's international links and the eventual formation of Mercosul, the Common Market of the South, with Argentina, Uruguay, and Paraguay. Chile and Bolivia have joined Mercosul as associate members. Regional economic integration is the fastest-growing topic in the literature on Brazil's foreign relations. Brazilian diplomats (who have taken a leading role in establishing Mercosul) and scholars are particularly prolific in this area. Unfortunately, the quality of that literature varies and often reads as little more than cheerleading. A number of U.S. scholars have focused on Brazil's regional links, and that literature has become more specialized, as in the article by Georges D. Landau on the treaty of Amazonian cooperation (1980). Robert E. Biles included an analysis of those links in his edited work, *Inter-American Relations: The Latin American Perspective* (1988). Riordan Roett edited the excellent *Mercosur: Regional Integration, World Markets* (1999), which includes both U.S. and Brazilian contributors. The security implications of integration are often neglected in the literature, but David Pion-Berlin addressed them adroitly in "Will Soldiers Follow? Economic Integration and Regional Security in the Southern Cone" (2000).

D. SECURITY, DEFENSE, MILITARY, AND NUCLEAR RELATIONS

A growing number of scholars, such as Sonny B. Davis, in *Brotherhood of Arms: Brazil–United States Military Relations, 1945–1977* (1996), began to study Brazil's military and security ties with other countries, Other authors looked more specifically at nuclear technology, such as Etel Solingen, in *Industrial Policy, Technology, and International Bargaining: Designing Nuclear Industries in Argentina and Brazil* (1996; see also Solingen 1989, 1994); Emanuel Adler, in *The Power of Ideology: The Quest for Technological Autonomy in Argentina and Brazil* (1991); George Quester, in *Brazil and Latin-American Nuclear Proliferation: An Optimistic View* (1979); and Paul L. Leventhal and Sharon Tanzer, editors of *Averting a Latin American Nuclear Arms Race: New Prospects and Challenges for Argentine-Brazilian Nuclear Cooperation* (1992). The literature on Brazil's nuclear programs and policies is some of the best in the field. The books by Solingen and Adler are among the most sophisticated analyses of nuclear issues in any country or region of the world. The best study of Brazil's nuclear programs and what they mean for international relations, however, is Michael Barletta's doctoral dissertation, "Ambiguity, Autonomy, and the Atom: Emergence of the Argentine-Brazilian Nuclear Regime" (2000). Barletta's study is cutting-edge in terms of theory, rigorous in terms of methodology, and seamlessly weaves technological and political issues. It stands as a model of what can be done in further study of Brazil's international relations.

Other scholars have focused on Brazil's space launch ties with other countries, such as Brian G. Chow, in *An Evolutionary Approach to Space Launch Commercialization* (1993), and Steven M. Flank, in his doctoral dissertation, "Reconstructing Rockets: The Politics of Developing Military Technology in Brazil, India, and Israel" (1993). These are also excellent studies in both their technological and political dimensions.

E. ENVIRONMENT

Brazil's environment has received increasing attention from international relations experts in both Brazil and abroad. For example, Ans Kolk and Peter Pennarts (photographer) published *Forests in International Environmental Politics: International Organizations, NGOs and the Brazilian Amazon* (1998). Andrew Hurrell and Benedict Kingsbury edited *International Politics of the Environment: Actors, Interests, and Institutions* (1992), which examines numerous issues and three case studies, including Brazil, under the chapter title "Brazil and the International Politics of Amazonian Deforestation." The chapter on Brazil analyzes the increasing importance of transnational environmental organizations. This "internationalization" of the Amazon has irked many Brazilian policy makers, who view such international meddling in the Amazon as a threat to Brazil's sovereignty. The

Amazonian environmental issue promises to generate some of the most theoretically insightful literature because of the multiplicity of actors involved in the Amazon. Hurrell and Kingsbury have taken an important step in exploring some of those theoretical implications.

VIII. Recent Trends

As we have seen, several disciplines (history, political science, sociology, economics) have been involved in the study of Brazil's international relations since the late nineteenth century, with one or another at different times taking the lead. Since 1945, the field has become increasingly multidisciplinary, especially since the mid-1980s. As a result, in addition to dealing with a vast array of real-world problems, scholars have been faced with a variety of competing philosophical, theoretical, and methodological approaches. For example, a new generation of international historians in the United States is moving away from traditional diplomatic history to social and cultural history. It remains to be seen what their impact will be on the study of international relations.

One of the major developments in the literature on Brazil's international relations has been the emergence of a new generation of Brazilian scholars, such as Monica Hirst. Whereas in the 1970s U.S. scholars accounted for most of the publications on Brazil's international relations, today Brazilian analysts on this subject have far surpassed the quantity and quality of the U.S. production. The Brazilian universities most prominently involved in this kind of research are the Universidade de Brasília (which benefits from its location in the nation's capital and its interaction with Itamaraty), the Pontifícia Universidade Católica in Rio de Janeiro (especially its Instituto de Relações Internacionais—IRI), and the Universidade de São Paulo. Such research has been bolstered by the availability of archival material. The Fundação Getúlio Vargas in Rio de Janeiro has such an archive.

Within the United States, expertise on Brazil's foreign relations is scattered geographically. As Robert Levine noted in chapter 2, U.S. scholars are generally expected to establish themselves as "Latin Americanists" first, given the broad demands of students. Few, if any, professors are given the luxury of specializing in Brazil—and especially in Brazil's foreign relations.

The U.S. journal that has most consistently published articles on Brazil's international relations has been the *Journal of Interamerican Studies and World Affairs*. The change of this journal's name to *Latin American Politics and Society* (starting in 2001) suggests that it is very difficult to sustain a journal that focuses exclusively on the international relations of Latin America. The *Latin American Research Review* has also been important. Other journals, such as *Foreign Affairs* and *International Organizations*, have occasionally included articles on Brazil.

The five most important U.S.-based professional associations for the literature on Brazil's international relations have been (in rough order of importance) the Latin American Studies Association (and especially its Brazil section), the American Political Science Association, the International Studies Association, the relatively new Brazilian Studies Association (BRASA), and the American Historical Association. With time, BRASA could become one of the most important associations in this area.

The Internet has revolutionized the ability of scholars to follow Brazil's foreign relations. In the 1980s, several universities, academic centers, and newspapers maintained files of articles on Brazil's foreign relations. In the 1990s, most of these institutions moved to an electronic mode. Within the United States, the electronic version of the *Handbook of Latin American Studies* has made it much easier to read reviews of major publications related to Brazil. Websites such as the Latin American Network Information Center, maintained by the University of Texas at Austin, provide superb access to important research materials. An excellent website is RelNet-Site Brasileiro de Referência em Relações Internacionais, at www.relnet.com.br/cgi-bin/WebObjects/RelNet. Such sites provide increasing opportunities for collaboration between U.S. and Brazilian scholars.

CONCLUSION

This chapter began by noting a resurgent interest in Brazil's international relations. Today, the literature on Brazil's international relations is richer, more specialized, and more abundant than it has ever been. Brazilian scholars have become more sophisticated and prolific in their analyses of Brazil's international relations, eclipsing U.S.-based scholarship. The broadening of themes is a welcome development, because the new themes tend to move away from a U.S.-centered view of Brazil in the world and toward recognition of Brazil's multiple facets in its international relations.

Despite these gains, there are still enormous gaps in the literature, especially in the area of applied theory. Robert Levine noted the reticence of "Brazilianists" to embrace cutting-edge theories. For example, despite its dominance in political science during the 1990s, rational choice theory has not been applied systematically to Brazil's international relations. There is also a need to further analyze Brazil's foreign relations from a substate level of analysis. Finally, the notion of "complex interdependence" has not been adequately applied to Brazil's foreign relations. G. Pope Atkins, in response to an earlier version of this chapter, wrote that there is a

> need in today's world for Brazilianists to embrace the pluralist concept of complex interdependence and to apply it to their analysis of Brazil's foreign relations. . . . Many of us in Latin American studies feel strongly that we are better served with multiple perspectives, which denies that any single theoretical construct can explain our world today or prescribe policies for dealing with it. To be specific: Pluralism properly challenges neorealism and rational choice theory as misleadingly simplistic rather than beneficially parsimonious, primarily because narrowly conceived state-centric assumptions are simply not equipped to deal with crucial transnational events and relationships. Pluralists admit they complicate the study of international relations but insist that pluralism is consonant with the complexities of the real world." (Atkins 2000)

This chapter has discussed some of the collaboration between U.S. and Brazilian scholars. In fact, such collaboration has been episodic. With the advent of the Internet, there is no reason why scholars in both countries should not collaborate on a broader and more sustained scale. A key impediment for further output of Brazilianists in the United States is the lack of funding for research in this area. In my experience, funds were made available to study the (perceived) "threats" of Brazil's conventional weapons, and nuclear and missile technology (Tollefson 1991). Once I concluded that Brazil's armaments, nuclear, and missile programs posed no threat to U.S. interests in the region, sponsors were no longer interested in funding further research related to Brazil's foreign relations. The few university centers in the United States that conduct research on Brazil's foreign relations (such as the Brazil Center at Johns Hopkins University's Paul H. Nitze School of Advanced International Studies) have received erratic support from both U.S. and Brazilian sponsors. Despite these obstacles, it is almost certain that there will be growing interest in the study of Brazil's foreign relations, as Brazil continues to assert itself internationally.

NOTES

1. Thanks to Wayne Selcher for his helpful comments on capability theory.

REFERENCES

Adler, Emanuel. 1991. *The Power of Ideology: The Quest for Technological Autonomy in Argentina and Brazil*. Berkeley: University of California Press.

Allison, Graham T. 1971. *Essence of Decision: Explaining the Cuban Missile Crisis*. Boston: Little, Brown.

Atkins, G. Pope. 2000. "Comments on Scott Tollefson, International Relations." Working Seminar on Brazilian Studies in the United States, 3 December, at Brazilian embassy, Washington, D.C.

Barletta, Michael. 2000. "Ambiguity, Autonomy, and the Atom: Emergence of the Argentine-Brazilian Nuclear Regime." Ph.D. diss., University of Wisconsin–Madison.

Beasley, Ryan K., Juliet Kaarbo, Jeffrey S. Lantis, and Michael T. Snarr, eds. 2001. *Foreign Policy in Comparative Perspective: Domestic and International Influences on State Behavior*. Washington, D.C.: Congressional Quarterly Press.

Becker, Bertha K., and Claudio A. G. Egler. 1992. *Brazil: A New Regional Power in the World Economy*. Cambridge: Cambridge University Press.

Berger, Mark T. 1995. *Under Northern Eyes: Latin American Studies and U.S. Hegemony in the Americas, 1898–1990*. Caribbean and Latin American Studies Series. Bloomington: Indiana University Press.

Biles, Robert E., ed. 1988. *Inter-American Relations: The Latin American Perspective*. Boulder, Colo.: Lynne Rienner.

Black, Jan Knippers. 1977. *United States Penetration of Brazil*. Philadelphia: University of Pennsylvania Press.

Burns, E. Bradford. 1966. *The Unwritten Alliance: Rio-Branco and Brazilian-American Relations*. New York: Columbia University Press.

Cardoso, Fernando Henrique, and Enzo Faletto. 1979. *Dependency and Development in Latin America*. Berkeley: University of California Press.

Child, Jack. 1985. *Geopolitics and Conflict in South America: Quarrels Among Neighbors*. New York: Praeger.

Child, Jack, and Philip Kelly, eds. 1988. *Geopolitics of the Southern Cone*. Boulder, Colo.: Lynne Rienner.

Chow, Brian G. 1993. *An Evolutionary Approach to Space Launch Commercialization*. Santa Monica, Calif.: Rand/National Defense Research Institute.

Cline, Ray S. 1980. *World Power Assessment: A Calculus of Strategic Drift*. Boulder, Colo.: Westview.

———. 1994. *The Power of Nations in the 1990s*. Lanham, Md.: University Press of America.

Cobbs, Elizabeth A. 1992. *The Rich Neighbor Policy: Rockefeller and Kaiser in Brazil*. New Haven, Conn.: Yale University Press.

Coffey, Peter, and Luiz Correa do Lago, eds. 1988. *EEC and Brazil: Trade, Capital Investment, and the Debt Problem*. New York: St. Martin's.

Council on Foreign Relations. 2001. *A Letter to the President and a Memorandum* on *U.S. Policy Toward Brazil*. Statement of an Independent Task Force. Stephen Robert, Chair; Kenneth Maxwell, Project Director. New York: Council on Foreign Relations.

Davis, Harold Eugene Davis, and Larman C. Wilson, eds. 1975. *Latin American Foreign Policies: An Analysis*. Baltimore: Johns Hopkins University Press.

Davis, Sonny B. 1996. *Brotherhood of Arms: Brazil–United States Military Relations, 1945–1977*. Boulder, Colo.: University of Colorado Press.

Desch, Michael C. 1993. *When the Third World Matters: Latin America and United States Grand Strategy*. Baltimore: Johns Hopkins University Press.

Due, John F., and Werner Baer. 1987. *Brazil and the Ivory Coast: The Impact of International Lending, Investment, and Aid*. Greenwich, Conn.: Jai.

English, Adrian J. 1987. "Brazil: A Super Power in the Making." *Defence* 18, no. 9:545–50.

Evans, Peter. 1979. *Dependent Development: The Alliance of Multinational, State and Local Capital in Brazil*. Princeton, N.J.: Princeton University Press.

Felder, Ellene A., and Andrew Hurrell. 1988. *U.S.-Brazilian Informatics Dispute*. FPI Case Studies, No. 13. Washington, D.C.: Foreign Policy Institute, School of Advanced International Studies, Johns Hopkins University.

Flank, Steven M. 1993. "Reconstructing Rockets: The Politics of Developing Military Technology in Brazil, India, and Israel." Ph.D. diss., Massachusetts Institute of Technology.

Fleischer, David V. 1985. "Relações Brasil-Cuba: uma reaproximação delicada." *Política e Estratégia* 3, no. 3:513–21.

Fontaine, Roger. 1974. *Brazil and the United States*. Washington, D.C.: American Enterprise Institute.

Fox, Annette Baker. 1976. *The Power of Attraction: Four Middle Powers and the United States*. New York: Columbia University Press.

Furtado, Celso. 1976. *Economic Development of Latin America: Historical Background and Contemporary Problems*. 2nd ed. Cambridge: Cambridge University Press.

Global Investment Business Center. 2000. *Brazil: Foreign Policy and Government Guide*. Washington, D.C.: International Business Publications.

Gordon, Lincoln, and Richard C. Leone. 2001. *Brazil's Second Chance: En Route toward the First World*. Washington, D.C.: Brookings Institution.

Graham, Richard, ed. 1991. *Brazil and the World System*. Austin: University of Texas Press.

Haines, Gerald K. 1989. *The Americanization of Brazil: A Study of U.S. Cold War Diplomacy in the Third World, 1945–1954*. Wilmington, Del.: Scholarly Resources Books.

Hartlyn, Jonathan, Lars Schoultz, and Augusto Varas, eds. 1992. *The United States and Latin America in the 1990s: Beyond the Cold War*. Chapel Hill: University of North Carolina Press.

Hilton, Stanley E. 1975. *Brazil and the Great Powers, 1930–1939: The Politics of Trade Rivalry*. Austin: University of Texas Press.

————. 1981. "The United States, Brazil, and the Cold War, 1945–1960: End of the Special Relationship." *Journal of American History* 68 (December): 599–624.

————. 1986. "Brazil's International Economic Strategy, 1945–1960: Revival of the German Option." *Hispanic American Historical Review* 66:287–318.

————. 1991. *Brazil and the Soviet Challenge, 1917–1945.* Austin: University of Texas Press.

Hollerman, Leon. 1988. *Japan's Economic Strategy in Brazil: Challenge for the United States.* Lexington, Mass.: Lexington Books.

Huggins, Martha. 1998. *Political Policing: The United States and Latin America.* Durham, N.C.: Duke University Press.

Hurrell, Andrew. 1992. "Brazil as a Regional Power: A Study in Ambivalence." In *Regional Great Powers in International Politics,* ed. Iver B. Neumann. New York: St. Martin's.

Hurrell, Andrew, and Benedict Kingsbury, eds. 1992. *International Politics of the Environment: Actors, Interests, and Institutions.* Oxford: Clarendon.

Kelly, Philip. 1997. *Checkerboards and Shatterbelts: The Geopolitics of South America.* Austin: University of Texas Press.

Kolk, Ans, and Peter Pennarts (photographer). 1998. *Forests in International Environmental Politics: International Organizations, NGOs and the Brazilian Amazon.* Utrecht, Netherlands: International Books.

Landau, Georges D. 1980. "The Treaty of Amazonian Cooperation: A Bold New Instrument for Development." *Georgia Journal of International and Comparative Law* 10, no. 3:463–89.

Lincoln, Jennie K., and Elizabeth G. Ferris. 1984. *Dynamics of Latin American Foreign Policies: Challenges for the 1980s.* Boulder, Colo.: Westview.

Leacock, Ruth. 1990. *Requiem for Revolution: The United States and Brazil, 1961–1969.* Kent, Ohio: Kent State University Press.

Leventhal, Paul L., and Sharon Tanzer, eds. 1992. *Averting a Latin American Nuclear Arms Race: New Prospects and Challenges for Argentine-Brazilian Nuclear Cooperation.* London: Macmillan.

Lowenthal, Abraham. 1986. *Brazil and the United States.* Washington, D.C.: Foreign Policy Association.

McCann, Frank D. 1973. *The Brazilian-American Alliance: 1937–1945.* Princeton, N.J.: Princeton University Press.

Mattos, Carlos de Meira. 1977. *A geopolítica e as projeções de poder.* Rio de Janeiro: Livraria José Olympio Editora.

Morris, Michael A. 1979. *International Politics and the Sea: The Case of Brazil.* Boulder, Colo.: Westview.

Nembhard, Jessica Gordon. 1996. *Capital Control, Financial Regulation, and Industrial Policy in South Korea and Brazil.* New York: Greenwood.

Oswald, J. Gregory, and Anthony J. Strover. 1970. *The Soviet Union and Latin America.* New York: Praeger.

Packenham, Robert A. 1992. *The Dependency Movement: Scholarship and Politics in Development Studies.* Cambridge: Cambridge University Press.

Pastor, Robert A. 1992. *Whirlpool: U.S. Foreign Policy Toward Latin America and the Caribbean.* Princeton, N.J.: Princeton University Press.

Perry, William. 1976. *Contemporary Brazilian Foreign Policy: The Strategy of an Emerging Power.* Beverly Hills, Calif.: Sage.

Pion-Berlin, David. 2000. "Will Soldiers Follow? Economic Integration and Regional Security in the Southern Cone." *Journal of Interamerican Studies and World Affairs* 42, no. 1:43–69.

Quester, George. 1979. *Brazil and Latin-American Nuclear Proliferation: An Optimistic View.* Los Angeles: Center for International Relations.

Raine, Philip. 1974. *Brazil, Awakening Giant.* Washington, D.C.: Public Affairs Press.

Roett, Riordan. 1972. *The Politics of Foreign Aid in the Brazilian Northeast.* Nashville, Tenn.: Vanderbilt University Press.

———. 1981. "Brazilian Foreign Policy: Options in the 1980s." In *Authoritarian Capitalism: Brazil's Contemporary Economic and Political Development,* ed. Thomas C. Bruneau and Philippe Faucher. Boulder, Colo.: Westview.

———. 1984. *Brazil: Politics in a Patrimonial Society.* 3rd ed. New York: Praeger.

———. 1989. "The Foreign Policy of Latin America." In *Foreign Policy in World Politics,* ed. Roy C. Macridis. 8th ed. Englewood Cliffs, N.J.: Prentice Hall.

———, ed. 1972. *Brazil in the Sixties.* Nashville, Tenn.: Vanderbilt University Press.

———. 1976. *Brazil in the Seventies.* Studies in Foreign Policy. Washington, D.C.: American Enterprise Institute.

———. 1999. *Mercosur: Regional Integration, World Markets.* Boulder, Colo.: Lynne Rienner.

Roett, Riordan, and Wolf Grabendorff, eds. 1985. *Latin America, Western Europe and the U.S.: Reevaluating the Atlantic Triangle.* New York: Praeger.

Roett, Riordan, and Susan Kaufman Purcell, eds. 1997. *Brazil Under Cardoso.* Boulder, Colo.: Lynne Rienner.

Roett, Riordan, and Scott Tollefson. 1986. "Brazil's Status as an Intermediate Power." *Third World Affairs* 2: 101–12.

Rohter, Larry. 2000. "Brazil Begins to Take Role on the World Stage." *New York Times,* 30 August.

Sanders, Thomas G. 1987. "Brazilian Geopolitics: Securing the South and North." *American Universities Field Staff International Reports,* no. 23.

Santos, Theotônio dos. 1970. "The Structure of Dependence." *American Economic Review* 60, no. 2:231–36.

Schneider, Ronald M. 1976. *Brazil: Foreign Policy of a Future World Power.* Boulder, Colo.: Westview.

Selcher, Wayne A. 1978. *Brazil's Multilateral Relations: Between First and Third Worlds.* Boulder, Colo.: Westview.

———. 1984. "Brazil's Foreign Policy: More Actors and Expanding Agendas." In *The Dynamics of Latin American Foreign Policies: Challenges for the 1980s*, ed. Jennie K. Lincoln and Elizabeth G. Ferris. Boulder, Colo.: Westview.

———. 1986. "Current Dynamics and Future Prospects of Brazil's Relations with Latin America: Toward a Pattern of Bilateral Cooperation." *Journal of Interamerican Studies and World Affairs* 28, no. 2:67–99.

———. 1988. "Brazil and the Southern Cone Subsystem." In *South America into the 1990s*, ed. G. Pope Atkins. Boulder, Colo.: Westview.

———, ed. 1981. *Brazil in the International System: The Rise of a Middle Power.* Boulder, Colo.: Westview.

Silva, Golbery do Couto e. 1967. *A geopolítica do Brasil.* 2nd ed. Rio de Janeiro: Livraria José Olympio Editora.

———. 1981. *Conjuntura política nacional: o poder executivo e geopolítica do Brasil.* Rio de Janeiro: Livraria José Olympio Editora.

Smith, Joseph. 1991. *Unequal Giants: Diplomatic Relations Between the United States and Brazil, 1889–1930.* Pittsburgh, Pa.: University of Pittsburgh Press.

Solingen, Etel. 1989. "Technology, Exports and Countertrade: Brazil as an Emerging Nuclear Supplier." In *International Nuclear Trade: The Challenge of the Emerging Suppliers*, ed. William C. Potter. New York: Lexington.

———. 1994. "Macropolitical Consensus and Lateral Autonomy in Industrial Policy: The Nuclear Sector in Brazil and Argentina." *International Organization* 47, no. 2:263–98.

———. 1996. *Industrial Policy, Technology, and International Bargaining: Designing Nuclear Industries in Argentina and Brazil.* Stanford, Calif.: Stanford University Press.

Tollefson, Scott D. 1991. "Brazilian Arms Transfers, Ballistic Missiles and Foreign Policy: The Search for Autonomy." Ph.D. diss., Paul H. Nitze School of Advanced International Studies, Johns Hopkins University.

Topik, Steven C. 1997. *Trade and Gunboats: The United States and Brazil in the Age of Empire.* Stanford, Calif.: Stanford University Press.

Wallerstein, Immanuel. 1974. *The Modern World-System: Capitalist Agriculture and the Origins of the European World-Economy in the Sixteenth Century.* New York: Academic Press.

Wesson, Robert. 1981. *The United States and Brazil: The Limits of Influence.* New York: Praeger.

∼

Geography

CYRUS B. DAWSEY III

INTRODUCTION

A large number of Brazil-focused geographical studies have been produced by Anglo-American scholars since 1945.[1] While these studies have contributed significantly to our knowledge of Brazil, describing this body of scholarship presents several unique challenges. Some are linked directly to the discipline itself, such as the broad differences in definition of the scope of the field held by those who call themselves geographers; or the dramatic, and some would say convulsive, paradigm shifts that have taken place as geography (and subfields) evolved during the second half of the twentieth century.

Other considerations relate to the position of geography within the broader galaxy of the social and physical sciences. Because of the internal diversity of the field, geographers sometimes find themselves more closely associated with colleagues in other disciplines than with other geographers. They often publish in nongeographical journals and teach in nongeographical university departments. Many geographers possess technical expertise that gives them a comfortable relationship with researchers in complementary disciplines but reduces these geographers' ability to communicate with other geographers who do not share the same interests. *Rediscovering Geography* (National Research Council 1997) provides a useful summary of the current status of the field of geography and its relationship to other disciplines.

Finally, the focus of this project on a spatial unit, Brazil, raises additional questions. While many geographical studies, especially within the regional tradition, have dealt explicitly with a recognized spatial area, much of the recent work has taken on a more systematic focus. Though a research project may have been conducted in Brazil, the major thrust of its report in the literature is likely to be a topic that transcends political boundaries or area definition. Much of the human-based information about Brazil is contained (buried?) in articles or books dealing with socio-economic conditions across Latin America or the Third World. Meanwhile, physical-based research on Brazil may appear in articles focused on tropical and subtropical environments published in journals in the physical, environmental, or biological sciences. The Brazil connection is not always evident in the title, abstract, or description of a report.

Before discussing these issues more thoroughly in the next section, I will present a general overview of the history of Brazil-centered geographical work. Following the discussion of the shifting trends in geography (and the resultant impact on studies about Brazil), some of the contributions of key individuals will be outlined. In the final section of the chapter I will attempt to provide a snapshot of important work produced in recent years and offer some comments regarding current directions and expectations for the future.

An important initial task is to define the core of the discipline. Three general conditions were used as starting points for identifying which scholarly works should be considered geographical. The criteria were not exclusive, however, and where it seemed useful, additional material was examined. A work was reviewed if (1) its author calls himself/herself a geographer; or (2) it appeared in a recognized geographical journal such as: the *Annals of the Association of American Geographers; Professional Geographer; Geographical Review; Yearbook of the Conference of Latin Americanist Geographers;* and others; or (3) the scope of the research appeared to conform to one of the mainline traditions in geography, including a focus on spatial relationships; the interaction between humans and the physical environment; or the general description of an area (regional tradition).

Meeting any of these conditions was sufficient reason for subjecting the work to review. Of course, these conditions were in addition to the criteria derived from the stated purpose of the project, namely, to examine research about Brazil conducted since 1945 by North America–based scholars. The literature survey focused on U.S.- and Canada-based publications, so articles written by residents of these nations but printed in foreign journals were usually not included. Though geographers in the United Kingdom have contributed greatly to English language scholarship on Brazil, the constraints of space and the stated objectives of the project have limited the references to our European colleagues. Among the many works thus omitted are those by Peter Furley, Anthony Hall, Joe Foweraker, Jay Mistry, John Dickenson, Michel Eden, Chris Barrow, and others. This study examined published English-language journal and book materials. A more exhaustive effort might include an evaluation of scholarship in other languages, especially Portuguese, as well as doctoral dissertations, university course titles, and course content as revealed through interviews with instructors.

I. General Description of the Studies of Brazil by U.S.- and Canada-based Geographers Since 1945

A. BACKGROUND: EARLY EXPLORATIONS AND DESCRIPTIONS

Much of what is considered to be early geographical writing is contained in descriptions produced by individuals who traveled to little-known (to Western society) exotic lands. Brazil was explored by many, including the German Alexander von Humboldt at the end of the eighteenth century and the Englishman Richard Burton who, in the 1860s, encountered English-speaking immigrants from the U.S. South in the São Francisco valley (Burton 1969). Louis Agassiz also spent time in Brazil, as did other, less famous, travelers. During the middle of the nineteenth century the Reverend James C. Fletcher (1845) published a book describing the wonders of Brazil. A later elaboration entitled *Brazil and the Brazilians*, jointly written with Daniel Kidder (Fletcher and Kidder 1856), became a major success and went through several printings through the 1870s. The book's glowing descriptions of an attractive agricultural environment and friendly people were major stimulants, leading thousands of disillusioned Americans from the Confederate states to relocate to Brazil after the American Civil War.

The output of descriptive books about Brazil has continued up to the present. This tradition includes great diversity, ranging from tales of early travels through the Northeast (Koster 1966) to journalistic observation (Gunter 1966) to photo-rich adventure tales (Schreider and Schreider 1970) to travel guides and tourist aids (Draffen, McAsey, Pinheiro, and Jones 1997). Though these and countless similar works might be characterized as geographical (regional description, elements of the physical geography, etc.), they fall outside the mainstream of scholarly work. Meanwhile, a small but committed group of professionals has worked over the years to build a substantial body of knowledge within the discipline of geography by using critical observation, scientific methodology, rational analysis, and peer-reviewed reporting.

B. MIDCENTURY REGIONAL STUDIES

By the end of the Second World War much of geography was focused on regions. Research involved describing conditions or analyzing problems associated with particular areas, and an important theme repeated in many reports was that these areas were unique or at least distinctive. Latin America was the focus of a substantial amount of interest. By this time major figures within the discipline had published work on Brazil, sometimes within the larger context of Latin or South America (Whitbeck, Williams, and Christians 1940; Wilgus 1943; Platt 1943). This period marked the emergence of a group of regional specialists who engaged in significant fieldwork in Brazil. Among the early group were Leo Waibel and Preston James, who would become the most prominent of all Latin Americanists focused on the study of Brazil. James's often-reprinted book, *Brazil* (1946), was the best regional treatise on that country, and it might be considered the geographical counterpart to sociologist T. Lynn Smith's *Brazil: People and Institutions* (1946) and (somewhat later) anthropologist Charles Wagley's *An Introduction to Brazil* (1963).

Works on regional geography were published in a variety of journals, but the most significant outlet for Anglo-American researchers was the *Geographical Review*. During the late 1940s and 1950s it ran articles describing settlement in northern Paraná (Dozier 1956), resource extraction and land use in the Amazon (Higbee 1951), Brazilian agricultural development (James 1953b), the siting of Brazil's proposed new capital (James and Faissol 1956), the basin of the São Francisco River (James 1948), and land use in the central plateau (Waibel 1948). Clarence Jones (1958) also contributed a general description of Brazil, and he and Preston James wrote the definitive summary of the field of geography of that day (James and Jones 1954). As might be expected, the work heavily emphasized regional research.

In the late 1950s two other geographers emerged as leading researchers: Hilgard O'Reilly Sternberg and Kempton Webb. Continuing in the tradition of their predecessors, they have devoted much of their efforts to the study of Brazil and Brazil-related topics. Through their positions at the University of California, Berkeley (Sternberg), and Columbia University in New York City (Webb), they were able to exert significant influence, not only within geography but also through interdisciplinary collaborative projects. Their active professionalism and commitment to Brazilian studies inspired many students, and several important present-day scholars benefited from their tutelage. These geographers remained focused on their area of interest even as a significant segment of the geographical discipline was diverted away from regional and human-environment interaction studies.

Though the regional tradition in geography has persisted, beginning in the 1960s researchers became more interested in analyzing specific problems or conditions than in describing defined areas of the earth's surface. The shift in focus was a response to changing values, improved investigative skills, developing computer technology, and increased familiarity with quantitative tools. During and since this period geographers have also become more concerned with social and environmental problems, a trend that parallels changes in other related social sciences. Studies have included prescriptions for redressing flaws in social or political structures. Geographers were among the most vocal early critics of the Brazilian government's policies (supported by international agencies) that encouraged increased population densities and the destruction of the natural vegetation of the Amazon region (Hiraoka 1982; Denevan 1973; Hecht and Cockburn 1989).

Much of the research on Brazil has also reflected an evolution and improvement in the way geographers conduct their craft. Moving beyond basic description, most contemporary studies are carried out within a framework of critical assessment, careful data collection, hypothesis testing, and quantitative analysis (where applicable). The technologies of geographic information systems (GIS) and remote sensing analysis are also beginning to affect studies by U.S. scholars working on Brazil. The impact, however, has not been as significant as might be expected, given the explosive increase in the use of these applications in the United States.

The preceding paragraphs have provided a brief sketch of the trends in geography research by Anglo-American scholars working in Brazil, and a more extensive discussion will follow over the next several pages. Though some scholars continue in the regional tradition of James, others have followed new paths. Over the decades, however, one element has remained constant. Geographers studying Brazil have continued to engage in fieldwork. It is certainly possible to conduct geographical research by relying on secondhand or remotely gathered information, but I am unaware of anyone who claims to be a Brazilianist geographer who has not had intimate and frequent contact with Brazil. Most Brazilianists use any excuse to travel to the field, attracted perhaps as much by the friendly hospitality of the Brazilian people as by the need to collect data.

II. ANALYSIS OF THE TRENDS IN SCHOLARSHIP
IN THE GEOGRAPHICAL STUDIES OF BRAZIL

A. SIGNIFICANCE OF THE FIELD OF GEOGRAPHY
WITHIN THE SOCIAL SCIENCES

The field of geography, which means description of the earth, has a long history. Over the years, however, our understanding of and description of the earth has changed. Though we trace geographical thought back to the ancient Greeks, many modern features of the discipline were established during the late nineteenth and early twentieth centuries. There is inadequate room here to elaborate on the sometimes compulsive self-examination that our discipline has undertaken in its attempts to define the scope of the field. Though geographers' understanding of their mission may vary, most have found a niche among the social sciences by becoming one or more of the following: (a) regional experts, (b) specialists on the complex relationship between humans and the physical environment, (c) developers and appliers of new quantitative and digital spatial analysis tools.

In these capacities geographers have been able to contribute significantly to knowledge about the world. Because the discipline is not limited to the study of a single category of event, geographers feel free to examine almost anything within an associated spatial or distributional context. For this reason geography is often considered a dimensional field (as history focuses on the temporal dimension) linked to two-dimensional space on the surface of the earth. This means that geographers frequently find themselves using and contributing to knowledge in other fields, including most of the social and some of the physical sciences. Geographers, sometimes referred to as spatial analysts, human ecologists, or other euphemisms, are often viewed as integrators and synthesizers of information developed outside the discipline.

B. CHANGING PARADIGMS IN GEOGRAPHY

1. Regional Description

For much of the twentieth century geography was considered to be, at its foundation, an ideographic field. In the tradition of Carl Sauer, Preston James, and others, it was believed that a geographer's most important contribution was to develop expertise on the unique characteristics of spatially distinguishable areas, described as regions. A region was conceived of as a portion of the earth's surface that possessed significant internal homogeneity and was substantially different from neighboring areas. Of course, deciding what variables would be used to identify homogeneity, and thus define a region, became a consuming task. From this perspective the most important differentiating characteristic among research reports was the area of study. A common set of systematic topics was applied to many different countries or regions within countries. Geographical presentations featured descriptions of far-flung areas, but most followed a standard outline: the physical landscape, the cultural or settlement history, population characteristics, important resources, agriculture. Every geographer was expected to possess a regional specialty and to become thoroughly familiar with her or his chosen area. Most geographers were also urged to develop good command of one or more foreign languages. Regional geographers had, to some extent, a point of view similar to that of many cultural anthropologists engaged in ethnographic case studies.

Regional specialization was abetted in the early 1960s by financial support from agencies such as the Ford Foundation's Social Science Research Council, the Guggenheim Foundation, and others. In the late 1940s the federal government of the United States established the Fulbright foreign fellowship program, and many graduate students completed research for their degrees by making use of the available funding. The Peace Corps also attracted idealistic young Americans to foreign areas, and Brazil received its share of volunteers. Several of these came back to the United States filled with enthusiasm and a desire to continue to study the country with which they had gained familiarity. They often went on to pursue graduate degrees as regional specialists.

2. Spatial Analysis Using Quantitative Methodologies

Beginning in the 1960s, geography pioneered new directions. Critical of the descriptive tradition and claiming that geography should attempt to be more scientific, a new generation of scholars applied sophisticated quantitative techniques to massive stores of data. They attempted to tease out sometimes obscure relationships and spatial patterns from complex sets of data by applying statistical analyses and the power of digital computers.

A parallel trend involved the extensive use of models based on simplifying assumptions, which reduced reality to a homogeneous plain populated by perfectly rational human beings. Land rent functions, hexagonal central place networks, and gravity-analogous interaction models became widespread in the literature. The new generation eventually hoped to discover universal laws and theories that could be used to predict human spatial behavior. Inevitable conflict arose between the advocates of the "new geography" and the "old-timers," and sometimes the differences surfaced in heated exchanges at professional meetings. Paralleling the quantitative movement in geography was a trend toward greater social awareness and responsibility. Reflecting the general political climate during the Vietnam War period, several geographers looked at events through the socialist/ Marxist lenses of oppression and class conflict. Rather than a means for discovering knowledge, research became a mechanism for advancing a social agenda. Of course, geography was not unique among the social sciences in this regard.

3. New Technology and Applied Geography Studies

During the decades since the 1960s and early 1970s, the paradigm lurches have given way to a more balanced evolution of the discipline. Some practitioners, still committed to the view that geography's greatest contribution lies in providing expert knowledge about foreign areas, continue in the regional tradition. Though this orientation does not come close to being as strong as it was earlier in the twentieth century, it is still recognized as a valid pursuit within the discipline.

Most geographical studies today, however, are not purely regional. They incorporate some elements expressed by the movements initiated thirty to forty years ago. Studies in land use or political geography, for example, often include the purpose of highlighting problems and suggesting better alternatives to current practices. Quantitative analysis has become more sophisticated, and, most important, the users of complex techniques have become much more skeptical of the quality of data available from public sources such as the census tables. Those who use these techniques have also developed a better knowledge of the limitations of the tools that are being employed.

Finally, the most significant development in recent years in geography has been the creation of new spatial analysis tools. GIS, or the analysis of sets of digitally integrated spatial information, has become the single most important subfield within the discipline. Coupled with the related areas of global positioning systems, computer cartography, and remote sensing analysis, GIS has made it possible for geographers to gain and apply knowledge in ways that were not possible in the past. New careers in the public as well as private sectors have opened up, and the ongoing improvements in computer hardware and software ensure that the field will continue to boom. Consequently, much of the research in geography has taken on a decidedly applied character. These powerful tools are used not only to uncover knowledge but to discover solutions to problems.

C. REFLECTION OF PARADIGM SHIFTS IN THE STUDIES OF BRAZIL

How have the changes in geography affected studies of Brazil? Before the quantitative revolution of the 1960s, geography's focus was primarily regional. Under this paradigm Brazil was a natural target of study. This large country with a broad range of physical and cultural landscapes has often captured the imagination of Anglo-Americans. The articles written for geographical journals dealt with many specific topics, but the subject was usually considered as an interesting, and perhaps unique, feature of this region known as Brazil (or Amazonia, or Northeast Brazil, etc.). Focus was on the area itself. Almost all the studies up through the 1950s followed in this tradition. Higbee's comprehensive description of human activity in the Amazon (1951), or Dozier's 1956 exposition on northern Paraná introduced these areas to their readers as unique and interesting places with particular sets of physical and human characteristics.

The regional perspective is still widely applied in studies of Brazil. General descriptions of the country in recent years, especially in some textbooks, have relied on the traditional themes of regional geography: physical bases, settlement history, land use, urbanization, resources, transportation, and so on (Momsen 1968; James and Minkel 1986; Morris 1987; Blouet and Blouet 1997). Much of the later research, however, has reflected a shift away from a focus on the area itself and toward the topic under consideration. For example, in 1951 Higbee described a wide variety of interesting aspects of human occupation of the Amazon, including information about vegetation, rubber extraction, settlement history, and the like. While more recent works about the Amazon still include a careful analysis of the special characteristics that differentiate the region from others, they seem to be primarily concerned with the systematic topic under consideration, be it the black earth (*terra preta*) areas, boomtown development, sex ratios, or the Trans-Amazonian Highway.

Interestingly, the new quantitative techniques were seldom applied by Anglo-American scholars in studies of Brazil. Great Britain's John Peter Cole (1965) produced a text on the social and economic geography of Latin America that incorporated some of the new methods. After visiting Brazil, trail-blazing quantifiers Peter Haggett and Brian Berry conducted research on soil erosion in the Serra do Mar (Haggett 1961), looked at soil sampling in Minas Gerais (Haggett 1963), and used principal components analysis to define homogeneous economic regions (Berry and Pyle 1972). Later, Dawsey (1979b) also applied principal components analysis to an examination of the relationship between destination *municipios* and the source states for migrants moving into southwest Paraná. These efforts were the exception rather than the rule. The regional specialist doing work in Brazil and familiar with the Portuguese language was usually not interested (nor perhaps trained) in quantitative models and statistics.

Additional technical problems came into play. The quantifiers were fond of mining data generated by government agencies, and Brazilian centers such as the Fundação Getúlio Vargas and the Instituto Brasileiro de Geografia e Estatística were good potential sources. These data, however, were not readily accessible to Anglo-Americans. Brazilian census tomes were available only in a few locations in the United States, and the collections were sometimes incomplete or out of date. Unreliable mail service in an era before electronic data transfer ensured that Anglo-American researchers who wanted to use Brazilian data almost had to go to Brazil to find it. Furthermore, few Anglo-American users of the quantitative techniques had a sufficient knowledge of Portuguese to work with the information once it had been obtained. Finally, serious questions were raised about the validity of some of the data collected for several of the Brazilian census reports. As a consequence of these conditions, the quantitative revolution was carried forth, not by Anglo-Americans but primarily in Brazil by the Brazilians themselves. Led by U.S.-trained scholars such as Speridião Faissol and Pedro Pinchas Geiger, Brazilian geography developed a core of practitioners who were knowledgeable in many of the techniques being used in the United States and Western Europe (Faissol 1980).

In a similar vein the new digital cartographic and GIS tools most often have been applied by Brazilian researchers rather than Anglo-Americans. Much of the applied GIS in the United States has moved from university campuses to planning agencies and private corporations. Spatial analysis in Brazil is being capably performed by foreign firms under contract and by local agencies such as the Centro de Análise e Planejamento Ambiental or the Instituto Nacional de Pesquisas Espaciais. The use of remotely sensed imagery in and of Brazil (including the radar mapping of the Amazon region under project RADAM Brasil), also more often has involved Brazilians rather than Anglo-Americans (Momsen 1979).

In summary the "Brazilianist geography" performed by Anglo-Americans is not as clear-cut today as it was during the period of regional specialization. Though some may work more or less exclusively on Brazilian topics, most present-day geographers would consider themselves to be systematic specialists, such as urban geographers, historical geographers, environmental geographers, and the like, who happen to have an interest in Brazil. As an example, Jock Galloway has written about the historical geography of Northeast Brazil (1968, 1975), but he has also studied sugar cane production in many other regions of the world (1989, 1996). Most geographers focus on themes that transcend the political boundaries of one country. So, while a significant amount of geography is being done by Anglo-Americans in and about Brazil, the work is not as directly linked to that region as might have been true a few decades ago.

D. OTHER FACTORS AFFECTING THE TRENDS

1. Economic and Political Developments in Anglo-America and Brazil

Political events inside and outside Brazil have helped shape Anglo-American studies of that country. The decade of the 1960s was an eventful period. In the United States the idealism of the Peace Corps returnees, the growing social consciousness among academics, and the unrest caused by the Vietnam War had an impact on scholarship. Meanwhile in Brazil the instabilities of the Quadros and Goulart governments, followed by the 1964 coup and subsequent military rule under General Castelo Branco and others, influenced the agenda of Anglo-American researchers. Political oppression, social differences, and injustice became important topics. Land tenure studies, stimulated in part by the Land Tenure Center at the University of Wisconsin, abounded. Rather than produce traditional land use maps of rural areas, some geographical research focused on comparing income among urban classes and highlighting the effects of the inequities in society (Oesterhoudt 1965; Ludwig and Taylor 1969; Land Tenure Center 1972). Cultural change in Brazil was the theme for the 1969 annual meeting of the Midwest Association for Latin American Studies (Rippy 1969).

Much of the zeal for social and political reform has been replaced by a concern about the destruction of the natural environment and disappearance of indigenous communities. The growing awareness of biological interdependencies, new signs of global warming, and increasing toxic pollution have spurred many studies. The growth of the environmental movement occurred during a period when the Brazilian government, supported by outside funding, was making a determined effort to bring economic development to the Amazon region. Population densities increased, much of the forest was leveled, indigenous societies were destroyed, and rivers were contaminated with mercury produced by mining activity. Events in Brazil have seriously endangered a significant portion of the earth's biological and cultural diversity. The Amazon region, therefore, has been the most important focal point for research by Anglo-American geographers since the 1980s.

Another factor that may have led Anglo-Americans to center their activity on northern Brazil is that most of the economic growth in the country has taken place in the core areas of the Southeast. The state of São Paulo and neighboring regions might easily be classified as part of the developed world. The industrial and service-based economy of this area, as well as the associated problems, are in many ways similar to those of regions in the United States and Western Europe. Though the Brazilian core certainly warrants continued study, it probably no longer captures the imagination of Anglo-Americans as it once did. This region may be perceived to be well-off (and therefore a less interesting research target) in comparison to the North or Northeast. Among Anglo-Americans there may be a notion that the people of Southeast Brazil possess sufficient financial and technical resources to study the important issues of that area. Finally, the problems of the Southeast (and there are many) are not viewed as having the global importance of those linked to the Amazon area. Destruction of the rain forest is presented as a threat to worldwide (and Anglo-American) well-being, while, for example, the pollution of the Tietê River might be viewed as a local issue of interest only to Brazilians. Though an objective examination has not been performed, this perception is likely reflected in the lack of research funding available for studies in the Southeast compared to those focused on the North.

2. Focus on Latin Americanist Instead of Brazilianist Geography

The percentage of geographers in Anglo-America who consider themselves to be predominantly regional specialists has dwindled, and within that group the portion interested in Brazil has also decreased. Academic programs (and perhaps region-based sections in government agencies) have been consolidated. Fewer university faculty are hired for their knowledge of distant lands, and among the regional positions still available, very few are reserved for Brazilianists. Most institutions, outside a handful of the very top graduate programs, will fill a position with a Latin Americanist geographer who has specialized in a Spanish-speaking region of the continent. Because that language is spoken in a large number of nations, and because of the Hispanic community resident in the United States, a non-Brazilian focus may be viewed as being more useful to an academic program. Of course, this ignores the overwhelming relative importance of Brazil among the nations of Latin America.

Portuguese is taught almost exclusively only at the college level in this country and then usually at the advanced undergraduate level in those limited schools where it is offered. Portuguese is almost always a second language (after Spanish) acquired by a graduate student contemplating fieldwork elsewhere in the Western Hemisphere. Travel to Brazil is more expensive than to nearer Latin American countries. The presence of many immigrants in the United States from Puerto Rico, Cuba, Mexico, and various Central American republics has created a sizable Spanish-speaking community, and this presence highlights the usefulness and relevance of that language as well as topics pertinent to those countries. More distant Brazil, in comparison, is erroneously perceived to be less significant.

3. Development of Geography at the Instituto Brasileiro de Geografia e Estatística and Brazilian Academic Centers

The native Brazilian discipline of geography has been remarkably active. To describe the evolution of the field and the many contributions of the Brazilians is beyond the scope of this essay, but there has been a relationship between this development and the activities of Anglo-American geographers. During the first half of the twentieth century, geography in Brazil was shaped by the French tradition. Pierre Deffontaines arrived in Brazil in 1934, and he was instrumental in establishing the Associação de Geógrafos Brasileiros in 1936. The *Revista Brasileira de Geografia* was organized during the same year under French influence, though the journal was modeled on the North American *Geographical Review*. Deffontaines was followed at the Universidade de São Paulo by Pierre Monbeig, who also greatly stimulated Brazilian geography (James 1972: 320).

During the 1940s and early 1950s Brazilian geographers came in contact with several Anglo-American researchers. Leo Waibel, a German-born immigrant to the United States, studied areas of the central plateau in Goiás, and during the period interacted with Brazilian colleagues. According to Speridião Faissol (1996), among Waibel's experiences in Brazil was an unhappy meeting with a German community in Goiás that had remained sympathetic to Nazism. Waibel had fled Hitler's regime. The most significant contacts between Brazilians and North Americans during this time occurred because of Preston James's interest in Brazil and his prominence in the United States. Faissol gained a scholarship and earned a doctoral degree at Syracuse University under James, and soon thereafter, Faissol returned to Brazil to become the head of the Conselho Nacional de Geografia (later renamed the Instituto Brasileiro de Geografia e Estatística, or IBGE) (Faissol 1996). Waibel, James, and Faissol worked together on one of the important geographical topics of the 1950s: where to locate the new capital of the country (James and Faissol 1956). Augelli (1963) later criticized the choice of the location in the interior state of Goiás.

The quantitative revolution of the 1960s arrived in Brazil with the visit of John Peter Cole from the University of Nottingham, England, and Brian J. L. Berry from the United States in 1969. Their presentations and scholarly output (Berry and Pyle 1972) were important stimulants to Brazilians such as Faissol, Pedro Pinchas Geiger, Marília Galvão, and others. The change in direction in Brazilian geography was reflected in the content of two comprehensive works that appeared during the 1970s. In the two-volume *Brasil: a terra e o homem,* edited by Aroldo de Azevedo (1970) and published by the Universidade de São Paulo press, the treatment of physical and human geography was still relatively traditional: rivers, mountains, population, ethnic groups, cities, and so on. Seven years later many of the chapters in the five-volume set *Geografia do Brasil,* produced by the IBGE (1977), included trend surfaces, principal components, and various other forms of quantitative analysis. Application of quantitative techniques continued into the 1980s and 1990s in a variety of physical and human geographical studies (Pinto 1986; USP 1993).

During subsequent years Brazilian geographers also developed competence in the use of air photography and satellite imagery (downloaded directly to Brazilian ground stations). The imagery was useful in Brazil where overland access to remote areas was difficult. Radar was especially valuable because of its ability to penetrate the persistent cloud cover of tropical areas. Use of GIS has also become widespread in Brazil. Applied to a variety of topics, the new technologies are being used to address some of Brazil's most pressing problems.

In summary, therefore, the discipline of geography in Brazil developed a solid base and has fared well in recent decades. Government-sponsored financing through CAPES, CNPq, FAPESP, and other agencies has supported education abroad as well as domestic investigations. Institutions of higher learning have continued to produce capable scholars and researchers who investigate a wide range of internal problems. Brazilian scholarship is healthy, and in comparison to their Anglo-American counterparts, Brazilian geographers have taken greater interest in the regions nearest at hand: the urbanized centers and the core agricultural areas of the Southeast. Though many Brazilian individual researchers, academic communities, and agencies are active in the Amazon region (often in partnership with Anglo-Americans), that area does not dominate geographical interest as it does for U.S.- and Canada-based investigators. To some extent, therefore, there has been a regional partitioning of research. Anglo-Americans concentrate their efforts in the tropical North, while Brazilians, though active throughout the country, focus on the Southeast. This division not only reflects a difference of interests but also relates to more mundane issues, such as the availability of funding for research, the location of major sources of data, familiarity with and access to the scholarly literature, travel experiences, and the residential location of the scholar.

The direction of Anglo-American research on Brazil has been shaped by more than paradigm shifts in the discipline, social currents in U.S. academia, and the emergence of Brazilian scholarship. It is also the result of personal interest and commitment. Though many scholars have devoted a large amount of energy to geographical studies in Brazil, three stand out because of their long-term impact: Preston James, Kempton Webb, and Hilgard O'Reilly Sternberg.

III. Important Academic Figures Who Shaped the Geographical Study of Brazil

A. PRESTON E. JAMES

Preston E. James was the earliest, and perhaps the most significant, of the Anglo-Americans to shape geographical research on Brazil. Born in Brookline, Massachusetts, in 1899, he completed a bachelor's degree at Harvard University and master's and doctoral degrees at Clark University. He was a member of the faculty at the University of Michigan for eighteen years before going into government service during the war years. After 1945 he moved to Syracuse University, where he went on to serve as department head and eminent scholar until his retirement in 1970. James published extensively on many Latin American areas, and his textbook, *Latin America* (latest edition: James and Minkel 1986), was the most important regional text for more than a generation. He also produced a general text on systematic geography (James 1966). James wrote about trends in geography (James and Jones 1954; James 1978), and his *All Possible Worlds* (James 1972; Martin and James 1993) has dominated studies of the history of geographic thought since the 1970s.

James's works on Brazil were numerous and wide ranging. He examined coffee production (1932), the embryonic iron industry (1939), and general patterns of industrialization in São Paulo (1935). He looked at rural areas of the Northeast (James 1952, 1953a), including the valley of the São Francisco River (1948), and he described the agriculture of the country as a whole (1953b). He investigated topics in physical geography and geomorphology as well as human geography (1959). His frequently reprinted text on Brazil (1946) was a landmark guide to anyone interested in the geography of that nation, and he often wrote essays for the *Handbook of Latin*

American Studies (James 1944) commenting on the development of geography in Brazil. James was certainly one of the most important geographers of his day (see descriptions of his work in Meinig 1971; Robinson 1980), and his interest in Brazil placed that country among the most popular targets for area studies. His textbooks impacted students as well as teachers, and his ideas greatly influenced the geographic thought of his day. His early connection with Faissol and other Brazilians helped to influence the direction of geography in Brazil.

B. KEMPTON WEBB

Kempton E. Webb was born in Malden, Massachusetts, in 1931, by which time Preston James had already spent eight years as a faculty member at the University of Michigan. Following in the footsteps of his fellow Massachusetts native, Webb also received his undergraduate degree from Harvard. He went on to complete a doctoral degree in 1958 under James at Syracuse. Following a brief period in Indiana, in 1961 Webb moved to Columbia University where he joined other Brazilianists, including anthropologist Charles Wagley, to form a strong Brazil-focused interdepartmental program. During most of the 1960s Webb served as the director of Columbia's Institute of Latin American Studies.

Webb's major scholarly contributions addressed highly specific matters, such as urban food supplies (1959b) and food production in Minas Gerais (1959a), but he also wrote on broader topics, including a comprehensive report on the evolution of the landscape in Northeast Brazil (1974). His general works on Brazil (1964, 1968, 1969, 1970, and 1980) and Latin America (Webb, Pohl, and Zepp 1967) were highly regarded, and they helped to shape U.S. academic views of the country.

As director of the Institute of Latin American Studies, Webb played an important role in developing interdisciplinary studies focused on Brazil. Perhaps the most significant (for Brazilianists) publication to be released by the institute was *Brazil: Field Research Guide in the Social Sciences,* edited by Robert Levine (1966). The volume included a comprehensive case study illustration of how a geographical investigation might be conducted in the state of Goiás (Mandell 1966). It is interesting that the outline of the article is firmly set in the regional tradition: demography, migration/colonization, settlement, economic activity in general, agriculture, and transportation. The quantitative movement was still a few years off.

Webb also wrote frequently for the *Handbook of Latin American Studies,* describing the status of Brazilian geography. Through his work at the institute and his personal connections to various organizations (Conference on Latin American History [CLAH], Latin American Studies Association [LASA], Ford Foundation, Consortium of Latin American Studies Programs), Kempton Webb exerted a strong influence on studies in and of Brazil. Perhaps one of his greatest contributions was his support of the idea that good research is accomplished by teams transcending disciplinary boundaries. Following his retirement from Columbia, Webb spent a brief period during the early 1990s as head of the department of geography and anthropology at William Paterson College in New Jersey.

C. HILGARD O'REILLY STERNBERG

Hilgard O'Reilly Sternberg is a Brazilian, born in Rio de Janeiro in 1917. Though a substantial portion of his professional career was spent in Brazil and though he has published extensively in Portuguese, a review of Sternberg's work is included here because of his impact on geography in the United States. He received advanced degrees in three countries: a doctoral degree from Louisiana State University in 1956; Doutor em Geografia from the Federal University of Rio de Janeiro in 1958; and the Docteur *honoris causa* from the University of Toulouse in 1964. Since 1964 Sternberg has held a position in one of the most prominent geography departments in this country, the University of California, Berkeley. During his long career (today his position is emeritus) Sternberg has published widely in the United States and abroad, held important positions in national and international organizations (including vice president of the International Geographical Union), and received significant awards, including the Order of Rio Branco from the Brazilian government in 1967.

Sternberg considers himself an "issues-oriented" geographer. He has a lengthy publication record on many different topics, but most of his work has dealt with various aspects of the human-physical interface. Among his most notable contributions are general works on Brazil (1948, 1955, 1956, 1965, 1970, 1975), reports on the status of geographic thought in Brazil (1951, 1959), studies of flooding in the Paraíba Valley (1949, 1950), research on drought in the Northeast (1952, 1958), and articles about the Amazon region (1981, 1987, 1995a and 1995b). Sternberg has shaped the course of Anglo-American scholarship through his students as well as his extensive research and publication record. As a prominent Brazilianist in a strong department with a historical commitment to studies of the relationship between people and their environment, Sternberg has attracted outstanding students with an interest in Brazil. Today, scholars from the Berkeley tradition such as Brian Godfrey, Nigel Smith, and Robert Voeks are among the most prolific publishers on the geography of Brazil. The influence of Sternberg has been carried forward to a new generation.

IV. RECENT GEOGRAPHICAL STUDIES OF BRAZIL

A. SUBFIELDS TARGETED BY U.S. AND CANADIAN GEOGRAPHERS IN RECENT YEARS

1. General Works

As discussed earlier in this essay, establishing a boundary between Brazil-focused geographical work and scholarship in other sciences is sometimes difficult. For example, the description of Minas Velhas in interior Bahia, which anthropologist Marvin Harris (1956) presented in *Town and Country in Brazil*, might easily be classified as regional geography. Likewise, sociologist T. Lynn Smith's 1946 chapters on agriculture, population distribution, migration, and land tenure are also geographical. Many contemporary works fall into a similar category. Following in the footsteps of geographer Leo Waibel (1950), historian Frederick Luebke (1987) wrote about German settlers in southern Brazil. Chapter 1 provided maps of the settlement pattern, house types, and several other characteristics within the domain of cultural geography. Historians Stanley Stein (1970) and Warren Dean (1969, 1976, 1987) also contributed significant geographical information about Brazil. Published after his untimely death, Dean's 1995 description of the destruction of the Mata Atlântica forest in Southeast Brazil raised public awareness of the consequences of environmental neglect. Drawing on property records, Brannstrom (2002) has shown that the biophysical category "Atlantic forest" used by Dean really consisted of a mixture of forest and savannah land types, each with a different perceived fertility and market value.

Several sources continue to provide fundamental geographical information about Brazil. General regional information is widely available in travel guides, dictionaries, encyclopedias, and on the Internet (at, among other places, the CIA's website: www.cia.gov/cia/publications/factbook/). Though most current geography textbooks on Latin America have adopted a systematic outline (separate chapters on physical landscapes, settlement history, population, agriculture, industrial development, etc.), some in recent years have followed the more traditional layout by allocating separate chapters to the various countries (James and Minkel 1986; Morris 1987). The chapter on Brazil by Galloway (1983) in the book by Blakemore and Smith (1983) provided a good summary of Brazil's historical geography.

Focus devoted an entire issue to an attractively illustrated and well-written article by Brian Godfrey (1999a) that presents one of the best concise descriptions of Brazil to appear in recent years.

Other information about Brazil is contained within the more specific topical literature on Latin America. Current popular textbooks follow this approach. Though the book by Blouet and Blouet includes a chapter by Gary Lobb (1997) on Brazil, most of the information on the country can be found in the earlier chapters on physical environment, aboriginal and colonial geography, agriculture, population, cities, and economic activity. In addition to the standard geographical topics, Clawson's 2000 text on Latin America (detailing much about Brazil) includes headings that are not commonly found elsewhere; he devotes space to chapters on religion, tourism, health, and social class. Caviedes and Knapp (1995) also use a systematic approach, and the chapters entitled "South America in the World Economy," "Settlement Networks and Urban Systems," "The South American State," and "Cultural and Ecological Survival" include substantial information on Brazil.

2. Historical, Cultural, and Political Geography

The remainder of this chapter will attempt to summarize important recent topical geographical research conducted in Brazil. Though grouped according to broad subdisciplinary categories, much of the work defies classification. By definition, geography is integrative and disrespectful of the boundaries among the sciences, and this applies to boundaries within the discipline as well. Though some examples of pioneering works are listed, most are drawn from research performed since the 1980s.

Many studies that have focused on specific ethnic groups or settlement communities might be classified as historical or cultural geography. Though not recent, Augelli's studies of Bastos, a Japanese colony (Augelli 1958a), and Varpa, a Latvian community (Augelli 1958b), contributed to our knowledge of the adaptation of immigrants in Brazil. Muller (1974) studied the pioneer settlement of Toledo in the southern state of Paraná. More recently, the small village of Marques in interior São Paulo was described by Dawsey (1989), and Gade (1994) wrote about change within the German ethnic communities of south Brazil. Another group subjected to study were the descendants of Anglo-Americans who emigrated to Brazil immediately after the Civil War (Dawsey 1993; Dawsey and Dawsey 1995).

Some geographers have focused on political topics and events. Caviedes (1984) analyzed the history of authoritarianism and the effect of immigration in Brazil and other nations of the Southern Cone. Hilgard Sternberg

(1987) showed that the Brazilian government's actions in the Amazon region have been heavily influenced by political interests, and Foresta (1991) contrasted the Amazon policies and motives of the post-1988 civilian government with those of the previous military regimes.

3. Migration, Social, and Urban Geography

Migration is fundamentally a spatial process, and internal human relocations in Brazil have been studied by many geographers (Dawsey 1992). The hope of land, gold, or commercial opportunity has attracted many migrants to frontier areas. The push and pull conditions leading to the rapid increase in settlement in southwest Paraná (Dawsey 1979b, 1981, 1983) and subsequent outmigration (Muller 1988b) have been examined. Momsen (1992) looked at similar migration motivators in the gold-mining areas of Pará.

Migrants have been attracted to cities as well as frontiers areas. The influx has helped to create problems in many urban areas where public resources are already stretched to breaking points, and increased crime rates have been one of the results (Dawsey 1986). The rapid growth of population within cities has placed pressure on the real estate markets, and policies designed to create affordable housing in Brazil (Rio de Janeiro) cannot rely on standard formulas developed elsewhere. Officials must take into account a variety of local demographic and spatial variables (Aryeetey-Attoh 1989). Urban growth in Brazil during the colonial period was less structured than in Spanish America (Godfrey 1991), and the continued growth of megacenters such as São Paulo has followed a different course from that of other important cities of the world (Wirth and Jones 1978). Despite growing use of the automobile in the 1970s, Brazilian cities were slow to take on the residential land use patterns typical of many Western centers (Dawsey 1979b, 1980) as many individuals from the high-income groups continued to reside near the city center, while the poor and unemployed remained at the periphery. Studies focused on the largest cities have shown that the provision of services has become spatially decentralized. These studies also show that the upper classes have moved away from the city center (Godfrey 1991).

The rapid growth of cities on the Brazilian frontier has also been the target of study. Boomtowns that are dependent on volatile patterns of resource extraction have emerged in the Amazon region (Godfrey 1990, 1992, 1999b), and Browder and Godfrey (1990) have proposed a theory of disarticulated urban development to account for differences between these and other types of communities such as the villages that appear overnight along major highways (Godfrey and Browder 1996, 1997). City growth and persistence do not appear to conform to a single model but may fit any of several different patterns.

4. Transportation and Economic Geography

Studies in transportation and economic geography have been relatively sparse compared to output earlier in the twentieth century. Textbooks by European scholars Peter Odell and David Preston (1979; Preston 1996) have contributed to our understanding of the economic geography of Latin America, but studies on Brazil have not been as frequent as for other subfields. Though first released in Brazil, Momsen's classic 1963 study of routes over the Serra do Mar gained circulation in the United States, and it has been followed by a description of the Trans-Amazonian Highway (Wozniewicz 1974) and criticism of the road-building and colonization programs in the Amazon (N. Smith 1976, 1982; Moran 1989). Anglo-American geographers appear to have shown little interest in nonhighway modes of transportation or in studies of the booming Southeast.

While geographers have conducted studies of economic activities in the primary sector, such as agriculture, mining, and forestry, relatively few have focused on manufacturing or services. Auty (1995) described the problems Brazil faces because of its attempts to develop a self-sufficient economy in contrast to the export-oriented development of East Asian nations. Meanwhile, Ohuallacháin and Wasserman (1999) studied the effect of liberalized economic policies on the Brazilian automobile industry and discovered that reducing sales taxes and tariffs on imported parts and vehicles caused small-scale independent parts suppliers to become vertically consolidated within the first-tier major manufacturing firms.

5. Environmental and Agricultural Geography

Physical geography is a strong subfield among Brazilian geographers, but few North America–based scholars have shown interest. Brannstrom and Oliveira (2000) have shown that underrepresentation of the post-settlement sedimentation caused by cotton and coffee production in the interior of the Southeast can have serious environmental management implications. Most studies of the physical environment have been tied to an examination of the human response to difficulties imposed by the climate, soil, or terrain, and many of these have addressed agricultural practices. Muller (1986, 1988a, 1988b, 1994) has looked at land ownership,

including the changes brought about by property consolidation and mechanization in western Paraná, and Brannstrom (2000) has proposed that
the relationship between laborers and land owners on coffee *fazendas*
was an important variable affecting the rate of forest clearing in interior
São Paulo.

From the days of Preston James (1948, 1952) drought in the Northeast
has stimulated investigations. Some have looked at the region as a whole
(Brooks 1971, 1973; Webb 1974; Markham 1975), while others have studied
particular crop alternatives or agricultural management practices (Johnson 1979; Voeks and Vinha 1988; Bicalho and Hoeffle 1989). Government
investments in irrigation projects have not altered traditional peasant
farming practices (Caviedes and Muller 1995), but the organization of a
cooperative was shown to have created benefits (Muller 1993).

No region of Brazil has received more attention from the Anglo-
American geography community than the Amazon. Scholars in the United
States have shown great concern about recent changes that have placed
the fragile environment under stress (Hecht 1985; Browder 1988; Hecht
and Cockburn 1989; Anderson 1990; Bendix and Liebler 1991). Hilgard
Sternberg (1964, 1995b), William Denevan (1973), Nigel Smith (1981, 1995,
1996), Smith and Schultes (1990), and Phillip Fearnside (1986, 1989, 1997a,
1997b, 2000) have carefully described the physical geography, vegetation,
soil, hydrology, and indigenous populations, and they also have detailed
the processes by which the resources and native cultures have been placed
in jeopardy.

One area of great particular interest to geographers has been the
examination of evidence of past agricultural practices among indigenous
groups. There is much uncertainty about the ultimate carrying capacity
of the lands of the Amazon region and about how many people lived in
the area at the time of first contacts with Europeans (Denevan 1976, 1992).
Past as well as current farming practices have been studied (Anderson and
Jardim 1989). The discovery of fertile "dark earths" (*terra preta*) within
the ubiquitously sterile soils of the tropical forest has intrigued researchers
in recent years. Nigel Smith (1980) proposed that the soils were anthro-
pogenic, a result of human intervention (Woods 1995). Denevan (1996,
1998) developed a model of prehistoric agriculture that included agricultural land use on bluffs (including the *terra preta*) combined with the
farming of areas in the *varzeas* of the floodplain. These studies and others
(Denevan and Hiraoka 1990) indicated that an earlier alternative agricultural technology may have allowed the region to support a greater number
of people than is possible using more recent subsistent practices.

B. AREAS THAT HAVE BEEN PARTIALLY IGNORED BY ANGLO-AMERICAN GEOGRAPHERS STUDYING BRAZIL

Anglo-American geographers appear to be neglecting some important subdisciplinary areas. Though important at one time, economic geography seems to have taken a backseat in recent decades. This may be due to changes within the subfield itself. During the period under consideration (1945–2003) the focus in economic geography has changed from the pure description of commodities and industries to an analysis of highly quantified theoretical landscapes to the modeling of the interaction between global core and periphery realms. Traditions in geography with strong regional foci to which someone interested in Brazil might be drawn may have lost some contact with the more recent directions within economic geography. Studies in economic geography are often heavily dependent on large quantities of good data, and the access to and comprehension of sources present in Brazil may be more difficult for many Anglo-Americans. Most geographical studies of Brazil by Anglo-Americans have relied on basic knowledge of the country and local conditions derived from careful field observations. Relatively few have sought to extract information by analyzing complex collections of data.

Similarly, relatively few transportation studies have been performed. Overland routes in the Amazon region have been examined, but these have often been cast as elements related to the more important variables of migration, settlement, and forest destruction. Interaction and gravity potential models, so widely used by transportation geographers in the United States, have not found their way into studies of Brazil. The nation possesses a well-developed highway network, a problem-laden rail system, and a booming commercial air business. Large metropolitan areas are supplied by streams of trucks. Intraurban congestion is legendary, and accident rates are high. The potential consequences of the recently announced Avança Brasil program warrant further study. Proposed improvement in navigation on the Paraguay River upstream of Corumbá in the Pantanal region has generated environmental opposition, and completion of the Paraná-Tietê *hidrovia* to the port of Artemis in interior São Paulo has been touted as an economic boon. The ultimate impact of these and similar programs is by no means certain. Engineers, economists, and developers sometimes are not as well equipped to investigate these types of developments within the broader social and environmental contexts so familiar to geographers.

Agriculture has attracted the attention of Anglo-American researchers, but most studies have dealt with small-scale peasant production systems. Studies in the Southeast by Dawsey (1979b, 1981, 1983) and Muller (1988a, 1988b, 1994) have focused on the developing frontier in western Paraná, near the Mato Grasso and Paraguay borders. Still lacking is research on the more established agricultural areas of northern Paraná, interior São Paulo, and Minas Gerais. Interesting changes, such as the replacement of coffee by citrus over large areas, the return of coffee to Minas Gerais, or the expansion of sugar cane acreage in response to the demands created by alcohol- and gasohol-burning automobile engines are potential topics for investigation.

Political and social geography are also underrepresented in the Anglo-American literature. During the second half of the twentieth century the nation experienced more than two decades of military domination followed by an eventful return to democratic rule. Recent years have included the death of a president-elect before he could assume office, the writing of a new constitution, numerous political scandals, and the impeachment of a sitting president. These national events, as well as the shifting political landscapes at the state and local levels, warrant geographical study. Similarly, dramatic social changes are taking place. Greater physical and economic mobility, the ever-increasing intrusion of mass media, the battle of original Brazilian music and film styles versus foreign invasion, changing lifestyles in the cities, and other social topics might be studied.

Finally, few Anglo-American geographers seem to be using the powerful analytical tools of GIS and remote sensing analysis in their studies of Brazil. These tools are applied in Brazil by local geographers (Pires and Novo 1991) and by technical experts from abroad. It is possible that Anglo-American geographers are also involved but that they are not publishing in the traditional geographical literature. The primary outlets may be journals in other fields such as agronomy, forestry, or ecology (Brondizio and Moran 1994; Moran, Brondizio, and Wu 1994; Brondizio Moran, Mausel, and Wu 1996; Bavia et al. 1999; McCracken et al. 1999; Nelson, Kimes, Salas, and Routhier 2000). The new technologies are being applied in Brazil by national government centers and agencies and under contract with foreign entities.

The apparent absence of Anglo-American geographers using GIS and other contemporary tools in the analysis of Brazilian topics may be due to any number of factors. It may pertain to the association of Brazilian geography, as taught and studied in the United States, with the tradition of regionalism. A second factor may relate to limited access in the past to sources of data. Possibly, geographers are working with new technology but releasing results through private reports or outlets outside the traditional geographical journals. Finally, research on Brazil is highly personal, and scholars pursue their own interests. These interests may not include the application of GIS or similar techniques.

V. Future Directions, Needs, and Possible Areas of Collaboration Between Anglo-American and Brazilian Scholars

It is difficult to predict future directions in the study of Brazil by Anglo-American geographers. Among the community of Latin Americanist geographers, the percentage that specializes in Brazil is small compared to those concentrating on other areas. Only a handful of articles have been published about Brazil in the major geographical journals in recent years. In 1985 (the most recent available data), 36 of the 286 (12.5 percent) Latin Americanist geographers listed in the *National Directory of Latin Americanists* (Library of Congress 1985) listed Brazil as their first regional area of interest.

The scholars within this limited group have usually selected a subject focus based on (1) the personal interests, experiences, and training of the researcher; (2) the relevance of the topic as perceived in the United States or Canada; and (3) access to the information necessary to conduct the study. Recent research has certainly reflected personal interest and training. Graduate students are attracted to faculty with compatible interests, and teachers in turn infect their students with their own passions. Consequently, succeeding generations of scholars often continue in the same lines of study.

The Amazon region has attracted an inordinate proportion of U.S. interest both within and without academia. Long neglected, this area is now the focus of much global concern, and that has been reflected in the amount of geographical scholarship. Several among the current generation have taken up the baton, so there is little indication that this emphasis will change in the near future. Most data used by geographers have been derived from painstaking personal collecting in the field. New options are becoming available. Brazilian census data, and GIS spatial data are now available on the Internet (for census data, see www.inpe.br). Electronic mail facilitates the communication with other scholars as well as informants in Brazil, and these changes should facilitate geographical research in some heretofore neglected areas.

Finally, there is little contact between Northern Hemisphere scholars

and potential Brazilian colleagues. Very few Anglo-Americans have published in Portuguese-language journals. This may be due to limited contact with Brazilian outlets, less facility with the language (though several
Brazilian journals accept manuscripts in English), or a perception that a
publication in Brazil is less significant (especially in the eyes of members
of tenure and promotion committees) than output in an Anglo-American
journal. It would be useful to attempt to develop mechanisms that will lead
to a greater interaction between Brazilian geographers and their Anglo-
American colleagues. In an era of tight travel budgets, attendance at common meetings is not always easy. The CLAGNET e-mail network (listserv)
serves as an effective means of communication among Latin Americanists, and an offshoot might be developed in order to serve the community
of Brazilianists. Similar networks exist among Brazilian geographers, so
cross-listings of resumes and e-mail addresses might be accomplished.

The discipline of geography in Anglo-America and in Brazil comes from
different traditions, and interaction would allow each group to broaden
its perspective on the field. Additional benefits might include sharing of
data, collaboration, avoidance of duplication, and an overall better understanding of the diversity of human and physical landscapes in Brazil. As
more and more scholars take advantage of the opportunities afforded
by modern communications technology, the separation between the disciplines in the Northern and Southern Hemispheres should become narrower. The study of Brazil has a rich tradition among Anglo-American
geographers, and we should make every effort to ensure continued interest.

NOTES

1. The author is grateful to the following people for reviewing this work
and offering comments: Tom Martinson, David Robinson, Brian Godfrey, William
Woods, Christian Brannstrom, Hilgard O'Reilly Sternberg, Keith Muller, Gilberto
Garcia, and Daniel Gade. The term "Anglo-American" is used throughout to indicate sources from the United States and Canada. Scholarship interchange between
the two nations is pervasive, yet works from other, non-English-speaking nations
of North America do not share the same outlets.

REFERENCES

Anderson, Anthony B., ed. 1990. *Alternatives to Deforestation: Steps Toward Sus-
    tainable Use of the Amazon Rain Forest.* New York: Columbia University Press.
Anderson, Anthony B., and Mario A. G. Jardim. 1989. "Costs and Benefits of
    Floodplain Forest Management by Rural Inhabitants in the Amazon Estuary:
    A Case Study of Açai Palm Production." In *Fragile Lands of Latin America:*

Strategies For Sustainable Development, ed. John O. Browder. Boulder, Colo.: Westview.

Aryeetey-Attoh, Samuel. 1989. "Housing Affordability Ratios in Rio de Janeiro, Brazil. " *Yearbook, Conference of Latin Americanist Geographers* 15: 49–58.

Augelli, John P. 1958a. "Cultural and Economic Changes of Bastos, a Japanese Colony on Brazil's Paulista Frontier." *Annals of the Association of American Geographers* 48, no. 1: 3–19

———. 1958b. "The Latvians of Varpa: A Foreign Colony on the Brazilian Pioneer Fringe." *Geographical Review* 48, no. 3: 365–87.

———. 1963. "Brasília: The Emergence of a National Capital." *Journal of Geography* 62, no. 6: 241–52.

Auty, Richard M. 1995. "Industrial Policy, Sectoral Maturation, and Postwar Economic Growth in Brazil: The Resource Curse Thesis." *Economic Geography* 71, no. 3: 257–73.

Azevedo, Aroldo de. 1970. *Brasil: a terra e o homem.* Vols. 1–2. São Paulo: Universidade de São Paulo.

Bavia, M. E., L. F. Hale, J. B. Malone, D. H. Braud, and S. M. Shane. 1999. "Geographic Information Systems, and the Environmental Risk of Schistosomiasis in Bahia, Brazil." *American Journal of Tropical Medicine and Hygiene* 60, no. 4: 566–72.

Bendix, Jacob, and Carol M. Liebler. 1991. "Environmental degradation in Brazilian Amazonia: Perspectives in U.S. News Media." *Professional Geographer* 43, no. 4: 474–85.

Berry, Brian J. L., and G. Pyle. 1972. "Grandes Regiões e Tipos de Agricultura no Brasil." *Revista Brasileira de Geografia* 32, no. 4: 5–39.

Bicalho, Ana Maria de Souza, and Scott William Hoeffle. 1989. "Urban Capital and the Pseudo-Modernization of Agriculture in Northeast Brazil." *Yearbook, Conference of Latin Americanist Geographers* 15: 35–48.

Blakemore, Harold, and Clifford T. Smith, eds. 1983. *Latin America: Geographical Perspectives.* New York: Methuen.

Blouet, Brian W., and Olwyn M. Blouet, eds. 1997. *Latin America and the Caribbean.* New York: John Wiley.

Branstrom, Christian. 2000. "Coffee Labor Regimes and Deforestation on the Brazilian Frontier, 1915–1965." *Economic Geography* 76, no. 4: 326–46.

———. 2002. "Rethinking the 'Atlantic Forest' of Brazil: New Evidence for Land Cover and Land Value in Western São Paulo, 1900–1930." *Journal of Historical Geography* 28, no. 3: 420–39.

Brannstrom, Christian, and Antônio Manoel dos Santos Oliveira. 2000. "Human Modification of Stream Valleys in the Western Plateau of São Paulo, Brazil: Implications for Environmental Narratives and Management." *Land Degradation and Development* 11, no. 6: 535–48.

Brondizio, Eduardo S., and Emilio F. Moran. 1994. "Land Use Change in the Amazon Estuary: Patterns of Caboclo Settlement and Landscape Management." *Human Ecology* 22, no. 3: 249–78.

Brondizio, Eduardo S., Emilio F. Moran, P. Mausel, and Y. Wu. 1996. "Land Cover in the Amazon Estuary: Linking of the Thematic Mapper with Botanical and Historical Data." *Photogrammetric Engineering and Remote Sensing* 62, no. 8: 921–29.

Brooks, Reuben H. 1971. "Human Response to Recurrent Drought in Northeastern Brazil." *Professional Geographer* 23, no. 1: 40–44.

———. 1973. "Drought and public policy in Northeast Brazil: alternatives to starvation." *Professional Geographer* 25, no. 4: 338–45.

Browder, John O. 1988. "Public Policy and Deforestation in the Brazilian Amazon." In *Public Policy and Misuse of Forest Resources*, ed. R. Repetto and M. Gillis. Cambridge: Cambridge University Press.

Browder, John O., and Brian Godfrey. 1990. "Frontier Urbanization in the Brazilian Amazon: A Theoretical Framework for Urban Transition." *Yearbook, Conference of Latin Americanist Geographers* 16: 57–66.

Burton, Richard F. [1869] 1969. *Explorations of the Highlands of the Brazil*. Reprint, New York: Greenwood.

Caviedes, César N. 1984. *The Southern Cone: Realities of the Authoritarian State*. Totowa, N.J.: Rowan and Allanheld.

Caviedes, César N., and Gregory Knapp. 1995. *South America*. Englewood Cliffs, N.J.: Prentice Hall.

Caviedes, César N., and Keith D. Muller. 1995. "Fruticulture and Uneven Development in Northeast Brazil." *Geographical Review* 84, no. 4: 380–94.

Clawson, David L. 2000. *Latin America and the Caribbean: Lands and Peoples*. Boston: McGraw Hill.

Cole, John P. 1965. *Latin America: An Economic and Social Geography*. London: Butterworth.

Dawsey, Cyrus B. 1979a. "Income and Residential Location in Piracicaba, São Paulo, Brazil." *Revista Geográfica* 89: 185–90.

———. 1979b. "Source of Settlers in Southwest Paraná." *Ecumene* 11: 6–11.

———. 1980. "A Bid-Price Model for Non-Western Cities: Revised Specification and Empirical Test: Income and distance to Work in a Latin American City." *American Journal of Economics and Sociology* NAPSD No. 03537.

———. 1981. "Push Factors in Recent Frontier Settlement in Southeast Brazil." In *Geographic Research on Latin America: Benchmark 1980*, ed. T. Martinson and G. Elbow. [Muncie, Ind.]: CLAG.

———. 1983. "Push Factors and Pre-1970 Migration to Southwest Paraná, Brazil." *Revista Geográfica* 98: 54–57.

———. 1986. "Distribution of Personal and Property Crime in Brazil." *Yearbook, Conference of Latin Americanist Geographers* 12: 51–55.

———. 1989. "Local Change at the Urban-Rural Fringe in Southeast Brazil." *Journal of Cultural Geography* 9, no. 2: 91–102.

———. 1992. "Migration in Brazil: Research During the 1980s." *Yearbook, Conference of Latin Americanist Geographers* 17–18: 109–17.

————. 1993. "An American Colony in Brazil, Revisited." *Geografia* 18, no. 1: 23–35.

Dawsey, Cyrus B., and James M. Dawsey, eds. 1995. *The Confederados: Old South Immigrants in Brazil.* Tuscaloosa: University of Alabama Press.

Dean, Warren. 1969. *The Industrialization of São Paulo 1880–1945.* Austin: Institute of Latin American Studies, University of Texas Press.

————. 1976. *Rio Claro: A Brazilian Plantation System, 1820–1920.* Stanford, Calif.: Stanford University Press.

————. 1987. *Brazil and the Struggle for Rubber: A Study in Environmental History.* Cambridge: Cambridge University Press.

————. 1995. *With Broadax and Firebrand: The Destruction of the Brazilian Atlantic Forest.* Berkeley: University of California Press.

Denevan, William M. 1973. "Development and the Imminent Demise of the Amazon Rain Forest." *Professional Geographer* 25, no. 2: 130–35.

————, ed. 1976. *The Native Population of the Americas in 1492.* Madison: University of Wisconsin Press.

————. 1992. *The Aboriginal Population of Amazonia.* Madison: University of Wisconsin Press.

————. 1996. "A Bluff Model of Riverine Settlement in Prehistoric Amazonia." *Annals of the Association of American Geographers* 86, no. 4: 654–81.

————. 1998. "Comments on Prehistoric Agriculture in Amazonia." *Culture and Agriculture* 20, no. 2–3: 544–59.

Denevan, William M., and M. Hiraoka. 1990. A Geographic Research on Aboriginal and Peasant Cultures in Amazonia, 1980–1990." *Yearbook, Conference of Latin Americanist Geographers* 17–18: 117–26.

Dozier, Craig. 1956. "Northern Paraná, Brazil: An Example of Organized Regional Development." *Geographical Review* 46, no. 3: 318.

Draffen, Andrew, Chris McAsey, Leonardo Pinheiro, and Robyn Jones. 1997. *Brazil.* Oakland, Calif.: Lonely Planet.

Faissol, Speridião. 1980. "Geography and spatial planning in Brazil." In *Studying Latin America: Essays in Honor of Preston E. James*, ed. David Robinson. Syracuse, N.Y.: Department of Geography, Syracuse University.

————. 1996. "Interview at the Universidade do Estado do Rio de Janeiro." www2.uerj.br/~dgeo/geouerj1h/faissol.htm (December 17, 2004).

Fearnside, Philip M. 1986. *Human Carrying Capacity of the Brazilian Rain-forest.* New York: Columbia University Press.

————. 1989. "Deforestation and Agricultural Development in Brazilian Amazonia." *Interciencia* 14, no. 6: 291–97.

————. 1997a. "Environmental Services as a Strategy for Sustainable Development in Rural Amazonia." *Ecological Economics* 20: 53–70.

————. 1997b. "Human Carrying Capacity Estimation in Brazilian Amazonia as a Basis for Sustainable Development." *Environmental Conservation* 24, no. 3: 271–82.

———. 2000. "Deforestation Impacts, Environmental Services and the International Community." In *Amazonia at the Crossroads: The Challenge of Sustainable Development,* ed. A. Hall. London: Institute of Latin American Studies.

Fletcher, James C. 1845. *Sketches of Residence and Travels in Brazil, Embracing Historical and Geographical Notices of the Empire and Its Several Provinces.* Philadelphia: Sorin and Ball.

Fletcher, James C., and Daniel P. Kidder. 1856. *Brazil and the Brazilians.* London: Sampson Low, Marston, Searle, and Rivington.

Foresta, Ronald. 1991. *Amazon Conservation in the Age of Development: The Limits of Providence.* Gainesville: University of Florida Press.

Gade, Daniel W. 1994. "Germanic Towns of Southern Brazil: Ethnicity and Change." *Focus* 44, no. 1: 1–6.

Galloway, J. H. 1968. "The Sugar Industry in Pernambuco During the Nineteenth Century." *Annals of the Association of American Geographers* 58: 285–303.

———. 1975. "Northeast Brazil, 1700–50: The Agricultural Crisis Reexamined." *Journal of Historical Geography* 1, no. 1: 21–38.

———. 1983. "Brazil." In *Latin America: Geographical Perspectives,* ed. Harold Blakemore and Clifford T. Smith. New York: Methuen.

———. 1989. *The Sugar Cane Industry: An Historical Geography from its Origins to 1914.* Cambridge: Cambridge University Press.

———. 1996. "Botany in the Service of Empire: The Barbados Cane-breeding Program and the Revival of the Caribbean Sugar Industry, 1880s–1930s." *Annals of the Association of American Geographers* 86, no. 4: 682–706.

Godfrey, Brian J. 1990. "Boom Towns of the Amazon." *Geographical Review* 80, no. 2: 103–18.

———. 1991. "Modernizing the Brazilian City." *Geographical Review* 81, no. 1: 18–35.

———. 1992. "Migration to the Gold-Mining Frontier in Brazilian Amazonia." *Geographical Review* 82, no. 4: 458–70.

———. 1999a. "Brazil, Brazil." *Focus* 45, no. 4: 1, 29.

———. 1999b. "Revisiting Rio de Janeiro and São Paulo." *Geographical Review* 89, no. 1: 94–121.

Godfrey, Brian J., and John O. Browder. 1996. "Disarticulated Urbanization in the Brazilian Amazon." *Geographical Review* 86, no. 3: 441–46.

———. 1997. *Rainforest Cities: Urbanization, Development and Globalization of the Brazilian Amazon.* New York: Columbia University Press.

Gunther, John. 1966. *Inside South America.* New York: Harper and Row.

Haggett, Peter. 1961. "Land Use and Sediment Yield in an Old Plantation Tract of the Serra Do Mar, Brazil." *Geographical Journal* 127, no. 1: 50–62.

———. 1963. "Regional and Local Components in Land-use Sampling: A Case Study from the Brazilian Triângulo." *Erdkunde* 17, no. 2: 108–14.

Harris, Marvin. 1956. *Town and Country in Brazil.* New York: Columbia University Press

Hecht, Susanna B. 1985. "Environment, Development, and Politics: Capital Accumulation and the Livestock Sector in Eastern Amazonia." *World Development* 13, no. 6: 663–84.

Hecht, Susanna, and Alexander Cockburn. 1989. *The Fate of the Forest: Developers, Destroyers, and Defenders of the Amazon.* New York: Verso.

Higbee, Edward C. 1951. "Of Man and the Amazon." *Geographical Review* 41, no. 3: 401.

Hiraoka, Mario. 1982. "The Development of Amazonia." *Geographical Review* 72, no. 1: 94–98.

IBGE (Instituto Brasileiro de Geografia e Estatística). 1977. *Geografia do Brasil.* Rio de Janeiro: Fundação IBGE.

James, Preston E. 1932. "Coffee Lands of Southeastern Brazil." *Geographical Review* 22, no. 2: 225–44.

———. 1935. "Industrial Development in São Paulo State, Brazil." *Economic Geography* 11: 258–66.

———. 1939. "Itabira Iron." *Quarterly Journal of Inter-American Relations* 1: 37–48.

———. 1944. "A Selective Guide to the Material Published in 1943 on Geography: Brazil." *Handbook of Latin American Studies* 9: 201–205. [Similar entries appeared in subsequent years.]

———. 1946. *Brazil.* New York: Odyssey.

———. 1948. "The São Francisco Basin: A Brazilian Sertão." *Geographical Review* 38, no. 4: 6–58.

———. 1952. "Observations on the Physical Geography of Northeast Brazil." *Annals of the Association of American Geographers* 42, no. 2: 153–76.

———. 1953a. "Patterns of Land Use in Northeast Brazil." *Annals of the Association of American Geographers* 43, no. 2: 98–126.

———. 1953b. "Trends in Brazilian Agricultural Development." *Geographical Review* 48, no. 3: 301.

———. 1959. "The Geomorphology of Eastern Brazil as Interpreted by Lester C. King." *Geographical Review* 49, no. 2: 240–46.

———. 1966. *A Geography of Man.* Waltham, Mass.: Blaisdell.

———. 1972. *All Possible Worlds.* Indianapolis: Odyssey.

———. 1978. *The Association of American Geographers: The First Seventy-Five Years, 1904–1979.* Easton, Conn.: AAG.

James, Preston E., and Speridião Faissol. 1956. "The Problem of Brazil's Capital City." *Geographical Review* 46, no. 3: 30, 3.

James, Preston E., and Clarence F. Jones, eds. 1954. *American Geography: Inventory and Prospect.* Syracuse, N.Y.: Syracuse University Press.

James, Preston E., and C. W. Minkel. 1986. *Latin America.* New York: John Wiley.

Johnson, Dennis. 1979. "Agroclimatological Zonation of Maize and Grain Sorghum in Northeast Brazil." *Revista Geográfica* (Mexico) 89: 37–43.

Jones, Clarence F. 1958. "Brazil." *Focus* 8, no. 6: 1–6.

Koster, Henry. 1966. *Travels in Brazil* (reprint edited by Gardiner, C. Harvey). Carbondale: Southern Illinois University Press.

Land Tenure Center of the University of Wisconsin. 1972. "Agrarian Reform in Brazil: A Bibliography (Part I and II)." *Training Methods Series* 18 and 19. Madison, Wis.: Land Tenure Center.

Levine, Robert, ed. 1966. *Brazil: Field Research Guide in the Social Sciences.* New York: Institute of Latin American Studies, Columbia University.

Library of Congress. 1966–85. *National Directory of Latin Americanists: Bibliographies.* Washington, D.C.: GPO.

Lobb, C. Gary. 1997. "Brazil." In *Latin America and the Caribbean*, ed. Brian W. Blouet and Olwyn M. Blouet. New York: John Wiley.

Ludwig, Armin K., and Harry W. Taylor. 1969. *Brazil's New Agrarian Reform: An Evaluation of its Property Classification and Tax Systems.* New York: Praeger.

Luebke, Frederick C. 1987. *Germans in Brazil.* Baton Rouge: Louisiana State University Press.

Mandell, Paul. 1966. "Goiás as a Case Study." In *Brazil: Field Research Guide in the Social Sciences*, ed. Robert Levine. New York: Institute of Latin American Studies, Columbia University.

Markham, Charles G. 1975. "Twenty-six-Year Cyclical Distribution of Drought and Flood in Ceará, Brazil." *Professional Geographer* 27, no. 4: 454–56.

Martin, Geoffrey, J., and James E. Preston E. 1993. *All Possible Worlds: A History of Geographical Ideas.* 3rd ed. New York: John Wiley.

McCracken, S., E. Brondizio, D. Nelson, E. F. Moran, A. Siqueira, and C. Rodriguez-Pedraza. 1999. "Remote Sensing and GIS at Farm Property Level: Demography and Deforestation in the Brazilian Amazon". *Photogrammetric Engineering and Remote Sensing* 65, no. 11: 1311–20.

Meinig, D. W. 1971. *On Geography: Selected Writings of Preston James.* Syracuse, N.Y.: Syracuse University Press.

Momsen, Richard P., Jr. 1963. "Routes over the Serra do Mar." *Revista Geográfica* 32: 5–167.

———. 1968. *Brazil: A Giant Stirs.* New York: Van Norstrand.

———. 1979. "Projeto Radam: A Better Look at the Brazilian Tropics." *Geojournal* 3, no. 1: 3–14.

———. 1992. "Migration to the Gold-mining Frontier in Brazil." *Geographical Review* 82, no. 4: 458–70.

Moran, Emilio F. 1989. "Government-Directed Settlement in the 1970s: An Assessment of the Transamazon Highway Colonization." In *The Human Ecology of Tropical Land Settlement in Latin America*, ed. Debra A. Schumann and William L. Partridge. Boulder, Colo.: Westview.

Moran, Emilio F., E. P. Mausel Brondizio, and Y. Wu. 1994. "Integrating Amazonian Vegetation, Land-Use and Satellite Data." *Bioscience* 44: 329–38.

Morris, Arthur. 1987. *South America.* Totowa, N.J.: Barnes and Noble.

Muller, Keith D. 1974. *Pioneer Settlement in South Brazil: The Case of Toledo, Paraná.* The Hague, Netherlands: Martinus Nijhoff.

———. 1986. "A Colonização pioneira no sul do Brasil: o caso de Toledo, Paraná," *Revista Brasileira de Geografia*, Brazilian Institute of Geography and Statistics (IBGE), 1 (January–March): 83–139.

———. 1988a. "The Impact of Agricultural Mechanization on Land Tenancy and Farm Size in South Brazil: The Example of West Paraná." *Latin American Studies* (Japan) 10: 181–219.

———. 1988b. "The Impact of Agricultural Mechanization on Population and Migration in South Brazil: The Example of West Paraná." *Latin American Studies* (Japan) 9: 58–86.

———. 1993. "Pindorama: European Agricultural Settlement Scheme, Coastal Northeast Brazil." *Papers and Proceedings of the Applied Geography Conferences* 16: 1–7.

———. 1994. "The Future of the Long-Lot in South Brazil: The Case of West Paraná." *Papers and Proceedings of the Applied Geography Conferences* 17: 129–34.

National Research Council. 1997. *Rediscovering Geography.* Washington, D.C.: National Academy Press.

Nelson, Ross F., Daniel S. Kimes, William A. Salas, and Michael Routhier. 2000. "Forest Age and Tropical Forest Biomass Estimation Using Thematic Mapper Imagery." *Bioscience* 50, no. 5: 419–32.

Odell, Peter R., and David A. Preston. 1979. *Economies and Societies in Latin America.* New York: John Wiley.

Oesterhoudt, Frank. 1965. "Land Titles in Northeast Brazil: The Use of Aerial Photography." *Land Economics* 41, no. 4: 387–94.

Ohuallacháin, Breandan, and David Wasserman. 1999. "Vertical Integration in a Lean Supply Chain: Brazilian Automobile Component Parts." *Economic Geography* 75, no. 1: 21–42.

Pinto, Maria Novaes. 1986. "Residuas de aplainamentos na 'chapada' dos Veadeiros-Goiás." *Revista Brasileira de Geografia* 48, no. 2:187–97.

Pires, J. S. R., and Evlyn M. L. M. Novo. 1991. "Use of TM/Landsat Data to Identify Silting Areas in the Tucuruí Reservoir." *Ciência e Cultura* 43: 385–87.

Platt, Robert S. 1943. *Latin America. Countrysides and United Regions.* New York: McGraw-Hill.

Preston, David A. 1996. *Latin American Development: Geographical Perspectives.* Burnt Mill, England: Longman.

Rippy, Merrill, ed. 1969. *Cultural Change in Brazil: Papers from the Midwest Association for Latin American Studies.* Muncie, Ind.: Ball State University.

Robinson, David, ed. 1980. *Studying Latin America: Essays in Honor of Preston E. James.* Syracuse, N.Y.: Department of Geography, Syracuse University.

Schreider, Helen, and F. Schreider. 1970. *Exploring the Amazon.* Washington, D.C.: National Geographic Society.

Smith, Nigel J. H. 1976. "Brazil's Transamazon Highway Settlement Scheme: Agrovilas, Agropoli, and Ruropoli." *Proceedings of the Association of American Geographers* 8: 129–32.

———. 1980. "Anthrosols and Human Carrying Capacity in Amazônia." *Annals of the Association of American Geographers* 70, no. 4: 553–56.

———. 1981. *Man, Fishes and the Amazon.* New York: Columbia University Press.

———. 1982. *Rainforest Corridors: Transamazon Colonization Scheme.* Berkeley: University of California Press.

———. 1995. *Amazonia: Resiliency and Dynamism of the Land and Its People.* New York: United Nations University Press.

———. 1996. *The Enchanted Amazon Rain Forest: Stories from a Vanishing World.* Gainesville: University Press of Florida.

Smith, Nigel J. H., and Richard Evans Schultes. 1990. "Deforestation and Shrinking Crop Gene-pools in Amazonia." *Environmental Conservation* 17, no. 3: 227–34.

Smith, T. Lynn. 1946. *Brazil: People and Institutions.* Baton Rouge: Louisiana State University Press.

Stein, Stanley J. 1970. *Vassouras: A Brazilian Coffee County 1850–1890.* New York: Atheneum.

Sternberg, Hilgard O'Reilly. 1948. "The Distribution of Water Power Resources in Brazil with Reference to Participation Ratio Concept." *Annals of the Association of American Geographers* 38, no. 2: 133–44.

———. 1949. "Enchentes e Movimentos Coletivos de Solo no Vale do Paraíba em Dezembro de 1948. Influência da explotação destrutiva das Terras." *Revista Brasileira de Geografia.* 11, no. 2: 223–61.

———. 1950. "Floods and Landslides in the Paraíba Valley, December, 1948." *Conservation in the Americas* 8: 2–20.

———. 1951. "The Status of Geography in Brazil." *Professional Geographer* 3, no. 3: 23–29.

———. 1952. "Land Use and the 1951 Drought in Ceará." *Proceedings of the International Geographical Congress* 17: 672–82.

———. 1955. "Agriculture and Industry in Brazil." *Geographical Journal* 121, no. 4: 488–502.

———. 1956. "Geography's Contribution to the Better Use of Resources." In *The Future of Arid Lands,* ed. Gilbert F. White. Washington D.C.: American Association for the Advancement of Science.

———. 1958. "Não Existe Ainda um Plano para o Problema das Sêcas." *Boletim Geográfico* 16, no. 144: 377–84.

———. 1959. "Geographic Thought and Development in Brazil." *Professional Geographer* 11, no. 6: 12–17.

———. 1964. "Land and Man in the Tropics." *Proceedings of the Academy of Political Science* Reprinted by the Center for Latin American Studies, University of California, Berkeley. Reprint 174.

———. 1965. "Brazil: Complex Giant." *Foreign Affairs* 43, no. 2: 297–311.

———. 1970. "A Geographer's View of Race and Class in Latin America." In *Race and Class in Latin America*, ed. Morner Magnus. New York: Columbia University Press.

———. 1975. *The Amazon River of Brazil*. Wiesbaden: Franz Steiner Verlag.

———. 1981. "The Green Lung." In *Abstracts* of the papers presented at the annual meeting of the Association of American Geographers, ed. P. Kane and D. Hornbeck. Los Angeles: AAG.

———. 1987. "Manifest Destiny and the Brazilian Amazon: A Backdrop to Contemporary Security and Development Issues." *Yearbook, Conference of Latin Americanist Geographers* 33: 25–35.

———. 1995a. "Proposals for a South American Waterway." In *Threatened Peoples and Environments in the Americas*, ed. M. Mörner and M. Rosendahl. Stockholm: Institute of Latin American Studies, University of Stockholm.

———. 1995b. "Waters and Wetlands of the Brazilian Amazon: an Uncertain Future." In *The Fragile Tropics of Latin America*, ed. T. Nishizawa and J. I. Uitto. Tokyo: United Nations University.

Universidade de São Paulo. 1993. Conferência Latinoamericana sobre Sistemas de Informação Geográfica, 4th. *Anais*. 2nd. Simpósio Brasileiro de Geoprocessamento: São Paulo: Escola Politécnica da Universidade de São Paulo.

Voeks, Robert A., and Sergion G. Vinha. 1988. "Fire Management of the Piassava Fiber Palm (*Attalea Funifera*) in Eastern Brazil." *Yearbook, Conference of Latin Americanist Geographers* 14: 7–13.

Wagley, Charles. 1963. *An Introduction to Brazil*. New York: Columbia University Press.

Waibel, Leo. 1948. "Land Use in the Planalto Central of Brazil." *Geographical Review* 38, no. 4: 529.

———. 1950. "European Colonization in Southern Brazil." *Geographical Review* 40: 529–47.

Webb, Kempton E. 1959a. "Origins and Development of a Food Economy in Central Minas Gerais." *Annals of the Association of American Geographers* 49, no. 4: 409–19.

———. 1959b. "Problems of Urban Food Supply in Brazil." *Annals of the Association of American Geographers* 49, no. 2: 218.

———. 1964. *Brazil*. Boston: Ginn.

———. 1968. "An Evolutionary View of the Brazilian Landscape." In *Portugal and Brazil in Transition*, ed. Raymond S. Sayers. Minneapolis: University of Minnesota Press.

———. 1969. "The Geography of Brazil's Modernization and Implications for the Years 1980 and 2000 A.D." In *The Shaping of Modern Brasil*, ed. Eric Baklanoff. Baton Rouge: Louisiana State University Press.

———. 1970. *Brazil*. Boston: Ginn.

———. 1974. *The Changing Face of Northeast Brazil*. New York: Columbia University Press.

———. 1980. "Developments in Brazilian Geography during the Twentieth Century." In *Studying Latin America: Essays in Honor of Preston E. James,* ed. David Robinson. Syracuse, N.Y.: Department of Geography, Syracuse University.

Webb, Kempton E., Irmgard Pohl, and Josef Zepp. 1967. *Latin America.* New York: E. P. Dutton.

Whitbeck, R. H., Frank E. Williams, and William F. Christians. 1940. *Economic Geography of South America.* New York: McGraw-Hill.

Wilgus, A. Curtis. 1943. *Latin America in Maps.* New York: Barnes and Noble.

Wirth, John D., and Robert L. Jones. 1978. *Manchester and São Paulo: Problems of Rapid Urban Growth.* Stanford, Calif.: Stanford University Press.

Woods, William I. 1995. "Comments on the Black Earths of Amazonia." *Papers and Proceedings of the Applied Geography Conferences* 18: 155–69.

Wozniewicz, Wenceslau D. 1974. "The Amazon Highway System." In *Man in the Amazon,* ed. Charles Wagley. Gainesville: University of Florida Press.

PART 3

≈

Counterpoints: Brazilian Studies
in Britain and France

CHAPTER 13

⌒

The British Contribution to the Study of Brazil

LESLIE BETHELL

This chapter on the British contribution to the study of Brazil begins with a survey of the (relatively few) firsthand descriptions of Brazil under Portuguese colonial rule written by British (and Irish) visitors from the middle of the sixteenth century to the first decade of the nineteenth century.[1] The survey ends with the first comprehensive history of colonial Brazil written by an Englishman, who never visited Brazil: the poet Robert Southey. The second section is a survey of the (many) books on Brazil by British writers during the nineteenth and early twentieth centuries—from 1808 when the Portuguese court arrived to take up temporary residence in Rio de Janeiro and opened Brazil to international trade (and foreign visitors), and especially from 1825 when Portugal recognized Brazil's independence, to the Second World War. These are both highly selective surveys.[2]

The main focus of this chapter, however, like the chapters on the U.S. contribution to the study of Brazil in the rest of the volume, is on the period from 1945 to 2003. The third section surveys British writing on Brazil from the end of the Second World War to circa 1970, beginning with an assessment of the work of Britain's greatest historian of colonial Brazil, Charles Boxer. The fourth section is a survey of Brazilian studies—teaching, research, and scholarly publications (mainly books) on Brazil—in British universities and research institutes since the implementation of the Parry report on the future of Latin American studies in the United Kingdom (1965).[3] Like the chapters on Brazilian studies in U.S. universities, this one concerns itself primarily with the humanities and social sciences, for the most part excluding the life, environmental, and medical sciences, except for multidisciplinary studies of Amazonia, a field in which British scholars have made a particularly notable contribution.

I. BRITISH AND IRISH ACCOUNTS OF BRAZIL
UNDER PORTUGUESE COLONIAL RULE

Having "discovered" Brazil in 1500, the Portuguese made every effort, not always successful, to keep out other Europeans, not least the British. Nevertheless, a number of British (and Irish) sailors, adventurers, privateers, and pirates landed on the Brazilian coast during the sixteenth and early seventeenth centuries. The journals and narratives that many of them wrote about what they found there are of great interest in themselves and of great value to historians of colonial Brazil. These observers include, for example, William Hawkins, who was three times in Brazil during the years 1530–32; his grandson Richard, who visited Brazil on his way to the South Seas in 1593; Richard's cousin William Hawkins and the Reverend Richard Madox, who were members of Edward Fenton's expedition of 1582–83; Thomas Cavendish, who, after becoming only the third European (after Magalhães and Drake) to circumnavigate the world (in 1586–88), sacked Santos and São Vicente in 1586 and São Vicente again in 1591, and James Lancaster, who did the same to Recife in 1595, during the period of Spanish domination of Portugal; Anthony Knivet who, after being shipwrecked following Cavendish's attack on São Vicente in 1591 and captured by the Portuguese, experienced for almost ten years "admirable adventures and strange fortunes" in Brazil; and the Irishman Bernard O'Brien, who lived on the lower Amazon in the 1620s. Their firsthand accounts of Brazil, and many others, can be found in Richard Hakluyt, *Principal Navigations* (1598), and Samuel Purchas, *Hakluytus Posthumus or Purchas His Pilgrimes* (1625).

In the middle of the seventeenth century, Richard Flecknoe is usually credited with having written the first book by an English-speaking traveler to Brazil: *A Relation of Ten Years Travells in Europe, Asia, Affrique and America* (1654). Flecknoe was an Irish Catholic priest, poet, and adventurer who traveled from Lisbon to Brazil in 1648 and spent eight months in Rio de Janeiro, January–August 1649. At the end of the seventeenth century, William Dampier, pirate, adventurer, explorer, and naturalist, left narratives of his several voyages. *A Voyage to New Holland . . . in the Year 1699* (1703, 1709), includes a description of a month-long visit to Bahia.

In the eighteenth century, an increasing number of British ships en route to the Pacific, India, and later Australia and China, via Cape Horn

and the Magellan Straits, made Brazil, and especially Rio de Janeiro and
Santa Catarina, a stopping place for wood, water, and fresh food. The
circumnavigation of the world by the ships *Duke* and *Duchess* in 1708–11
produced two books that include accounts of Brazil: Woodes Rogers, *A
Cruising Voyage Round the World* (1712) and Edward Cooke, *A Voyage to
the South Sea and Round the World* (1712). Several accounts of George
Anson's circumnavigation of the world (1740–44) during the war with
Spain, perhaps the most important voyage of exploration between those
of Sir Francis Drake and Captain James Cook, include descriptions of
the island of Santa Catarina, which Anson's fleet of five ships touched
in December 1740 on its outward journey to the Pacific "to distress the
Spaniards in those parts." The fullest account is *A Voyage Round the World
in the Years 1740, 41, 42, 43, 44 by George Anson Esq., commander in chief
of His Majesty's ships sent upon an expedition to the South Seas* (1748), a
volume compiled from Anson's papers by Richard Walter, the chaplain of
the HMS *Centurion*.

Mrs. Nathaniel Kindersley was the first woman known to have written
an account of a visit to Brazil: *Letters from the island of Teneriffe, Brazil,
the Cape of Good Hope, and the East Indies* (1777). She called at Salvador
(Bahia) on her way to India in 1764. Commodore John Byron, grandfather
of the poet, describes in *A Voyage Round the World in HMS Dolphin* (1767)
a visit to Rio de Janeiro in September–October 1764. In his *Oriental Memoirs* (1813) James Forbes describes a visit on his way to India in June to
October 1765.

At the beginning of the first of its famous voyages of circumnavigation
(1768–71), HMS *Endeavour* under Captain James Cook spent a month in
Brazil, November–December 1768. See *An Account of the Voyages Undertaken by Order of His Present Majesty for Making Discoveries in the Southern
Hemisphere*, edited at the request of the Admiralty by John Hawkesworth
(1773). Cook was accompanied by the young botanist (and future president of the Royal Society, 1778–1820) Joseph Banks and two official artists,
Alexander Buchan and the twenty-two-year-old Sydney Parkinson, both
of whom died before the voyage was completed. Parkinson left *A Journal
of a Voyage to the South Seas* (1773), as well as the first significant body of
scientific drawings of the flora and fauna of Brazil (now in the Natural
History Museum, London). See *Sydney Parkinson: Artist of Cook's Endeavour Voyage* (edited by D. J. Carr 1983).

Several descriptions of Rio de Janeiro resulted from the visit in August–
September 1787 of the "First Fleet" under the command of Sir Arthur
Phillip (eleven ships transporting more than seven hundred convicts to

New South Wales), which initiated the colonization of Australia. These include Phillip's own account, *Voyage of Governor Phillip to Botany Bay* (1789), Watkin Tench's *Narrative of an Expedition to Botany Bay* (1789), John White's *Journal of a Voyage to New South Wales* (1790), and John Hunter's *An Historical Journal* (1793). Lord Macartney's three-week visit to Rio de Janeiro in November–December 1792, on his way to China as Britain's first ambassador, also produced some interesting accounts of Brazil. Most noteworthy is Sir George Staunton's *An Authentic Account of an Embassy from the King of Great Britain to the Emperor of China* (1797)—Staunton was Macartney's secretary—and, above all, John Barrow's *Voyage to Cochinchina in the Years 1792 and 1793* (1806). The fourth chapter of Barrow's narrative is devoted to Rio de Janeiro, the fifth to Brazil in general.

In the early years of the nineteenth century, Thomas Lindley wrote about Bahia in *Narrative of a Voyage to Brazil* (1805). Lindley was imprisoned there for a year in 1802 on charges of smuggling—rather casually imprisoned, since he was given opportunities to explore the city. The Irish naval officer James Tuckey spent twenty days in Brazil in May–June 1803 en route to Australia on HMS *Calcutta* and wrote interestingly about it in his *An account of a voyage to establish a colony at Port Phillip . . . New South Wales* (1805). Sir George Mouat Keith, author of *A Voyage to South America and the Cape of Good Hope* (1810), describes a visit to Bahia and Rio de Janeiro on HMS *Protector* in 1805. Admiral Sir Sidney Smith arrived in Rio de Janeiro in May 1808 to take command of the British fleet stationed there, following the transfer of the Portuguese court from Lisbon to Rio in 1807–8 during the Napoleonic Wars. He remained there until July 1809. His *Memoirs,* edited by Edward Howard (1839), provide an interesting account of Rio at the time.

Andrew Grant, *History of Brazil, comprising a geographical account of that country, together with a narrative of the most remarkable events which have occurred there since its discovery* (1809), provides in six of its twelve chapters an overview of Brazil's history, and especially of the Dutch occupation of Northeast Brazil in the first half of the seventeenth century. It is, however, more a guide for travelers and merchants than a history, with severe warnings about the climate (Grant, who had never visited Brazil, was a doctor).

The first history of Brazil under Portuguese colonial rule to treat the entire three centuries, from the beginning of the sixteenth century to the early nineteenth century, and to be based on extensive research, was written by the young English revolutionary poet (and future poet laureate) Robert Southey, who had also never visited Brazil. The first volume of what became a three-volume history was published in 1810, but Southey had begun work on the project more than a decade earlier.

In 1796, when he was twenty-two, Southey spent three and a half months visiting his uncle the Reverend Herbert Hill, Anglican chaplain to the British factory (the community of British merchants) in Lisbon. Southey returned for fifteen months in 1800–1. Hill was a great collector of rare Portuguese books and manuscripts. And it was in Hill's library—and back in England at his house in Keswick in the Lake District, which he shared with Samuel Taylor Coleridge—that Southey began to write "[a] great historical work, the History of Portugal." "On Portugal I am probably better informed than any other foreigner, and as well informed as any Portuguese," he claimed in 1806. He planned an eleven- or twelve-volume history of Portugal itself and of the Portuguese in Asia and Brazil, the Jesuits in Japan, the literary history of Spain and Portugal, and the history of the monastic orders. Work on the history of the Portuguese in the New World was brought forward after the British capture of Buenos Aires in 1806 and the flight of the Portuguese court to Rio de Janeiro in 1807–8. It became the first part of a projected history of Portugal to be published—and, although he continued to work on it until his death in 1843, the only part.

The three quarto volumes of Southey's *History of Brazil* (1810, 1817, 1819) ran to more than twenty-three hundred pages (with a concluding "View of the State of Brazil" alone nearly two hundred pages). The first volume deals with the territorial occupation of Brazil by the Portuguese (to 1640); the second with the Dutch occupation of Northeast Brazil in the second quarter of the seventeenth century, the expulsion of the Dutch in 1654, and Portuguese relations with the Brazilian Indians; the third with territorial expansion north, south, and west in the eighteenth century and the expulsion of the Jesuits, social institutions, and the roots of what Southey saw as a future autonomous nation-state. A revised edition of the first volume, published in 1822, added a hundred pages more. "What I have done," Southey wrote in 1818, "is in many parts imperfect; it is nevertheless even now a great achievement . . . and centuries hence, when Brazil shall have become a great and prosperous country which one day it must be, I shall be regarded there as the first person who ever attempted to give a consistent form to its crude, unconnected and neglected history."

Southey's great *History*, first published in Portuguese, reduced and in an inaccurate translation by Luiz Joaquim de Oliveira e Castro (1862), was much admired by later historians of colonial Brazil such as Capistrano de Abreu and Oliveira Lima. There is no modern critical edition of Southey's *History of Brazil* in either English or Portuguese.

II. British Accounts of Brazil in the
Nineteenth and Early Twentieth Centuries

In the nineteenth and early twentieth centuries, Britain was the preeminent political and economic power in Brazil and also had significant social, cultural, and intellectual influence. The books written during this period by British visitors to Brazil and British residents in Brazil—mineralogists, merchants, naval officers (and their wives), diplomats, naturalists, clergy and missionaries, doctors, newspaper owners, editors and reporters, employees of railway and navigation companies, civil engineers, explorers, travelers and travel writers—are a fundamental source for the history of Brazil.

The following is a highly selective list of the most notable:

- John Mawe, *Travels in the interior of Brazil, particularly in the gold and diamond districts of that country* (1812). Mawe, a mineralogist from Derbyshire was the first foreigner allowed to visit the gold and diamond mines of Minas Gerais following the opening of the Brazilian ports to world, especially British, trade in 1808.
- John Luccock, *Notes on Rio de Janeiro and the southern parts of Brazil taken during a residence of ten years in that country from 1808 to 1818* (London, 1820), described by the great nineteenth-century Brazilian historian Varnhagen as "the most faithful portrayal of the material, moral and intellectual state of the capital of Brazil on the arrival of the Royal Family and of its progress during these years." Luccock was a cloth merchant from Leeds who was importing textiles and other manufactured goods from West Yorkshire.
- Henry Koster, *Travels in Brazil, in the years from 1809 to 1815* (1816). Koster was a British merchant who had grown up in Portugal and established himself in Pernambuco in 1809 for health reasons. This classic book, which Robert Southey urged him to write—Koster used Southey's library and dedicated the book to him—focuses on Koster's experience as a sugar planter but also describes many other aspects of life in Pernambuco as well as his travels to other parts of the Brazilian Northeast.
- William Swainson, *Zoological Illustrations* (1820–33), *The ornithological drawings of William Swainson: Series I: The birds of Brazil* (1834), and *A selection of the birds of Brazil and Mexico* (1841). A botanist, ornithologist, and ornithological illustrator, Swainson was the first British scientist to visit Brazil after 1808. He arrived in Pernambuco in December

1816 and stayed with Koster. He also traveled to the São Francisco River, to Bahia, and finally Rio de Janeiro in 1818. Swainson is considered the best illustrator of the flora and fauna of Pernambuco since the Dutch artists who were resident there in the middle of the seventeenth century.

- Henry Chamberlain, *Views and costumes of the city and neighbourhood of Rio de Janeiro, Brazil, from drawings taken by Lieutenant Chamberlain, Royal Artillery, during the years 1819 and 1820, with descriptive explanations* (1822), whose watercolors formed the basis of a famous album of thirty-six lithographs, was the son of the British consul-general in Rio. He visited Brazil in 1819–20 when he was twenty-two.

- James Henderson, *A History of the Brazil comprising its geography, commerce, colonisation, aboriginal inhabitants, etc., etc., etc.* (1821). This is an impressive work of more than five hundred pages, with illustrations by the author, based on a visit to Rio de Janeiro, Bahia, Pernambuco, and Maranhão in 1819–20. It is, however, like Grant's *History of Brazil* (1809), more travelogue and geography than history.

- Maria Graham, *Journal of a voyage to Brazil and residence there during part of the years 1821, 1822, 1823* (1824). Graham, née Dundas, later Lady Callcott, was the wife of a British naval officer. This is one of the best— and most quoted—accounts of Brazil at the time of independence.

- Robert Walsh, *Notices of Brazil in 1828 and 1829* (1830). Walsh, an Irish Anglican clergyman, was chaplain to the British mission in Rio de Janeiro.

- John Armitage, *The History of Brazil, from the period of the arrival of the Braganza family in 1808 to the abdication of Dom Pedro the First in 1831* (1836). Planned as a sequel to Southey's *History*, this was the first history of the period 1808–31, including Brazil's independence from Portugal and the abdication of Brazil's first emperor, that was based on state documents and other primary sources and, unlike Southey's *History*, also based on firsthand knowledge of the country. Armitage spent eight years in Brazil, from 1828 to 1835. Translated into Portuguese in 1837 his *History of Brazil* remained a fundamental text for all later historians of the period. There is no modern critical edition in English or in Portuguese.

- Charles Darwin, *Journals and remarks 1832–6* (1839), the third volume of Robert Fitzroy's four-volume *Narrative of the surveying voyages of His Majesty's Ships 'Adventure' and 'Beagle' between the years 1826 and 1836* (1839). Darwin's volume was published separately as *Journal of researches into the geology and natural history of the various countries visited during the voyage of H.M.S. Beagle round the world* (1840). Darwin was twice in Brazil during the second voyage of HMS *Beagle* (December 1831–October 1836)—in Bahia in February and Rio de Janeiro during April–June 1832, sending home by naval vessel consignments of carefully labeled specimens, and briefly in Bahia and Recife again on the return journey in August 1836.

- George Gardner, *Travels in the interior of Brazil principally through the northern provinces and the gold mining districts during the years 1836–41* (1846). Gardner, who was later superintendent of the Royal Botanical Gardens of Ceylon, went to Brazil to collect botanical specimens and penetrated parts of southeastern, central, and northeastern Brazil rarely visited by foreigners.

- The letters, journals and books of the three great British naturalists who contributed so much to the exploration and scientific discovery of the Amazon in the mid-nineteenth century—Alfred Russel Wallace, cofounder with Darwin of the theory of evolution by natural selection; Henry Walter Bates; and Richard Spruce—are especially important for our knowledge and understanding of Brazil. Wallace and Bates, aged twenty-five and twenty-three, respectively, traveled to Pará in 1848 to collect for private dealers and for Kew Gardens, which had been reorganized in 1841 and formally recognized as the national botanic garden under the direction of Sir William Hooker (and later his son Sir Joseph Hooker). Wallace and Bates remained together for two years, parting company in 1850. Wallace spent two more years on the Rio Negro and the Orinoco, Bates another nine years on the Solimões and Upper Amazon.

  Returning to England in 1852, Wallace lost most of his notes, sketches and, worst of all, his collections in a shipboard fire but nevertheless published the following year *A narrative of travels on the Amazon and Rio Negro* (1853). As an appendix to the volume, Wallace included notes on the natural history, geography, and geology of the Amazon valley and its aboriginal tribes, with vocabularies of Amazonian languages, which represent a mere fragment of the physical history of the Amazon that he had planned to write. Bates was encouraged by Darwin to publish his classic *A naturalist on the River Amazons* (1863) after Bates returned home in 1859. Darwin believed Bates was second only to Humboldt in his knowledge of tropical forests. Darwin regarded Bates's book as "the best book of natural history travels ever published in England." Bates became for thirty years the first (paid) secretary of the Royal Geographical Society, which had been founded in the 1830s.

  Wallace and Bates were primarily entomologists, Spruce a botanist (though all three, it should be said, were also explorers, geographers, geologists, anthropologists, linguists, and much else besides). Spruce, then thirty-two—though with an established reputation for his work in Yorkshire and the Pyrenees—went to the Amazon in 1849, a year after Wallace and Bates. Spruce stayed in northern Brazil, Peru, and Ecuador for fifteen years until 1864, like Bates, Spruce sacrificed his health for his research. On his return he published his *Palmae Amazonicae* (1869) and much later his monumental *Hepaticae Amazonicae et Andinae* (1884–85). Fifteen years after Spruce's death, his friend Wallace collected and edited his *Notes of a botanist on the Amazon and the Andes* (1908).

- William Hadfield, *Brazil, the River Plate and the Falkland Islands* (1854), is a history of the region, a guidebook, and a travelog. Hatfield was secretary of the South American and General Steam Navigation Company. See also by Hadfield, *Brazil and the River Plate in 1868* (1869) and *Brazil and the River Plate 1870–76* (1877).

- William D. Christie, *Notes on Brazilian Questions* (1865). Christie was British minister from 1859 to 1863 and the cause of one of the most famous diplomatic incidents in Brazilian history (the "Christie affair"), which led to the suspension of diplomatic relations until 1865. This important book deals with this and many other "Brazilian questions" of the time, including slavery, abolition, and commercial relations with Britain.

- William Scully, *Brazil; Its Provinces and Chief Cities, the Manners and Customs of the People, Agriculture, Commerce and Other Statistics . . .* (1866). Scully was the Irish-born proprietor and editor of the *Anglo-Brazilian Times,* published in Rio de Janeiro from 1865 to 1884. His book was essentially a prospectus for investors and immigrants.

- Sir Richard Burton, *Explorations of the Highlands of Brazil* (1869), which includes an account of his descent of the Rio São Francisco ("Brazil's Mississippi") in 1867, and *Letters from the Battlefields of Paraguay* (1870). The great "orientalist" and explorer was British consul in Santos in 1865–68. He traveled to Paraguay to report on the War of the Triple Alliance (the Paraguayan War) in 1868 and 1869. Apart from travel, Burton's other great passion was translation. His favorite language, after Arabic, was Portuguese, which he learned in Goa. While in Brazil, besides translating Camões's *Lusiads,* Burton translated several Brazilian works, including José Basilio da Gama's epic poem (5 cantos, 1,400 lines) *O Uruguai* and two contemporary novels, J. M. Pereira da Silva's *Manuel de Moraes* and José de Alencar's *Iracéma.*

- Henry Alexander Wickham, *Rough Notes of a Journey Through the Wilderness from Trinidad to Para, Brazil* (1872). Wickham was an itinerant naturalist whose book, generally poor, was valuable for the information on rubber that it contained and eventually famous for the impact that it had, through Kew Gardens, on rubber production in Southeast Asia and the eventual collapse of Amazonian rubber production. See also his *On the Plantation, Cultivation and Curing of Para Indian Rubber* (1908).
- Michael G. Mulhall, *Rio Grande do Sul and Its German Colonies* (1873), (with Edward T. Mulhall) *Handbook of Brazil* (1877), and *Journey to Matto Grosso* (1879). The Mulhalls were the owners of the *Standard*, an English newspaper in Buenos Aires.
- Charles Barrington Brown and William Lidstone, *Fifteen Thousand Miles on the Amazon and Its tributaries* (1878). Brown, a geologist, and Lidstone, a civil engineer, were employees of the Amazon Steam Navigation Company in 1873–75. They were accompanied on their expedition up the Amazon by James William Helenus Trail, a young botanist. From 1877 Trail was a professor of botany at the University of Aberdeen and contributed a series of important articles to the *Journal* of the Royal Geographical Society.
- Thomas Plantagenet Bigg-Wither, *Pioneering in South Brazil: Three Years of Forest and Prairie Life in the Province of Paraná* (1878). Bigg-Wither was a railway surveyor in Paraná in the early 1870s.
- James W. Wells, *Exploring and Travelling Three Thousand Miles Through Brazil from Rio de Janeiro to Maranhão* (1886). Wells was a civil engineer who made this journey in 1873–75. His route overlapped in many places with that taken earlier by George Gardner and Richard Burton.
- J. P. Wileman, *Brazilian Exchange: The Study of an Inconvertible Currency* (1896). Wileman was a British civil engineer who lived in Rio Grande do Sul for many years and died in Rio in 1914. His book was the first systematic analysis of Brazil's financial history, covering the period from 1860 to 1894, and a major influence on the governments of the new Brazilian Republic. He also founded the weekly *Brazilian Review* in 1898 (edited from 1915 to 1941 by his son H. F. Wileman under the title *Wileman's Brazilian Review*), an important source of economic, financial, and business news aimed at subscribers abroad.
- J. C. Oakenfull, *Brazil in 1909* (1910), *Brazil in 1910* (1911), and similar volumes, including *Brazil: Past, Present and Future* (1919), an eight-hundred-page volume with firsthand descriptions of parts of the country not usually covered in books of this kind. The chapters on different

sectors of the economy replaced the yearbooks published until the First World War.

- Charles W. Domville-Fife, *The United States of Brazil* (1910). Domville-Fife was an "explorer" and journalist, mainly for the *Times* of London. The book is divided into two parts, the first a historical survey, the second an examination of contemporary Brazil. Domville-Fyfe later published *Among Wild Tribes of the Amazons: An Account of Exploration and Adventure* (1924).

- H. M. Tomlinson, *The Sea and the Jungle (being the narrative of the voyage of the tramp steamer Capella, 1909 and 1910)* (1912), an account of a journey from England to Pará, and along the Amazon and Madeira rivers and back again, is considered a travel literature classic.

- Reginald Lloyd et al., eds., *Twentieth Century Impressions of Brazil: Its History, People, Commerce, Industries and Resources* (1913), a thousand-page large format directory.

- William Henry Koebel, *The Great South Land. The River Plate and Southern Brazil of Today* (1919). Koebel was a journalist and author of numerous books on Central and South America. *The Great South Land* is the book that contains the most on Brazil, contrasting the level of development of Brazil's south and southeast with Argentina and Uruguay, countries of which the British public had rather greater knowledge. Koebel's most enduring legacy, however, was *The Anglo-South American Handbook* (1920), which after his death in 1923 reappeared as the *South American Handbook*. The *Handbook* was maintained as an annual publication, even during the Second World War, and is still considered the best and most detailed guide to the region as a whole, including Brazil. There has also been since 1998 a separate *Brazil Handbook*.

- R. B. Cunninghame Graham, *A Brazilian Mystic: The Life and Miracles of Antonio Conselheiro* (1920), which draws heavily on Euclides da Cunha's classic, *Os sertões* (1902).

- Rudyard Kipling, *Brazilian Sketches* (1927), a record of the famous writer's impressions of Brazil which he visited early in 1927 when he was sixty-two.

- Kenneth Grubb, *The Lowland Indians of Amazonia* (1927), is basically a linguistic survey but includes information on foreign missionary societies. Grubb enlisted in the World-wide Evangelization Crusade after the First World War and spent "four years of lonely exploration of the Upper Amazon," studying more than two hundred Indian languages. See also his *The Republic of Brazil; A Survey of the Religious Situation*

(1932), with Erasmo Braga, on evangelical Protestant missions in Brazil. Grubb also wrote two useful travel books largely about Brazilian Amazonia: *Amazon and Andes* (1930) and *From Pacific to Atlantic* (1933).

- Peter Fleming, *Brazilian Adventure* (1933), was the book about Brazil most read by the British public in the interwar period. It has much useful material on Indians.
- James A. Williamson, *English Colonies in Guiana and on the Amazon, 1604–1668* (1933), is one of the earliest scholarly works on Brazil by a British historian. Williamson was a master at Westminster City School who wrote many books—both scholarly and popular—on early voyages of exploration.
- Evelyn Waugh, *92 Days* (1934), a book about British Guiana by the famous novelist. Much of it describes a visit across the frontier to Boa Vista and elsewhere in northern Roraima.
- Ernest Hambloch, *His Majesty the President: A Study of Constitutional Brazil* (1935), is one of the most perceptive contemporary analyses of the Brazilian political system during the First Republic (1889–1930) and the provisional government of GetúlioVargas (1930–34). Hambloch first went to Brazil in 1910 when he was twenty-four to replace Roger Casement, the consul-general who was going on extended leave. Hambloch spent the next four years there, followed by a further twenty years from 1916, first in the consular and diplomatic service (until his resignation in 1927), then as coffee planter, Reuters correspondent in São Paulo, and correspondent of the London *Times* in Rio. He was forced to leave after the publication of his controversial book, which was seen in Brazil as an attack not on presidentialism per se but on President Vargas—by an agent of British capitalism. Also interesting, not least about the reception of his earlier book, are Hambloch's *British Consul: Memories of Thirty Years' Service in Europe and Brazil* (1938) and *Here and There: A Medley of Memories* (1968).

III. British Writing on Brazil 1945–ca. 1970

British scholarship relating to Brazil in the immediate postwar period was dominated by the historian of the Portuguese empire Charles R. Boxer (1904–2000). Boxer came to the study of colonial Brazil via the study of the Dutch and Portuguese languages in order to better to understand the history of Japan. He wrote all his early works while serving in the British Army, mostly in the Far East, on East Asia and particularly Japan in the sixteenth and seventeenth centuries. Although he had no conventional academic credentials, after the Second World War (during which he was a Japanese prisoner of war in Hong Kong for four years), he accepted an appointment in 1947 as Camoens Professor of Portuguese at King's College, London (a chair founded in 1917 and held from 1923 to 1936 by Edgar Prestage, a specialist on the diplomatic history of seventeenth-century Portugal). Boxer made his first visit to Brazil in April 1949 for the fourth Congresso Nacional de História held in Rio de Janeiro and published his first (minor) essays on Brazilian colonial history during the following twelve months.

For two months, September–October 1948, Boxer served as a consultant at the Library of Congress in Washington, D.C., and played a principal role in the preparation of the first International Colloquium on Luso-Brazilian Studies, which took place in Washington in October 1950 under the auspices of the library, which was then celebrating its 150th anniversary, and Vanderbilt University, which had recently established its Institute of Brazilian Studies. Boxer took responsibility (with Engel Sluiter of Berkeley) for the panel on instruments of scholarship and wrote one of the eight principal papers submitted to that panel, "Some Considerations on Portuguese Colonial Historiography," later published in the colloquium's *Proceedings/Atas* (1953). Boxer was the only British scholar to present a paper at the colloquium.

In the preface to his first monograph dealing in part with colonial Brazil, *Salvador de Sá and the Struggle for Brazil and Angola, 1602–1686* (1952). Boxer wrote, "English ignorance of Brazilian history can only be described as abysmal. . . . Hardly a line has been written in this country on the colonial period of Brazilian history since Robert Southey published his three volume history in 1810–1819." Following a second visit to Brazil in 1954, Boxer published a second monograph on colonial Brazilian history: *The Dutch in Brazil, 1624–1654* (1957) and lecture, *A Great Luso-Brazilian Figure: Padre Antônio Vieira SJ, 1608–1697* (1957). Unfortunately, he postponed (and never returned to) his plan to write a full-scale biography of Vieira. Two further visits to Brazil in 1959 enabled Boxer to complete the research for a third monograph, *The Golden Age of Brazil, 1695–1750: Growing Pains of a Colonial Society* (1962).

Another visit to Brazil in 1963 was less successful, and Boxer vowed that it would be "the last for a long time." In fact, he returned only twice—in 1972 for a conference and in 1986 to receive the Dom Pedro II gold medal of the Instituto Histórico e Geográfico Brasileiro. And apart from his Taylorian lecture in 1967, *Some Literary Sources for the History of Brazil in the 18th Century* (1967), Boxer did not write again specifically on Brazil.

However, two general works, *The Dutch Seaborne Empire, 1600–1800* (1965) and *The Portuguese Seaborne Empire, 1415–1825* (1969), and many of his later publications on Portuguese colonial history (mostly based on lecture series delivered in the United States)—*Race Relations in the Portuguese Colonial Empire, 1415–1825* (1963); *Four Centuries of Portuguese Expansion, 1415–1825: A Succinct Survey* (1965); *Portuguese Society in the Tropics: The Municipal Councils of Goa, Macau, Bahia, Luanda, 1510–1800* (1965); *Women and Iberian Expansion Overseas, 1415–1815* (1975); *The Church Militant and Iberian Expansion, 1440–1770* (1978)—included much of interest on colonial Brazil. Boxer had resigned from the Camoens chair of Portuguese at King's College in 1967 and, although continuing to base himself in England, accepted a series of posts at universities in the United States, including Yale, where he was Professor of the History of the Expansion of Europe Overseas from 1969 to 1972. He was a great collector of books and manuscripts, and in 1965 had agreed to sell his library to the Lilly Library of Indiana University. Half was transferred between 1965 and 1969, the rest only in 1997.

There is now an excellent biography of Boxer by the U.S. historian Dauril Alden, *Charles R. Boxer: An Uncommon Life* (2001). For a complete list of Boxer's writings, see George West, *A List of the Writings of Charles Ralph Boxer Published Between 1926 and 1984* (1984) and Alden, *Boxer*, appendix 7, "The Writings of Charles Boxer, 1985–1996."

Besides Boxer, the only British scholar to attend the first International Colloquium on Luso-Brazilian Studies in Washington in 1950 was H. V. (Harold) Livermore. Livermore taught Portuguese at Cambridge immediately after the war before becoming education officer at Canning House (the Hispanic and Luso-Brazilian Councils). He was primarily a scholar of Portuguese literature and history, publishing *A History of Portugal* (1947) and *A New History of Portugal* (1966), and from the late fifties teaching at the University of British Columbia in Vancouver. He did, however, edit (with W. J. Entwistle) the only book published in Britain during the immediate postwar period that attempted, at least in part, to treat modern Brazil, that is to say, Brazil since independence, in a serious way. *Portugal and Brazil: An Introduction* (1953) included eight chapters on Brazil, four of them by British authors: Kenneth Grubb on land and people; R. A. Humphreys, who since 1948 had held the only chair of Latin American history in a British university (London), on monarchy and empire; Livermore himself on the republic; and Ann Livermore on music.

Another British scholar, John Bury, although unable to attend the Luso-Brazilian Colloquium in Washington, had submitted a paper to the fine arts panel ("Portuguese and Brazilian Architecture of the 17th and 18th Centuries"), which was, like Boxer's paper on Portuguese colonial historiography, eventually published in the *Proceedings/Atas* (1953). Bury, however, settled on a business rather than an academic career. Nevertheless, he continued to write and research and made a distinguished contribution to the study of colonial Brazilian art and architecture. The more important of his essays, including a chapter on the art and architecture of colonial Brazil in volume 2 of the *Cambridge History of Latin America* (1984), were published in *Arquitetura e arte no Brasil colonial* (1990).

Apart from Brazil's colonial history (largely occupied by one man—Boxer), only the Amazon attracted British scholars to Brazil in the postwar period. Anthropology in British universities remained primarily focused on Africa and Asia, but Amazonia became an important field of research at this time, largely as a result of the powerful influence of Claude Lévi-Strauss on Rodney Needham at Oxford and Edmund Leach at Cambridge.

Francis Huxley was the first to do fieldwork among the indigenous peoples of Brazilian Amazonia. His *Affable Savages: An Anthropologist Among the Urubu Indians of Brazil* (1956), a pioneering study of the Urubu Indians (now generally known as the Kaapor) in Maranhão and Pará, was based on fieldwork in 1951 (alongside the young Brazilian anthropologist Darcy Ribeiro) and in 1953 for his doctoral degree from Oxford. However, after a brief spell at Cambridge, and failing to secure a post at Oxford, Huxley moved out of mainstream academic life.

David Maybury-Lewis, a student of Needham's, worked in central Brazil in the late 1950s and wrote the popular *The Savage and the Innocent* (1965) and the scholarly *Akwe-Shavante Society* (1967). But Maybury-Lewis had moved to Harvard in 1961 immediately after completing his doctoral degree at Oxford—and remained at Harvard. His later edited volumes, *Dialectical Societies: The Ge and Bororo of Central Brazil* (1979) and *The Attraction of Opposites: Thought and Society in the Dualistic Mode* (essays on Brazilian Indians) (1989), might be said to belong more properly to the U.S. contribution to Brazilian studies.

Peter Riviere, another student of Needham's, went to Brazil for the first time in 1957 with the Oxford and Cambridge South American Expedition. He returned to Oxford and remained there for the rest of his academic career, mainly researching the Indians of Guiana but writing on Brazil (both anthropology and history, see the end of this section) and guiding many research students working on Brazil at Oxford.

John Hemming, an Oxford history graduate, was a member of the ill-fated 1961 expedition to the Amazon in which Richard Mason lost his life at the hands of the Kreen-Akrore Indians (now called the Panara). Hemming went into the family business but continued to research and write on Brazil, becoming Britain's leading specialist on the Amazon, particularly the history of its indigenous peoples (see the end of this section).

The botanical artist Margaret Mee had visited Brazil for the first time in 1952, made the first five of her journeys to the Amazon between 1956 and 1967, and published the most important of her many well-known studies of Brazilian flora, *Flowers of the Brazilian Forests*, in 1968. (Her fifteenth and final visit to Brazil was in 1988, the year in which the diaries and sketchbooks of all her journeys were published as *In Search of Flowers of the Amazon Forest*, edited by Tony Morrison.)

An expedition organized and led jointly by the Royal Geographical Society and the Royal Society (at the invitation of the Brazilian government) in 1969, the first British multidisciplinary venture of its kind produced (besides a mass of research papers, particularly in the new field of *cerrado* studies) an excellent general book by the writer and broadcaster Anthony Smith, *Mato Grosso: Last Virgin Land* (1971).

Two young British scholars who were to play a significant role in the development of Brazilian studies in British universities, Giovanni Pontiero and myself, had visited Brazil for the first time in 1960 (indeed, we traveled there together—by ship, steerage) in 1969. Pontiero, twenty-eight, was researching for a doctoral degree in literature at Glasgow University (under the supervision of Professor William C. Atkinson, head of the Department of Hispanic Studies and author of the Penguin *History of Spain and Portugal*, 1960, who always laid great stress on the study of Portugal and Brazil). I was then twenty-three, and a doctoral student in history at University College London (under the supervision of Professor R. A. Humphreys). A pamphlet written by W. C. Atkinson for the British Council in the early seventies, *British Contributions to Portuguese and Brazilian Studies* (1974)—a revised and updated version of a pamphlet originally published in 1945—is mainly concerned with Portugal. On Brazil it finds worthy of note in the entire thirty years since the end of the Second World War only Boxer's monographs, the volume of essays edited by Livermore and Entwistle, Pontiero's first book, *An Anthology of Brazilian Modernist Poetry* (1969), and my own first book, *The Abolition of the Brazilian Slave Trade: Britain, Brazil and the Slave Trade Question, 1807–1869* (1970). In fact, by this time, several other young scholars had also published their first monographs: A. J. R. Russell-Wood, *Fidalgos and Philanthropists: The Santa Casa de Misericórdia of Bahia, 1550–1775* (1968); Emanuel de Kadt, *Catholic Radicals in Brazil* (1970); Peter Rivière, *The Forgotten Frontier:*

Ranchers of Northern Brazil (1972); and Kenneth Maxwell, *Conflicts and Conspiracies: Brazil and Portugal, 1750–1808* (1973).

IV. Brazilian Studies in British Universities Since the Parry Report (1965)

As in the United States, the early 1960s represented a turning point in the study of Latin America, including Brazil, at British universities. Before then only isolated individuals studied Latin America, and none of the leading figures studied Brazil, with the singular exception of Charles Boxer, who was soon to leave British academic life—and had always made a point of saying that he knew nothing of Brazil after its separation from Portugal in 1822. The committee set up in October 1962 by the University Grants Committee under the chairmanship of Professor J. H. Parry (and including among its members both Boxer and R. A. Humphreys) had for its terms of reference "to review development in the Universities in the field of Latin American Studies and to consider and advise on proposals for future developments." It presented its report in August 1964. The opening sentences of chapter 1, "Summary of Findings and Recommendations," reads: "The state of Latin American studies in British universities entirely fails to reflect the economic, political and cultural importance of Latin America. It reflects, instead, a lack of interest in, and a general ignorance about, this great area in Great Britain."

The *Report on the Future of Latin American Studies in the UK* (the Parry Report) (1965) led to the creation of Institutes/Centres of Latin American Studies during the late 1960s at five universities: London, Cambridge, Glasgow, Liverpool, and Oxford. "Named posts" (lectureships in Latin American politics, economics, sociology, etc.) were established, research and travel funds made available, master's degrees in Latin American studies created, and students for doctoral degrees accepted. As a result, teaching and research on Latin America at British universities with Parry institutes or centers was gradually transformed.

The University of London established its Institute of Latin American Studies with R. A. Humphreys as its first director. Humphreys was not a "Brazilianist," but many of his books had much to say about Brazil, notably *Latin America and the Second World War* (1981–82). From the beginning, the London Institute was expected to play a national role in the development of Latin American studies in the United Kingdom. Of those appointed to the several new named posts created jointly between the institute and the colleges of the university, two had Brazilian interests:

David Goodman (economics) at University College and Colin Lewis (economic history) at the London School of Economics, although the latter was primarily a specialist on Argentina. As director (1987–92), I attempted to establish within the institute a Centre for Contemporary Brazilian Studies. I failed. However, I initiated, and my successors, Victor Bulmer-Thomas and James Dunkerley, continued to support a series of conferences on Brazil coordinated by Maria D'Alva Kinzo of the University of São Paulo, the proceedings of which were published by the Institute: Maria D'Alva Kinzo, ed., *Brazil: The Challenges of the 1990s* (1993); Maria D'Alva Kinzo and Victor Bulmer-Thomas, eds., *Growth and Development in Brazil: Cardoso's Real Challenge* (1995); D'Alva Kinzo and James Dunkerley, eds., *Brazil Under Democracy: Economy, Polity and Society Since 1995* (2003). In 1998 the Institute also held a major conference on Amazonia, the proceedings of which were also published: Anthony Hall, ed., *Amazonia at the Crossroads: The Challenge of Sustainable Development* (2000). In 1996 the first master's degree in Brazilian studies in the United Kingdom was launched at the institute. It was, however, suspended in 2000.

Other academics in the University of London with Brazilian research interests and linked to the Institute of Latin American Studies were based in the various colleges of the university.

At University College London, I was appointed in 1966 to the first post established in a British university specifically to include Brazil in its title, a Lectureship in Hispanic American and Brazilian History. I held the Lectureship (later Readership) until I was appointed to the University of London Chair of Latin American History in 1986. During these years I taught one of the few courses in a British university specifically on Brazil—"Brazil: Empire and Republic, 1822 to the Present Day"—to both undergraduates and postgraduate students of Latin American history. In addition to publishing *Abolition of the Brazilian Slave Trade* (1970), I began editing the *Cambridge History of Latin America*. The first five volumes were published while I was at University College: volumes 1 and 2 *Colonial Latin America* (1984), volume 3 *Latin America from Independence to c. 1870* (1985), volumes 4 and 5 *Latin America: c. 1870 to 1930* (1986). The chapters in volumes 1 to 5 of the *Cambridge History on Brazil* were also published separately as *Colonial Brazil* (1987) and *Brazil: Empire and Republic (1808–1930)* (1989). As director of the Institute of Latin American Studies, I continued work on the *Cambridge History*. Three more volumes included a good deal on Brazil: volume 6 *Latin America Since 1930: Economy, Society and Politics*, part 1: *Economy and Society* and part 2: *Society and Politics* (1994), and volume 10 *Latin America Since 1930: Ideas, Culture and Society* (1995). *Bibliographical Essays* (1995) includes eighteen essays on Brazil.

At the London School of Economics, besides Colin Lewis (economic history) and Emanuel de Kadt (sociology), until he left for the University of Sussex in 1969; Peter Gow (social anthropology—though more a specialist on the Peruvian than the Brazilian Amazon); Ian Roxborough (sociology), until he left for the United States; Anthony Hall (social planning/ sustainable development); and, more recently, Francisco Panizza (politics) have all researched on Brazil. Anthony Hall has become the United Kingdom's leading specialist on the economic, social, and environmental problems of the Brazilian Northeast and Amazonia. He is the author of *Drought and Irrigation in North-east Brazil* (1978), *Developing Amazonia: Deforestation and Social Conflict in Brazil's Carajas Programme* (1989), and *Sustaining Amazonia: Grassroots Actions for Productive Conservation* (1997), and (with David Goodman) he edited *The Future of Amazonia: Destruction or Sustainable Development?* (1990).

Brazilianist David Treece (literature and culture) has been at King's College London since 1987, joined more recently by Nancy Naro (history). Treece is the author of *The Gathering of Voices: The Twentieth Century Poetry of Latin America* (1992), with Mike Gonzalez, and *Exiles, Allies, Rebels: Brazil's Indianist Movement, Indigenist Politics and the Imperial Nation-State* (2000). He is also a highly respected translator into English of the works of João Guimarães Rosa, Caio Fernando Abreu, Ana Cristina Cesar, and João Gilberto Noll. Naro, a U.S. historian with a doctoral degree from the University of Chicago, spent most of her academic career in Brazil. She is the author of *A Slave's Place, A Master's World: Fashioning Dependency in Rural Brazil* (2000). King's College's Department of Portuguese and Brazilian Studies established the Centre for the Study of Brazilian Society and Culture in 1996 and appointed David Treece its first director. The center concentrates on research into Brazilian popular culture.

Also teaching, researching, and publishing on Brazil were, at Royal Holloway College, Michael Eden (geography), author of *Ecology and Land Management in Amazonia* (1990), who died in 1998, and Duncan McGregor (geography); and at Goldsmith's College, Stephen Nugent (anthropology), author of *Amazonian Caboclo Society: An Essay on Invisibility and Peasant Economy* (1993).

At Cambridge University the Centre for Latin American Studies has had relatively few Brazilianists attached to it, although David Joslin, the pioneer of Latin American studies in Cambridge, included a great deal on Brazil in his history of the Bank of London and South America, *A Century of Banking in Latin America* (1963). The center published an important collection of papers on Amazonia, edited by Françoise Barbira-Scazzocchio, *Land, People and Planning in Contemporary Amazonia* (1980). David Lehmann, a social anthropologist with Brazilian as well as Andean research interests and author of *Struggle for the Spirit: Religious Transformation and Popular Culture in Brazil and Latin America* (1996) was director of the center throughout the 1990s. After completing his doctoral degree at Oxford (1987) with Peter Rivière and after taking up research fellowships at Glasgow and Edinburgh, David Cleary, author of *Anatomy of the Amazon Gold Rush* (1990), was a research officer at the center 1991–96 before moving first to Harvard and then to Brazil. John Wells (economics) did important work on income distribution in Brazil early in his career. Maria Manuel Lisboa, a Portuguese scholar, has recently strengthened the teaching of Brazilian literature at Cambridge. And the cultural historian Peter Burke and his wife, Maria Lucia Pallares-Burke, are writing an intellectual biography of Gilberto Freyre.

Four Brazilians have held the prestigious Simon Bolivar Chair in Latin American Studies at Cambridge: Celso Furtado, 1973–74; Fernando Henrique Cardoso, 1976–77; José de Sousa Martins, 1993–94; and Eduardo Viveiros de Castro, 1997–98.

Cambridge University Press has played a fundamental role in the development of Latin American, including Brazilian, studies in the United Kingdom. First, it established a Latin American studies monograph series in 1967, and three British scholars contributed volumes on Brazil to the series in its first decade or so: Bethell (1970), Maxwell (1973), and Hall (1978). Second, it publishes the *Journal of Latin American Studies,* founded jointly by the five Parry centers in 1969. The *JLAS* has established itself as one of the leading journals in the field and has published many articles, indeed several special issues, on Brazil. Finally, there are the Cambridge histories. The twelve-volume *Cambridge History of Latin America,* of which I am editor, will eventually include twenty-four chapters on Brazil (a third of them by British historians). The *Cambridge History of Latin America* is being published in Portuguese in Brazil by Editora da Universidade de São Paulo as well as in Spanish by Editorial Crítica, Barcelona, and Chinese by the Chinese Academy of Social Sciences, Beijing. Volume 3 of the three-volume *Cambridge History of Latin American Literature* (1996) is devoted to Brazilian literature and includes chapters by Giovanni Pontiero on poetry from modernism to the 1990s and John Gledson on prose from 1940 to 1980. The first two parts of the third volume of the three-volume

Cambridge History of the Native Peoples of the Americas (1999) are devoted to South America and include two chapters on the native peoples of Amazonia: by Neil L. Whitehead, a British anthropologist (former student of Rivière's at Oxford) at the University of Wisconsin–Madison, on the sixteenth to nineteenth centuries, and by David Maybury-Lewis on the twentieth century.

At the University of Oxford, Herminio Martins (sociology), Alan Angell (politics), and Rosemary Thorp (economics), all members of the Latin American Centre and fellows of St. Antony's College, have supervised Brazilian graduate students. Thorp's *Progress, Poverty and Exclusion: An Economic History of Latin America in the Twentieth Century* (1998) has much of interest on Brazil. Peter Rivière (Linacre College, social anthropology), Donald Hay (Jesus College, economics), Andrew Hurrell (Nuffield College, international relations), Laurence Whitehead (Nuffield College, politics/political economy), and recently Claudia Pazos-Alonso (Wadham College, literature) have also played a role in the development of Brazilian studies. Besides *Forgotten Frontier* (1972), Rivière published *Individual and Society in Guiana: A Comparative Study of Amerindian Social Organisation* (1984), much of which relates to the native peoples of Brazil, and *Absent Minded Imperialism: Britain and the Expansion of Empire in Nineteenth Century Brazil* (1995), a study of the drawing of the border between Guiana and Brazil. Whitehead is the coauthor (with Lourdes Sola and Eduardo Kugelmas) of *Banco Central. Autoridade política e democratização—um equilíbrio delicado* (2002).

In 1993 the Baring Foundation established at St. Antony's College a Senior Research Fellowship in Brazilian Studies, which was affiliated with the Latin American Centre. The college appointed me to the post. Following the collapse of Barings Bank in 1995, the fellowship came to an untimely end a year later. In 1997, however, the University of Oxford established the Centre for Brazilian Studies, independent of the Latin American Centre, and appointed me as its first director. Among my recent publications is an edited volume, *Brasil: fardo do passado, promessa do futuro. Dez ensaios sobre política e sociedade brasileira* (2002).

With the creation of the Oxford Centre, the study of Brazil has for the first time a strong institutional base in the United Kingdom. The center began with an academic staff of director and one postdoctoral Research Fellow in Economics, Edmund Amman, author of *Economic Liberalisation and Industrial Performance in Brazil* (2000), who left to take up a post in the University of Manchester in 2000. By 2001–2002 the center had four postdoctoral research fellows—in economics, politics, international political economy, and the politics of human rights. The center also appoints visiting research fellows (funded by the center) and visiting research associates (self-funded) from Brazil for periods of one term to one year. And the center brings to Oxford each year forty to fifty Brazilian scholars, intellectuals, and policy makers for its seminars, workshops, and conferences. At the end of the academic year 2002–2003 the center had about two dozen conference and workshop reports, six research papers, and forty-six working papers on-line at www.brazil.ox.ac.uk. The center published its first reference book, Oliver Marshall, *Brazil in British and Irish Archives* (2002), and its first monograph, *The New Brazilian Cinema*, edited by Lucia Nagib (2003). For the center's activities since 1997, see its published *Annual Reports* and *The First Five Years, October 1997–June 2002* (August 2002).

The Institute of Latin American Studies at Liverpool University has been able to count on the support of several Brazilianists, especially in its early years, when it had some claim to be the leading center of Brazilian studies in the United Kingdom. The staff included Giovanni Pontiero, who taught literature there for four years until he went to Manchester in 1970; Peter Flynn, who taught politics for four years until he returned to Glasgow in 1972; and, especially, Colin Henfrey (social anthropology), John Dickenson (geography), and John Gledson (literature), who were on the faculty until their early retirements in the 1990s. Before moving to Canada, Joyce Lorimer published an important monograph: *English and Irish Settlement on the River Amazon, 1550–1646* (1989). A recent addition to the faculty is Claire Williams, who specializes in Brazilian literature; with Claudia Pazos-Alonso at Oxford, she edited *Closer to the Wild Heart: Essays on Clarice Lispector* (2002).

John Dickenson published two studies on Brazilian geography: *Studies in Industrial Geography: Brazil* (1978) and *Brazil* (1982) as well as an important contribution to Brazilian bibliography, *Brazil* (1997).

John Gledson, who was to become the leading British specialist on Brazilian literature and culture (and the supervisor of a great many doctoral theses), first visited Brazil in 1970 as a graduate student at Princeton. He published three important studies on Brazilian literature in the 1980s: *Poesia e poética de Carlos Drummond de Andrade* (1981), *The Deceptive Realism of Machado de Assis: A Dissenting Interpretation of Dom Casmurro* (1984), and *Machado de Assis: ficção e história* (1986). He has edited two volumes of Machado's *Bon dias! Crônicas, 1888–1889* (1990) and *A Semana, 1892–1932* (1996) as well as *Contos: Uma antologia* (1999). Gledson also is an internationally recognized translator of Brazilian literature and of one of Brazil's leading literary essayists, Roberto Schwarz.

At the University of Glasgow, Peter Flynn replaced W. C. Atkinson as director of the Institute of Latin American Studies in 1972 and retained the post until the closure of the institute in 1997. Flynn, who was to become Britain's leading specialist on Brazilian politics and author of *Brazil: A Political Analysis* (1978), had gone to Brazil for the first time in 1965 as a graduate student at St. Antony's College, Oxford. Even more than Atkinson, Flynn explicitly adopted a policy of giving high priority to Brazil in research appointments, visiting fellowships (Regis de Castro Andrade was there for eight years), research strategy, and publications (almost a third of more than sixty working papers published during the 1970s and 1980s were on Brazilian topics). Brazilianists at Glasgow have included Simon Mitchell (sociology/social anthropology), who edited a collection of essays entitled *The Logic of Poverty: The Case of the Brazilian Northeast* (1981); Francis Lambert (modern history); John Parker (literature); Arthur Morris (geography); Jackie Roddick (development and environmental studies); Elizabeth Allen (geography/development studies); and, more recently, Liam Kane (education).

Elizabeth Allen played a leading role in the establishment of the Centre for Amazonian Studies (mainly social and natural sciences) within the institute in 1989. Although it is located in Glasgow, the center draws on specialists at other universities and research institutes, especially but not exclusively, those in Scotland. It publishes working papers on Amazonia and is compiling a register and database of researchers working on Amazonia. Outside universities with designated "Parry" Institutes/Centres of Latin American Studies, individual scholars and groups of scholars in departments of history, geography, anthropology, and so on, as well as in departments of modern languages, romance languages, and Spanish and Portuguese, continued to pursue the study of Brazil in teaching and research.

The University of Essex (founded in 1965) did not receive Parry funding, but it nevertheless established a center for Latin American studies that was generally regarded as a sixth Parry center. Christian Anglade (politics), Joe Foweraker (sociology), Dawn Ades and Valerie Fraser (art history), and recently Mathias Rohrig Assunção (history) have all contributed to Brazilian studies within the Latin American center. Foweraker is the author of *The Struggle for Land: A Political Economy of the Pioneer Frontier in Brazil from 1930 to the Present Day* (1981) and *Citizenship Rights and Social Movements: A Comparative and Statistical Analysis* (1997), on Spain, Mexico, Chile, and Brazil. Ades is the author of *Art in Latin America. The Modern Era, 1820–1980* (1989) and *Siron Franco* (1995), a study of one of Brazil's leading contemporary artists. Fraser is the author of *Building a New World: Studies in the Modern Architecture of Latin America, 1930–1960* (2000), which has much to offer on the building of Brasília. Laurence Hallewell was the founding librarian of Essex's Latin American library before moving to Brazil and the United States. He is the author of *Books in Brazil: A History of the Publishing Trade* (1982).

At the University of Manchester, where Giovanni Pontiero taught literature until his untimely death in 1992, Paul Cammack (politics), Paul Henley, (Granada Centre for Visual Anthropology) and, more recently, Hilary Owen (literature) and Edmund Amman (economics) have all produced important work on Brazil. Besides his *Anthology of Brazilian Modernist Poetry* (1969), Giovanni Pontiero wrote *Carlos Nejar: poeta e pensador* (1984), *Os Personae—poemas de Carlos Nejar* (1986), and *Manuel Bandeira (visão geral de sua obra)* (1986). He was also a prize-winning translator of Clarice Lispector (three novels and three collections of short stories), Manuel Bandeira, Ana Miranda, and other Brazilian writers, as well as the Portuguese novelist José Saramago.

At the University of Edinburgh, Alan Tormaid Campbell (social anthropology), Peter Furley (geography), and Gordon MacMillan (geography/ development economics) are all specialists on Brazil. Campbell is the author of *To Square with Genesis: Casual Statements and Shamanic Ideas in Wayapi* (1989) and *Getting to Know Waiwai: An Amazonian Ethnography* (1995); Furley the editor of *The Forest Frontier: Settlement and Change in Brazilian Roraima* (1994); and MacMillan is the author of *At the End of the Rainbow? Gold, Land and People in the Brazilian Amazon* (1995).

At Bristol University, David Brookshaw (history and literature), who took up his post in 1978 after a spell at Queen's University, Belfast, has published two studies of Brazilian literature: *Raça e côr na literatura brasileira* (1983) and *Paradise Betrayed: Brazilian Literature of the Indian* (1989). In 2002 Lorraine Leu (popular culture/music) also joined the faculty at Bristol.

At Leeds University, Lisa Shaw (literature and cultural studies) and Stephanie Dennison (history and cultural studies)—both students of John Gledson's at Liverpool—have developed a strong interest in Brazil. Shaw is the author of *The Social History of the Brazilian Samba* (1999)

At Southampton University, Frank Colson (history) and Mark Dinneen (literature) have specialized in Brazil. Dinneen is the author of *Listening and the People's Voice: Erudite and Popular Literature in Northeast Brazil* (1996) and editor of *Brazilian Woodcut Prints* (2001)

St. Andrews University has a center for indigenous American studies.

Its director, Joanna Overing, a leading U.S.-trained anthropologist, is more a specialist on Venezuelan than Brazilian Amazonia. But Mark Harris (anthropology), author of *Life on the Amazon: The Anthropology of a Brazilian Peasant Village* (2000), specializes in Brazil.

At the Institute of Development Studies, Sussex University, Emmanuel de Kadt (sociology), John Humphrey (sociology), and Hubert Schmitz (economics) have all published on Brazil. Humphrey is the author of two important books: *Capitalist Control and Workers' Struggle in the Brazilian Auto Industry* (1982) and *Gender and Work in the Third World: Sexual Divisions in Brazilian Industry* (1987).

At Exeter University, Joseph Smith (history) has published *Unequal Giants: Diplomatic Relations Between the United States and Brazil, 1889–1930* (1991) and *A History of Brazil, 1500–2000* (2002).

Nottingham University claims to have the highest number of undergraduates in Portuguese and Brazilian studies in the United Kingdom, and its Postgraduate School of Critical Theory and Cultural Studies, headed since 1995 by Bernard McGuirk (comparative literature/critical theory), is beginning to attract Brazilian students and researchers. With Solange Ribeiro de Oliveira, McGuirk edited *Brazil and the Discovery of America: Narrative, History, Fiction, 1492–1992* (1996). A number of British Brazilianists have pursued their academic careers at universities and research institutions outside Britain.

After completing his doctoral degree at Oxford and publishing *Fidalgos and Philanthropists* (1968), A. J. R Russell-Wood moved to Johns Hopkins University in 1971 and remained there. His many important publications in the field of colonial Brazilian history—*The Black Man in Slavery and Freedom in Colonial Brazil* (1982); *Society and Government in Colonial Brazil, 1500–1822* (1992); *A World on the Move: The Portuguese in Africa, Asia and America, 1415–1808* (1992)—form part of the U.S. contribution to the study of Brazil.

After taking his first degree at Cambridge, Kenneth Maxwell wrote his doctoral thesis at Princeton under the supervision of Stanley Stein. It was published as *Conflicts and Conspiracies* (1973). Maxwell then remained in the United States (at the University of Kansas, the Tinker Foundation, Columbia University, the Council on Foreign Relations, and Harvard), as much a specialist on Portugal as on Brazil.

After completing a doctoral degree in social anthropology at University College London, Peter Fry went to Brazil in 1970 and has remained there, first at UNICAMP, then at the Universidade Federal do Rio de Janeiro (UFRJ). He is the author of *Para inglês ver: identidade e política na cultura brasileira* (1982), and, with Carlos Vogt, *Cafundó: A África no Brasil: linguagem e sociedade* (1996).

After taking his doctoral degree at Berkeley in 1970, Roderick J. Barman settled in Canada and teaches at the University of British Columbia in Vancouver. He is the author of *Brazil: The Forging of a Nation, 1798–1852* (1988), *Citizen Emperor: Pedro II and the Making of Brazil, 1825–1891* (1999), and *Princess Isabel of Brazil, Gender and Power in the Nineteenth Century* (2002).

After completing her doctoral degree at the University of California, Los Angeles, in 1971, Nancy Leys Stepan also remained in the United States, teaching mainly at Columbia University. She is the author of *The Beginnings of Brazilian Science: Oswaldo Cruz, Medical Research and Policy, 1890–1920* (1975), *"The Hour of Eugenics": Race, Gender and Nation in Latin America* (1991), and *Picturing Tropical Nature* (2001).

Nigel J. H. Smith, a biogeographer—and author of *Rainforest Corridors: The Transamazon Colonisation Scheme* (1982), *The Amazon River Forest: A Natural History of Plants, Animals and People* (1999), and *Amazon Sweet Sea: Land, Life and Water at the River's Mouth* (2002)—has made his career at the University of Florida, Gainesville.

Stephen Grant Baines (whose 1988 doctoral degree is based on his research on the Waimiri-Atroari); Vanessa Rosemary Lea (*Parque indígena do Xingú*, 1997, and *Area indígena Kapoto*, 1997) a student of Peter Rivière, the late Peter Silverwood-Cope (*Os maku: povo caçador do noreste da Amazônia*, 1990) a student of Edmund Leach's at Cambridge, and Kenneth Taylor (research on the Yanomami) have all, like Peter Fry, made their careers at Brazilian universities.

Finally, there has also been considerable research activity on Brazil in the United Kingdom outside the universities:

• The Royal Botanic Gardens, Kew, has carried out important research on Brazil since the nineteenth century. In recent decades the research effort has been led by Simon Mayo, Ray Harley, and many others. The appointment of Ghillean Prance as director in 1989 gave research on Brazil a great boost. Prance, a distinguished botanist (coauthor, with M. F. da Silva, of *Arvores de Manaus* [1976]; coeditor, with Thomas Lovejoy, of *Amazonia* [1985], and author of *Tropical Forests and World Climate* [1986] and *Manual da botánica económica do Maranhão* [1988]), was the first director of postgraduate studies at Instito Nacional de Pesquisas da Amazônia (INPA) in Manaus in the mid-1970s and curator of Amazonian botany and coordinator of the Projeto Flora Amazônica at the New York Botanical Garden (1977–87) before moving to Kew. He retired in 2000. Kew's current major involvement in Brazil is through the Plantas do Nordeste project.

- At the Royal Botanic Garden, Edinburgh, James Ratter (botany), one of the world's leading authorities on the *cerrado*, Sam Bridgewater (botany), and William Milliken (botany/ethnology) have all made important contributions to the study of Brazil. Milliken is the author (with others) of *The Ethnobotany of the Waimiri Atroari Indians of Brazil* (1992) and (with Bruce Albert) *Yanomami, A Forest People* (1999), both published by the Royal Botanic Gardens, Kew.

- Like the Royal Botanic Gardens, Kew, the Royal Geographical Society in London has been interested in Brazil since the first half of the nineteenth century. Its most recent involvement was the Maracá Rainforest Project (Projeto Maracá) in 1987–88, which was organized at the invitation of the Brazilian Secretaria Especial do Meio Ambiente (SEMA— now part of Instituto Brasileiro do Meio Ambiente [IBAMA]) in partnership with INPA in Manaus. The project set out to record and document the ecological structure of a relatively undisturbed section of the Brazilian rain forest. With more than two hundred scientists and technicians led by John Hemming, the society's director and secretary, it was the largest research effort ever mounted by a European country in Amazonia. It produced a number of important publications, including John Hemming, James A. Ratter, and Angelo A. dos Santos, *Maracá* (1988); William Milliken and James A. Ratter, eds., *The Vegetation of the Ilha de Maracá* (1989); John Hemming and James A Ratter, *Maracá— Rainforest Island* (1993); John Hemming, ed., *The Rainforest Edge: Plant and Soil Ecology of Maracá Island, Brazil* (1994); and James A. Ratter and William Milliken, eds., *Maracá: The Biodiversity and Environment of an Amazonian Rainforest* (1998).

Hemming was director and secretary of the Royal Geographical Society for more than twenty years (1975–96). During that time he published two fundamental works on the history of Brazil's indigenous peoples: *Red Gold: The Conquest of the Brazilian Indians, 1500–1760* (1978), and *Amazon Frontier: The Defeat of the Brazilian Indians* (1987), on the late eighteenth and nineteenth centuries. A third and final volume has now been published: *Die If You Must: Brazilian Indians in the Twentieth Century* (2003). Hemming also wrote chapters on the Indians of Brazil in 1500 and Brazilian Indians under Portuguese colonial rule for the first two volumes of the *Cambridge History of Latin America* (1984) and edited an important two-volume collection of papers on contemporary Amazonia: *Change in the Amazon Basin:* Vol. 1, *Man's Impact on Forests and Rivers,* and Vol. 2, *The Frontier After a Decade of Colonisation* (1985).

• The British Museum has published Elizabeth Carmichael, *The Hidden Peoples of the Amazon* (1985), a guide to its ethnographic collections, and Colin McEwan, Cristiana Barreto, and Eduardo Neves, eds., *Unknown Amazon: Culture in Nature in Ancient Brazil* (2001), the scholarly catalog of a path-breaking exhibition held there in 2001.

NOTES

1. The author wishes to thank the many British colleagues, especially John Hemming, John Dickenson and Oliver Marshall, who provided information and commented on an earlier version of this essay.

2. For a more comprehensive guide to books on Brazil by British and Irish authors from the mid-sixteenth century to the mid-twentieth century, with brief descriptions of the contents of each volume and references to modern editions and Portuguese translations, see Leslie Bethell, *Brazil by British and Irish Authors* (Oxford, Centre for Brazilian Studies, 2003).

3. For books on the history, culture, ecology, economy, society, and politics of Brazil written by journalists, travel writers, and independent scholars since circa 1970, again see Bethell, *Brazil by British and Irish Authors.*

∽

CHAPTER 14

Comparative Development of the Study of Brazil in the United States and France

Edward A. Riedinger

It became commonplace at the end of the twentieth century to observe in international studies and relations that the United States had emerged as the world's only superpower. The United States had defeated its great military and ideological nemesis, the Soviet Union. Rarely observed and hardly considered, however, was that several decades earlier the United States had defeated another superpower, this one in cultural terms. That was France.[1] The cultural imperium of France emerged in Europe in the seventeenth century. Replacing the declining Renaissance ardor of Florence and Rome, it advanced around the globe into the twentieth century. Its allure of elite refinement and distinction swept over Germanic and Slavic states, North and West Africa, the Middle East, Southeast Asia, and Latin America. Indeed, the idea that there was an America that was "Latin" was French. The gaze that the world cast toward France was reciprocated by a French focus that studied all areas of the world. Within the Western Hemisphere, France gave special attention to Brazil. When U.S. culture superseded that of the French around the world, it did so not only in character but also scale. In many respects, indeed, the U.S. character *was* its scale. It was a culture of open access for the majority, not of restricted refinements for an elite. Although U.S. study of Brazil has been on a larger scale, it differs from the French in duration and character. Brazil shares with the a hemisphere with the United States, but with France it shares *uma mentalidad, une mentalité.*

I. FRANCE AND BRAZIL

Throughout the five centuries of the history of Brazil, four major countries have been keenly interested and influential in its development. During the first three centuries Portugal dominated, interrupted by Spanish and Dutch interventions during the first part of the seventeenth century. In the last half of the twentieth century the United States has been most significant. During the first half of the twentieth century and throughout the nineteenth century, Britain and—even more so—France were foremost in interest and influence. It should be noted that, because of immigration, Italian culture and sociopolitical influence were important from the end of the nineteenth century to the middle of the twentieth.

In reviewing the accumulated study of and research on Brazil in the United States, it is of crucial importance to be able to place such a review within a comparative reference. Major countries and cultures with other interests, influence, and changing perspectives have preceded U.S. study. The latter has been both quite extensive and intensive. However, it is only the most recent and relatively the briefest of several phases in the history of foreign study of and interest in Brazil. Over the course of the nineteenth century and well into the twentieth century, British and French research and interest dominated.

British attention and concerns were primarily of a commercial and technical nature. During the nineteenth century, railroads, ports, shipping, wholesaling, some aspects of finance and insurance, electrical communications, and athletic activities followed British patterns. A medical doctor, Andrew Grant, wrote the earliest history in English of Brazil. Published in London in 1809, Dr. Grant's *History of Brazil, Comprising a Geographical Account of that Country, Together with a Narrative of the Most Remarkable Events Which have Occurred* appeared just after British merchants were given preferential trading privileges in the country.[2] It was prepared to caution readers about the region's insalubrious climate. The author, however, intrigued by the vast exotic realm, wrote about it with an engaging thoroughness (somewhat anticipating the first tourist guides of Thomas Cook). Shortly after the English edition was published, versions in French (*Histoire du Brésil*, 1811) and German (*Beschreibung von Brasilien*, 1814) appeared. The French edition was actually completed in Russia. Czar Alexander I later financed a monumental expedition through the interior of Brazil during 1821–29. German-born Baron Georg Heinrich von Langsdorf, the Russian consul in Brazil, headed this expedition.

It was France, however, as leader of the "Latin" cultural world, that had greater interest and influence. Brazil was indeed one of the largest and, increasingly, one of the most promising of the Latin countries. The term "Latin America" originated from the pan-Latin ideas of the French economist Michel Chevalier during the early part of the reign of Napoleon III (who occupied Mexico while the United States was engaged in its Civil War). The French sought to lead a Latin cultural bloc as a geopolitical pawn against Anglo, Germanic, and Slavic blocs. During the same period France promoted a "Latin" monetary union of itself, Belgium, Switzerland, and Italy (an effort defeated by the profligacy of Vatican state accounts). From the time of Maurice Ravel and Georges Bizet on, French composers created a Latin repertoire against the Germanic Wagnerian advance. They elaborated some of the most memorable Spanish themes in classical music. Moreover, they adapted Italian opera to French.

With the opening of the port of Rio de Janeiro in 1808 and until after the Second World War, French structures and standards dominated the Brazilian professions, especially medicine, sanitation, engineering, diplomacy, and law. Architecture and interior design, whether public or private, reflected, successively, the French neoclassical, Beaux Arts, art nouveau, and art deco styles. Banking, luxury retailing, elite social and culinary manners, and leisure indulgences were French. In education, the administrative model and the second language of the school curricula were French. as was the organization of music and art education, libraries, museums, and fine arts exhibitions. Literature (belles-lettres) and publishing were French. Exceptions to this influence, other than the British, occurred in religious architecture and in clerical culture. In their upper hierarchical and urban manifestations these were Italian, quite specifically Roman, yet with some Gallican Church variations. Military organization and engineering changed at the turn of the twentieth century from French to German.

Unlike Brazilian studies in the United States, French interest in and focus on Brazil has roots almost as deep as Brazilian history itself. Indeed, before there was even an English presence in the Americas, the French were studying and publishing on Brazil. The French attempt in the mid-sixteenth century to create "France Antarctique" in the Bay of Guanabara prompted the Portuguese to eradicate the French settlement and found Rio de Janeiro. One of the expelled leaders, Jean de Léry, wrote the first French classic on the country, *Histoire d'un Voyage fait en la terre du Brésil* (1580). Earlier André Thévet had included Brazil in his *Les singularitez de la France antarctique, autrement nommée Amerique: & de plusieurs terres & isles decouvertes de nostre temps* (1557). A woodcut of 1551 that portrays a triumphal procession into Rouen by Henry II and his consort, Catherine of Medici, includes a "Figure des Brisilians," depicting life and warfare between Tupinamba and Tapajó natives.

This initial French relation with the origins of Brazil has received significant recent French scholarly attention. Frank Lestringant, a prolific historian on the French Renaissance and Reformation, has written *Jean de Léry, ou, L'invention du sauvage: Essai sur l'Histoire d'un voyage faict en la terre du Brésil*" (1999), *D'encre de Brésil: Jean de Léry, écrivain (1999)*, and *André Thevet, cosmographe des derniers Valois* (1991) and has annotated an authoritative edition of *Les singularitez de la France antarctique*. Françoise Argod-Dutard has edited a collection of conference presentations, *Histoire d'un voyage en la terre du Brésil: Jean de Léry: Journées d'etude (10 et 11 décembre 1999)* (2000).

At the beginning of the seventeenth century, a priest, Yves d'Evreux, wrote of his travels in northern Brazil in *Voyage dans le nord du Brésil fait durant les années 1613 et 1614*. It appeared in Portuguese only in 1874, as *Viagem ao norte do Brasil feita nos annos de 1613 a 1614*, published in Maranhão. In the early seventeenth century, the French attempted to establish a "France Équatoriale" east of the mouth of the Amazon River. In 1612 the French established the city of São Luís in Maranhão. This incursion prompted the Portuguese (then under Spanish rule) to expel the French two years later. The Portuguese drove the French west of the river and took over the French settlement. Maurice Pianzola has re-created this period in *Des Français à conquête du Brésil—XVIIè siècle* (1991).

During the early eighteenth century two French Capuchin missionaries aided nascent anthropological and linguistic interests regarding Brazilian native populations. In 1707 Father Martin de Nantes published the *Relation succinte et sincere de la mission . . . dans le Brezil parmy les Indiens appellés Cariris*. Two years later Father Bernardo de Nantes published the *Katecismo indico da lingua kariris, acrescentado de varias praticas doutrinaes, & moraes, adaptadas ao genio, & capacidade dos indios do Brasil*. The pioneer scientific findings of Charles-Marie de La Condamine regarding the Amazon were presented in his *Relation abrégée d'un voyage fait dans l'intérieur de l'Amérique méridionale, depuis la côte de la mer du Sud, jusqu'aux côtes du Brésil et de la Guiane, . . .* (1745).

With the seat of the Portuguese monarchy settled in Brazil after 1808, King João VI invited a group of French artists and technicians to embellish and survey his vast realm. This undertaking has been described in *A missão artística de 1816* (1956) by Afonso de Escragnolle Taunay, a Brazilian descendant of one of the leading members of the mission. Along with Grant's history of Brazil in French, there shortly appeared additional histories in French by Alphonse de Beauchamp (1815 and 1824, on the country's recent independence), Hippolyte Taunay (1822), and Ferdinand Denis (1825). The first doctoral dissertations at the Sorbonne on Brazil appeared in 1823: "Géographie de la province cis-platine du Brésil" and "Hygiène publique à Rio de Janeiro." They follow the social-utilitarian scientific focus that was the purpose of the new doctoral degrees then resulting from Napoleonic reforms of higher education. A recounting of French travelers' observations during this period has been made by Jeanine Potelet in *Le Brésil, vu par les voyageurs et les marins français, 1816–1840: Témoignages et images* (1993). Earlier the same author wrote *Les indiens du Brésil, 1816–1833: Littérature de voyage et réalité* (1975).

An early economic study of Brazil, more than three hundred pages long, by a classic liberal French economist, Horace Say (younger brother of Jean-Baptiste, he of "Say's Law") is of special curiosity. In *Histoire des relations commerciales entre la France et le Brésil et considérations générales sur les monnaies, les changes, les banques et le commerce extérieur* (1839), Horace Say advances neoliberal arguments still occurring today among international bankers, funding agencies, and the Brazilian government. For the end of the nineteenth century, Jeffrey Needell has detailed the intensity of French influence in *A Tropical Belle Epoque: Elite Culture and Society in Turn-of-the-Century Rio de Janeiro* (1987).

As late as 1905 French gunboats in the mouth of the Amazon challenged Brazilian sovereignty over Amapá, which borders French Guyana. In 1909 Pierre Denis published *Le Brésil au XXe siècle*. The year before he had written on one of the earliest Brazilian coffee crises, "La crise du café au Brésil et la valorisation," in the Parisian *Revue politique et parlementaire*. Brazil resolved other border disputes at this time under the tutelage of its renowned foreign minister, the Baron of Rio Branco, José Maria da Silva Paranhos. One of the lasting contributions he made to Brazil's role in international relations was to organize the professional training of its diplomats, establishing this tutelage within the dominant French model. He collaborated with Emile Levasseur in editing *Le Brésil* on the occasion of the Paris Exposition Universelle in 1889.

The ideological axis for the abolition of slavery and the establishment of the republic originated from French positivism. The Brazilian republican movement sang as its anthem *La Marseillaise*. Marc Ferrez, Brazilian born but of French descent and education, pioneered photography in Brazil during the latter half of the nineteenth century and in 1907 inaugurated the Pathé cinema in Rio de Janeiro. Joaquim Maria Machado de Assis founded (1897) the Brazilian Academy of Letters, modeling it on the French institution, replicating even the uniforms of "*les imortelles.*" France singularly influenced the concentrated development of modernism in Brazil. Heitor Villa-Lobos spent the 1920s in Paris, obtaining access to Parisian music publishers and impresarios through Arthur Rubinstein. Darius Milhaud composed many pieces with themes originating from his years in Brazil. Brazilian organ compositions by Amaral Vieira, Alberto Nepomuceno, and Henrique Oswald followed patterns of César Franck, Charles-Marie Widor, and Marcel Dupré.

The Brazilian painters Anita Malfatti, Tarsila do Amaral (a student of Fernand Léger's), José Lins do Rego, Emiliano DiCavalcanti, and Cândido Portinari regularly exhibited in Paris salons and were distinguished members of the École de Paris. The sculptors Victor Brecheret and Bruno Giorgi studied with or followed Auguste Rodin and Aristide Maillol (along with the Italian Arturo Dazzi). The Archives Nationales de France sponsored a major exposition of Brazilian art in 1955; its catalog was entitled *France et Brésil.*

Writers such as Paul Claudel, Blaise Cendrars, and Georges Bernanos lived and traveled in Brazil, later writing about these experiences. Le Corbusier (the Franco-Swiss architect Charles-Edouard Jeanneret) was the key mentor of Oscar Niemeyer, who designed the Parisian headquarters of the Communist Party of France. The emergence of modern Brazilian drama followed innovations appearing in Parisian theater. A specialized study of the relation between Brazilian and French theater is *Louis Jouvet et le Théâtre de l'Athénée: "Promeneurs de rêves" en guerre de la France au Brésil* (2000) by Denis Rolland. Since 1963 Molière Prizes, based on the Paris theater critics' prize of the same name, have been annually awarded for outstanding performance in Brazilian theater. These are presented at Rio de Janeiro's Municipal Theater, which was modeled on the Opéra de Paris (Palais Garnier). One of the earliest Brazilian films to achieve international prominence, *Orfeu Negro*, was a joint Franco-Brazilian production (Marcel Camus, 1959)

The long history of French and Brazilian cultural interchange has recently been narrated by Mario Carelli in *Cultures croisées: Histoire des échanges culturels entre la France et le Brésil, de la découverte aux temps modernes* (1993), published in Portuguese as *Culturas cruzadas: Intercâmbios culturais entre França e Brasil* (1994). In *Aspects de la coopération franco-brésilienne: Transplantation culturelle et stratégie de la modernité* (1982), Guy Martinière further studies this cultural relationship in terms of modernism. The force of the influence of French thinking on modern Brazilian culture and society is studied in Monica Leite Lessa's *L'influence intellectuelle française au Brésil, 1886–1930* (2001) and Sérgio Miceli's *Intelectuais e classe dirigente no Brasil, 1920–1945* (1979), translated as *Les intellectuels et le pouvoir au Brésil, 1920–1945* (1981). The presentations at a Paris roundtable of 1989 on French and Brazilian mutual perceptions appeared in *Images réciproques du Brésil et de la France = Imagens recíprocas do Brasil e da França* (1991), edited by Solange Parvaux and Jean Revel-Mouroz. Moreover, aspects of mutual Brazilian-French social perceptions are presented in *Usages sociaux de la mémoire et de l'imaginaire au Brésil et en France* (2001), compiled by Jean Baptiste Martin and others from the papers of a conference at Lyon in 2000.

In the last half of the twentieth century, the French role in Brazil declined, and France itself succumbed to extensive U.S. influence. (This changed position is reviewed in *Les attitudes françaises face à l'influence des Etats-Unis au Brésil, 1944–1960* [2000] by Georgete Medleg Rodrigues.) Nevertheless, because of France's long interest and historic cultural role in Brazil, modern French academic study of Brazil, from the 1930s to the present, has been considerable, significant, and growing.

II. Modern French Study of Brazil

A. THE UNIVERSIDADE DE SÃO PAULO, THE 1930S

The founders of the Universidade de São Paulo (USP) in 1934 resolved that the quality of the institution would depend upon attracting the finest young scholars from European universities. Simon Schwartzman, in *A Space for Science: The Development of the Scientific Community in Brazil* (1991), has written that

> [While] there is no single register [at USP] of the persons invited, those who actually came, or the duration of their stay . . . the first group included, from France, Paul Arbusse Bastide (sociology), Emile Coornaert (history of civilization), Robert Garric (French literature), Pierre Deffontaines (geography), Etienne Borne (philosophy and psychology), and Michel Berveiller (Greco-Roman literature); from Italy, Francesco Picollo (Latin), Luigi Fantappié (mathematical analysis, integral and differential calculus), Ettore Onorato (mineralogy), and Gleb Wataghin (theoretical physics); from Germany, Ernest Breslau (zoology), Heinrich Rheinboldt (chemistry), Felix Rawitscher (botany); and from Portugal, Francisco Rebelo Gonçalves (Portuguese literature).
>
> Besides those, the Faculdade's first yearbook, for 1934–35, lists Jean Mougé, Pierre Monbeig, Fernand Braudel, Claude Lévi-Strauss, Edgar Otto

Gothsch, and Pierre Hourcade, all from France. . . . A second wave brought
Ernst Marcus, Paul Vanorden Shaw, François Perroux, Luigi Galvani, Gia-
como Albanese, Giuseppe Ungaretti, Georges Readers, and Ottorino de Fiori
Cropani. Marcus was to replace Breslau, who died suddenly. Most professors
came for a short period and returned after the first year. Others from the
same country often replaced them, such as Jean Gagé, Pierre Fromont, Roger
Bastide, Alfred Bonzon, Karl Arens, and Atílio Venturi.

Classes started on 11 March 1935 with forty-six students in philosophy,
twenty-nine in mathematics, ten in physics, twenty-nine in chemistry, fifteen
in the natural sciences, sixteen in geography and history, eighteen in the
social and political sciences, five in classical literature and Portuguese, and
nine in other foreign languages.[3]

As can be seen, the major contingent of scholars was French. Those
involved with the social sciences were influenced by the concept of the *science de l'homme*, the study of humankind based on an integrated perspective of psychology, sociology, and anthropology, together with philosophy
and economics. The extent of such French study in field research in Africa
and Asia gave it a particular focus on tropical lands and environments and
on stages of culture and civilization among a vast array of native peoples.

To select young French academics, the USP founders consulted with
specialists in philosophy, psychology, and anthropology such as Georges
Dumas, Pierre Janet, and Paul Rivet. The young scholars whom these
French consultants recommended determined what and how the French
have studied Brazil, even until today. Their role in the development of USP
represents the high point of French influence on Brazil's academic culture.
The principal members of the USP generation of French academics writing on Brazil comprised:

- Paul Arbousse-Bastide. Writing primarily on positivist educational philosophy, his principal work related to Brazilian education was *For-
  mando o homem: Contribuição para o plano de um ginásio ideal* (1944),
  with an introduction by the singular Brazilian educator Fernando de
  Azevedo. Arbousse-Bastide also wrote an introduction for a book by
  Gilberto Freyre.
- Roger Bastide. With pioneering social and psychological studies of
  Afro-Brazilian religion, he produced such important works as *Images
  du Nordeste mystique en noir et blanc* (1945), *Brésil, terre des contrastes*
  (1957), *Le candomblé de Bahia, rite Nagô, et autres essais* (1958), *Les
  religions africaines au Brésil; vers une sociologie des interpénétrations*

de civilisations (1960). Bastide's work on African culture and religion in Brazil was given continuity in that of Pierre Verger and numerous scholars since.

- Fernand Braudel. The great *Annales* historian began his university career at USP, in residence from 1935 to 1938. He published little, however, on Brazil. Imprisoned after the start of World War II, he spent his time writing his famous work on the Mediterranean during the reign of Philip II. An economic research institute is named after Braudel at USP, inaugurated in 1987. The focus of the *Annales* school on the *longue durée*, of viewing historical development within fundamental, unchanging structures of geography and climate, appears recently once more in *Brésil: Une geohistoire* (2001) by Martine Droulers. This author has also written on Brazil's great identifying geographical phenomenon, *L'Amazonie*.
- Pierre Deffontaines. A geographer and topographer of wide-ranging interests in the Americas, Europe, and Asia, his principal works concerning Brazil were *Geografia humana do Brasil* (1940, 1952) and *El Brasil, la tierra y el hombre* (1944, 1960). He also wrote studies of native tribes (Mascatis and Guaycurus) and the development of Brazilian air transport.
- Pierre Fromont. A noted agricultural economist, his works on international rural economics studied Brazil only in comparative terms in relation to his principal specializations in France, Europe, Egypt, and the Middle East.
- Robert Garric. A scholar of French letters and organizer of the social worker profession in France, he did little work directly on Brazil. However, he wrote the preface for Antônio Carneiro Leão's *Victor Hugo no Brasil* (1960).
- Pierre Hourcade. A specialist in Brazilian and Portuguese literature, he was one of the early translators into French of Jorge Amado, publishing *Bahia de Tous les Saints [Jubiabá]* (1938). The Brazilian embassy in Paris has published *Auteurs brésiliens en français = Autores brasileiros em francês* (1998) by Inês Fonseca, a description of Brazilian authors and their works translated into French, with supplementary material related to the literary activities in the two countries.[4]
- Claude Lévi-Strauss. In developing structural anthropology, he focused much of his work on Brazil, such as *La vie familiale et sociale des Indiens Nambikwara* (1948), *Le cru et le cuit* (1964), and the classic *Tristes tropiques* (1955).
- Pierre Monbeig. He advanced numerous broad theories on regional and national aspects of geography in relation to frontier and borderland areas. In this regard he wrote about Brazil in *Pionniers et planteurs de*

São Paulo (1952), *La Croissance de la ville de São Paulo* (1953), *Le Brésil* (1954), and *Novos estudos de geografia humana brasileira* (1957).

- Charles Morazé. A comparative political specialist, he wrote extensively on the development of modern Europe. In *Les trois âges du Brésil: Essai de politique* (1954) he analyzed from a structuralist perspective the development of Brazil in relation to the Western world.
- François Perroux. A prolific writer on economic planning, market economies, and developing countries, he wrote little specifically on Brazil, although several of his works were translated to Portuguese, including *Lições de economia política*, 1936, and *O capitalismo*, 1974.
- George Readers. Of particular relevance to French-Brazilian intellectual relations was his article "Dom Pedro II, ami et protecteur des savants et écrivains français" in the *Revista da Universidade Católica de São Paulo* (June 1955).

B. AFTER USP AND THE SECOND WORLD WAR

The publications on Brazil of the French scholars from USP began to appear in the late 1940s and throughout the 1950s. With the appearance of these works, an additional contingent of French scholars began to emerge, also focusing on Brazil.

- Germain Bazin. The author of many dozens of volumes of art history, he concentrated especially on the baroque and modern periods. Consequently, he was drawn to the distinct nature of baroque art in Brazil, writing the two-volume *L'Architecture religieuse baroque au Brésil* (1956–58), and *Aleijadinho et la sculpture baroque au Brésil* (1963). Bazin's work in this regard was indebted to the accomplishments during the preceding decades of the newly organized Instituto do Patrimônio Histórico e Artístico Nacional (IPHAN) under Rodrigo Mello Franco.

The architectural and artistic accomplishments of IPHAN were complemented by the work of the German architect-turned-musicologist Franz Kurt Lange (as a naturalized Uruguayan, he latinized his name to Francisco Curt Lange), who made numerous discoveries in regard to Brazilian baroque music. Recently, he has paid further attention to the Brazilian baroque, in the context of that period in Portugal, in *L'or des tropiques: Promenades dans le Portugal et le Brésil baroques* (1993), translated as *O ouro dos trópicos: Passeios pelo Portugal e o Brasil barrocos* (1996). A continuation of interest in the Brazilian baroque occurred most recently in an exhibition of such art at the Petit Palais in Paris during 1999–2000.

- Yves Bruand. An arts librarian at the National Library of France, he was appointed professor of modern art at the University of Toulouse. He is one of the foremost authorities on modern Brazilian architecture and the author of *L'architecture contemporaine au Brésil* (1971), translated as *Arquitetura contemporânea no Brasil* (1981, 1997).
- Raymond Cantel. Noted for his multiedition Portuguese grammar in French, *Précis de grammaire portugaise*, he also specialized in the writings of Padre Antônio Vieira, bringing out *Les sermons de Vieira: Étude du style* (1959) and *Prophétisme et messianisme dans l'oeuvre d'Antonio Vieira* (1960). In addition, he published two works on *literatura de cordel*.
- Jacques Chonchol. His work on Brazil has focused on Brazil within the context of agricultural and land reforms in Latin America and Indian rights. Two of his many books have appeared in Portuguese, *Metodologia para formular un programa de desarrollo agrícola* (1966) for the Superintendência do Desenvolvimento do Nordeste (the federal agency for the development of the Northeast), and *Crise e transformação dos regimes autoritários* (1986).
- Benjamin Coriat. Coriat focuses on theories of enterprise, such as Fordism and Taylorism, and the exercise of entrepreneurial culture in France and Japan; he also has written on socioeconomic implications of robotics and electronics. On Brazil he wrote *Alcool: Enquête au Brésil sur un programme agro-énergétique de substitution au pétrole* (1982), about the innovative way in which Brazil, a petroleum-poor country, came to substitute sugarcane alcohol for gasoline in motors.
- Frédéric Mauro. A prolific economic historian, he wrote on the expansion of modern Europe, especially in the Americas and the Atlantic. In relation to Brazilian history, he produced volumes on its economic development, *Études économiques sur l'expansion portugaise, 1500–1900* (1970), *Brasil: do Pau Brasil ao açucar, estruturas económicas e instituições políticas: 1530–1580* (1971), *La Formation économique du Brésil: de l'époque coloniale aux temps modernes* (1974); volumes on each century of its development, *Le Brésil au XVIIe siécle: documents inédits relatifs à l'Atlantique portugais* (1961), *Le Brésil du XVe à la fin du XVIIIe siècle* (1977), *La Vie quotidienne au Brésil au temps de Pedro Segundo : 1831–1889* (1981), *Le Portugal, le Brésil et l'Atlantique au XVIIe siècle: 1570–1670: étude économique* (1983), *La Préindustrialisation du Brésil: essais sur une économie en transition: 1830/50–1930/50* (1984), *O Império luso-brasileiro: 1620–1750* (1991); and a multiedition, standard, one-volume history of Brazil, *Histoire du Brésil* (1973, 1979, 1994).

- Kátia Mytilineou de Queirós Mattoso. A Brazilian scholar in France, she has held the only chair in Brazilian history at a French university (Paris-IV—Sorbonne). She is the author of numerous insightful books in French and Portuguese on slavery, Bahia, and colonial Brazil. One of her most influential and intriguing has been *Être esclave au Brésil: XVIe–XIXe* (1979), translated as *To Be a Slave in Brazil, 1550–1888* (1986). François Crouzet, Philippe Bonnichon, and Denis Rolland prepared *Pour l'histoire du Brésil: Hommage à Katia de Queirós Mattoso* (2000) on her work. She has been succeeded in the Sorbonne chair by another Brazilian historian, Luiz Felipe de Alencastro. Also a specialist in the Atlantic slavery system, he is the author of *O trato dos viventes: Formação do Brasil no Atlântico Sul* (2000). He contributed to *Antropologia da escravidão: O ventre de ferro e dinheiro* (1995). This is the Brazilian version of the widely translated work of Claude Meillassoux, *Anthropologie de l'esclavage: Le ventre de fer et d'argent* (1986), which has been translated into several languages, including English: *The Anthropology of Slavery: The Womb of Iron and Gold* (1991).

  Together with the Brazilian diplomat Paulo Roberto de Almeida, Mattoso published *Brésil: Cinq siècles d'histoire* (1995). Among Almeida's publications in French is one on Southern Cone economic integration, *Le Mercosud: Un marché commun pour l'Amérique du Sud* (2000). This topic, together with Brazil as a regional power and emerging world power, appears in recent works of several other authors: *Le Brésil* (1985, 2000) and *Pouvoir et territoire au Brésil, de l'archipel au continent* (1996) by Hervé Théry; *La genèse du Mercosud: Dynamisme interne, influence de l'Union Européene et insertion internationale* (2000) by Marcelo Medeiros; and *Histoire de l'Amazonie* (2000) by Jean Soublin.
- Daniel-Henri Pageaux. Although a specialist in Portuguese literature, his Latin American interests include authors such as Ernesto Sábato and Aimé Césaire. He also has an interest in comparative literature, through which he studies Brazilian literature in relation to Latin America and the Lusophone world.
- Raymond Pébayle. A specialist in the rural economic geography of Rio Grande do Sul, he has written *Le centre du plateau rio-grandense: Une région rurale en mutation* (1970), *Les gauchos du Brésil: Éleveurs et agriculteurs du Rio Grande do Sul* (1977), and *Les Brésiliens, pionniers et bâtisseurs* (1989). With Monbeig he wrote a descriptive account of mid-century Brazil, *Le Brésil* (1968), that has been reprinted several times in the popular *Que sais-je?* series (vol. 628).
- Jean Roche. A specialist on the history of Rio Grande do Sul, he wrote

La colonisation allemande et le Rio Grande do Sud (1959) [*A colonização alemã e o Rio Grande do Sul*] (1969) and *L'administration de la province du Rio Grande do Sul de 1829 à 1847 d'après les rapports inédits du président du Rio Grande do Sul devant le Conseil Général, puis l'Assemblée Législative Provinciale* (1961).

- Michel Rochefort. A geographer specializing in rivers and South America, Brazil, Senegal, and Alsace, he wrote *Rapports entre la pluviosité et l'écoulement dans le Brésil subtropical et le Brésil tropical Atlantique, étude comparée des bassins du Guaïba et de Paraïba do Sul* (1958).
- Ignacy Sachs. Sachs, a leading economist who specializes in strategies for Third World economic development and environmental preservation, is the author of *Resources, Employment, and Development Financing: Producing Without Destroying: The Case of Brazil* (1989) and the UNESCO publication *Extractivism in the Brazilian Amazon: Perspectives on Regional Development* (1994). He was a leader at the 1992 Rio Conference. He wrote the preface for *Le Brésil après le miracle* (1987) by Celso Furtado.

Classics of Brazilian scholarship have also appeared in French, among them, *Racines du Brésil* (1998) [*Raízes do Brasil* (1936)] by Sérgio Buarque de Holanda and *Maîtres et esclaves* (1952) [*Casa-grande e senzala* (1933)] by Gilberto Freyre. Roger Bastide translated the latter; the *Annaliste* historian Lucien Febvre wrote the preface.

French study and writing on Brazil are centuries old; French intellectual and cultural influence was paramount in Brazil even during much of the nineteenth century and into the twentieth century. In relation to later U.S. study of Brazil, what has distinguished the French perspective? Several characteristics present themselves. First, French work is primarily in the social sciences or socially relevant physical sciences. However, French scholars rarely focus exclusively on Brazil. In part this could be due to fewer academic or research positions in France that concentrate exclusively on Brazil. Generally, Brazil is studied only as a "case" within the context of a particular disciplinary focus or hypothesis such as the psychology of religion, literature in Portuguese, Third World economies, tropical native peoples, agriculture, ecology, and so on. The approach is integrated more horizontally than vertically. Nonetheless, the term *brésilianiste* has begun to appear. However, the spelling preserves the "a" of the English term, a recondite example of franglais.

Second, although the volume of French work on Brazil is smaller than the American, the historical extent of it is centuries old, going back to the very beginning of Brazil. Production since 1945 is of a wide, integrative nature; several works, especially in anthropology and social psychology, have become classics. Third, in relation to economic theory, the dependency paradigm and recognition of a key role for the state hold much stronger sway among French theorists (as with Brazilian economists) than among current neoliberal Anglo-American professionals. Fourth, the weight of the *Annales* school of historiography is apparent in the work of French historians and social scientists relating the Brazilian past. Special attention to the *longue durée*, especially to the geographic setting, and to quantitative description is apparent. A further and deeply important aspect of this orientation is that France has historically been both an Atlantic and Mediterranean power. Indeed, some of the most defining characteristics of French culture lie in Roman Mediterranean civilization. The origins of Brazilian patriarchal families, sociopolitical patronage, code law, papal hierarchical religion, and Romance language lie as they do for France, in Roman concepts of pater familias, the *patronus-clientus* relationship, curial law, pontifical and priestly collegial religion, and the Latin language.

Fifth, as a result of the modern Francophone community and the preceding French empire, French social scientists have generations of experience in working in subtropical or tropical environments, such as the Caribbean, West Africa, the Middle East, and Southeast Asia. Moreover, there has been the French conception of and respect for negritude, the originality of African art and culture, and the adaptive, integrative character of French *civilisation*. Sixth, contemporary French and Brazilian scholars share many traditions beyond just a Latin culture. There is often an ideological and social camaraderie of "subaltern elites," allowing them to operate as gadflies to the Anglophone, neoliberal social science establishment. Seventh, ironically (yet understandably—even transparently— for Pierre Bourdieu and his followers), the weight, indeed the allure, of French influence in Brazil was related to its elite associations. The influence was associated with refined intellectual and cultural pursuits, luxury consumption, and restricted social activities and endeavors. The weight and allure of U.S. culture in Brazil, and indeed the world, since the middle of the twentieth century, have been the contrary. The United States is perceived as representing mass access to cultural and economic consumption, political and social participation, and educational opportunity.

Eighth, unlike the United States, where most graduate students studying Brazil are American, most current graduate-level specialization on Brazil in France is done not by French but Brazilian students. However, because of scholarship funding and changing interests in fields of study, the number of such students is declining. Ninth, French works that analyze Brazil as a regional or emerging world power tend to emphasize its role as a Latin rival or counter to that of U.S. power rather than an ally of it. U.S. analyses see Brazil as a potential rival but also as a surrogate or complement to it. And, finally, there is an interesting parallel of late twentieth-century paradigm shifts between liberal French scholars and Latin American Catholic theologians. As the role of both has lessened among Latin American elites, they have tended to identify themselves with mass-oriented positions. The French scholars have assumed positions favoring antiglobalization, *antimondialisation.* The Latin American theologians have adopted a "preferential option for the poor" with liberation theology. Contemporary French interests in Brazil intersect with a number of new and traditional interests. The French position regarding globalization mixes various concerns. Its exports must be able to penetrate world markets, to regain, maintain, or expand global market share. Moreover, the French position is concerned about preservation of natural resources and the integrity of the environment. These concerns dominate throughout Europe, an area densely populated and wanting in natural resources. The region of the Amazon, its rain forests, rivers, and native peoples, are of interest both for these factors and the long-standing French interest in geography and ethnic cultures, particularly in tropical areas.

III. Current Conditions and Resources

In addition to the scholarly works of the postwar period, a considerable increase has occurred in recent decades in the production of doctoral dissertations on Brazil at French universities. The *Catalogue général des thèses sauternes en France sur le Brésil, 1823–1999,* published in 2000 as an extra issue of the *Cahiers du Brésil Contemporaine,* indicates that 1,344 theses or dissertations (doctoral and *troisième cycle,* the latter being a kind of advanced master's degree requiring a thesis) have been presented at French universities. (See summary information at www.ehess.fr/centres/crbc/cbc-thes/sommaire.html#som.) The volume has an insightful preface by its editor, Anita Pires-Saboia. More than 98 percent of the theses appeared from 1945 to 1999. Most significantly, 95 percent have appeared since 1970 and 54.9 percent since 1985. At the heart of this increase was one that also affected the United States, the expansion of higher education. Almost half (49.9 percent) of the dissertations have appeared in the disciplines of economics (22.6), sociology (14.1), and geography (13.2). Another three fields, literature (12.4), education (8), and history (7.5), bring total coverage to 77.8 percent. The remaining areas are anthropology (6.3), law (5.5), the arts (4.3), political science (3.6), and psychology (2.3). The social sciences overwhelmingly dominate, along with the tradition of *science de l'homme.*

The expansion of study of Brazil resulted from several factors. Within French higher education, the number of universities increased by approximately 150 percent after the student uprisings of May 1968. Just in Paris during the 1970s, the Université de Paris became thirteen different institutions, with the Sorbonne remaining as a core remnant. Located throughout the city, the new universities adopted more modern curricula, including such things as business administration, and reformed degree programs, especially the doctorate. Throughout the country the number of students, programs, and institutions increased. As more university positions in more varied fields became available in France, a greater number of Brazilian students sought them. The growing repression of the military regime after 1964 forced numerous young Brazilian radicals into exile. As students enrolling in French universities, particularly in Paris, they swelled the number of theses written on Brazil. Brazilian enrollment in French sociology departments vastly increased; that discipline was virtually forbidden then in Brazil. Furthermore, the Brazilian military government gave priority to improving the country's level of higher education as a fundamental vehicle for national development. It sponsored more financial aid through thousands of scholarships for doctoral study abroad. These were offered principally through the Conselho Nacional de Pesquisa (CNPq, Ministry of Science and Technology) and the Coordenação de Aperfeiçoamento de Pessoal de Nível Superior (Ministry of Education and Culture). Although most students with these grants chose to study in the United States, their second choice, especially in the 1980s, was France. Thus a further increase in French doctoral dissertations on Brazil appeared.

The Associação dos Pesquisadores e Estudantes Brasileiros na França was established in 1984. Ten years later the Rede Santos-Dumont was founded, a network that coordinated exchange programs between Brazilian and French universities at the doctoral and postdoctoral levels. (There is a gateway to websites related to Franco-Brazilian educational and professional cooperation at www.cendotec.org.br/assoc.shtml.) The Université Aix-Marseille II hosts the Comité Français d'Evaluation de la Coopération Universitaire avec le Brésil (Comitê Francês de Avaliação da Cooperação Universitária com o Brasil) with a website at www.egide.asso.fr/fr/programmes/cofecub/. The publication *France-Brésil: Vingt ans de coopération—science et technologie* (1989), edited by Luiz Claudio Cardoso et

Guy Martinère, recounts in considerable detail the number of cooperative projects in scientific and technical areas that have occurred between the two countries. Academic relations are part of a larger people-to-people exchange operation functioning through the Centre International d'Amitié Franco Brésilien.[5] On a regional level, university exchanges with Brazil occur through the Réseau d'appui à la coopération en Rhône-Alpes, in Grenoble (its website is at www.resacoop.org/).

Tracing study and research on Brazil in France has been greatly enhanced by the database FRANCIS. Produced by L'Institut de l'Information Scientifique et Technique du Centre National de la Recherche Scientifique, it "indexes multilingual, multidisciplinary information published in over 4,200 journals covering the humanities (67%), social sciences (30%), and economics (3%). The database is strong in religion, the history of art, psychology, and literature (with particular emphasis on current trends in European and world literature). It contains bilingual (English-French) subject descriptors. Particularly noteworthy is the inclusion of abstracts in 80% of the records. FRANCIS represents a wide range of materials, including serials, journal articles, books, book chapters, conference papers, French dissertations, exhibition catalogs, legislation, teaching materials, and reports."[6] FRANCIS allows subject and keyword searching in French. Moreover, it allows limiting of searches by location to publications in France. In this way, a search for a Brazilian subject or keyword allows a fairly precise count of what has been the French research on that topic since roughly the mid-1980s. In terms of where in France research is and can be done on Brazil, there are several key libraries and centers. While most are in Paris, several exist in cities of the provinces. What follows is a list of current resources. For earlier sources of such information, see the *Répertoire des Recherches latino-américanistes en France*, no. 1 (1979) and the *Répertoire des Recherches latino-américanistes en France*, no 2. (1982), edited by the Groupe de Recherches sur l'Amérique Latine at the Université de Toulouse-le-Mirail; *Latinoamericanistas en Europa: Registro bio-bibliográfico de 1990* by Jean Stroom; and *Latinoamericanistas en Europa: Registro bio-bibliográfico de 1995*, from the Centro de Estudios y Documentación Latinoamericanos in Amsterdam.

I. PARIS

1. Ambassade du Brèsil, Bibliothèque, 34, cours Albert—1er, Hôtel Schneider, 75008 Paris; telephone: 01 45 61 63 65; fax: 01 42 89 03 45; e-mail: Biblioteca@bresil.org; website: www.bresil.org/db/RECHERCH.ASP.

The Brazilian embassy in Paris has a public, circulating library with more than seven thousand cataloged items. It consists of books, periodicals, and audiovisual materials on Brazil or Franco-Brazilian relations in the arts, humanities, and social sciences. The collection can be searched via an on-line catalog at the website. In addition to the library, the embassy also provides information on Brazil-related activities and organizations in France in the section titled "le Brésil en France" at www.bresil.org/.

2. Bibliothèque Nationale de France, Quai François-Mauriac, 75706 Paris Cédex 13; telephone: 01 53 79 59 59; website: http://www.bnf.fr.

Material on Brazil at the National Library of France (both the old site, Rue Richelieu, and the new, Mauriac) can be found through the English-language work *Resources for Brazilian Studies at the Bibliothèque Nationale* [de France] (1980) by William Vernon Jackson. Although the new national library has been built since this title was published, nonetheless, the book is still quite useful since it describes holdings in subject classification groupings. Materials transferred from the Richelieu to the Mauriac site are still grouped by the same classification. By using the National Library, one can also find out about materials on Brazil at almost four thousand libraries and research centers in France. The Catalogue Collectif de France, accessible at www.ccfr.bnf.fr. It is somewhat similar to the WorldCat database of the Online Computer Library Center or the Research Libraries Information Network.

3. Centre de Recherches sur le Brésil Contemporain (CRBC), École des Hautes Études en Sciences Sociales, Maison des Sciences de l'Homme, 54 Bd. Raspail, 75270 Paris Cédex 06; telephone: 01 49 54 20 85; fax: 01 45 48 83 53; e-mail: crbc@ehess.fr; website: www.ehess.fr/centres/crbc/accueil.html.

The CRBC is housed in the Maison des Sciences de l'Homme, founded by Fernand Braudel. The library of the Maison houses the premier collection of *science de l'homme* research resources, with more than 100,000 volumes and about two thousand current periodicals. In conjunction with the Presses Universitaires de France, the CRBC publishes a monograph series on Brazil, the *Collection Brasília*, begun in 1981 (in addition, the publisher L'Harmattan has a *Série Brésil* within its collection, *Recherches et Documents Amérique Latine*). Former Brazilian president Fernando Henrique Cardoso published *Les Idées à leur place* (1984), in the CRBC series. The CRBC has published the journal *Cahiers du Brésil Contemporain (CBC)* since 1987 and maintains a databank, Banque de données France-Brésil, and a small library. Founded in 1985 by Ignacy Sachs, it is the principal Brazilian studies center in France. Issues of the *CBC* may be searched on line at www1.msh-paris.fr/revues/Home.asp.

Complementing the library of the CRBC is that of the Institute des Hautes Études d'Amérique Latine (IHEAL, part of the Université de Paris–III), the 100,000-volume Bibliothèque Pierre Monbeig. It is located at 28, rue Saint-Guillaume (75007; telephone: 44 39 86 76; fax:: 45 48 79 58; website: www.iheal.univ-paris3.fr/documentation/index. html). IHEAL has also maintained a publishing enterprise since 1957, Éditions de l'IHEAL.

4. Centre de Recherche sur les Pays de Langue Portugaise (CREPAL), Bibliothèque Université de Paris III—Sorbonne Nouvelle, 17, rue de Sorbonne, Esc. C—2e étage 75005 Paris; telephone: 01 40 46 29 17; fax:: 01 43 25 74 71; website: bucensier.univ-paris3.fr/.

The holdings of the library of CREPAL are primarily in Brazilian, Portuguese, and Lusophone African literature and the Portuguese language. The collection consists of about thirty thousand volumes and nearly four hundred periodicals. Additional related resources are located in the adjoining building of the interuniversity library of the Sorbonne and the Bibliothèque Sainte Geneviève (10, Place de Panthéon).

5. Centre d'Études des Pays de Langue Portugaise, Université de Paris VIII, 2, rue de la Liberté, 93526 Saint-Denis Cédex 02; telephone: 01 49 40 66 83; website: www.univ-paris8.fr/article.php3?id_article=368.

The University of Paris VIII is on the northern edge of the city (Vincennes–St. Denis). Its Portuguese instruction resources depend on the university libraries in central Paris, in the Sorbonne and Panthéon areas.

6. Musée de l'Homme, Bibliothèque, Fonds Bastide, Palais de Chaillot, Place du Trocadéro, 75016 Paris; telephone: 01 44 05 72 06; website: www.paris.org/Musees/Homme/info.html.

The Bastide Collection within the library of this museum holds some of the richest French resources on Brazilian ethnology and anthropology.

7. Further Sources

That list describes collections, centers, and guides specifically focusing on Brazil. There are, however, general resources with important materials related to Brazil. Among these are the general libraries of the Université de Paris, especially in the Sorbonne. Important among the university-related libraries is the Bibliothèque Sainte-Geneviève, on the Place de Panthéon. Interesting for colonial documentation is the Bibliothèque Mazarine, at the Institut de France; the Archives Nationales, in the Hôtel de Rohan; and the library of the Musée de la Marine, in the Palais de Chaillot. Useful for studying Brazil within the context of the Lusophone world is the Centre Calouste Gulbenkian, on the Avenue d'Iena. A number of specialized libraries are located within schools, museums, research centers, institutes, and foundations for music and dance, fine and decorative arts, theater, photography, cinema, architecture, political science, international relations, and comparative law. Their addresses and telephone numbers are listed in the section on France in *The World of Learning* (2004).

II. PROVINCES

8. Rennes, Bretagne: Département de Portugais et d'Études Portugaises, Brésiliennes et de l'Afrique Lusographe, Université Rennes 2—Campus Villejean, Pôle Langues, bâtiment L et bâtiment E 6, av. Gaston Berger, 35043 Rennes; telephone: 02 99 14 16 52; e-mail: dominique. bellier@ uhb.fr; website: www.uhb.fr/enseignement/UFRLangues/index.htm.

   The interest of this Breton university in Portuguese, and hence Brazil, is in relation to Celtic or Gaelic culture. Celtic culture, which has existed in Europe since before the Roman empire, extends from Ireland and western Scotland into Wales (País de Gales, in Portuguese); Brittany, in northwest France; the old Gaul parts of France; Galicia, in northwest Spain; and Portugal (name derived from the "port of the Gauls," i.e., Celts).

9. Toulouse, Gascogne: Institut Pluridisciplinaire pour les Études sur l'Amérique Latine—Toulouse (IPEALT), Université de Toulouse—Le Mirail, Maison de la Recherche, 5, Allées Antonio Machado, 31058 Toulouse Cédex 01; telephone: 05 61 50 43 93; fax: 05 61 50 36 25 e-mail: ipealt@univ-tlse2.fr; website: www.univ-tlse2.fr/ipealt/.

   IPEALT publishes the journal *Caravelle: Cahiers du monde hispanique et luso-bresilien*, founded in 1963 by Frédéric Mauro and other scholars. Indexes for this journal are available on line at www.istitutodatini.it/biblio/riviste/a-c/carav.htm. The Université de Toulouse is located in southern France, near the Pyrenees, a neighbor to Andorra, Spain, and Portugal.

10. Tours, Centre: Institut d'Études Hispaniques et Portugaises, Faculté des Lettres, Université de Tours, 3, rue des Tanneurs, Bureaux 5 à 11, 37041 Tours Cédex 01; telephone: 02 47 36 65 89; fax: 02 47 36 65 53; e-mail: bourreau@univ-tours.fr; website: www.univ-tours.fr/espagnol/institut.htm.

   This institute has a small program, at a university in the Loire region, for Portuguese literature, which includes Latin American studies.

11. Aix-en-Provence, Provence: Département d'Études Luso-Brésiliennes (Portugal, Brésil et Afrique de langue portugaise), Université de Provence—Aix-Marseille I, 29, av. Robert Schuman, Bureau 327, 13621 Aix-en-Provence; telephone: 04–42–95–30–30; fax: 04–42–59–42–80; website: www.up.univ-mrs.fr/~werlaos.

This department publishes the *Cahiers d'Études Romanes* for Spanish, Catalan, and Latin American studies. This publication and the department focus on Portuguese, and hence Brazil, as part of the Roman and Mediterranean world. Beyond Aix-en-Provence, the Université de Provence has a location in Marseilles and is a member of the Conférence Française des Universités de l'Arc Méditerranéen.

Notes

1. Curiously, all the U.S. allies from the Second World War, Britain, the Soviet Union, and France, saw themselves replaced in succeeding decades, economically, militarily, ideologically, and culturally, by the United States.

2. Ironically, Andrew Grant's was the shortest entry in the first edition of the *Dictionary of National Biography*.

3. Simon Schwartzman, *A Space for Science—The Development of the Scientific Community in Brazil* (University Park: Pennsylvania State University Press, 1991), chapter 5, available on-line at www.schwartzman.org.br/simon/space/chapter5. htm#_1_7.

4. It can be read at http://www.bresil.org/Litterature_en_francais/livro7derncor. pdf.

5. B.P. 2218; 51081 Reims Cedex; tel. 33 3 26 36 44 26; fax 33 3 26 40 26 89; e-mail: services@ciafb.com; web: http://www.ciafb.com/.

6. From Research Libraries Group statement.

PART 4

∾

Bibliographic and Reference Sources

CHAPTER 15

A Chronology of U.S.–Brazil Relations and Academic Publications, 1945–2003

PAULO ROBERTO DE ALMEIDA

Selective Bibliography and Chronology

	Domestic, hemispheric, and international events, U.S.–Brazil bilateral relations	Academic production in each country related to the study of Brazil or about U.S.–Brazil bilateral relations (books and articles, excluding dissertations)
1945	• Inter-American conference of Chapultepec (Argentina not invited). • Creation of the United Nations at the San Francisco conference. • Death of Franklin D. Roosevelt, inauguration of Harry Truman. • Brazil takes part in World War II and recognizes the USSR at the demand of the United States (and as a stake for possible acceptance as a permanent member of the U.N. Security Council [UNSC]). • End of the war in Europe and Asia (atomic bomb droppd on Hiroshima and Nagasaki). • Coup d'état against Vargas returns democracy to Brazil; general elections held.	• Hispanic Division of the Library of Congress: *Handbook of Latin American Studies* (published since 1936 and since 1939 by the LOC). • Pierson, Donald, *Survey of the Literature on Brazil of Sociological Significance Published up to 1940.* • Brown, Rose, *American Emperor: Dom Pedro II of Brazil.* • Cunha, Euclides da, *Rebellion in the Backlands.* • Verissimo, Erico, *Brazilian Literature: An Outline.* • Freyre, Gilberto, *Brazil: An Interpretation.*

1946
- First signs of the Cold War: peace conferences divide war allies, and Winston Churchill warns that an "iron curtain" is dividing Europe.
- Brazil: inauguration of General Dutra, whose government will strictly follow the leadership of the United States during the first phase of the Cold War.
- Juan Perón becomes president of Argentina, campaigning against the U.S. ambassador (with the slogan "Braden or Perón").

- Smith, T. Lynn, *Brazil, People and Institutions.*
- James, Preston E., *Brazil.*
- Freyre, Gilberto, *The Masters and the Slaves.*

- President Truman signs Fulbright Act (Bill 584), creating an exchange program for international cooperation in cultural, technical, and educational matters.

1947
- Independence of India and Pakistan; decolonization in the Third World gains support of the United States against European "old" colonialism.
- Trade negotiations in Geneva give rise to the multilateral trading system (GATT—General Agreement on Tariffs and Trade).
- Secretary of State George C. Marshall announces a plan to assist Europe; United States approves the establishment of the Organization for European Economic Cooperation (OEEC), basis of the future OECD.
- Conference of Petrópolis approves the Inter-American Treaty for Reciprocal Assistance, a conceptual framework for what would become NATO.

- Hill, Lawrence F., ed. *Brazil.*
- Tavares de Sá, Hernane, *The Brazilians: People of Tomorrow.*
- Landes, Ruth, *The City of Women.*

- Institutes of Latin American studies established at the universities of Texas and North Carolina, as well as at Tulane and Vanderbilt (Brazil).

1948
- Creation of the State of Israel; Ghandi is assassinated in India.
- Hardening of the Cold War in Europe and Asia as a result of communist coups; the blockade

- Putnam, Samuel, *Marvelous Journeys: A Survey of Four Centuries of Brazilian Writing.*
- Roosevelt, Theodore, *Nas Selvas do Brasil* (Brazilian edition of

of West Berlin confirms the 1946 alert by Winston Churchill about the "iron curtain"; George Kennan's containment doctrine becomes an official U.S. policy.

• Creation of the Organization of American States (OAS) at conference in Bogotá; Brazil breaks diplomatic relations with the USSR and outlaws the Communist Party.

• United Nations Conference on Trade and Employment approves the Havana Charter, instituting an international trade organization (which never took effect because U.S. did not ratify).

Through the Brazilian Wilderness, 1914).

• Florida University Press begins to publish, for the Hispanic Division of the Library of Congress, the *Handbook of Latin American Studies* (this continues till 1966, when the *Handbook* becomes the responsibility of University of Texas at Austin).

1949
• Creation of North Atlantic Treaty Organization (NATO), a common defense alliance of Western countries to counter Soviet forces in Central Europe; Germany is officially divided.

• The Soviet Union detonates its first atomic bomb.

• Communists seize power in continental China; U.S. supports Taiwan as an official permanent member of the U.N. Security Council.

• Creation of the Joint Brazil–U.S. Economic Commission

• Wagley, Charles, *The Tenetehara Indians of Brazil.*
• Hunnicutt, B. M., *Brazil: World Frontier.*
• Wythe, George, *Brazil: An Expanding Economy.*

• Creation of Escola Superior de Guerra (modeled after the National War College).

1950
• War in Korea: intervention by United States (by UNSC resolution) and China (by sending in "voluntary troops").

• Creation of the European Payments Union within the framework of the OEEC.

• Azevedo, Fernando de, *Brazilian Culture.*
• Costa, Sérgio Corrêa da, *Every Inch a King: A Biography of Dom Pedro I.*
• Nabuco, Carolina, *The Life of Joaquim Nabuco.*

- Perón announces the "third way" in foreign policy.
- Brazil: Vargas returns to power, democratically elected, supported by organized labor and reformist parties.

- The First Luso-Brazilian Colloquium is held at the Library of Congress and Vanderbilt University.

1951
- Nationalization of the oil industry in Iran causes intervention by the CIA against the Mossadegh regime.
- Brazil refuses to send troops to Korea under the aegis of the U.N.
- Creation of the European Community of Carbon and Steel, the basis for a deeper integration process.
- Perón is reelected in Argentina.
- Reform of the tariff policy in Brazil.

- Smith, T. Lynn, and Alexander Marchant, eds., *Brazil: Portrait of Half a Continent.*
- Pierson, Donald, *Cruz das Almas: A Brazilian Village.*

1952
- Eisenhower becomes president of the United States; coup d'état in Egypt overthrows monarchy.
- Death of Eva Perón in Argentina; insurrection in Bolivia; Batista's military coup in Cuba; dictatorship of Pérez Jiménez in Venezuela.
- U.S.-Brazil military agreement (in effect until 1997).

- Wagley, Charles, *Race and Class in Rural Brazil.*

1953
- Death of Stalin in the USSR starts a new phase in the Cold War; Soviet troops quell anti-Communist workers' revolt in East Berlin.
- Reform of the exchange system in Brazil.

- Wagley, Charles. *Amazon Town.*

1954
- Nasser seizes power in Egypt, as does Alfredo Stroessner in Paraguay.

- Joint Brazil–U.S. Economic Development Commission, *Brazilian Technical Studies, The Development of Brazil.*

- France entangled in colonial insurrections in Indochina and Algeria.
- Political and military crises in Brazil: restrictions against foreign capital and the suicide of Vargas.

- Kiemen, Mathias C., *The Indian Policy of Portugal in the Amazon Region, 1614–1693*.
- Creation of Instituto Brasileiro de Relações Internacionais at the Ministry of Foreign Relations (Rio de Janeiro).

1955
- Creation of the Warsaw Pact: military alliance of communist countries dominated by the Soviet Union.
- Independence of Morocco and Sudan.
- Coup d'état overthrows Perón in Argentina.
- Opening of Brazilian market to foreign capital.

- Kuznets, Simon, ed., *Economic Growth: Brazil, India, Japan*.
- Costa, Hipólito José. *Diário de minha viagem para Filadélfia, 1798–1799*.

1956
- Nationalization of the Suez Canal by Egypt's Gamal Abdel Nasser provokes a crisis: intervention by British and French troops and war against Israel (Brazil sends in troops under U.N. flag).
- Anticommunist uprising in Hungary repressed by Soviet tanks.
- Kubitschek administration promotes industrialization with foreign capital participating in Brazil.

- Harris, Marvin, *Town and Country in Brazil*.
- Release of *Revista Brasileira de Estudos Políticos*.
- Creation of Instituto Superior de Estudos Brasileiros.

1957
- Rome treaties establish the European Economic Community (common market) and European Atomic Energy Community; launching of *Sputnik* puts USSR at forefront of space race.
- Broad reform of customs duties in Brazil; foreign auto makers start industrial production in Brazil.

- Stein, Stanley J., *The Brazilian Cotton Manufacture* and *Vassouras: A Brazilian Coffee County*.

1958
- Formation of the United Arab Republic (Egypt, Syria, Yemen).
- Creation of the International Atomic Energy Agency (Vienna).
- U.S. Vice President Richard Nixon's disastrous trip to Latin American countries.
- Brazil proposes Pan-American Operation and starts negotiations with the International Monetary Fund (IMF) for a short-term loan.

- Morse, Richard M., *From Community to Metropolis: A Biography of São Paulo, Brazil.*
- Haring, C. H., *Empire in Brazil: A New World Experiment with Monarchy.*
- Moraes, Rubens B. de, *Bibliographia Brasiliana.*

- Release of *Revista Brasileira de Política Internacional.*

1959
- Revolt against China in Tibet; Antarctic Treaty.
- Cuba: Fidel Castro seizes power after three years of guerrilla war against Fulgencio Batista's dictatorship.
- Creation of the Inter-American Development Bank.
- Kubitschek administration suspends negotiations with the IMF.

- Reichmann, Felix, *Sugar, Gold and Coffee: Essays on the History of Brazil.*
- Fujii, Yukio and T. Lynn Smith, *The Acculturation of the Japanese in Brazil.*
- Freyre, Gilberto, *New World in the Tropics: The Culture of Modern Brazil.*

1960
- Election of John F. Kennedy in the United States.
- Creation of the Organisation for Economic Cooperation and Development (OECD) and Organization of Petroleum Exporting Countries (OPEC); Treaty of Montevideo creating the Latin American Free-Trade Association (LAFTA); creation of the Centro-American Common Market (CACM).
- IMF grants loan to Brazil.

- Hutchinson, Harry W., *Field Guide to Brazil.*
- Wiznitzer, Arnold, *Jews in Colonial Brazil.*

1961
- Berlin crisis (because of massive population outflows) leads to the erection of the wall dividing the eastern and western parts of the

- Schurz, William L., *Brazil: The Infinite Country.*
- Quadros, Jânio, "Brazil's New Foreign Policy," *Foreign Affairs.*

city; U.S.-sponsored invasion of Cuba (Bay of Pigs) by anti-Castro forces.

- Creation of Non-Aligned Movement for neutral and developing countries.
- "Alliance for Progress" in the Americas proposed by the United States because of the impact of the Cuban Revolution on Latin America.
- Independent foreign policy of Brazilian president Jânio Quadros; exchange rate reform.

1962
- Independence of Algeria; border conflict between India and China.
- Missile crisis in Cuba: U.S. president Kennedy orders naval blockade to prevent Soviet shipments of nuclear missiles; Inter-American Conference of Punta del Este decides to expel Cuba from the inter-American system of the OAS; Brazil adopts a legalist approach.
- Brazilian Congress discusses a bill on foreign capital.

- Boxer, Charles R., *The Golden Age of Brazil, 1695–1750.*
- Bishop, Elizabeth, *Brazil.*
- Gordon, Lincoln, and E. Grommers, *U.S. Manufacturing Investment in Brazil.*
- Rodrigues, José Honório, "The Foundations of Brazil's Foreign Policy," *International Affairs* (London).
- American Catholic Historical Association chooses as its president Manoel Cardozo, curator of Oliveira Lima Library.

1963
- Détente between United States and Soviet Union; Kennedy is assassinated.
- Independence of Malaysia; creation of the Organization of African Unity.
- Treaty banning nuclear weapons testing within the atmosphere, under water, and in space.
- "Lobster War" between France and Brazil; Brazil's foreign policy: establishment of economic and commercial ties with socialist countries.

- Wagley, Charles, *An Introduction to Brazil.*
- Dos Passos, John, *Brazil on the Move.*
- Robock, Stefan, *Brazil's Developing Northeast.*
- Calógeras, João Pandiá, *A History of Brazil.*
- Freyre, Gilberto, *Brazil.*
- Freyre, Gilberto, *The Mansion and the Shanties.*
- Furtado, Celso, *The Economic Growth of Brazil.*

1964 • China detonates its first atomic bomb; United States increases its intervention in Vietnam.
• First conference of the U.N. Conference on Trade and Development (UNCTAD) in Geneva.
• Military coup expels João Goulart, aligns Brazil with United States, and breaks ties with Cuba and other socialist countries.

• Jackson, William V., *Library Guide for Brazilian Studies.*
• Horowitz, Irving L., ed., *Revolution in Brazil.*
• Manchester, Alan K., *British Preeminence in Brazil: Its Rise and Decline* (2nd ed.).
• Vianna Moog, Clodomir, *Bandeirantes and Pioneers.*
• Cruz Costa, João, *A History of Ideas in Brazil: The Development of Philosophy in Brazil and the Evolution of National History.*

1965 • Political-military crisis in the Dominican Republic: intervention by U.S. forces (supported by OAS), with the participation of Brazilian troops.
• Kashmir war between India and Pakistan.
• IMF loan granted to Brazil.

• Morse, Richard M., ed., *The Bandeirantes: The Historical Role of the Brazilian Pathfinders.*
• Marchant, Anyda, *Viscount of Mauá and the Empire of Brazil.*
• Baer, Werner, *Industrialization and Economic Development in Brazil.*
• Rodrigues, José Honório, *Brazil and Africa.*
• Furtado, Celso, *Diagnosis of the Brazilian Crisis.*
• Release of *Civilização Brasileira* and *Política Externa Independente.*

1966 • China launches the Cultural Revolution; France withdraws from the military arrangements of NATO and develops an autonomous foreign policy outside the U.S. nuclear umbrella.
• Military coup in Argentina; Castro's Cuba brings logistic help and political support to armed guerrilla movements engaged in insurrections in Latin America (CIA detects Ché Guevara in Bolivia).

• Baklanoff, Eric, ed., *New Perspectives of Brazil.*
• Simmons, Charles W., *Marshal Deodoro and the Fall of Dom Pedro II.*
• Burns, E. Bradford, ed., *A Documentary History of Brazil.*
• Levine, Robert M., ed., *Brazil: Field Research Guide in the Social Sciences.*
• Bello, José Maria, *A History of Modern Brazil, 1889–1964.*
• Castro, Josué de, *Death in Northeast.*

• Creation of Instituto Universitário de Pesquisa em Ciências Sociais do Rio de Janeiro, Universidade Cândido Mendes.

1967 • Six Day War in the Middle East: Israel confronts various Arab countries.
• Military coup in Greece: dictatorship overthrows the monarchical regime.
• Inter-American Conference of Punta del Este: commitment to integration.
• Tlatelolco Treaty bans nuclear weapons in Latin America.

• Daland, Robert T., *Brazilian Planning.*
• Dulles, John W. F., *Vargas of Brazil.*
• Hopper, Janice H., ed., *Indians of Brazil in the Twentieth Century.*
• Skidmore, Thomas E., *Politics in Brazil, 1930–1964: An Experiment in Democracy.*
• Young, Jordan M., *The Brazilian Revolution of 1930 and the Aftermath.*
• Frank, Andre G., *Capitalism and Underdevelopment in Latin America.*
• Pierson, Donald, *Negroes in Brazil* [reissued].
• Prado, Caio, Jr., *The Colonial Background of Modern Brazil.*
• Rodrigues, José Honório, *The Brazilians: Their Character and Aspirations.*
• Cardoso, F. H., and Enzo Faletto, *Dependência e desenvolvimento na América Latina.*

1968 • Soviet intervention in Czechoslovakia illustrated through a "socialism with human face"; students revolt in France, Mexico, and Brazil.
• Massive demonstrations in the United States against intervention in Vietnam.
• Non-Proliferation Treaty, proposed by nuclear states (U.S., U.K., and USSR), refused by

• Burns, E. Bradford, *Nationalism in Brazil: A Historical Survey.*
• Graham, Richard, *Britain and the Onset of Modernization in Brazil, 1850–1914.*
• Leff, Nathaniel H., *The Brazilian Capital Goods Industry, 1929–1964.*
• Poppino, Rollie E., *Brazil: The Land and People.*
• Collier, Richard, *The River That God Forgot: The History of the Amazon Rubber Baron.*

Brazil, France, and China as being discriminatory.

- Momsen, Richard P., Jr., *Brazil: A Giant Stirs.*
- Jaguaribe, Hélio, *Economic and Political Development: A Theoretical Approach and a Brazilian Case Study.*
- Vellinho, Moyses, *Brazil South: Its Conquest & Settlement.*

1969
- Man lands on the moon: the United States leads the space race.
- Negotiations on strategic weapons between the United States and Soviet Union.
- Creation of the Andean Group; Plata Basin Treaty among Argentina, Brazil, Bolivia, Paraguay, and Uruguay.
- Brazil: military junta seizes power and promotes a hardening of the regime, outlaws opposition leaders.

- Dean, Warren, *The Industrialization of São Paulo.*
- Graham, Richard, *A Century of Brazilian History Since 1865.*
- Hahner, June, *Civilian-Military Relations in Brazil, 1889–1898.*
- Baer, Werner, *The Development of the Brazilian Steel Industry.*
- Fernandes, Florestan, *The Negro in Brazilian Society.*

1970
- Rupture in the communist movement between China and Soviet Union; crisis in the Middle East: Palestinians are expelled from Jordan (to Lebanon).
- Generalized system of preferences (GSP) introduced in the world trading system (GATT/UNCTAD).
- Brazil: military dictatorship rounds up academic figures from universities and forces them into exile (sociologist Fernando Henrique Cardoso among them); urban guerrilla movements fail in their attempt to expand the political opposition.
- Brazil claims sovereignty over offshore sea territory (200 miles)

- Stein, Stanley. and Barbara Stein, *The Colonial Heritage of Latin America.*
- Levine, Robert M., *The Vargas Regime: The Critical Years, 1934–1938.*
- Bergsman, J., *Brazil-Industrialization and Trade Policies.*
- Macaulay, Neill, *The Prestes Column: Revolution in Brazil.*
- Della Cava, Ralph, *Miracle at Joaseiro.*
- Dulles, John W. F., *Unrest in Brazil: Political-Military Crises, 1955–1964.*
- Tomlinson, Regina J., *The Struggle for Brazil: Portugal and the "French Interlopers."*

raising opposition in the United States.
- Brazil and Paraguay devise Itaipú dam; Brazil is world soccer champion for the third time in Mexico.

1971
- Communist China replaces Taiwan in the U.N. and its Security Council (Brazil votes against it).
- End of the Bretton Woods monetary system by unilateral decision of the United States.
- Military coup in Bolivia; treaty on the denuclearization of the seabed.
- Political and military crack down in Brazil; creation of the National Institute for Space Policy; new Industrial Property Code introduces various types of exclusions to patent protection, creating conflicts with the United States.
- Energy cooperation with Paraguay causes a political-diplomatic crisis with Argentina regarding the water resources of the Paraná River.
- Official state visit of Brazil's President Garrastazu Médici to the United States, where President Nixon acknowledges leadership of Brazil in Latin America.

- Love, Joseph, *Rio Grande do Sul and Brazilian Regionalism, 1882–1930.*
- Degler, Carl N., *Neither Black nor White: Slavery and Race Relations in Brazil and the United States.*
- Stepan, Alfred, *The Military in Politics: Changing Patterns in Brazil.*
- Meggers, Betty J., *Amazonia: Man and Culture in a Counterfeit Paradise.*

1972
- Nixon visits China, opens formal relations; SALT I agreement tries to reduce nuclear arms race by limiting U.S. and USSR antiballistic missile systems.
- First U.N. Conference on Environment held in Sweden.

- McCann, Frank, *The Brazilian-American Alliance, 1937–1945.*
- Toplin, Robert B., *The Abolition of Slavery in Brazil.*
- Conrad, Robert E., *The Destruction of Brazilian Slavery, 1850–1888.*

- Socialist government in Chile nationalizes the U.S. company ITT.
- Brazil maintains its support of Portugal's colonial policy; external groups pressure Brazil on human rights.
- Maoist guerrillas in Araguaia; launching of the first Brazilian computer.

- Young, Jordan M., *Brazil, 1954–1964: End of a Civilian Cycle.*

1973
- War in the Middle East hastens the oil crisis; Perón returns to Argentina; Salvador Allende is overthrown and killed in Chile; GATT's Multifiber Arrangement is implemented.
- Deterioration of the trade balance: boost to exports and limitation on imports (law of similar products); official government candidate for opposition to the Brazilian presidency.

- Dulles, John W. F., *Anarchists and Communists in Brazil, 1900–1935.*
- Bandeira, Moniz, *Presença dos Estados Unidos no Brasil: dois séculos de história.*

1974
- Nixon resigns; revolution in Portugal marks the end of the colonial empire.
- Ernesto Geisel becomes president of Brazil, begins expansion of the political spectrum; opposition wins seats in Congress; Nuclebrás (Nuclear Vessel Manufacturing Co.) created; government advocates "responsible pragmatism"; Brazil pushes Third World–oriented foreign policy.

- Selcher, Wayne, *The Afro-Asian Dimension of Brazilian Foreign Policy, 1956–1972.*
- Skidmore, Thomas E., *Black into White: Race and Nationality in Brazilian Thought.*
- Bruneau, Thomas C., *The Political Transformation of the Brazilian Catholic Church.*
- Chilcote, Ronald. H., *The Brazilian Communist Party.*
- Eisenberg, Peter, *The Sugar Industry in Pernambuco.*
- Muller, Keith D., *Pioneer Settlement in South Brazil: The Case of Toledo, Paraná.*

1975
- End of Vietnam War; independence of Suriname; Tokyo round of GATT negotiations; creation

- Stanley Hilton, *Brazil and the Great Powers, 1930–1939: The Politics of Trade Rivalry.*

of SELA (Latin American Economic System).

- Brazil-Germany agreement for nuclear cooperation; adoption of Antarctic Treaty; Brazil creates National Fuel Ethanol Program; institutes risk contracts in the oil sector; petrochemical industry in Brazil expands rapidly

1976 • Death of Mao Tse-Tung; redemocratization of Spain begins; coup deposes Isabel Perón in Argentina.
- Brazil: design of information technology policy; U.S. pressure regarding the nuclear issue; trade tensions (shoes, soy); disenfranchisement of congressional representatives; censorship law on political adds; attacks from extreme right.

1977 • Peace negotiations between Israel and Egypt; Stroessner becomes president of Paraguay for life.
- Brazil: crises in the relationship with United States on nuclear issues and human rights; accusations regarding the 1952 military pact; public demonstrations for democracy; Geisel shuts down Congress,

1978 • John Paul II becomes "Polish pope"; Sandinista guerrillas in Nicaragua spark popular uprising.
- Brazil: constitutional amendment no. 11 revokes AI-5 and other

- Hilton, Stanley. *Brazil and the International Crisis: 1930–1945.*
- Holloway, Thomas H., *The Brazilian Coffee Valorization of 1906.*
- Forman, Shepard L., *The Brazilian Peasantry.*
- Martins, Carlos E., *Brasil-Estados Unidos: dos anos 60 aos 70.*

- Perry, William, *Contemporary Brazilian Foreign Policy: The International Strategy of an Emerging Power.*
- Martins, Luciano, *Pouvoir et développement économique: Formation et évolution des structures politiques au Brésil.*

- Schneider, Ronald, *Brazil: Foreign Policy of a Future World Power.*
- Wirth, John D., *Minas Gerais in the Brazilian Federation, 1889–1937.*
- Davis, Shelton H., *Victims of the Miracle: Development and the Indians of Brazil.*
- Erickson, Kenneth Paul, *The Brazilian Corporative State and the Working-Class Politics.*
- Black, Jan Knippers, *United States Penetration of Brazil.*

- Levine, Robert M., *Pernambuco in the Brazilian Federation, 1889–1937.*
- Dulles, John W. F., *Castello Branco: The Making of a Brazilian President.*

institutional acts; Amazon Cooperation Treaty signed; seventy years of Japanese immigration to Brazil celebrated.
• United States cancels development of neutron bomb.

1979 • United States and China formally establish diplomatic relations; Soviet Army invades Afghanistan; Anastasio Somoza of Nicaragua and the Shah of Iran are overthrown; second oil crisis begins; Tokyo round of GATT ends.
• Itaipú-Corpus Accord signed by Brazil, Argentina, and Paraguay; Brazil and Argentina sign nuclear cooperation agreement; João Figueiredo becomes president of Brazil: grants political amnesty, interventions in labor unions; inflation accelerates.

1980 • U.S.-Iran crisis erupts: hostages taken at U.S. embassy in Tehran; reform era in China begins.
• Ronald Reagan is elected U.S. president; U.S. and others boycott Moscow Olympics.
• Independent trade union, Solidarity, in Poland defies Communist power.
• Creation of Associação Latino-Americano de Integração (ALADI) to replace Asociación Latinoamericana de Libre Comercio (ALALC) means preferential tariffs instead of free trade area; amendment to constitution reestablishes direct elections for state governors in Brazil.

• Chandler, Billy J., *The Bandit King: Lampião of Brazil.*
• Hemming, John, *Red Gold: The Conquest of the Brazilian Indians, 1500–1760.*

• Evans, Peter, *Dependent Development: The Alliance of Multinational, State and Local Capital in Brazil.*
• Malloy, James, *The Politics of Social Security in Brazil.*
• Flynn, Peter, *Brazil: A Political Analysis.*

• Love, Joseph, *São Paulo and the Brazilian Federation, 1889-1937.*
• Dulles, John W. F., *President Castello Branco: A Brazilian Reformer.*

1981 • Anwar Sadat is assassinated in Egypt; martial law imposed in Poland.
• Brazil: pursues development-oriented diplomacy; asserts the South's interests; suffers right-wing terrorist attacks; makes adjustments in exchange rate policy.

• Wesson, Robert G., *The United States and Brazil: Limits of Influence.*
• Holloway, Thomas H., *Immigrants on the Land: Coffee and Society in São Paulo, 1886–1934.*
• McDonough, Peter J., and Amaury de Souza, *The Politics of Population in Brazil.*
• Conniff, Michael L., *Urban Politics in Brazil: The Rise of Populism, 1925–1945.*
• Hilton, Stanley, *Hitler's Secret War in South America.*
• Seeger, Anthony, *Nature and Society in Central Brazil: The Suya Indians of Mato Grosso.*

1982 • North-South dialogue pushes a new economic world order; Convention on the Law of the Sea takes place; foreign debt crisis begins in Latin America.
• Brazil lends diplomatic support to Argentina during the Falkland/Malvinas War; Reagan visits Brazil; Itaipú hydroelectric power plant inaugurated; fuel subsidies are removed, as requested by the IMF.

• Russell-Wood, Anthony J. R., *The Black Man in Slavery and Freedom in Colonial Brazil.*
• Hallewell, Laurence, *Books in Brazil: A History of the Publishing Trade.*

1983 • U.S. intervenes in Grenada; Argentina undergoes redemocratization.
• Brazil: sends letter of intent to the IMF; economic difficulties mark beginning of a period of stagnation.

• Conrad, Robert E., *Children of God's Fire: A Documentary History of Black Slavery in Brazil.*

1984 • Assassination of Indira Gandhi; Argentina judges military junta members.

• Hahner, June E., *Women in Brazil: Problems and Perspectives.*

- OAS General Assembly meets in Brasília; law of information technology causes tensions with the United States; first Brazilian rocket, Sonda IV, launched.

- Hollist, W. Ladd, *Dependency Transformed: Brazil in a Global and Historical Perspective.*

1985
- Mikhail Gorbachev begins economic and political reforms in Soviet Union.
- Reagan and Gorbachev hold summit meeting; U.S. declares total trade embargo against Nicaragua.
- Brazil returns to democracy with indirect election of Tancredo Neves; José Sarney takes office as president; Iguazu Declaration marks beginning of nuclear tensions with Argentina.

- Schwartz, Stuart B., *Sugar Plantations in the Formation of Brazilian Society.*
- Ludwig, Armin K., *Brazil: A Handbook of Historical Statistics.*
- Hirst, Mônica. org., *Brasil-Estados Unidos na transição democrática.*

1986
- Nuclear incident at Chernobyl; fall of "Papa Doc" Duvalier in Haiti and Ferdinand Marcos in the Philippines; GATT Uruguay round begins in Punta del Este.
- Brazil-Argentine economic cooperation begins; Brazil reestablishes diplomatic relations with Cuba; United States threatens trade sanctions against Brazil due to information technology issues; Cruzado Plan, which replaced the cruzeiro with a new currency, fails and is replaced with the Cruzado II Plan.

- Mainwaring, Scott, *The Catholic Church and Politics in Brazil, 1916–1985.*
- Macaulay, Neill, *Dom Pedro: The Struggle for Liberty in Brazil and Portugal, 1798–1834.*
- Kuznesof, Elizabeth, *Household Economy and Urban Development: São Paulo, 1765–1836.*
- Moura, G., *Tio Sam chega ao Brasil: a penetração cultural americana.*

1987
- Uprising in territories occupied by Israel.
- Brazil: bilateral disagreements with United States regarding information technology, pharmaceutical patents; market reserve

- Dean, Warren, *Brazil and the Struggle for Rubber: A Study in Environmental History.*
- Hemming, John, *Amazon Frontier: The Defeat of the Brazilian Indians.*

maintained by Brazilian software law; unilateral moratorium is declared for foreign debt; other economic plans are issued: Bresser, "*Verão*" Plans; Congress to draft new Brazilian constitution.

1988 • Iran-Iraq War ends; Soviets leave Afghanistan; United States and Soviet Union sign disarmament agreement.
• Integration treaty: Brazil and Argentina make plans for a bilateral common market; new nationalistic Brazilian constitution promulgated; Brazil negotiates with its commercial creditors.

1989 • Massacre of dissidents in China; Palestinian Liberation Organization recognizes the State of Israel; United States invades Panama; coup ousts Stroessner in Paraguay; Group of 15 (G-15) created; United States and Canada sign free trade treaty.
• Fall of the Berlin Wall triggers the end of socialism.
• In the U.N. and the G-8 conference Sarney criticizes debt policies of rich countries; first direct elections for president held in Brazil since 1960s: Fernando Collor beats Luis Inácio "Lula" da Silva in the second round of

• Needell, Jeffrey D., *A Tropical Belle Epoque.*
• Topik, Steve, *The Political Economy of the Brazilian State, 1889–1930.*
• Griggs, William C., *The Elusive Eden: Frank McMullan's Confederate Colony in Brazil.*

• Skidmore, Thomas, *The Politics of Military Rule in Brazil, 1964–85.*
• Stam, Robert, *Tropical Multiculturalism: A Comparative History of Race in Brazilian Cinema and Culture.*
• Barman, Roderick, *Brazil: The Forging of a Nation, 1798–1852.*
• Fritsch, Winston, *External Constraints on Economic Policy in Brazil, 1889–1930.*
• Creation of the Camões Center for the Study of the Portuguese-Speaking World, at Columbia University, New York.

• Haines, Gerald K., *The Americanization of Brazil: A Study of U.S. Cold War Diplomacy in the Third World, 1945–1954.*
• Hayes, Robert A., *The Armed Nation: The Brazilian Corporate Mystique.*
• Hecht, Susanna, and Alexander Cockburn, *The Fate of the Forest: Developers, Destroyers, and Defenders of the Amazon.*
• Bandeira, Moniz. *Brasil-Estados Unidos: a rivalidade emergente, 1950–1988.*
• Eakin, Marshall C., *British Enterprise in Brazil: The St. John d'el Rey Mining Company and the*

elections; inflation at record levels.

Morro Velho Gold Mine, 1830–1960.

1990 • Fall of socialist regimes in Central and Eastern Europe; beginning of German unification.
   • Meeting in Buenos Aires: Brazil-Argentina integration accelerated; Chile and Uruguay demand information about the bilateral process and integration of Paraguay in the "multilateral-ization" process; Collor promotes an open economy and trade liberalization.
   • President George Bush introduces his "Initiative for the Americas," a proposal for a free-trade area extending from Alaska to Patagonia; proposal faces criticism in Latin America.

• Chilcote, Ronald. H., *Power and the Ruling Classes in Northeast Brazil: Juazeiro and Petrolina in Transition.*
• Hahner, June E., *Emancipating the Female Sex: The Struggle for Women's Rights in Brazil.*
• Graham, Richard, *Patronage and Politics in Nineteenth-Century Brazil.*
• Leacock, Ruth, *Requiem for Revolution: The United States and Brazil, 1961–1969.*
• Moura, Gerson, *O Alinhamento sem recompensa: a política externa do governo Dutra.*
• Miceli, Sergio, *A Desilusão americana: relações acadêmicas entre Brasil e Estados Unidos.*

1991 • Gulf War: Coalition against Iraq after the invasion of Kuwait.
   • Soviet reformer Gorbachev resigns from office, under pressure of the new reformists: Soviet Union collapses ending 74 years of communism and is replaced by Commonwealth of Independent States (CIS); new independent countries emerge in Europe and Central Asia.
   • Asuncion Treaty establishes Mercosul, Uruguay and Paraguay join the Brazil-Argentina plan; Brazil unilaterally abandons its nuclear weapons program.

• Smith, Joseph, *Unequal Giants: Diplomatic Relations Between the United States and Brazil, 1889–1930.*
• Andrews, George Reid, *Blacks and Whites in São Paulo, 1888–1988.*
• Dulles, John F. W., *Carlos Lacerda, Brazilian Crusader.*
• Da Matta, Roberto, *Carnivals, Rogues, and Heroes: An Interpre-tation of the Brazilian Dilemma.*

1992 • Conference on Environment and Development in Rio de Janeiro: several action plans and

• Levine, Robert M., *Vale of Tears: Revisiting the Canudos Massacre in Northeastern Brazil, 1893–1897.*

environmental protection programs approved.

- Tripartite negotiations for the
creation of North American Free
Trade Agreement (NAFTA:
United States, Canada, and
Mexico).
- Initiatives for the creation of a
free-trade area, linking Chile and
Andean countries to Mercosul.
- Nuclear cooperation with
Argentina and the creation of
Agência Brasileiro Argentina de
Contabilidade e Controle de
Materias Nucleares (ABACC);
impeachment of Collor; Vice
President Itamar Franco takes
office.

- French, John D., *The Brazilian
Workers' ABC: Class Conflict and
Alliances in Modern São Paulo.*
- Cobbs, Elizabeth A., *The Rich
Neighbor Policy: Rockefeller and
Kaiser in Brazil.*
- Graham, Sandra L., *House and
Street: The Domestic World of
Servants and Masters in
Nineteenth-Century Rio de
Janeiro.*
- Keck, Margaret E., *The Workers'
Party and Democratization in
Brazil.*
- Massi, Fernanda P., and H. A.
Pontes, *Guia biobibliográfico dos
brasilianistas.*
- Cervo, A. L., and C. Bueno,
*História da política exterior do
Brasil.*
- Release of *Política Externa.*

1993
- The Area de Libre Comercio
Suramericana (ALCSA) initiative
is launched by Brazil seeking the
integration of South America.
- Brazil sponsors the creation of
the Association of Coffee-
Producing Countries.
- The Brazilian Institute of
International Relations, publisher
of *Revista Brasileira de Política
Internacional (RBPI)*, is restruc-
tured in Brasília (it was created
in Rio de Janeiro, in 1954).

- Holloway, Thomas H., *Policing
Rio de Janeiro: Repression and
Resistance in a Nineteenth-
Century City.*
- Chernela, Janet, *A Sense of Space:
The Wanano Indians of the
Brazilian Amazon.*
- Randall, Laura, *The Political
Economy of Brazilian Oil.*
- First edition of the Brasília series
of *RBPI.*

1994
- The final meetings of the
Uruguay round and the creation
of WTO in Marrakech; in
December, the Mexican crisis
initiates financial crises in other
Latin American countries;
NAFTA goes into effect.

- Hanchard, Michael, *Orpheus and
Power: The Movimento Negro of
Rio de Janeiro and São Paulo,
Brazil, 1945–1988.*
- Ridings, Eugene W., *Business
Interest Groups in Nineteenth-
Century Brazil.*

• Summit of the Americas held in Miami: negotiations to create hemispheric free trade by 2005 begin.
• Brazil has concerns with FTAA plans; Ouro Preto Protocol confirms the intergovernmental structure of the Mercosul.
• Brazil reaches agreement on debt with private creditors; becomes world soccer champion for fourth time; Fernando H. Cardoso is elected in the first round of presidential elections in Brazil.

• Shapiro, Helen, *Engines of Growth: The State and Transnational Auto Companies in Brazil.*

1995 • WTO goes into effect; first ministerial meeting to create hemispheric trade bloc in Denver: United States pushes for results by 2000. U.S. Congress denies "fast track" authority to include Chile in NAFTA.
• Fiftieth anniversary of the Bretton Woods institutions (IMF and Inter-American Development Bank [BIRD]).
• Cardoso takes office; institutes policy of international affirmation; begins constitutional reforms, especially in the economic area. Mercosul customs union goes into effect: the Common External Tariff to be managed by the Mercosul Trade Commission; special treatment given to automobiles and sugar.

• Dean, Warren, *With Broadax and Firebrand: The Destruction of the Brazilian Atlantic Forest.*
• Lesser, Jeffrey, *Welcoming the Undesirables: Brazil and the Jewish Question.*
• Page, Joseph A., *The Brazilians.*
• Nelson, Roy C. *Industrialization and Political Affinity: Industrial Policy in Brazil.*
• Dawsey, Cyrus B. *The Confederados: Old South Immigrants in Brazil.*
• Rodrigues, José H., and Ricardo Seitenfus. *Uma História diplomática do Brasil.*

1996 • Algeria: the Islamic extremists' civil war; treaty bans nuclear tests (Comprehensive Test Ban Treaty [CTBT]).

• Topik, Steve, *Trade and Gunboats: The United States and Brazil in the Age of Empire.*
• Schneider, Ronald, *Brazil: Culture*

- First WTO Ministerial Conference in Singapore.
- Chile and Bolivia join Mercosul as associate members.
- Brazil amends its constitution, especially in the economic sector; privatization process opened for foreign capital.

and Politics in a New Industrial Powerhouse.
- Davis, Sonny B., *A Brotherhood of Arms: Brazil–United States Military Relations, 1942–1977.*
- Dulles, John F. D., *Carlos Lacerda, Brazilian Crusader: The Years 1960–1977.*
- Plank, David N., *The Means of Our Salvation: Public Education in Brazil, 1930–1995.*

1997
- Financial crisis in Asia and repercussions in Brazil.
- Brazil decides to join the Nuclear Non-Proliferation Treaty (NPT) (after thirty years of refusal); constitutional amendment puts an end to petroleum monopoly by the Brazilian government; Cardoso travels toUnited States for high-level talks with President Bill Clinton.

- Eakin, Marshall C., *Brazil: The Once and Future Country.*
- Hunter, Wendy, *Eroding Military Influence in Brazil: Politicians Against Soldiers.*
- Weinstein, Barbara, *For Social Peace in Brazil: Industrialists and the Remaking of the Working Class in São Paulo, 1920–1964.*
- Pereira, Anthony W., *The End of the Peasantry: The Rural Labor Movement in Northeast Brazil, 1961–1988.*
- Schwam-Baird, David M., *Ideas and Armaments: Military Ideologies in the Making of Brazil's Arms Industries.*
- Godfrey, Brian J., and John O. Browder, *Rainforest Cities: Urbanization, Development, and Globalization of the Brazilian Amazon.*

1998
- Crisis in Iraq inspection system brings military attack by the United States.
- Second WTO ministerial conference in Geneva: fiftieth anniversary of the multilateral trading system.
- Worsening of international financial crisis and Russian

- Weschler, Lawrence, *A Miracle, a Universe: Settling Accounts with Torturers.*
- Cohen, Thomas M., *The Fire of Tongues: António Vieira and the Missionary Church in Brazil and Portugal.*
- Butler, Kim D., *Freedoms Given, Freedoms Won: Afro-Brazilians in*

defaults: Brazil signs a standby agreement with the IMF, including US$41.5 billion in financial help and a fiscal adjustment program (with no changes in the exchange rate policy); Cardoso is reelected in the first round of elections in Brazil.

Post-Abolition São Paulo and Salvador.

1999 • Introduction of the Euro in the European Union (eleven countries); Brazilian monetary crisis forces changes in its exchange rate policy (new agreement with the IMF).
• Massacre in Kosovo and NATO intervention against Serbia; Poland, Czech Republic, and Hungary join NATO, celebrating its fiftieth anniversary.
• Europe–Latin America Conference in Rio de Janeiro: Mercosul and the EU decide to negotiate an association agreement; trade ministerial meeting in Toronto decides to finalize a draft treaty for Free Trade Area of the Americas (FTAA); market access and exceptions will be discussed at a later date, during the co-presidency of the United States and Brazil (2003–2005).
• Third WTO ministerial meeting in the Seattle fails to launch a new round of multilateral trade negotiations (the Millenium round).

• Skidmore, Thomas E., *Brazil.*
• Levine, Robert M., *Brazil: A History.*
• Lesser, Jeffrey, *Negotiating National Identity: Immigrants, Minorities, and Struggle for Ethnicity in Brazil.*
• Hanchard, Michael, ed., *Racial Politics in Contemporary Brazil.*
• Barman, Roderick J., *Citizen Emperor: Pedro II and the Making of Brazil, 1825–1891.*
• Anderson, Robin L., *Colonization as Exploitation in the Amazon Rain Forest, 1758–1911.*
• Mainwaring, Scott P., *Rethinking Party Systems in the Third Wave of Democratization: The Case of Brazil.*
• Kingstone, Peter R., *Crafting Coalitions for Reform: Business Preferences, Political Institutions, and Neoliberal Reform in Brazil.*
• Peard, Julyan G., *Race, Place, and Medicine: The Idea of the Tropics in Nineteenth-Century Brazilian Medicine.*
• Almeida, Paulo R. de. *O Estudo das relações internacionais do Brasil.*
• The Brazilian embassy in Washington, D.C., promotes a meeting of Brazilianists, to discuss issues connected with

Brazilian studies in the United
States.

2000 • End of the Kuomintang regime
in Taiwan increases tensions with
continental China; meeting of
the presidents of North and
South Korea; Alberto Fujimori
secures a third term, highly
contested, in Peru; Ecuador's
president is removed from power
and economy is "dollarized"
amid a serious financial crisis.
• China seeks admission into the
WTO.
• Mercosul experiences trade fric-
tions with a new administration
in Argentina (radical president
Fernando De La Rúa).
• U.S. Vice President Albert Gore
(winner of the popular election)
and George W. Bush (governor
of Texas and winner in the
Electoral College), dispute the
U.S. presidential elections
(Supreme Court interrupts ballot
recount in Florida, declaring
Bush the winner); Chile and
United States announce negotia-
tions for a free-trade agreement
(Chile's negotiations with Merco-
sul fall apart).

• Green, James N., *Beyond
Carnival: Male Homosexuality in
Twentieth-Century Brazil.*
• Font, Mauricio, *Brazil: Develop-
ment, Industrialization and Social
Transformation.*
• Treece, Dave, *Exiles, Allies, Rebels:
Brazil's Indianist Movement,
Indigenist Politics, and the
Imperial Nation-State.*
• Foster, David William, *Gender
and Society in Contemporary
Brazilian Cinema.*
• Summerhill, William R., *Order
Against Progress: Government,
Foreign Investment, and Railroads
in Brazil, 1854–1913.*
• Triner, Gail D., *Banking and
Economic Development: Brazil,
1889–1930.*
• Costa, Emilia V. da, *The Brazilian
Empire: Myths and Histories.*
• Oliveira, Lúcia Lippi, *Americanos:
representações da identidade
nacional no Brasil e nos EUA.*
• The Brazilian embassy in
Washington, D.C., promotes
a second meeting of Brazil-
ianists, to discuss the draft
chapters for *Guide to the Study
of Brazil in the United States,
1945–2000.*
• Embassy also promotes the
establishing of a program of
Brazilian studies at the
Georgetown University, as well
as the "Project Brasil" at the
Woodrow Wilson Center for
International Scholars,
Washington, D.C.

2001 • George W. Bush takes office;
unilateralism and slowing of
economic activity in the United
States affirmed.
• Brazil: economic crisis in
Argentina has an impact on
Brazil; Brazil receives new IMF
financial assistance package.
• Terrorist attacks in New York
and Washington, D.C., in
September create new
dimensions to international
security; United States attacks
Taliban rule in Afghanistan;
Brazil supports U.N. Security
Council's resolutions.
• First meeting between Cardoso
and Bush; Third Summit of the
Americas held in Québec,
Canada: disputes over timing of
negotiations, for creation of free
trade zone for the Americas.

• Gordon, Lincoln, *Brazil's Second
Chance: En Route Toward the
First World.*
• Eakin, Marshall C., *Tropical
Capitalism: The Industrialization
of Belo Horizonte, Brazil.*
• Barman, Roderick J., *Princess
Isabel of Brazil: Gender and Power
in the Nineteenth Century.*
• Baer, Werner, *The Brazilian
Economy: Growth and Develop-
ment,* 5th ed.
• Williams, Daryle, *Culture Wars in
Brazil: The First Vargas Regime,
1930–1945.*
• Schultz, Kirsten, *Tropical
Versailles: Empire, Monarchy, and
the Portuguese Royal Court in Rio
de Janeiro, 1808–1821.*
• Beattie, Peter M., *The Tribute of
Blood: Army, Honor, Race, and
Nation in Brazil, 1864–1945.*
• Ames, Barry, *The Deadlock of
Democracy in Brazil.*
• Almeida, Paulo R. de, *Formação
da diplomacia econômica no
Brasil.*
• Brazilian embassy in Washington,
D.C., organizes a seminar on
U.S.-Brazil relations.
• Embassy promotes the creation
of the Center for Brazilian Stud-
ies at Columbia University, in
New York.

2002 • U.S. adopts safeguard measures
against imported steel (Brazil);
issues raised in WTO regarding
farm subsidies, orange juice,
and steel restrictions; Brazilian
general elections; Quito
ministerial meeting of the FTAA:

• Publication in Brazil of *O Brasil
dos brasilianistas; um guia dos
estudos sobre o Brasil nos Estados
Unidos, 1945–2000.*
• DeWitt, John, *Early Globalization
and the Economic Development of
the United States and Brazil.*

Brazil and United States preside jointly over the final phase of FTAA negotiations, 2003–2005.

2003 • Luiz Inácio Lula da Silva inagurated as president for 2003–2007.
 • Brazilian Congress passes major reforms to social security and pension systems.
 • Currency and economy grow stronger throughout the year.

• Brazilian embassy in Washington, D.C., organizes a third seminar on Brazilian studies in the U.S.: Guide to U.S. Archives on Brazil (in Portuguese).

• Davila, Jerry, *Diploma of Whiteness: Race and Social Policy in Brazil, 1917–1945.*
• Lewin, Linda, *Surprise Heirs.*
• MacLachlan, Colin M., *A History of Modern Brazil.*
• Samuels, David, *Ambition, Federalism, and Legislative Politics in Brazil.*
• Summerhill, William R., *Order Against Progress: Government, Foreign Investment, and Railroads in Brazil, 1854–1913.*

CHAPTER 16

~

Brasiliana in the United States: Reference Sources and Documents

ANN HARTNESS

INTRODUCTION

Many reference sources about Brazil were published in the United States in the twentieth century,[1] beginning with a few books and pamphlets early in the period and gaining steady momentum as Brazilian studies developed and expanded. Most were produced by university professors and other scholars focusing on Brazil from the viewpoint of various academic disciplines; by librarians specializing in Latin American studies, often with Brazil as a subspecialty; or by staff members of the government agencies that sponsored certain publications. Although the earliest reference work about Brazil cited here (*A List of Books, Magazine Articles, and Maps Relating to Brazil, 1800–1900* by Phillips)[2] was published in 1901, and others followed in the first half of the twentieth century, publications proliferated in the 1970s and 1980s when the critical mass of scholars and students interested in Brazil provided both individuals qualified to compile them and those who needed the information that they imparted.

Several categories of sponsors or publishers issued these reference sources. The U.S. government played an important publishing role from the time that Phillips's book was published through today. Through the agency of the Library of Congress, the government has been responsible for some of the most important and comprehensive publications, such as the *Handbook of Latin American Studies,* which is compiled at the Library's Hispanic Division.

Through their presses and their Latin American studies centers or institutes, universities also played an important role in sponsoring and/or publishing these sources. An examination of the bibliography accompanying this essay reveals that universities in the Southwest and California were the leading academic publishers of reference materials about Latin America in general and about Brazil. For example, *HAPI: Hispanic American Periodicals Index,* began publication at the University of Arizona but shortly thereafter moved to the University of California, Los Angeles, where it has been compiled and published under the auspices of the Latin American Center ever since. UCLA's Latin American Center also publishes the *Statistical Abstract of Latin America.* In the realm of cyberspace, the Latin American Network Information Center (LANIC) was developed at the Institute of Latin American Studies at the University of Texas at Austin, and it continues there. It is described later, under "Electronic Resources."

Since the mid-1980s the University of New Mexico has published two series of guides intended to introduce readers to various aspects of Brazilian studies: the Brazilian Curriculum Guide Specialized Bibliography and the Brazilian Curriculum Guide Specialized Bibliography, Series II, with Jon. M. Tolman as the general editor. The Ministério das Relações Exteriores provides support for the latter series; each of the six bibliographies published thus far bears the rubric "Produced pursuant to a grant from the Brazilian Ministry of Foreign Affairs." Brasa-net, the Internet listserv for scholars interested in Brazil, also originated at the University of New Mexico.

The scholarly interchange between England and the United States has also resulted in important contributions by U.S. scholars to reference works originating in England, notably several published by Cambridge University Press and published simultaneously in London and New York. *The Cambridge History of Latin America* (Bethell 1984–) is one example. Brazilian authors and those of other nationalities whose works have been published in the United States are cited here, because of their contributions to Brazilian studies in this country. Rubens Borba de Moraes is an example.

Commercial publishers have also played an important role in the production of reference books about Latin America and, specifically, Brazil. The importance of the G. K. Hall Company of Boston is outlined in the section on "Bibliographies." ABC-Clio Information Services, Scarecrow Press, Greenwood Press, and Gale Research are others that have issued bibliographies and other reference books about Brazil.

To make primary source materials accessible to scholars in the United States, the microfilming of large sets of documents related to Brazil paralleled the accelerated publication of reference works. Again, the U.S.

government, acting through the Library of Congress and the National Archives, played the premier role because these institutions already held copies of many materials that needed to be filmed; the logistics of filming them were formidable; the financial resources required were considerable; and their commercial viability was questionable, at best. In addition, these institutions, with important clienteles from the academic and library worlds, were in a good position to identify materials needed as scholarly resources and at the same time had the responsibility to preserve scarce materials in their care. The Latin American Microform Project (LAMP) also became an important participant at the end of the 1970s, when it began a major microfilming project in cooperation with the Biblioteca Nacional, Rio de Janeiro.

Reference and documentary sources in electronic formats (CD-ROMs and databases accessed through the Internet) were the major development of the 1990s. The following discussion will point out print sources, which are also available electronically, and new sources that made their debuts in cyberspace.

BIBLIOGRAPHIES

The U.S. government, represented by the Library of Congress, has been a leader in the publication of bibliographies related to Brazil. Its efforts go back to the beginning of the twentieth century with *A List of Books, Magazine Articles, and Maps Relating to Brazil, 1800–1900,* by Philip Lee Phillips (1901), which was reissued in a facsimile edition in 1970 by University Microfilms. Publications of the Brazilian government were the subject of *Brazil: A Guide to the Official Publications,* by John De Noia (1948), as part of its series, Official Publications of the Other American Republics; it is discussed in the section called "Political Science and Law." But the crowning achievement of the Library of Congress is the *Handbook of Latin American Studies (HLAS),* the bibliographic bible of Latin American studies.

This annual publication, launched in 1935, was sponsored first by the Committee on Latin American Studies of the American Council of Learned Societies and then by the Joint Committee on Latin American Studies. It has had three academic publishers: the Harvard University Press, the University of Florida Press, and, since 1979, the University of Texas Press. It is now in its fifty-ninth edition (2003), and the Hispanic Division of the Library of Congress has been responsible for its preparation since 1943, assisted by many volunteer subject specialists from the academic world who review the publications received by the library and write the annotations describing and evaluating them. The *HLAS* concentrates on the humanities and social sciences, although it includes publications about a broad range of related subjects: art and architecture are examples. It cites monographs, journal articles, reports, serials, and other publications from all the countries of Latin America. Brazil figures prominently in its coverage, in keeping with its importance in the region, the scholarly interest in it, and its active publishing world. In addition to print format, the *HLAS* is available online (http://lcweb2.loc.gov/hlas/) and on CD-ROM.

The Library of Congress Office in Rio de Janeiro has compiled useful lists of the commercial, institutional, and government publications that it acquired from 1975 through 1992, when its two publications, *Accessions List, Brazil and Uruguay* (volumes 1–14, 1975–88, were entitled *Accessions List, Brazil*) and *Accessions List, Brazil and Uruguay: Cumulative List of Serials* (published annually 1983–88, under the title, *Accessions List, Brazil: Cumulative List of Serials*), were suspended. These unannotated lists were important sources of bibliographical data about Brazilian publications of interest to scholars, because they cited only those within the scope of the library's acquisitions policies.

The G. K. Hall Company of Boston, has been the most important commercial publisher of Brazilian bibliography as well as of Latin American bibliography in general. In the 1960s it began to issue a series of publications that reproduced the catalog cards of major library collections devoted to Latin America, including Brazil, or to specific countries or topics. An example of the former is the University of Texas's *Catalog of the Latin American Collection* (1969), issued in an original set of thirty-one volumes and three supplements totaling sixteen volumes, and its successor, *Bibliographic Guide to Latin American Studies*, an annual catalog that cites the publications cataloged for the Benson Latin American Collection at the University of Texas and for the Library of Congress. Because both these libraries have important collections of Brasiliana, the *Guide*, which cites books by author, title, and subject, is a useful source of Brazilian bibliography. G. K. Hall has also published several catalogs focusing on Brazil or on Portugal and Brazil: *A Catalogue of the Greenlee Collection, the Newberry Library, Chicago; Catalog of the Oliveira Lima Library, the Catholic University of America; Catalog of Brazilian Acquisitions of the Library of Congress, 1964–1974*; and the *Luso-Brazilian Catalogue* of the Canning House Library, London, and its supplement.

Access to periodical literature was greatly facilitated by the debut of *HAPI: Hispanic American Periodicals Index*, in the 1970s. It indexes academic journals focusing on the humanities and social sciences that are published in Latin America or that are published elsewhere but specialize in Latin American topics. It continues today, and at this writing includes thirty Brazilian journals. It is published in both print and electronic formats; many academic libraries subscribe to the online version.

The Brazilian holdings of the University of New Mexico libraries were the subject of two catalogs: Gillett and McIntyre's *Catalog of Luso-Brazilian Material in the University of New Mexico Libraries* (1970) and *Shelflist of the Brazilian Small Press Collection, University of New Mexico General Library* (1991). The university also published three general bibliographies in its first series, The Brazilian Curriculum Guide Specialized Bibliography: *Brazilian Studies: A Guide to the Humanities Literature,* by Conniff and Sturm (1986?); *Brazilian Reality Through the Lens of Popular Culture* by Levine (1984?); and *Women in Brazil: Problems and Perspectives* by Hahner (1984). A second edition of the latter, also entitled *Women in Brazil,* was published in 1998 in its second series.

A variety of other general bibliographies published from the mid-1970s to the early 1990s focused on various aspects of Brasiliana. A revised and enlarged edition of the classic work by one of Brazil's best-known librarians, bibliographers, and book collectors, Rubens Borba de Moraes, *Bibliographia brasiliana,* the standard reference source for rare books about Brazil, was published jointly by the University of California, Los Angeles, and the Livraria Kosmos, Rio de Janeiro, with annotations in English (1983). It also incorporated entries from his 1969 *Bibliografia brasileira do período colonial. Brazil: A Working Bibliography in Literature, Linguistics, Humanities, and the Social Sciences,* by Ronald M. Harmon and Bobby J. Chamberlain (1975), emphasized basic works about Brazil published since the mid-1960s and classic older works readily available in the United States. *Brazil,* by Solena V. Bryant (1985), which is volume 57 in the World Bibliographical Series of Clio Press, followed the plan of that series by providing annotated citations for more than eight hundred contemporary books (1970s and early 1980s) in all subject areas, with the focus on the humanities, social sciences, and fine arts, and the emphasis on books for the English-language reader. Its second edition (1997) by John P. Dickenson, with 903 entries, focused on materials published since the first edition. My *Brazil in Reference Books, 1965–1989: An Annotated Bibliography* (1991) covered 1,669 reference books for twenty-nine subjects, published in Brazil and elsewhere, with emphasis on the humanities, social sciences, and fine arts.

Bibliographies or other reference books devoted to a single Brazilian state or region have seldom been published in the United States, but a notable departure from that generalization is Muricy's *The Brazilian Amazon: Institutions and Publications* (1991?). This guide, published by the Seminar on the Acquisition of Latin American Library Materials (SALALM), serves as a directory to 162 of the most important institutional publishers in the region. It cites 296 titles that these institutions publish: subject-oriented and cultural periodicals, monographic series, and selected monographs and pamphlets. Its timely publication, the year before the United Nations Conference on Environment and Development held in Rio de Janeiro in 1992, came during a period of high foreign interest in Amazonia, and it remains a valuable source for those interested in the bibliography of that region.

Laurence Hallewell's *Books in Brazil: A History of the Publishing Trade* (1982), although not a bibliography, is an important source for the study of Brazilian bibliography. This detailed history of publishing, from its tentative beginnings during the colonial period to its contemporary vigor, is not a reference book strictly speaking, but it is easy to consult for reference purposes, because of the many topical headings within chapters and its excellent index. A revised and updated Portuguese edition, *O livro no Brasil: sua história,* was published in São Paulo in 1985.

General Works

Few general reference books about Brazil alone have been published in the United States. The U.S. government has been responsible for the one most widely available, *Brazil, a Country Study,* which has been published in five editions as part of its Area Handbook Series, the first four from 1964 to 1983 with varying titles—American University's *U.S. Army Area Handbook for Brazil* (1964); Weil's *Area Handbook for Brazil* (1971 and 1975); and *Brazil: A Country Study,* published in 1983 under the aegis of the U.S. Army and in 1998 by the Library of Congress. These handbooks describe contemporary Brazil in terms of its history, social and economic conditions, politics, and military situation, and each edition provides a bibliography that emphasizes publications in English. In addition to its print version, *Brazil: A Country Study* is also available online (http://hdl. loc.gov/loc.gdc/cntrystd.br).

Brazil is well represented in several encyclopedias encompassing all the countries of Latin America. The five-volume *Encyclopedia of Latin American History and Culture* (1996), edited by Tennenbaum, has many long articles and shorter, dictionary-style entries devoted to Brazilian topics. *Latin America, History and Culture: An Encyclopedia for Students* (1999), culled from the *Encyclopedia of Latin American History and Culture* but rewritten and updated by Tennenbaum for secondary school students, also has many references to Brazil and includes entries based on current events, as well as entries on historical topics and culture. Brazil also figures prominently in *The Encyclopedia of Latin America* (1974), edited by Helen Delpar, a one-volume publication with entries that are necessarily shorter but offer both contemporary and historical information. For example, it was current enough to include entries for presidents Arthur da Costa e Silva and Ernesto Geisel, who served in the late 1960s and early 1970s. Although *The Cambridge Encyclopedia of Latin America and the Caribbean* (1985, and 2nd ed., 1992) originated in England, both editions by Collier, Skidmore, and Blakemore were published simultaneously in New York. One of its three general editors, Thomas Skidmore, is a well-known U.S. historian of Brazil, and other prominent U.S. *brasilianistas* contributed essays to it.

Quantitative data about Brazil is available in the *Statistical Abstract of Latin America,* which has been published annually since 1955. Its most recent edition, volume 38, was issued in 2002. It presents a wide variety of economic, social, and cultural data supplied by the country in question. Sources of the tables (usually the Instituto Brasileiro de Geografia e Estatística—IBGE in the case of Brazil) are identified. It also issues frequent supplements devoted to single topics, such as land reform, urbanization, and elections. Sources of historical statistics are discussed in the "History" section.

A pioneer guide for academics, *Brazil: Field Research Guide in the Social Sciences,* was compiled by Levine in 1966 at a time when the number of U.S. researchers (usually graduate students) was rapidly increasing in Brazil, and there were few academic mentors with in-country experience. It is telling that the average age of its ten contributors was twenty-six— the typical age of an advanced graduate student. The guide is comprised of essays devoted to research opportunities and problems in six academic disciplines, preceded by an essay on general problems of research in Brazil. Appendixes deal with research facilities, living conditions, and other topics. Although this guide is now outdated, it still contains useful observations and information, and it provides a fascinating glimpse of Brazil as seen through the eyes of the first sizable wave of budding Brazilianists.

HISTORY AND GEOGRAPHY

Interest in Brazilian history generated more bibliographies than any other academic discipline, with most of the bibliographical production concentrated in the late 1970s and early 1980s. Two bibliographies devoted to

Latin American history in general were precursors of those focused exclusively on Brazil. Charles Griffin's *Latin America: A Guide to the Historical Literature* (1971) devoted several sections to Brazil, while Cortes Conde and Stein's *Latin America: A Guide to Economic History, 1830–1930* (1977) allotted more than 100 of its 685 pages to it. Slavery in Brazil, with its counterpart in U.S. history, is a frequent subject of historians from the United States. It was the subject of the first bibliography dedicated exclusively to Brazilian history that was published during this period: *Brazilian Slavery: An Annotated Research Bibliography* (1977) by Conrad. In addition to monographs and journal articles, it listed selected primary sources: propaganda pamphlets, travel accounts, speeches, censuses, and others.

Three bibliographies covering broad historical periods followed in the early 1980s. Francis A. Dutra's *A Guide to the History of Brazil, 1500–1822: The Literature in English,* made the bibliography of Brazil's colonial history accessible to the reader limited to English-language proficiency. Robert Levine's two bibliographies, *Brazil, 1822–1930: An Annotated Bibliography for Social Historians* (1983), and *Brazil Since 1930: An Annotated Bibliography for Social Historians* (1980), defined social history broadly and provided a bibliographical overview of Brazil from the beginning of the empire well into the twentieth century.

A particular aspect of history was highlighted in *Urban Labor History in Twentieth Century Brazil,* by French and Fortes (1998), a well-annotated bibliography preceded by an introduction to the topic, issued as part of the University of New Mexico's series, Brazilian Curriculum Guide Specialized Bibliography, Series II.

The most comprehensive general reference work that included Brazilian history and its bibliography was the *Cambridge History of Latin America* (*CHLA*), a multivolume work edited by Leslie Bethell that began publication in 1984. It is an example of a publication originating in England but published also in the United States. Several Americans were among the international group of scholars who contributed articles to its sections about Brazil. *Colonial Brazil* (1988) and *Brazil: Empire and Republic, 1822–1930* (1989), also edited by Bethell, are books comprised of chapters reprinted from various volumes of the *CHLA.*

The most comprehensive reference work dealing with Brazil alone was Robert M. Levine's *Historical Dictionary of Brazil* (1979), which had entries for people, events, popular culture, sports, politics, and other topics about contemporary and historical Brazil. The others were chronologies: Fitzgibbon's *Brazil: A Chronology and Fact Book, 1488–1973* (1974) was comprehensive in its chronological scope, while Young's *Brazil, 1954–1964: End of a Civilian Cycle* (1972) dealt with a series of events of considerable interest in the United States.

Brazilian history is well represented in several general encyclopedias of Latin America. The excellent five-volume *Encyclopedia of Latin American History and Culture* (1996), which was discussed in "General Works," thoroughly covers many events and individuals associated with Brazil. Published forty years earlier, the one-volume *Encyclopedia of Latin-American History* (1956) by Martin and Lovett included many briefer entries for Brazil. The second edition in 1968 was characterized in the introduction as an effort "to bring up to date the earlier version by incorporating events that have transpired in Latin America since 1956." However, it did not include many major political figures of the period such as presidents Juscelino Kubitschek, Jânio Quadros, and João Goulart, although it identified some of the earlier presidents of Brazil.

Historical statistics were the focus of several works published from the mid-seventies to the mid-eighties. These works were undoubtedly a response to developments taking place in academe and in the wider world of which it is a part. Quantitative history was in vogue, and demography as an academic discipline was expanding. Brazil was undergoing strong economic growth, and the scholars who studied it and who sometimes served as consultants or advisers to projects there, needed facts and figures, including long-term statistical series. Ludwig's *Brazil: A Handbook of Historical Statistics* (1985) provided series of demographic, economic, and social statistics for the nineteenth and twentieth centuries. My *Subject Guide to Statistics in the Presidential Reports of the Brazilian Provinces, 1830–1889* (1977) was an index to statistics found in the annual reports of the provincial presidents to the legislative assemblies during the empire. Usually referred to as *relatórios* or *fallas*, the statistics found in them spanned a wide variety of subjects: agricultural production, crime, trade, slavery, population, and education are only a few. I also provided a bibliography of the 1,085 reports that I examined. *The Handbook of National Population Censuses: Latin America and the Caribbean, North America, and Oceania* by Goyer and Domschke (1983) included Brazil and listed all known national population censuses. *The Demographic History of Brazil* by Merrick (1984) was a contribution to the University of New Mexico's Brazilian Curriculum Guide Specialized Bibliography series.

In contrast to the situation in Brazilian history, very few reference books included geography. Palmerlee's *A Glossary of Portuguese & Brazilian Map Terms & Abbreviations* (1968), replacing a shorter version, *A Portuguese-English Glossary of Map Terms* (1962), was compiled to facilitate the study of Portuguese and Brazilian maps by English speakers. It included "terms and abbreviations from . . . maps and atlases, including specialized economic, geologic, climatic and vegetation maps" (p. i).

Brazilian place names were the subject of the U.S. Office of Geography's *Brazil: Official Standard Names Approved by the United States Board on Geographic Names* (1963), as part of its Gazetteer series, which covers many countries, and of the *Supplement to Brazil Gazetteer*, published in 1992. The 62,500 entries of the former identify and locate places (cities, vilas, etc.) and named physical features (atolls, rivers, mountains), giving their standard names with cross-references from variants, and their Universal Transverse Mercator (UTM) grid coordinates, based principally on maps published by the Instituto Brasileiro de Geografia e Estatística. Although the federal agency responsible for this publication was established in 1890 "to provide for uniform usage of geographic names throughout the Federal Government," (p. iii), it is also a useful source for scholars seeking to identify or locate obscure places, to clarify their status, or to distinguish between places and physical features with the same name.

POLITICAL SCIENCE AND LAW

Identifying and locating the official publications of governments, with their complex structures comprised of many agencies, has always been difficult, and Brazilian official publications are no exception. In 1945 the Library of Congress began a series of bibliographies of the government publications of the other American republics, and John De Noia's *Brazil: A Guide to the Official Publications* (1948) was the third volume in the series, based on publications held by the Library of Congress. They were listed under the agencies and offices of each branch of the Brazilian government— executive, legislative, and judicial—and as a result, this work also served as an informal, but incomplete, guide to the Brazilian government for the English-language reader.

Serial publications issued by government agencies—periodicals, statistical yearbooks, annual reports of the president and the ministries, budgets, and many others—were the focus of two later publications that addressed the ongoing need for information about official publications by increasing numbers of researchers. *Brazil* (1968) by Rosa Q. Mesa was the second in a series of twelve volumes, Latin American Serial Documents. It specifically addressed the needs of North American researchers, since it identified official Brazilian serial publications located in libraries in the United States and Canada.

Brazilian Serial Documents: A Selective and Annotated Guide (1974) by Mary Lombardi covered official serial publications through 1971. In addition to basic bibliographic data, it often included notes about the history of the publication or about its contents. It also summarized information about each government agency included, such as a brief history, name changes, and laws or decrees pertaining to the name changes.

Guide to Official Publications of Foreign Countries (2nd ed. 1997), sponsored by the Government Documents Round Table of the American Library Association, covered most countries of the world, including Brazil, listing the major publications of the executive (chief executive officer and ministries), legislative, and judicial branches of government, as well as certain categories of particular interest, such as statistics, long-term economic or development plans, and human rights statements.

Understanding the law and legal philosophies of other countries has also challenged those concerned with them: attorneys, judges, legislators, scholars, businessmen, and others. Therefore, it is not surprising that the U.S. government, again through the efforts of the Library of Congress, began early in the twentieth century to make this information available in a series of book-length bibliographical essays. Borchard's *Guide to the Law and Legal Literature of Argentina, Brazil and Chile*, published in 1917, was the fourth guide in the series. *Legal Codes of the Latin American Republics* (1942), also issued by the Library of Congress, briefly surveyed the legal codes of each country, including Brazil, in a trilingual edition (English, Portuguese, and Spanish). The Library of Congress also focused explicitly on making Latin American legislation accessible in the United States through the *Index to Latin American Legislation, 1950–1960*, and its three supplements covering the years 1961 through 1975. In the case of Brazil, it indexed legislation published in the *Diário oficial*.

The politics of a country, influenced by the interplay of its history, culture, economic situation, geography, and myriad other factors, creates another challenge to outsiders (as well as to its own citizens) interested in research. Frances Hagopian's chapter, "Brazil," in the *Handbook of Political Science Research on Latin America: Trends from the 1960s to the 1990s* (1990), presented an overview of the field with many bibliographical references, which were based on her work as a contributing editor to the *Handbook of Latin American Studies*. *Latin American Politics: A Historical Bibliography* (1984) was the bibliography with the broadest coverage, both chronologically (1914–early 1980s) and ideologically. Its chapter on Brazil cited almost four hundred articles that appeared in a variety of Brazilian and foreign periodicals between 1973 and 1982 and abstracted their content.

Several bibliographies related to Brazilian politics and some of the ideologies that informed it focused on the military regime (1964–85) and leftist movements, although some of these bibliographies treated other aspects of political life. Cold War concerns in the United States undoubtedly nurtured this emphasis. An effort to provide a contemporaneous bibliography about the political events of 1964 and the years immediately following was assembled by the Latin American Research Program at the University of California, Riverside, probably in response to the needs of students and researchers: Sousa's *Annotated Bibliography of the Brazilian Political Movement of 1964* (1966) was a fifteen-page annotated bibliography citing 103 books and articles published from 1964 to August 1966. *Bibliographical Notes for Understanding the Brazilian Model: Political Repression & Economic Expansion* (1974) focused on both political and economic aspects of 1964–74, and *The Political Economy of Contemporary Brazil* by Evans, Liedke, and Liedke Filho (1984) did the same for the early 1980s. Chilcote, the author of *Brazil and Its Radical Left: An Annotated Bibliography on the Communist Movement and the Rise of Marxism, 1922–1972* (1980), described his list of books, pamphlets, articles, and periodicals as "a comprehensive compilation of materials relating to the Communist, Socialist, and Anarchist movements in Brazil over a period of half a century" (1).

Brazilian political parties have been the subject of chapters in several general reference works. Greenwood Press has published two related works with chapters devoted to Brazil: Alexander's *Political Parties of the Americas: Canada, Latin America, and the West Indies* (1982) and Ameringer's *Political Parties of the Americas, 1980s to 1990s: Canada, Latin America, and the West Indies* (1992). Both contain essays summarizing Brazil's political history and glossaries of its political parties, the former for the nineteenth and twentieth centuries and the latter for its recent political history. A work with a similar title, Coggins and Lewis's *Political Parties of the Americas and the Caribbean: A Reference Guide* (1992), was published in England and widely distributed in the United States by a U.S. publisher of reference materials, Gale Research.

Interest in political movements, particularly those involving dissident groups, resulted in several reference works of varying quality and thoroughness that identified and described these movements. Treatment of Brazil was generally superficial, an unsurprising outcome in works encompassing many countries, with limited and often indirect sources of information about the groups included. Degenhardt's *Political Dissent: An International Guide to Dissident Extra-Parliamentary, Guerrilla, and Illegal Political Movements* (1983) devoted only four pages to twelve Brazilian groups representing both the Right and the Left, while the second edition, entitled *Revolutionary and Dissident Movements: An International Guide* (1988), which was published in England but distributed in the United States, summarized the contemporary political situation in Brazil in less than one page and did not identify specific dissident groups. Similarly, *Latin American Political Movements*, edited by O'Maolain (1985), devoted eight pages to Brazil in a work that the introduction characterizes as presenting "basic factual information on political parties and alliances, guerrilla movements, pressure groups and other legal and illegal organizations currently active" (vii). *Latin American Revolutionaries: Groups, Goals, Methods*, by Radu and Tismaneanu (1990), presents a "Handbook of Revolutionary Organizations of Latin America" in part 2. The section covering Brazil deals with four groups.

U.S. reference sources have provided limited biographical information about Brazilian political leaders; coverage usually has been limited to some, but not all, presidents and a few other prominent leaders, such as Rui Barbosa. Emphasis has been on the past, rather than on contemporary leaders. *The Biographical Dictionary of Latin American and Caribbean Political Leaders*, edited by Alexander (1989), is an example. This work, with entries for about 450 leaders, includes only twenty-three Brazilians, fourteen of whom were active before 1950. It also illustrates a characteristic of many reference books that cover Latin America in general: Brazil is underrepresented. In spite of Brazil's obvious importance as a political and economic power, five countries (Argentina, Bolivia, Chile, Peru, and Venezuela) are represented with more entries.

ETHNOLOGY

The black presence in Brazilian society has dominated U.S. publications related to ethnology, reflecting the significance of race as a major theme in U.S. society. When combined with the publications related to slavery cited in the section entitled "History" in this essay, the number of publications makes it clear that the African presence in Brazil has been an important focus of interest and scholarship in the United States.

In light of the recent high interest, in the United States and elsewhere, in the indigenous peoples of the Amazon region, it is surprising that no major bibliographies or other reference works have been published in almost forty years. The landmark seven-volume *Handbook of South American Indians*, by Steward (1963), is still the major reference source in this field. It devotes considerable attention to indigenous groups in Brazil in volumes 1 and 3, *The Marginal Tribes* and *The Tropical Forest Tribes*, respectively, as well as in other volumes dealing with comparative ethnology of South American Indians, physical anthropology, linguistics, and other topics. It also includes an extensive bibliography. The multivolume *Cambridge History of the Native Peoples of the Americas* (1996–2000) contains one volume (in two parts) with various chapters on people of Brazil (vol. 3, parts 1–2, 1999).

Apart from this exception, however, most books in this field published in the United States are about blacks. *Afro-Braziliana: A Working Bibliography,* by Dorothy B. Porter (1978), also known as Dorothy Porter Wesley, is the most extensive bibliography on the subject. It is a selective, partially annotated list of books, pamphlets, and periodical publications by or about Afro-Brazilians. Two publications in the Brazilian Curriculum Guide Specialized Bibliography series of the University of New Mexico also have contributed to the bibliography of the field: *Race Relations in Modern Brazil* by Hasenbalg (1984?) and *Slavery and Race Relations in Brazil* by Andrews (1997). *Afro-Brazilian Religions: A Selective, Annotated Bibliography 1900–1997* by Oliver (1998) is a specialized bibliography with 1,192 references emphasizing scholarly publications in English and Portuguese; it includes a sampling of popular literature on the subject.

Three general reference works supply information about various aspects of Afro-Brasiliana, along with those about other racial and ethnic groups in Brazil and throughout Latin America. The *Dictionary of Afro-Latin American Civilization* by Nuñez (1980) is a useful source, although its emphasis is on the Caribbean Islands, which the author terms the "focal point of the African Diaspora" (xii). He describes the book as "a historical and descriptive dictionary [with 4500 entries] of terms and phrases, with selected biographies of Afro-Latin political leaders, writers, and other important personalities" (xiii). *Race and Ethnic Relations in Latin America and the Caribbean: An Historical Dictionary and Bibliography* (1980) by Levine emphasizes the countries where "racial themes have played unusually important roles" (vii)—Brazil among them—according to the introduction. Levine identifies or defines names, events, and terms that relate to relations among races and ethnic groups; slavery, race relations, prejudice and discrimination, and racial themes in formal and popular culture and daily life are the subjects of many entries. The *Dictionary of Latin American Racial and Ethnic Terminology* by Stephens (1999) focuses on words used to designate racial and ethnic groups. Part 2 (143 pages) is devoted to Brazilian Portuguese terms, an increase of thirty-one pages over its first edition in 1989.

LITERATURE AND LANGUAGE

The *MLA International Bibliography of Books and Articles on the Modern Languages and Literatures,* which has been published since 1921 by the Modern Language Association of America, is a key source of information in the fields of Brazilian literature and the Portuguese language. It is available online and on CD-ROMs, as well as in print. Many academic libraries subscribe to it in electronic format. Chamberlain's *Portuguese Language and Luso-Brazilian Literature: An Annotated Guide to Selected Reference Works* (1989) focuses on 538 reference books dealing with both topics.

Interest in Brazilian literature resulted in the publication of a number of important bibliographies and biobibliographies in the United States. In the period before the 1970s, these publications were few and far between. In 1931, *A Tentative Bibliography of Brazilian Belles-lettres* by Ford, Whittem, and Raphael was published under the auspices of the Harvard University Council on Hispano-American Studies. It focused on the works of writers of poetry, drama, and fiction. A quarter of a century later, Topete's *A Working Bibliography of Brazilian Literature* (1957) cited reference works, anthologies, general critical studies, essays, journalism, biography, fiction, poetry, and the theater, the works of authors in each genre and critical references about them, and selected English and Spanish translations. It was followed in 1969 by Gerrit De Jong's *Four Hundred Years of Brazilian Literature,* which covered ninety authors from the colonial period to Afrânio Peixoto (1876–1947) and the major literary movements of the same period.

The publication in 1974–75 of Claude Hulet's three-volume work, *Brazilian Literature,* initiated a series of valuable works on that topic published from the mid-1970s to the early 1990s. It surveyed literary production from 1500 to 1960 by means of biobibliographies of important authors, excerpts from their works, brief critical comments, suggestions for further reading, and other bibliographical references for each one.

Living authors were highlighted in Foster and Reis's *Dictionary of Contemporary Brazilian Authors* (1981), which provided biobibliographical data and some critical commentary. Foster and Rela's *Brazilian Literature: A Research Bibliography* (1990) cited secondary sources: general works about Brazilian literature and historical/biographical/ critical publications for about 150 authors. The University of New Mexico's series, Brazilian Curriculum Guide Specialized Bibliography, included Tolman and Paiva's *Brazilian Literature and Language Outlines* (1986?), an overview and bibliography of the subject.

The contemporary literary landscape was the focus of Stern's *Dictionary of Brazilian Literature* (1988). Its approximately three hundred entries covered "the most significant writers, literary schools, and related cultural movements in Brazilian literary history, with an emphasis on twentieth century and very contemporary figures" (v). Additional material included a historical/literary chronology and a glossary of frequently used literary terms.

Brazilian vanguardism had a prominent place in *Vanguardism in Latin American Literature: An Annotated Bibliographical Guide,* by Forster and Jackson (1990), because the longest chapter in the book was devoted to it. Described as a "scholarly guide for the first phase of vanguardist expression in Brazilian literature, and its relationship to international vanguard movements and the avant-garde aesthetic" (64), the book's 369 entries cited the most significant works published after 1971 and those not listed in Placer's *Modernismo brasileiro: bibliografia (1918–1971).*

Brazilian literature was an important presence in *Latin American Writers* (1989), edited by Carlos Solé. This scholarly, three-volume work, with its long biobibliographical and critical articles devoted to individual authors, included twenty-seven Brazilians, beginning with Gregório de Mattos (1636–1695) and ending with Ariano Vilar Suassuna (b. 1927).

Popular literature in the form of *literatura de cordel* was the subject of a useful work by Hallewell and McCarthy, "Bibliography of Brazilian Chapbook Literature," compiled as an appendix to a paper entitled "Brazilian Chapbook Literature," presented at meeting of the Seminar on the Acquisition of Latin American Library Materials (SALALM) in 1985. Its 251 entries cite publications on all aspects of *cordel:* history, criticism, origins, illustrations, covers, production, publication, and distribution, although it does not cite the works themselves.

Several good dictionaries assisting English speakers with Portuguese have been published in the United States. Taylor's *A Portuguese-English Dictionary* (1958) is a classic. Two bilingual dictionaries were published in the 1990s: *The Random House Portuguese Dictionary* (1991) edited by Chamberlain, and the two-volume *Dicionário brasileiro* (1993) by Houaiss and Avery. Idiomatic Portuguese is the subject of *A Dictionary of Informal Brazilian Portuguese with English Index* (1983) by Chamberlain and Harmon. Its purpose was to acquaint the English speaker with the informal language used in Brazilian society and in contemporary Brazilian literature, in contrast to the language as it is learned in the classroom.

Finally, the indigenous languages of Brazil (a total of 236), as well as the Portuguese language, are covered in Grimes's *Ethnologue: Languages of the*

World, which has been published in fourteen print editions and is now available on CD-ROM and online (www.ethnologue.com). It identifies the languages used in each country of the world, including Brazil, and for each gives its name and variant names, and number of speakers. Both formats include a language map of Brazil.

ART AND ARCHITECTURE

Brazilian art in its varied manifestations has been the subject of several reference works published in the United States. In addition, three important works provide access to the extensive bibliography. *A Guide to the Art of Latin America,* edited by Smith and Wilder (1948), was the pioneer bibliography in this field. Brazilian art and architecture were represented in 904 (18.5%) of its 4,896 entries, which cover twenty-one countries. The *Handbook of Latin American Art: A Bibliographic Compilation* (1984–86), edited by Joyce Waddell Bailey, covers the colonial period and the nineteenth and twentieth centuries. Its sections on Brazil were compiled by Aracy Abreu Amaral and total more than two hundred pages (Brazilian art during the colonial period is covered in vol. 2, while the art of the nineteenth and twentieth centuries is covered in vol. 1, part. 2). Neistein's *A arte no Brasil* is based on work done for the *Handbook of Latin American Studies,* beginning in the early 1970s and continuing for about twenty-five years. Its bilingual text with 1,690 entries is wide ranging in its coverage: painting, sculpture, graphic and decorative arts, folk art, Afro-Brazilian and indigenous art and folkloric traditions, architecture, urban planning, cinema, and others.

The University of New Mexico published *Architecture and Sculpture in Brazil* (1985) by Ottaviano C. De Fiore, as well as two editions of *Modern Brazilian Painting* (1986 and 1997) by Stella de Sá Rego and Marguerite Harrison, which survey nineteenth- and twentieth-century painting and provide good bibliographies. Each edition of the latter also includes a brief section devoted to photography, and an image list, citing books in which works of specific artists are reproduced.

The most outstanding general reference book is *Encyclopedia of Latin American & Caribbean Art* (2000), edited by Jane Turner and published simultaneously in England and the United States, with an international list of more than two hundred contributors, many Americans among them. This well-illustrated encyclopedia, an updated spin-off of the multivolume set *The Dictionary of Art* (1996), covers the arts from the European conquest to the present. The Encyclopedia's twelve hundred signed entries include biographies of artists; articles on indigenous art; articles on general topics, such as Latin American women artists and Latin American artists in the United States; and articles about art in each country. The twenty-five pages of the article devoted to Brazil in general attest to the significant place that it has in this publication. Brazilian art and architecture are well represented in entries throughout the book, and there are articles about art in several Brazilian cities.

Interest in Brazilian popular art and indigenous art has also resulted in publications in the United States: Rodman's *Genius in the Backlands: Popular Artists of Brazil* (1977) gives biographical data and descriptions of the works of twenty-one popular painters, sculptors, and woodcarvers, among others, accompanied by portraits and by illustrations of their work. *Arts of the Amazon* (1995), edited by Braun, documents the art of the entire region, including the Brazilian Amazon, covering ceramics, basketry, textiles, carvings, feather art, body decoration, masks, and other forms, with excellent photographs and extensive descriptive and interpretive text.

Music

Excellent overviews of Brazilian music are available in three surveys. Appleby's *The Music of Brazil* (1983) is a survey from colonial days to the late twentieth century, replete with information about composers, performing artists, musical forms, and instruments. A glossary of musical terms peculiar to Brazil is a very useful feature. Béhague's *Music in Latin America: An Introduction* (1979), covering roughly the same period, deals with a wider geographic area, but coverage of Brazil is extensive. Both books give many musical examples and have good bibliographies and detailed indexes that facilitate their use as reference sources. An earlier classic work, *Music of Latin America*, by Nicolas Slonimsky (1945, reprinted in 1972), included a survey of Brazilian popular and art music and a "Dictionary of Latin American Musicians, Songs and Dances, and Musical Instruments," which identified many of Brazil's musicians and defined many terms associated with its music. Other more modest publications have also surveyed Brazilian music. An early effort, *The Music of Brazil* by Luper (1943), was issued by the Music Division of the Pan-American Union as part of its Music Series, and it included "A partial list of Brazilian music obtainable in the United States."

The University of New Mexico's two series contributed four items: *Classical Music of Brazil* by Peter J. Schoenbach, and *MPB: Contemporary Brazilian Popular Music* by Enylton de Sá Rego and Charles A. Perrone, both published in the mid-1980s; *Folk and Popular Music of Brazil* (1997) by Perrone and Crook; and Coelho's *Brazilian Classical Music* (1998). These short works (twenty to thirty-nine pages) provide basic information about each topic, as well as bibliographies and discographies.

Brazil's internationally celebrated contributions to popular music, samba and bossa nova, are highlighted in *The Brazilian Sound: Samba, Bossa Nova, and the Popular Music of Brazil* by McGowan and Pessanha, first published in 1991 by a publisher specializing in the field of entertainment and issued in a new edition in 1998 by a university press. It is an illustrated guide to the history, styles, interpretations, instruments, and international influence of Brazilian popular music and includes biographical data for musicians, a glossary, a bibliography, and a discography with one thousand entries. Heitor Villa-Lobos, one of Brazil's best-known composers, whose music is frequently performed and recorded in the United States, is the subject Appleby's *Heitor Villa-Lobos: A Bio-Bibliography* (1988). In addition to biographical data and a bibliography of works about him, it includes a list of his works and their premières, and a discography.

Documentary Sources

The need for accessible primary source materials for scholarly research in the United States paralleled the expanding need for reference sources, and it prompted the microfilming of many collections of important documents related to Brazil. Among them were official publications of both the Brazilian and the U.S. governments, publications of Brazilian and U.S. organizations, and Brazilian newspapers.

The single most useful source for locating microfilm related to Brazil produced in the United States is "Resources in Latin American and Hispanic Studies," the sales catalog issued by Scholarly Resources Inc. (104 Greenhill Avenue, Wilmington, DE 19805-1897; 1-800-772-8937; sales@scholarly.com), a company that distributes film produced by the Library of Congress, the National Archives, some academic institutions, and private organizations and in some cases publishes microfilm in cooperation with organizations. Although Scholarly Resources has a website, www.scholarly.com, its listing of available microfilm is far from complete, and much of its microfilm related to Brazil is not yet listed there.

One of the most innovative microfilm products in terms of its content is the *Brazil's Popular Groups* series. The inauguration of the Nova República in 1985 gave impetus to many grassroots movements, which published pamphlets, periodicals, and posters, and other ephemera to provide information and to advocate for their causes. The Library of Congress Field Office in Rio de Janeiro began collecting representative publications of the groups involved in many of these movements, and indeed of those that went back as far as the mid-1960s, sending them to Washington, D.C., for microfilming. The set of microfilm covering the earliest years, *Brazil's Popular Groups, 1966–1986*, was described in promotional literature as "a collection of materials (2,271 pieces) issued by socio-political, religious, labor, and minority grass-roots organizations in Brazil between 1966 and 1986" and was comprised of thirty-two reels. The second set, covering only a three-year period, 1987–89, occupied forty-three reels of microfilm, due in part to intensive collection of publications at that time by the staff of the Library of Congress Field Office but also reflecting the intensity of grass-roots activity during this period. This project is ongoing, and at the time of this writing microfilm covering 1966–2003 was available. A broad range of human concerns is covered in this series; it reflects the evolution of Brazilian society with the addition of new issues and interests, and changes in emphases over the years. Those included from 1966 to 1996 (although not all topics are included in all years) are agrarian reform, blacks, Indians, other ethnic groups, children, ecology, education and communication, homosexual and bisexual groups, human rights and civil rights, the labor movement, political parties and issues, religion and theology, urban issues, and women. As of this writing, three sets of microfilm focusing on specific groups, women, blacks, and homosexuals and bisexuals, had also been produced with material taken from the larger sets of *Brazil's Popular Groups* and others were planned. Detailed information is available at http://www.loc.gov/acq/ovop/rio/bpg/. It should also be noted that the *Princeton University Library Latin American Microfilm Collection* has amassed a group of sixty-two microfilm rolls of Brazilian pamphlets, serials, broadsides, fliers, and posters that deal with some of the same subjects as *Brazil's Popular Groups* but do not duplicate items included there. A detailed listing of microfilm is available in the printed sales catalog of Scholarly Resources, the distributor for both institutions.

The Library of Congress is also responsible for microfilming the *Diário oficial*, Brazil's official gazette, complete from 1892 to 1993, and for the earlier nineteenth century (parts of the 1820s and 1830s), in an ongoing project that has thus far produced more than twenty-two hundred rolls of microfilm. The New York Public Library and the University of Wisconsin Library have also microfilmed parts of it. One of Brazil's most important and long-lived newspapers, *O Estado de São Paulo* (1890–present), and its predecessor, *A Província de São Paulo* (1875–89), have also been filmed by the Library of Congress.

The National Archives has produced a great deal of microfilm based on records of the U.S. Department of State regarding Brazil. Those originating in the nineteenth century include *Diplomatic Instructions* (1833–1906), *Diplomatic Despatches* (1809–1906), *Notes from the Brazilian Legation* (1824–1906), and consular despatches from Salvador (1808–49), Bahia (1850–1906), Maranhão, Pará, Pernambuco, Rio Grande do Sul, Rio de Janeiro, Santa Catarina, and Santos. The U.S. Navy is also represented in nineteenth-century materials microfilmed by the National Archives: *Letters Received by the Secretary of the Navy from Commanding Officers of Squadrons, 1841–1886: Brazil Squadron, 1841–1861*.

Twentieth-century Department of State records filmed by the National Archives include *Records of the Department of State Relating to the Internal Affairs of Brazil* from 1910 to 1959, *Records of the Department of State Relating to Political Relations between the United States and Brazil*, covering 1930–59, and *Records Relating to Political Relations between Brazil and Other States*, from 1910 to 1944. Microfilming of most of these records is ongoing, continuing into the twenty-first century. For example, *Records of the Department of State Relating to Internal Affairs of Brazil, 1960–1963*, was issued in 2001.

Many Brazilian official publications were microfilmed in an important cooperative project carried out by the Latin American Microform Project (LAMP), associated with the Center for Research Libraries, Chicago, and the Biblioteca Nacional, Rio de Janeiro, in association with the Plano Nacional de Microfilmagem de Periódicos Brasileiros. This project, initiated by LAMP, began in 1978 and concluded several years later. It microfilmed a large quantity of material, including all available annual reports (*relatórios* or *fallas*) of the presidents of the provinces during the empire, and of the state governors who succeeded them to 1930 to the *assembléias legislativas*; the annual reports of the president to Congress, 1889–1993; the annual reports of the ministries at the national level, 1821 to 1960, and the *Almanak administrativo, mercantil e industrial do imperio do Brazil*—"Almanak Laemmert"—1844–89. Microfilm for these publications is located at both the Center for Research Libraries and the Biblioteca Nacional. Between 1995 and 1999 all these materials were digitized, and they are available online: http://wwwcrl.uchicago.edu. The project to digitize these resources is discussed in more detail under the heading "Electronic Resources."

Protestant churches began sending missionaries to Brazil in the nineteenth century, and they are a rich source for records on microfilm. These sources contribute to studies in many areas of the social sciences and humanities, in addition to their obvious importance to the history of their religious denominations and of missionary activity in Brazil. They include correspondence to and from the mission boards in the United States, reports of missionary interactions with major political figures, accounts of slavery and abolition, descriptions of mission stations, summaries of meetings and conferences, information on the establishment of many educational institutions and hospitals, diaries, inventories of supplies, and much more. Two notable collections distributed by Scholarly Resources are *Presbyterian Board of Foreign Missions,* and *Methodist Episcopal Church Board Missionary Correspondence, 1846–1912.* Both collections, which include various Latin American countries, include correspondence and reports from Brazil.

As previously stated, most of the microfilm collections described here, as well as several other smaller collections pertaining to Brazil, are fully described in the Scholarly Resources sales catalog. The exception is the collection of official documents microfilmed by the LAMP/Biblioteca Nacional cooperative project. Information about them can be obtained from the Center for Research Libraries, but since these official publications are now available online, they can be readily obtained in that format.

Electronic Resources

Several electronic resources for Brazilian studies have already been noted under the subjects related to them: the *Handbook of Latin American Studies,* the *MLA Bibliography,* and the *Ethnologue* are examples. In addition, the catalogs of many U.S. libraries with significant holdings of publications from and about Brazil are accessible through the Internet.

Other notable multidisciplinary resources for Brazilian studies in electronic format include the LANIC (Latin American Network Information Center) system, an online central clearinghouse connecting users to Internet resources, both free and commercial, that pertain to Latin America. It is managed by the Teresa Lozano Long Institute of Latin American Studies at the University of Texas and is available to all Internet users. It provides a link to each country of Latin America, including Brazil (www.lanic.utexas.eduhttp://lanic.utexas.edu/la/brazil/) and through it to the web pages of a variety of resources: government agencies, newspapers, library catalogs, and others.

The Latin American Microfilm Project's Brazilian Government Document Digitization Project at the Center for Research Libraries was funded by the Andrew W. Mellon Foundation to digitize executive branch serial documents issued by Brazil's national government from 1821 to 1993 and by its provincial/state governments from the earliest available for each province to 1930. The project provides Internet access (wwwcrl.uchicago. edu,http://wwwcrl.uchicago.edu; click on "Search collection databases") to documents that are not widely accessible in print format to facilitate their scholarly use. Although the project's usefulness for historians is obvious, its chronological coverage, extending to the early 1990s for some documents, and the many subjects that they encompass, make it a valuable resource for many academic disciplines.

The Latin Americanist Research Resources Pilot Project, sponsored by the Association of Research Libraries (ARL) with funding from the Andrew W. Mellon Foundation, and the participation of more than forty ARL-member libraries, although still evolving, is already functioning. One of its components is known informally as the "tables of contents project," or LAPTOC. Its website (www.lanic.utexas.edu/project/arl) lists the tables of contents of the issues of about four hundred periodicals—mostly academic journals—published in Argentina, Brazil, and Mexico since 1995, for which the participating libraries take collecting responsibility. This responsibility includes acquiring each issue of the periodical and making copies of its articles available upon demand through rapid delivery interlibrary service. Seven university libraries have taken responsibility for collecting the sixty-nine Brazilian periodicals included in the project. The University of Texas at Austin has collecting responsibility for 71 percent, or forty-nine of them, while Rice University has ten, and the National Agriculture Library; the Interamerican Development Bank; New York University; the University of California, Los Angeles; the University of California, San Diego; and Vanderbilt University have one or two each.

Conclusion

Many more reference sources covering Brazil than might be immediately apparent were published in the United States from 1945 to 2003, with the majority appearing since the 1960s. They vary widely in subject matter, depth of coverage, and the quality of information supplied. The publication of bibliographies predominated in the earlier years of interest in Brazilian studies in the United States, paralleling a similar trend in the field of Latin American studies in general. Bibliographies have been published with some regularity up to the present, reflecting the constant need to identify and locate materials related to Brazil and to impose some sort of order on the proliferation of these publications. They comprise the single largest group of reference materials discussed in this essay. The "Bibliographies" section of the reference list that follows cites twenty-eight general bibliographies about Brazil or with significant Brazilian content, and most subject sections list additional ones. For example, "History and Geography" cites ten, and several other historical reference books have substantial bibliographical components.

During the period of intensive development of Latin Americans studies programs in U.S. universities in the 1960s and 1970s, more general reference works devoted to Latin America, such as encyclopedias, appeared than in the earlier period. Many included entries about Brazil, although some were limited to what they often referred to as "Hispanic America," the Spanish-speaking countries of the region. During the same period, the Cold War and political upheavals in Latin America and elsewhere probably inspired certain government publications such as the Area Handbook Series and the Gazeteer series; Brazil was represented in both series. By the late 1970s and continuing to the present, many reference works focusing on specific subjects as they related to Brazil appeared, and commercial publishers often issued them, although university presses, institutes of Latin American studies, and academic departments continued to play an important role as publishers. In the academic world, materials to support courses on Brazil were also being issued. Microfilming projects proliferated in the 1970s and have continued to the present, preserving U.S. government documents related to Brazil, as well as many Brazilian official publications, newspapers, and periodicals, and a variety of more specialized records and publications associated with Brazil, in a format that facilitated access to them in a way that print copies, available in a limited number of large libraries, could never do.

New technologies, which made possible on-line reference sources and CD-ROMs, came into general use in the 1990s and have already made some information much more accessible than previously. That trend will continue and accelerate. We can anticipate the ongoing expansion of electronic reference sources, although, like publications in print format, they can be expected to vary greatly in the depth of their coverage and in the quality of information provided.

Perhaps the greatest lacuna is contemporary biographical data in English for Brazilian political, academic, business, cultural, educational, and scientific leaders. A publication in a "who's who" format, incorporating succinct biographical notes for leaders in all fields of endeavor, updated on a regular basis, would be a valuable addition to the bibliography of reference sources about Brazil. A work identifying the many acronyms used in Brazil for organizations, institutions, and government agencies and programs would be another priority for development. Indeed, works of this type would be well suited to an on-line format, because of the need for regular updating. Information in English about Brazilian national and regional holidays, festivals, and customs would also be a welcome addition to reference sources about Brazil.

NOTES

1. The dictionary definition of "reference book"—a "book containing useful facts or specially organized information, as an encyclopedia, dictionary, atlas, yearbook, etc.," according to the *Random House Dictionary*—has been expanded for purposes of this essay to include bibliographies.

2. Complete bibliographic citations for all reference books cited in this essay are listed at the end under their section headings.

REFERENCES

BIBLIOGRAPHIES

Accessions List, Brazil. 1975–1988. Rio de Janeiro: Library of Congress Office, Brazil.

Accessions List, Brazil and Uruguay. 1989–1992. Vol. 15, no. 1–vol. 18, no. 6. Rio de Janeiro: Library of Congress Office.

Accessions List, Brazil and Uruguay: Cumulative List of Serials. 1989–1992. Rio de Janeiro: Library of Congress Office.

Accessions List, Brazil: Annual List of Serials. 1975–1988. Rio de Janeiro: Library of Congress Office.

Accessions List, Brazil: Cumulative List of Serials. 1975–1980. Rio de Janeiro: National Program for Acquisitions and Cataloging, Library of Congress Office.

Bibliographic Guide to Latin American Studies. 1978–. Vols. 1–. Boston: G. K. Hall.

Bryant, Solena. 1985. *Brazil.* World Bibliographical Series vol. 57. Santa Barbara, Calif.: Clio.

Conniff, Michael, and Fred Gillette Sturm. 1986? *Brazilian Studies: A Guide to the Humanities Literature.* Brazilian Curriculum Guide Specialized Bibliography. Albuquerque: Latin American Institute, University of New Mexico.

Dickenson, John P. 1997. *Brazil.* Rev. ed. World Bibliographical Series vol. 57. Santa Barbara, Calif.: Clio.

Gillett, Theresa, and Helen McIntyre. 1970. *Catalog of Luso-Brazilian Material in the University of New Mexico Libraries.* Metuchen, N.J.: Scarecrow.

Hahner, June Edith. 1984? *Women in Brazil: Problems and Perspectives.* Brazilian Curriculum Guide Specialized Bibliography. Albuquerque: Latin American Institute, University of New Mexico.

———. 1998. *Women in Brazil.* Brazilian Curriculum Guide Specialized Bibliography. Series II. Albuquerque: Latin American Institute, University of New Mexico.

Hallewell, Laurence. 1982. *Books in Brazil: A History of the Publishing Trade.* Metuchen, N.J.: Scarecrow.

———. 1985. *O livro no Brasil: sua história.* Rev. e atualizada. São Paulo: Editora da Universidade de São Paulo.

Handbook of Latin American Studies, no. 1–. 1935–. Austin: University of Texas Press. Available online at http://lcweb2.loc.gov/hlas/ (December 14, 2004).

HAPI: Hispanic American Periodicals Index. 1970/74–. Los Angeles: Latin American Center Publications, University of California. (Reference Series).

Harmon, Ronald M., and Bobby J. Chamberlain. 1975. *Brazil: A Working Bibliography in Literature, Linguistics, Humanities, and the Social Sciences.* Special Studies, no. 14. Tempe: Center for Latin American Studies, Arizona State University.

Hartness, Ann. 1991. *Brazil in Reference Books, 1965–1989: An Annotated Bibliography.* Metuchen, N.J.: Scarecrow.

Hispanic and Luso-Brazilian Councils. Canning House Library. 1967. *Canning House Library, Hispanic Council, London: Author Catalogue (and Subject Catalogue).* 4 vols. Boston: G. K. Hall.

———. 1973. *Canning House Library, Hispanic and Luso-Brazilian Councils, London: Author Catalog and Subject Catalog: Supplement.* 2 vols. Boston: G. K. Hall.

Levine, Robert M. 1984 or 1985. *Brazilian Reality through the Lens of Popular Culture.* Brazilian Curriculum Guide Specialized Bibliography. Albuquerque: Latin American Institute, University of New Mexico.

Library of Congress. 1977. *Catalog of Brazilian Acquisitions of the Library of Congress, 1964–1974* (Catálogo de aquisições brasileiras da Library of Congress, 1964–1974). Comp. William V. Jackson. Boston: G. K. Hall.

Moraes, Rubens Borba de. 1969. *Bibliografia brasileira do período colonial; catálogo comentado das obras dos autores nascidos no Brasil e publicadas antes de 1808.* São Paulo: Universidade de São Paulo, Instituto de Estudos Brasileiros.

———. 1983. *Bibliographia brasiliana: Rare Books About Brazil Published from 1504 to 1900 and Works by Brazilian Authors of the Colonial Period.* Reference Series, vol. 10. 2 vols. Rev. and enlarged ed. Los Angeles: Latin American Center Publications, University of California.

Muricy, Carmen M. 1991? *The Brazilian Amazon: Institutions and Publications.* Bibliography and Reference Series, 28. Albuquerque: SALALM Secretariat, General Library, University of New Mexico.

Newberry Library. 1970. *A Catalogue of the Greenlee Collection, the Newberry Library, Chicago.* 2 vols. Boston: G. K. Hall.

Oliveira Lima Library. 1970. *Catalog of the Oliveira Lima Library, the Catholic University of America.* 2 vols. Boston: G. K. Hall.

Phillips, Philip Lee. 1901. *A List of Books, Magazine Articles, and Maps Relating to Brazil, 1800–1900.* Washington, D.C.: GPO.

————. [1901]. 1970. *A List of Books, Magazine Articles, and Maps Relating to Brazil, 1800–1900.* Facsimile ed. Washington, D.C.: GPO.

Shelflist of the Brazilian Small Press Collection, University of New Mexico General Library. 1991. Intro. Todd Hollister and Russ Davidson. Albuquerque: General Library, University of New Mexico.

University of Texas. Library. Latin American Collection. 1969. *Catalog of the Latin American Collection.* 31 vols. (plus 16 supplemental vols.). Boston: G. K. Hall.

GENERAL WORKS

American University. Foreign Areas Studies Division. 1964. *U.S. Army Area Handbook for Brazil.* Washington, D.C.: GPO.

Brazil: A Country Study. Area Handbook Series. 1983. 4th ed. Washington, D.C.: U.S. Army.

Brazil: A Country Study. Area Handbook Series. 1998. Edited by Rex A. Hudson. 5th ed. Washington, D.C.: Federal Research Division, Library of Congress.

Collier, Simon, Thomas E. Skidmore, and Harold Blakemore, eds. 1985. *The Cambridge Encyclopedia of Latin America and the Caribbean.* Cambridge: Cambridge University Press.

————. 1992. *The Cambridge Encyclopedia of Latin America and the Caribbean.* 2nd ed. Cambridge: Cambridge University Press.

Delpar, Helen, ed. 1974. *Encyclopedia of Latin America.* New York: McGraw-Hill.

Levine, Robert M. 1966. *Brazil: Field Research Guide in the Social Sciences.* New York: Institute of Latin American Studies, Columbia University.

Statistical Abstract of Latin America. 1955–. Los Angeles: Committee on Latin American Studies, University of California. Annual.

Tenenbaum, Barbara A., ed. 1996. *Encyclopedia of Latin American History and Culture.* 5 vols. New York: Scribner's .

————. 1999. *Latin America, History and Culture: An Encyclopedia for Students.* 4 vols. New York: Scribner's.

Weil, Thomas E. 1971. *Area Handbook for Brazil.* Washington, D.C.: GPO.

————. 1975. *Area Handbook for Brazil.* 3rd ed. Washington, D.C.: GPO.

HISTORY AND GEOGRAPHY

Bethell, Leslie, ed. 1984–. *The Cambridge History of Latin America.* Cambridge: Cambridge University Press.

————. 1988. *Colonial Brazil.* Cambridge: Cambridge University Press.

————. 1989. *Brazil: Empire and Republic, 1822–1930.* Cambridge: Cambridge University Press.

Conrad, Robert Edgar. 1977. *Brazilian Slavery: An Annotated Research Bibliography.* Boston: G. K. Hall.

Cortes Conde, Roberto, and Stanley J. Stein, eds. 1977. *Latin America: A Guide to Economic History, 1830–1930.* Berkeley: University of California Press.

Dutra, Francis A. 1980. *A Guide to the History of Brazil, 1500–1822: The Literature in English.* Santa Barbara, Calif.: ABC-Clio.

Fitzgibbon, Russell Humke. 1974. *Brazil: A Chronology and Fact Book, 1488–1973.* Dobbs Ferry, N.Y.: Oceana.

French, John D., and Alexandre Fortes. 1998. *Urban Labor History in Twentieth Century Brazil.* Brazilian Curriculum Guide Specialized Bibliography. Series II. Albuquerque: Latin American Institute, University of New Mexico.

Goyer, Doreen S., and Elaine Domschke. 1983. *The Handbook of National Population Censuses: Latin America and the Caribbean, North America, and Oceania.* Westport, Colo.: Greenwood.

Griffin, Charles C. 1971. *Latin America: A Guide to the Historical Literature: A Selective Bibliography with Critical Annotations.* Austin: Published for the Conference on Latin American History by the University of Texas Press.

Hartness, Ann. 1977. *Subject Guide to Statistics in the Presidential Reports of the Brazilian Provinces, 1830–1889.* Austin: Institute of Latin American Studies, University of Texas.

Levine, Robert M. 1979. *Historical Dictionary of Brazil.* Metuchen, N.J.: Scarecrow.

———. 1980. *Brazil Since 1930: An Annotated Bibliography for Social Historians.* New York: Garland.

———. 1983. *Brazil, 1822–1930: An Annotated Bibliography for Social Historians.* New York: Garland.

Ludwig, Armin K. 1985. *Brazil: A Handbook of Historical Statistics.* Boston: G. K. Hall.

Martin, Michael Rheta, and Gabriel H. Lovett. 1956. *An Encyclopedia of Latin-American History.* New York: Abelard-Schuman.

———. 1968. *Encyclopedia of Latin-American History.* Rev. ed. by L. Robert Hughes. Indianapolis, Ind.: Bobbs-Merrill.

Merrick, Thomas William. 1984. *The Demographic History of Brazil.* Brazilian Curriculum Guide Specialized Bibliography. Albuquerque: Latin American Institute, University of New Mexico.

Palmerlee, Albert Earl. 1962. *A Portuguese-English Glossary of Map Terms.* Lawrence: Department of Geography, University of Kansas.

———. 1968. *A Glossary of Portuguese & Brazilian Map Terms & Abbreviations.* Cleveland: MicroPhoto Division, Bell and Howell.

U.S. Board on Geographic Names. 1992. *Supplement to Brazil Gazetteer: Names Approved by the United States Board on Geographic Names.* Washington, D.C.: Defense Mapping Agency.

U.S. Office of Geography. 1963. *Brazil: Official Standard Names Approved by the United States Board on Geographic Names.* Gazetteer no. 71. Washington, D.C.

Young, Jordan M. 1972. *Brazil, 1954–64: End of a Civilian Cycle.* New York: Facts on File.

POLITICAL SCIENCE AND LAW

Alexander, Robert J., ed. 1982. *Political Parties of the Americas: Canada, Latin America, and the West Indies,* vol. 1. Westport, Conn.: Greenwood.

———. 1988. *The Biographical Dictionary of Latin American and Caribbean Political Leaders.* New York: Greenwood.

Ameringer, Charles D., ed. 1992. *Political Parties of the Americas, 1980s to 1990s: Canada, Latin America, and the West Indies.* Westport, Conn.: Greenwood.

Bibliographical Notes for Understanding the Brazilian Model: Political Repression and Economic Expansion. 1974. Washington, D.C.: CoDoC International Secretariat.

Borchard, Edwin Montefiore. 1917. *Guide to the Law and Legal Literature of Argentina, Brazil and Chile.* Washington, D.C.: GPO.

Chilcote, Ronald H. 1980. *Brazil and Its Radical Left: An Annotated Bibliography on the Communist Movement and the Rise of Marxism, 1922–1972.* Millwood, N.Y.: Kraus International.

Coggins, John, and D. S. Lewis. 1982. *Political Parties of the Americas and the Caribbean: A Reference Guide.* Harlow, Essex, U.K.: Longman.

Degenhardt, Henry W., ed. 1983. *Political Dissent: An International Guide to Dissident, Extra-Parliamentary, Guerrilla, and Illegal Political Movements.* Detroit: Gale Research.

———. 1988. *Revolutionary and Dissident Movements: An International Guide.* 2nd ed., rev. and updated. Harlow, Essex, U.K.: Longman.

De Noia, John. 1948. *Brazil: A Guide to the Official Publications.* Guide to the Official Publications of the Other American Republics, vol. 3. Latin American Series, no. 35. Washington, D.C.: Library of Congress.

Evans, Peter, Elida Rubini Liedke, and Enno D. Liedke Filho. 1984. *The Political Economy of Contemporary Brazil: A Study Guide.* Brazilian Curriculum Guide Specialized Bibliography. Albuquerque: Latin American Institute, University of New Mexico.

Guide to Official Publications of Foreign Countries. 1997. 2nd ed. Bethesda, Md.: CIS.

Hagopian, Frances. 1990. "Brazil." In *Handbook of Political Science Research on Latin America: Trends from the 1960s to the 1990s,* ed. David W. Dent. New York: Greenwood.

Index to Latin American Legislation, 1950–1960. 1961. 3 supplements, each in 2 vols.: 1961–65, 1966–70, and 1971–75. Compiled in the Hispanic Law Division, Law Library, Library of Congress. Boston: G. K. Hall.

Latin American Politics: A Historical Bibliography. 1984. Santa Barbara, Calif.: ABC-Clio,

Legal Codes of the Latin American Republics. 1942. Latin American Series, no. 1. Washington, D.C.: Library of Congress.

Lombardi, Mary. 1974. *Brazilian Serial Documents: A Selective and Annotated Guide.* Bloomington: Indiana University Press.

Mesa, Rosa Quintero. 1968. *Brazil.* Latin American Serial Documents, vol. 2. Ann Arbor, Mich.: University Microfilms.

O'Maolain, Ciaran, ed. 1985. *Latin American Political Movements,* ed. New York: Facts on File.

Radu, Michael, and Vladimir Tismaneanu, eds. 1990. *Latin American Revolutionaries: Groups, Goals, Methods.* Washington, D.C.: Pergamon-Brassey's International Defense Publishers.Sousa, Amaury. 1966. *Annotated Bibliography of the Brazilian Political Movement of 1964.* Riverside: Latin American Research Program, University of California.

ETHNOLOGY

Andrews, George Reid. 1997. *Slavery and Race Relations in Brazil.* Brazilian Curriculum Guide Specialized Bibliography. Series II. Albuquerque: Latin American Institute, University of New Mexico.

Hasenbalg, Carlos Alfredo. 1984?. *Race Relations in Modern Brazil.* Brazilian Curriculum Guide Specialized Bibliography. Albuquerque: Latin American Institute, University of New Mexico.

Levine, Robert M. 1980. *Race and Ethnic Relations in Latin America and the Caribbean: An Historical Dictionary and Bibliography.* Metuchen, N.J.: Scarecrow.

Nuñez, Benjamin. 1980. *Dictionary of Afro-Latin American Civilization.* Westport, Conn.: Greenwood.

Oliver, Eileen C. 1998. *Afro-Brazilian Religions: A Selective Annotated Bibliography, 1990–1997.* Austin, Tex.: SALALM Secretariat.

Porter, Dorothy B. 1978. *Afro-Braziliana: A Working Bibliography.* Boston: G. K. Hall.

Stephens, Thomas M. 1999. *Dictionary of Latin American Racial and Ethnic Terminology.* 2nd ed. Gainesville: University Press of Florida.

Steward, Julian Haynes, ed. 1963. *Handbook of South American Indians.* 7 vols. New York: Cooper Square.

LITERATURE AND LANGUAGE

Literature

De Jong, Gerrit. 1969. *Four Hundred Years of Brazilian Literature: Outline and Anthology.* Provo, Utah: Brigham Young University Press.

Ford, J. D. M., Arthur F. Whittem, and Maxwell I. Raphael. 1931. *A Tentative Bibliography of Brazilian Belles-lettres.* Cambridge, Mass.: Harvard University Press.

Forster, Merlin H., and K. David Jackson, eds. 1990. *Vanguardism in Latin American Literature: An Annotated Bibliographical Guide.* New York: Greenwood.

Foster, David William, and Roberto Reis. 1981. *A Dictionary of Contemporary Brazilian Authors.* Tempe: Center for Latin American Studies, Arizona State University.

Foster, David William, and Walter Rela. 1990. *Brazilian Literature: A Research Bibliography*. New York: Garland.

Hallewell, Laurence, and Cavan McCarthy. 1987. "Bibliography of Brazilian Chapbook Literature." In *Latin American Masses and Minorities: Their Images and Realities: Papers of the Thirtieth Annual Meeting of the Seminar on the Acquisition of Latin American Library Materials, Princeton University, 1985*, vol. 2, ed. Dan C. Hazen. Madison: SALALM Secretariat, University of Wisconsin.

———. 1987. "Brazilian Chapbook Literature." In *Latin American Masses and Minorities: Their Images and Realities: Papers of the Thirtieth Annual Meeting of the Seminar on the Acquisition of Latin American Library Materials, Princeton University, 1985*, vol. 1, ed. Dan C. Hazen. Madison: SALALM Secretariat, University of Wisconsin.

Hulet, Claude L. 1974–75. *Brazilian Literature*. 3 vols. Washington, D.C.: Georgetown University Press.

Modern Language Association. 1970–. *MLA International Bibliography of Books and Articles on the Modern Languages and Literatures*. Library ed. New York: Modern Language Association of America.

Placer, Xavier. 1972. *Modernismo brasileiro: bibliografia, 1918–1971*. Rio de Janeiro: Biblioteca Nacional, Divisão de Publicações e Divulgação (Coleção Rodolfo Garcia. Série B, Catálogos e bibliografias.)

Solé, Carlos, ed. 1989. *Latin American Writers*. 3 vols. New York: Scribner's.

Stern, Irwin, ed. 1988. *Dictionary of Brazilian Literature*. New York: Greenwood.

Tolman, John, and Ricardo Paiva. 1986? *Brazilian Literature and Language Outlines*. Brazilian Curriculum Guide Specialized Bibliography. Albuquerque: Latin American Institute, University of New Mexico.

Topete, José Manuel. 1957. *A Working Bibliography of Brazilian Literature*. Gainesville: University of Florida Press.

Language

Chamberlain, Bobby J. 1989. *Portuguese Language and Luso-Brazilian Literature: An Annotated Guide to Selected Reference Works*. New York: Modern Language Association of America.

———, ed. 1991. *The Random House Portuguese Dictionary: Portuguese-English, English-Portuguese, Português-Inglês, Inglês-Português*. New York: Random House.

Chamberlain, Bobby J., and Ronald M. Harmon. 1983. *A Dictionary of Informal Brazilian Portuguese with English Index*. Washington, D.C.: Georgetown University Press.

Grimes, Barbara F., ed. 2000. *Ethnologue: Languages of the World*. 14th ed. 2 vols. Dallas: SIL International. Available online at www.ethnologue.com (December 14, 2004).

Houaiss, Antônio, and Catherine B. Avery, eds. 1993. *Dicionário brasileiro*. 2 vols. Englewood Cliffs, N.J.: Prentice-Hall.

Taylor, James L. 1958. *A Portuguese-English Dictionary*. Stanford, Calif.: Stanford University Press.

ART AND ARCHITECTURE

Bailey, Joyce Waddell, ed. 1984–86. *Handbook of Latin American Art (Manual de arte latinoamericano: A bibliographic compilation)*. Volume/regional editor—Brazil, Aracy Abreu Amaral. 3 vols. Santa Barbara, Calif.: ABC-Clio.

Braun, Barbara, ed. 1995. *Arts of the Amazon*. Text by Peter G. Roe. New York: Thames and Hudson.

De Fiore, Ottaviano C. 1985. *Architecture and Sculpture in Brazil*. Brazilian Curriculum Guide Specialized Bibliography. Albuquerque: Latin American Institute, University of New Mexico.

Neistein, Jose. 1997. *A arte no Brasil: dos primórdios ao século vinte, uma bibliografia seleta, anotada (Art in Brazil from Its Beginnings to Modern Times: A Selected, Annotated Bibliography)*. Washington, D.C.: Brazilian-American Cultural Institute.

Rego, Stella de Sá, and Marguerite Itamar Harrison. 1986. *Modern Brazilian Painting*. Brazilian Curriculum Guide Specialized Bibliography. Albuquerque: Latin American Institute, University of New Mexico.

———. 1997. *Modern Brazilian Painting*. Brazilian Curriculum Guide Specialized Bibliography. Series II. 2nd ed. Albuquerque: Latin American Institute, University of New Mexico.

Rodman, Selden. 1977. *Genius in the Backlands: Popular Artists of Brazil*. Old Greenwich, Conn.: Devin-Adair.

Smith, Robert Chester, and Elizabeth Wilder, eds. 1948. *A Guide to the Art of Latin America*. Library of Congress, Latin American Series no. 21. Washington, D.C.: GPO.

Turner, Jane, ed. 1996. *The Dictionary of Art*. 34 vols. New York: Grove's Dictionaries.

———. 2000. *Encyclopedia of Latin American & Caribbean Art*. New York: Grove's Dictionaries.

MUSIC

Appleby, David P. 1983. *The Music of Brazil*. Austin: University of Texas Press.

———. 1988. *Heitor Villa-Lobos: A Bio-Bibliography*. New York: Greenwood.

Béhague, Gerard. 1979. *Music in Latin America: An Introduction*. Englewood Cliffs, N.J.: Prentice-Hall.

Coelho, Tadeu. 1998. *Brazilian Classical Music*. Brazilian Curriculum Guide Specialized Bibliography. Series II. Albuquerque: Latin American Institute, University of New Mexico.

Luper, Albert T. 1943. *The Music of Brazil*. Music Series, no. 9. Washington, D.C.: Music Division, Pan-American Union.

McGowan, Chris, and Ricardo Pessanha. 1991. *The Brazilian Sound: Samba, Bossa Nova, and the Popular Music of Brazil*. New York: Billboard.

————. 1998. *The Brazilian Sound: Samba, Bossa Nova, and the Popular Music of Brazil.* New ed. Philadelphia: Temple University Press.

Perrone, Charles A., and Larry N. Crook. 1997. *Folk and Popular Music of Brazil.* Brazilian Curriculum Guide Specialized Bibliography. Series II. Albuquerque: Latin American Institute, University of New Mexico.

Rego, Enylton José de Sá, and Charles A. Perrone. 1985. *MPB: Contemporary Brazilian Popular Music.* Brazilian Curriculum Guide Specialized Bibliography. Albuquerque: Latin American Institute, University of New Mexico.

Schoenbach, Peter J. 1984? *Classical Music of Brazil.* Brazilian Curriculum Guide Specialized Bibliography. Albuquerque: Latin American Institute, University of New Mexico.

Slonimsky, Nicolas. [1945] 1972. *Music of Latin America.* New York: T. Y. Crowell. Reprint, with a new foreword and addenda by the author. New York: Da Capo.

DOCUMENTARY SOURCES

U.S. Department of State

U.S. Department of State. 1963. *Records of the Department of State Relating to Internal Affairs of Brazil, 1910–29.* Washington, D.C.: National Archives and Records Service, General Services Administration. 54 microfilm reels.

————. 1963. *Records of the Department of State Relating to Political Relations Between Brazil and Other States, 1910–29.* Washington, D.C.: National Archives, National Archives and Records Service, General Services Administration. 2 microfilm reels.

————. 1986. *Records of the Department of State Relating to Internal Affairs of Brazil, 1930–39.* Washington, D.C.: National Archives and Records Administration. 48 microfilm reels.

————. 1986. *Records of the Department of State Relating to Internal Political and National Defense Affairs of Brazil, 1950–1954.* Washington, D.C.: National Archives and Records Administration. 14 microfilm reels.

————. 1987. *Records of the Department of State Relating to Internal Affairs of Brazil, 1940–1944.* Washington, D.C.: National Archives and Records Administration. 84 microfilm reels.

————. 1987. *Records of the Department of State Relating to Internal Affairs of Brazil, 1945–1949.* Washington, D.C.: National Archives and Records Administration. 48 microfilm reels.

————. 1987. *Records of the Department of State Relating to Internal Political and National Defense Affairs of Brazil, 1955–1959.* Washington, D.C.: National Archives and Records Administration. 8 microfilm reels.

————. 2001. *Records of the U.S. Department of State Relating to Internal Affairs of Brazil, 1960–1963.* Wilmington: Scholarly Resources. 21 microform reels.

————. Consulate (Belem, Brazil). 1960. *Despatches from United States Consuls in*

Pará, 1831–1906. Washington, D.C.: National Archives, National Archives and Records Service, General Services Administration. 9 microfilm reels.

———. Consulate (Recife, Brazil). 1960–62. *Despatches from United States Consuls in Pernambuco, 1817–1906*. Washington, D.C.: National Archives, National Archives and Records Service, General Services Administration. 17 microfilm reels.

———. Consulate (Rio Grande do Sul, Brazil). 1957. *Despatches from United States Consuls in Rio Grande do Sul, 1829–1897*. Washington, D.C.: National Archives, National Archives and Records Service, General Services Administration. 7 microfilm reels.

———. Consulate (Salvador, Brazil). 1960. *Despatches from United States Consuls in St. Salvador, 1808–1849*. Washington, D.C.: National Archives, National Archives and Records Service, General Services Administration. 4 microfilm reels.

———. Consulate (Salvador, Brazil). 1959–61. *Despatches from United States Consuls in Bahia, 1850–1906*. Washington, D.C.: National Archives, National Archives and Records Service, General Services Administration. 8 microfilm reels.

———. Consulate (Santa Catarina, Brazil). 1962. *Despatches from United States Consuls in Santa Catarina (St. Catherine), 1831–50*. Washington, D.C.: National Archives, National Archives and Records Service, General Services Administration. 2 microfilm reels.

———. Consulate (Santos, São Paulo, Brazil). 1959–62. *Despatches from United States Consuls in Santos, 1831–1906*. Washington, D.C.: National Archives, National Archives and Records Service, General Services Administration. 6 microfilm reels.

———. Consulate (São Luís do Maranho, Brazil). 1960. *Despatches from United States Consuls in Maranham, 1817–1876*. Washington, D.C.: National Archives, National Archives and Records Service, General Services Administration. 3 microfilm reels.

———. Consulate General (Rio de Janeiro, Brazil). 1959. *Despatches from United States Consuls in Rio de Janeiro, 1811–1906*. Washington, D.C.: National Archives, National Archives and Records Service, General Services Administration. 33 microfilm reels.

———. Embassy in Brazil. 1943–51. *Notes from the Brazilian Legation in the United States to the Department of State, 1824–1906*. Washington, D.C.: National Archives. 8 microfilm reels.

———. Embassy in Brazil. 1947–51. *Despatches from United States Ministers to Brazil, April 3, 1809–August 10, 1906*. Washington, D.C.: National Archives. 74 microfilm reels.

Library of Congress

Brazil's Popular Groups, 1966–1986. 1988. Washington, D.C.: Library of Congress Photoduplication Service. 32 microfilm reels.

————. 1991. *Supplement, 1987–1989*. Washington, D.C.: Library of Congress Photoduplication Service. 43 microfilm reels.

————. 1994. *Supplement 2, 1990–1992*. Washington, D.C.: Library of Congress Photoduplication Service. 70 microfilm reels.

————. 1995. *Supplement 3, 1993*. Washington, D.C.: Library of Congress Photoduplication Service. 32 microfilm reels.

————. 1995. *Supplement 4, 1994*. Washington, D.C.: Library of Congress Photoduplication Service. 18 microfilm reels.

————. 1996. *Supplement 5, 1995*. Washington, D.C.: Library of Congress Photoduplication Service. 28 microfilm reels.

————. 1998. *Supplement 6, 1996*. Washington, D.C.: Library of Congress Photoduplication Service. 24 microfilm reels.

————. 1998. *Supplement 7, 1997*. Washington, D.C.: Library of Congress Photoduplication Service. 26 microfilm reels.

————. 2000. *Supplement 8, 1998*. Washington, D.C.: Library of Congress Photoduplication Service. 23 microfilm reels.

————. 2000. *Supplement 9, 1999*. Washington, D.C.: Library of Congress Photoduplication Service. 18 microfilm reels.

————. 2001. *Supplement 10, 2000*. Washington, D.C.: Library of Congress Photoduplication Service. 18 microfilm reels.

————. 2003. *Supplement 11, 2001*. Washington, D.C.: Library of Congress Photoduplication Service. 15 microfilm reels.

————. 2004? *Supplement 12, 2002*. Washington, D.C.: Library of Congress Photoduplication Service. 17 microfilm reels.

————. 2004. *Supplement 13, 2003*. Washington, D.C.: Library of Congress Photoduplication Service. 18 microfilm reels.

Brazil's Popular Groups: Blacks. 1994–. Washington, D.C.: Library of Congress Photoduplication Service.

Brazil's Popular Groups: Homosexual and Bisexual. 1994–. Washington, D.C.: Library of Congress Photoduplication Service.

Brazil's Popular Groups: Women. 1988–. Washington, D.C.: Library of Congress Photoduplication Service.

MISCELLANEOUS

Brazil. 1823–1969. *Diário oficial*. Washington, D.C.: Library of Congress Preservation Microfilming Program.

Methodist Episcopal Church Board Correspondence, 1884–1915. 1999?–. Rolls 78–86 (Latin America). Wilmington, Del.: Scholarly Resources. 9 microfilm reels.

Methodist Episcopal Church Board Missionary Correspondence, 1846–1912. 1999?–. Rolls 22, 23, 25–28 (South America). Wilmington, Del.: Scholarly Resources. 6 microfilm reels.

Missionary Files: MECS, 1897–1940. 1999?–. Wilmington, Del.: Scholarly Resources. 13 microfilm reels.

Missionary Files. 2001? Rolls 24–35, Misfiles, Latin America: Methodist Episcopal Church, 1912–1949. Wilmington, Del.: Scholarly Resources. 12 microfilm reels.

O Estado de São Paulo. 1890–. Washington, D.C.: Library of Congress. Microfilm.

Presbyterian Board of Foreign Missions, 1833–1911. 1956?–. Rolls 78–86 (Latin America). Wilmington, Dell.: Scholarly Resources. Microfilm.

Princeton University Library Latin American Microfilm Collection. Princeton, N. J.: Photographic Services, Princeton University Library. 62 microfilm reels.

A Província de São Paulo. 1875–1889. Washington, D.C.: Library of Congress. 15 microfilm reels.

U.S. Navy. 1951. *Letters Received by the Secretary of the Navy from Commanding Officers of Squadrons, 1841–1886: Brazil Squadron, 1841–1861.* Washington, D.C.: National Archives and Records Service. 17 microfilm reels.

CHAPTER 17

~

Selective Bibliography
and Chronology

PAULO ROBERTO DE ALMEIDA

Note: This bibliography, mainly concerned with well-known works in the social sciences, contains journal articles and essays compiled in edited collections (chapters on Brazil often appear in general works on Latin America), theses, or dissertations; some entries refer to Brazilian original editions or translations, when relevant to the bilateral relations or important in the context of further academic work in the United States.

Alden, Dauril. 1968. *Royal Government in Colonial Brazil with special reference to the Administration of the Marquis of Lavradio, Viceroy, 1769–1779.* Berkeley: University of California Press.

———. 2001. *Charles R. Boxer: An Uncommon Life, Soldier, Historian, Teacher, Collector, Traveller.* Portugal: Fundação Oriente.

———, ed. 1973. *Colonial Roots of Modern Brazil.* Berkeley: University of California Press.

Alexander, Robert J. 1957. *Communism in Latin America.* New Brunswick, N.J.: Rutgers University Press.

———. 1962. *Labor Relations in Argentina, Brazil, and Chile.* New York: McGraw-Hill.

———. 1965. *Latin-American Politics and Government.* New York: Harper and Row.

Almeida, Paulo R. 1998. *Relações internacionais e política externa do Brasil: dos descobrimentos à globalização.* Porto Alegre: Editora da UFRGS.

———. 1999. *O Brasil e o multilateralismo econômico.* Porto Alegre: Livraria do Advogado.

———. 1999. *O estudo das relações internacionais do Brasil.* São Paulo: Unimarco.

———. 2001. *Formação da diplomacia econômica no Brasil: as relações econômicas internacionais no Império.* São Paulo: Senac.

————. 2002. *Os primeiros anos do século XXI: o Brasil e as relações internacionais contemporâneas*. São Paulo: Paz e Terra.

Alvarez, Sonia E. 1990. *Engendering Democracy in Brazil: Women's Movement in Transition Politics*. Princeton, N.J.: Princeton University Press.

Alves, Maria Helena Moreira. 1985. *State and Opposition in Military Brazil*. Austin: University of Texas Press.

Ames, Barry. 1973. *Rhetoric and Reality in a Militarized Regime: Brazil Since 1964*. Beverly Hills, Calif.: Sage.

————. 2001. *The Deadlock of Democracy in Brazil*. Ann Arbor: University of Michigan Press.

Anderson, Robin L. 1999. *Colonization as Exploitation in the Amazon Rain Forest, 1758–1911*. Gainesville: University Press of Florida.

Andrews, George Reid. 1991. *Blacks and Whites in São Paulo, 1888–1988*. Madison: University of Wisconsin Press.

Appleby, David P. 1983. *The Music of Brazil*. Austin: University of Texas Press.

Armitage, John. 1836. *The History of Brazil from the Period of the Arrival of the Bragança Family in 1808 to the Abdication of Dom Pedro the First in 1831*. 2 vols. London: Smith, Elder.

Astiz, Carlos A., ed. 1969. *Latin American International Politics: Ambitions, Capabilities and the National Interests of Mexico, Brazil and Argentina*. Notre Dame, Ind.: University of Notre Dame Press.

Atkins, G. Pope. 1977. *Latin America in the International System*. New York: Free Press.

————. 1995. *Latin America in the International Political System*. 3rd ed. Boulder, Colo.: Westview.

Azevedo, Fernando de. 1950. *Brazilian Culture*. Trans. William Rex Crawford. New York: Macmillan.

Baer, Werner. 1965. *Industrialization and Economic Development in Brazil*. Homewood, Ill.: Richard D. Irwin.

————. 1969. *The Development of the Brazilian Steel Industry*. Nashville, Tenn.: Vanderbilt University Press.

————. 1990. *The Political Economy of Brazil*. Austin: University of Texas Press.

————. 1996. *A economia brasileira*. São Paulo: Nobel.

————. 2001. *The Brazilian Economy: Growth and Development*. 5th ed. Westport, Conn.: Praeger.

Baklanoff, Eric, ed. 1966. *New Perspectives of Brazil*. Nashville, Tenn.: Vanderbilt University Press.

————, ed. 1969. *The Shaping of Modern Brazil*. Baton Rouge: Louisiana State University Press.

Bandeira, Manuel. 1958. *Brief History of Brazilian Literature*. Trans. Ralph Edward Dimmick. Washington, D.C.: Pan-American Union.

Barbosa, Rubens A. 1991. *América Latina em perspectiva*. São Paulo: Aduaneiras.

Barbosa, Rubens A., Marshall C. Eakin, and Paulo Roberto de Almeida. orgs. 2002. *O Brasil dos brasilianistas: um guia dos estudos sobre o Brasil nos EUA, 1945–2002.* São Paulo: Editora Paz e Terra.

Barickman, B. J. 1998. *A Bahian Counterpoint: Sugar, Tobacco, Cassava, and Slavery in the Recôncavo, 1780–1860.* Stanford, Calif.: Stanford University Press.

Barman, Roderick J. 1988. *Brazil: The Forging of a Nation, 1798–1852.* Stanford, Calif.: Stanford University Press.

———. 1999. *Citizen Emperor: Pedro II and the Making of Brazil, 1825–1891.* Stanford, Calif.: Stanford University Press.

———. 2001. *Princess Isabel of Brazil: Gender and Power in the Nineteenth Century.* Wilmington, Del.: SR Books.

Bastide, Roger. 1978. *The African Religions of Brazil: Toward a Sociology of the Interpenetration of Civilizations.* Trans. Helen Sabba. Baltimore: Johns Hopkins University Press.

Beattie, Peter M. 2001. *The Tribute of Blood: Army, Honor, Race, and Nation in Brazil, 1864–1945.* Durham, N.C.: Duke University Press.

Becker, Bertha K., and Cláudio A. G. Egler. 1992. *Brazil: A New Regional Power in the World Economy.* Cambridge: Cambridge University Press. Brazilian edition: *Brasil: uma nova potência regional na economia-mundo.* Rio de Janeiro: Bertrand Brasil, 1993.

Bello, José Maria. 1966. *A History of Modern Brazil, 1889–1964.* Trans. James Taylor, with a new concluding chapter by Rollie E. Poppino. Stanford, Calif.: Stanford University Press.

Bergsman, J. 1970. *Brazil-Industrialization and Trade Policies.* Oxford: Oxford University Press.

Besse, Susan K. 1996. *Restructuring Patriarchy: The Modernization of Gender Inequality in Brazil, 1914–1940.* Chapel Hill: University of North Carolina Press.

Bethell, Leslie. 1970. *The Abolition of the Brazilian Slave Trade: Britain, Brazil and the Slave Trade Question, 1807–1869.* Cambridge: Cambridge University Press. Brazilian edition: *Abolição do tráfico de escravos no Brasil: a Grã Bretanha, o Brasil e a questão do tráfico de escravos, 1807–1869.* Trans. Vera Nunes Neves Pedroso. Rio de Janeiro: Expressão e Cultura, 1976.

———, ed. 1984–96. *The Cambridge History of Latin America.* 12 vols. Cambridge: Cambridge University Press. (Many chapters on Brazil written by American Brazilianists)

———, ed. 1987. *Colonial Brazil,* selection of essays from vols. 1 and 2 of *The Cambridge History of Latin America.* Cambridge: Cambridge University Press.

———, ed. 1989. *Brazil, Empire and Republic, 1822–1930,* selection of essays from vols. 3 and 5 of *The Cambridge History of Latin America.* Cambridge: Cambridge University Press.

Bieber, Judy. 1999. *Power, Patronage, and Political Violence: State Building on a Brazilian Frontier, 1822–1889.* Lincoln: University of Nebraska Press.

————. 2001. *History of Brazil*. Brazilian Curriculum Guide Specialized Bibliography, Series II. Albuquerque: Latin American and Iberian Institute, University of New Mexico.

Bishop, Elizabeth. 1962. *Brazil*. New York: Time.

Black, Jan Knippers. 1977. *United States Penetration of Brazil*. Philadelphia: University of Pennsylvania Press.

Bom Meihy, José Carlos Sebe. 1984. *Introdução ao nacionalismo acadêmico: os brasilianistas*. São Paulo: Brasiliense.

————. 1990. *A Colônia brasilianista: história oral da vida acadêmica*. São Paulo: Nova Estella Editorial.

Borges, Dain E. 1992. *The Family in Bahia, Brazil, 1870–1945*. Stanford, Calif.: Stanford University Press.

Boxer, Charles R. 1952. *Salvador de Sá and the Struggle for Brazil and Angola, 1602–1686*. London: University of London.

————. 1957. *The Dutch in Brazil, 1624–1654*. Oxford: Clarendon.

————. 1962. *The Golden Age of Brazil, 1695–1750: Growing Pains of a Colonial Society*. Berkeley: University of California Press. Brazilian edition: *A idade de ouro do Brasil: dores de crescimento de uma sociedade colonial*. 2nd. ed. rev. São Paulo: Companhia Editôra Nacional, 1969.

————. 1965. *Portuguese Society in the Tropics: The Municipal Councils of Goa, Macao, Bahia and Luanda, 1510–1800*. Madison: University of Wisconsin Press.

————. 1967. *Some Literary Sources for the History of Brazil in the Eighteenth Century*. London: Oxford University Press.

————. 1969. *The Portuguese Seaborne Empire, 1415–1825*. New York: Alfred A. Knopf.

Brown, Rose. 1945. *American Emperor: Dom Pedro II of Brazil*. New York: Viking.

Bruneau, Thomas C. 1974. *The Political Transformation of the Brazilian Catholic Church*. London: Cambridge University Press. Brazilian edition: *Católicismo brasileiro em época de transição*. São Paulo: Loyola, 1974.

Bulmer-Thomas, Victor. 1993. *The Economic History of Latin America Since Independence*. New York: Cambridge University Press.

Burns, E. Bradford. 1966. *The Unwritten Alliance: Rio Branco and Brazilian-American Relations*. New York: Columbia University Press.

————. 1968. *Nationalism in Brazil: A Historical Survey*. New York: Praeger.

————. 1970. *A History of Brazil*. New York: Columbia University Press.

————. 1980. *The Poverty of Progress: Latin America in the Nineteenth Century*. Berkeley: University of California Press.

————, ed. 1966. *A Documentary History of Brazil*. New York: Alfred A. Knopf.

————, ed. 1967. *Perspectives on Brazilian History*. New York: Columbia University Press.

Butler, Kim D. 1998. *Freedoms Given, Freedoms Won: Afro-Brazilians in Post-Abolition São Paulo and Salvador*. New Brunswick, N.J.: Rutgers University Press.

Calogeras, João Pandiá. 1963. *A History of Brazil.* Trans. Percy Alvin Martin. New York: Russell and Russell. Original edition: *Formação Histórica do Brasil.* Rio de Janeiro: P. de Mello, 1930.

Capistrano de Abreu, João. 1997. *Chapters in Brazil's Colonial History, 1500–1800.* Trans. Arthur Brakel. New York: Oxford University Press.

Cardoso, Fernando Henrique. 1969. *Sociologie du développement en Amérique latine.* Paris: Éditions Anthropos.

———. 1971. *Politique et développement dans les sociétés dépendantes.* Trans. Mylène Berdoyes. Paris: Éditions Anthropos.

———. 1973. *Dependency Revisited.* Austin: Institute of Latin American Studies, University of Texas.

———. 1977. *The Originality of the Copy: ECLA and the Idea of Development.* Cambridge: Centre of Latin American Studies, University of Cambridge.

———. 1978. *On the Characterisation of Authoritarian Regimes in Latin America.* Cambridge: Centre of Latin American Studies, University of Cambridge.

———. 1979. *Development Under Fire.* Buenos Aires: Centro de Economía Transnacional, Instituto para América Latina.

———. 2001. *Charting a New Course: The Politics of Globalization and Social Transformation.* Ed. Mauricio Font. Lanham, Md.: Rowman and Littlefield.

Cardoso, Fernando Henrique, and Enzo Faletto. 1979. *Dependency and Development in Latin America.* Trans. Marjory Mattingly Urquidi. Berkeley: University of California Press.

Castro, Josué de. 1966. *Death in Northeast.* New York: Random House. Original edition: *Sete palmos de terra e um caixão; ensaio sôbre o Nordeste, área explosiva.* São Paulo, Editora Brasiliense, 1965.

Chandler, Billy Jaynes. 1972. *The Feitosas and the Sertão dos Inhamuns: The History of a Family and a Community in Northeast Brazil, 1700–1930.* Gainesville: University of Florida Press. Brazilian edition: *Os Feitosas e o sertão dos Inhamuns: a história de uma família e de uma comunidade do Nordeste do Brasil, 1700–1930.* Rio de Janeiro–Fortaleza: Civilização Brasileira–Universidade Federal do Ceará, 1980.

———. 1978. *The Bandit King: Lampião of Brazil.* College Station: Texas A&M University Press. Brazilian edition: *Lampião, o rei dos cangaceiros.* Rio de Janeiro: Paz e Terra, 1 981.

Chernela, Janet. 1993. *The Wanano Indians of the Brazilian Amazon: A Sense of Space.* Austin: University of Texas Press.

Chilcote, Ronald. H. 1974. *The Brazilian Communist Party: Conflict and Integration, 1922–1972.* New York: Oxford University Press. Brazilian edition: *O Partido Comunista Brasileiro: conflito e integração, 1922–1972.* Rio de Janeiro: Graal, 1982.

———. 1980. *Brazil and Its Radical Left: An Annotated Bibliography on the Communist Movement and the Rise of Marxism, 1922–1972.* Millwood, N.Y.: Kraus International.

————. 1990. *Power and the Ruling Classes in Northeast Brazil: Juazeiro and Petrolina in Transition*. Cambridge: Cambridge University Press.

Clements, Benedict J. 1988. *Trade Strategies, Employment and Income Distribution in Brazil*. New York: Praeger.

Cline, Howard Francis, comp. and ed. 1967. *Latin American History: Essays on Its Study and Teaching, 1898–1965*. 2 vols. Austin: Conference on Latin American History, University of Texas Press.

Cline, William. 1987. *Informatics and Development: Trade and Industrial Policy in Argentina, Brazil and Mexico*. Washington, D.C.: Economics International.

Cobbs, Elizabeth A. 1992. *The Rich Neighbor Policy: Rockefeller and Kaiser in Brazil*. New Haven, Conn.: Yale University Press.

Cohen, Thomas M. 1998. *The Fire of Tongues: António Vieira and the Missionary Church in Brazil and Portugal*. Stanford, Calif.: Stanford University Press.

Coes, Donald V., Jorge Garcia, and Julie J. Nogues. 1991. *Liberalizing Foreign Trade: Brazil, Colombia and Peru*. Oxford: Blackwell.

Colby, Gerard, and Charlotte Dennett. 1995. *Thy Will Be Done: The Conquest of the Amazon: Nelson Rockefeller and Evangelism in the Age of Oil*. New York: HarperCollins. Brazilian edition: *Seja feita a vossa vontade: a conquista da Amazônia: Nelson Rockefeller e o evangelismo na idade do petróleo*. Trans. Jamari França. Rio de Janeiro: Record, 1998.

Collier, Richard. 1968. *The River That God Forgot: The Story of the Amazon Rubber Boom*. New York: E. P. Dutton.

Conniff, Michael L. *Urban Politics in Brazil: The Rise of Populism, 1925–1945*. Pittsburgh: University of Pittsburgh Press.

Conniff, Michael L., and Frank D. McCann Jr., eds. 1989. *Modern Brazil: Elites and Masses in Historical Perspective*. Lincoln: University of Nebraska Press.

Conrad, Robert E. 1972. *The Destruction of Brazilian Slavery, 1850–1888*. Berkeley: University of California Press. Brazilian edition: *Os últimos anos da escravatura no Brasil, 1850–1888*. Rio de Janeiro: Civilização Brasileira, 1975.

————. 1986. *World of Sorrow: The African Slave Trade to Brazil*. Baton Rouge: Louisiana State University Press.

————, ed. 1983. *Children of God's Fire: A Documentary History of Black Slavery in Brazil*. Princeton, N.J.: Princeton University Press.

Cooke, M. L. 1944. *Brazil on the March: A Study of International Cooperation*. New York: McGraw-Hill.

Costa, Emília Viotti da. 1985. *The Brazilian Empire: Myths and Histories*. Chicago: University of Chicago Press.

Costa, Hipólito José. 1955. *Diário de minha viagem para Filadélfia, 1798–1799*. Rio de Janeiro: Publicações da Academia Brasileira.

Costa, Sérgio Corrêa da. 1950. *Every Inch a King: A Biography of Dom Pedro I*. New York: Macmillan. Original edition: *As quatro coroas de d. Pedro I*. Rio de Janeiro: Civilização Brasileira, 1942.

Coutinho, Afrânio. 1969. *An Introduction to Literature in Brazil*. Trans. Gregory Rabassa. New York: Columbia University Press.

Cruz Costa, João. 1964. *A History of Ideas in Brazil: The Development of Philosophy in Brazil and the Evolution of National History*. Trans. Suzette Macedo. Berkeley: California University Press.

Cunha, Euclides da. 1945. *Rebellion in the Backlands*. Trans. Samuel Putnam. Chicago: Chicago University Press.

Daland. Robert T. 1967. *Brazilian Planning: Development, Politics and Administration*. Chapel Hill: University of North Carolina Press.

Da Matta, Roberto. 1991. *Carnivals, Rogues, and Heroes: An Interpretation of the Brazilian Dilemma*. Trans. John Drury. Notre Dame, Ind.: University of Notre Dame Press.

Danaher, Kevin, and Michael Shellenberger, eds. 1995. *Fighting for the Soul of Brazil*. New York: Monthly Review Press.

Davis, Shelton H. 1977. *Victims of the Miracle: Development and the Indians of Brazil*. New York: Cambridge University Press. Brazilian edition: *Vítimas do milagre: o desenvolvimento e os índios do Brasil*. Rio de Janeiro: Zahar, 1978.

Davis, Sonny B. 1996. *A Brotherhood of Arms: Brazil–United States Military Relations, 1942–1977*. Niwot: University of Colorado Press.

Dawsey, Cyrus B., and James M. Dawsey. eds. 1995. *The Confederados: Old South Immigrants in Brazil*. Tuscaloosa: University of Alabama Press.

Dean, Warren. 1969. *The Industrialization of São Paulo, 1880–1945*. Austin: University of Texas Press. Brazilian edition: *A industrialização de São Paulo, 1880–1945*. São Paulo: Difel, 1971.

———. 1976. *Rio Claro: A Brazilian Plantation System, 1820–1920*. Stanford, Calif.: Stanford University Press. Brazilian edition: *Rio Claro: um sistema brasileiro de grande lavoura, 1820–1920*. Rio de Janeiro: Paz e Terra, 1977.

———. 1987. *Brazil and the Struggle for Rubber: A Study in Environmental History*. Cambridge: Cambridge University Press.

———. 1995. *With Broadax and Firebrand: The Destruction of the Brazilian Atlantic Forest*. Berkeley: University of California Press. Brazilian edition: *A Ferro e fogo: a destruição da floresta atlântica*. São Paulo: Companhia das Letras, 1997.

———, ed. 1985. *Diplomatic Claims: Latin American Historians View the United States*. New York: University Press of America. (Chapter by Moniz Bandeira: "Getúlio Vargas and the United States: Two Confrontations," pp. 257–90)

Degler, Carl N. 1971. *Neither Black Nor White: Slavery and Race Relations in Brazil and the United States*. New York: Macmillan; 2nd ed.: Madison: University of Wisconsin Press, 1986. Brazilian edition: *Escravidão e relações raciais no Brasil e nos Estados Unidos*. Rio de Janeiro: Labor do Brasil, 1976.

Della Cava, Ralph. 1970. *Miracle at Joaseiro*. New York: Columbia University Press. Brazilian edition: *Milagre em Joaseiro*. Rio de Janeiro: Paz e Terra, 1977.

DeWitt, John. 2002. *Early Globalization and the Economic Development of the United States and Brazil*. Westport, Conn.: Praeger.

Dos Passos, John. 1963. *Brazil on the Move*. New York: Doubleday.

Dulles, John W. F. 1967. *Vargas of Brazil: A Political Biography*. Austin: Texas University Press. Brazilian edition: *Getúlio Vargas: biografia política*. Trans. Sérgio e Marisa Bath. Rio de Janeiro: Editora Renes, 1977.

————. 1970. *Unrest in Brazil: Political-Military Crises, 1955–1964*. Austin: Texas A&M Press.

————. 1973. *Anarchists and Communists in Brazil, 1900–1935*. Austin: Texas A&M Press. Brazilian edition: *Anarquistas e comunistas no Brasil, 1900–1935*. Trans. Cesar Parreiras Horta. Rio de Janeiro: Nova Fronteira, 1977.

————. 1978. *President Castello Branco: The Making of a Brazilian President*. College Station: Texas A&M University Press. Brazilian edition: *Castelo Branco: o caminho para a presidência*. Trans. R. Magalhães Júnior. Rio de Janeiro: Editora José Olympio, 1979.

————. 1980. *President Castello Branco: A Brazilian Reformer*. College Station: Texas A&M University Press. Brazilian edition: *Castelo Branco, o presidente reformador*. Trans. Heitor A. Herrera. Brasília: Editora da UnB, 1983.

————. 1983. *Brazilian Communism, 1935–1945: Repression During World Upheaval*. Austin: University of Texas Press. Brazilian edition: *O Comunismo brasileiro, 1935–1945: repressão em meio ao cataclismo mundial*. Trans. Raul de Sá Barbosa. Rio de Janeiro: Nova Fronteira, 1985.

————. 1986. *The São Paulo Law School and the Anti-Vargas Resistance*. Austin: University of Texas Press. Brazilian edition: *A Faculdade de Direito e a resistência anti-Vargas, 1938–1945*. São Paulo–Rio de Janeiro: Edusp–Nova Fronteira, 1984.

————. 1991. *Carlos Lacerda, Brazilian Crusader*. College Station: Texas A&M University Press. Brazilian edition: *Carlos Lacerda: vida de um lutador*. Trans. Vanda Mena Barreto de Andrade. Rio de Janeiro: Nova Fronteira, 1992.

————. 1996. *Carlos Lacerda, Brazilian Crusader: The Years 1960–1977*. College Station: Texas A&M University Press.

Eakin, Marshall C. 1989. *British Enterprise in Brazil: The St. John d'el Rey Mining Company and the Morro Velho Gold Mine, 1830–1960*. Durham, N.C.: Duke University Press.

————. 1997. *Brazil: The Once and Future Country*. New York: St. Martin's.

————. 2001. *Tropical Capitalism: The Industrialization of Belo Horizonte, Brazil*. New York: Palgrave.

Eisenberg, Peter. 1974. *The Sugar Industry in Pernambuco: Modernization Without Change, 1840–1910*. Berkeley: University of California Press. Brazilian edition: *Modernização sem mudança: a indústria açucareira em Pernambuco, 1840–1910*. Rio de Janeiro– Campinas: Paz e Terra–Unicamp, 1977.

Eltis, David. 1987. *Economic Growth and the Ending of the Transatlantic Slave Trade*. New York: Oxford University Press.

Erickson, Kenneth Paul. 1977. *The Brazilian Corporative State and the Working-Class Politics*. Berkeley: University of California Press.

————. 1979. *Labor in the Political Process in Brazil: Corporatism in a Modernizing Nation.* Ann Arbor, Mich.: University Microfilms. Brazilian edition: *Sindicalismo no processo político do Brasil.* São Paulo: Brasiliense, 1979.

Evans, Peter. 1979. *Dependent Development: The Alliance of Multinational, State and Local Capital in Brazil.* Princeton, N.J.: Princeton University Press. Brazilian edition: *A Tríplice aliança: as multinacionais, as estatais e o capital nacional no desenvolvimento dependente brasileiro.* Rio de Janeiro: Zahar, 1980.

Fausto, Boris. 1999. *A Concise History of Brazil.* Cambridge: Cambridge University Press. Abridged translated version of *História do Brasil.* São Paulo: Edusp, 1995.

Fernandes, Florestan. 1969. *The Negro in Brazilian Society.* Trans. Jacqueline D. Skiles, A. Brunel, and Arthur Rothwell. Ed. Phyllis B. Eveleth. New York: Columbia University Press. Brazilian edition: *A Integração do negro na sociedade de classes.* São Paulo: Dominus Editora, 1965.

Flory, Thomas. 1981. *Judge and Jury in Imperial Brazil, 1808–1871: Social Control and Political Stability in the New State.* Austin: University of Texas Press.

Flynn, Peter. 1979. *Brazil: A Political Analysis.* Boulder, Colo.: Westview.

Font, Mauricio A. 1990. *Coffee, Contention, and Change in the Making of Modern Brazil.* Cambridge: Basil Blackwell.

Fontain, P.-M., ed. 1985. *Race, Class, and Power in Brazil.* Los Angeles: Center for Afro-American Studies, University of California.

Fontaine, Roger W. 1975. *Brazil and the United States.* Washington, D.C.: American Enterprise Institute.

Forman, Shepard L. 1975. *The Brazilian Peasantry.* New York: Columbia University Press. Brazilian edition: *Camponeses: sua participação no Brasil.* Rio de Janeiro: Paz e Terra, 1978.

Foster, David William. 2000. *Gender and Society in Contemporary Brazilian Cinema.* Austin: University of Texas Press.

Frank, Andre Gunder. 1967. *Capitalism and Underdevelopment in Latin America: Historical Studies of Chile and Brazil.* New York: Monthly Review Press.

French, John D. 1992. *The Brazilian Workers' ABC: Class Conflict and Alliances in Modern São Paulo.* Chapel Hill: University of North Carolina Press.

Freyre, Gilberto. 1945. *Brazil: An Interpretation.* New York, Alfred A. Knopf.

————. 1946. *The Masters and the Slaves: A Study in the Development of the Brazilian Society.* Trans. Samuel Putnam. New York: Alfred A. Knopf. Brazilian edition: *Casa-grande e senzala.* Rio de Janeiro: José Olympio, 1933.

————. 1959. *New World in the Tropics: The Culture of Modern Brazil.* New York: Alfred A. Knopf.

————. 1963. *Brazil.* Washington, D.C.: Pan-American Union.

————. 1963. *The Mansion and the Shanties.* Trans. Harriet de Onís. New York: Alfred A. Knopf. Brazilian edition: *Sobrados e mocambos.* 1946.

Furtado, Celso. 1963. *The Economic Growth of Brazil: A Survey from Colonial to Modern Times.* Berkeley: University of California Press. Brazilian edition: *Formação econômica do Brasil.* São Paulo: Companhia Editora Nacional, 1959.

————. 1965. *Diagnosis of the Brazilian Crisis.* Berkeley: University of California Press.

Garfield, Seth. 2001. *Indigenous Struggle at the Heart of Brazil: State Policy, Frontier Expansion, and the Xavante Indians, 1937–1988.* Durham, N.C.: Duke University Press.

Godfrey, Brian J., and John O. Browder. 1997. *Rainforest Cities: Urbanization, Development, and Globalization of the Brazilian Amazon.* New York: Columbia University Press.

Gordon, Lincoln. 2001. *Brazil's Second Chance: En Route Toward the First World.* Washington, D.C.: Brookings Institution Press. Brazilian edition: *A Segunda chance do Brasil: a caminho do Primeiro Mundo.* São Paulo: Editora Senac, 2002.

Gordon, Lincoln, and Englebert Grommers. 1962. *U.S. Manufacturing Investment in Brazil.* Boston: Harvard Graduate School of Business Administration.

Graham, Lawrence S. 1968. *Civil Service Reform in Brazil: Principle Versus Practice.* Austin: University of Texas Press.

Graham, Lawrence S., and Robert H. Wilson, eds. 1990. *The Political Economy of Brazil: Public Policies in an Era of Transition.* Austin: University of Texas Press.

Graham, Richard. 1968. *Britain and the Onset of Modernization in Brazil, 1850–1914.* Cambridge: Cambridge University Press. Brazilian edition: *Grã-Bretanha e a modernização do Brasil.* São Paulo: Brasiliense, 1973.

————. 1969. *A Century of Brazilian History Since 1865.* New York: Borzoi.

————. 1990. *Patronage and Politics in Nineteenth-Century Brazil.* Stanford, Calif.: Stanford University Press.

————, ed. 1992. *Brazil and the World System.* Austin: University of Texas Press.

Graham, Sandra Lauderdale. 1992. *House and Street: The Domestic World of Servants and Masters in Nineteenth-Century Rio de Janeiro.* Austin: University of Texas Press.

Gregor, Thomas. 1977. *Mehinaku: The Drama of Daily Life in a Brazilian Indian Village.* Chicago: University of Chicago Press. Brazilian edition: *Mehináku: o drama da vida diária em uma aldeia do Alto Xingu.* São Paulo: Companhia Editora Nacional-INL-MEC, 1982.

Griggs, William C. 1987. *The Elusive Eden: Frank McMullan's Confederate Colony in Brazil.* Austin: University of Texas Press.

Haber, Stephen, ed. 1997. *How Latin America Fell Behind: Essays on the Economic Histories of Brazil and Mexico, 1800–1914.* Stanford, Calif.: Stanford University Press.

Hagopian, Frances. 1996. *Traditional Politics and Regime Change in Brazil.* New York: Cambridge University Press.

Hahner, June Edith. [1967]. 1984. *Women in Brazil: Problems and Perspectives.* Albuquerque: Latin American Institute, University of New Mexico. Brazilian edition: *A Mulher no Brasil.* Rio de Janeiro: Civilização Brasileira, 1978.

————. 1969. *Civilian-Military Relations in Brazil, 1889–1898.* Columbia: University of South California Press. Brazilian edition: *Relações entre civis e militares no Brasil, 1889–1898.* São Paulo: Pioneira, 1975.

————. 1986. *Poverty and Politics: The Urban Poor in Brazil, 1870–1920.* Albuquerque: University of New Mexico Press.

————. 1990. *Emancipating the Female Sex: The Struggle for Women's Rights in Brazil.* Durham, N.C.: Duke University Press.

————. 1998. *Women in Brazil.* Brazilian Curriculum Guide Specialized Bibliography. Series II. Albuquerque: Latin American Institute, University of New Mexico.

Haines, Gerald K. 1989. *The Americanization of Brazil: A Study of U.S. Cold War Diplomacy in the Third World, 1945–1954.* Wilmington, Del.: Scholarly Resource Books.

Hallewell, Laurence. 1982. *Books in Brazil: A History of the Publishing Trade.* Metuchen, N.J.: Scarecrow. Brazilian edition: *O Livro no Brasil: sua história.* São Paulo: T. A. Queiroz–Edusp, 1985.

Hanchard, Michael. 1994. *Orpheus and Power: The Movimento Negro of Rio de Janeiro and São Paulo, Brazil, 1945–1988.* Princeton, N.J.: Princeton University Press.

————, ed. 1999. *Racial Politics in Contemporary Brazil.* Durham, N.C.: Duke University Press.

Handbook of Latin American Studies. Cambridge, Mass.: Harvard University Press, 1936–47; Gainesville: University of Florida Press, 1948–66; Austin: University of Texas Press, 1967–present; URL: http://lcweb2.loc.gov/hlas.

Hanson, Carl A. 1973–74. "Dissertations on Luso-Brazilian Topics: A Bibliography of Dissertations Completed in the United States, Great Britain, and Canada, 1892–1970," *Americas* 30:251–67; 373–403.

Harding, Rachel E. 2000. *A Refuge in Thunder: Candomblé and Alternative Spaces of Blackness.* Bloomington: Indiana University Press.

Haring, C. H. 1958. *Empire in Brazil: A New World Experiment with Monarchy.* Cambridge, Mass.: Harvard University Press.

Harris, Marvin. 1956. *Town and Country in Brazil.* New York: Columbia University Press.

Hartner, Eugene C. 1985. *The Lost Colony of the Confederacy.* Jackson: University Press of Mississippi.

Hartness, Ann. 1991. *Brazil in Reference Books, 1965–1989: An Annotated Bibliography.* Metuchen, N.J.: Scarecrow.

Hayes, Robert A. 1989. *The Armed Nation: The Brazilian Corporate Mystique.* Tempe: Arizona State University.

Hecht, Susanna, and Alexander Cockburn. 1989. *The Fate of the Forest: Developers, Destroyers, and Defenders of the Amazon.* New York: Verso.

Hemming, John. 1978. *Red Gold: The Conquest of the Brazilian Indians, 1500–1760.* Cambridge, Mass.: Harvard University Press.

————. 1987. *Amazon Frontier: The Defeat of the Brazilian Indians.* Cambridge, Mass.: Harvard University Press.

————. 2003. *Die If You Must: Brazilian Indians in the Twentieth Century.* London: Macmillan.

Herndon, William Lewis. 2000. *Exploration of the Valley of the Amazon, 1851–1852, Made under Direction of the Navy Department, Washington.* Edited with a foreword by Gary Kindir. New York: Grove Press. Original edition: Washington: R. Armstrong, 1853–54.

Hewlett, Sylvia Ann. 1980. *The Cruel Dilemmas of Development: Twentieth-Century Brazil.* New York: Basic Books.

Hill, Lawrence F. 1971. *Diplomatic Relations Between Brazil and the United States.* New York: AMS Press. Original edition: Durham, N.C.: Duke University Press, 1932.

————, ed. 1947. *Brazil.* Berkeley: California University Press.

Hilton, Stanley E. 1975. *Brazil and the Great Powers, 1930–1939: The Politics of Trade Rivalry.* Foreword by José Honório Rodrigues. Austin: University of Texas Press. Brazilian edition: *O Brasil e as grandes potências: os aspectos políticos da rivalidade comercial, 1930–1939.* Rio de Janeiro: Civilização Brasileira, 1977.

————. 1975. *Brazil and the Internacional Crisis: 1930–1945.* Baton Rouge: Louisiana State University Press. Brazilian edition: *O Brasil e a crise internacional (1930–1945).* Rio de Janeiro: Civilização Brasileira, 1977.

————. 1977. *Suástica sobre o Brasil: a história da espionagem alemã no Brasil, 1939–1944.* Rio de Janeiro: Civilização Brasileira.

————. 1981. *Hitler's Secret War in South America.* Baton Rouge: Louisiana State University Press. Brazilian edition: *A Guerra secreta de Hitler no Brasil: a espionagem alemã e a contra-espionagem aliada no Brasil, 1939–1945.* Rio de Janeiro: Nova Fronteira, 1983.

————. 1982. *A Guerra civil brasileira: história da Revolução Constitucionalista de 1932.* Rio de Janeiro: Nova Fronteira.

————. 1986. *A Rebelião vermelha.* Rio de Janeiro: Editora Record.

————. 1987. *O Ditador & o embaixador.* Rio de Janeiro: Editora Record.

————. 1991. *Brazil and the Soviet Challenge, 1917–1947.* Austin: University of Texas Press.

————. 1994. *Oswaldo Aranha, uma biografia.* Rio de Janeiro: Objetiva.

Hirst, Mônica, org. 1985. *Brasil–Estados Unidos na transição democrática.* Rio de Janeiro: Paz e Terra.

Hollist, W. Ladd. 1984. *Dependency Transformed: Brazil in a Global and Historical Perspective.* New York: St. Martin's.

Holloway, Thomas H. 1975. *The Brazilian Coffee Valorization of 1906: Regional Politics and Economic Dependence.* Madison: University of Wisconsin Press. Brazilian edition: *Vida e morte do Convênio de Taubaté: a primeira valorização do café.* Rio de Janeiro: Paz e Terra, 1978.

————. 1981. *Immigrants on the Land: Coffee and Society in São Paulo, 1886–1934.*

Chapel Hill: University of North Carolina Press. Brazilian edition: *Imigrantes para o café: café e sociedade em São Paulo, 1886–1934.* Rio de Janeiro: Paz e Terra, 1984.

———. 1993. *Policing Rio de Janeiro: Repression and Resistance in a Nineteenth-Century City.* Stanford, Calif.: Stanford University Press.

Hopper, Janice H., ed. 1967. *Indians of Brazil in the Twentieth Century.* Washington, D.C.: Institute for Cross-Cultural Research.

Horowitz, Irving Louis, ed. 1964. *Revolution in Brazil: Politcs and Society in a Developing Nation.* New York: E. P. Dutton.

Huggins, Martha K. 1985. *From Slavery to Vagrancy in Brazil: Crime and Social Control in the Third World.* New Brunswick, N.J.: Rutgers University Press.

Hunnicutt, B. M. 1949. *Brazil: World Frontier.* New York: Van Nostrand.

Hunter, Wendy. 1997. *Eroding Military Influence in Brazil: Politicians Against Soldiers.* Chapel Hill: University of North Carolina Press.

Hutchinson, Harry W. 1960. *Field Guide to Brazil.* Washington, D.C.: National Research Council.

Iggers, George G., and Harold T. Parker, eds. 1979. *International Handbook of Historical Studies: Contemporary Research and Theory.* Westport, Conn.: Greenwood.

Jackson, William Vernon. 1964. *Library Guide for Brazilian Studies.* Pittsburgh: University of Pittsburgh Book Centers.

Jaguaribe, Hélio. 1968. *Economic and Political Development: A Theoretical Approach and a Brazilian Case Study.* Cambridge, Mass.: Harvard University Press.

James, Preston E. 1946. *Brazil.* New York: Odyssey.

Joint Brazil–United States Economic Development Commission. 1955. *Brazilian Technical Studies.* Washington, D.C.: Institute of Inter-American Affairs.

———. 1954. *The Development of Brazil.* Washington, D.C.: Institute of Inter-American Affairs.

Karasch, Mary C. 1987. *Slave life in Rio de Janeiro, 1808–1850.* Princeton, N.J.: Princeton University Press. Brazilian edition: *A vida dos escravos no Rio de Janeiro, 1808–1850.* Trans. Pedro Maia Soares. São Paulo: Companhia das Letras, 2000.

Keck, Margaret E. 1992. *The Workers' Party and Democratization in Brazil.* New Haven, Conn.: Yale University Press.

Kiemen, Mathias C. 1954. *The Indian Policy of Portugal in the Amazon Region, 1614–1693.* Washington, D.C.: Catholic University Press.

Kingstone, Peter R. 1999. *Crafting Coalitions for Reform: Business Preferences, Political Institutions, and Neoliberal Reform in Brazil.* University Park: Pennsylvania State University Press.

Klein, Herbert. 1986. *African Slavery in Latin America and the Caribbean.* New York: Oxford University Press. Brazilian edition: *A Escravidão africana: América Latina e Caribe.* São Paulo: Brasiliense, 1987.

Kuznesof, Elizabeth. 1986. *Household Economy and Urban Development: São Paulo, 1765–1836.* Boulder, Colo.: Westview.

Kuznets, Simon, ed. 1955. *Economic Growth: Brazil, India, Japan*. Durham, N.C.: Duke University Press.

Landes, Ruth. 1947. *The City of Women*. New York, Macmillan. Brazilian edition: *A Cidade das mulheres*. Rio de Janeiro: Civilização Brasileira, 1967.

Lang, James. 1979. *Portuguese Brazil: The King's Plantation*. New York: Academic Press.

Leacock, Ruth. 1990. *Requiem for Revolution: The United States and Brazil, 1961–1969*. Kent, Ohio: Kent State University Press.

Leacock, Ruth, and Seth Leacock. 1972. *Spirits of the Deep: A Study of an Afro-Brazilian Cult*. New York: Doubleday Natural History Press, American Museum of Natural History.

Leeds, Anthony, and Leeds, Elizabeth. 1978. *A Sociologia do Brasil urbano*. Rio de Janeiro: Zahar.

Leff, Nathaniel H. 1968. *The Brazilian Capital Goods Industry, 1929–1964*. Cambridge, Mass.: Harvard University Press.

———. 1968. *Economic Policy-Making and Development in Brazil, 1947–1964*. New York: John Wiley.

Léry, Jean de. 1990. *History of a Voyage to the Land of Brazil*. Trans. and introd. by Janet Whatley. Berkeley: University of California Press.

Lesser, Jeffrey. 1995. *Welcoming the Undesirables: Brazil and the Jewish Question*. Berkeley: University of California Press. Brazilian edition: *O Brasil e a Questão Judaica: imigração, diplomacia e preconceito*. Rio de Janeiro: Imago, 1995.

———. 1999. *Negotiating National Identity: Immigrants, Minorities, and Struggle for Ethnicity in Brazil*. Durham, N.C.: Duke University Press.

Levine, Robert M. 1970. *The Vargas Regime: The Critical Years, 1934–1938*. New York: Columbia University Press. Brazilian edition: *O Regime Vargas: os anos críticos, 1934–1938*. Rio de Janeiro: Nova Fronteira, 1970.

———. 1978. *Pernambuco in the Brazilian Federation, 1889–1937*. Stanford, Calif.: Stanford University Press. Brazilian edition: *A Velha usina: Pernambuco na federação brasileira,1889–1937*. Rio de Janeiro: Civilização Brasileira, 1980.

———. 1979. *Historical Dictionary of Brazil*. Metuchen, N.J.: Scarecrow.

———. 1980. *Brazil Since 1930: An Annotated Bibliography for Social Historians*. New York: Garland.

———. 1983. *Brazil, 1822–1930: An Annotated Bibliography for Social Historians*. New York: Garland.

———. 1992. *Vale of Tears: Revisiting the Canudos Massacre in Northeastern Brazil, 1893–1897*. Berkeley: University of California Press.

———. 1997. *Brazilian Legacies*. New York: M. E. Sharpe.

———. 1998. *Father of the Poor? Vargas and His Era*. New York: Cambridge University Press.

———. 1999. *Brazil: A History*. Westport, Conn.: Greenwood.

———, ed. 1966. *Brazil: Field Research Guide in the Social Sciences*. New York: Institute of Latin American Studies, Columbia University Press.

Levine, Robert M., and John J. Crociotti, eds. 1999. *The Brazil Reader: History, Culture, Politics*. Durham, N.C.: Duke University Press.

Levine, Robert M., and José Carlos Sebe Bom Meihy. 1995. *The Life and Death of Carolina Maria de Jesus*. Albuquerque: University of New Mexico Press.

Lewin, Linda. 1987. *Politics and Parentela in Paraiba: A Case Study of Family-Based Oligarchy in Brazil*. Princeton, N.J.: Princeton University Press.

Love, Joseph. 1971. *Rio Grande do Sul and Brazilian Regionalism, 1882–1930*. Stanford, Calif.: Stanford University Press. Brazilian edition: *O Regionalismo gaúcho e as origens da Revolução de 1930*. São Paulo: Perspectiva, 1975.

————. 1980. *São Paulo and the Brazilian Federation, 1889–1937*. Stanford, Calif.: Stanford University Press. Brazilian edition: *A Locomotiva: São Paulo na federação brasileira, 1889–1937*. Rio de Janeiro: Paz e Terra, 1982.

————. 1996. *Crafting the Third World: Theorizing Underdevelopment in Rumania and Brazil*. Stanford, Calif.: Stanford University Press. Brazilian edition: *A Construcao do Terceiro Mundo: teorias do subdesenvolvimento na Romenia e no Brasil*. Trans. Patricia Zimbres. São Paulo: Editora Paz e Terra, 1998.

Love, Joseph, and Nils Jacobsen, eds. 1988. *Guiding the Invisible Hand: Economic Liberalism and the State in Latin American History*. New York: Praeger.

Lowenthal, Abraham F. 1986. *Brazil and the United States*. Washington, D.C.: Foreign Policy Association.

Luebke, Fredrick C. 1987. *Germans in Brazil: A Comparative History of Cultural Conflict During World War I*. Baton Rouge: Louisiana State University Press.

Ludwig, Armin K. 1985. *Brazil: A Handbook of Historical Statistics*. Boston: G. K. Hall.

Macaulay, Neill. 1974. *The Prestes Column: Revolution in Brazil*. New York: New Viewpoints. Brazilian edition: *A Coluna Prestes: revolução no Brasil*. São Paulo: Difel, 1977.

————. 1986. *Dom Pedro: The Struggle for Liberty in Brazil and Portugal, 1798–1834*. Durham, N.C.: Duke University Press.

McCann, Frank D., Jr. 1973. *The Brazilian-American Alliance, 1937–1945*. Princeton, N.J.: Princeton University Press. Brazilian edition: *Aliança Brasil–Estados Unidos, 1937–1945*. Rio de Janeiro: Biblioteca do Exército, 1995.

————. 1981. "Brazilian Foreign Relations in the Twentieth Century." In *Brazil in the International System: The Rise of a Middle Power*, ed. Wayne Selcher. Boulder, Colo.: Westview.

————. 1982. *A nação armada: ensaios sobre a história do exército brasileiro*. Recife: Guararapes.

McDonough, Peter J., and Amaury de Souza. 1981. *The Politics of Population in Brazil*. Austin: University of Texas Press. Brazilian edition: *A Política de população no Brasil*. Rio de Janeiro: Paz e Terra, 1984.

Mainwaring, Scott P. 1986. *The Catholic Church and Politics in Brazil, 1916–1985*. Stanford, Calif.: Stanford University Press. Brazilian edition: *Igreja Católica e política no Brasil*. São Paulo: Brasiliense, 1989.

————. 1999. *Rethinking Party Systems in the Third Wave of Democratization: The Case of Brazil.* Stanford, Calif.: Stanford University Press.

Malloy, James. 1979. *The Politics of Social Security in Brazil.* Pittsburgh, Pa.: University of Pittsburgh Press. Brazilian edition: *A Política de previdência social no Brasil.* Rio de Janeiro: Graal, 1986.

Manchester, Alan K. 1933. *British Preëminence in Brazil: Its Rise and Decline: A Study in European Expansion.* Chapel Hill: University of North Caroline Press; 2nd ed., New York: Octagon Books, 1964. Brazilian edition: *Preeminência inglesa no Brasil.* São Paulo: Brasiliense, 1973.

Maram, Sheldon L. 1974. "Anarchists, Immigrants and the Brazilian Labor Movement, 1890–1920." Ph.D. diss., University of California, Berkeley. Brazilian edition: *Anarquistas, imigrantes e movimento operário brasileiro.* Rio de Janeiro: Paz e Terra, 1979.

Marchant, Alexander. 1942. *From Barter to Slavery: The Economic Relations of Portuguese and Indians in the Settlement of Brazil, 1500–1800.* Baltimore: Johns Hopkins University Press. Brazilian edition: *Do escambo à escravidão: as relações econômicas de portugueses e índios na colonização do Brasil, 1500–1800.* São Paulo: Companhia Editora Nacional, 1943.

Marchant, Anyda. 1965. *Viscount of Mauá and the Empire of Brazil.* Berkeley: University of California Press.

Margolis, Maxine L. 1973. *The Moving Frontier.* Gainesville: University Presses of Florida.

Massi, Fernanda Peixoto, and Heloísa André Pontes (com a colaboração de Maria Cecília Spina Forjaz). 1992. *Guia biobibliográfico dos brasilianistas: obras e autores editados no Brasil entre 1930 e 1988.* São Paulo: Editora Sumaré–FAPESP.

Mattoso, Katia M. de Queirós. 1979. *Être esclave au Brésil.* Paris: Hachette. American edition: *To Be a Slave in Brazil, 1550–1888.* New Brunswick, N.J.: Rutgers University Press, 1986. Brazilian edition: *Ser escravo no Brasil.* São Paulo: Brasiliense, 1982.

Maxwell, Kenneth. 1973. *Conflicts and Conspiracies: Brazil and Portugal, 1750–1808.* Cambridge University Press. Brazilian edition: *A devassa da devassa: a Inconfidência Mineira, Brasil-Portugal, 1750–1808.* 3rd ed. São Paulo: Paz e Terra, 1985.

————. 1995. *Pombal: Paradox of the Enlightenment.* Cambridge: Cambridge University Press.

————. 1999. *Chocolate, piratas e outros malandros: ensaios tropicais.* São Paulo: Paz e Terra.

Meade, Teresa A. 1997. *"Civilizing" Rio: Reform and Resistance in a Brazilian City, 1889–1930.* University Park: Pennsylvania State University Press.

Meggers, Betty J. 1971. *Amazonia: Man and Culture in a Counterfeit Paradise.* Chicago: Aldine Atherton; rev. ed.: Washington, D.C.: Smithsonian Institution Press, 1996. Brazilian edition: *Amazônia: a ilusão de um paraíso.* Rio de Janeiro: Civilização Brasileira, 1977.

Meggers, Betty J., and Clifford Evans. 1957. *Archaelogical Investigations at the Mouth of the Amazon.* Washington, D.C.: GPO.

Merrick, Thomas W., and Douglas H. Graham. 1979. *Population and Economic Development in Brazil, 1808 to the Present.* Baltimore: Johns Hopkins University Press.

Metcalf, Alida. 1992. *Family and Frontier in Colonial Brazil: Santana de Parnaíba, 1500–1822.* Stanford, Calif.: Stanford University Press.

Miceli, Sergio. 1990. *A Desilusão americana: relações acadêmicas entre Brasil e Estados Unidos.* São Paulo: Ed. Sumaré.

———, coord. 1993. *A Fundação Ford no Brasil.* São Paulo: Ed. Sumaré–FAPESP.

Momsen, Richard P., Jr. 1968. *Brazil: A Giant Stirs.* Princeton, N.J.: Van Nostrand.

Moniz Bandeira, L. A. 1973. *Presença dos Estados Unidos no Brasil: dois séculos de história.* Rio de Janeiro: Civilização Brasileira. 2nd. ed., rev.: *Relações Brasil-EUA no contexto da globalização: I—Presença dos EUA no Brasil.* São Paulo: Editora SENAC–São Paulo, 1998.

———. 1989. *Brasil–Estados Unidos: a rivalidade emergente, 1950–1988.* Rio de Janeiro: Civilização Brasileira. 2nd. ed., rev.: *Relações Brasil-EUA no contexto da globalização: II—Rivalidade emergente.* São Paulo: Editora SENAC–São Paulo, 1999.

———. 1993. *Estado nacional e política internacional na América Latina: o continente nas relações Argentina-Brasil (1930/1992).* São Paulo: Ensaio.

———. 1998. *De Marti a Fidel: a revolução cubana e a América Latina.* Rio de Janeiro: Civilização Brasileira.

Moog, Vianna Clodomir. 1964. *Bandeirantes and Pioneers.* Trans. by L. Barret. New York: Braziller. Brazilian edition: *Bandeirantes e pioneiros: paralelo entre duas culturas.* Porto Alegre: Livraria O Globo, 1954.

Moraes, Rubens Borba de. 1958. *Bibliographia Brasiliana: A Bibliographical Essay on Rare Books About Brazil Published from 1504 to 1900 and Works of Brazilian Authors Published Abroad Before the Independence of Brazil in 1822.* Rio de Janeiro: Colibris Editora. Rev. and enlarged edition: *Bibliographia Brasiliana: Rare Books About Brazil Published from 1504 to 1900 and Works by Brazilian Authors of the Colonial Period.* 2 vols. Los Angeles: University of California, 1983.

Morel, Edmar. 1965. *O Golpe começou em Washington.* Rio de Janeiro: Civilização Brasileira.

Morris, Michael A. 1979. *International Politics and the Sea: The Case of Brazil.* Boulder, Colo.: Westview.

Morse, Richard M. 1958. *From Community to Metropolis: A Biography of São Paulo, Brazil.* Gainesville: University of Florida Press; new and enlarged edition: New York: Octagon Books, 1974. Brazilian edition: *Formação histórica de São Paulo: da comunidade à metrópole.* São Paulo: Difel, 1970.

———, ed. 1965. *The Bandeirantes: The Historical Role of the Brazilian Pathfinders.* New York: Alfred A. Knopf.

Moura, Gerson. 1980. *Autonomia na dependência: a política externa brasileira de 1935 a 1942*. Rio de Janeiro: Nova Fronteira.

———. 1986. *Tio Sam chega ao Brasil: a penetração cultural americana*. São Paulo: Brasiliense.

———. 1991. *Sucessos e ilusões: relações internacionais do Brasil durante e após a Segunda Guerra Mundial*. Rio de Janeiro: Fundação Getúlio Vargas.

———. 1995. *História de uma história: rumos da historiografia norte-americana no século XX*. São Paulo: Edusp.

Muller, Keith D. 1974. *Pioneer Settlement in South Brazil: The Case of Toledo, Paraná*. The Hague: Nijhoff.

Nabuco, Carolina. 1950. *The Life of Joaquim Nabuco*. Trans. Ronald Hilton. Stanford, Calif.: Stanford University Press.

Nabuco, Joaquim. 1977. *Abolitionism: The Brazilian Antislavery Struggle*. Trans. Robert Conrad. Urbana: University of Illinois Press.

Napoleão, Aluizio. 1947. *Rio-Branco e as relacões entre o Brasil e os Estados Unidos*. Rio de Janeiro: Ministério das Relações Exteriores.

Nazzari, Muriel. 1991. *Disappearance of the Dowry: Women, Families and Social Change in São Paulo, Brazil, 1600–1900*. Stanford, Calif.: Stanford University Press.

Needell, Jeffrey D. 1987. *A Tropical Belle Epoque: Elite Culture and Society in Turn-of-the-Century Rio de Janeiro*. Cambridge: Cambridge University Press.

Neistein, José. 1997. *Art in Brazil from its Beginnings to Modern Times: A Selected, Annotated Bibliography*. Washington, D.C.: Brazilian-American Cultural Institute. Brazilian edition: *A Arte no Brasil: dos primórdios ao século vinte, uma bibliografia seleta, anotada*. São Paulo: Livraria Kosmos Editora, 1997.

Nelson, Roy C. 1995. *Industrialization and Political Affinity: Industrial Policy in Brazil*. London: Routledge.

Nist, John A. 1967. *The Modernist Movement in Brazil: A Literary Study*. Austin: University of Texas Press.

Normano, João Frederico. 1931. *The Struggle for South America, Economy and Ideology*. Boston: Houghton Mifflin.

———. 1935. *Brazil: A Study of Economic Types*. Chapel Hill: University of North Carolina Press. Brazilian edition: *Evolução econômica do Brasil*. São Paulo: Companhia Editora Nacional, Brasiliana, 1939.

Nunes Leal, Vitor. 1977. *Coronelismo*. Trans. June Henfrey. New York: Cambridge University Press. Original edition: *Coronelismo, enxada e voto*. Rio de Janeiro: José Olympio, 1949.

Oliveira, Lúcia Lippi. 2000. *Americanos: representações da identidade nacional no Brasil e nos EUA*. Belo Horizonte: UFMG.

Oliveira Lima, Manuel de. 1899. *Nos Estados Unidos: impressões sociaes e políticas*. Leipzig: Brockaus.

———. 1914. Edited with introduction and notes by Percy Alvin Martin. *The Evolution of Brazil Compared with That of Spain and Anglo-Saxon America*.

Stanford, Calif.: Stanford University Press; new ed.: New York: Russell and Russell, 1966. Brazilian edition: *América Latina e América inglesa: a evolução brazileira comparada com a Hispano-Americana e com a Anglo-Americana*. Rio de Janeiro: Garnier, s.d. [1913].

―――. 1980. *Pan-Americanismo: Monroe, Bolivar, Roosevelt*. Facsimile edition: Brasília: Senado Federal. Original edition, Rio de Janeiro: H. Garnier, 1907.

Page, Joseph A. 1972. *The Revolution That Never Was: Northeast Brazil, 1955–1964*. New York: Grossman. Brazilian edition: *A Revolução que nunca houve: o Nordeste do Brasil, 1955–1964*. Rio de Janeiro: Record, 1989.

―――. 1995. *The Brazilians*. Reading, Pa.: Addison-Wesley.

Pang, Eul-Soo. 1978. *Bahia in the First Brazilian Republic: Coronelismo and Oligarchies, 1889–1934*. Gainesville: University Press of Florida. Brazilian edition: *Coronelismo e oligarquia (1889–1934): a Bahia na Primera República brasileira*. Rio de Janeiro: Civilização Brasileira, 1979.

―――. 1988. *In Pursuit of Honor and Power: Noblemen of the Southern Cross in Nineteenth-Century Brazil*. Tuscaloosa: University of Alabama Press.

Parker, Phyllis R. 1977. *Separate but Equal?: U.S. Policy Toward Brazil, 1959–1964*. Austin: University of Texas.

―――. 1979. *Brazil and the Quiet Intervention: U.S. Policy Prior to the Brazilian Coup of 1964*. Austin: University of Texas Press. Brazilian edition: *1964: o papel dos Estados Unidos no Golpe de Estado de 31 de março*. Rio de Janeiro: Civilização Brasileira, 1977.

Parker, Richard G. 1991. *Bodies, Pleasures and Passions: Sexual Culture in Contemporary Brazil*. Boston: Beacon.

Peard, Julyan G. 1999. *Race, Place, and Medicine: The Idea of the Tropics in Nineteenth-Century Brazilian Medicine*. Durham, N.C.: Duke University Press.

Pereira, Anthony W. 1997. *The End of Peasantry: The Rural Labor Movement in Northeast Brazil, 1961–1988*. Pittsburgh, Pa.: University of Pittsburgh Press.

Perrone, Charles A. 1989. *Masters of Contemporary Brazilian Song: MPB, 1965–1985*. Austin: University of Texas Press.

Perry, William. 1976. *Contemporary Brazilian Foreign Policy: The International Strategy of an Emerging Power*. Beverly Hills, Calif.: Sage.

Pierson, Donald. 1942. *Negroes in Brazil: A Study of Race Contact at Bahia*. Chicago: University of Chicago Press; 2nd ed.: Carbondale, Southern Illinois University Press, 1967. Brazilian edition: *Pretos e brancos na Bahia: estudo do contato racial*. São Paulo: Companhia Editora Nacional, 1945.

―――. 1945. *Survey of the Literature on Brazil of Sociological Significance Published up to 1940*. Cambridge, Mass.: Harvard University Press.

―――. 1951. *Cruz das Almas: A Brazilian Village*. Washington, D.C.: Government Printing Office. Brazilian edition: *Cruz das Almas*. Rio de Janeiro: José Olympio, 1966.

Plank, David N. 1996. *The Means of Our Salvation: Public Education in Brazil, 1930–1995*. Boulder, Colo.: Westview.

Pontes Nogueira, Sizinio. 1964. *A Mission of Friendship: Jose Silvestre Rebello in Washington, 1824.* Washington, D.C.: Brazilian American Cultural Institute.

Poppino, Rollie E. 1968. *Brazil: The Land and People.* New York: Oxford University Press.

Prado, Caio, Jr. 1967. *The Colonial Background of Modern Brazil.* Trans. Suzette Macedo. Berkeley: University of California Press. Original edition: *Formação do Brasil contemporâneo, v. 1: Colônia.* São Paulo: Livraria Martins, 1942.

Price, Robert E. 1964. *Rural Unionization in Brazil.* Madison: Land Tenure Center, University of Wisconsin.

———. 1965. *The Brazilian Land Reform Statute.* Madison: Land Tenure Center, University of Wisconsin.

Purcell, Susan Kaufman, and Riordan Roett, eds. 1997. *Brazil Under Cardoso.* New York: Americas Society.

Putnam, Samuel. 1948. *Marvelous Journeys: A Survey of Four Centuries of Brazilian Writing.* New York: Alfred A. Knopf.

Rady, Donald Edmund. 1973. *Volta Redonda: A Steel Mill Comes to a Brazilian Coffee Plantation.* Albuquerque: printed privately.

Randall, Laura. 1977. *A Comparative Economic History of Latin America, 1500–1914.* Vol. 3, *Brazil.* New York: Institute of Latin American Studies, Columbia University.

———. 1993. *The Political Economy of Brazilian Oil.* Westport, Conn.: Praeger.

Reichmann, Felix. 1959. *Sugar, Gold and Coffee: Essays on the History of Brazil Based on Francis Hull's Books.* Ithaca, N.Y.: Cornell University Press.

Ridings, Eugene W. 1994. *Business Interest Groups in Nineteenth-Century Brazil.* Cambridge: Cambridge University Press.

Robock, Stefan H. 1963. *Brazil's Developing Northeast: A Study of Regional Planning and Foreign Aid.* Washington, D.C.: Brookings Institution.

Rodrigues, José Honório. 1965. *Brazil and Africa.* Berkeley: University of California Press. Original edition: *Brasil e África: outro horizonte.* Rio de Janeiro: Civilização Brasileira, 1961.

———. 1967. *The Brazilians: Their Character and Aspirations.* Trans. Ralph Edward Dimmick. Austin: University of Texas Press. Original edition: *Aspirações nacionais: interpretação histórico-política.* Rio de Janeiro: Civilização Brasileira, 1963.

Rodrigues, José Honório, and Ricardo A. S. Seitenfus. 1995. *Uma História diplomática do Brasil (1531–1945).* Rio de Janeiro: Civilização Brasileira.

Roett, Riordan. 1972. *The Politics of Foreign Aid in the Brazilian Northeast.* Nashville, Tenn.: Vanderbilt University Press.

———. 1984. *Brazil: Politics in a Patrimonial Society.* 3rd ed. New York: Praeger.

———, ed. 1976. *Brazil in the Seventies.* Washington, D.C.: American Enterprise Institute for Public Research. Brazilian edition: *O Brasil na década de 70.* Rio de Janeiro: Zahar, 1978.

Roosevelt, Theodore. 1914. *Through the Brazilian Wilderness.* New York: C. Scribner's Sons. Brazilian edition: *Nas selvas do Brasil.* Trans. Luiz Guimarães Jr., Rio de Janeiro: Serviço de Informação Agrícola, do Ministério da Agricultura, 1943.

Rose, R. S. 2000. *One of the Forgotten Things: Getúlio Vargas and Brazilian Social Control, 1930–1954*. Westport, Conn.: Greenwood.

Rosenn, Keith S. 1991. *Foreign Investment in Brazil*. Boulder, Colo.: Westview.

Russell-Wood, Anthony John R. 1968. *Fidalgos and Philanthropists: The Santa Casa da Misericórdia of Bahia, 1550–1775*. Berkeley: University of California Press. Brazilian edition: *Fidalgos e filantropos: a Santa Casa da Misericórdia da Bahia, 1550–1775*. Brasília: Editora da UnB, 1981.

———. 1975. *From Colony to Nation: Essays on the Independence of Brazil*. Baltimore: Johns Hopkins University Press.

———. 1982. *The Black Man in Slavery and Freedom in Colonial Brazil*. New York: St. Martin's.

———. 1992. *Society and Government in Colonial Brazil*. Aldershot, U.K. Variorum Collected Studies Series.

———. 1992. *A World on the Move: The Portuguese in Africa, Asia and America, 1415–1808*. New York: St. Martin's.

Sable, Martin H. 1989. *Guide to the Writings of Pioneer Latinamericanists of the United States*. New York: Haworth.

Sayers, Raymond S. 1956. *The Negro in Brazilian Literature*. New York: Hispanic Institute. Brazilian edition: *O Negro na literatura brasileira*. Rio de Janeiro: Edições o Cruzeiro, 1958.

Schmitter, Philippe. 1971. *Interest Conflict and Political Change in Brazil*. Stanford, Calif.: Stanford University Press.

Schneider, Ronald. 1971. *The Political System in Brazil: Emergence of a "Modernizing" Authoritarian Regime, 1964–1970*. New York: Columbia University Press.

———. 1976. *Brazil: Foreign Policy of a Future World Power*. Boulder, Colo.: Westview.

———. 1991. *"Order and Progress": A Political History of Brazil*. Boulder, Colo.: Westview.

———. 1996. *Brazil: Culture and Politics in a New Industrial Powerhouse*. Boulder, Colo.: Westview.

Schultz, Kirsten. 2001. *Tropical Versailles: Empire, Monarchy, and the Portuguese Royal Court in Rio de Janeiro, 1808–1821*. New York: Routledge.

Schurz, William L. 1961. *Brazil: The Infinite Country*. New York: E. P. Dutton.

Schwam-Baird, David Michael. 1997. *Ideas and Armaments: Military Ideologies in the Making of Brazil's Arms Industries*. Lanham, Md.: University Press of America.

Schwartz, Stuart B. 1973. *Sovereignty and Society in Colonial Brazil: The High Court of Bahia and Its Judges, 1609–1751*. Berkeley: University of California Press. Brazilian edition: *Burocracia e sociedade no Brasil colonial: a Suprema Corte da Bahia e seus juízes*. São Paulo: Perspectiva, 1979.

———. 1985. *Sugar Plantations in the Formation of Brazilian Society: Bahia, 1550–1835*. New York: Cambridge University Press. Brazilian edition: *Segredos internos:*

engenhos e escravos na sociedade colonial brasileira, 1550–1835. São Paulo: Companhia das Letras–CNPq, 1988.

———. 1992. *Slaves, Peasants, and Rebels: Reconsidering Brazilian Slavery*. Urbana-Champaign: University of Illinois Press.

Seeger, Anthony. 1981. *Nature and Society in Central Brazil: The Suya Indians of Mato Grosso*. Cambridge, Mass.: Harvard University Press.

Selcher, Wayne. 1974. *The Afro-Asian Dimension of Brazilian Foreign Policy, 1956–1972*. Gainesville: University of Florida Press.

———. 1978. *Brazil's Multilateral Relations: Between First and Third Worlds*. Boulder, Colo.: Westview.

———, ed. 1981. *Brazil in the International System: The Rise of a Middle Power*. Boulder, Colo.: Westview.

———, ed. 1986. *Political Liberalization in Brazil: Dynamics, Dilemmas and Future Prospects*. Boulder, Colo.: Westview.

Shapiro, Helen. 1994. *Engines of Growth: The State and Transnational Auto Companies in Brazil*. Cambridge: Cambridge University Press.

Shirley, Robert W. 1971. *The End of a Tradition: Culture Change and Development in the Municipio of Cunha*. New York: Columbia University Press. Brazilian edition: *O Fim de uma tradição: cultura e desenvolvimento no Município de Cunha*. São Paulo: Perspectiva, 1977.

Sikkink, Kathryn. 1991. *Ideas and Institutions: Developmentalism in Brazil and Argentina*. Ithaca, N.Y.: Cornell University Press.

Simmons, Charles W. 1966. *Marshal Deodoro and the Fall of Dom Pedro II*. Durham, N.C.: Duke University Press.

Simpson, Lesley Byrd. 1949. "Thirty Years of the HAHR," *Hispanic American Historical Review*, 29 (May 1949): 188–204. Reprinted in volume I of Howard Francis Cline, comp. and ed., *Latin American History: Essays on Its Study and Teaching, 1898–1965*. 2 vols. Austin: Conference on Latin American History, University of Texas Press, 1967.

Skidmore, Thomas E. 1967. *Politics in Brazil, 1930–1964: An Experiment in Democracy*. New York: Oxford University Press. Brazilian edition: *Brasil: de Getúlio Vargas a Castelo Branco, 1930–1964*. Rio de Janeiro: Saga, 1969; 10th ed.: São Paulo: Ed. Paz e Terra, 1996.

———. 1974. *Black into White: Race and Nationality in Brazilian Thought*. New York: Oxford University Press. Brazilian edition: *Preto no branco: raça e nacionalidade no pensamento brasileiro*. Rio de Janeiro: Paz e Terra, 1976.

———. 1988. *The Politics of Military Rule in Brazil, 1964–85*. New York: Oxford University Press. 3rd Brazilian edition: *Brasil: de Castelo Branco a Tancredo Neves*. Rio de Janeiro: Paz e Terra, 1989.

———. 1999. *Brazil: Five Centuries of Change*. New York: Oxford University Press.

Smith, Joseph. 1991. *Unequal Giants: Diplomatic Relations Between the United States and Brazil, 1889–1930*. Pittsburgh, Pa.: University of Pittsburgh Press.

Smith, T. Lynn. 1946. *Brazil: People and Institutions*. Baton Rouge: Louisiana State

University Press. 1963 Brazilian edition: *Brasil: povo e instituições*. Trans. José Arthur Rios. Rio de Janeiro: Bloch-AID, 1967.

Smith, T. Lynn, and Yukio Fujii. 1959. *The Acculturation of the Japanese Immigrants in Brazil*. Gainesville: University of Florida Press.

Smith, T. Lynn, and Alexander Marchant, eds. 1951. *Brazil: Portrait of Half a Continent*. New York: Dryden.

Southey, Robert. 1817–22. *History of Brazil*. 3 vols. London: Longman, Hurst, Rees, Orme and Brown.

Stam, Robert. 1998. *Tropical Multiculturalism: A Comparative History of Race in Brazilian Cinema and Culture*. Durham, N.C.: Duke University Press.

Stein, Stanley J. 1957. *The Brazilian Cotton Manufacture: Textile Enterprise in a Underdeveloped Area, 1850–1950*. Cambridge, Mass.: Harvard University Press. Brazilian edition: *Origens e evolução da indústria têxtil no Brasil, 1850–1950*. Rio de Janeiro: Campus, 1979.

———. 1957. *Vassouras: A Brazilian Coffee County, 1850–1900*. Cambridge, Mass: Harvard University Press; new U.S. edition: *Vassouras, A Brazilian Coffee County, 1850–1900: The Roles of Planter and Slave in a Plantation Society*. Princeton, N.J.: Princeton University Press, 1985. Brazilian edition: *Grandeza e decadência do café no vale do Paraíba. Com referência especial ao Município de Vassouras*. São Paulo: Brasiliense, 1961.

Stein, Stanley J., and Barbara H. Stein. 1970. *The Colonial Heritage of Latin America: Essays in Economic Dependence in Perspective*. New York: Oxford University Press. Brazilian edition: *A Herança colonial da América Latina: ensaios de dependência econômica*. Rio de Janeiro: Paz e Terra, 1976.

Stepan, Alfred. 1971. *The Military in Politics: Changing Patterns in Brazil*. Princeton, N.J.: Princeton University Press. Brazilian edition: *O Militares na política: as mudanças de padrões na vida brasileira*. Rio de Janeiro: Artenova, 1975.

———. 1988. *Rethinking Military Politics: Brazil and the Southern Cone*. Princeton, N.J.: Princeton University Press.

———, ed. 1973. *Authoritarian Brazil: Origins, Policies and Future*. New Haven, Conn.: Yale University Press.

———, ed. 1989. *Democratizing Brazil: Problems of Transition and Consolidation*. New York: Oxford University Press. Brazilian edition: *Democratizando o Brasil*. Rio de Janeiro Paz e Terra, 1988.

Stepan, Nancy. 1975. *The Beginnings of Brazilian Science: Oswaldo Cruz, Medical Research and Policy, 1890–1920*. New York: Science History Publications. Brazilian edition: *Gênese e evolução da ciência brasileira: Oswaldo Cruz e a política de investigação científica e médica*. Rio de Janeiro: Artenova, 1976.

———. 1991. *The Hour of Eugenics: Race, Gender, and Nation in Latin America*. Ithaca, N.Y.: Cornell University Press.

Summerhill, William R., III. 2000. *Order Against Progress: Government, Foreign Investment, and Railroads in Brazil, 1854–1913*. Stanford, Calif.: Stanford University Press.

Tavares de Sá, Hernane. 1947. *The Brazilians: People of Tomorrow.* New York: J. Day.

Tomlinson, Regina Johnson. 1970. *The Struggle for Brazil: Portugal and the "French Interlopers."* New York: Macmillan.

Topik, Steven. 1978. *The Evolution of the Economic Role of the Brazilian State, 1889–1930.* Austin: Office for Public Sector Studies, Institute of Latin American Studies, University of Texas.

———. 1985. *State and Economy: Brazil Under the Empire and the Republic.* Austin: Office for Public Sector Studies, Institute of Latin American Studies, University of Texas.

———. 1987. *The Political Economy of the Brazilian State, 1889–1930.* Austin: University of Texas Press.

———. 1996. *Trade and Gunboats: The United States and Brazil in the Age of Empire.* Stanford, Calif.: Stanford University Press.

Toplin, Robert Brent. 1972. *The Abolition of Slavery in Brazil.* New York: Atheneum.

Triner, Gail D. 2000. *Banking and Economic Development: Brazil, 1889–1930.* New York: Palgrave.

Uricoechea, Fernando. 1980. *The Patrimonial Foundations of the Brazilian Bureaucratic State.* Berkeley: University of California Press.

Vellinho, Moyses. 1968. *Brazil South: Its Conquest & Settlement.* Preface by Erico Verissimo; Trans. Linton Lomas Barrett and Marie McDavid Barrett. New York: Alfred A. Knopf. Brazilian edition: *Capitania d'El-Rei: aspectos polêmicos da formação rio-grandense.* Porto Alegre: Editôra Globo, 1964.

Verissimo, Erico. 1945. *Brazilian Literature: An Outline.* New York: Macmillan. New edition: New York: Greenwood, 1969.

Wagley, Charles. 1952. *Race and Class in Rural Brazil.* Paris, France: UNESCO.

———. 1953. *Amazon Town: A Study of Man in the Tropics.* New York: Macmillan. Brazilian edition: *Uma Comunidade amazônica: estudo do homem nos trópicos.* São Paulo: Companhia Editora Nacional, 1957.

———. 1963. *An Introduction to Brazil.* New York: Columbia University Press, 1963; rev. ed., 1971.

———. 1977. *Welcome of Tears: The Tapirapé Indians of Central Brazil.* New York: Oxford University Press. Brazilian edition: *Lágrimas de boas-vindas: os índios Tapirapé do Brasil Central.* Belo Horizonte-São Paulo: Itatiaia-Edusp, 1988.

Wagley, Charles, and Eduardo Galvão. 1949. *The Tenetehara Indians of Brazil: A Culture in Transition.* New York: Columbia University Press. Brazilian edition: *Os Índios Tenetehara: uma cultura em transição.* Rio de Janeiro: Ministério da Cultura, 1961.

Warren, Jonathan W. 2001. *Racial Revolutions: Antiracism and Indian Resurgence in Brazil.* Durham, N.C.: Duke University Press.

Weinstein, Barbara. 1983. *The Amazon Rubber Boom, 1850–1920.* Stanford, Calif.: Stanford University Press. Brazilian edition: *A Borracha na Amazonia: expansão e decadência, 1850–1920.* Trans. Lolio Lourenço de Oliveira. São Paulo: Hucitec-EDUSP, 1993.

————. 1996. *For Social Peace in Brazil: Industrialists and the Remaking of the Working Class in São Paulo, 1920–1964.* Duke: University of North Carolina Press. Brazilian edition: *(Re)formação da classe trabalhadora no Brasil.* São Paulo: Cortez Editora–Universidade São Francisco, 2000.

Weis, W. Michael. 1993. *Cold Warriors & Coups d'Etat: Brazilian-American Relations, 1945–1964.* Albuquerque: University of New Mexico Press.

Weschler, Lawrence. 1998. *A Miracle, a Universe: Settling Accounts with Torturers.* Chicago: University of Chicago Press.

Wesson, Robert G. 1981. *The United States and Brazil: Limits of Influence.* New York: Praeger.

Weyland, Kurt. 1996. *Democracy Without Equity: Failures of Reform in Brazil.* Pittsburgh, Pa.: University of Pittsburgh Press.

Williams, Daryle. 2001. *Culture Wars in Brazil: The First Vargas Regime, 1930–1945.* Durham, N.C.: Duke University Press.

Wirth, John D. 1970. *The Politics of Brazilian Development, 1930–1954.* Stanford, Calif.: Stanford University Press. Brazilian edition: *A Política de desenvolvimento na era Vargas.* Rio de Janeiro: Editora da FGV, 1973.

————. 1977. *Minas Gerais in the Brazilian Federation, 1889–1937.* Stanford, Calif.: Stanford University Press. Brazilian edition: *O Fiel da balança: Minas Gerais na Federação Brasileira, 1889–1937.* Rio de Janeiro: Paz e Terra, 1982.

Wiznitzer, Arnold. 1960. *Jews in Colonial Brazil.* New York: Columbia University Press.

Wolfe, Joel. 1993. *Working Women, Working Men: São Paulo and the Rise of Brazil's Industrial Working Class, 1900–1955.* Durham, N.C.: Duke University Press.

Worcester, Donald E. 1973. *Brazil: From Colony to World Power.* New York: Scribner's.

Wright, Antônia Fernanda P. de Almeida. 1972. *Desafio americano à preponderância britânica no Brasil: 1808–1850.* Rio de Janeiro: Imprensa Nacional.

————. 1978. *Testando o Leviathan: a presença dos Estados Unidos nos debates parlamentares de 1828 a 1837.* São Paulo: Perspectiva.

Wythe, George. 1949. *Brazil: An Expanding Economy.* New York: Twentieth-Century Fund

Young, Jordan M. 1967. *The Brazilian Revolution of 1930 and the Aftermath.* New Brunswick, N.J.: Rutgers University Press.

————. 1972. *Brazil, 1954–1964: End of a Civilian Cycle.* New York: Facts on File, 1972. Brazilian edition: *Brasil, 1954–1964: fim de um ciclo civil.* Rio de Janeiro: Nova Fronteira, 1974.

NOTES ON
CONTRIBUTORS

Paulo Roberto de Almeida has a doctoral degree in social sciences and has been a Brazilian career diplomat since 1977. He served as minister-counselor at the Brazilian embassy in Washington, D.C. (1999–2003), and is on assignment at the Strategic Issues Group of the presidency, in Brasília. His research interests are Brazil's economic history and international economic relations. He is the author of, among other books, *Relações internacionais e política externa do Brasil* (2004), *A Grande mudança* (2003), *Une histoire du Brésil* (2002), *Formação da diplomacia econômica no Brasil* (2001), *Le Mercosud: un marché commun pour l'Amérique du Sud* (2000), *O Estudo das relações internacionais do Brasil* (1999), *O Brasil e o multilateralismo econômico (1999)*, and *Mercosul: fundamentos e perspectivas* (1998). He is deputy editor of the *Revista Brasileira de Política Internacional*. The address of his website is www.pralmeida.org.

Werner Baer is professor of economics at the University of Illinois at Champaign-Urbana. A prolific writer on economic development and international economics, he has published hundreds of books, articles, and essays on Brazil's economy. His books include *Industrialization and Economic Development in Brazil* (1965), *The Development of the Brazilian Steel Industry* (1970), and the *Brazilian Economy: Growth and Development* (2001). He has taught at the Fundação Getúlio Vargas and lectured at many other Brazilian institutions, including the Universidade de São Paulo and the Pontifícia Universidade Católica in Rio de Janeiro. His e-mail address is w-baer@uiuc.edu.

Rubens Antônio Barbosa served as Brazil's ambassador to the United States from 1999 to 2004. In his previous assignment he was Brazil's ambassador to the United Kingdom (1994–99). He has served as Brazil's representative to the Latin American Integration Association and was Brazilian national coordinator for the Mercosul integration process. He is the author of *América Latina em perspectiva: a integração regional da retórica à realidade* (1991), *Panorama visto de Londres* (1998), and *Mercosul Codes* (2000). His e-mail address is rubarbosa@terra.com.br.

Leslie Bethell is Professor Emeritus of Latin American History at the University of London; Professorial Fellow of St. Antony's College, Oxford; and director of the Centre for Brazilian Studies, Oxford University (since 1997). He is the author of *The Abolition of the Brazilian Slave Trade* (1970); coauthor of *Latin America Between the Second World War and the Cold War, 1944–1948* (1992) and *A Guerra do Paraguai* (1995); and editor of *Brasil: O Fardo do passado, A promessa do futuro* (2002). He is the general editor of the eleven-volume *Cambridge History of Latin America* (1984–95), which is also being published in Spanish, Chinese, and Portuguese. His e-mail address is leslie.bethell@brazilian-studies.oxford.ac.uk.

Judy Bieber is associate professor of history at the University of New Mexico. Her research has focused on the social and political dynamics of the frontier in Brazil. She is the author of *Power, Patronage, and Political Violence: State Building on a Brazilian Frontier, 1822–1889* (1999). She is the editor of *Plantation Societies in the Era of European Expansion* (1997). Her e-mail address is jbieber@unm.edu.

Janet M. Chernela is a professor in the Department of Anthropology and the Latin American Studies Center at the University of Maryland, College Park, and formerly was a member of the faculty at the Instituto Nacional de Pesquisas da Amazônia and Florida International University. She has written more than seventy articles and the book *The Wanano Indians of the Brazilian Amazon: A Sense of Space* (1993). She has conducted fieldwork in the Amazon basin of Brazil since 1978 and is an appointed member of the American Anthropological Association's Commission on Indigenous Peoples of South America. Her e-mail address is chernela@ umd.edu.

Cyrus B. Dawsey III is a professor of geography at Auburn University, where he has served as director of the Institute for Latin American

Studies. He specializes in computerized cartography, urban models, historical geography, and the cultural geography of Brazil. He is coeditor of *Confederados: Old South Immigrants in Brazil* (1995) and author of more than fifty articles and reviews. His e-mail address is dawsecb@auburn.edu; website: www.auburn.edu/~dawsecb.

MARSHALL C. EAKIN is a professor of history at Vanderbilt University and executive director of the Brazilian Studies Association. His work focuses on industrialization and nation building. He is the author of *Tropical Capitalism: The Industrialization of Belo Horizonte, Brazil* (2001), *Brazil: The Once and Future Country* (1997), and *British Enterprise in Brazil: The St. John d'el Rey Mining Company and the Morro Velho Gold Mine, 1830–1960* (1989). His e-mail address is marshall.c.eakin@vanderbilt.edu.

ROBERTO GUIMARÃES is from Pernambuco. He did his graduate work at the University of Illinois, Champaign-Urbana and is on the staff of the International Monetary Fund.

ANN HARTNESS is director of the Nettie Lee Benson Latin American Collection at the University of Texas at Austin. She is a specialist on Brazilian bibliography, with a special emphasis on reference works and government publications. She is the author of *Brasil, obras de referência, 1965–1998* (1999) and *Subject Guide to Statistics in the Presidential Report of the Brazilian Provinces, 1830–1889* (1977), and the editor of *Continuity and Change in Brazil and the Southern Cone: Research Trends and Library Collections for the Year 2000* (1992). In 2003 the Brazilian government bestowed upon her its National Order of the Southern Cross. Her e-mail address is hartness@mail.utexas.edu.

K. DAVID JACKSON is a professor of Portuguese at Yale University. He specializes in the modernist movement in Brazil, especially the work of Oswald de Andrade. Jackson is the author of *Portugal: As primeiras vanguardas* (2003); *Camões and the First Edition of Os Lusíadas, 1572* (2003); *A Vanguarda literária no Brasil* (1998); *Os Construtores dos oceanos* (1998); *A Hidden Presence* (1995); *Sing Without Shame* (1990); and *A Prosa vanguardista: Oswald de Andrade* (1978). His e-mail adress is k.jackson@yale.edu.

ROBERT M. LEVINE died on April 1, 2003, after a long struggle with cancer. At his death he was a professor of history at the University of

Miami, where he had also served as director of the Latin American Studies Program. Perhaps the most prolific Brazilianist in the United States, he was the author of many books, including *The Vargas Regime: The Critical Years, 1934–1938* (1970), *Pernambuco in the Brazilian Federation, 1889–1937* (1978), *Vale of Tears: Revisiting the Canudos Massacre in Northeastern Brazil, 1893–1897* (1992), *Father of the Poor? Vargas and his Era* (1998), *Brazil: A History* (1999), and, with José Carlos Sebe Bom Meihy, *The Life and Death of Carolina Maria de Jesus.* (1995). Levine was also coeditor of the *Luso-Brazilian Review.*

JOSÉ NEISTEIN has been the executive director of the Brazilian-American Cultural Institute since 1970. He has taught at the University of Pennsylvania (1990–96) and has been a collaborating editor (art in Brazil) for the *Handbook of Latin American Studies* since 1972. He is the author of *Psychologie des brasilianische Portugiesisch* (1963); *Modern Brazilian Poetry* (1972); *Axl Leskoschek's Brazilian Miniatures* (1974); *Feitura das artes* (1981); *Leskoschek's Illustrations to Dostoievsky* (1984); and *Art in Brazil, from the Beginnings to Modern Times: An Annotated Bibliography* (1997). His email address is info@bacidc.org; website: www.bacidc.org.

EDWARD A. RIEDINGER is director of the Latin American Library at Ohio State University. He is the author of *Como se faz um presidente: a campanha de J. K.* (1988). He was the secretary for English-language correspondence for Juscelino Kubitschek (1972–76). Riedinger's e-mail address is riedinger.4@osu.edu; website: www.lib.ohio-state.edu/latweb/LATHOME.HTML.

CARMEN CHAVES TESSER is a professor of Spanish and Portuguese at the University of Georgia. She is also director of the Portuguese School at Middlebury College. Her research focuses on issues of language and theory, and translations of Spanish and Portuguese into English. She is the author of *Las Máscaras de la apertura: un contexto literario* (1998) and many articles for *Foreign Language Annals, Hispania, Georgia Review,* and the *Dictionary of Literary Biography,* among others. She has served as president of the American Association of Teachers of Spanish and Portuguese and is president of the National Federation of Associations of Teachers of Modern Languages. Her e-mail address is carmem@uga.edu.

SCOTT D. TOLLEFSON is an assistant professor of political science at Kansas State University, where he directs the master's degree program. He works on civil-military relations in Argentina, Brazil, and Chile, as well as international relations and security in Brazil and Latin America. He is the author of numerous articles and book chapters and serves as the international relations (Brazil) editor for the *Handbook of Latin American Studies*. His e-mail address is tollef@ksu.edu; webpage: www.ksu.edu/polsci.

Theodore Robert Young is dean of the Languages Division at Pasadena City College, California, and a research associate with the Latin American and Caribbean Center at Florida International University. He holds a doctoral degree in Romance languages and literatures from Harvard University and researches contemporary Brazilian film and literature in the twentieth century. He is the author of *O Questionamento da história em 'O Tempo e o vento' de Erico Verissimo* (1997) and coeditor of *A Twice-told Tale: Reinventing the Old World–New World Encounter in Latin American Literature and Film* (2000). His e-mail address is tryoung@pasadena.edu.

INDEX

Abad, Peter, 74
Abraham, Richard D., 94
Abreu, Caio Fernando, 115
Abreu, Capistrano de, 162, 183, 186,
    351, 464
Abreu, Maria Isabel, 82, 89
Academia Brasileira de Letras, 6
Adams, Mildred, 99
Ades, Dawn, 369–70
Adler, Emanuel, 300, 304
Afolabi, Niyi, 125
Africa, 31, 47, 53, 109, 178, 293, 295, 299,
    361, 375, 388, 405
Afro-Brazilians and Afro-Brazilian
    culture, 139–40, 143, 146, 150, 152,
    267, 382–83, 437
Agassiz, Louis, 4, 30, 49, 50, 311
Agosin, Marjorie, 119, 126
Aiex, Anoar, 121
Aires, Jorge Cardoso, 117
Albuquerque, Severino, 104, 105, 108,
    116, 120, 125
ALCANCE Project, 86
Alden, Dauril, 164, 186, 360, 460
Alencar, José de, 115, 355
Alencastro, Luiz Felipe de, 386
Alexander, Robert J., 12, 23, 436, 452, 460

Allegretti, Mary, 214
Allen, Elizabeth, 369
Allen, J. H. D., 94, 95
Alliance for Progress, 11, 42, 96, 98,
    269, 405
Almeida, Manuel Antônio de, 114, 115
Almeida, Onésimo, 53
Almeida, Paulo Roberto de, xiii, xvi,
    231, 386, 399, 420, 422, 460–61, 462,
    485
Alphonsus, João, 104
Alston, Lee, 252, 259
Alvarez, Sonia, 276, 279, 281, 461
Alves, Maria Helena Moreira, 60, 67
Amado, Jorge, 37, 50, 99, 100, 103, 104,
    113, 114, 116, 383
Amann, Edmund, 251, 257, 259, 367,
    370
Amaral, Aracy A., 137, 138, 154, 440
Amazon and Amazonia, 30, 31, 32, 37,
    53, 105, 120, 123, 133, 178, 182, 203,
    252, 275, 299, 300–301, 312, 313, 317,
    319, 320, 325, 328, 329, 330, 331, 333,
    348, 354, 355, 356, 357, 358, 361, 362,
    363, 365, 368, 369, 370, 371, 372,
    373–74, 378, 379, 383, 412, 429, 436,
    441, 486

American Association of Teachers of Spanish and Portuguese (AATSP), 54, 74, 77, 87, 97, 111, 488

American Council of Learned Societies, 8, 79, 426

American Council on the Teaching of Foreign Languages (ACTFL), 82, 84, 85

American Historical Association, 6, 41, 44, 170, 172

American Philosophical Society, 41

American Political Science Association, 265, 302

American Portuguese Studies Association, 97, 102, 110, 111

Ames, Barry, 277–78, 281–82, 422, 461

Amora, Antônio Soares, 100, 107

Anderson, Anthony B., 330, 334–35

Anderson, Robin L., 19, 23, 178, 186, 420, 461

Andrade, Ana Luiza, 108, 121, 125

Andrade, Carlos Drummond de, 100, 103, 104, 112, 113, 117, 119, 121, 368

Andrade, Mário de, 38, 100, 104, 113, 114, 115, 117, 120, 151, 152, 154–55

Andrade, Oswald de, 100, 104, 112, 113, 114, 117, 118, 487

Andrews, George Reid, 19, 23, 60, 67, 167, 179, 184, 186, 416, 453, 461

Andrews, Norwood, 103, 124

Ângelo, Ivan, 113, 115

ANPUH (National Association of University History Professors), 171, 172, 183

Anson, George, 349

Antelo, Raul, 107

anthropology, xiv, 39, 58, 66, 203–40, 361

Appleby, David P., 122, 123, 126, 145, 148, 155, 441, 442, 455, 461

Araújo, Virgínia de, 117

Arbousse-Bastide, Paul, 382

Argentina, 10, 43, 105, 167, 291, 299, 300, 356, 364, 403, 406, 408, 411, 412, 413, 414, 415, 416, 417, 421, 422, 436, 446, 489

Arizona State University, 56, 66, 103, 135

Armitage, John, 353, 461

Armstrong, Piers, 37, 49, 50, 182, 186

Army Specialized Training Program (ASTP), 79–80, 81

Asia, 109, 362, 375, 383, 388, 399, 416, 419

Assis, Joaquim Maria Machado de, 99, 100, 102, 104, 110, 111, 113, 114, 115, 116, 118, 119, 120, 121, 368, 379

Assunção, Mathias Rohrig, 369

Athayde, Roberto, 117

Atkins, G. Pope, 303, 304, 461

Auburn University, 167, 486

audio-lingual method (ALM), 81–83

Aufderheide, Patricia Ann, 178, 179, 187

Augelli, John P., 321, 327, 335

Australia, 37, 348, 350

Avelar, Idelber, 104, 105, 125

Ayres, Miriam, 105, 108, 125

Azevedo, Aluísio de, 99, 114, 115

Azevedo, Aroldo de, 322, 335

Azevedo, Fernando de, 99, 126, 267, 382, 401, 461

Azevedo, Luiz Heitor Corrêa, 144, 147, 151, 155

Azevedo, Thales de, 204

Baden, Nancy, 121, 126

Baer, Werner, xv, 10, 45, 50, 60, 69, 241, 244–45, 246, 247, 248, 250, 251, 252, 253, 254, 255, 256, 257, 258, 259–60, 261, 299, 305, 406, 408, 422, 461, 485

Baerle, Kaspar Van, 137

Bagby, Albert I., 116

Bahia, 96, 140, 142, 146, 172, 174, 176, 177, 178, 181, 204, 267, 326, 349, 350, 353, 354, 386, 444

Baker, Cynthia, 104, 126
Baklanoff, Eric, 246, 260, 406, 461
Baldus, Herbert, 206
Balée, William, 204, 209, 214–15, 232
Bamberger, Joan, 206, 231, 232
Bandeira, Manuel, 102, 104, 117, 118, 121, 126, 461
Barata, Mário, 134
Barbosa, Maria Somerlate, 104, 108, 125
Barbosa, Francisco de Assis, 4, 107
Barbosa, João Alexandre, 107, 118
Barbosa, Rubens Antônio, 45, 231, 461–62, 486
Barbosa, Rui, 172
Bardi, Pietro Maria, 134, 155, 158
Barickman, Bert, 181, 182, 186, 187, 462
Barletta, Michael, 300, 304
Barman, Roderick, 19, 23, 163, 165, 177, 181, 184, 186, 187, 372, 415, 420, 422, 462
Barr, Lois Baer, 119, 131
Barreto, Lima, 99, 100, 103, 113, 114
Barreto, Tobias, 121
Barrett, Linton L., 95, 99, 116
Barroso, Ary, 123
Barrutia, Richard, 81
Barthes, Roland, 182
Basso, Ellen, 151, 154, 155, 216, 217, 218, 222–23, 229, 230, 232
Bastide, Roger, 133, 134, 139, 155, 281, 382–83, 387, 393, 462
Basualdo, Carlos, 138
Batchelor, Malcolm, 95
Bates, Henry Walter, 354–55
Bates, Margaret, 99
Baum, Emmi, 116
Bayón, Damián, 136, 155
Bazin, Germain, 384
Beattie, Peter M., 40, 48, 178, 180, 187, 422, 462
Becker, Bertha K., 60, 67, 292, 304, 462
Becker, Howard S., 118
Beckerman, Paul, 254, 255, 259

Béhague, Gérard, 122, 126, 145, 146, 147, 148, 149, 150, 151, 152, 153, 156, 441, 455
Beiguelman, Paula, 175, 187
Belém, 147, 226
Bell, Stephen, 182, 187
Bello, José Maria, 14, 23
Benjamin, Walter, 39
Berardinelli, Cleonice, 107
Bergad, Laird, 174, 187
Berger, Mark T., 289, 304
Bergsman, Joel, 245, 247, 248, 249, 260, 408, 462
Bernucci, Leo, 105, 108, 121, 125
Berrien, William, 76, 89, 96, 126
Besse, Susan M., 178, 187, 462
Bethell, Leslie, xvi, 60, 68, 110, 163, 173, 174, 175, 187, 347, 362, 363, 366, 374, 425, 431, 450, 462, 486
Bieber, Judy, xv, 162, 181, 184, 186, 187, 462–63, 486
Bird, Pamela G., 116
Bishop, Elizabeth, 100, 112, 116, 117, 118, 127, 405, 463
Black, Jan Knippers, 289, 304, 411, 463
Bledsoe, Robert, 104, 124
Bloch, Pedro, 117
Boas, Franz, 185, 203, 205
Boehrer, George, 164, 171, 172, 185, 187–88
Bolivia, 299, 408, 409, 419, 436
Bonpland, Aimé, 30
Borges, Dain, 167, 178, 188, 280, 463
Borim, Dario, 104, 105, 125
Bork, Albert, 116
Bosi, Alfredo, 100
Boxer, Charles R., 4, 109, 127, 162, 347, 358–60, 361, 362, 363, 405, 463
Braga-Pinto, César, 104, 105, 125
Branche, Jerome, 125
Brandão, Ignácio de Loyola, 115
Brandeis University, 124
Branner, John Casper, 30, 74, 94, 127

Brannstrom, Christian, 329, 330, 334, 335

Brasil, Emanuel, 113, 127

Brasília, 226, 245, 297, 370, 414, 417, 485

Bratcher, Joe, 112

Braudel, Fernand, 182, 381, 383, 392

Brazilian-American Cultural Institute, 138, 488

Brazilian Anthropology Association (ABA), 214

Brazilian Association of Comparative Literature (ABRALIC), 102

Brazilian embassy, projects, ix–xiii, 420–21, 423

Brazilian History Recovery Project (Resgate-EUA), xi

brazilianist, brasilianista, brazilianism, ix, xi, xiii, 3–5, 17, 31–32, 33–34, 35, 37, 38, 39, 40, 43, 46, 48, 58, 96, 103, 163, 259, 269, 296, 302–3, 313, 318, 320, 324, 420–21

Brazilian Studies Association (BRASA), 97, 162, 183, 302, 487

Brazilian studies centers and programs, ix, xi, 8, 34, 53, 56, 101, 364, 365, 367–68, 392–95, 422

Briesemeister, Dietrich, 109

Brigham Young University, 124

Bristol University, 370

Brito, Paulo Henriques, 118

Brookshaw, David, 110

Brow, William, 125

Brown, Donald, 99

Brown, Harry W., 116

Brown, Timothy, 102, 124

Brown University, 53, 56, 66, 108, 110, 111, 125, 126, 166, 295

Bruand, Yves, 385

Bruneau, Thomas, 270, 273, 277, 282, 410, 463

Bruneti, Almir Campos, 107

Bueno, Eva Paulino, 125

Bulmer-Thomas, Victor, 60, 364, 463

Bunker, Stephen, 275, 282

Burdick, John, 179, 188, 267, 277, 278, 282

Burke, Peter, 366

Burnham, John W., 94

Burns, E. Bradford, 14, 23, 53, 60, 68, 165, 166, 167, 168, 171, 177, 185, 188, 289, 304, 406, 407, 463

Burton, Sir Richard, 311, 336, 355

Bury, John, 360–61

Bush, George W., 290, 421, 422

Butler, Kim, 19, 23, 179, 188, 419–20, 463

Butterman, Steven, 126

Cabrera Infante, Guillermo, 105, 120

Cal, Ernesto da, 102

Caldwell, Helen, 95, 100, 102–3, 116, 119, 127

California State University, Long Beach, 124

Callado, Antônio, 104, 113, 114, 117

Calógeras, João Pandiá, 13, 23, 405, 464

Câmara, Dom Helder, 45

Câmara, Joaquim Mattoso, Jr., 80, 82

Cambridge History of Latin America, 364–65, 366, 425, 431, 486

Cambridge University Press, 366–67

Cammack, Paul, 370

Camões, 94, 99, 105, 109, 355, 359, 360, 415

Campbell, Alan Tormaid, 370

Campos, Augusto de, 107, 118

Campos, Haroldo, 107, 110, 114, 118

Canada, 37, 43, 163, 311, 322, 326, 333, 334, 368, 372, 415, 417, 422, 433, 435

Cândido, Antônio, 100, 107, 118, 127, 281

Cantel, Raymond, 385

Canudos, 179, 183

Cardoso, Ciro Flamarion, 175, 176, 188

Cardoso, Eliana A., 254, 260

Cardoso, Fernando Henrique, 16, 23, 41, 162, 175, 188, 271, 272, 274, 281, 282, 293, 304, 366, 392, 407, 408, 418, 419, 420, 422, 464
Cardoso, Lúcio, 114
Cardoso, Manoel S., 32, 50, 164, 171, 172, 184, 185, 188, 193, 405
Carelli, Mário, 110
Caribbean, 8, 65, 73, 291, 388, 437
Carnegie Endowment and Carnegie Institute, 32, 79, 206
Carneiro, Cecílio, 115
Carneiro, Edison, 188
Carneiro, Robert L., 211, 212–13, 229, 232
Carson, James S., 75
Carson-Leavitt, Joyce, 125
Carter, Henry Hare, 94, 95, 96
Carter, Jimmy, 77
Carter, Rosalind, 45
Carter, William, 204, 236
Carvalho, José Geraldo Vidigal de, 176, 188
Carvalho, José Murilo de, 183
Carvalho, Marcus, 174–75, 188
Casa Rui Barbosa, 108, 172
Cascudo, Luís da Câmara, 151, 156
Castedo, Leopoldo, 135
Castelo, José Aderaldo, 100
Castelo Branco, Humberto, 18, 319
Castro, Antônio Barros de, 176, 189
Castro, Eduardo Viveiros de, 366
Castro, Fidel, 11, 22, 165, 268, 404, 406
Castro, Hebe Maria Mattos de, 176, 177, 189
Castro, Josué de, 13–14, 24, 115, 406, 464
Castro, Maria de Magalhães, 123
Catholic Church, 179, 270, 275, 277, 389
Catholic University of America, 164, 166, 427
Caulfield, Sueann, 40, 178, 189
Cavendish, Thomas, 348

Center for Applied Linguistics, 86
Central America, 8, 34, 57, 291, 321, 411, 412, 414
Central Intelligence Agency (CIA), 38, 50, 326, 402, 406
Centro Interdisciplinar de Estudos Contemporâneos, 108
Certeau, Michel de, 39, 47
Chaloub, Sidney, 176, 180, 189
Chamberlain, Bobby, 84, 89, 91, 111, 428, 438, 439, 449, 454
Chamberlain, Henry, 353
Chandler, Billy Jaynes, 177, 184, 189, 412, 464
Chang, Linda, 125
Chapman, Frank Michler, 30
Chase, Gilbert, 122, 144–45, 156
Chasteen John, 178, 189
Chernela, Janet M., xv, 203, 209–10, 214, 216–17, 222, 231, 233, 417, 464, 486
Chilcote, Ronald, 19, 47, 410, 416, 435, 452, 464–65
Child, Jack, 295, 296, 304
Chile, 11, 38, 293, 369, 410, 416, 418, 419, 421, 436, 489
China, 31, 47, 348, 401, 404, 405, 406, 408, 409, 411, 412, 415, 421
Chomsky, Noam, 78, 80, 82, 89–90
Chonchol, Jacques, 385
Christensen, Asher N., 265
Christian-based communities, 34, 48
Christie, William D., 355
Cioffari, Vicenzo, 79, 90
City College of New York, 95, 124
City University of New York, 213, 214
Clark, Fred, 103, 119, 120, 124
Clay, Jason, 225
Clay, Jennifer, 134
Cleary, David, 225, 233, 366
Clements, Benedict J., 253, 260, 465
Cline, Ray S., 292, 304
Cobbs, Elizabeth A., 290, 304, 417, 465

Cockburn, Alexander, 313, 330, 339, 415, 470

Coelho, Joaquim-Francisco, 103, 108, 121, 124

Coes, Donald V., 245, 253, 254, 255–56, 257, 259, 260, 465

Cohen, Thomas M., 419, 465

Colasanti, Marina, 106

Colby, Gerard, 38, 49, 50, 465

Colchie, Thomas, 116, 117

Cold War, 5, 21, 34, 42, 163, 165, 275, 288, 290–91, 292, 298, 299, 400, 435, 447

Cole, John Peter, 317, 322, 336

Coleman, Algernon, 79

College of Charleston, 108, 125

Collier, David and Ruth, 273, 276, 282

Collins, Randall, 217, 233

Colson, Frank, 370

Columbia University, xi, 33, 34, 37, 74, 95, 98, 99, 101, 102, 124, 164, 165, 166, 167, 168, 170, 203, 204, 208, 241, 312, 324, 325, 371, 372, 415, 422

Committee on Latin American History, 8

communism, 12, 15

Companhia Vale do Rio Doce (CVRD), 226

Condamine, Charles-Marie de la, 378

Confederates and Confederacy, 31, 311, 327

Conference on Latin American History (CLAH), 34, 50, 162, 170, 183, 325

Conklin, Beth, 220–21, 224, 233

Connecticut College, 103

Conniff, Michael, 167, 177, 179, 189, 413, 428, 448, 465

Conrad, Robert, 18, 24, 173, 174, 175, 177, 184, 189, 409, 413, 431, 451, 465

Conselho Nacional de Pesquisa (CNPq), 390

Contestado Rebellion, 179

Cook, Cecil, 206

Cook, James (Captain), 348, 349

Cooke Mission, 9, 244, 262

Coordenação de Aperfeiçoamento de Pessoal de Nível Superior (CAPES), 390

Corção, Gustavo, 115

Coriat, Benjamin, 385

Cornell University, 125, 167

Cortesão, Jayme, 151–52, 157

Costa, Emilia Viotti da, 60, 68, 162, 166, 168, 175, 186, 189–90, 421, 465

Costa, Hipólito José de, 6–7, 24, 403, 465

Costa, Iraci del Nero da, 173, 176, 185, 190

Costa, Sérgio Corrêa da, 99, 127, 401, 465

Costigan, Lúcia Helena, 54

Council for Advanced Professional Training (CAPES), 20

Council on International Educational Exchanges (CIEE), 64

Coutinho, Afrânio, 100, 103, 107, 118, 127, 466

Courteau, Joanna, 104, 108, 124

Couty, Louis, 4

Covington, Paula, 111, 127

Cowles, Maria Antônia, 86

Crawford, William Rex, 99

Crocker, Christopher, 206

Crocker, William H. and Jean, 206, 234

Cruz Costa, João, 13, 24, 406, 466

Cuba, 43, 44, 57, 291, 321, 402, 404, 405, 406, 414

Cuban Revolution, 4, 5, 11, 21, 34, 98, 268, 404

Cunha, Euclides da, 9, 24, 48, 99, 105, 114, 121, 268, 282, 357, 399, 466

Cunha, Manuela Carneiro da, 190

Curitiba, 35, 62

Curran, Mark, 103, 120, 121, 124

Curtis, Gerald, 104, 124

Daland, Robert, 266, 270, 282, 407, 466
Damasceno, Leslie, 104, 120, 121, 125
Da Matta, Roberto, 182, 206, 207, 234, 416, 466
Dampier, William, 348
Daniel, Mary L., 103, 116, 121, 124
Dantas, Audalio, 118
Dartmouth College, 32, 108, 125
Darwin, Charles, 353–54
Dassin, Joan, 104, 121, 124, 277, 282
Dávila, Jerry, 179, 180, 190, 423
Davis, Shelton, 223, 225, 234, 411, 466
Davis, Sonny B., 299–300, 305, 419, 466
Dawsey, Cyrus, xvi, 309, 317–18, 327, 328, 332, 336–37, 418, 466, 486
Dean, Warren, 15, 18, 24, 166, 168, 177, 182, 184, 185, 190, 200, 243, 244, 246, 260, 326, 337, 408, 414, 418, 466
Debret, Jean Baptiste, 137, 157
Deffontaines, Pierre, 321, 381, 383
Degler, Carl, 60, 68, 174, 176, 178, 190, 409, 466
De Jesus, Carolina Maria, 118, 179
De Jong, Gerrit, 119, 127, 281, 438, 453
Della Cava, Ralph, 15, 24, 177, 179, 184, 190, 277, 282, 408, 466
Denevan, William, 212, 313, 330, 337
Denis, Pierre, 379
Dennett, Charlotte, 38, 49, 50, 465
Dennis, Ron, 104, 124
Denslow, David, 243, 260
dependency theory, 16, 19, 38, 271–75, 288, 293–95
Derrida, Jacques, 47, 182
DeWitt, John, 466
Diacon, Todd, 179, 182, 186, 190
DiAntonio, Robert, 119, 120, 127
Dias, Eduardo Mayone, 60, 68
Dias, Maria Odila Leite da Silva, 179, 190
Dickenson, John, 311, 368, 374, 428, 448
Diégues, Manuel, Jr., 267
Diffie, Bailey, 95

Dimmick, Ralph E., 95, 99, 102, 116, 131
Dineen, Mark, 370
Dixon, Paul, 105, 119
Dixon, Sandra, 125
Doherty Foundation, Henry L. and Grace, 41
Dominican Republic, 34, 406
Dornbusch, Rudiger, 254, 260
Dos Passos, John, 96, 127, 405, 467
Dourado, Autran, 113, 114
Downes, Leonard, 112, 127
Dozier, Craig, 317, 337
Driver, David, 99, 120, 124, 128
Drummond, John, 134
Duke University, 65, 125
Dulles, John W. F., 15, 18, 24, 96, 128, 177, 190–91, 407, 408, 410, 411, 412, 416, 419, 467
Dunkerley, James, 364
Dunn, Chris, 105, 123, 125, 128
Dutch, 137, 172, 350, 351, 353, 358, 359, 360, 376
Dutra, Francis, 184, 191, 431, 451
Dwyer, John P., 116
Dzidzienyo, Anani, 184

Eakin, Marshall C., xiii, xv, 19, 24–25, 60, 68, 96, 128, 167, 180, 183, 191, 231, 264, 269, 282, 415–16, 419, 422, 462, 467, 487
Earth Summit (1992), 142, 429
Eco, Humberto, 39
economics, 37, 58, 66, 241–63
Eden, Michael, 365
education, 38, 48, 66, 152–53, 180
Edwards, William Henry, 30
Egler, Claudio A. G., 60, 67, 292–93, 304, 462
Eisenberg, Peter, 15, 25, 36, 173, 174, 175, 184, 191, 410, 467
Elkins, Stanley, 173, 185, 191
Ellenbogen, Bert, 270, 282
Elliott, L. E., 96, 128

Ellis, E. Percy, 116
Ellison, Fred P., 53, 74, 81, 88, 90, 102, 116, 118, 120, 124, 128
Engel, Magali, 178, 191
England. *See* United Kingdom
English, Adrian, 292, 305
Enlace: The Newsletter of the American Association of Teachers of Spanish and Portuguese, 68
Erickson, Kenneth, 273, 283, 411, 467–68
Espírito Santo, 176
Estado Novo, 32
Esteves, Martha Abreu, 178, 191
Europe, 20, 36, 41, 109–10, 124, 151, 163, 269, 288, 291, 293, 295, 299, 311, 318, 320, 375, 401, 402, 406, 416, 420
Evans, Clifford, 211–13, 236, 475
Evans, Peter, 247, 261, 274, 275, 278, 283, 295, 305, 412, 452, 468
Exeter University, 371

Faissol, Speridião, 312, 318, 321, 322, 324, 337, 339
Faletto, Enzo, 271–72, 274, 293, 304, 407, 464
Farias, José, 104, 125
Faucher, Philippe, 273
Faulkner, William, 105
Fausto, Boris, 60, 68, 468
Fearnside, Phillip, 330, 337–38
Feldman, David, 81, 91
Felix, Regina Rogerio, 126
Ferguson, R. Brian, 209, 234
Fernand Braudel Center, 46
Fernandes, Florestan, 17, 19, 162, 274, 283, 408, 468
Fernandez, Oscar Lorenzo, 123
Ferreira, Débora, 104, 105, 126
Ferrez, Marc, 379
Figueiredo, Guilherme, 117
Figueiredo, João, 223, 412
Filho, Eurídice Silva, 125

Fisher, William, 219–20, 222–23, 226, 229, 234
Fishlow, Albert, 37, 244, 249, 252–53, 254, 255, 261
Fitz, Earl E., 116, 119, 130
Fitzgibbon, Russell, 96, 128, 265, 431, 451
Flasche, Hans, 109
Flecknoe, Richard, 348
Fleischer, David, 36, 46, 273, 281, 283, 297, 305
Fleming, Peter, 358
Fletcher, James C., 30–31, 50, 311, 338
Florentino, Manolo, 176, 191
Florida International University, 56, 61, 66, 125, 486, 489
Flory, Thomas, 177, 181, 184, 191, 468
Flowers, Nancy, 213–14, 234, 238, 240
Flynn, Peter, 273, 283, 368, 369, 412, 468
Folha de São Paulo, 36, 46
Fonseca, Eduardo Giannetti da, 60, 69
Fonseca, Rubem, 113, 115
Font, Mauricio, 468
Fontaine, Roger, 289, 305, 468
Ford Foundation, 11, 20, 37, 41, 45, 81, 98, 108, 124, 268, 315, 325
Ford, J. D. M., 94, 111, 128, 453
foreign policy and international relations, 22, 288–308
Fortaleza, 63
Foster, David William, 421, 438, 453, 454, 468
Fostini, John, 116, 117
Foucault, Michel, 39, 47, 182
Foweraker, Joe, 311, 369
Fox, Annette Baker, 290, 305
France and French, 5, 20, 21, 39, 105, 110, 122, 133, 174, 182, 206, 321, 345, 375–95, 403, 405, 406, 407, 408
FRANCIS (database), 391
Franconi, Rodolfo, 104, 108, 121, 125
Franklin, John Hope, 174, 191

Franssen, Paul, 119, 128
Fraser, Valerie, 369–70
Freitas, Décio, 176, 177, 182, 191–92
French, John, 168, 180, 184, 192, 417, 431, 451, 468
Freyre, Gilberto, 6, 9, 13, 17, 25, 36, 99, 100, 106, 118, 128, 162, 172–73, 176, 182, 191, 267, 268, 283, 366, 382, 387, 399, 400, 404, 405, 468
Frizzi, Adria, 116, 125
Fromont, Pierre, 383
Fry, Peter, 371–72
Fryer, Peter, 60–61, 68
Fulbright programs, 11, 42, 50, 98, 108, 268, 315, 400
FUNAI (National Indian Foundation of Brazil), 225
Fundação Getúlio Vargas, 301, 318, 485
Fundação Joaquim Nabuco, 108
Fundação Roberto Marinho, 86
Furley, Peter, 370
Furtado, Celso, 13, 17, 25, 293, 305, 366, 387, 405, 406, 468–69

Galiza, Luiz, 117
Gall, Norman, 46
Galloway, J. H., 326, 338
Galvão, Eduardo, 203–4, 239, 483
Galvão, Marília, 322
Galvão, Patrícia, 115
Galvão, Walnice Nogueira, 36, 107
Galves, Charlotte, 88
García, Frederick, 103, 124
Gardner, George, 354
Garfield, Seth, 182, 191, 469
Garric, Robert, 383
Gasparian, Fernando, xi
Gebara, Ademir, 176, 192
Geiger, Pedro Pinchas, 318, 322
gender, women, and sexuality studies, 38, 39, 44, 47, 179, 183, 210, 276, 279, 371
Genovese, Eugene, 174, 192, 200

George, David S., 104, 120, 121, 125
Georgetown University, xi, 65–66, 82, 83, 84, 85, 86, 88, 101, 108, 124, 164, 421
Germans and Germany, 5, 20, 31, 32, 45, 109, 295, 299, 321, 326, 376, 377, 411, 415, 416; Ibero-americanisches Institut, 109
Giacomelli, Eloah F., 116
Ginway, Elizabeth, 104, 105, 125
Gledson, John, 110, 366, 368
Glickman, Nora, 119
Goals 2000, 86–87
Godfrey, Brian, 326, 327, 328, 329, 334, 335, 338, 419, 469
Góes, José Roberto, 176
Goiás, 163, 182, 321, 324
Goldberg, Isaac, 98–99, 112, 119, 128
Goldsmith, W., 245, 261
Gomes, Antônio Carlos, 147, 154
Gomes, Flávio dos Santos, 177, 192, 199
Gomez, Gale Goodwin, 225
Gomez, Mercio, 204
Gomez, R. A., 268, 283
Gonçalves, Marcos Augusto, 36, 50
Gonzalez, Mike, 365
González Echevarría, Roberto, 116, 117
Goodman, David, 364, 365
Gordon, Lincoln, 35, 246, 247, 261, 288, 297, 305, 405, 422, 469
Gordon, Richard Allen, 126
Gorender, Jacob, 175, 192
Goulart, João, 12, 38, 319, 406, 432
Gow, Peter, 365
Graham, Douglas H., 252, 261
Graham, Laura, 151, 154, 157, 216, 220–21, 222, 229, 233, 235
Graham, Lawrence S., 270, 283, 469
Graham, Maria, 353
Graham, R. B. Cunninghame, 357
Graham, Richard, 14, 19, 25, 157, 163, 165, 168, 174, 175, 177, 181, 185, 192, 294, 305, 407, 408, 416, 469

Graham, Sandra Lauderdale, 19, 25, 168, 173, 178, 192, 417, 469
Gramsci, Antonio, 38, 39
Grant, Andrew, 350, 353, 376, 378, 395
Graves, Mortimer, 79
Great Britain. *See* United Kingdom
Green, James, 19, 40, 178, 183, 184, 421
Greenfield, Gerald, 178, 182, 192–93
Greenleaf, Richard E., 135, 157
Gregor, Thomas, 209, 210, 229, 235, 469
Greimas, Algirdas, 80
Griffin, Charles C., 96, 128, 157, 431, 451
Grinberg, Keila, 176, 193
Grommers, Engelbert L., 246, 247, 261
Gross, Daniel, 203, 213–14, 225, 229, 234, 235, 238, 240
Grossman, William F., 116
Grubb, Kenneth, 357–58, 360
Guarnieri, Camargo, 148
Guggeheim Foundation, 41, 315
Guillermoprieto, Alma, 61, 68
Guimarães, Bernardo, 103
Guimarães, Roberto, xv, 241, 487
Gulbenkian Foundation, Calouste, 61, 136, 394

Haber, Stephen, 60, 68, 243, 261, 469
Haberly, David, 103, 116, 120, 124
Haddad, Eduardo, 258, 260, 261
Hadfield, William, 355
Haggett, Peter, 317, 338
Hagopian, Frances, 272, 276, 278, 279, 280, 283, 434, 452, 469
Hahner, June, 19, 167, 177, 178, 180, 184, 193, 408, 413, 416, 428, 449, 469–70
Haines, Gerald, 19, 25, 291, 305, 415, 470
Haiti, 34, 57, 414
Hall, Anthony, 311, 365, 366
Hall, John R., 294, 364
Hall, Michael, 36
Hall Company, G. K., 427
Hallewell, Laurence, 370, 413, 429, 439, 449, 454, 470

Hambloch, Ernest, 358
Hamilton, D. Lee, 99
Hamilton, Russell, 103, 124
Hanchard, Michael, 19, 267, 278, 283, 417, 420, 470
Handbook of Latin American Studies (HLAS), 8–9, 135, 142, 145–46, 164, 171, 184, 265, 266, 280, 302, 323–24, 399, 401, 424, 426–27, 440, 445, 449, 470, 488, 489
Hanke, Lewis, 96, 128
Harding, Rachel, 179, 193, 470
Harding, Timothy, 178, 193
Hargis, Kent, 258, 260
Haring, Clarence, 33, 164, 404, 470
Harris, Mark, 371
Harris, Marvin, 10, 49, 204, 231, 239, 326, 338, 403, 470
Harrison, Marguerite, 105, 125, 440, 455
Hartness, Ann, xvi, 111, 128, 184, 193, 424, 428, 432, 449, 451, 470, 487
Harvard University, 7, 9, 33, 56, 57, 74, 94, 95, 96, 98, 102, 103, 108, 124, 125, 164, 165, 206–7, 213, 217, 229, 323, 324, 361, 366, 371, 426, 438, 489
Hasenbalg, Carlos Alfredo, 176, 193, 437, 453
Hastings, Kim, 105, 125
Hatoum, Milton, 106, 115
Hawkins, William and Richard, 348
Heapy, Dorothy, 116
Hecht, Susanna B., 313, 330, 339, 415, 470
Hecht, Tobias, 48, 50
Heckenberger, Michael, 213, 235
Hemming, John, 361–62, 373–74, 412, 414, 470–71
Henderson, James, 353
Henfrey, Colin, 368
Hensey, Frederick G., 81
Herkenhoff, Paulo, 138
Herndon, William Lewis, 6, 25, 30, 471

Herron, Robert, 103, 124
Herskovits, Melville J., 152, 157, 185
Hertelendy, Susan, 116
Hewings, Geoffrey, 258, 260, 261
Higbee, Edward C., 317, 339
Higgins, Kathleen, 174, 178, 193
Hill, Lawrence, 96, 128, 164, 184, 193, 400, 471
Hilton, Ronald, 95, 99
Hilton, Stanley, 18, 25, 35, 177, 184, 194, 289, 292, 305–6, 410, 411, 413, 471
Hirst, Mônica, 301, 414, 471
Hispania, 74, 111
Hispanic American Historical Review, 6, 8, 32, 46–47, 162, 167, 170, 174, 183
Hispanic American Periodicals Index (HAPI), 425, 427–28, 449
history, 39, 40, 42, 43, 44, 56, 58, 66, 222
Hobsbawm, E. J., 38
Hodge, Henry, 81
Hoffnagel, Judith, 36
Hoffnagel, Marc, 36
Holanda, Heloísa Buarque de, 107, 122
Holanda, Sérgio Buarque de, 17, 36, 107, 162, 182, 183, 387
Hollingsworth, Margaret Richardson, 114
Holloway, Thomas, 19, 25, 167, 179, 184, 194, 411, 413, 417, 471–72
Holton, Kimberly DaCosta, 125–26
Horowitz, Irving Louis, 270, 284, 406, 472
Horton, Rod W., 116
Hourcade, Pierre, 383
Howard, Catherine, 225
Hower, Alfred, 102, 109, 112, 116, 124, 128
Huddle, Donald, 245, 247, 248, 261
Huggins, Martha, 289, 306, 472
Hulet, Claude, 53, 119, 128, 438, 454
Humboldt, Alexander von, 4, 30, 311
Humphrey, John, 371

Humphreys, R. A., 360, 363
Hunnicut, Benjamin, 96, 128, 401, 472
Hunter, Wendy, 276, 279, 280, 284, 419, 472
Hurrell, Andrew, 293, 298, 301, 305, 306, 367
Hutchinson, Harry W., 13, 25, 404, 472
Huxley, Francis, 361

Ianni, Octávio, 176, 194
Igel, Regina, 97, 104, 108, 121, 124, 128
India, 44, 300, 348, 400, 405, 406
Indiana University, 63, 106, 107, 108, 124, 125, 126, 166, 324, 360
Indians and indigenous peoples, 146, 151, 186, 203–40, 373, 377–78, 385, 436–37
Instituto Histórico e Geográfico Brasileiro (IBGE), 170, 172, 318, 321, 339, 359, 430, 433
Inter-American Development Bank, 11, 12, 404, 418, 446
Inter-American Foundation, 274
International Association of Lusitanists, 97, 102, 110
International Colloquium on Luso-Brazilian Studies, 96, 97, 126, 172, 182–83, 359, 360–61, 402
International Conference Group on Portugal, 97
Iowa State University, 88, 124
Ishimatsu, Lori, 104, 116, 120, 125
Israel, 37, 300
Istoé, 38
Itamarati, 106, 297–98, 403
Ivo, Lêdo, 115

Jackson, Edwina, 137
Jackson, Elizabeth, 105, 116, 125
Jackson, K. David, xiv, 93, 103, 116, 118, 121, 124, 129, 439, 453, 487
Jackson, William V., 13, 26, 111, 129, 392, 406, 472

Jakobson, Roman, 80
James, Preston, 10, 26, 129, 281, 312, 313, 317, 321, 323–4, 326, 330, 339, 400, 472
Japan and Japanese, 32, 37, 41, 53, 179, 185, 299, 327, 351, 358–59, 385, 412
Jensen, John, 60, 69, 86, 88, 91
Jesuits, 172, 351
Jews and Jewish studies, 73, 121, 179
João VI, Dom, 378
Jobim, Tom, 123
Johns Hopkins University, 31, 45, 107, 165, 166, 168, 170, 279, 303
Johnson, John J., 12
Johnson, Orna, 209
Johnson, Randal, 60, 68, 104, 118, 120, 121, 122, 124, 129
Joint Brazil-United States Economic Development Commission, 10, 26, 401, 402, 472
Jones, Chester Lloyd, 75, 90
Jones, Clarence, 312, 339
Jones, Willis Knapp, 117
Joslin, David, 365–66
Journal of Latin American Studies, 366

Kadt, Emanuel de, 362, 365, 371
Kahl, Joseph, 270, 284
Kanitz, Stephen, 60, 68
Kaplan, L. C., 116
Karasch, Mary, 167, 173, 174, 178, 182, 184, 186, 194, 472
Karnoff, Neel, 116
Karpa-Wilson, Sabrina, 104, 108, 125
Kasten, Lloyd, 94, 95, 108
Kato, Mary, 88
Keck, Margaret, 276, 279, 284, 417, 472
Keith, Henry, 116
Kelly, Philip, 296, 306
Kelm, Orlando, 85, 90, 91
Kennedy, Bryan, 126
Kennedy, John F., 12, 269, 404, 405
Kerstentzsky, Isaac, 247, 254, 260

Keys, Kerry Shawn, 116, 117
Kidder, Daniel P., 30–31, 50, 96, 129, 311, 338
Kiddy, Elizabeth, 179, 194
Kiemen, Mathias C., 403, 472
Kindersley, Mrs. Nathaniel, 349
Kinzo, Mari D'Alva, 60, 68, 364
Kipling, Rudyard, 357
Kirkendall, Andrew, 181, 194
Kirschenbaum, Leo, 99
Kittleson, Roger, 181, 194
Klein, Herbert, 166–67, 168, 173, 174, 181, 186, 194, 196
Knight, Peter T., 251, 254, 261
Knivet, Anthony, 348
Knowlton, Edgar G., 116
Knox, John, 102, 116
Knox College (Illinois), 66
Koebel, William Henry, 357
Koike, Dale, 84, 90, 92
Koster, Henry, 311, 340, 352, 353
Kottak, Conrad Phillip, 123, 227, 231, 235
Kowarick, Lúcio, 176, 194
Kraay, Hendrik, 179, 180, 194
Kracke, Waud, 210, 229, 235
Krapohl, Kern, 116
Kubitschek, Juscelino, 12, 403, 404, 432, 488
Kuznesof, Elizabeth, 173, 178, 184, 194, 414, 472

labor movements and labor relations, 12, 15, 66, 180, 276
Lacerda, Carlos, 18
Lacey, E. A., 116
Lado, Robert, 82
Lago, Luiz A. Corrêa do, 176, 194, 299, 304
Lake Forest College, 125
Lambert, Jacques, 166, 284
Landau, Georges D., 299, 306
Landers, Clifford, 116

Landers, Vanda Bonafini, 121, 125
Landes, Ruth, 33, 35, 96, 129, 185, 194, 400, 473
Lane, Helen R., 116
Lang, Henry, 94
Lange, Francisco Curt, 146, 158, 384
Langfur, Hal, 181, 182, 194
Langoni, Carlos Geraldo, 253, 261
Langsdorf, Georg Heinrich von, 376
LAPTOC, 446
Lathrap, Donald, 212, 235
Lathrop, Thomas A., 60, 68
Latin American Microfilm Project (LAMP), 426, 444, 445, 446
Latin American Studies Association (LASA), 97, 183, 302, 325
Lauerhass, Ludwig, 53
Lave, Jean Carter, 206, 217, 231, 235
Leach, Edmund, 361, 372
Leacock, Ruth, 19, 26, 289, 306, 416, 473
Leeds University, 370
Leff, Nathaniel, 10, 242–43, 245, 250, 262, 407, 473
Lehmann, David, 366
Lehnen, Leila, 63
Leite, Dante Moreira, 107
Leite, Paulo Moreira, 35, 49, 50
Leroy, Claude E., 60, 68
Léry, Jean de, 4, 377–78, 473
Lesser, Jeffrey, 19, 26, 36, 60, 68, 179, 180, 183, 184, 195, 278, 284, 418, 420, 473
Levi, Darrell, 178, 180, 184, 195
Levine, Robert M., xiv, xvi, 13, 14, 18, 26, 30, 35, 50, 52, 53, 60, 68, 118, 164, 165, 166, 177, 179, 180, 183, 184, 185, 195, 301, 302, 324, 340, 406, 408, 411, 416, 420, 428, 430, 431, 437, 449, 450, 451, 453, 473–74, 487–88
Lévi-Strauss, Claude, 80, 205, 207, 219, 236, 361, 381, 383
Lewin, Linda, 167, 177, 178, 184, 195, 423, 474

Lewis, Colin, 364, 365
Libby, Douglas, 163, 174, 195
Libecap, Gary D., 252, 259
Library of Congress, 95, 112, 144, 172, 185, 265, 280, 333, 340, 359, 402, 426, 427, 433, 434, 442, 443, 444, 449; Hispanic Division, 8, 133, 135, 138, 142, 399, 401, 424, 426
Lima, Alceu Amoroso, 6
Lima, Emma Eberlein O.F., 60, 68
Lima, Jorge de, 104, 117
Lima, Lana Lage da Gama, 177, 195
Lima, Luiz Costa, 107, 118, 129
Lindley, Thomas, 350
linguistics, 39, 73–92, 99–100
Lins, Osman, 100, 113, 114, 115, 117, 121
Linz, Juan, 273, 284
Lisansky, Judith, 204, 222, 225, 226, 236
Lispector, Clarice, 104, 106, 113, 115, 117, 119, 120, 368, 370
literature, 37, 42, 52, 56, 58, 66, 93-132
Livermore, Harold, 109, 129, 360, 362
Lobo, Luísa, 107
Loewenstein, Karl, 32, 50, 96, 129, 265, 266, 268, 284
Lokensgaard, Mark, 104, 125
Lombardi, Mary, 178, 195, 434, 453
London School of Economics, 364, 365
Loos, Dorothy, 102, 116, 120, 124, 129
Lopes, Albert, 96, 99, 104
Lopes, Francisco Caetano, Jr., 105, 108, 125
Lopes, Maria Angélica, 108, 125
Louisiana State University, 33, 266, 325
Love, Joseph, 14, 26, 165, 166, 177, 185, 196, 281, 284, 409, 412, 474
Lowe, Elizabeth, 105, 116, 120, 124
Lowenthal, Abraham F., 290, 306, 474
Lowie, Robert H., 205–6, 236
Lowrie, Samuel H., 267, 280
Lucas, Fábio, 107
Luccock, John, 352

Ludwig, Armin K., 319, 340, 414, 432, 451, 474
Luebke, Frederick, 326, 340, 474
Luna, Francisco Vidal, 173, 174, 176, 181, 196
Lunes, Samira A., 60, 68
Luso-Brazilian Review, 47, 103, 110, 111, 162, 179, 183, 196, 488
Luso-Brazilian studies, 95, 98, 106, 109

MacArthur Foundation, 41–42, 294
Macaulay, Neill, 18, 26, 166, 408, 414, 474
Machado, Aníbal, 104
Machado, José Bettencourt, 118, 129
Machado, Lourival Gomes, 136
MacLachlan, Colin, 171, 423
Macmillan, Gordon, 370
Mac Nichol, Murray, 104, 124
McBride, Maria-Odilia Leal, 125
McCann, Bryan, 180, 196
McCann, Frank D., 46, 165, 177, 180, 184, 196, 289, 306, 409, 465, 474
McDonough, Peter, 19, 273, 284, 413, 474
McGowan, Chris, 61, 68, 150, 158, 442, 455–56
McGregor, Duncan, 365
McGuirk, Bernard, 119, 371
McNelis, Paul D., 255, 262
Madox, Richard, 348
Magrans, Ramon, 125
Mainwaring, Scott, 277, 278, 284–85, 414, 420, 474–75
Maligo, Pedro, 105, 108, 120, 125, 129
Malkiel, Yakov, 94
Malloy, James M., 273, 284, 412, 475
Maloney, William, 258, 260
Manaus, 147, 373
Manchester, Alan K., 164, 184, 196, 406, 475
Mandel, Paul, 37
Maracá Rainforest Project, 373–74

Maram, Sheldon, 178, 196, 475
Marchant, Alexander, 10, 32, 33, 50, 95, 96, 164, 171, 172, 184, 185, 196, 267, 280, 281, 284, 286, 402, 475
Marchant, Elizabeth, 104, 106, 125
Marcos, Plínio, 120
Margolis, Maxine, 204, 236, 475
Mark, Murillo, 136
Marques, Oswaldino, 107
Marsh, Laurence C., 247, 262
Marshak, Stephen, 58
Marshall, Oliver, 368, 374
Martin, Percy Alvin, 106, 184
Martins, Amilcar, 174, 196
Martins, Heitor, 107, 121
Martins, José de Souza, 366
Martins, Lêda, 225
Martins, Roberto, 174, 196
Martins, Wilson, 35, 100, 107, 112, 118, 120, 121, 129
Martius, K. F. P. von, 4, 151
Marx, Roberto Burle, 141, 142
Marxism, 34, 38, 41, 44, 175, 207, 271, 316
Mason, Richard, 361–62
Massi, Fernanda, 96, 129, 163, 170, 197, 417, 475
Mate, Herbert, 99, 124
Mato Grosso, 32, 332, 362
Matos, Francisco Gomes de, 81, 88
Matos, Gregório de, 99
Mattos, Carlos de Meira, 295, 306
Mattos, Sérgio, 123
Mattoso, Kátia M. de Queirós, 176, 197, 386, 475
Mauro, Frédéric, 385, 394
Mawe, John, 352
Maxwell, Kenneth, 163, 164, 178, 181, 184, 197, 305, 363, 366, 371, 475
Maybury-Lewis, David, 206–8, 225, 229, 236, 361, 367
Mazzara, Richard, 116, 119
Meade, Teresa, 47, 180, 197, 475

Mecham, J. Lloyd, 265
Medeiros, Paulo de, 110
Mee, Margaret, 142, 158, 362
Meggers, Betty, 211–14, 229, 236, 409, 475–76
Meghreblian, Caren Ann, 137, 158
Mehrtens, Cristina Peixoto, 48, 180, 198, 267, 285
Meihy, José Carlos Sebe Bom, 35, 40, 49, 96, 103, 118, 127, 163, 183, 184, 195, 197, 463, 474, 488
Meireles, Cecília, 100, 104, 106, 117, 120
Meireles, Cildo, 138
Melatti, Julio Cezar, 206, 236
Mello, Evaldo Cabral de, 183
Mello, Kátia, 38, 50
Mellon Foundation, Andrew W., 446
Melo Neto, João Cabral de, 104, 117, 121
Mendes, Leonardo Pinto, 125
Mendes, Murilo, 100, 105
Menton, Seymour, 112
Mercosul, 299, 417, 418, 419, 420, 421, 486
Merrim, Stephanie, 105, 119, 120
Mesa-Lago, Carmelo, 109, 129
Messner, Dieter, 110
Metcalf, Alida, 173–74, 178, 186, 197, 476
Mexico, 6, 8, 10, 31, 32, 40, 43, 47, 53, 54, 57, 58, 67, 164, 243, 266, 270, 290, 321, 369, 407, 409, 417, 446
Meyers, Robert, 105, 125
Miceli, Sérgio, 381, 416, 476
Michigan State University, 38, 108, 125
Middlebury College, 61, 79, 488
Middle East, 299, 375, 383, 388, 404, 407, 408, 410, 413, 414, 415, 416, 418, 419, 422
Miller, Charles R. D., 96
Miller, Edgar H., 116
Miller, Shawn, 181, 182, 197
Milleret, Margo, 63, 85, 92, 104, 125

Minas Gerais, 95, 146, 174, 176, 177, 178, 182, 276, 317, 324, 332, 352
Mindlin, Henrique E., 134, 141, 158
Modernism and Modern Art Week, 98, 103, 137, 143
Modern Language Association (MLA), 76, 77, 82, 84, 87, 94, 97, 438, 445, 454
Moisés, Carlos Felipe, 107
Moisés, Massaud, 100, 107
Momsen, Richard P., Jr., 317, 318, 328, 329, 340, 408, 476
Monbeig, Pierre, 321, 381, 383–84, 386
Moniz, Naomi Hoki, 105, 108, 121, 124
Moniz Bandeira, L. A., 476
Monteiro, Adolfo Casais, 107
Monteiro, John, 163, 186, 193, 197
Monteiro Lobato, José, 102, 116
Moog, Clodomir Vianna, 13, 26, 102, 118, 129, 406, 476
Moore, Barrington, 271, 285
Moraes, Rubens Borba de, 96, 404, 425, 428, 449, 476
Moran, Emilio F., 204, 211, 226, 236, 329, 332, 335–36, 340
Morazé, Charles, 384
Moreira, Luci de Biaji, 104, 108, 125
Moreira, Luiza, 108, 125
Morley, Helena, 118, 129
Morley, Samuel, 246–47, 248, 249, 254, 262
Morris, Fred, 45
Morris, Michael A., 297, 306, 476
Morse, Richard, 10, 14, 38, 50–51, 96, 129–30, 164, 165, 166, 167, 183, 197, 404, 406, 476
Moser, Gerald, 95
Moser, Robert, 126
Mosher, Jeffrey Carl, 181, 197
Mota, Carlos Guilherme, 162, 183
Mott, Luiz, 176, 197
Motta, José Flávio, 176, 197
Moura, Clóvis, 176, 197

Mueller, Bernardo, 252, 259
Mulhall, Michael G., 356
Muller, Keith D., 328, 329–30, 332, 334, 341, 410, 477
Mulvey, Patricia, 179, 186, 197
Murphy, Robert and Yolanda, 204, 208–10, 229, 237

Nabuco, Joaquim, 7, 99, 106, 172, 175, 401, 477
Naro, Antony, 36, 88
Naro, Nancy, 36, 174, 197, 365
Nascimento, Milton, 150
Natal, 46
National Council for Scientific and Technological Development (CNPq), 20
National Defense Education Act (1958), 5, 21, 75, 77, 96, 98, 268, 281; Foreign Language and Area Studies fellowships, 64–65, 98; Title VI, 57, 61, 64–65, 77, 86, 98, 103, 106–7, 165
National Endowment for the Arts, 42
National Endowment for the Humanities, 42, 55
Nazmi, Nader, 254, 255, 256, 257, 262
Nazzari, Muriel, 178, 198, 477
Needell, Jeffrey, 19, 26, 167, 180, 184, 198, 379, 415, 477
Needham, Rodney, 361
Neistein, José, xv, 113, 130, 133, 159, 440, 455, 477, 488
Neme, Mario, 137
Nery, Adalgisa, 99
Ness, Walter L., 252, 262
Neto, José Maia, 118
Neto, Mário Cravo, 138
Neves, Margaret A., 116
Newfarmer, Richard S., 247, 262
Newton, Dolores, 206, 231, 237
New York University, 35, 66, 95, 98, 102, 103, 107, 108, 124, 125, 165, 166, 168, 170, 446

Nicholls, William H., 251, 262
Niebuhr, Ralph, 116
Niemeyer, Oscar, 141, 380
Nimuendajú, Curt (née Curt Unkel), 205–6, 213, 237
Nishida, Mieko, 174, 198
Nist, John, 103, 112, 116, 117, 120, 130, 477
Nixon, Richard M., 12, 404, 409, 410
Noda, Roberto, 104, 130
Noll, João Gilberto, 106
Normano, João Frederico, 9, 26, 477
Northwestern University, 95, 124, 126
Notre Dame University, 56, 279; Kellogg Institute, 56
Nottingham University, 371
Novais, Fernando, 182, 198, 294
Nowell, Charles, 95
Nugent, Stephen, 229, 231, 237, 365
Nunes, Benedito, 107
Nunes, Jairo, 88
Nunes, Maria Luísa, 111, 120, 130

Oakenfull, J. C., 356–57
O'Donnell, Guillermo, 271, 272, 275, 285
Ohio State University, 54, 57, 83, 488
Olinto, Antônio, 115
Oliveira, Celso de, 108, 119, 124
Oliveira, Emanuelle Karen Felinto de, 126
Oliveira, Myriam Ribeiro de, 136
Oliveira Lima, Manuel de, 6–8, 26–27, 106, 111, 127, 351, 405, 427, 450, 477–78
Oliver, Elide, 107
Onís, Harriet, 112, 116, 117, 130
Operation Pan America, 11, 12, 404
Organization of American States (OAS), 106, 401, 405, 406, 414
Ornstein, Jacob, 76, 90
Orton, James, 30
Ouseley, Sir William Gore, 137, 159

Owen, Hilary, 118
Owensby, Brian, 180, 198

Pace, Richard, 204, 227–29, 237
Packenham, Robert A., 295, 307
Page, Joseph, 19, 96, 130, 270, 285, 418, 478
Pageaux, Daniel-Henri, 386
Paiva, Clotilde, 173, 194
Paiva, Ricardo, 60, 69, 85, 86, 104, 108, 111, 124, 131, 438
Paiva, Rui Miller, 251, 262
Pan-Americanism, 32, 74
Pan-American Union, 75, 144
Pang, Eul-Soo, 15, 27, 177, 181, 184, 198, 478
Panizza, Francisco, 365
Pará, 176, 226, 357, 361, 444
Paraguay, 34, 299, 332, 355, 402, 408, 409, 411, 412, 415, 416
Paraíba, 176, 177
Paraná, 312, 317, 318, 327, 329, 332, 356
Paraná River, 32, 409
Park, Robert E., 267, 281
Parker, Richard, 49, 51, 478
Parkinson, Sydney, 349
Parris, Lori A., 116
Parry, J. H., 363, 366, 369
Parsons, Nivea, 60, 69, 86
Pastor, Robert A., 291
Patai, Daphne, 34, 51, 104, 105, 120, 124
Payne, Judith, 105, 120, 125, 130
Payne, Leigh, 279, 282, 285
Pazos-Alonso, Claudia, 119, 367
Peace Corps, 11, 34, 315, 319
Peard, Julyan, 179, 198, 420, 478
Pébayle, Raymond, 386
Pedro II, Dom, 31, 99, 143, 359, 384
Peixoto, Afrânio, 99, 438
Peixoto, Marta, 104, 108, 116, 119, 120, 121, 124, 129
Pena, Martins, 117
Penna, João Camillo, 125

Pennsylvania State University, 125
Peppercorn, Lisa M., 122, 129, 148, 159
Pereira, Anthony, 280, 419, 478
Pereira, Antônio Olavo, 115
Pereira, Leonardo Affonso de Miranda, 176
Perez, Marilu, 126
Perkins Commission (President's Commission on Foreign Languages and International Studies), 77–78
Perlman, Janice, 277, 285
Pernambuco, 137, 146, 173, 174, 176, 177, 182, 352, 353, 444, 487
Perrone, Charles, 61, 68, 112, 116, 120, 121, 123, 125, 130, 150, 159, 160, 441–42, 456, 478
Perrone-Moisés, Leyla, 107
Perroux, François, 384
Perry, William, 292, 307, 411, 478
Pessanha, Ricardo, 61, 68, 150, 158, 442, 455–56
Peterson, Loida Pereira, 126
Petrópolis, 172, 400
Phillips, June K., 87, 90
Picchio, Luciana Stegagno, 109, 130
Pierson, Donald, 10, 27, 33, 35, 51, 96, 130, 185, 267, 268, 280, 285, 399, 402, 407, 478
Pinho, Clemente Segundo, 107
Piñón, Nélida, 106, 108, 115, 121
Pinsdorf, Marion K., 178, 198
Pinto, Cristina Ferreira, 108, 117, 121, 125
Pion-Berlin, David, 299, 307
Plank, David, 19, 419, 478
political science, 37, 42, 53, 56, 58, 66, 264–87
Pontes, Heloísa, 163, 170, 197, 417, 475
Pontes, Joel, 107
Pontiero, Giovanni, 110, 117, 362, 366, 368, 370
Pontifícia Universidade Católica, Rio de Janeiro, 63, 64, 301, 485

Poore, Dudley, 116
Poppino, Rollie, 96, 130, 407, 479
Porter, Dorothy Burnett (also known as Dorothy Porter Wesley), 111, 130, 139, 159, 437, 453
Portes, Alejandro, 274, 286
Portinari, Cândido, 133, 137, 159
Portugal, 37, 105, 110, 122, 133, 146, 152, 172, 177, 347, 348, 351, 360, 362, 376, 384, 410, 427
Portuguese: language programs, x, 52, 54–55, 58, 61–65; language instruction, 60, 66, 73–92, 94, 320–21; second-language acquisition, 82
Posey, Darrell, 214–15, 221, 232, 237–38
postcolonial studies, 40, 44
postmodernism, 39–40, 47
Potter, Norman, 105, 107, 125
Pottier, Bernard, 80
Power, Tim, 276, 277, 280, 284, 286
Prado, Caio, Jr., 14, 17, 27, 162, 407, 479
Prado, Paulo, 33, 36, 182
Prata, Mônica, 126
Prebish, Raúl, 11, 271
Prescott, William Hickling, 5–6, 27
Preto-Rodas, Richard A., 109, 112, 120
Price, David, 223–24, 229, 238
Princeton University, 34, 95, 108, 124, 164, 166, 368, 443
Purdue University, 111, 251
Putnam, Samuel, 99, 100, 114, 116, 119, 130, 400, 479

Qorpo Santo, 104
Quadros, Jânio, 12, 319, 404–5, 432
Quaglino, Maria Ana, 126
queer studies, 39, 47
Queirós, Dinah Silveira, 119
Queiroz, Maria Isaura Pereira de, 33
Queiroz, Rachel de, 81, 113, 114
Queiroz, Suely Robles Reis de, 176, 198
Quinlan, Susan, 104, 105, 120, 121, 125, 130

Rabassa, Gregory, 102, 103, 104, 114, 116, 117, 124, 130
Rabben, Linda, 225, 238
race and race relations, 13, 34, 38, 109, 110, 120, 178–79, 267, 278, 437
Raine, Philip, 292, 307
Rainey, Marvin, 95
rain forest, 34, 105, 141, 214, 300, 373
Rameh, Cléa, 82, 89
Ramos, Arthur, 152, 160, 266, 281
Ramos, Donald, 173, 178, 198
Ramos, Graciliano, 100, 103, 104, 113, 114, 119
Randall, Laura, 19, 479
Raphael, Alison, 179, 199
Ratcliff, Dillwyn F., 116, 117
Readers, George, 384
Reagan, Ronald, 42, 412, 414
Recife, 46, 354
Rector, Mônica, 88, 107, 111, 131
Rego, Enylton de Sá, 108, 121, 125, 150, 160
Rego, José Lins do, 100, 102, 113, 114, 380, 441, 456
Reis, João José, 174–75, 176, 177, 199
Reis, Letícia Vidor de Sousa, 176
Reis, Raul Franco dos, 123
Reis, Roberto, 107, 162, 438, 453
Rey, Marcos, 115
Ribeiro, Darcy, 115, 361
Ribeiro, João Ubaldo, 114, 115
Ricardo, Cassiano, 104
Richards, Stanley, 116
Ridings, Eugene W., 19, 27, 184, 417, 479
Riedinger, Edward A., xvi, 375, 488
Riggio, Edward, 116
Rio Branco, Baron of (José Maria da Silva Paranhos), 7, 172, 379
Rio de Janeiro, 35, 37, 41, 45, 46, 62, 63, 102, 145, 146, 147, 151, 171, 172, 173, 174, 176, 179, 180, 181–82, 225, 301, 325, 328, 347, 348, 349, 350, 351, 353,

354, 355, 359, 377, 380, 403, 407, 416, 417, 420, 426, 427, 428, 429, 443, 444
Rio Grande do Sul, 176, 177, 178, 182, 251, 356, 386–87, 444
Rivière, Peter, 361, 362–63, 367, 372
Roberts, Kimberly, 94
Rocha, João Cezar de Castro, 112, 126
Roche, Jean, 386–87
Rochefort, Michel, 387
Rockefeller Foundation, 8, 11, 41, 76, 268
Rodman, Selden, 140, 160, 441, 455
Rodrigues, José Honório, 13, 27, 131, 162, 182, 199, 405, 406, 407, 418, 479
Rodrigues, Nelson, 104, 119, 120
Rodríguez Monegal, Emir, 120, 121
Roett, Riordan, 45, 270, 286, 296, 297, 298, 299, 307, 479
Rogers, Francis M., 77, 95, 97
Rolland, Denis, 380
Rondon, Cândido, 32
Roosevelt, Anna, 212, 213, 214, 229, 238
Roosevelt, Franklin, 106
Roosevelt, Theodore, 32, 51, 400–401, 479–80
Rosa, Alberto Machado da, 102
Rosa, Guimarães, 103, 105, 113, 114, 116, 119, 120, 121, 365
Rose, Stanley, 95
Rose, Theodore, 102, 124
Roxborough, Ian, 365
Rubião, Murilo, 117
Ruffinelli, Jorge, 112
Russell-Wood, A. J. R., 18, 27, 32, 49, 51, 163, 166, 167, 168, 174, 179, 181, 183, 184, 199, 362, 371, 413, 480
Russo, Harald, 94
Rutgers University, 124, 125

Sá, Lúcia, 105, 108, 125
Sable, Martin, 96, 131, 480
Sachs, Ignacy, 387, 393
Sacks, Norman P., 95

Sadler, J. T. W., 116
Sadlier, Darlene, 104, 117, 120, 124
Said, Edward, 39, 47
St. Andrew's University, 370–71
St. Clair, David, 118
St. John's University (New York), 64
St. Louis University, 103, 124
Salles, Antônio, 107
Salvador, 62, 63, 104, 147, 172, 349
Sanchez, Kathryn, 126
Sanders, Thomas G., 295–96, 307
San Diego State University, 65, 124
Sant'Anna, Affonso Romano de, 107
Santiago, Silviano, 106, 107, 112, 115
Santos, Luís Delfino dos, 103
Santos, Ronaldo Marcos dos, 176, 199
Santos, Theotônio dos, 293, 307
Santos, Vivaldo, 126
São Francisco River, 323, 353, 355
São Paulo, 35, 46, 48, 62, 67, 96, 112, 137, 138, 147, 148, 171, 172, 174, 177, 178, 179, 180, 181–82, 243, 320, 323, 327, 328, 330, 331, 332, 358, 384, 429, 444
Saraiva, Arnaldo, 109
Saunders, John, 116
Saunders, John Van Dyke, 270, 286
Say, Horace, 379
Sayers, Raymond, 102, 104, 109, 116, 120, 124, 131, 480
Schadl, Suzanne Michele, 126, 178, 179, 199
Scheper-Hughes, Nancy, 34, 51, 60, 68
Schil, Mary, 104, 125
Schmidt, Afonso Frederico, 104
Schmink, Marianne, 204, 205, 226–28, 229, 238
Schmitt, Jack, 116, 124
Schmitter, Philippe, 15, 27, 270, 273, 275, 285, 286, 480
Schneider, Ronald, 10, 15, 19, 27, 60, 69, 270, 273, 281, 286, 292, 307, 411, 418, 480

Schoenbach, Peter, 104, 105, 124, 149, 160, 441, 456
Scholarly Resources, 442–43, 445
Schuh, G. Edward, 251, 262
Schultz, Kirsten, 181, 199, 422, 480
Schurz, William L., 404, 480
Schwarcz, Lilia Moritz, 176, 179, 199–200
Schwartz, Jorge, 107
Schwartz, Stuart, 18, 27, 35, 165, 166, 167, 174, 183, 184, 200, 414, 480–81
Schwartzman, Simon, 381–82, 395
Schwartzman, Steve, 225
Schwarz, Roberto, 107, 108, 182, 368
Scliar, Moacyr, 106, 113, 115
Scully, William, 355
Seckinger, Ron, 184
Seeger, Anthony, 151, 160, 216, 225, 229, 238, 239, 413, 481
Selcher, Wayne, 273, 286, 292, 296, 297, 303, 307–8, 410, 481
Seminar on the Acquisition of Latin American Library Materials (SALALM), 429, 439
Sena, Jorge de, 107, 108, 109
Serbin, Ken, 179, 200
Setúbal, Paulo, 114
Sevcenko, Nicolau, 107
Shapiro, Helen, 250, 262, 418, 481
Shapiro, Judith, 209
Sharpe, Peggy, 120, 121, 124, 131
Shaw, Lisa, 370
Shaw, Paul Vanorden, 267, 382
Sheinin, David, 119, 131
Shelby, Barbara, 116, 117
Sikkink, Kathryn, 279, 481
Silva, André Cavazotti, 123
Silva, Eduardo, 176, 199
Silva, Golbery do Couto e, 295, 308
Silva, Magda, 126
Silverman, Malcolm, 104, 119, 121, 124
Simões, Antônio, 85, 90, 91
Simonsen, Mário H., 246, 254, 260

Simonsen, Roberto, 9
Simpson, Amelia, 123, 179, 200
Skidmore, Thomas E., 4, 14, 18, 27–28, 35, 53, 60, 69, 96, 116, 131, 165, 177, 178–79, 184, 200, 273, 276, 286, 407, 410, 415, 420, 430, 450, 481
Slater, Candace, 34–35, 51, 116, 117, 120
slavery, 13, 31, 33, 34, 172–77
Slavinsky, Barbara, 104, 125
Slenes, Robert, 163, 173, 174, 176, 178, 200
Sluiter, Engel, 95, 359
Slutzkin, Herman, 102, 124
Smallman, Shawn, 180, 200
Smith, Alfred, 81, 90
Smith, Carlton Sprague, 95
Smith, Gordon W., 246–47, 248, 251, 263
Smith, Joseph, 19, 28, 290, 308, 371, 416, 481
Smith, Nigel, 326, 329, 330, 342, 372
Smith, Peter S., 177, 200
Smith, Robert C., 32, 51, 90, 95, 133–34, 135, 136, 138, 143, 160, 440, 455
Smith, Russell E., 255, 263
Smith, T. Lynn, 10, 28, 33, 35, 51, 95, 96, 131, 266–67, 268, 274, 281, 286, 312, 326, 342, 400, 402, 404, 481–82
Smith, William, 53, 113, 127
Smith College, 125
Smithsonian Institution, 205, 206, 211
Soares, Luís Carlos, 294
Sobral, Patrícia, 105, 108, 125
Social Science Research Council, 8, 41, 165, 268, 274, 315
Sociedade Brasileiro pelo Progresso da Ciência (SBPC), 97
sociology, 56, 58, 66, 264–87
Soeiro, Susan, 178, 200
Soihet, Rachel, 178, 200
Solingen, Etel, 300, 308
Solt, Mary Ellen, 113, 131
Sommer, Barbara Ann, 182, 186, 200

Sousândrade, Joaquim de, 104, 121
Southampton University, 370
Southey, Robert, 4, 28, 163, 347, 350–51, 352, 359, 482
Souza, Inglês de, 99
Souza, Laura de Mello e, 179, 182, 200–201
Souza, Márcio, 113, 115
Souza, Ronald, 116, 118
Sovereign, Marie, 104, 124
Soviet Union, 11, 275, 288, 289, 290, 292, 375, 395, 399, 401, 402, 403, 405, 407, 408, 409, 412, 414, 415, 416
Spain, 105, 369, 411
Spanish, 101, 320–21
Spitzer, Leo, 94
Spix, J. B. von, 151
Spruce, Richard, 354–55
Sputnik, 11, 268, 403
Staden, Hans, 137, 151
Stam, Robert, 60, 69, 120, 122, 129, 131, 415, 482
Standards of Foreign Language Learning in the Twenty-first Century, 87
Stanford University, 30, 34, 56, 57, 63, 66, 86, 94, 95, 106, 108, 112, 124, 125, 126, 164, 166, 170, 174, 241
State University of New York: Albany, 167; Binghamton, 125; Stony Brook, 107, 166
Stein, Barbara Hadley, 33, 408, 482
Stein, Stanley, 10, 14, 28, 33, 34, 60, 69, 95, 164, 165, 174, 181, 183, 201, 250, 263, 326, 342, 371, 403, 408, 431, 451, 482
Stepan, Alfred, 15, 17, 28, 60, 69, 270, 273, 276, 286–87, 409, 482
Stepan, Nancy Leys, 178, 201, 372, 482
Stephens, Thomas, 88, 92, 453
Stern, Irwin, 111, 131, 439, 454
Sternberg, Hilgard O'Reilly, 237, 281, 312, 323, 325–26, 327–28, 330, 334, 342–43
Sternberg, Ricardo, 104, 108, 119, 124
Stevenson, Robert, 146, 147, 151, 153, 160
Steward, Julian, 205, 208, 211, 212, 238–39, 436, 453
Strand, Mark, 116, 117
Suassuna, Ariano Vilar, 104, 117, 439
Summerhill, William, 19, 28, 181, 201, 421, 423, 482
Sussekind, Flora, 107, 108, 118, 131
Sussex University, 371
Swainson, William, 352–53
Sweet, David, 178, 201
Syracuse University, 321, 323, 324
Syvrud, Donald E., 245, 249, 254, 263
Szoka, Elzbieta, 112, 120

Tannebaum, Frank, 33, 173, 185, 201
Tanner, Evan, 254–55, 256–57, 263
Taunay, Afonso de Escragnolle, 99, 114, 378
Taylor, James L., 116, 439, 455
Taylor, L. L., 116
Taylor, Philip B., Jr., 265
Telles, Lygia Fagundes, 113, 115, 117
Tendler, Judith, 250, 263, 277, 287
Tesser, Carmen, xiv, 67, 73, 488
Texas Tech University, 103, 125
Teyssier, Paul, 110
Thévet, André, 4, 151, 377
Thomas, Earl W., 83, 90, 95, 281
Thompson, Douglas, 104, 125
Thompson, Robert Ferris, 140, 157, 160
Thorau, Henry, 109
Thorp, Rosemary, 367
Tinker Foundation, 294, 371
Tollefson, Scott, xvi, 288, 296, 303, 308, 488
Tolman, Jon, 53, 60, 69, 86, 91, 104, 111, 124, 131, 162, 425, 438, 454
Tomlins, Jack E., 100, 116, 117, 118
Tomlinson, H. M., 357
Topete, José Manuel, 111, 131, 438, 454

Topik, Steven, 19, 28, 167, 177, 181, 184, 185, 201, 244, 263, 290, 308, 415, 418, 483

Toplin, Robert Brent, 173, 177, 184, 201, 409, 483

Trebat, Thomas J., 252, 263

Treece, David, 110, 365, 421

Trevisan, Dalton, 117

Trevisan, João Silvério, 106

Triner, Gail, 48, 181, 201, 421, 483

Trinity University, San Antonio, 125

Tsuchida, Nobuya, 178, 201

Tulane University, 10, 56, 98, 107, 108, 122, 125, 145, 166, 400

Tulchin, Joseph, 60, 69

Turner, Doris, 103, 124

Turner, Terence, 206, 207, 221, 239

Twain, Mark (Samuel Clemens), 31

Twine, France Winddance, 267, 278, 287

Tyler, William G., 258, 263

Tyson, Brady, 45

UNICAMP, 88, 174, 371

United Kingdom, 5, 37, 105, 162, 163, 170, 177, 310, 322, 345, 347–74, 376, 395, 403, 407, 425, 486

United Nations Economic Commission for Latin America (ECLA), 11, 244, 248, 271

United States Agency for International Development (USAID), 38, 42, 241

United States Department of Education, 42, 85; Fund for the Improvement of Post-secondary Education (FIPSE), 86; U.S.-Brazil Partnerships for Educational Binational Dialogue, 66

United States Military Academy, 103

United States National Archives, 426, 442, 444

United States Naval Academy, 76

Universidade Católica de Brasília, 64

Universidade de Brasília, 46, 213–14, 297, 301

Universidade de Pernambuco, 135

Universidade de São Paulo (USP), 11, 35, 36, 63–64, 133, 166, 170, 175, 186, 206, 267, 294, 301, 321, 322, 343, 364, 366, 381–84, 485

Universidade do Brasil, 145

Universidade Estadual do Rio de Janeiro, 125, 126

Universidade Federal da Bahia, 174

Universidade Federal de Pernambuco, 174–75

Universidade Federal de Santa Catarina, Florianópolis, 125, 213

Universidade Federal do Acre, 205

Universidade Federal do Rio de Janeiro, 80, 88, 325, 371

Universidade Federal Fluminense, 178, 294

Université de Aix-Marseille, 390

University of Arizona, 56, 66, 425

University of British Columbia, 372

University of California: Berkeley, 55, 56, 61, 63, 66, 84, 95, 96, 102, 106, 107, 117, 124, 125, 126, 164, 165, 166, 167, 170, 206, 241, 295, 312, 325, 359, 372; Davis, 167, 294; Irvine, 167; Los Angeles (UCLA), 53, 56, 61, 63, 88, 95, 98, 124, 125, 126, 146, 153, 165, 166, 168, 170, 184, 265, 269, 372, 425, 428, 446; Riverside, 435; San Diego, 63, 65, 167, 446; Santa Barbara, 61, 63, 107, 109, 125, 126, 166; Santa Cruz, 279

University of Cambridge, 361, 363, 365–66, 371, 372

University of Chicago, 79, 166, 167, 174, 267, 365

University of Edinburgh, 370

University of Essex, 369, 370

University of Florida, 9, 56, 61, 62, 66, 95, 98, 103, 124, 125, 165, 166, 167, 170, 204–5, 267, 269, 372, 401, 426

University of Georgia, 125, 126, 488

University of Glasgow, 363, 368, 369

University of Illinois, 45, 57–58, 94, 95, 124, 125, 126, 164, 166, 174, 241, 485, 487

University of Iowa, 103, 108, 125, 148, 149

University of Kansas, 117, 164, 371

University of Liverpool, 363, 368

University of London, 363, 364, 486

University of Manchester, 367, 370

University of Maryland, 63, 108, 110, 486

University of Massachusetts, Amherst, 57, 61, 124

University of Massachusetts, Dartmouth, 54, 56, 97, 112, 125

University of Miami, 53, 108, 124, 126, 152, 153, 166, 487–88

University of Michigan, 125, 184, 323, 324

University of Minnesota, 125, 166, 174, 251, 266, 279

University of Mississippi, 125

University of Missouri, 126, 153

University of New Hampshire, 97

University of New Mexico, 8, 53, 56, 62–63, 66, 83, 84, 88, 99, 124, 125, 126, 165, 166, 167, 170, 184, 425, 428, 432, 437, 438, 440, 441, 486

University of North Carolina, 10, 65, 96, 99, 103, 107–8, 124, 125, 126, 400

University of Oxford, 110, 166, 206, 361, 363, 366, 367–68, 369, 371, 374, 486

University of Paris, 386, 390

University of Pennsylvania, 75, 86, 94, 95, 96, 488

University of Pittsburgh, 56, 66, 125, 167

University of Salzburg, 110

University of South Carolina, 108, 124, 125

University of Southern California, 38

University of South Florida, 62, 167

University of Sussex, 365

University of Tennessee, Knoxville, 125

University of Texas, 8–9, 10, 34, 53, 56, 61, 66, 83, 84, 85, 86, 88, 98, 101, 106, 107, 108, 123, 124, 125, 126, 139, 145, 152, 165, 166, 168, 170, 241, 265, 269, 279, 294, 400, 401, 426, 427, 446, 487; UT-LANIC, 46, 302, 425, 445

University of Toronto, 108, 124

University of Toulouse, 385, 394

University of Trier, 109

University of Utrecht, 110

University of Virginia, 74, 103

University of Wisconsin, 8, 56, 61, 66, 83, 94, 95, 96, 98, 102, 103, 107, 108, 110, 111, 124, 125, 126, 166, 167, 279, 319, 367, 443

Urban, Greg, 139, 160, 216–17, 222, 229, 239

Uruguay, 299, 408, 414, 416, 417

Vainfas, Ronaldo, 176, 179, 182, 201

Valente, Luiz, 53, 105, 108, 125

Valenzuela, Arturo, 271–72, 274, 280, 287

Valladares, Clarival do Prado, 136, 161

Van den Dool, Karin, 86

Vanderbilt University, 10, 34, 45, 95, 96–97, 103, 125, 167, 172, 241, 267, 279, 359, 400, 402, 446, 487

Vargas de Amaral Peixoto, Alzira, 46, 165

Vargas, Getúlio, 32, 38, 46, 96, 171, 177, 180, 183, 185, 265, 268, 358, 399, 402, 403

Varnhagen, Adolfo de, 4, 28, 162, 352

Vasconcellos, Mauro de, 115

Vasconcellos, Selma, 177, 201

Vasconcellos, Sylvio de, 136, 161
Veiga, J. J., 113, 117
Veloso, Caetano, 150
Verger, Pierre, 383
Veríssimo, Érico, 9, 99, 104, 106, 113, 114, 118, 121, 131, 399, 483
Vermette, Mary T., 84
Versiani, Ivana, 107
Vessels, Gary, 104, 125
Vieira, Nelson H., 53, 109, 120, 131
Vietnam War, 34, 44, 319, 406, 407, 410
Villa-Lobos, Heitor, 122–23, 148, 380, 442
Villela, Annibel, 243, 247, 253, 260
Vincent, Jon, 119
Voeks, Robert, 326, 330, 343
Votre, Sebastião, 88

Wager, Willis, 116, 117
Wagley, Charles, 10, 14, 33, 37, 49, 60, 69, 95, 96, 131, 185, 203–5, 208, 227–28, 231, 239, 280, 281, 287, 312, 324, 343, 401, 402, 405, 483
Waibel, Leo, 312, 321, 326, 343
Waldemar, Thomas, 104, 125
Walden, Stephen Thomas, 123, 125
Wallace, Alfred Russel, 354–55
Wallerstein, Immanuel, 38, 294, 308
Wallis, Marie, 99, 124
Walsh, Robert, 353
Walther, Don, 95–96, 99, 124
Warner, Ralph, 99
Washington University, 103
Wasserman, Renata, 108, 120, 124
Watson, Ellen, 116
Wayne State University, 108, 124
Webb, Kempton, 312, 323, 324–25, 330, 343–44
Weinstein, Barbara, 19, 28, 34, 40, 44, 47, 48, 50, 51, 167, 168, 180, 182, 202, 419, 483–84
Welch, Cliff, 182, 202
Welch, John H., 252, 263

Wells, James W., 356
Wells, John, 366
Wenger, Etienne, 217, 235
Wenner-Gren Foundation, 41, 268
Werner, Dennis, 213, 240
Wesleyan University, 125
Wesson, Robert, 289–90, 308, 413, 484
Weyland, Kurt, 277, 278, 280, 287, 484
Wheeler, Douglas, 84, 91
Whitehead, Laurence, 367
Whitehead, Neil, 186, 217, 240, 367
Wiarda, Howard, 273, 287
Wickham, Henry Alexander, 356
Wilder, Elizabeth, 135, 440, 455
Wileman, J. P., 356
Wilkening, Eugene, 270, 287
Wilkins, Lawrence A., 74, 91
Williams, Daryle, 40, 180, 202, 422, 484
Williams, Edwin B., 75, 94, 95, 131
Williams, Emmett, 113, 132
Williams, Frederick G., 104, 119, 121, 124
Williamson, James A., 358
Willems, Emilio, 96, 281
Willumsen, Maria, 60, 69
Wilson, Clotilde, 99
Wilson, R., 245, 261
Wirth, John D., 14, 15, 29, 166, 177, 185, 202, 270, 287, 328, 344, 411, 484
Wolfe, Joel, 180, 202, 484
Wood, Charles, 204, 226–28, 229, 238
Woodbridge, Benjamin, 96, 99, 124
Woodrow Wilson Center for International Scholars, xi, 274, 421
Worcester, Donald, 96, 132, 484
World Bank, 221–22, 225, 253
World War II, 9, 32, 170, 171, 246, 249, 265, 312, 347, 377, 383, 384, 395, 399
Wright, Robin, 217–19, 222–23, 230, 240
Wyatt, James L., 81
Wynia, Gary, 269, 287

Xavier, Ismail, 122, 132

Yale University, 34, 55, 94, 95, 103, 106, 107, 110, 124, 125, 164, 165, 166, 168, 170, 241, 360, 487
Young, Jordan, 183, 407, 410, 431–32, 452, 484

Young, Theodore, xiv, 52, 104, 121, 125, 489

Zarur, Jorge, 204
Zenith, Richard, 117
Zubatsky, David S., 111, 132
Zweig, Stefan, 33, 51, 96, 132